By the same author

Nineteenth-Century Printing Practices and the Iron Handpress
Printing on the Iron Handpress
A Sampler of Leaves
Problem Solving and Printing on the Cast-Iron Handpress
Seven Aspects of Solitude
The Emperor's Lion
The Ill-Timed Lover
1945–1965: An Evaluation of Two Decades of Self-Deception
Eight Parting Poems

Translations

Cantata of Bomarzo
The Woman with Her Mouth Open

FANTASIES & HARD KNOCKS

for Nova
with a ~~little~~ few martinis
and negronis, you fly on
a magic carpet through my
life.

Gabriel

Gabriel leaning against his Washington press in the via Duomo studio, Verona, Italy, 1973. (Photo by Guido Trevisani, courtesy of PWP Archives.)

Fantasies & HardKnocks

My Life as a Printer

BY

Richard-Gabriel Rummonds

Embellished with over 450 images & 65 recipes

EX OPHIDIA PRESS

PORT TOWNSEND ◆ 2015

Copyright © 2015 by Richard-Gabriel Rummonds

All rights reserved
First Edition

Published by Ex Ophidia Press
724 Tyler Street, Suite 3
Port Townsend, WA 98368
http://fantasiesandhardknocks.com
Gabriel Rummonds, Publisher
rummonds@msn.com
360-385-9966

John D. Wagner, Business Manager and Public Relations
1jdwagner@gmail.com
919-796-9984

Title-page lettering by Jerry Kelly. Edited by James T. Jones.
Set in Adobe Minion by Bradley Hutchinson and printed at C & C Offset Printing
in China on Gold HuaSheng Premium Ivory wood-free paper.

Rummonds, Richard-Gabriel, 1931–
    Fantasies and hard knocks : my life as a printer / Richard-Gabriel Rummonds
       p.   cm.
    Includes indexes.
Hardcover ISBN: 978-0-692-36404-8

Subject headings supplied by the publisher.

1. Rummonds, Richard-Gabriel—Memoir. 2. Handpress. 3. Printing, Practical. 4. Handpress printers—Gay. 5. Private Presses—Plain Wrapper Press. 6. Private Presses—Ex Ophidia. 7. Authors—20th century. 8. Artists—20th century. 9. Expatriates, American—Italy. 10. Cooking, Italian. 11. University of California at Berkeley—1950s. 12. Book Arts Programs, American. I. Title.

To the memory of D. Steven Corey (1947–1991)

Contents

The books are listed in chronological order of publication by imprint with Plain Wrapper Press books first, followed by Ex Ophidia books. Note: the numbers preceding the book titles are item numbers, not chapter numbers.

Preface   xiii
A Prelude to Printing: Before New York   3
A Prelude to Printing: New York and Beyond   23

PLAIN WRAPPER PRESS
Quito, Ecuador   39
  1. *Eight Parting Poems*   55

Buenos Aires, Argentina   69
    Peopleology of Richard Rummonds   83
  2. *1945–1965: An Evaluation of Two Decades of Self-Deception*   89

New York, New York   117
  3. *The Dog Bite: A Dream Narrative*   149

Verona, Italy: Via Duomo, 15   161
  4. *Images & Footsteps*   179
  5. *Ten Poems & Ten Reflections*   205
  6. *Le Streghette*   213
  7. *Ballata delle Madri*   223
  8. *Some Things from Jack*   231

Verona, Italy: The Vespa   245
  9. *Didascalie*   253
  10. *Poesie dal Tappeto Volante*   263
  11. *The Ill-Timed Lover*   271
  12. *Tre Poesie d'Amore*   279
  13. *Pronto Soccorso: The Pucci-Parigi Book*   287

ix

Verona, Italy: The Lull before the Storm 297

14. *Siete Poemas Sajones / Seven Saxon Poems* 313
15. *A Lost Poem* 339
16. *Three Poems of Passion* 351
17. *Géographie du Regard* 363
18. *Society of Private Printers: Third Exchange* 373
19. *The Emperor's Lion* 387
20. *Will and Testament: A Fragment of Biography* 411
21. *Le Stagioni* 435
22. *A Christmas Recipe* 439

Verona, Italy: Via Carlo Cattaneo, 6 443

23. *Six Printers Mottos: A Spectrum Specimen* 451
24. *Stella Variabile* 465
25. *Circhi e Cene / Circuses and Suppers* 477
26. *La Donna con la Bocca Aperta / The Woman with Her Mouth Open* 487
27. *Lo Stemma Cittadino* 497
28. *Six Poems* 503
29. *Wooings* 509
30. *Cantata de Bomarzo* 521
31. *Cantata di Bomarzo* 535

Verona, Italy: Getting the Word Out 543

32. *Verona e i Suoi Fiumi* 585
33. *The Ship of Sounds* 597
34. *The River* 603
35. *Suite Lirica / Lyric Suite* 613
36. *Il Cinque Maggio / Der Fünfte Mai* 625

Cottondale, Alabama: Settling In 633

37. *Prima Che Tu Dica "Pronto" / Before You Say "Hello"* 649
38. *Seven Aspects of Solitude* 667

EX OPHIDIA

Cottondale, Alabama: Ex Ophidia 681

39. *Dal Vero* 689
40. *Could I Ask You Something?* 697

Table of Contents   xi

41. *Atlantic Crossing* 713
42. *Journeys in Sunlight* 725

Postscript, October 1988 735
Afterword, September 2014 737
Appendix I: Notes on "The Mr. Wilson Story" 749
Appendix II: An Aborted Faulkner Project 753
Acknowledgements 757
Credits and Permissions 761
Recipes Index 765
General Index 767

Preface

> Man's most valuable trait is a judicious sense of what not to believe.
> – Euripides

Truth and Myth

Memoirs can never avoid being part truth, part myth. *Truth*, as the Japanese filmmaker Akira Kurosawa so aptly demonstrated in his 1950 film *Rashomon*, is in the eye of the beholder. And *myth*, often regarded as an intellectually acceptable device for embellishing and reconstructing events, is in the mind of the storyteller. I have deliberately tried to avoid contributing to my own myth in this memoir. If I have erred or let the fantasies sometimes prevail, I can only plead forgetfulness or out-and-out mischievousness.

Giovanni Mardersteig Interview

I was privileged to be the last person to formally interview Giovanni (Hans) Mardersteig, the distinguished German/Italian handpress printer, at his Officina Bodoni in Verona, Italy, shortly before he died at the age of eighty-five on December 27, 1977. At that time I also lived and worked in Verona, which was why Sandra Kirshenbaum, the editor and publisher of *Fine Print: A Review for the Arts of the Book*, asked me to approach Mardersteig printer-to-printer for an interview. In spite of the fact that he was quite ill at the time, he graciously consented to see me. Even though he wouldn't allow me to record the interview, he had no objection to my bringing along a colleague to take notes. Prior to meeting with Mardersteig, I carefully prepared a list of forty questions that I felt would best reveal Mardersteig the printer, rather than his better-known persona as a scholar/publisher. His response to my first question demonstrated that he was still very much in possession of his sharp wit. Noting that his press was acknowledged as the oldest existing handpress in continuous operation, I asked him to what he attributed its longevity. His reply was, "My long life!" We were up and running. My questions ranged from "What had originally inspired you to take up printing?" to "What was the extent of your involvement in the development of your famous typefaces, such as Dante and Fontana?"

I was quite pleased with the results and later showed Mardersteig's responses to my questions to Franco Riva, the vice director of the Biblioteca Civica di Verona (Verona Civic Library). Franco, who was also a private press printer and one of my mentors in Verona, was very dismayed by the interview, indicating that Mardersteig's answers were all part of a well-orchestrated fabrication. I was stunned. Franco then proceeded, response by response, to call into question the accuracy of the interview.

A few weeks later, I was still pondering what to do with the interview when I had a visit from Hans Schmoller, the English typographer and book designer. He was in Verona working on the translation of Mardersteig's *The Officina Bodoni: An Account of a Hand Press, 1923–1977* (1980). I also showed him Mardersteig's responses to my questions and expressed my concern about Franco's comments. Sadly, Hans confirmed many of the points that Franco had made. When I asked Hans why Mardersteig would have misled me, he tried to justify the great printer's responses, "It is the way he wants to be perceived, to be remembered; and those who love him and admire his work would do nothing to alter the image he has of himself." I was shattered, but even though I, too, admired his work, I decided not to contribute to his myth, and so my interview was never published. Mardersteig's view of himself certainly influenced how I would write my own "myth."

García Márquez Interview

In an article written by Anthony Day and Marjorie Miller in the September 2, 1990, issue of the *Los Angeles Times Magazine*, Gabriel García Márquez said he was writing his memoirs, organizing them by theme rather than chronology. He favored this methodology, saying, it "allows me to skip over the themes that don't interest me, or that are not in my interest to write." By being selective about which events to include, he created an explicit myth of himself by omission.

I mention Mardersteig and García Márquez because they represent the conflicting ideas of truth and myth in memoirs. But I did, in fact, perpetrate many of my own myths during my life. I repeated some of them so many times that I also came to believe they were true. In this memoir, I identify these myths as fantasies and explain their relevance to the story. After all, there is no need to burden a good story with facts.

Preface xv

The Arrangement of My Text

Influenced by what García Márquez said in the interview, I have arranged this memoir of my life as a printer by "themes," that is, a separate chapter for each of the forty-two items I printed and published with the Plain Wrapper Press and Ex Ophidia imprints between 1966 and 1988. Each chapter begins with its own chronology of events. In addition, there are a few interludes to help make a smooth transition from one location or event to another in order to provide background information not necessarily germane to a particular book. There are also many people, some of whom played important roles at the Plain Wrapper Press, whom I don't care to mention, and so they have – to use a metaphor from the film industry – ended up on the cutting-room floor.

Memoir Title Changes

The title went through at least three changes, each reflecting my state of mind at the time. The first was *The Plain Wrapper Press: An Exercise in Frustration*, with a proposed foreword by Anthony Rota, the English bookseller, or Plain Wrapper Press authors Anthony Burgess or Brendan Gill. From my notes on the text, it appears that this was to be an annotated bibliography rather than a memoir. It was to be penned by Gabriel Precio, one of my many *noms de plume*, who also wrote the introductions to *Peopleology of Richard Rummonds* and *1945–1965: An Evaluation of Two Decades of Self-Deception*.

The second title, *Fantasies and Cold Hard Facts*, was the provisional title for a thwarted memoir/bibliography to be published by W. Thomas Taylor. In 1993, Tom published *Plain Wrapper Press: 1966–1988*, an illustrated bibliography with a foreword by Decherd Turner and bibliographic descriptions by Elaine Smyth.

Before the memoir component of the project was abandoned, Michael Bixler, the typesetter, had cast many galleys of the text in Monotype Dante. Tom later sold much of that unprinted type to Coriander Reisbord at her Skeptical Press in El Cerrito, California. For many years afterwards, I ran into people who had read bits and pieces of the proofs, all of them curious about the rest of the text.

Once I decided to return to a memoir, I changed the title to *Fantasies & Hard Knocks* – the third and final title – at Harry Duncan's suggestion. Harry was a fine press printer and another of my printing mentors.

Notes on the Text

A summary of the literary and artistic contents is given below the title of each item, followed by the number of pages, the dimensions, the number of copies, and the publication date. The pagination is counted from the recto of the first leaf to the verso of the last leaf. Dimensions are leaf sizes, with height by width calculated to the next highest half-centimeter.

The editors of *Fine Print* once referred to me as the "*enfant terrible* of fine printing" since I never hesitated to speak my mind when discussing the book arts or talking about myself. Nor will I refrain from doing so in this memoir. There are frequent interruptions in the narrative, but that is how I have always found life and conversation to be.

I have interspersed comments relevant to the books, as well as some pertaining to the general development of the Press. But even more important are those comments that I have added concerning my growth as a printer and my feelings about my work, including some of the accompanying frustrations, tempered by moments of genuine satisfaction.

I was probably the first openly gay fine press printer and have included many extracts intended to give the reader an indication of the types of texts that interested me as a publisher and to provide the reader with additional insights regarding the texts I wrote myself. Few of the latter texts are available elsewhere. It may have been presumptuous of me to have interwoven five relatively minor items of my own work among so much fine literature by internationally acclaimed authors, but in the beginning, printing my own poems and stories *was* the *raison d'être* of the Plain Wrapper Press.

All my texts and correspondence quoted in the text have been silently edited to correct errors of spelling, punctuation, syntax, grammar, capitalization, and spacing, as well as typographical errors. Some of the obvious spelling errors are due to my dyslexia, and these are retained since they indicate how I pronounced and wrote these words. A few of the words in the short stories were simply made up.

Abbreviations Used in the Text

I use RPR and RGR throughout and refer to Richard Price Rummonds (the name I used prior to my baptism in the Roman Catholic Church on April 9, 1966) and Richard-Gabriel Rummonds (the name I used after my baptism).

Preface   xvii

I use PWP and EXO throughout to refer to the Plain Wrapper Press and Ex Ophidia, respectively. All my books were issued using one of these two imprints.

Notes on the Recipes

Traditionally printers have been addicted to strong drink and good food, with a little wenching and chasing after handsome young boys thrown in for good measure. Among the most vivid memories carried away by many of the collaborators and visitors to the press are those of the wonderful local wines and meals that I served in my apartment at via Duomo, 15, or in the side courtyard at the via Carlo Cattaneo, 6, studio, as well as in many local trattorias and restaurants. For this reason, I have included recipes for many of the culinary delights we offered our friends, guests, and collaborators.

Cooking in Italy

I did not start cooking seriously until I moved to Italy in 1970. The kitchen at via Duomo, 15, was primitive by comparison with American kitchens. There was a large shallow porcelain sink, a small three-burner gas stove with two medium-sized burners and a smaller one to accommodate a Moka coffee pot, and a miniature oven. In addition, there was a small refrigerator, the type that fits under a counter. At that time, Italians didn't need large refrigerators or freezers since they usually shopped every day for what they were putting on the table that day. I fell right in step with this custom, and even today, visitors to Port Townsend are amazed to find my refrigerator almost empty.

I didn't have any cookbooks in Verona; I just relied on friends to give me their recipes, or I reconstructed dishes I enjoyed in restaurants. The recipes in this book come from these early recipes, which in some cases have been rewritten with an occasional glance at my Italian cookbooks. For the most part, they are traditional recipes from the Veneto. However, I have always been inventive in the kitchen and often improvised with the ingredients on hand. Remember: taste is paramount in any dish.

Printing and Eroticism

In March 1977, filling in at the last minute for James D. Ramer, the dean of the library school at the University of Alabama, I gave a lecture, "In the Footsteps of William Morris," for Dr. Robert L. Leslie's Heritage of the Graphic Arts series in New York. It was the first of many in which I would discuss my work in minute detail. Half in jest, I prefaced my talk by saying "For me, printing has always been an erotic experience." Then I launched into my prepared text. My professional and erotic lives very quickly became fused into a single pursuit.

I am indebted to Gore Vidal, Paul Zweig, and Larry Rivers, even though of different sexual orientations, for their frankness when discussing their own sexual escapades in their respective memoirs. In *What Did I Do?: The Unauthorized Autobiography of Larry Rivers* (1992), Rivers wrote, "Despite my smoking of pot and sucking of cunt and the occasional cock . . ." If he can express his sexuality so candidly, I see no reason why I can't do the same.

A Final Note to the Reader

I have made every effort to verify the material presented in this memoir. I have relied on images and documents to ascertain the exact facts of these events that I describe. In the end this story simply presents my life as a printer as I remember it.

FANTASIES & HARD KNOCKS

Richard from the *Review 1949* – his high school yearbook – Sacramento, CA, 1949. He was selected as one of the ten most popular seniors in his class. Yearbook caption: Dick Rummonds – wacky, but sincere in all that he undertakes. (Photo by Oliver Livoni, courtesy of PWP Archives.)

A Prelude to Printing: Before New York

> What is important for a memoirist is not the factual
> accuracy of the account but its symmetry.
> – Orhan Pamuk, *Istanbul: Memories and the City*

The Demise of the Plain Wrapper Press

It is ironic that as I now attempt to sort out my fantasies and to document my thoughts concerning my life as a printer, I am no longer one. Late in the summer of 1988, soon after I finished printing *Seven Aspects of Solitude*, a keepsake and the last publication to bear the Plain Wrapper Press imprint, I sold all of my equipment to Gregor G. Peterson at the Huckleberry Press in Incline Village, Nevada, and moved from Cottondale, Alabama, to Los Angeles, California, to pursue a career in screenwriting. The first item I printed, *Eight Parting Poems*, was issued in 1965. It was also a keepsake. In all, thirty-eight items were printed at the Plain Wrapper Press and four at Ex Ophidia, the latter number including two commissions for the Whitney Museum of American Art in New York. A grand total of forty-two items – not a very impressive opus for twenty-three years of hard knocks.

Family

My father, Newton Price Rummonds, was not a printer. Though trained as an architect, he was primarily engaged in the construction business. My mother, Geraldine Rummonds, *née* Westenhaver – after a brief flirtation with the movies – settled for a less glamorous life as homemaker and mother. I was their firstborn, coming into this world on April 26, 1931, in Long Beach, California, where both my parents had been raised. Thirteen months later, another son, Robert Newton, was born, followed by Thomas Chester in 1935. My youngest brother William Lee was born in 1946 when I was fifteen. Both Robert and Bill became architects, and Tom, a successful illustrator.

In point of fact I can't think of anyone in my family who might have been even remotely connected with the printing industry, nor did I ever seriously consider printing as a profession until becoming immersed in the craft in the early seventies.

Richard in his father's arms, flanked on the left by his mother and on the right by his paternal grandparents, Long Beach, CA, 1931. (Photographer unknown, courtesy of PWP Archives.)

Left to right: Robert, Tom, mother, and Richard at the World's Fair of the Golden Gate International Exposition, Treasure Island, CA, 1939. (Photographer unknown, courtesy of PWP Archives.)

A Prelude to Printing: Before New York

Emotionally, I was born an orphan, shunning my peers, preferring to read and daydream, so I won't dwell on my early family life. Needless to say, I was a high-strung, insecure, introverted child who escaped into a world of make-believe, easily stimulated by books and movies. The first book I bought with my own pocket money was *The Prince and the Pauper* by Mark Twain. Ten-cent Saturday matinees with double features, serials, newsreels, and cartoons nourished my excitable imagination.

Memories of Teenage Eroticism

I was never confused about my sexuality because I didn't think I was any different from the other boys at school. But when I was about fifteen, I had two very vivid experiences that frightened me.

The first was in the public library near my house where I was doing my homework at one of the long tables. A guy who looked like a high school jock came over and sat down next to me and offered me some comic books if I would touch his penis. I could see he had an erection and I wanted to touch it, but I was afraid. Instead, I got up and walked away, pretending that I didn't see it. I returned to the library several days in a row, hoping to see him again. Even though I wasn't interested in the comic books, I would have touched his penis.

The second involved my friend Jim from high school, a fellow scout who would sometimes give me a lift home on his bicycle. As my elbow kept drifting into his crotch, he put his hand on my shoulder and said, "If you don't stop that, you're gonna hafta to suck my dick." I was terrified. I realize now that it wasn't sex I was looking for. I was just curious about his body.

Allure of Printing

I can trace my fascination with printing back to early childhood, but this inquisitiveness shouldn't be mistaken for an interest in printing as a career. I wanted to take print shop classes in junior high school in Sacramento, California, but my advisor wouldn't allow it because I was enrolled in the college preparatory program. In 1946, students were segregated by their career goals: trade, secretarial, and college preparatory.

Knowing of my budding interest in printing, my high school English teacher, Elizabeth Schwartz, gave me a small piece printed by Raymond Duncan. Like his sister Isadora, he was a dancer, most often dressed in flow-ing Greek tunics and sandals. Miss Schwartz had visited him at his Paris atelier, where in addition to his interest in dance he had also designed a typeface, cutting each letter individually in wood. Using these letters he printed several little books and ephemeral pieces that he sold to curious tourists. Miss Schwartz brought me one of these as a souvenir from Paris.

Early Recollections of Printing

I have only four early recollections directly associated with the act of printing or print shops, two of which took place in Oakland, California, during World War II. The first is a vague memory of having produced numerous hectographic codebooks for my brothers and fellow "secret agents" on a spirit duplicator.

The second – which also ranks among my earliest erotic memories – is the smell of printing ink. I was in the habit of scrounging through the trash bins behind a neighborhood print shop, looking for offcuts of paper and discarded cans of ink. One day the printer caught me red-handed. When I finished explaining why I wanted the paper, he said, "Come on inside, kid." I obediently followed him into the dark, mysterious pressroom, where the smell of ink was so overpowering that I had what I realized years later was an orgasm. The very accommodating printer gave me as much paper as I could carry and continued to furnish me with an endless supply of offcuts. It is no wonder that I've always lusted after printers.

A small rubber-stamp printing kit I had received as a birthday present was the third. I used it to print tickets for my backyard marionette shows in Sacramento in the mid-forties.

The last is of an incident that occurred in the summer of 1949, after I graduated from high school, in the architectural office of one of my father's associates. One of the chores I performed there was to feed huge sheets of paper into a blueprint machine. Floating the paper into position and then retrieving it as it completed its cycle brought back vivid and tantalizing memories of the pre-adolescent eroticism I had experienced in the print shop in Oakland.

I had a premonition of the erotic attraction that printing would later hold for me: the intoxication of the ink and the sensuous touch of the paper, and, much later in Verona, of fastening the dampened sheets to the tympan, inking the form with a handheld roller, and pulling the bar to make the impression – the tactile manual labor associated with operating a handpress.

In my youth I never really seriously considered becoming a printer, but once I became one I couldn't imagine myself engaged otherwise. All of this amounts to a meager anecdotal beginning for someone whose professional career would primarily be identified with the craft of fine printing.

An Early Interest in Theater

While still a junior high school student, I turned one of our garages into a marionette theater. I worked alone because I couldn't find anyone among my peers who shared my enthusiasm for puppets. It was truly a one-kid operation. I made all the puppets, including their costumes, and constructed the sets for these backyard entertainments, which I also wrote. Since I played all the parts, I would often have to juggle two or three marionettes at the same time – trying to keep one hand free to run the music cues on an old wind-up Victrola.

My interest in puppets had been sparked in the summer of 1946 during a family vacation to Laguna Beach, California, where I saw several shows performed by a professional company of traveling puppeteers. I wrote to Robert Gray, the company's director, saying that I would like to join his troupe and was free to wander the country with him – the troupe members traveled together in a station wagon. Much to my surprise, he accepted me as an apprentice, but withdrew the offer upon discovering that I was only fifteen years old. Undaunted by Gray's unreasonable rejection, I continued producing my own marionette shows until I left Sacramento to attend college.

The theater was my first love – not acting in it, but designing for it. My only acting experience was playing Biondello, a servant in Shakespeare's *The Taming of the Shrew*, put on by the seniors in my high school in June 1949. Even though I was a cutup during rehearsals, when we performed the play, I couldn't deliver my few lines without stammering.

Theater at Syracuse University

I attended Syracuse University in upstate New York during the academic year 1949–1950. I chose it because of its art and theater departments and because I had fallen in love with the photograph of Crouse College on the

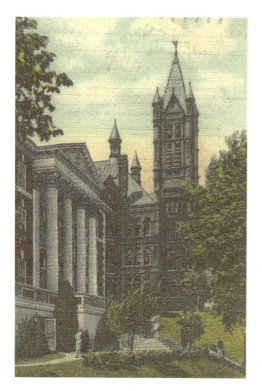

Vintage postcard of Crouse College, Syracuse University, Syracuse, NY, date unknown. (Photographer unknown.)

Left to right: Richard with Bob Prach and Bob Kelly at Skytop, the freshmen dorm at Syracuse University, Syracuse, NY, 1949. (Photographer unknown, courtesy of PWP Archives.)

A Prelude to Printing: Before New York 9

cover of the catalog. Inspired by the grandeur of the French Renaissance, this magnificent structure is a fine example of nineteenth-century American architecture; it also housed the art department. Another factor in selecting Syracuse was its location. It was about as far away from home as a rebellious youth from California could go without leaving the country. Even though my parents indulged me, I was anxious to take my first steps toward independence. In retrospect, I should have gone to Carnegie Institute of Technology (now Carnegie Mellon University) or Yale, both of which had better set and costume design curriculums.

During my first semester at Syracuse, I took a required figure drawing class. It was the first time I had ever seen a naked woman. I was very nervous about the class and deliberately went early so I could settle in before the other students arrived. However, I went to the wrong classroom. When I finally did arrive at my assigned section, the class had already started. I opened the door, and as I came around the screen that shielded the model from the hallway, I came face-to-face with Cora, the model, looking at me from between her legs. I dropped my art gear and nearly fainted. She sensed that I was shy, so during her break, Cora, with a loose Japanese silk kimono barely covering her nakedness, came over to look at my sketch. She took my chin in her hand and said, "Aren't you kind of young to be drawing pictures of naked women?" On top of everything else, the instructor, Maurice Douek, kept yelling at me, "You need to look at the model if you are going to draw her."

The Children's Theatre

I had been at Syracuse for only a couple of weeks when I saw an article in the school paper about the Syracuse University Children's Theatre. The article mentioned that the theater was recruiting teachers and production assistants, so I went down to the Boar's Head Playhouse, the venue for student productions, to volunteer my services. By early October I was teaching children how to make marionettes, and together we wrote a short play about Rumpelstiltskin, which was performed for the children's families and friends.

I must have been the only applicant for the production assistant position because a few days after my interview I received a call from Stanley Raiff, a fellow student and director of the Children's Theatre, offering me a job as the theater's technical director. At first I was quite elated by his offer, but

One of Richard's costume sketches for *The Little Princess*, Syracuse, NY, 1950. (Courtesy of the University of Utah.)

Richard's lion costume for *Androcles and the Lion*, New York, NY, 1963. (Photographer unknown, courtesy of PWP Archives.)

A Prelude to Printing: Before New York

11

back in my dorm room, when I realized I would be working in the real world of make-believe, I began to have second thoughts about accepting the position. After all, my only experience in the theater consisted of my marionette shows and a few plays and variety shows I had worked on during two semesters of scene shop in high school. Having never been one to be intimidated by lack of experience, I accepted his offer.

My first assignment was to design a new production of *The Wizard of Oz* adapted by Stan. Starting in mid-November, I designed dozens of costumes, which, fortunately for me, the mothers of the child actors were asked to make. I was so inexperienced as a set designer that during the opening performance, when Dorothy ran into the house and slammed the door behind her, the set fell over, coming to rest in a cloud of dust on the apron of the stage. All the kids in the audience loved it; they thought a twister was actually blowing the house away. Until I learned how to secure the cutout trees with stage braces, I had to position some of the stagehands behind the trees to hold them up.

I hovered in the wings, ready to yank any stage-frightened child off the set. Just as the curtain was about to open, one or two of them would invariably start to pee, with blue dye from their muslin and crêpe paper Munchkin costumes running down their legs. Nevertheless, three succesful performances of the play were given in mid-February 1950.

In May 1950, I also designed the sets and costumes for another Children's Theatre production, *The Little Princess* by Frances Hodgson Burnett. Much later in 1963, I designed and made the set and costumes for another of Stan's productions for children: the off-Broadway staging of Aurand Harris's *Androcles and the Lion*, done in the style of the commedia dell'arte.

Theater at the University of California

After a year at Syracuse with its deep snows and freezing temperatures, I moved back to sunny California and enrolled at the University of California at Berkeley in the fall of 1950, where I remained on and off through the spring of 1954. Even though I was an English major, I found time in my last year to design sets and costumes for plays produced by the Department of Dramatic Art in the Studio Theater. These included *The Affected Ladies* by Molière in November 1953 and *A Phoenix Too Frequent* by Christopher Fry in March and April 1954.

Richard's set and costumes for *A Phoenix Too Frequent*, Berkeley, CA, 1954. (Photo by Richard Capp, courtesy of PWP Archives.)

My fascination with the theater never completely waned. In the summer of 1956, I designed sets and costumes for Leonard Altobell's Litchfield Summer Theatre in Connecticut. And then in February and March of 1960, I designed sets for Richard Charlton's Sombrero Playhouse in Phoenix, Arizona. This was a star-studded experience, with such stage luminaries as Helen Hayes, Fay Bainter, Faye Emerson, Wendell Corey, Jerome Cowan, June Havoc, Hugh Marlowe, Kathryn Grayson, and David Poleri. After six productions, I resigned. Even though my designs were well received – one reviewer said, "The silent star of the show was the magnificent set" – I couldn't take the emotional stress of sixteen-hour days and unrealistic expectations for a new theatrical extravaganza every seven days.

An Interlude

As early as the spring of 1951, I had become a full-fledged "bohemian." I was frequently seen on and off campus dressed in an assortment of weird outfits that included an orange sailor suit and purple gauze cape – often barefoot with flowers in my hair. During my first year at Berkeley, I was trying to "find" myself, answer questions about my sexuality, and determine what I wanted to do with the rest of my life. My mother and father thought I was not getting the college education they were paying for. They terminated my allowance, and I

A Prelude to Printing: Before New York

left the University of California in June 1951. I decamped to my parents' home in Sacramento to be tamed. I was bored. The situation was further aggravated by my ambivalence about my sexual orientation, which was continually being put to the test. I couldn't stand it at home any longer, so I enlisted in the U.S. Navy on June 26 and was promptly sent to San Diego, California – where I would prove my manhood. But after a battery of psychological tests, the Navy decided that I would not survive the rigors and pressures of military life, and so I returned home, this time in quasi-disgrace.

How right the Navy was. I should have known myself when I stepped on that bus to San Diego with a copy of Gertrude Stein's *Four Saints in Three Acts* (1934) and a postcard of a print from Picasso's *Metamorphosis*, that I wasn't Navy material.

Before leaving for the Navy, I went to see my old Berkeley girlfriend, Tracy. We had been in Thomas Parkinson's English 41B class. I loved looking at her. She had a long thin neck, exposed on all sides by her very short hair. When she heard I had enlisted, she asked me to come by her place, where she told me we should have sex. I was too nervous to get an erection despite her efforts. Later that evening we went over to San Francisco to the hungry i, which at that time was located in the basement of the Columbus Tower in North Beach. She regaled her lesbian friends, describing in great detail my failure. They looked across the room and laughed at me as I sat alone, leaning against the wall, drinking a ginger beer. I was so angry that I wanted to whip out my penis and jerk off in front of them, but it was still uncooperative.

Running Away

I tried living in Sacramento with my parents again, but it didn't work out. I was very unhappy so I ran away from home without telling anyone where I was going. One night in early January 1952, I ran into an old friend, Harrison Starr, a film buff, at a drinking party in Berkeley. Half joking, he suggested that I join the Merchant Marine. The next day, we drove over to San Francisco so I could enlist, only to find the office closed due to a longshoremen's strike. Before returning to Berkeley, we decided to call on Isabel Freud, a mutual friend from our university days. She told me I could stay with her at 554 Lombard Street until the strike was over. A few days later, I moved in with Isabel, but the longshoremen's strike showed no signs of being settled soon. As the

Isabel Freud and Richard, Santa Rosa, CA, 1963. (Photographer unknown, courtesy of PWP Archives.)

weeks turned into months, a warm and affectionate sibling-like relationship developed between Isabel and me. We became almost inseparable.

But my life didn't have any direction, so I decided to look for a job. By now I had traded in my assortment of weird Berkeley outfits for a wardrobe of somber black clothes; white tennis shoes were the only concession I made to nonconformity. Having no real qualifications I found a job shaving Dictaphone cylinders at the Family and Children's Agency, which was housed in a beautiful Bernard Maybeck building on Gough Street. I worked there through the first week in February.

In the fall of 1952 Isabel started seeing a steady boyfriend, so I moved out and into a series of rooming and boarding houses. With the exception of one on Nob Hill, each one was more depressing and degrading than the previous. I spent my free time going to movies and painting a series of imaginary portraits in oils. I also painted portraits of Isabel and Wanda Rose Christiansen, a young woman I worked with at the Family and Children's Agency. Wanda Rose gave me twenty dollars for her portrait.

A Prelude to Printing: Before New York 15

Jack Werner Stauffacher at his Greenwood Press, San Francisco, CA, 1949. (Photographer unknown, courtesy of Jack Werner Stauffacher.)

Greenwood Press

Harrison also introduced me to Brandt Sloane, an Englishman, who was starting a new film society called the Kinesis Group in San Francisco. It was through this society that I met Jack Werner Stauffacher, who printed the first program for the society at his Greenwood Press. Being a film enthusiast, I spent a lot of time helping out at Kinesis.

Jack took me under his wing, treating me like a kid brother. I found myself spending more and more of my free time with the Stauffachers. I would often babysit for them, or Jack would let me tag along to some film event. Some of the most memorable excursions were visits to Jean Varda's barge across the Golden Gate Bridge in Sausalito, where the Greek-born artist hosted what I thought at the time were wild parties. This was a time of great disillusionment for me. I discovered at Varda's that many of my literary heroes were quite fallible. Dylan Thomas really did drink himself blind in public.

I have always associated personal printing and publishing with Jack's Greenwood Press, which represented to me a perfect balance between a private and a commercial press. His shop, with its cozy corner filled with books and memorabilia, was a social and intellectual meeting place where some of my favorite authors at the time, such as Kenneth Patchen, would just drop in, and where Jack could become emotional – without feeling self-conscious – when talking about the shape of a comma or a capital "J." He introduced me to the music of Gustav Mahler and the novels of Hermann Hesse, both of whom were discussed as casually as the small talk indulged in by others in more mundane settings. But most importantly, it was where the act of printing gave me a tremendous physical and intellectual sense of well-being. Feeling so strongly about the Greenwood Press, it's surprising I never helped Jack print. Perhaps I was intimidated by his orderly shop and his gigantic Victoria platen press. Even so, there always seemed to be time to stop and talk, have a glass of wine, or go see a film together.

My First Trip to Mexico

In the summer of 1952, Kenneth Pettitt, a fellow student at the University of California, wrote to me from Mexico City describing how exciting it was to live in a foreign country. He had met many expatriate writers, and was sure I would fit right in. Since I had vacation time due from the Family and Children's Agency, I decided to use it for a trip to Mexico City.

Before my departure in October, Isabel and I decided to commemorate the occasion with a cake. We both loved white wedding cake, and so I ordered one from a very charming neighborhood bakery run by two elderly spinsters. First I picked out a small cake; it was to be an intimate wedding. Then I selected a bride and groom to go on top of the cake. One of the spinsters suggested a few words on the cake might be appropriate. George Starbuck, the poet, had been one of my housemates in Berkeley in the spring of 1951. He was known as a skirt-chaser and reputed to sing the refrain from Woody Guthrie's song "So Long, It's Been Good to Know Yuh" after seducing a girl. I requested these words for the cake. Giving me a dirty look, both ladies gasped, "You must be kidding." "No," I said, "I am quite serious." "Well, in that case, you will have to pay for the cake in advance." "Of course. I came prepared to do so." As I turned to leave, I said, "On second thought, leave the groom off the cake." When I came back to retrieve the cake, both ladies gave me a very cold stare. When I

A Prelude to Printing: Before New York

reached Isabel's and opened the box, the groom was in a small cellophane bag next to the cake.

Upon my return from Mexico in November, I moved to Berkeley. In the spring of 1953, I enrolled again at the University of California to continue my studies, which came to an abrupt end in the spring of 1954 when I was expelled from the university for perpetrating a hoax in *Occident*, the student literary magazine.

Exiled in Santa Rosa and a Second Trip to Mexico

I returned to my family, who had moved to Santa Rosa, California, staying with them until October 1955, except for four months away in Mexico in the fall of 1954.

When I first moved to Santa Rosa, I did a lot of heavy, late-night drinking in a bar that had been one of Jack London's hangouts. I drank straight Scotch and never spoke to anyone. One night my father invited me to go with him for a drink at London's old bar; he had heard from his drinking buddies about an eccentric character and thought we might check him out. I found some excuse to decline his invitation and never went back to that bar again because I didn't want to embarrass my father.

After a few months living at home, I found a rundown penthouse apartment on the roof of an old bank building next door to Corrick's, a stationery/gift store where I worked as a window dresser. The apartment was huge, but I only occupied the front room, kitchen, and bath. A thick mat on the floor served as both a bed and sofa. The only other piece of furniture was a low table with a couple of cushions around it.

I had a terrible crush on Tom Lofgren, one of my co-workers at Corrick's. He was a very shy young man with pale, Nordic blond hair and deep-set eyes. He lived with his widowed father. I never met his father, but apparently he was very high maintenance. Tom loved Beethoven string quartets and brought recordings of them over to my place so we could listen to them together on my stereo. I would fix a nice dinner, and then we sat on the mat with our backs to the wall, lost in a world of our own as the music filled the room. We often held hands or intertwined our arms. I wanted to lean over and kiss him, but I was afraid he would reject me, perhaps never talk to me again. A few years later my mother wrote to tell me that Tom committed suicide, leaving his father to look after himself.

A Brief Return to Berkeley

By early October 1955 I was sharing an apartment at 2317 Virginia Street in Berkeley with my brother Robert. We gave a New Year's Eve party. At midnight, Robert grabbed my girlfriend Carmelita and began kissing her passionately. I was so distraught that I rushed out of the apartment and wandered round in the Berkeley hills until dawn.

I am not sure where Carmelita and I met. She was a journalism major. Since I was still very shy around girls, our relationship was quite chaste, although I always mustered enough presence of mind to kiss her goodnight after our dates. She was very beautiful; her mother was Mexican and her father Basque. She went to New York around the same time I did, where she was an intern at *Mademoiselle* magazine.

Jack Pooler

Even though I thought of Carmelita as my girlfriend, at the same time I began a passionate and sexually active affair with Jack Pooler. I had first met him in the fall of 1953 when he was still a library school student working in the same section that I was. We immediately became close friends.

On my return to Berkeley, Jack found me a job in the stockroom at Fraser's, a high-end retail store in Berkeley. I helped him dress the windows for Christmas, suggesting that we spray the trees green. The trees were decorated with only green balls attached with green ribbons. They were the perfect foil for the Christmas merchandise.

Jack Pooler, Palo Alto, CA , 1964. (Photographer unknown, courtesy of Jack Pooler.)

A Prelude to Printing: Before New York

Jack was the most refined young person I had met up to that time. His taste was impeccable. From him, I learned to relax while making love.

Getting Out of Town

Once I had calmed down after the New Year's Eve fiasco, I decided to leave Berkeley and try my luck again as a set and costume designer, hoping to find work in one of the numerous summer stock theaters on the East Coast. One night at Terrence O'Flaherty's house in San Francisco, I told him about my determination to go east. Terry, the TV critic for the *San Francisco Chronicle*, knew everyone. If I planned to go through New Orleans, he would ask his friend Lucius Beebe, the travel writer and train historian, to give me a lift to New York on the *Virginia City*, Beebe's private, turn-of-the-century railway car.

Early in February 1956 I stuck out my thumb and started hitchhiking east. Even though I had been terrified of sex as a student, I didn't hesitate to have impersonal sex along the way as long as I wasn't obliged to climax. I would do anything that would get me closer to Phoenix, El Paso, New Orleans, and eventually New York.

New Orleans

I arrived in New Orleans on February 13, the day before Mardi Gras, and went directly to the train station to meet up with Beebe. When he opened the train car door to greet me, his dog – a Great Dane – leaped down, knocking me off my feet. Beebe was very apologetic. His partner, Charles Clegg, corralled the dog, but I was still shaken and refused to climb aboard. I could hear the animal prowling around inside. I made up some excuse as to why I couldn't accept his generous offer, knowing I had probably forfeited the adventure of a lifetime. I called my parents and explained what had happened. They agreed to wire me the bus fare to New York.

In the meantime, for some unknown reason, I decided to look for a job as a dishwasher. I sat down on a bench in front of the train station and perused the help-wanted ads. Not knowing New Orleans, I didn't have the faintest idea where these jobs were located. A handsome young Nicaraguan approached me, and I asked him in Spanish where a certain street was. "*Muy lejos*," he said. When I told him I was looking for a job until my parents' money arrived, he told me it would be impossible to find one for just a few days. He suggested that I go home with him. I could stay at his house as long as I wanted. He lived in one of those buildings near Elysian Fields. It was like a scene out of Tennessee Williams's *A Streetcar Named Desire*. The fellow left me with his mother, and I never saw him again. She made up a comfortable bed for me and fed me. With nothing to do but wait, I wandered around the French Quarter, trying to immerse myself in the Mardi Gras festivities, but New Orleans depressed me; I was broke, and to make things worse, it rained most of the time.

I used to tell people I took a green crêpe paper costume (a weeping willow tree) in a brown paper bag with me to New Orleans for Mardi Gras, and that I changed into it at the Greyhound Bus station. I think I did take a costume with me to New Orleans, but I don't think I ever wore it. After all, I was staying with the Nicaraguan fellow's mother and wouldn't have wanted to make a spectacle of myself in front of her.

A Prelude to Printing: Before New York

Philadelphia Cream Cheese Pie

Serves 8

Isabel Freud wanted to impress Lou Hanson, her boyfriend, with a home-cooked dinner. The problem was she didn't know how to cook. I did all the cooking. While Isabel entertained Lou in the living room, I prepared a dinner culminating with a Philadelphia Cream Cheese Pie – my mother's recipe. When all was ready, I snuck out the backdoor, only to return later as a guest for dessert.

For the crust
   6 ounces Graham cracker crumbs, finely rolled
   ¼ cup sugar
   4 tablespoons unsalted butter, softened

For the filling
   12 ounces Philadelphia Cream Cheese
   ½ cup sugar
   2 large eggs
   1 teaspoon vanilla
      Pinch of salt

For the topping
   8 ounces sour cream
   ⅓ cup sugar
   1 teaspoon vanilla
      Pinch of salt

The crust: Preheat the oven to 350 degrees. Combine all the ingredients. Press the mixture into the bottom and sides of a 9-inch pie pan.

The filling: Cream cheese and sugar. Add eggs one at a time. Add vanilla and salt and blend well. Pour the mixture into unbaked Graham cracker shell. Bake for 30 minutes. Remove from the oven and cool for 5 minutes.

The topping: Cream all the ingredients together. Pour on top of the filling. Bake for 10 minutes. Cool and then place in the refrigerator for at least 8 hours or until very firm.

Richard with a Japanese waitress at a Cherry Blossom festival, Japan, 1957. (Photographer unknown, courtesy of PWP Archives.)

Prelude to Printing: New York and Beyond

A memoir is how one remembers one's own life,
while an autobiography is history.
– Gore Vidal, *Palimpsest*

New York

Shortly after I arrived in New York in late February 1956, I moved in with Ken Wollitz, a college friend who had studied music at Berkeley and had preceded me to New York by only a couple of months. He lived in a $37.50-a-month Greenwich Village walk-up with the bathtub in the kitchen and a communal toilet in the hallway. The place was at 65 Carmine Street, just off Hudson, and sparsely furnished. We slept on a big, floppy mattress on the floor in the back room, snuggling up to keep warm. Without his glasses Ken was almost blind, and like all people with vision problems, he was very tactile. Lying close together, we would kiss and jerk each other off. We took our meals at a low table with sawed-off legs, the only piece of furniture in the front room. We sat on cushions, Japanese style, and consumed a lot of tea while listening to classical music for hours on end, or we strolled through the Village making new friends and drinking Italian coffee at the San Remo, a popular Bohemian hangout on Bleecker Street. I was soon engaged to design sets for a summer stock theater in Litchfield, Connecticut, which was to open on June 16 and run for eleven weeks.

Søren Agenoux

Before leaving for Connecticut I managed to fall in and out of love several times. I soon left Ken in March and moved in with Søren Agenoux, another Berkeley friend and aspiring poet.

Søren was a frail, fair-haired young man with an insatiable appetite for sex. He gave good head, and as we said back then, he loved "to scrape the plaster off the ceiling with his toes." Søren, whose birth name was Frank Hansen, had invented the name "Agenoux," which he claimed meant "on your knees" in French. He thought that I should have a *nom d'artiste*, and renamed me Ruiseart Rath-dorcha, which I used on all my summer stock

Søren Agenoux, New York, NY, 1967. (Photo by Fred W. McDarrah.)

applications. Søren told me the name meant something improbable, like "a boy caught in a tree of night" in Gaelic.

In the meantime I found a job in a small packaging studio and eked out enough money to pay the rent and feed us. One day I came home to find our belongings had either been impounded by the City Marshall or tossed out on the sidewalk, including my model theater, which I was able to rescue. This model theater was essential to my work, because I always made models of the sets I designed. I called it the Faeries' Garden Theatre. It was made of painted balsa wood and was twenty-four inches wide, twelve inches deep, and twenty-four inches high. It had a cardboard drop curtain, which could be lowered and raised, on which I had painted a garden filled with cherubs and fairies. On the back of the curtain I had written the names of friends and acquaintances for each of the fairies. It was also equipped with colored Christmas tree lights, which gave the stage an almost real theatrical glow.

Ecossaise

    for Ruiseart, on April 26, 1956, his birthday

The collars of the trees
Frayed by white nightengales [sic],
                /my hope,
Plaid [sic] to the cross of regret,
    Crack where you pull them off
    To the ground
    On new checkmates.
    Strange hope to be swallowed
    Like a star along with
    A dish of cream . . .
    Longed for to be patient.
    Stay as they will, these trees
    Can only be what they seem.
    Fastened to the landscape,
    Gardening in the
    ground,
    Feathers pushing music
    Around them for sound,
Steeples and knights
And turrets on elephants
Advancing to chants
As in a dream,
Stay as they will,
These trees
Can only be
What they seem.

– Søren

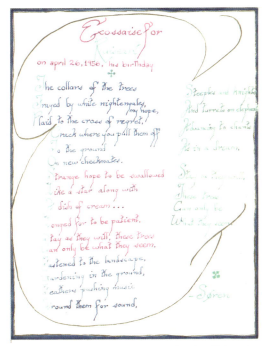

Søren Agenoux's poem for Ruiseart [Richard] (1956).
(Courtesy of PWP Archives.)

It turned out that Søren had not paid the rent, even though I had given him the money for it every month. We had been evicted. For a while we stayed at the Hotel Albert, a cheap residential hotel in Greenwich Village. After that, Julian Beck and Judith Malina let us sleep on the bare stage of their Living Theatre, which was in a loft at Broadway and One-Hundredth Street on the Upper West Side. Because the Department of Buildings had closed the theater, it was empty and the electricity had been turned off, so we slept surrounded by candles. I eagerly looked forward to returning to New York because Julian and I had discussed the possibility of my designing sets and costumes for The Living Theatre later that fall.

Søren knew many writers in New York, so we would occasionally see Edward Albee or join Allen Ginsberg with his friends in a coffee shop on the Upper West Side. It was wonderfully invigorating to be with people around my own age who spent hours talking about or reading poetry. I felt that I had nothing to contribute to the conversation since my poetry was so timid and without the energy or dynamics of theirs.

Ginsberg and I met again at Tom and Ariel Parkinson's in Hampstead, London, in August 1958. He came into the living room dressed only in white Jockey shorts and plopped himself down in a large chair. Even though the Parkinsons had already retired, Allen and I continued drinking and talking until quite late. When he got up to go upstairs, I noticed his shorts had unsightly skid marks on them. I was glad he didn't make a pass at me; he wasn't my type. In addition to his deplorable personal hygiene, he was too hairy.

Gordon Fraser

Before I had left for New York, Jack Pooler gave me a letter of introduction to Gladys E. Hares, Gordon Fraser's administrative assistant. They had worked together at Fraser's, a retail store that Gordon had started in Berkeley in 1947. He had studied decorative arts in Germany prior to World War II and was an early champion of the Bauhaus concept of design in the States.

In late February I went to see Gladys at Fraser's Inc., where she introduced me to Gordon, who was now a successful importer of contemporary tablewares. Gordon was in his early forties, very tall and extremely thin with wavy strawberry blond hair. He was an eccentric who carried only crisp, new one-dollar bills in his wallet and emptied his pockets of any loose change each night. Gordon was also a health nut and drank a quart of fresh calves' blood

Prelude to Printing: New York and Beyond

Gordon Fraser near Portofino, Italy, 1960. (Photographer unknown, courtesy of Gordon Fraser.)

every morning before leaving for his office. He must have liked me, because he invited me to come to his apartment for supper that same night, where I met his twenty-three-year-old lover, Philip Baker, a blond cherub from Boston.

Bronchitis

Unaccustomed to cold winters, I came down with a severe case of bronchitis. I wasn't sure how I was going to manage, because I had no one to turn to. In a moment of desperation, I called Gordon. He rescued me and moved me into his apartment overlooking the Hudson River near the Cloisters in Fort Tryon Park. When I first met him, he was investigating the possibility of having a line of dinnerware manufactured in Japan exclusively for his company. To humor me and give me something to occupy my days, in addition to accompanying Philip to the theater, concerts, and museums, Gordon asked me to play around with some ideas for a contemporary line of casual dinnerware. He never tired of saying, "Richard, since you'll always be a Plain Jane, you're going to have to learn to live by your talents." I ended up making hundreds of sketches for him. "Yes, Gordon, I am on my way to living by my talents."

Fraser China designed by Richard in 1956. (Photographer unknown, courtesy of The New York Public Library.)

Fraser China

I arrived at the summer theater in Litchfield the first week in June 1956. Soon after, Gordon showed my designs to Oliver Roberge, the general merchandise manager at Bloomingdale's. He saw great potential in my sketches and was eager to launch the project. Gordon called me at the theater, begging me to cut short the season. He wanted me to fly to Japan at once to work with the ceramic engineers at the Maruichi China factory in Nagoya, so I left Litchfield before designing the sets for the last show. The designs I had done for him, as a whim, had become a reality.

This dinnerware, known commercially as Fraser China, was considered very daring for the mid-fifties: it was the first to remove the metallic bands on Japanese china and became the prototype for all chinaware that combined solid colors with bold geometric patterns that soon flooded the market. I made two trips to Japan, the first in November and December 1956, and the second in March through June 1957. Once there I designed all the shapes, as well as their surface decorations. Before long Fraser China was on the shelves of stores throughout the country. It grossed more than one million dollars in sales the first year.

Prelude to Printing: New York and Beyond

Philip Baker, seated, and Richard in Fort Tryon Park, New York, NY, 1959. (Photo by Rolf Nelson, courtesy of PWP Archives.)

Philip Baker and Me

By June 1956 Philip Baker and I were having more sex together than he was having with Gordon, who was frequently away on business. We continued these trysts well into the sixties. On the other hand I had sex with Gordon only once, in July 1957, when Philip was visiting his family in Boston. Gordon thought we should "do it," but it was very perfunctory.

Philip and I liked to entertain, so we arranged for a private performance of *Miss Chicken Little*, an opera by Alec Wilder, at the Rockland Opera Company in the Old Piermont Methodist Church in Piermont, New York. After the performance, we invited all the singers, musicians, and guests back to Gordon's place for cocktails and a buffet. As I remember Andy Warhol and Harry Partch, who had missed the performance, but came to the party. I had seen Partch's production of Sophocles's *Oedipus the King* at Mills College, in Oakland, California, in 1952. Partch designed all the instruments,

Old Piermont Methodist Church in Piermont, NY, 1959. (Photo by William Rothschild, courtesy of the Nyack Library Local History Room.)

including his famous Cloud Chamber Bowls. The choreography was by Edith Wiener, who was very much influenced by Martha Graham.

Industrial Design

With the success of Fraser China, I established myself as an industrial designer. Many doors opened to me as a result, even though I had no formal training in the field. Before long I was engaged by many of the leading tableware manufacturers throughout the world, most often for factories in Japan, Germany, Sweden, and Italy, where I spent extended periods of time developing new products for the American market.

Industrial design provided me with a new lifestyle and new friends, such as Anthony Strilko, the composer. Tony and I met at a harpsichord recital hosted by Winthrop Kelly Edey in his ersatz Edward Gorey townhouse on West 83rd Street, which was filled with rare antique clocks. Tony groped me, and we left the party to jump into bed at his place on West 79th Street. In the early 1960s Tony and I often exchanged boyfriends and tricks; they were not anemic twinkies or toned hustlers, but well-educated boys who

Prelude to Printing: New York and Beyond

Tony Strilko and Richard, Nantucket, MA, 1964. (Photo by David Kent, courtesy of PWP Archives.)

enjoyed museums, art galleries, the theater, opera, good food and wines, and traveling, as well as having a good time in bed. During this period in New York, for the first time in my life I was surrounded by people who shared my sexual orientation.

Success also meant, among other things, being able to rent a house with Tony on Nantucket Island, Massachusetts, for the summer of 1964. I was working on a new line for Noritake China Company, and Tony was orchestrating Samuel Barber's *Antony and Cleopatra* for its debut at the inauguration of the new Metropolitan Opera House in Lincoln Center. We got up early and worked on our projects until noon, sending the results down to the boat with our houseboy, David Kent. The rest of the day and night was given over to pleasure. Tony wrote a duet for piano and recorder for me. My part consisted mostly of "toot, toot" as he dexterously moved his hands over the keyboard.

Carlos Cárdenas, New York, NY, 1963. (Photo by RPR, courtesy of PWP Archive.)

Carlos Cárdenas

I am also indebted to Kelly for introducing me to Carlos Cárdenas in November 1962. Carlos was the great love of my life. Kelly, with his proclivity for working-class Latinos, took me along with him one night to one of the dancing bars on the Lower West Side where these guys hung out. Carlos was sitting alone at the bar, and I started a conversation in Spanish with him. He asked me to dance, which I did even though I was never a very good dancer. I was smitten instantly. I asked him home, but he said that although he couldn't come with me that night, he would see me the following Saturday.

Even though I never expected him to show up at the bar, he did, and we went directly to my apartment at 315 East 69th Street. We were all over each other before the door was unlocked. We made passionate love that first night. Our bodies just seemed to fit together. One of the poems in *Eight Parting Poems* is dedicated to Carlos.

Carlos was so beautiful. He had the wiry body of an athlete, with slim, delicate fingers and smooth, flawless skin. His only imperfection was his crooked teeth, which were an erotic turn-on for me.

He had learned English very fast. Because of his communication and typing skills, Pan Am employed him in corporate sales. Years later when we were no longer lovers, he came to Verona on extended visits. One of my fantasies about Carlos was that he was my cousin – that his mother had been married to my mother's brother at one time, and I frequently referred to him as my "Cuban cousin."

Avery Russell

Kelly was also responsible for another sexual liaison in the spring of 1963 when he introduced me to Avery Russell, a petite redhead from North Carolina. Avery and I would frequently go out to dinner, take in a movie or a play, and occasionally end up at an Egyptian nightclub with belly dancers. Most often we stopped at an Irish pub near her apartment on West 57th Street for a nightcap. It was in this pub that I learned about the pleasures of Jameson Irish Whiskey.

I would walk Avery home, expecting to stay over, but she usually found an excuse to prevent me from going upstairs, so I would hail a cab and go home to my apartment, usually getting there around three in the morning. I'd crawl into bed, jerk off, and fall asleep. Half an hour later, the doorman would call to ask if it was all right to let my redheaded girlfriend in. Avery would come in, strip, and get into bed. She would try to arouse me, but by then it was too late, so we just slept curled up in each other's arms.

A Last Fling in New York

In 1964 Jack Lowery, an interior designer and one of my professional colleagues, gave a small dinner party for eight: four women and four men, although three of the men were homosexuals. There were two tables of four. Halfway through the multicourse dinner, the gentlemen got up and changed tables. The only guests I remember were Vera, a famous scarf designer, and Arnold Scaasi, the couturier. After walking Vera home Arnold suggested that we go back to his place on Central Park South. We both loved to kiss. In those days I was very flexible in bed, usually doing whatever my partner wanted. I never tired of waking up in Arnold's big bed and seeing Central Park spread out below. I occasionally met Arnold at his showroom, waiting in the small reception area while he directed the staff to sew seed pearls and sequins on gowns for celebrity clients. Then we were off to dinner and another night of sex at his place.

Nagging Compromises

Even though I had all the accoutrements of success, I was very unhappy; the more famous I became as an industrial designer, the more compromises I had to make to keep my designs in the forefront. Insecure about my talent from the beginning, I found myself pandering to the demands of market researchers and sales representatives. I became a successful industrial designer by default, much as I would become a handpress printer years later. By the mid-sixties I had moved from working in the theater and as an industrial designer to exploring printing, first as a hobby, and then as a profession.

Beef Tolstoy

Serves 6

On one of my trips to Tokyo, I discovered a tiny Russian restaurant called Tolstoy. The cook told me he had escaped from Russia during the Revolution and that his father had been Tolstoy's cook at Yasnaya Polyana, where he had created a dish called Beef Tolstoy, claiming it was better than Beef Stroganoff. I must have been very gullible because I believed his story. Tolstoy was a vegetarian toward the end of his life, although that doesn't necessarily rule out the fact that the father of the restaurateur had been a cook for Tolstoy. I left with the following recipe and have it made dozens of times since.

    8 tablespoons unsalted butter, divided
 1½ pounds mushrooms, sliced
 1½ pounds beef tenderloin, thinly sliced across the grain and cut into
        3-inch strips
    Salt and freshly ground black pepper to taste
    Dash freshly grated nutmeg
    6 ounces yellow onion, finely chopped
    3 tablespoons beef broth or dry white wine
    8 ounces sour cream

Melt 2 tablespoons of the butter in a 3-quart sauté pan over medium-high heat. When butter begins to bubble, add half the mushrooms and brown. Transfer them to a bowl and set aside. Repeat with the remaining mushrooms. Melt 1½ tablespoons of the butter in the pan. When butter begins to bubble, add half the meat and quickly brown on one side, then turn over and brown on the other side, sprinkling with salt, pepper, and nutmeg before transferring them to the bowl. Repeat with the remaining meat. Add the remaining tablespoon of butter to the sauté pan. When the butter begins to bubble, add onion and brown until golden. Deglaze the pan with broth or wine and add cream. Stir until cream begins to bubble, then return meat and mushrooms to the pan. Cook on low heat for about 5 minutes, stirring occasionally. Serve on wide noodles or rice.

PLAIN WRAPPER PRESS

Richard in the Andes, Ecuador, 1965. (Photographer unknown, courtesy of PWP Archives.)

Quito, Ecuador

> And identity is funny being yourself is funny as you are never
> yourself or yourself except as you remember yourself
> and then of course you do not believe yourself.
> – Gertrude Stein, *Everybody's Autobiography*

The Devil's First Appearance

I have seen the Devil twice: the first time early in 1965 in New York, when I was abed with fever, and the second, a few years later in Quito, while caught in a lover's embrace. Both times I was sufficiently shaken to take immediate steps to alter my lifestyle.

The first time, I awoke from a deep sleep during a prolonged illness to be confronted by the Devil stealthily coming toward me. One of my neuroses in those days was to leave the bedroom door slightly ajar so the light I left on in the vestibule at the other end of the hall would cast a faint ray of light on the companion single bed closest to the door. The Devil was not in his theatrical red suit; he had no features at all, being more like one of those phantasms in an etching by Goya, a nebulous presence. As I stared in horror, he turned and vanished.

The fever, along with the lights and shadows ever present in New York, even in the darkest of rooms, had everything to do with my hallucination. I know the Devil doesn't exist, but I couldn't convince my psyche. As soon as I was well, I began looking for a way to leave town, to get back in touch with what I perceived as my real self and perhaps to regain a part of that youthful innocence I had lost when I began hitchhiking across the country. I told myself that part of my quest for a reformed way of life demanded that I also do something significant for those less fortunate than myself. I had always felt a little confused and guilty about my comfortable middle-class upbringing.

An Unexpected Opportunity

Shortly after the Devil's visit, my lawyer and business manager, Lee Epstein, told me about an opportunity in Quito with the United States Agency for International Development (USAID), a program under the auspices of the

Alliance for Progress. He mentioned it casually, thinking I might know a colleague who would be interested. I doubt he would have said anything to me about it if he thought for a moment that I might consider it for myself. After all I was one of his brightest stars, and he had a vested interest in keeping me in New York. The Quito project sounded exactly like what I was looking for, and as an added plus, it would enable me to relive the carefree days spent in Mexico – an important time in my life, a time of self-discovery and coming to grips with my sexual identity. For many years I indulged in the fantasy that I had been raised in Mexico; however, the two short trips mentioned earlier were the extent of the time I spent there.

Going to Ecuador would also give me an opportunity to rekindle the fascination I have always had for living a bilingual existence. In addition I wanted to get away from the promiscuous lifestyle and degrading behavior to which I had become accustomed, including sexual favors from travel agents' messenger boys, curtain installers, and liquor and grocery store delivery boys. Such were the perks of being rich and gay in New York in the early sixties.

Once I decided to leave New York, I was faced with the unpleasant tasks of buying back contracts from my clients – and forfeiting all future royalties for the products I had designed – saying goodbye to the people who had worked with me, and trying to convince my friends that I was not crazy. When all was said and done, I was $6,000 in debt, although by November 15, 1966, I had paid it off.

Ecuador and My First House

I arrived in Ecuador on April 1, 1965. Over nine thousand feet high in the Andes, Quito was one of the most beautiful cities I had ever seen, a veritable paradise. The temperature stayed around fifty-five degrees most of the year – high forties in the winter and low sixties in the summer. Before long I was ensconced in a large modern house on the edge of town. The rent was $150 per month, and for an additional $55 I had three servants, including a houseman and a cook, although they didn't last long. They were opportunistic hustlers. During one of my absences, they broke into my locked storeroom and took off with all the alcoholic beverages. A former chef for the President of Ecuador soon replaced them. Though he was an excellent cook, he ignored my menu suggestions, preferring to make his own dishes. We continued this agonizing tug-of-war until I moved into my second house in November.

Quito, Ecuador

Richard's first house in Quito, Ecuador, 1965. (Photo by RPR, courtesy of PWP Archives.)

Early in June I began to renovate the living room. I had the glass ceiling removed to expose the beams and had all the rooms in the house repainted in vibrant colors. Around that time I also hired a couple of men to put in a vegetable garden. My belongings from New York didn't arrive until mid-August, although until then I had the basic government-issued necessities. In the meantime I began to take part in the social and cultural life of the city.

Getting Involved in Quito's Social Life

In June I started playing basketball with some of my Ecuadorean friends on Sunday mornings. One evening, I took some of the guys to a burlesque show from Argentina, which was very disappointing. Only one of the strippers could compare with those I had seen in Chicago and on San Pablo Boulevard in Berkeley in the fifties, strippers like Tempest Storm and Lili St. Cyr. I found it more interesting to watch the men in the audience. They all sat on the edge of their upturned seats to get a better view of the strippers while fondling themselves.

Guillermo Ramos

In addition to everything else, I was having a torrid affair with Guillermo Ramos, a young Ecuadorean I had met in June. He worked in the photographic section of the American Embassy. Our relationship was stormy, full

Guillermo Ramos at a swimming pool near Quito, Ecuador, 1965. (Photo by RPR, courtesy of PWP Archives.)

of deceit, treachery, and thievery. I was always on the verge of a nervous breakdown. Even though the sex was frequent, it was not particularly satisfying. I was very smitten with him and continually forgave his transgressions. I wanted to believe him, even when he lied about owning a farm. We once visited a farm a few hours from Quito that he said was his, but I could easily see the people who worked the farm didn't know him. I had fantasies about retiring in Ecuador and living with Guillermo on this farm, growing our own food, and living the bucolic life.

Winthrop Kelly Edey's Visit

Kelly came for a week in July 1965 after a visit to Lima, Peru. Since I was going to Lima to attend an international trade fair in November, he gave me the names of two of his friends, Carlos Flores-Veloso and Javier Barba-Vera. I visited them a second time on my way to Argentina in July 1966.

The first night Kelly was in Quito, we went to a festival held in front of a magnificent colonial church, La Iglesia de la Compañía de Jesús. There was a huge display of fireworks with numerous three- and four-story towers made

Quito, Ecuador

Winthrop Kelly Edey at his home, New York, NY, 1964. (Photographer unknown, courtesy of Winthrop Kelly Edey.)

out of bamboo wired with rockets and sparklers, by far the most spectacular aspect of the festival. The rockets shot off in all directions, and part of the adventure was dodging or jumping over them. In the square, many young boys made bamboo frames representing bulls and other animals. These, too, were wired with sparklers. The boys zigzagged through the crowd, yelling and screaming. Hot-air tissue paper balloons called *globos* filled the sky.

Work

The slow pace of life in Quito suited my temperament. I immersed myself in my work helping native artisans, mostly Indians, utilize their numerous indigenous skills to produce handicrafts out of traditional materials for a world market. This often meant going to the villages to work directly with them – usually a very pleasurable aspect of my work, since the artisans, who were very poor, would excitedly try anything I suggested. In those days I got around in a beautiful white Triumph Spitfire – which had arrived on August 10. Until that time I used a government-issued jeep. The Spitfire was, I suppose, a bit ostentatious for a mid-level civil servant.

One of the drawbacks of going native – spending the night in a sleeping bag on the floor of a hut or at a volunteer's insect-infested place, bathing in the open air with cold water, and eating meals from local vendors that were so bad I was always afraid the food would kill me – was that I was always sick, constantly plagued and treated for amoebas and parasites. During this period I lost 20 pounds, weighing in at 110.

Richard sitting on the fender of his Triumph Spitfire, on the road to Guayaquil, Ecuador, 1965. (Photo by Guillermo Ramos, courtesy of PWP Archives.)

The Peace Corps

The program relied on Peace Corps volunteers such as Sarah Scattergood to monitor the projects in the field. They were also the paymasters, which occasionally presented some problems. Many of the Peace Corps volunteers set themselves up as "Little Caesars." They distributed the handicraft orders and paid for them on delivery. All of the volunteers seemed to be political extremists, of either left or right. Those on the left were usually associated with agricultural projects and the establishment of cooperatives, those on the right with educational and artisan projects. I always had to spend the first couple of hours after my arrival in a village holding court, listening to the complaints of the artisans against the volunteers. These complaints varied. Perhaps a hat weaver hadn't been given any orders because her husband was a communist, or another had failed to complete an

Quito, Ecuador

Sarah Scattergood with fellow Peace Corps volunteers, Ibarra, Ecuador, 1965. (Photo by RPR, courtesy of PWP Archives.)

earlier order on time because of a sick child. I was much more lenient than the volunteers in such cases and always recommended giving the women another chance.

Even though I received a lot of support from my immediate superior, Ben Bernstein, and believed wholeheartedly in the project, I had a hard time adjusting to the mentality of the Foreign Service. Fortunately, because of my interest in art, music, and literature, I had an entrée into Ecuadorean society with similar tastes. Consequently, I didn't have to rely on the small and mostly dull American community for company.

Soon after moving into my first house, I began dashing from one party to the next. Two girls from the American Embassy threw big drinking parties almost every weekend. I went a couple of times, but soon tired of the company, mostly young secretaries and single men. Most of the men were old "aunties" in their forties or older.

In May 1965 there was talk of an amateur production of *Guys and Dolls*, for which I was asked to design the sets and costumes. Fortunately nothing came of this project because it would have been a great distraction from my work. Also in May I went to a cocktail party honoring Galo Plaza Lasso, the former president of Ecuador. I carried his calling card in my wallet until I left Quito. When caught speeding late at night, I pulled it out and told the policeman to call the person on the card. Instead of calling Plaza Lasso, the

Hat weavers, Sigsig, Ecuador, 1965. (Photo by RPR, courtesy of PWP Archives.)

policeman would return the card and send me on my way, recommending that I drive more slowly in the future.

In addition to the cocktail and dinner parties, often in the homes of Ecuadoreans or European diplomats, there were musical *soirées*. In June I attended a performance of a concerto for two pianos by Alberto Ginastera at the Argentine Embassy and an evening of jazz at the German Embassy.

The Art Scene

I especially enjoyed visiting Wilson Hallo Granja at his Galería Siglo XX. That summer I bought a magnificent Enrique Tábara painting from him. In October 1965 I opened my house for a private showing of three-dimensional assemblages by the Columbian artist Hernando Tejada, which was attended by members of the diplomatic corps, including the American ambassador, Wimberley Coerr, and his wife, along with several prominent Ecuadoreans.

Calle Las Casas

By November I got tired of haggling with my landlord about needed repairs and moved into a charming colonial-style house owned by the Ecuadorean ambassador to Sweden. This house, on Calle Las Casas, had a music room into which the sun poured every afternoon. I painted it mustard yellow. I redecorated the dining room too, painting the ceiling mauve and wall-

Quito, Ecuador

papering the walls with the foil linings of cigarette packages I purchased from shoeshine boys.

Domestic Help

The trials and tribulations caused by domestic help were a favorite topic of conversation at most diplomatic gatherings. One evening, also early in November, at the house of the Mexican ambassador, when I casually complimented his wife on the delicious meal, she began to recount the sad story of Anita Carrión, her cook. Apparently, Anita's husband, Ricardo Fabara, worked at the Panamanian Embassy, so the two had to live apart, rarely seeing each other or their children, who were with relatives in the country. The ambassador's wife said she would do anything to reunite Anita's family. I boldly suggested that they could both work for me because there was a small servant's cottage behind the backyard. So before long Anita, Ricardo, their children, and their servants arrived to look after me. Their indulgence allowed me to live the life of a gentleman, and later, toward the end of my stay in Quito, with their help I was able to finish printing *Eight Parting Poems*.

The Devil's Second Appearance

The second time I saw the Devil was in November. I was sitting in the living room with Guillermo. Anita and Ricardo had retired for the night. The only illumination in the room came from a fire in the fireplace and a few candles. As we embraced I looked toward the arched entry into the vestibule, and let out a little gasp. Guillermo asked, *"¿Qué pasa? Parece que viste al Diablo."* Well, he was right; I had just seen the Devil. The same nebulous presence that had visited me in New York was now stalking me in Quito.

In those days I had a naive theory that the Devil could not take a soul if his intended victim was looking directly at him. "He takes us when we least expect him, when we are caught off guard," I used to say. I felt that I had been spared a second time, but I didn't want to press my luck. If I were going to do something to save my soul, I had to act quickly and decisively.

An Unexpected Tryst

Many people not connected with the government visited Quito, and it was possible to occasionally have a fling with one or another of them, echoing my promiscuous lifestyle in New York.

One night at a party early in November 1965, I met a man in his early forties who was an auditor with the Chase Bank. He kept maneuvering me into a corner, and as we drank and talked, he very causally, slyly groped me. Finally, he said, "Let's go to your place and fuck." And we did. We got together a few more times while he was still in Quito. Knowing that I would soon be in Lima around the same time that he would, he gave me the bank's address.

When I got to Lima, I went to the Chase Bank and asked for him. He had been delayed. They were very surprised to hear that he was due there, since his arrivals were always kept secret. I decided it would not be judicious to seek him out again.

Allen Tate

My first guest from the States at Calle Las Casas was Allen Tate – the artist, not the poet. He was a New York friend of many years, originally from Alabama, who taught at the Parsons School of Design. He arrived on December 18, 1965, and left shortly after New Year's. While he was in Ecuador,

Allen Tate, Hugo García, and an unidentified boy at a market in Ambato, Ecuador, 1965. (Photo by RPR, courtesy of PWP Archives.)

Quito, Ecuador 49

we traveled to the Equator Monument, where he sat on the steps with one foot in the Northern Hemisphere and the other in the Southern. With Hugo García, a Cuban seminarian I had befriended in the fall, we also visited several native markets where Allen bought crafts from the local artisans. We met up with Guillermo in Guayaquil for a few days of sun and seafood. Allen was later to illustrate *1945–1965: An Evaluation of Two Decades of Self-Deception*.

Entertaining at Calle Las Casas

I gave a costume party on January 5, 1966. Four of the guests, including the architect/sculptor Milton Barragán and his wife Jocelyn, and Edward Morrow Jr. and his wife Barbara, came dressed as the Beatles. Another evening I hosted a pre-concert dinner party for a group of us that were going to attend a performance of the National Symphony of Chile. As the hour for the concert drew closer, I worried about arriving late and mentioned my concern to one of the other guests. She reminded me that there was nothing to worry about; the conductor was at the table with us. So many diplomatic and church leaders were frequent guests at my house that it was rumored I was really a CIA agent.

The Temptation of Catholicism

For some time, I had toyed with the idea of giving up the secular life altogether and pursuing a contemplative one. I had read Thomas Merton's books in the early fifties and was drawn to the mystical and bucolic life of the Trappist monks he described, perhaps only romantically then – certainly never considering the church as a vocation. But after the Devil's second visit, a life of contemplation seemed like a viable *modus vivendi* for achieving the salvation of my soul. In January I wrote to several friends that I was thinking about entering a monastery in Spain.

Both my paternal grandfather and great-grandfather had been moderators of the Quaker church. My own father, though a man of high moral principles, had been something of a rake in his youth, turning his back on organized religion. Even after he married and settled down, he did not return to the fold, although his children regularly attended the neighborhood Presbyterian Church. I suppose I was also subconsciously attracted to the Catholic Church in part by its ritualistic "theater," but the decisive factor was the miracle of the mass, the Holy Communion.

Baptism

On April 9, 1966, during the Easter Vigil on Holy Saturday in the Santa Iglesia Catedral de Quito, Pablo Muñoz-Vega, the coadjutor archbishop of Quito, baptized and received me into the Roman Catholic Church. I took my seat on the altar dais with a young boy who was also being baptized that night. All the lights in the church were turned off. Then from the rear of the church, Muñoz-Vega, holding a lighted candle, approached the altar with his bishops. He lit the candles of his bishops and mounted the dais. He motioned for me to come to him and lit my candle, and I, in turn, began to light other candles, and soon everyone in the church was holding a lighted candle. The young boy and I approached the baptismal font. Muñoz-Vega poured water over my head. Then he placed a white tunic on me and anointed my head with oil. During the Holy Communion, because I was an adult, I drank from the chalice after Muñoz-Vega. With the singing of the "Gloria," all the church bells in Quito began to ring. Following the Mass we went into the sacristy; the ceremony had been so beautiful and highly emotional for me, I began to cry. Muñoz-Vega embraced me. He said, "Do not cry, you should be happy; we are for you."

Unidentified seminarian, Richard, and Hugo García in the front garden of the house on Calle Las Casas, Quito, Ecuador, 1965. (Photo by Allen Tate, courtesy of PWP Archives.)

Quito, Ecuador

Curiously, I incorrectly printed the month as March instead of April on the little baptismal announcement I sent out to commemorate the occasion. It was set in Weiss Italic on Strathmore Grande paper, which I had cut from a promotional folder I had designed while still in New York.

One result of my conversion was a dramatic change in my social life. I broke off the affair I had been having since February with Marta, a married Ecuadorean woman who was always leaving jewelry and intimate apparel strewn about my bedroom. Anita would return Marta's jewelry, but refused to touch her lingerie. I would have to return it to her myself.

New Friends

I started to develop new friendships, mostly with a number of seminarians I had met through Hugo. I enjoyed the chaste company of these seminarians, and more importantly, I decided to join them in a life devoted to God by presenting myself to a Trappist monastery in Argentina that I had read about in *Jubilee*, a Catholic lay magazine.

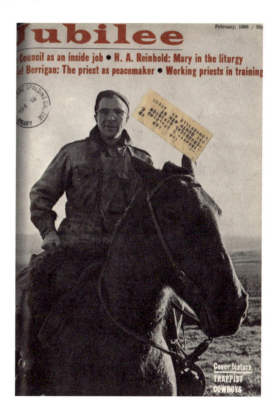

Cover of *Jubilee*, February 1966. (Photo by William E. Barksdale.)

However, old habits die slowly, and I would sometimes cruise the streets of Quito late at night with Hugo, the *padrecito*, picking up young boys who wanted to take a ride in a luxury sports car in exchange for sexual favors.

Quito, Ecuador

Ceviche de Pescado
Raw Fish Appetizer

Serves 6

On November 18, 1965, while still lovers, Guillermo and I drove down to Guayaquil, a port city, where we planned to fish in the Pacific Ocean and camp out on the beach for twelve days. I had borrowed camping equipment from Wimberley Coerr. We went out early in the morning with the local fishermen in their small boats, usually catching white sea bass. We would keep one for ourselves and give the rest to the crew. For dinner, we dug a shallow hole in the sand and make a small fire. Once the coals were red, we put the fish, wrapped in banana leaves, on top of the coals and cover everything with sand.

Sometimes the fishermen made ceviche and gave us a plastic bag of it to eat later. I have eaten ceviche in Ecuador, Peru, Chile, and Argentina, but my favorite is this simple recipe made by Ecuadorean fishermen. Ceviche can be made from any firm white fish, as well as other seafood, such as shrimp, squid, and scallops.

1½ pounds white sea bass, cut in bite-size pieces
1½ cups bitter Seville orange or Key lime juice
2 large garlic cloves, finely chopped
2 fresh ajíes amarillos (yellow chiles), seeded and finely chopped
½ teaspoon sea salt
⅛ teaspoon white pepper
1 red onion (about 9 ounces), thinly sliced
½ cup cilantro, finely chopped

Soak fish in a large bowl in lightly salted water. Cover and let stand for 1 hour in the refrigerator. Drain fish and pat dry with paper towels. Return fish to the bowl and add juice, garlic, chiles, salt, and pepper. Cover with plastic wrap and put in a cool place for 4½ hours, stirring from time to time. Store in the refrigerator for an hour before serving. Drain fish. And add onion and cilantro and lightly toss. Serve in cocktail glasses.

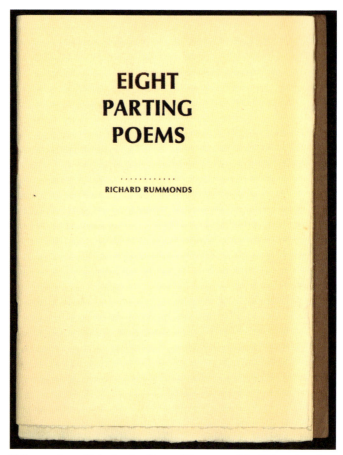

Title page from *Eight Parting Poems*. (Courtesy of the University of Oregon Libraries.)

Item 1. *Eight Parting Poems*

An introduction, seven poems in English,
and a Spanish translation of Sara Teasdale's poem
"When I Am Not with You" by Richard Rummonds.
16 pages. 20 x 14.5 cm. 35 copies. 1966.

Assembling My Equipment

Just before I moved to Quito, I had bought my first printing press, a vertical-platen Superior press with an inside chase measurement of 6½ x 10 inches, and enough accessories from the American Printing Equipment & Supply Company to set up shop. I did all this with the intention of printing just a few pieces of ephemera for my own amusement.

Purchasing Type

As an industrial designer I was always looking for ways to become more physically involved in the production of my graphic designs. Beginning in 1960 I started buying single fonts of European foundry type, mostly from Bauer Alphabets and Amsterdam Continental Types. Just for the pleasure of handling type, I frequently set a letterhead, albeit in a rather primitive way, since I had no type stick or spacing materials of my own. I would give

Superior Press from the Craftsmen Machinery Catalog (1955). (Courtesy of the University of Utah.)

my composition to a job printer, who added the word and line spaces. He then printed directly from my type or used it to pull proofs for offset plates.

In June 1961 the Phoenix Art Museum mounted an exhibition of stationery I had designed between 1956 and 1961. The catalog referred to me as a *graphiker*, the German term for graphic designer.

Arrival of the Press

The press arrived in Quito in mid-August 1965, shipped courtesy of the U.S. Government along with most of my other personal effects. I was so distracted by the newness of my surroundings and getting adjusted to the challenges of the new job that the press was left unused, sitting in a box on the floor in the corner of a spare bedroom in my first house.

Mario Léon

Shortly after I arrived in Quito, I developed a crush on Mario Léon, a young Ecuadorean poet married to an American woman. We spent many late nights in low-life bars and clubs, carousing, drinking, and talking about poetry. Mario was a tease. He would often whisper in my ear, adding little kisses or putting his hand high up on the inside of my thigh almost touching my crotch.

One night he took off his wedding ring, putting it under a napkin; he didn't want any of the girls in the bar to know he was married. I retrieved the ring and slipped it into my pocket. Even though I saw him frantically looking for it, I didn't say a word. The next night, after having had a lot to drink, I returned the ring to him. He was so relieved that he gave me a big kiss on the lips. At that point, he was so drunk and delirious that he didn't know what he was doing.

Earlier that summer, even before the press was operative, I wrote to friends in New York and Copenhagen that I was planning to print two projects with Mario on my little press. I sometimes got together with a few young artists who were forming a "group," for which Mario was writing a manifesto. With two other Ecuadoreans, Mario and I also discussed starting a little magazine, which we would print on my press. Fortunately, he moved to California with his wife before anything could be finalized. Only after I started printing *Eight Parting Poems* – one of the poems in this keepsake is dedicated to Mario – did I realize how impractical it would have been to print a magazine on the Superior press.

Item 1. Eight Parting Poems 57

Getting Ready to Print

On September 15, 1965, I wrote to Lee Epstein, my former lawyer, that I still had not started to print. Some of the fonts of type had arrived as they had come from the factory, still tied with string in paper wrappers; however, much of it had arrived "pied," the typographic term for loose, mixed up type. I also mentioned that it would take ages to get the type sorted before I could use it. Eventually, I was able to distribute all the type into small plastic boxes with multiple compartments. Even so, I had to wait several more months to print while I figured out how to operate my new toy.

In spite of the fact that my only manual was John Ryder's *Printing for Pleasure* (1955), which is primarily useful for owners of Adana horizontal-platen presses, I did manage to glean a few insights into the machinations of my Superior press. I started out by setting and printing a few lines of type for invitations to late-night suppers and cocktail parties, as well as the baptismal announcement mentioned earlier; of these, only the last has survived.

In October I met the publisher of the most important newspaper in Ecuador, who was also an amateur printer and gave me several tips on where to locate printing materials. I was thus able to buy some much-needed wooden furniture from a local job printer.

My First PWP Publication

If my life had taken the turn I expected it would after I left Ecuador, *Eight Parting Poems* would have been the only PWP publication. I have always had an innate sense of drama – after all, my first love was the theater. Like all children of fantasy, I needed to create something special, something that would be a fitting and dramatic exit from one phase of my life to the next. As the date of my departure for Argentina and, by extension, my entrance into the monastery drew closer, I thought more about printing a small keepsake for my friends as a farewell gesture, albeit a somewhat maudlin one considering the circumstances. Certainly, it was one tinged with self-pity, because along with the new spiritual well-being I felt, I also harbored faint traces of guilt about again abandoning my friends. I remembered some of the poems I had written for former lovers after we were no longer intimate and had long since parted, and a couple of poems for straight friends whom I adored. It seemed like the appropriate content for the keepsake.

The short poems of unrequited love in *Eight Parting Poems* reflected, in most cases, a reaction to the pain or frustration that real incidents in my life evoked. Because of the intimate nature of the poems, I could not have chosen a more apt text for a farewell keepsake. Not having a lot of time to devote to this project, I knew it would have to be brief; I selected seven of the many poems I had written over a period of ten years, plus a translation, my first into Spanish, of "When I Am Not with You," a poem by Sara Teasdale originally published in *Dark of the Moon* (1926).

Jack Spicer

I knew very little about the forms of poetry before meeting the poet Jack Spicer – first as a teaching assistant in Thomas Parkinson's English 141 class at the University of California in the spring of 1953, then as a friend, and briefly as a lover. Jack wanted to read everything I had ever written, in particular the stories from Syracuse, written in 1949 and 1950, and those from Thomas Parkinson's English 41B class in the spring of 1951. Jack and I used to meet at a coffee shop on Telegraph Avenue, a block away from where I lived at 2415 Haste Street. I drank a strange concoction of black coffee and

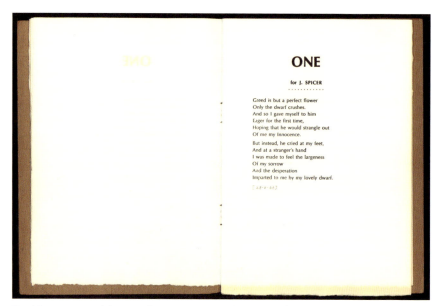

Double-page spread from *Eight Parting Poems*. (Courtesy of the University of Oregon Libraries.)

Item 1. Eight Parting Poems   59

instant cocoa while he discussed the pros and cons of my prose. Under Jack's
tutelage I began to try my hand at verse.

The poem dedicated to Jack was originally written as part of an assignment for Tom's class and later revised for this keepsake. Jack had asked me
to incorporate the word "greed" in a poem. Here it is as it appears in *Eight
Parting Poems:*

[*Greed*]
>   For J. Spicer

Greed is but a perfect flower
Only the dwarf crushes.
And so I gave myself to him
Eager for the first time,
Hoping that he would strangle out
Of me my innocence.

But instead, he cried at my feet,
And at a stranger's hand
I was made to feel the largeness
Of my sorrow
And desperation
Imparted to me by my lovely dwarf.

Even though I had never designed a book before this one, I had designed
several promotional brochures and catalogs while living in New York. I felt
I could successfully tackle this project. Of my fifty-odd foundry typefaces
– all in one-font assortments – I selected Optima. Some of the other choices
included Columbia (the first typeface I bought), Melior, Standard, Weiss,
Microgramma, Eurostyle, and Futura Inline. The chase of the press was
large enough to print two pages at once; however, because of the limited
number of characters at my disposal, I was forced to print each page individually. Much to my regret, I actually had to rewrite the poem dedicated
to Dietrich Leube while setting it because I ran out of lowercase roman *y*'s.
In my own copy of this item, I later noted the changes in pencil, as well as
correcting all the other typos. Below is the poem for Dietrich, with the original line from the manuscript in italic, following the printed line as it appears in the keepsake:

I do believe I shall drown this very night
Like Narcissus kissing his own eyes,
For under my body lies yours in flight
Of ecstasy, deaf to my pleading cries.
Before shutting your eyes, lifting you
Before you shut your eyes, lifting you
Far beyond our proximity, I saw
Reflected an old degenerate who knew
That his life was lost, that his sin would gnaw
At your soul, until at last, you hated him.
You did not know that I was almost dead
When you gave your love, perhaps as a whim,
And left it at the edge of a soiled bed.

Go on alone, I have ceased to exist.
You have nothing left to fear or resist.

Dietrich Leube and Germany

In a letter, dated August 21, 1966, to Dietrich from Buenos Aires I wrote
that *Eight Parting Poems* "was printed very quickly and I am sorry to say
there are many errors. . . . It was a work of love if ever I made a work of love
with the exception of your first poem book" – a reference to "A Sonnet for
Dietrich," produced in one copy and given to him in May 1958. It was a
simple typescript with one of my own tempera illustrations and was bound
in a modified accordion-style binding between covers, reminiscent of
Japanese books.

I met Dietrich on his sixteenth birthday in September 1957 at a party
given for him by the daughter of the Director of the Württembergische
Metallwarenfabrik (WMF) in Geislingen/Steige, Germany, where I worked
as a designer of stainless-steel tableware. We became fast friends, and then
lovers, although we never consummated our relationship sexually, even
though we often slept in each other's arms.

In addition to Dietrich I was romantically involved with Isolde, who was
also my secretary at the factory. We went to movies, parties, and on long
hikes with a picnic basket full of German goodies and bottles of wine. We
never had sex, but we did do a lot of petting and kissing. I wanted to marry

Item 1. Eight Parting Poems

Dietrich Leube, Geislingen/Steige, Germany, 1957. (Photo by Hannes Heldele, courtesy of Dietrich Leube.)

her, and I told her that once I was resettled in New York I would send for her, but after a lengthy correspondence, one day we just stopped writing.

Starting to Print

The little hand-lever press, which looked very much like a one-armed bandit, was set up on a bureau in a corner near the baby grand piano in the music room in Quito. In December 1965 I wrote to my parents, "I have my press working now." I had intended to print some Christmas cards on it, but I never got around to it. It was not until early the following spring that I started to print *Eight Parting Poems*. In a letter, dated May 28, 1966, I mentioned to my parents that "I have been printing and have made quite a bit of progress on my little book. . . . I really enjoy printing and since there is no urgency about getting [the book] finished, I can fuss over it as long as I want." This, of course, wasn't the case once I decided to leave Quito for Buenos Aires.

Setting Type

Even though I had often seen Jack Werner Stauffacher set type at his Greenwood Press in San Francisco in the early fifties, I couldn't remember exactly how it was done. I tried in vain to reconstruct from memory what I had seen him do. For some reason, which I still can't explain, I picked each piece of type out of its compartment with a pair of tweezers instead of using my fingers. I had ample spacing material for each of the point sizes, but I hadn't had the foresight to order leads or slugs, so I used strips of index cards and laundry cardboard to separate the lines. My composing stick was the narrow end of a cardboard shoebox lid.

O'Day's Printing Company

In the late fifties and early sixties, while living in Arizona, I had two experiences directly related to practical printing. The first was a series of elaborate sales kits I designed for Ted Washburn. He lived in Phoenix and was one of those sexual encounters I had while hitchhiking to New York in 1956. We stayed in touch, and in September 1959, he hired me to design the corporate identity for Glassart Stained Glass, a company he managed in Scottsdale. The kit consisted of a number of large mat boards, each with a color photograph of a stained-glass window and a caption describing it. I set the captions in a large sans serif typeface. I also imposed the forms, and Andy at O'Day's Printing Company printed the dozen or so kits on a vertical-platen press. Since we worked after hours, the shop was nice and quiet. Andy talked a lot about his young wife, who was pregnant at the time. I fell in love with him, or perhaps with what he represented to me, the eroticism of printers and printing. The kits, incidentally, were a great success.

John Ball's Printing Company

The second experience, in which I had an opportunity to actually print on a press, came in 1961 at John Ball's Printing Company, when I was graphics director at Operation Reach in Phoenix. We were asked to make a single-copy presentation kit for a real estate developer, so I suggested that we do something like the kit I had designed for Glassart. I should have realized from the beginning that the project was doomed. We were working on a very tight budget. To help keep costs down I volunteered to come in nights and weekends to do the printing. John set up the press, a Chandler & Price

Item 1. Eight Parting Poems   63

vertical-platen press, and then I printed the sheets. Why we didn't use one of the Vandercook proof presses for the job, I don't know. The results were worse than a high school print shop exercise. Thinking back, I don't recall how I did it. John left me alone in the shop. I had never printed before, but had, of course, watched him print. In the end the client refused to accept the kit, and the design studio was very unhappy because we had lost so much time and money on it.

Finding the Right Paper

I wanted to print my keepsake on "fancy" paper, not exactly an easy thing to find in Quito. After weeks of searching, I finally located some T.H. Saunders paper in a small dark shop that sold stationery, as well as house paint, spices, and herbs. I cut the paper down to size, and then using the top of the piano as a work surface, I started printing, not realizing that this type of heavily sized paper should have been dampened before printing. The daybed, below Ariel Parkinson's large painting of angels, received the overflow of printed sheets.

Printing the Keepsake

I must have been pretty good at locking up the chase because I don't remember pieing any of the forms. The keepsake was printed in two colors, using inks that came with the press. I managed to print all of the forms in black and was ready to start on the forms in brown when my troubles began. I couldn't get all the black ink off the gelatine rollers; the solvent I used made them swell, so they wouldn't rotate properly. In desperation I went to a local job printer and explained my problem; he advised me to dry the rollers out with talcum. This seemed to work – up to a point. The swelling went down, but I couldn't get all the talcum off without rewiping the rollers with a solvent-doused cloth. In retrospect I probably could have wiped the talcum off with a damp rag. Losing patience I went ahead and inked-up, only to have the brown ink turn into paste when mixed with the small amount of talcum that remained on the rollers. On the sheet the brown ink looked thick enough to chip off the page. The uneven inking throughout this item is sufficient evidence that I didn't have the foggiest notion of what I was doing.

As my frustration mounted, my deadline grew closer. Halfway through I had to enlist Anita Carrión and Ricardo Fabara to help me feed the press and distribute the type. They also helped with the folding. After several weeks of frantic work, the printing was finished. I took the loose sheets and the printed Kraft paper wrappers to the reproduction services section at the American Embassy, where they let me use their equipment to staple the keepsakes together.

Jack Spicer had once put a personalized doodle in each copy of a book he had written, so I decided that I would do the same with mine; however, once I discovered that I was incapable of making spontaneous doodles, I abandoned the idea. I barely finished printing and distributing the keepsakes before the movers arrived.

Printing on a Mimeograph Machine

In the *Proceedings of the Fine Printing Conference at Columbia University* (1983), I am quoted as saying, "I would have started printing on a mimeograph machine if I had one, but I didn't, I started on a Washington handpress." I suppose it was my good fortune that one wasn't available, or I might never have discovered the iron handpress. It wasn't the craft that initially attracted me. Some of Jack Spicer's early books were published in mimeographed editions.

I came to printing through writing, using the former as a means of sharing my ideas – or more accurately, my feelings – with my friends. This is especially apparent in the first two items from the PWP, both of which were printed for distribution to a very particular and sympathetic audience. The atmosphere in which they were produced was almost as rarified as their contents.

Leaving Ecuador

It was now time to pack up and leave. I donated the press and type to the School of Journalism at the Pontificia Universidad Católica del Ecuador. The gift included all the printed ephemera I had collected over a period of fifteen years, including a complete set of Adrian Wilson's theater programs for The Interplayers and some Greenwood Press items. I was still distributing keepsakes on my last day in Quito.

I left Ecuador on June 28, 1966, thinking of myself as a published author – albeit self-published, but then most of my idols, the "precious" avant-garde women writers between the two wars whom I had read voraciously as a student, had occasionally been self-published: Gertrude Stein, Laura Riding, Djuna Barnes, and Mary Butts. On my way to Buenos Aires, I stopped off

Item 1. Eight Parting Poems 65

in Lima, again visiting Winthrop Kelly Edey's friends, and then went on to Santiago, boasting to my friends of my literary success. My first book was already out of print!

Origin of the Press's Name

By printing this keepsake, primitive as it was, I partially realized a fantasy that had been buried deep inside me since my college days at Berkeley: I had become a publisher. I even had an imprint. But there was one question about this imprint that I could never answer satisfactorily. Why did I decide to call it "Plain Wrapper"? In the 1970s both Anthony Rota, the London bookseller, and Lewis M. Allen, the California handpress printer, were very critical of the name, but by then it was too late to change it. I have often tried – without success – to pinpoint my reason for giving the press this name. It was certainly an appropriate name for this first item, which was issued in plain Kraft paper wrappers without the title printed on the cover. Of course, I knew the prurient implications of "plain brown wrapper," but certainly the contents of my poems, though homoerotic, were not then or now particularly scandalous. Gertrude Stein's Plain Edition publications may have been an influence, but probably most decisive of all was the fact that I saw this choice as a private joke similar to the literary hoax that I had perpetrated at the University of California in the spring of 1954. It was intended to be "precious," shocking. My friends would appreciate the plain wrapper inference but also probably let out one more sigh of exasperation with my pranks and self-indulgence.

Plain Wrapper Press: Five

Bibliographers have been exasperated with me for another reason. The first two items from the press are numbered in a rather misleading way. This first item is "Plain Wrapper Press: Five," and the second, *1945–1965: An Evaluation of Two Decades of Self-Deception,* is "Plain Wrapper Press: Eleven." The "Five" indicates my fifth appearance in print, not the fifth publication from the press. My first four appearances in print were all in *Occident*: first, "The Green Lift" (under the *nom de plume* Denise More) in the Fall 1950 issue; second, "The Little Boy in the Bell Glass" in the Spring 1951 issue; third, "Mrs. Bebe Bear and the Announcing Angel's Egg" in the Spring 1953 issue (and reprinted at the PWP in Item 2; and fourth, "The Emperor's Lion" (under the *nom de plume* Cora C. Fletcher) in the Spring 1954 issue (and later reprinted at the PWP as Item 19.

The Primitive Precursors

In *A Checklist of Books Printed by Richard-Gabriel Rummonds at the Plain Wrapper Press: 1966—1972*, printed in Verona in 1973, I referred to *Eight Parting Poems* and the next two items as "the primitive precursors of the books . . . printed in Verona." None of the three demonstrates any real skill or artistry, but I learned a great deal from the mistakes I made while producing them.

Despite my expatriate feelings, mentally I functioned like a typical American, proceeding as if anything were possible – in this case, printing a book – with just a little patience and a lot of determination, disregarding the obvious necessity of first acquiring at least a modicum of skill. I continued to blunder along for many more years before I gained any real technical proficiency and confidence. Until the end, I set type with my left hand, cupping the fixed end of the composing stick in my right palm.

Regardless of the praise I received from critics such as Anthony Rota, who wrote in the January 1977 issue of *Fine Print*, "It is seldom that editorial, typographical, and practical printing skills are as evenly matched and as successfully combined as they are in the fortunate case of Mr. Richard-Gabriel Rummonds," I was never able to produce a single book that totally met all my expectations. In the beginning I made mistakes out of ignorance or bad judgments. Later mistakes I made out of inexperience, and in the final years I made mistakes because I wasn't capable of performing alone every detail of every operation required to produce the sort of books I so fervently dreamed of making.

Item 1. Eight Parting Poems 67

Filetto al Pepe Verde
Filet Mignon with Green Peppercorns

Serves 4

Most of the food and drink consumed by Americans working in Ecuador came from the PX, but they also relied on La Favorita, a high-end supermarket, for fresh meat. My favorite cut was filet mignon, which I prepared using the following recipe.

   6 tablespoons green peppercorns in brine, rinsed and drained
   4 filets mignons (5 to 6 ounces each)
   2 tablespoons unsalted butter
      Salt to taste
   2 ounces shallots, minced
   4 tablespoons cognac
   ½ cup heavy cream or crème fraîche
      Fresh marjoram sprigs for garnish

Put peppercorns on a plate and lightly mash them with a fork. Press peppercorns onto both sides of the meat. Melt butter in a heated 3-quart sauté pan over medium high heat. When butter begins to bubble, add meat and cook uncovered for 2 minutes on each side for rare, lightly salting the second side. Transfer meat to a plate and loosely cover with aluminum foil to keep warm. Add shallots to the pan and cook on high heat for 2 minutes. Add cognac and set aflame, shaking the pan until flame dies out. Deglaze the pan with cream, cooking until cream thickens, about 2 minutes. Place meat on individual plates and spoon the sauce over them. Garnish with small sprigs of marjoram.

Entrance to the former Seminario Menor Metropolitano Sagrado Corazón de Jesús in the Villa Devoto neighborhood of Buenos Aires. It is presently the Colegio Episcopal de Buenos Aires Sagrado Corazón de Jesús, Buenos Aires, Argentina, 2009. (Photo by Mary Manous, with permission of the photographer.)

Buenos Aires, Argentina

> El recuerdo es nítido, pero no hay ninguna posibilidad
> de que sea cierto.
> – Gabriel García Márquez, *Vivir para Contarla*

A New Country, A New City

I arrived in Buenos Aires on July 11, 1966 – in the middle of the Argentine winter. It was cold and I was unsure what to expect so far away from the world I knew. I came armed with letters of introduction from three influential benefactors in Ecuador: don Italo Carlos Viglierchio, the Argentine ambassador; Monsignor Giovanni Ferrofino, the papal nuncio; and Monsignor Pablo Muñoz-Vega, the coadjutor archbishop of Quito – all requesting that their counterparts treat me kindly.

Since the monastery I was planning to enter was located in a remote part of the pampa, the archbishop of Buenos Aires entrusted me to Father Daniel José Keegan, the rector of the Seminario Menor Metropolitano Sagrado Corazón de Jesús (Minor Seminary) in Buenos Aires. It was decided I would live in the seminary until I was ready to be received as a novice by the Trappists, whose community was so small that the monastery didn't have the personnel to instruct novices formally. Padre Alejandro, the father superior, decided I should study at the seminary in Buenos Aires and come to Azul, the closest village to the monastery, for spiritual retreats during school breaks.

Establishing a New Routine

I was given a private room with a bath in the seminary. I also took most of my meals in the faculty dining room. The food was exceptionally good, steak twice a day and lots of fruit and cheese. Each morning and afternoon there was a *merienda* (a snack) consisting of *café con leche* and bread rolls with butter and jam. Little by little I gained back some of the weight I had lost in Quito.

In August I began teaching English three days a week to twelve- to fifteen-year-old boys in the Minor Seminary. The following January I went

A group of Gabriel's students on retreat at Punta Indio, Argentina, 1967. *Left to right:* Leopoldo Messer, Víctor Malkevicius, Mario Barboza, Carlos Capurro, Gabriel Sada, and Carlos Malkevicius. (Photographer unknown, courtesy of Leopoldo Messer.)

with the students on a retreat to the Estancia Santa Rita, accompanying two of the boys, Leopoldo Messer and Gabriel Sada, on the bus. It was during this retreat that the only photograph of me during my stay in Argentina was taken. Unfortunately, my eyes were closed.

Gabriel at Punta Indio, Argentina, 1967. (Photographer unknown, courtesy of Leopoldo Messer.)

The Monastery

My first visit to the monastery of Nuestra Señora de los Ángeles in late July 1966 was quite naturally very emotional, and I felt from the moment I crossed the threshold that I was destined to join their order. The community consisted of about twenty-five monks, mainly from the United States, Chile, and Argentina. Like all Trappists they supported themselves off the land; these were *gaucho* monks, who herded cows and sheep.

The Chapel at the monastery of Nuestra Señora de los Ángeles, near Azul, Argentina, from *Jubilee*, February 1966. (Photo by William E. Barksdale.)

A Second Retreat

My visits to the monastery became more frequent. On October 9 I left Buenos Aires for a four-day retreat there. A few weeks before my departure, I took a vow of chastity to reconfirm my commitment to a religious life.

Christmas at the Monastery

When school was out for the Christmas break, I returned to the monastery on December 23. In 1966 Trappists didn't ordinarily converse; however, I was told that two years before Pope Paul VI had given the Trappists a special dispensation for a two-hour recreation period on Christmas Day. The day before the holiday, I went out in the woods and chopped down a small pine tree, setting it up in the refectory and decorating it with chains and stars cut from plain white paper and brown paper bags. It was a festive tree even though it had no lights or candles, just the stark white and brown against the green of the pine boughs. Cookies were baked and a punch was made out of fresh strawberries from the monastery garden.

Even though I was only a guest at the monastery and excluded from fraternizing with the monks, Father Alejandro invited me to join him and the other monks in the library on Christmas Day. He and I passed the refreshments, pausing to chat with each monk, but no one could think of anything to say. In a cloistered environment without telephones, radio, television, movies, and books, without gossip, affairs, family and work problems, with everyone sharing the same beliefs, goals, and ideals, there is nothing to chat or argue about, so we spent most of the social period listening to recorded Christmas carols.

The next day we were back in the fields. The monks were harvesting oats, and I was in the berry patch, picking strawberries. This was the good life I had always dreamed of. A few days later I returned to Buenos Aires very happy. Father Alejandro had told me that the order had decided to accept me as a novice the following December, a little less than a year away.

Exploring Buenos Aires

Buenos Aires was an enormous city of five million inhabitants. Getting to the center of it from Villa Devoto was in itself quite a chore. It required a train ride and two subways. Fortunately, the trains and subways ran late into the night. There were many things to see and do in Buenos Aires: museums, libraries, and wonderful English-style tearooms.

Even though I had a few letters of introduction from friends in Lima to people in Buenos Aires, I resolved not to become involved in any new friendships. This was easier said than done. I did look up two of these referrals, Heriberto Goldsmith, a homosexual friend of Carlos Flores-Veloso and Javier Barba-Vera, and Ed Shaw and his Argentine wife María, friends of an American woman from San Francisco I had met in Lima. Ed had also been instrumental in setting up the artisan program in Ecuador.

When I called Heriberto he invited me to come by for a drink. Even though I arrived at the appointed hour, he came to the door dripping wet, wrapped in a towel. He asked me to follow him into the bathroom,

Buenos Aires, Argentina 73

where he finished his bath. He was obese, not exactly my type. During drinks he asked me to stay over. I realized that we had different things in mind concerning a potential friendship, so nothing more came of the encounter.

A few weeks later I had dinner with Ed and María, and we talked about the early days of the artisan program and my involvement with it before coming to Buenos Aires. We really didn't have any other interests in common, so we never got together again.

I was acquainted with two seminarians in the Major Seminary who spoke English, Jorge Lynch and Juan Carlos Leardi. Even though Jorge lived in the Major Seminary, he took classes in the Minor. He was around my age and had also had a late calling to the religious life, having previously had a successful career in commerce. He lived in a fashionable part of the city in a wonderful apartment which was tastefully appointed with English antiques, art, and books. I spent several enjoyable evenings in his company discussing literature and the religious life in English. Juan Carlos was in his twenties. We would frequently get together in his room in the seminary to chat in English or read and discuss inspirational tracts. With both of these seminarians, there seemed to be side glances with not-so-concealed meanings, but I pretended not to notice them.

I had very few social contacts outside of the seminary. José Prado, a Spaniard who was a secular professor of Greek and Latin at the Minor Seminary, invited me to have supper with his family one night. He and I often chatted about world events during the *meriendas* in the faculty dining room. He was also my Latin teacher.

Ricardo Palou

On my first retreat at the monastery I shared a guest room with a young man named Ricardo Palou, who was also an aspirant to the Trappist order. He lived in Buenos Aires, and we quickly became intimate friends. Ricardo frequently stopped by my room in the seminary, where we would talk or read together in Spanish, since he didn't know any English. I was fascinated by him. He was short and very skinny with a small mouth, spitting saliva as he talked. He would often stand next to my desk, flirtatiously sporting what I assumed was a semi-erection. Under the circumstances I was too frightened to touch it or to make a direct pass at him.

Most weekends Ricardo and I went out to dinner and sometimes to a movie. There were many enormous and very modern movie palaces in Buenos Aires. One had to purchase tickets in advance. Each ticket had the seat number printed on it. It was more like going to the theater. We saw *Doctor Zhivago* and a lot of silly Spanish-language movies with Sarita Montiel and the popular Spanish singer Raphael.

After the movie, we would go to a neighborhood *parrilla*, a working-class restaurant, for charbroiled steaks, four by nine inches and three-quarters of an inch thick. The meat was so tender it could be cut with a fork. The dinner came with sliced fresh tomatoes, French fries, and wine – all for sixty cents. Ricardo and I continued to see each other through November. He may have moved away; I am not sure, but I don't remember seeing him again that year, maybe because I had less free time. On Saturday nights I joined a small group of seminarians to review Sunday's Bible lesson. In addition my studies were very demanding since all my classes were conducted in Spanish.

The Paulinos

I once casually mentioned my interest in printing to Ricardo and described the keepsake I had produced in Quito. He, too, had a background in printing and suggested we visit his old school, where he had been educated by the Paulinos at the Pía Sociedad de San Pablo in Florida, a suburb of Buenos Aires. As part of their vocation, the Paulinos operated an extensive publishing program. Ricardo and I went to visit them in late August 1966. I'll never forget the sight of seven-year-old boys nimbly carrying tied-up pages from the composing room to the pressroom, or twelve-year-olds, standing on skids, operating high-speed automatic presses. I didn't realize it at the time, but this visit would shortly involve me in another printing project of my own.

The Paulinos were very friendly, and because they had heard of my extensive travels from Ricardo, they were curious about my life and in particular why I had decided to become a Trappist. When they discovered I had also designed commercial graphics, they asked if I would design some book jackets for them. Even though I had no previous experience in this field, I accepted the challenge. Because of my special talents, the father superior asked me to consider joining the Paulinos. (My options were expanded even more when I met several Hermanos Cristianos, who hoped I would come to them and teach English in one of their schools.)

Buenos Aires, Argentina

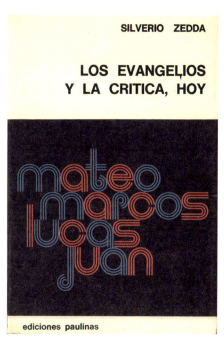

Left: Cover designed by Gabriel for *¿Control de la natalidad después del Concilio?* (1967) by Jakob David. (Courtesy of the University of Utah.)

Right: Cover designed by Gabriel for *Los evangelios y la crítica, hoy* (1967) by Silverio Zedda. (Courtesy of Patricio Gatti.)

Mario Aguirre Mac-Kay

One day in September during the Argentine spring, I was in the composing room working with Marcelo Gudiño and Ángel Rojas, the brothers in charge of the printing operation. They introduced me to the Chilean publisher Mario Aguirre Mac-Kay, who was living in exile in Argentina. He published books on Chilean history – nothing subversive, however. He had just published his first book in a new series and was not very happy with its typography, although he did like the book jacket I had designed for it. He asked if I would be interested in designing the basic format for the series he was planning to issue. I ended up designing six more titles in this series for him before I left Argentina.

Designing Books for Editorial Francisco de Aguirre

Mario offered to pay me for my work, but I told him I couldn't accept any remuneration since what I would be doing for him was in effect for the

Paulinos. I had never designed a trade book before. The numerous catalogs and brochures I had done commercially didn't follow any formal book formats, and the design of *Eight Parting Poems* was most likely taken from one of the poetry books in my library in Quito. I visited the United States Information Service and checked out *Bookmaking* (1965) by Marshall Lee, absorbing everything I thought I would need to know about book design. Poor Mario. He got a rather bizarre design. It had running heads and folios on most of the pages in the front matter, including the blanks. He still used this design long after I left Argentina. I may have failed him as a book designer, but the logo I created for his imprint was quite handsome. He was extremely proud of it, and I have always considered it to be one of my finest corporate identity designs.

Life in the Seminary

I was determined to enter the monastery as soon as possible; however, everyone concerned thought I should first complete my studies in Latin, Greek, and theology in the Minor Seminary.

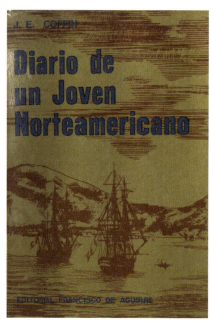 

Left: Cover designed by Gabriel for *Diario de un joven norteamericano* (1967) by J. E. Coffin. (Courtesy of the University of Utah.)

Right: Title-page spread from the above. (Courtesy of the University of Utah.)

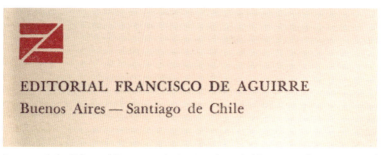

Pressmark for Editorial Francisco de Aguirre (1967). (Courtesy of Patricio Gatti.)

Since I was no longer drinking and whoring, I had a lot of extra time on my hands, during which I single-handedly cataloged the entire Minor Seminary library of eight thousand titles using the Dewey Decimal System. The books were originally arranged by size and color, not subject. A librarian at the United States Information Service gave me an outdated copy of Dewey's manual to help me with the classifications.

I was getting more exercise in Buenos Aires than I had in Quito. I played volleyball for forty-five minutes almost every day after lunch, and sometimes, when one of the soccer teams needed an extra player, I joined in. The most difficult part of the game for me was to not touch the ball with my hands. At one point enrollment in the seminary dropped down to twenty-eight students. I joked with the fathers that if we didn't have enough students for two teams we would have to close up shop, and this eventually happened after I left Argentina. In 1968 the seminary was closed and reestablished as the Colegio Episcopal de Buenos Aires Sagrado Corazón de Jesús, a private co-educational secondary school.

Inner Turmoil

My contentment with my new life was occasionally fraught with turmoil. I had discussed the possibility of visiting my parents in California at Christmas, but there were too many unresolved issues to settle before I could face them. I described the gravity of the situation in a letter, dated November 18, to my parents :

> All day yesterday I stewed. I just could not seem to settle all the problems battling in my head. . . . I paced around my room or tried to busy myself with work, but to no avail. I then took a hot bath, still great

therapy for me. I soaked in the tub until the water got cold and then got out and lay down on my bed in just my underwear and closed my eyes, wanting to fall asleep, black out everything. It was like the old days. Close your eyes and it will disappear. But I don't want problems to "disappear" any more. I want to solve them.

Working with the Paulinos

I continued to design books and book jackets for the Paulinos, but because they were always short-handed they put me to work in the composing room. Before long I found myself spending whole days dividing galleys into pages, adding running heads and folios, pulling proofs for dummies, laying out imposition schemes, and marking copy for the Linotype compositor. All of this hands-on experience would eventually pay off once I started printing *1945– 1965: An Evaluation of Two Decades of Self-Deception*. In a letter, dated November 30, to my father, I mentioned that I was earning $20 a month from the Paulinos, enough to cover my laundry and postage stamps.

Unwanted Temptations

Even though I tried to get my mind off sex, I was put through several distressful and saddening ordeals. I traveled to and from the seminary to the Paulinos on a small crowded yellow bus. One evening coming back to the seminary, I was seated on the aisle, when a young man unintentionally kept brushing his genitals against my shoulder. My body was so sensitive to his touch that I had an orgasm without even getting an erection.

Not Masturbating or Having Sex

I was alone in the seminary the week after Christmas; all the students had left for the holidays. So on New Year's Eve I went into the center of Buenos Aires. Being the height of the summer, with most people away at the beach or in the mountains, the city was deserted. I saw a young man from Paraguay wandering the streets. We had met a few days earlier at the customs office, where both of us had gone to pick up packages. His name was Rufino Grossi; he recognized me and asked if he could buy me a glass of champagne. We went to the only café still open and toasted the New Year. As we got up to leave, he said he was staying in a hotel nearby and wondered if I would like to come up to his room for another glass of champagne. As much as I would

Buenos Aires, Argentina

have liked to go with him, I knew I would break my recent vow of chastity if I went with him. I went back to the seminary, miserable, wondering if I really was a fit candidate for the monastery.

Here is another story of unwanted sexual attention. I often assisted Father Keegan at Sunday Mass in the English Church. After the service we were always invited to lunch by one of the parishioners. One Sunday after lunch the host asked if I would like a swim in his pool, and he offered me a swimsuit. While we were in the water, leaning against the edge of the pool, he groped me, holding on until I managed to wrestle away from his clutches. He wanted to know what we did for sex in the monastery.

These were rough experiences for someone who had led a very promiscuous life before coming to Buenos Aires, but now I found that I had a very low sex drive. They must have put saltpeter in the food at both the seminary and the monastery.

A Change of Plans

In the meantime, Father Alejandro thought it would be best for me to "test" my vocation by living for a year in the secular world. I seemed to be trying too hard to atone for my past. He suggested that I go to Rome, where I could continue to work with the church. If, after that time, I felt I still had a vocation, I would always be welcome at the monastery. I would soon be leaving Argentina, but not before I had an opportunity to print a little book of my short stories.

Cannelloni con Ripieno di Gamberi
Cannelloni Stuffed with Shrimp

Serves 8

Aside from the wonderful Argentine meat dishes, I especially enjoyed the Italian Cannelloni con Ripieno di Gamberi, found in the many Italian-style pizzerías in Buenos Aires. Father Keegan's mother also made this dish at a retreat I went on with some of the seminarians at the Estancia Santa Rita in Punta Indio. Even though I never had an opportunity to cook in Argentina, I learned to make this dish in Verona and frequently served it as a first course. Here is my version of the recipe.

For the stuffing
   2 tablespoons unsalted butter
   3 ounces yellow onion, finely chopped
1½ pounds medium shrimp, peeled and deveined
   1 large garlic clove, finely chopped
   ½ cup Marsala wine
   ½ cup heavy cream
   1 large egg
   2 tablespoons flat-leaf parsley, finely chopped
   2 ounces Parmigiano-Reggiano cheese, freshly grated
   ½ teaspoon salt

For the pasta
   1 pound dry lasagna
   2 tablespoons cold unsalted butter

For the béchamel sauce
   3 tablespoons unsalted butter
   3 tablespoons all-purpose flour
   3 cups milk
   ½ teaspoon salt
   1/16 teaspoon saffron threads

Buenos Aires, Argentina 81

The stuffing: Preheat the oven to 400 degrees. Melt butter in a large skillet over medium heat. When butter begins to bubble, add onion and cook until translucent, about 5 minutes. Raise the heat to high and add shrimp and garlic. Cook until shrimp are light pink on all sides, about 1 minute, and set aside. Deglaze the pan with wine and add cream. Cook the sauce until reduced to about 3 tablespoons. Put shrimp and sauce in a food processor and pulse until shrimp are minced. Transfer the mixture to a bowl and add egg, parsley, Parmigiano-Reggiano, and salt and mix well.

The pasta: Use fresh pasta if available. If not, cook dry pasta according to the directions on the package. As you remove pasta from boiling water, place it in a bowl of cold water to stop the cooking. Pat dry with kitchen towels. Cut into 5 x 5 inch squares. The crimped edge can be cut off. Spread 3 table-spoons of the stuffing down the middle of the square, then fold over the parallel edges, making a tube. Place in a buttered baking dish, seam side down. Leave a little space between each cannelloni.

The béchamel sauce: Add butter to a saucepan over low heat. When butter begins to bubble, add flour and continue stirring with a wooden spoon until butter and flour are completely combined, about 1 to 3 minutes. Remove the pan from the heat and cool for 15 minutes. In another saucepan, heat milk over medium high heat until it is very hot, but not boiling. Return the pan with the butter and flour mixture over medium-high heat and add all the milk at once. Cook about 10 minutes until the sauce is smooth and thick. Add salt and saffron. Cover cannelloni with the béchamel sauce. Dot cannelloni with butter and place baking dish on the middle rack. Bake until cannelloni are bubbly and golden brown, about 10 minutes. Allow to cool for 2 minutes before serving.

BYNNER
54

NEWBAUER, J & M : STANLEY
56 : 63

ASKIN,
50

PETTITT : GODDARD
50 : 50

SHEDD : LINCOLN
MEX. 52 : 54
MEXICO

RICHARDS
BERK. 53

BURT
53

O'HANORAHAN
52

LOPEZ*
54

JONES
56

STARR : STAUFFACHER
51 : 53

KARIM : COOPER
50 : 53

LIBRARY : BLASER
53

Leaf from Gabriel's proposed *Peopleology of Richard Rummonds*, Buenos Aires, Argentina, 1966. (Courtesy of PWP Archives.)

Peopleology of Richard Rummonds

Including family, friends, acquaintances, lovers
and a few indiscretions by Richard Rummonds;
with an introduction by Gabriel Precio
[Richard-Gabriel Price Rummonds.]

An Incomplete Project

In October 1966 Father Keegan let me keep the library's Smith-Corona electric typewriter in my room. I spent much of my free time compiling what I called a *Peopleology*. It was to be issued as a typescript in one copy and published as Plain Wrapper Press: 6. The project, which had reached fifteen pages, was abandoned when I decided instead to work on an edition of my short stories.

Gabriel Precio

Since I wanted to talk about myself objectively, I extrapolated from my full name, Richard-Gabriel Price Rummonds, the "Gabriel" and the "Price" and translated them into Spanish. That is how Gabriel Precio – the man in the middle – came to compile and edit this project, as well as *1945–1965: An Evaluation of Two Decades of Self-Deception.*

Precio's introduction also contained a long, convoluted description of the evolution of the *Peopleology of Richard Rummonds*. He mentioned my compulsive need to save every scrap of paper, every address book, and lists of all residences and sexual encounters. The *Peopleology* traces almost everyone I could remember, linking each back to a common "ancestor," much like the format used in creating a genealogy. It was a monstrous project that deserved to be abandoned, although the names and dates in it were essential to the writing of this memoir.

The *Peopleology* was very self-indulgent, as can be gathered from the following two paragraphs of the introduction from the edited draft "written" by Gabriel Precio:

In the summer of 1945 a very sad and confused boy moved with his family to Sacramento. He was fourteen and until that time he had had only one friend he could call his own. His playmates had always been his brother Bobby's friends. He usually entertained himself, mostly in a world of make-believe. He built model airplanes, collected stamps, drew, dressed up in costumes and gave plays, wrote stories, and planted a garden. He was not athletic and shied away from competitive sports.

The summer of 1945 brought to a head a long series of traumatic experiences that resulted in the family deciding that a complete change of environment was the only solution. This was rather symptomatic of Richard's behavior because he continued to make geographic changes with each traumatic experience he was to face in adult life. If he had had any friends in the years before 1945, they would hardly have recognized him after the family moved to Sacramento, California. He decided that he would have to proceed on his own. He had discovered that summer that his brother Bobby was not his friend, but in fact an adversary, and little did he realize that until the end of his secular life he would have to do battle with him. From a shy, inhibited boy who would cry if you looked at him, would cry if he failed, would cry

Richard, who was president of the Art Club, is seated in the front row in this group photo from the *Review 1949*, Sacramento, CA, 1949. (Photo by Oliver Livoni, courtesy of PWP Archives.)

Peopleology of Richard Rummonds   85

if he could not have his way, he suddenly stopped crying. . . . He laughed and made friends, he joined clubs, he led clubs. From that time on he was obsessed with people and keeping track of them. His address books grew each year because he could not let go of the past.

A Fragile Life: 1943–1945

What Precio failed to mention in his introduction above was the "long series of traumatic experiences" that happened to me in Vallejo, California, between 1943 and 1945. Beginning in 1943 and continuing through the next year, I was waylaid by a gang of bullies from my school. They dragged me into a vacant lot and stripped me; they called it "pantsing" in those days. Leaving me naked, they took off with my clothes, scattering them along the sidewalk as they ran away. What had I done to them? It was not a sexual attack, but it left me feeling humiliated and sexually violated. Retrieving my clothes and slipping them on as best I could without pausing, I ran down the street in a state of fear and anxiety. No one came to my rescue.

Once home I tried to tell my mother, blurting out what had happened, but she was getting ready to go out for the evening. "Honey, this is not the best time to talk to me." My mother and I never broached the subject again. Most devastating of all, my brother Bobby was part of the gang.

In the summer of 1945, my parents sent Bobby, Tommy, and me (called Dickie in those days) to Camp Gualala, run by the Berkeley YMCA. I immediately developed a crush on Pierre, one of the cabin councilors for the younger boys, who was probably a high school student. We would take long, solitary hikes in the woods and read to each other. He would let me wear his T-shirts, which practically came down to my knees. We started sleeping together, spoon-style, in his bunk, and there were snide remarks about a sore ass and a quarter on my stomach.

It was an idyllic experience. We held hands as we walked, hugged when we stopped to rest. I doubt that we ever kissed, not even on the cheek or neck. I am fairly confident we never had any genital contact. If we had, I am sure it would have freaked me out, because I was still in denial about my own genitals. When I think back on this encounter, it was nothing more than an insecure boy's crush on a sympathetic youth.

This special relationship suddenly came to an end one afternoon in the mess hall. Gesturing toward me, all the campers started to sing "Dixie."

I reacted by smashing everything in sight. Again, in another instance of fraternal betrayal, Bobby was the ringleader. He led the singing.

A couple of the senior councilors restrained me, sequestering me in their cabin until my parents came to get me. Later they talked with the principal of my school. He suggested a change of schools, perhaps even a military academy. Each of these humiliating experiences left me feeling more isolated from my peers and family. I may have been socially withdrawn in Vallejo, but after we moved to Sacramento, I blossomed into a healthy, extroverted boy and student.

Peopleology of Richard Rummonds

Cabbage Stuffed with Meat

Serves 4

I seem to remember that the food at Camp Gualala was pretty bland. I would have been happy with a large helping of my mother's cabbage stuffed with meat. At least it was tasty and filling. I occasionally served her recipe when I was too poor to buy a nice cut of meat.

- 2 pound head of cabbage
- 1 pound beef, veal, pork, and liver in equal parts mixed together
- 3 tablespoons yellow onion, finely chopped
- 2 tablespoons flat-leaf parsley, finely chopped
- ¾ teaspoon salt
- ½ teaspoon fresh thyme
- 1 large garlic clove finely chopped
- 2 tablespoons wine vinegar
- 3 tablespoons brown sugar
- 1 teaspoon capers

Preheat the oven to 375 degrees. Remove the outer leaves and stem of cabbage. Cook it, uncovered, in 2 quarts of boiling water until barely tender and slightly crisp. Drain well and scoop out the inside, leaving a 1½-inch shell. Place the shell in a greased ovenproof dish. Combine the remaining ingredients in a bowl. Coarsely chop the removed parts of the cabbage and add them to the stuffing. Fill the cabbage shell with the stuffing. Bake for 50 minutes.

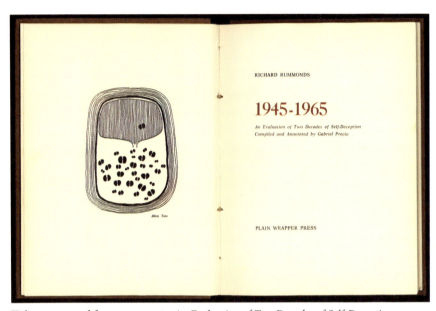

Title-page spread from *1945–1965: An Evaluation of Two Decades of Self-Deception*. (Courtesy of the University of Oregon Libraries.)

Item 2. 1945–1965: *An Evaluation of Two Decades of Self-Deception*

Seven short stories by Richard Rummonds;
compiled and annotated by Gabriel Precio
[Richard-Gabriel Price Rummonds].
With a linecut reproduction of a pen and ink
drawing by Allen Tate. 84 pages. 20 x 15 cm. 32 copies. 1967.

Beginning of the Plain Wrapper Press

I came to printing through creative writing, an interest I have had since high school, but didn't explore seriously until a student at Syracuse University, and later at the University of California. Writing was never a career I pursued with any real determination, primarily because my poems and stories had very limited appeal. They were generally quite subjective and often written in a self-conscious style that was then, and still is, derogatorily described as "precious." I started the Plain Wrapper Press in order to print my own poems and stories, using them as a means of sharing my feelings with my friends.

Creative Writing

The first story I remember writing was called "The Mushroom Hunt," for Miss Schwartz's English class in the fall of 1946. But I didn't begin writing stories in earnest until I enrolled at Syracuse University during the 1949–1950 school year, first in Katherine Aston's freshman English class and later in Raymond Raimondi's English 5 class. Miss Aston encouraged my whimsy, letting me subvert assignments in order to experiment with language and form. She praised my writing for its "artistic" bent and suggested that we meet outside of class to discuss my potential as a writer. On the other hand Mr. Raimondi, in his exposition class, was very critical and complained bitterly that I could not write a "straight" piece of prose.

The Purple Place

In the fall of 1953, after a little more than two years away from the university, I moved back to Berkeley from Richmond, California, where I had spent the summer teaching in a school for emotionally disturbed children. Now that I was on my own again, I needed a place to live and a job. I found a small (160 square feet) one-room cottage in a garden behind a large shingled house at 1106 Oxford Street on the north side of campus. It was sparsely furnished, and I referred to it as the Purple Place because I painted the walls a deep royal purple. Soon after, I took a job as a page in the Social Science Research Service at the university's main library.

The Purple Place at 1106 Oxford Street, Berkeley, CA, 2003. Richard's house in 1953. (Photo by RGR, courtesy of PWP Archives.)

Item 2. 1945–1965: An Evaluation of Two Decades of Self-Deception 91

Small as it was, the Purple Place was a great location, with its large rambling garden for big parties. One of the most memorable occurred the night I served my infamous Purple Punch, a concoction of gin and Welch's grape juice. Joan Fisher, one of my classmates in Thomas Parkinson's English 141 creative writing class, showed up. She was my idealized woman: I loved her. The party ended well after one or two in the morning, but I hadn't seen Joan leave. Standing on the porch I heard a faint murmur coming from the berry brambles at the bottom of the garden. It was Joan, drunk and all scratched up. Somehow I managed to disentangle her and put her on the old psychiatrist's couch across the room from my bed. In those days the milkman put the bottles of milk in the refrigerator. I looked up at him as he walked past me and said, "What am I doing on the couch?" He replied, "Beats me." When Joan got up, she explained that when I had gotten up to pee, I put her in the bed, and then fell asleep on the couch.

English 106A

Among my courses that fall semester was Mark Schorer's English 106A class, a creative writing workshop. Of all my university writing courses, this one turned out to be the most productive. In all I wrote twenty-two completed stories while a student at the University of California, of which eleven were written for Schorer's class.

Before the fall of 1953, all my stories were very autobiographical. In Schorer's class I began to write about other people, although I never completely escaped including certain personal traits in one or more of the characters. Many of my stories were so personal that their meaning was often entirely lost on those who didn't know me. I *am* the stories. In most cases they failed as literature simply because I could never completely extricate myself from them, but they provided a key to my personality, and certainly clues to my sexuality. One of the curious things about the stories from Schorer's class is that all of them were about heterosexual, not homoerotic, relationships. However, by the spring of 1954, I had stopped writing stories and began to live the experiences I had written about.

Getting into Schorer's Class

Mark Schorer selected about ten students for his writing workshops by having each of the applicants incorporate into a "fragment" of fiction one of several sentences he put on the blackboard. Although Schorer didn't identify any of the authors, I was quite sure the sentence I had selected was from a novel by Henry James, one of my favorite authors at the time. Who else could have written: "My dear young lady, . . . you don't want to be ruined for picturesqueness' sake?" I was mistaken; it didn't come from one of James's novels, but from one of his short stories, "Four Meetings," first published in the November 1877 issue of *Scribner's Monthly*. I wove this sentence into a short story about a shy young girl who dated a rakish library school student. In James's story the protagonist is warning the young lady not to risk financial ruin by spending all of her hard-earned savings on picturesque views.

My story in its entirety follows. The superscript numbers refer to the notes for "The Mr. Wilson Story," which appear in this book in Appendix I on page 749.

A Novel
in Which It Was
Too Tedious to Write
the Beginning or the End
and So the Middle
Will Have to Suffice[1] *or*
The Mr. Wilson[2] Story

. . . The two of them, that is to say Lucy[3] and Mr. Wilson, felt quite like Greeks at harvest time, for from high up, up above the cities and the university and the library[4] where they both worked, they were alone in the piedmonts that had matured into autumn. And there was a great clatter of sun color, and a clatter it was, because the gold and orange of the yellow-white beeches and the red-violet of the eucalyptus were alive in that one false moment before winter. Lucy had prepared a lovely lunch, and the two of them, alone in the oak-treed canyon, had eaten the lunch and had drunk the wine which Mr. Wilson had insisted upon bringing as no outing was ever complete without this, oh so autumnal, beverage.

Mr. Wilson was not really the proper name to call this gentleman, for he was just a library student, but he had an eloquence and a way, or

Item 2. 1945–1965: An Evaluation of Two Decades of Self-Deception

Richard, the year before he took Schorer's class, San Francisco, CA, 1952. (Photo by Isabel Freud, courtesy of PWP Archives.)

perhaps to say a style, which made everyone think of him as being an older man even though he was just a library student and probably not more than twenty-three as this was, in fact, his first year as a library student. Consequently, when Lucy first met Mr. Wilson, he was introduced to her as Mr. Wilson since he was some sort of supervisor in the loan department where she worked. Lucy was, herself, so shy and said that she was shy although not to many people because she really was shy, really too shy to even talk about being shy, that she had never ventured to ask him his first name, and he, after being called Mr. Wilson for so long, did not venture to give it. They only came close to talking about important things like names once, and that was soon after Mr. Wilson first started to ask Lucy out, and this was soon after Mr. Wilson discovered that Lucy was from a small copper mining town in Montana[5] and that she had never gone out with boys, let alone men. They had just begun to talk one day and it seemed that Mr. Wilson had been to nearly every big amusement park[6] in the West and even some on the east coast and it also seemed that Lucy had never been to any at all, not even a circus one; so Mr. Wilson said, There is a fine one, although not a very large one, in San Francisco. We could go some time if you like, I mean, I would like to take you some time.

And so it was arranged and they went. And one of the things they saw that most impressed Lucy was a tattooed lady. Lucy was really quite fascinated by this creature and to herself said, She is not at all shy. And she said to Mr. Wilson, still rather talking to herself, If I were a tattooed lady, what name would I go by and what sort of tattoos do you think I should have?

My dear young woman, Mr. Wilson said, you don't want to be ruined for picturesqueness' sake, do you?[7]

And Lucy thought for a moment and looked at the happyhappy-happy smile of the tattooed lady and then said, No.

And yet Lucy knew that there were less exhibitory ways of ruining herself, and eating and drinking on Sunday afternoons with Mr. Wilson was really quite a picturesque way of ruining herself without really ruining herself in the nasty meaning of ruining herself because her shyness was a nastiness and to ruin it was to take a geranium out-of-doors...[8]

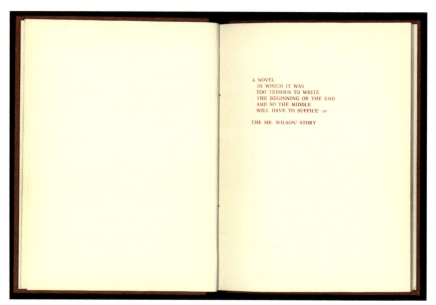

Part-title spread from *1945–1965: An Evaluation of Two Decades of Self-Deception.* (Courtesy of the University of Oregon Libraries.)

Writing for Schorer

I was extremely anxious to be admitted to Schorer's class. Because he was known as an ultra-conservative, and by 1953 I had acquired a certain notoriety in campus literary circles as an avant-garde bad boy, I was afraid he wouldn't accept me.

All the other students who had selected the Henry James sentence picked up on its sexual innuendo. Perhaps Schorer thought he saw in me an original talent – only to be disappointed when none of my pieces ever exceeded a page or two in length. Commenting on one of my "precious" little stories, he wrote, "Mr. Rummonds ... you can't go on this way." But I did, and seven of the resulting stories, which mirrored the vivid fantasy life of a late bloomer, became the text for *1945–1965 An Evaluation of Two Decades of Self-Deception*.

Structurally, my stories are like swings. They almost always start out with a sense of reality. As they gain momentum, they evolve into a world of fantasy, but by the end of the story, they swing back to the reality of the beginning. They are full of latent erotic feelings usually disguised in poetic imagery, and the few people who read them often found them rather silly.

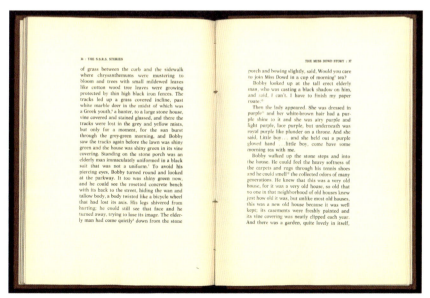

Double-page spread from *1945–1965: An Evaluation of Two Decades of Self-Deception*. (Courtesy of the University of Oregon Libraries.)

Schorer considered these stories playful exercises and pleaded with me to set them aside and write a "serious" story. Contrary to his opinion, I *did* think of these as serious stories. He once said that he felt that I first composed a title and then wrote a story to go with it. I was often inspired by seemingly insignificant sources, sometimes just a word or two overheard in passing. But it was more likely that I imaged the whole thing. I was quite fond of self-pitying daydreams.

I have always been a perfectionist, especially when it came to my stories. I often labored for days over even the shortest of stories. Most of my critics thought that I just sat down and wrote until I got tired and then turned in what I had written. This is certainly an unfair criticism. The number of surviving drafts proves just the opposite.

Once I had finished writing the S.S.R.S. Stories, I more or less lost interest in Schorer's class. Toward the end of the semester I was trying hard just to meet the word requirement for his class. Each story had to be completely retyped until it was error-free since the professors would not accept any papers with handwritten corrections. One weekend, because I typed very slowly, I enlisted Isabel Freud's help to retype some of my drafts.

Unlike other creative writing classes at the university, Schorer's class failed to produce a group of writers who would continue to see each other to read and criticize each other's work. I published the stories and poems of many of my classmates the following year when I was the editor of *Occident*. The one student I continued to see was Virginia Mowry. We continued to correspond long after we left the university.

Themes

Eating is one of the major themes that runs through all the stories in this collection. I always associated eating with both pleasure and frustration. In "The Mr. Wilson Story," it takes the form of picnics, which I always managed to turn into lavish productions. They were never a matter of mere sandwiches and Cokes. They required careful planning of both menu and guests. Eating in the open air with someone I was close to was one of the most intimate exchanges I allowed myself. I fondly remember the picnics I had with Joan Fisher on campus in the fall of 1953, and those in the late sixties in New York with Barbara Knight in Central Park.

Item 2. 1945–1965: An Evaluation of Two Decades of Self-Deception   97

Another recurring theme is self-discovery and the desire to belong. In "The Mr. Wilson Story," Lucy is striving to overcome her shyness so that she can eventually experience love, perhaps even marriage. I always thought one of my basic problems in relating to people was that I had never been an adolescent, but seemingly went directly from being a child to an adult.

In all my stories the protagonists have compulsive routines. Mr. Wilson and Lucy have their Sunday afternoon picnics. Bebe Bear and her husband always have sex in the morning. Miss Dowd always serves Bobby tea in the afternoon. Miss Suds always works in her garden *after* washing out her nylons and underthings.

An important influence on my writing can be traced to Paul B. Schaeffer's Medieval Culture course. It was one of my favorite courses, and I imitated certain mannerisms and speech colorations from his lectures. As he did, I still touch my right hand lightly to my left shoulder. He turned historical facts about kings, saints, and devil-possessed maidens into fanciful stories, which he narrated as if he were actually witnessing the events.

Corsberg's Criticism

In the fall of 1955, I was staying with my parents, who had recently moved from Sacramento to Santa Rosa to be nearer my father's work. Primarily as an excuse to get out of the house, I enrolled in a creative writing class at the community college. At our first session, Ken Corsberg, the instructor, asked all the students to bring an autobiographical sketch with them to the next class. I balked at this assignment and in lieu of it turned in a rather pompous note, which said in part: "So you will not be at a complete loss about me, I am enclosing several little pieces," which included four from *1945–1965*. His comments on them were quite similar to Schorer's. Corsberg wrote of another of the stories in the same book:

> [The Miss Dowd Story] is the most puzzling story of all. It seems to verge on the edge of meaning and yet it never quite comes forth. I think you were definitely uncertain in your own mind just what you wanted to say and just how you felt about the characters involved and obviously uncertain about how they felt. If you were writing this just

to expel some morbid thoughts that creep into your own mind, it may have accomplished its purpose. As a manuscript to communicate some meaning to the reader it falls way short.

None of the negative remarks from Schorer or Corsberg ever discouraged me from wanting to write more stories. Shortly after submitting "Pictures and a Poem," a story that I had written for Corsberg, I dropped out of his class and returned to Berkeley, moving in with my brother Robert in October.

Planning a Typescript of Stories Written for Schorer

Inasmuch as the date for my entering the monastery had been postponed indefinitely, I remained at the seminary through most of 1967, continuing my studies, which I completed by the middle of September, as well as working with the Paulinos. Not content with these commitments, I figured that I would probably have just enough time to prepare another little book in the form of a typescript. It would consist of a selection of short stories I had written for Schorer.

I was planning to issue them in an annotated edition of only one copy, bound in black leather, for my brother Tom, who had recently moved from Germany to Holland. Of my three brothers I am closest to him. When I lived in Verona in the seventies, I frequently visited him and his wife Elfie and their two children in Munich, where they eventually settled. They also liked to vacation in Italy, often near Verona.

The extant sample pages show the text typed on the Smith-Corona typewriter in a sans serif, caps-and-small-caps face in black and red with justified margins on mouldmade paper. The project was even more complicated by the fact that I was imposing the pages in eight-page signatures as I typed them.

I had started to edit the stories, but I needed some objective, perhaps even professional, help to get them in shape for my project. In a letter, dated December 12, 1966, I wrote to Allen Tate, outlining the scope of the project, to which I added a subtitle: *An Evaluation of Two Decades of Self-Deception.* In the same letter I had asked him if he would be interested in editing the manuscript, explaining that neither Precio nor I could spell or write a decent sentence. I also noted, "It's going to be one of those *I tell all* type of memoirs.

Item 2. 1945–1965: An Evaluation of Two Decades of Self-Deception   99

That's why it is being limited to one copy." Allen replied that it was more than he could handle.

Gladys E. Hares

Next I contacted Gladys E. Hares. At the time I wrote to her from Buenos Aires in 1967, she had retired and moved to California. She said she would be pleased to help me. In February I sent her the first installment of the project. We were soon sending edited versions of the text back and forth, and in April Gladys returned the final draft of the edited manuscript.

Gladys E. Hares in Fort Tryon Park for Richard's twenty-eighth birthday, New York, NY, 1959. (Photo by Arto Szabo, courtesy of PWP Archives.)

The Dedication

Like the stories, the dedication was subjective and self-indulgent. I loved the name Rainer. It was a throwback to my time in Germany with Dietrich Leube, and I felt it suited my personality. The date is my birthday.

Gabriel Precio's Introduction

In his introduction to "The Open Edition," Precio wrote:

> These stories *Spiccato Spectres Related Silenticiously*, usually referred to simply as *The S.S.R.S. Stories* ... were written for Mark Shorrer's [sic] 106A creative writing course at the University of California at Berkeley in the fall of '53. The stories appear here, for the most part, exactly as they were submitted to Shorrer with the addition of the always necessary corrections in spelling, punctuation, and grammar. In the years which followed, Richard continued to change a word here and there and to unravel some of the more ambiguous sentences; however, he did not attempt to rewrite the stories, and left what even he recognized as bad or trite writing intact, maintaining that his purpose in altering the stories was not to retouch them, but to focus them.

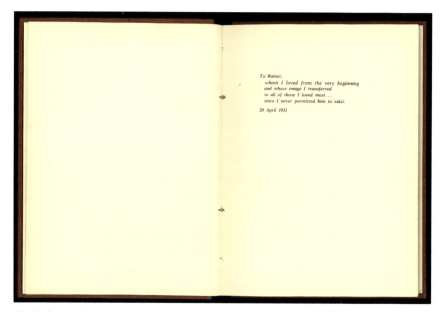

The dedication from *1945–1965: An Evaluation of Two Decades of Self-Deception.* (Courtesy of the University of Oregon Libraries.)

Item 2. 1945–1965: An Evaluation of Two Decades of Self-Deception 101

The stories from this class were his favorites, and even though he was always very protective, often secretive, about all his stories, he would occasionally read some of these to his closest friends. As he became more reticent, especially towards the second decade, he seldom mentioned or read the stories. No more than a dozen of his friends after '54 were even aware of them and probably very few of those who were actually heard or read any of them.

During the school year '53–'54, Richard worked part time as a page in the Social Sciences Research Section [i.e. Social Science Reference Service] of the university library. He was always intrigued by "busy work," possibly because it afforded him ample opportunity to escape into his world of daydreams. It is, therefore, not surprising that the SSRS would appear in his writing; however, what is surprising is his complete involvement in this detached, yet influential, environment which directly or indirectly is present in all of these stories. After having written a story dedicated to Mr. [Patrick] Wilson, Richard made a "project" out of writing a story for each of the other members of the permanent staff, even though his contact with them, except for Mr. Wilson, was impersonal and did not extend beyond the library. The results could hardly be considered truly inspired by or faithful to any of them. He used their names more as an element of "style" than of sentiment, and their personalities and habits became springboards for his fantasies only when they were related to his own experiences.

Since the stories are so subjective and of questionable literary value, only twenty copies are being distributed among his friends. The editor apologizes if he has whetted the curiosity of the reader concerning the additional information in The Closed Edition; however, because of the intimate and frank nature of this material, it was deemed prudent to omit these sections from The Open Edition.

One of the things Precio does not mention, although he hints at it, is the crush I had on Pat, who was in charge of the Map Room, a division of the SSRS, where I was often assigned to work with him.

Thinking About Printing Another Keepsake

It had occurred to me earlier while pulling galley proofs for the Paulinos, that with a little more effort I could use the same proof press to print another little keepsake, in this case a book of my short stories, for my friends instead of limiting the project to a single typescript copy.

One day at the Pía Sociedad de San Pablo, I casually mentioned my type-script project to Mario Aguirre Mac-Kay. He thought I should issue these stories in a limited edition and even offered to help me financially with the project in appreciation for all the help I had been to him. He said that he would talk to the Paulinos to see if they would set the type and let me use one of their proof presses during the two-week semester break, a time when most of the activity in the pressroom came to a standstill. Surely they would do it as a token of their appreciation for all I had done for them.

The Paulinos very kindly indulged me by letting me use their facilities. I am still not quite sure why I wasn't planning to go to the monastery during this period. Printing was taking precedence over saving my soul.

Putting the Project Together

Profiting from the mistakes I had made designing Mario's books, I chose a rather understated design for this one. Again I planned to use two colors: this time black and terra cotta. At the time the stories were written, I had a beautiful terra-cotta lambswool V-neck sweater that I often wore over my bare torso. It made me feel very sexy – not that anyone ever paid any atten-tion to me. I was just another young, skinny kid. In part because of the early sensuous association I had for this and other earth tones, I frequently used these colors at the PWP.

Setting the Type

Even when this project was still conceived of as a typescript, I knew I would not be able to issue it as a single-signature pamphlet. I prepared a dummy, imposing it for gatherings just as I had done on projects for the Paulinos. Mario insisted on paying for the composition, which was set in Linotype Simoncini Aster, and the materials. I suppose it is fortunate that the compositor didn't understand English or he might have balked at setting such a silly text.

The compositor and I didn't hit it off in the beginning – I think he was an atheist, even though he worked for a religious order – but more to the point, he made fun of the way I spoke Spanish. At first I thought he was referring to my American accent, but I later discovered that he was

Item 2. 1945–1965: An Evaluation of Two Decades of Self-Deception   103

mimicking my Mexican accent. After all, I had learned to speak Spanish in Mexico. So in addition to having a comical accent by Latin American standards, my vocabulary was liberally sprinkled with Mexican words.

In a letter dated May 30, 1967, to Paul Secon, I wrote:

> I have been working very hard on my little book project. This week I worked with the typesetter and we got the [text] . . . set up in type. I expect to pull the proofs this week and with luck start to hand print it the following week. . . . One thing it has done, it has shot me full of new energy. Even the sex organs are itchy, but I am ignoring this, at least for the time being. We have only four more weeks of classes until the semester break and I expect to make real headway on the project then. . . . Now I am afraid. A priest asked me today when I expected to enter the monastery and I said next January like I always say, but today I knew that I was lying. . . . The other night I was saying my prayers and I could hear someone playing *Der Rosenkavalier* and I was so unhappy. Your side [the secular world] gained a point at half-time.

Paul, the founder of the Pottery Barn, had been a friend since the late fifties, when I was still an industrial designer in New York. We had often worked together to develop new products for his store. One of the poems in *Eight Parting Poems* is dedicated to him.

Getting Down to Printing

Unlike Quito, Buenos Aires offered an abundance of fully stocked upscale art supply stores, where I selected the Canson Ingres paper. In mid-June I said in letters to Gladys and my parents that I would start to print the following week; however, a month later in a letter to my parents, I mentioned that I had started printing and would be printing for the next two weeks. I also asked them for $25 to help cover some of the expenses.

After cutting the paper down to size, I inked up the Reprex proof press and began printing in quarto. For some reason I didn't feel it was necessary to pull positioning proofs on newsprint before starting the run, so I ruined a lot of the Canson paper due to faulty backup. The image on the heavily sized paper wasn't as sharp as I thought it should be. While I was wondering how I could improve the impression, the compositor, who was watching me print at a distance, suggested that I try dampening the paper, without explaining how to do it. I followed my instincts: first I laid a sheet of paper down on the feed board and passed a dripping sponge over the surface I was about to print; then I wiped away any water that hadn't already run off onto the floor before I printed the sheet. The inking was still uneven, over- and under-inked, most of the time on the same page, but fine printing at last! The bulk of the book was printed during this period.

Leandro Velasco

Once I was committed to printing the text instead of typing it, I decided to add a frontispiece image. On June 20 I asked Leandro Velasco, a Colombian artist and former lover in New York, to make a small pen and ink drawing for the book. One of the poems in *Eight Parting Poems* is dedicated to Leandro. In 1964 he lived with another Colombian, with whom he was also having sex. For several months we played gonorrhea Ping-Pong. Leandro kept writing that he was working on the project, but I never received anything from him. The book was paginated and printed in a way that the frontispiece illustration would appear on a two-page tip-in, so I could print the text before I had the illustration. In desperation I decided that I would illustrate the book myself, so I began experimenting with engraved Lucite. I made dozens of sketches I thought I might be able to use for intaglio prints.

Leandro Velasco in Central Park, New York, NY, 1964.
(Photo by RGR, courtesy of PWP Archives.)

Item 2. 1945–1965: An Evaluation of Two Decades of Self-Deception   105

In the meantime I had mentioned the problems I was having with Leandro to Allen. Within a short time he sent me several pen and ink drawings, one of which I liked very much; it abstractly conveyed the ideas of isolation and creativity.

Binding the Book

After the text was printed, I wasn't quite sure what my next step would be, except I knew that I did not want to attempt to bind the book myself. Quite by chance, Father Keegan sent me on an errand to retrieve some periodicals he was having bound. The binder used a corrugated shed behind his house as a studio. It was in a terrible mess – not unlike most of the small trade binderies I later saw in Italy. But in all that clutter there was one thing that instantly attracted my attention. I couldn't take my eyes off the exquisite marbled papers that were hung up to dry all over the studio. Sensing my curiosity, the binder showed me how he made them. I stood in awe as he sprinkled the colors onto a thick liquid base, whisking them around with a broom straw. When he was satisfied with the pattern, he would lower the sheet of paper onto the prepared surface and then slowly roll it back, revealing the floating colors that had adhered to it in a marbled pattern. I commissioned him that afternoon to bind my small book on the condition that he use one of his marbled papers for the endsheets. I was very pleased with the results. His papers were suggestive of the midnight sky described in one of the stories.

It wasn't until many years later, as the books started to come apart, that I realized he had bound them on rough cords like the periodicals he was accustomed to binding.

By the time I received Allen's drawing, the book had already been printed and bound. I had a linecut made of it, which I printed separately. I took these pages to the binder to be tipped into the books.

Frustrations

In a letter, dated September 4, to Allen I lamented, "The book has many mistakes, but I had to draw the line somewhere as it was driving me crazy." I spent days trying to get the lines to backup. It was off due to the erratic system I used to dampen the paper. I was learning how to print by printing. This last problem was one of the first to be resolved by more experience once I started printing on the handpress in Italy.

Armando Braun Menéndez

Once the book was finished, I felt more sociable, and so one night, like many earlier ones, Mario and I went to visit Armando Braun Menéndez, one of Argentina's most prominent landowners and head of Emecé Editores. I presented him with a copy of my book, and he praised it like any dear godfather would, still commenting on its shortcomings, "So much effort, though not yet refined, for such a slight text." Setting my gift aside, he turned and began pulling books, the likes of which I had never seen before, off his shelves. There were many limited editions with original graphics that had been printed on antique handpresses. Many of the texts were by the most renowned living authors, including Jorge Luis Borges. Several of the books in Armando's library had been printed by Francisco Colombo and his successors Emilio and Osvaldo Colombo, the most famous family of handpress printers in Latin America.

There existed in Argentina and Chile in the sixties several bibliophile groups. Unknown to me at the time, Armando represented the type of collector I sought out years later and came to depend on for the survival of the Plain Wrapper Press. Many of the volumes in his collection were private

Armando Braun Menéndez in his library, Buenos Aires, Argentina, date unknown. (Photographer unknown, courtesy of Patricio Gatti.)

Item 2. 1945–1965: An Evaluation of Two Decades of Self-Deception 107

press books, and seeing them made me realize just how beautiful books could be when they were also conceived as art objects. Armando said that if I ever decided to print another book, he would bring me together with Borges, an author he was sure would be delighted to give me a text. I also realized that to print such large format books I would need a bigger press and the skill to operate it.

The Reality of *1945–1965: An Evaluation of Two Decades of Self-Deception*

I immediately sensed that what I had worked so hard on was in reality quite insignificant by comparison to the books I had seen in Armando's library, and I was crushed. As I strove to improve the craftsmanship in my books in later years, my complete lack of any formal training in printing became more evident and often led to even greater frustration. In a letter, dated August 22, 1967, to my brother Tom I made a complaint that I repeated over and over again for the next twenty years: the book "took so long to print and ended up being terribly costly, but R-G doesn't know how to do things simply. It is filled with mistakes [mostly uneven inking and bad backup], with evidence that I cannot be perfect."

Armando and his magnificent library had opened my eyes to the future. I already knew that if I were to continue publishing, my own texts would be pretentious in such luxurious formats. For the first time I gave serious thought to what and who I wanted to print, especially if I intended to sell what I printed, hoping that through the selection of the material and the printing of it, I would be able to make a personal statement that could be identified as having come only from me. This was a real turning point in the editorial policy of the PWP, as well as the first link in the chain of events that eventually led to the publication of the author responsible for the international reputation of the Press: Borges. That evening I ceased to be a vanity press and started on a circuitous course that would establish the PWP as a fine literary press.

Departing Buenos Aires

Shortly before leaving Buenos Aires, I was feeling melancholy and confused about what lay ahead. I lapsed into the old New York habit of going to a bathhouse. In the early sixties my doctor innocently suggested I go to the baths to release some of the tension and anxiety brought on by my work.

Little did he know that I would frequent the Everard baths on West 28th Street almost every Wednesday night and stay until dawn.

I had heard about a bathhouse in Buenos Aires, but didn't know its exact location. After wandering around in the neighborhood where it was supposed to be, I eventually found it. It was enormous and dirty, filled with cockroaches with four-inch wingspans. I entered the unoccupied stream room and spread out on a deckchair. After awhile an attractive young man in his early twenties came in. We were alone. He pressed his towel-draped hard penis against my shoulder. Without saying a word he reached under my towel and found my already erect penis. Holding tight he pulled me to my feet. He said he wanted to be fucked – it would be his first and last time – before getting married on the weekend. He bent over, holding onto the back of the deckchair, and I entered him. Suddenly he pulled away, having come almost instantly. I said, "Hey, I haven't come yet." But he didn't care. Without saying another word, we both headed for the showers. The steaming water must have loosened his tongue; he began to chat. What was my name? Where did I live? I told him I lived in Villa Devoto (well known as the location of the seminary). His puzzled face suddenly turned to fear. He dropped to his knees and said, "Are you a priest?" I took my revenge. "Yes, my son." He was so upset that he threw up on my stomach. I washed myself off, and he followed me into the steam room. I felt sorry for him and gave him some practical advice about his sexuality and advised him never to tell his wife about what had just happened between us.

The Last Two Nights in Buenos Aires

Mario was a real angel. He put me up in a hotel for two nights before I sailed to Europe. The first night we had a quiet supper. Both of us, on the verge of tears, reminisced about all that had transpired since we first met. During our last few meetings, I sensed that Mario was also coming on to me, curious about my lifestyle. On the second night, however, he left me on my own to extricate myself from my Buenos Aires adventure. The next day he alone saw me off. There were a lot of seminarians on board the ship on their way to study in Rome. They had been told that I was from the seminary in Buenos Aires, so they asked me to join their reciting of the rosary twice a day.

I set sail on September 15 for Barcelona on the Italia Line's *Augustus* and arrived in Barcelona two weeks later. From there I went by train to

Item 2. 1945–1965: An Evaluation of Two Decades of Self-Deception 109

Amsterdam where I visited with my brother Tom and his family. The photograph below shows me bronzed and in good health.

After a week in Amsterdam, I continued by train to Copenhagen where I spent five days with Berta Moltke and Paul Secon before arriving in mid-October at my ultimate destination, Rome.

Letter to My Parents
The following letter, dated October 25, to my parents describes my first week in Rome:

> I am finally settled in Rome and so I want to get a short letter off to let you know that I am well and working. . . . My job is very interesting and I am doing most of the work in the American college (that's the seminary for Americans studying in Rome). I also see my friends from Latin America from time to time at their college. I receive $30 a week and after I pay for my board and room, I have four dollars left for everything else. It will be a bit difficult but I must learn to make sacrifices. Also it will only be until the 13th of December. I have checked into flights. There is an Alitalia flight directly from Rome to

Gabriel with his niece Christiane Rummonds, Amsterdam, The Netherlands, 1967. (Photo by Thomas Rummonds, courtesy of PWP Archives.)

New York on Wed. the 13th. I would like to take it and then have a reservation on to California on the 19th of December. I have lost track of what our money situation is but I think there is enough left to cover this flight. If not, I have some savings, about $500. Would you please let me know what the flight would cost if you bought it at that end. . . . I have come to the conclusion in the last few months that I am psychologically unbalanced, much more seriously than I had even dared to let myself admit. I do not know where to turn to even find help, medical help that is. The self-destructive element is now so strong within me that I am less capable every day of mixing in society. By self-destructive, I do not mean physically. I mean emotional and social. It is so strange. I have none of the "normal" vices. I do not drink, I do not take drugs, as a matter of fact, I have never tried even a simple drug like marijuana. [This is not exactly true.] I don't even have sex anymore. I thought that spending the time in Europe would open me up, and it did to a certain extent when I was with Tom and Elfie and later in Denmark with friends, but even they noticed it. Now in Rome, I am alone. I wanted to find a pleasant place to live but I chose an ugly one and I cannot bring myself to move. My excuse is that it is close to where I work. Please be patient with me when I come to visit. I will not stay long. I still have my vows. I keep telling myself that I will go to a priest and ask for release from them, but I do not. I go to mass but I say fewer prayers now. Partly there is little time. One works until eight in the evening in Rome. My friend in Denmark asked me to write a movie and I wrote the first draft of one and send it to him. He wants me to do it for two reasons: one he thinks it will be good therapy and two he talked to his agent about it and he liked it. Rome is quite interesting. It does not have the beautiful parkways and gardens with flowers like Barcelona or Copenhagen, but the fountains are truly magnificent. Fortunately there are many free things to do here, because I will not have any money to go out. Movies are $1.65. That's practically half my allowance for the week. I will use the nights to study Italian.

I must close now. I have some things I must attend to now.

Item 2. 1945–1965: An Evaluation of Two Decades of Self-Deception   111

Rome

Once in Rome, thanks to Father Jorge María Mejía, an old friend from Buenos Aires, I was under the wing of the Argentine legation to the Vatican. Soon after I was sent to work at Information Documentation on the Conciliar Church (IDO-C), a Catholic organization housed in a convent in via di S. Maria dell'Anima.

During the day as I worked at compiling a bibliography of secular periodicals that routinely cited the Catholic Church, I looked down from my small round attic window at the carefree populace enjoying the sun and drinking coffee in the cafés of Piazza Navona. At night I worked the banks of the Tiber River for small sums of money. Through a Turkish friend, Semin Sayit, I made contact with the Italian film industry and was working on a number of screenplays, one intended as a vehicle for Alida Valli, a great favorite of mine. These activities and other distractions only widened the gap between a secular and a spiritual life that inevitably led to my decision not to pursue a contemplative life in a Trappist monastery.

Piazza Navona, Rome, Italy, 2009. The small round window on the right was Gabriel's office in 1967. (Photo by RGR, courtesy of PWP Archives.)

One More Unfulfilled Fantasy

Toward the end of my stay in Rome, I lived in a fantasy world completely out of touch with reality. One more unfulfilled fantasy, an unrealistic and grandiose project, illustrates just how crazy I was, considering that I had no money or any real experience printing on a handpress. I wrote in a letter, dated November 12, to Kenneth Pettitt about the most far-fetched project I have ever conceived. The letter has been heavily edited and corrected.

Recently, I have been thinking about printing a large sized, literary and art magazine, *Plain Wrapper Press Notebook*, in an edition of 250 copies. It would be for bibliophiles and hand printed from handset types on handmade paper. Probably two issues a year at a cost of $5 a year. Each issue would be devoted to one writer and one artist. The masthead, etc., would be printed on an overlay which can be torn out, leaving, in effect, a limited edition book, each numbered and signed, etc. I plan to devote one issue to Neruda, the Chilean poet, another to Borges, the Argentine writer; and also one to Cortázar. I know their Latin American publishers very well, and so it would be quite simple, I think. I would want unpublished material, but the author would retain all rights to the material after publication. I would publish the material in the language of the author. The introductions, bibliographies, etc. would be in English. I feel I should start out in English which brings me to YOU [I wanted to start by printing some of Kenneth's poems]. . . . Since the edition is so limited I can not pay for the poems, but will give the authors 15 copies. Subscriptions won't be much of a problem because only 200 will have to be sold, primarily to collectors of limited editions (with, I hope, good literary taste). I will probably print the first two numbers here in Italy. Where it is printed is of very little concern to me. I am more interested in how it is printed and of course the quality of the contents. I have friends all over the world who are writers or painters and I feel it is time for me to stop being so self-indulgent in my publications and do something of literary value.

I was lucky no one took me seriously. The letter is another example of how unhinged I was.

Item 2. 1945–1965: An Evaluation of Two Decades of Self-Deception 113

Thoughts about Returning to Europe

Before leaving Rome, I wrote to Paul and Berta that I wanted to return to Europe, but not to IDO-C.

> I am still very confused about the future. One moment I say I won't come back, the next I want to come back. Printing is probably the only field I could work in and make a decent salary right now. Berta, don't say come to Copenhagen unless you really mean it, because I just might surprise you if nothing else works out. It would be a more logical place than Italy for printing since more printing is done in English there than here. Or at least I would assume so. Although Holland is probably better.

Locro de Betty
Argentine Meat and Vegetable Stew

Serves 15

This is a popular winter comfort food in Latin America. Each household has its own family recipe. The ingredients also vary from country to country. This particular one comes from Fabiana Gadano, whose mother Betty is responsible for this recipe as made in Buenos Aires.

6 tablespoons olive oil, divided
1 pound boneless pork ribs, cut into bite-sized pieces
1 pound rump roast, trimmed of fat and cut into bite-sized pieces
½ pound salt pork, cut into ½-inch cubes
1 pound chorizo sausage, cut into ½-inch pieces
2 large yellow onions (about 3 pounds), coarsely chopped
6 scallions (green onions), white parts only sliced cross-wise
3 large garlic cloves, finely chopped
6 large sprigs of flat-leaf parsley, (about ⅛ ounce) finely chopped
4 cups chicken broth, divided
1 pound dried hominy, soaked in 6 cups of water overnight
1 pound dried white beans soaked in 6 cups of water overnight
½ pound carrots, peeled and sliced into bite-sized pieces
1 pound baking potatoes, peeled and coarsely chopped
1 pound yams, peeled and coarsely chopped
1 pound acorn squash after peeling and seeding, coarsely chopped
1 large tomato, peeled and coarsely chopped
1 teaspoon paprika
½ teaspoon ground cumin
1 bay leaf
½ teaspoon crushed red pepper flakes
4 ears yellow sweet corn, cut off the cob
1 teaspoon salt
½ teaspoon freshly ground black pepper

Item 2. 1945–1965: An Evaluation of Two Decades of Self-Deception   115

In a large Dutch oven over medium heat, add 2 tablespoon of the oil. When oil is hot, add pork ribs and brown. Transfer to a plate until needed. Add 2 more tablespoons of the oil to the Dutch oven and repeat process with beef. Transfer to a plate until needed. Add remaining oil to the Dutch oven and sauté sausage and salt pork. When salt pork is translucent, add onions, scallions, garlic, and parsley. Deglaze the pan with 1 cup of the chicken broth. Return meats and their juices to the pan. Add hominy, beans, and remaining broth. Add carrots, potatoes, yams, squash, tomato, and spices. Bring to a boil, then turn heat down to simmer and cover the Dutch oven. Cook for 1 hour, stir frequently. Add corn and simmer for an additional ½ hour. Season with salt and pepper.

32 Union Square, New York, NY, 1992. This was the first location of the PWP in New York in 1968. (Photo by RGR, courtesy of PWP Archives.)

New York, New York

> We live by selected fictions.
> – Lawrence Durrell, *Balthazar*

Return to New York

By mid-December 1967 I found myself back in New York, arriving from Rome with nothing more than a few clothes and the return-trip portion of my ticket. Ostensibly I was passing through on my way to California to spend Christmas with my family, whom I had not seen in several years. Knowing of the ill will that had already existed for many years between my brother Robert and myself, Charles McNab and Allen Tate urged me to call my parents to see if the "Strawberry Bitch" had also been invited for the holidays. This was the name used by my friends as well as my brother Tom and his children to refer to Robert. Carlos Cárdenas and I went to Philadelphia for a weekend, where we stayed with Robert in an old tea warehouse he had renovated on Strawberry Street. Carlos and I slept on a sofa bed in his living room. Early in the morning, Robert came stomping out of his bedroom, complaining of the noise the two of us were making as we had sex. He threw us out. Carlos turned to me and said, "I never want to see that fucking Strawberry Bitch again." We spent the rest of the day happily visiting museums and shopping before returning to New York.

Later that year a psychiatrist friend of mine who lived in New York went to Philadelphia to party. There was a guy holed up in a closet servicing anyone who would enter his lair. Yes, it was the Strawberry Bitch.

As soon as I asked my mother if Robert would be there, she burst into tears. She only wanted to bring her sons together. I told her that under the circumstances I would not be coming home for Christmas. When Robert heard that I wasn't coming home, he decided to go skiing in Aspen, leaving our parents alone to face the miserable holiday they deserved. Instead of being depressed by their misguided plans for a reconciliation, I felt unexpectedly elated, even liberated. My parents had not been able to intimidate me this time. I was free.

Letter to My Parents

In the following letter, dated December 29, 1967, I vented my frustration and disappointment that they had not understood how emotionally fragile I felt when I wrote to them from Rome a few weeks earlier. The letter, full of self-pity and melodrama, often doesn't even make sense.

> What can I say? I feel our letters must now be reduced to mediocrities. I so carefully tried to explain the delicate balance of sanity, which now exists in my brain – but my warnings went unheeded. Is this what you call family love? For your so-called "democratic" attitudes you have succeeded in "killing" this one. I have lost all confidence in you – all trust. I have no desire to ever see you again on YOUR TERRITORY. If we are to visit again – and I hope we will (although it can't be soon) you will have to come to me. I am so used to disappointments that after the shock of what you had done – or what you would not do – passed through me – I felt nothing. I was not sad at Christmas – I had no guilt feelings. I made very simple plans – plans which I could trust – and so Allen and I had a quiet dinner and watched TV, and I went to bed about 10:30. Your presents arrived on Saturday. They were perfect. Exactly what I had asked for. How eager you were to please me materially – why was it so difficult to give me the one thing I came so far to receive from you? It is impossible to wrap love up in boxes. It doesn't fit under trees – only in hearts – even wicked, sinful, bitter, pride filled hearts. . . . There is nothing that I can now not lose.
>
> . . .
>
> I have seen my Cuban friend Carlos several times since I have been back. It is always a mixture of intense pleasure and pain to be with him. I saw him the night I spoke to you. I felt so lost. We took a long walk and I had my arm through his and I am always on fire next to him. I asked him to sleep with me (not for sex) but he said, "no." How well I remember his small smooth body all entwined with mine – sleeping soundly like two brothers.

I never wrote to my parents again about my personal life or intimate concerns.

New York, New York

Reassessing the Future

Once I had eliminated the tempting possibility of returning to Rome, I resigned myself to the necessity of remaining in New York, a city with which I have always had a love/hate relationship. I realized it would be easier to support myself and the press in New York than in Rome. With this in mind I decided to give myself a year and then go back to Europe, preferably Spain, once I learned to print.

There I was; I would have to make the best of a bad situation. It also meant that I would have to start all over again. I had little more than the clothes on my back and no possessions to speak of, but on the plus side, I had no debts. I asked myself: What do you really want to do with your life? The answer I received – even though it was just a faint or imagined whisper – was to print. I originally anticipated that I might have to stay in New York for one year, but unfortunately my estimate was way off, and it would be almost three before I returned to Europe. This was a period in my life filled with unprecedented frustration and setbacks. Aside from never having enough money, my chief source of frustration came from not being able to get my Press set up, and once it was operative, having to cope with the setbacks caused by my complete lack of training as a printer.

Job Search

Back in 1961 when I had returned to New York from Arizona – with few job opportunities – I had asked Betty Binns, a noted textbook designer, if she could help me find some freelance book work. Through Betty I prepared dummies and layouts for a number of publishers.

The first order of business was to find a job. I knew I didn't want to return to product design, so I went to see Pete Landa, one of the art directors who had also given me a few paste-up jobs. He was now an art director at Dover Publications. I must have felt destiny was looking after me, because even though Pete didn't have any openings he suggested that I go see Robert Scudellari at Random House, which was known in those days as "the revolving door of publishing" because of the constant turnover in junior editors and book designers.

Random House

When I went to see Bob early in February 1968, a cold wind was blowing, chilling me to the quick. I was dressed in the only suit I owned, one of those thin black cotton suits worn by seminarians in Rome. I was too broke even to think about acquiring a topcoat, let alone any new clothes. When I arrived at Random House no one paid any attention to my incongruous appearance because New York was so full of oddballs and eccentrics.

When I showed Bob my portfolio, he didn't know quite what to make of it. It was completely unlike the impressive portfolios that ordinarily came across the desks of New York art directors. Mine contained one trade book (a play in Spanish I had designed for a small publishing house shortly after my return to New York), the two little PWP books I had printed in South America, and a few photographs of products I had designed in the fifties and sixties. Fortunately I didn't have any examples of the books I had worked on for the Ediciones Paulinas or Editorial Francisco de Aguirre, which would have instantly revealed my incompetence as a book designer. I tried to convince him that there really wasn't any difference between designing tableware and designing books; it was all a matter of making the right aesthetic decisions. In 1968, book designers' salaries started out at around $6,000 – a far cry from the $50,000 a year (the equivalent of $378,322 in 2014) that I had been earning as an industrial designer a few years earlier.

He seemed to like me, but he also didn't trust me. Why did I want to be a low-paid book designer instead of a high-paid industrial designer? I told him that I wanted to learn everything there was to know about book design and production so I could start my own private press.

A couple of weeks after the interview, I had a call from Bob offering me a job. I've never understood why, considering the meagerness of my portfolio, but perhaps he saw in me such a sincerity and determination regarding book-making that he decided to take a chance on me. I was a real workaholic, working long hours, usually starting around seven in the morning and leaving the office around seven in the evening. I designed a lot of books that first year.

In December my salary was raised to $10,500 based on my productivity. Even though the extra money would have been a godsend, I asked for a four-day week at my old pay, feeling that the extra day at my own press would mean the difference between completing the projects I had already

New York, New York　　　　　　　　　　　　　　　　　　　　121

undertaken or giving up altogether on the idea of ever becoming a fine printer. Bob didn't want to "set a precedent," so I quit. By this time, printing had become my primary concern, and I falsely assumed that I would be able to support myself with free-lance book design commissions until the PWP could become self-sufficient.

Golda Fishbein

When I started at Random House, I was put in a cubicle where I shared a telephone with Golda Fishbein, the calligrapher and book designer who would later play a major role at the PWP. Golda had only recently started as a staff designer for the Alfred A. Knopf imprint, reporting to Betty Anderson, one of the really great book designers of our generation. On the other hand I reported to Leon Bolognese, the competent but dull art director for the College Department imprint at Random House. Most of what I learned about book design and production I picked up from Betty and Leon.

I pretty much kept to myself, uninterested in making new friends. One day Golda came into work and said she wouldn't be in the next day. I said in a flippant way, "Where are you going? To Mexico? To get a divorce?" That was exactly what she was going to do. Having discovered that we were probably tuned in on the same wavelength, we became close friends. Knowing Golda those first months in New York made my life at Random House considerably more bearable.

My immediate plan was to learn as much as I could about publishing in a year and then cut out for Spain. I had selected Spain because I thought the cost of living would be within my means and I already spoke the language. However, an even more important factor was that I had decided – influenced by my recent sojourn in Latin America – to publish bilingual editions of Spanish and Latin American authors exclusively.

Charles McNab

Shortly after New Year's Charles invited me to stay with him; however, I was soon looking for my own place. I moved into a horrible cockroach-infested tenement at 506 East 82nd Street. With a lot of determination, I managed to turn it into a palace. (Years later when I was living in a real palace in Verona, Charles, during a visit, commented that I had succeeded in turning it into a tenement.)

I first met Charles under an overpass in Yorkville in 1963. I was waiting around to get my cock sucked. Charles was on his knees at the end of a long line of guys waiting to be serviced. When he got to me, he said, "I need a breather. Come back to my place." I liked Charles. For all his sexual bravado, he was actually a very shy guy. He was the administrative assistant to the head of Warner Brothers in their New York office. We both loved movies, and he always had passes to all the openings. In 1964 we saw the opening of the Beatles' *A Hard Day's Night* at the Tran-Lux East on Third Avenue.

Charles McNab in Central Park, New York, NY, 1970. (Photo by RGR, courtesy of PWP Archives.)

Searching for a Printing Press

From what I have just said, it may not appear that my primary objective was to find a printing press with a large bed and a studio in which to put it. In March 1968 I heard that Bret Rohmer at the Brownstone Press on East 21st Street wanted to sell his Vandercook 14 proof press. I took down the specifications as Bret described the press over the phone. He told me the bed measured 17 x 28 inches; however, the actual measurement was 14 x 26 inches. Bret must have seen how green I was because he unflinchingly asked $450 for the press, and I eagerly gave it to him – in installments – without even attempting to negotiate a better price. Now I had a press, but no place to put it, which caused another problem.

New York, New York

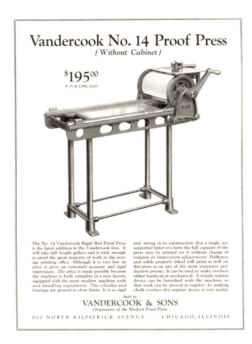

Vandercook No. 14 Proof Press, from an early 1930s Vandercook & Sons catalog. (Courtesy of Paul Moxon)

A Grisly Murder

Many years later in April under the same overpass where I had met Charles McNab, I met a young man whom I liked very much. We decided to go to a bar in the Village. Philip Baker had given me a birthday party earlier that evening, and I had some presents that I wanted to drop off at my place first. I asked him if he wanted to come with me, but he said that he would wait for me along the promenade. About ten minutes later I found him lying on the ground, severely beaten. I rushed to the emergency room of a nearby hospital and told them that there was a man who had been badly beaten on the promenade.

The young man died. The police were looking for information, and another guy I casually knew from the promenade gave them my name. They called me at Random House and took me down to the station to look at mug shots. They wanted me to pin the murder on any one of the kids in the photographs. They all looked so sad, I started to cry. I started having a recurring dream in which I was being stalked. A young man would stop me on the street and say, "I know you saw me kill your friend." Then he would pull out a knife and kill me. I would wake up screaming. Finally, I told the police I couldn't help them anymore. Fortunately they stopped calling.

Unrequited Love

I wasn't always successful with the guys I pursued. I was very aggressive when it came to casual sex, but I became very shy with people I had a serious crush on. Tom Stuart was a good example. I had met him through friends and fell in love with him instantly. He was some kind of scientist. We would go out to eat or to a movie, always parting on the street. When I couldn't take it any longer, I wrote him the following letter, dated June 28, 1968:

> –T–
>
> Yes, this is one of "those" letters.
>
> My life seems to be destined to letters of passion and pain instead of the reality of sensuality and the joy of physical commitments, long or short. I keep telling myself that I will not spoil our evenings by prodding you about going to bed, making love. How wearisome to you I must have become! How unfortunate we did not just make a one-night stand out of the first night and let it go at that. Your finger touching mine on the bar certainly kindled within me the desire to give myself completely to you. At the same time, YOU frighten me. Were you serious, or just playing, or even worse, were you teasing me? I still do not know. It was too quick . . . I wanted to know you first as the intellectually probing young man who was in evidence on the surface and then ultimately, I suppose, I had hoped to know you sexually, to lie next to you all night, hardly sleeping, yet sleeping, to touch your shoulders with mine, to caress your chewed fingers, to kiss the little bumps on your lips, to run my tongue over your erratic teeth, without glasses to look closely into your uncovered eyes, to feel you swell and come into heat. NOW you are afraid of me. And I realize that I shall never experience these things with you . . . which is why I am suggesting that we do not see each other for awhile. Taking leave of you hurts me too much. My whole body aches as if I had been trying to run and WIN in a fantastically impossible race. When I leave you, I say it doesn't matter, I'll pick up someone, anyone, and a boy may appear who under any other circumstances would be attractive to me but I lower my head and hurry off. The beer in my stomach and too much air in my lungs give me chest pains Just wanting to make love to you, makes everyone else unacceptable. I crawl into bed and lightly pinch my nipples or run my

hand down onto my cock and it does not respond. It too will not settle for fantasies or substitutes. Perhaps once I start printing, I shall become so engrossed, so inverted again, that I shall be immune to personal involvements, then we can see each other again without the threat of "affair tension." I do not see any other solution. I did not want it to go so far, but from the moment I saw you, I was drawn to you. I tried not to have to face the truth that part of the attraction was physical. I have a long history of either abstaining altogether or having sex with people who repulse me. When I meet someone I like, I freeze up and usually become impotent. The pain of impersonal sex discolors what should be healthy passion and the desire for sexual pleasure. You are right, of course, you know that I would not content myself with going to bed with you just once (that is reserved for the anonymous, the undesirable strangers). The change from stranger to intimate is usually too great for me, and I tend to fail, and failing, I fall and lose. Without even having gotten close to you, I have probably lost you. I hope that I will still have you as a friend after I am able to pull myself back together.

Until another time,

-R-

Poor Health

I was always sick in New York. During the brutal winter, I suffered several bouts of bronchitis, as well as unexplained psychosomatic venereal diseases. But more alarming was my weight loss. I used to attend Mass at a Hungarian church in my neighborhood before going in to work. I followed along in my Spanish missal because I didn't like the Mass in English. One morning I fainted. When I came to in the sacristy, they said it was probably just malnourishment; I needed to eat more.

Making New Contacts

But I was relatively happy in New York, partly because I believed I would soon be leaving, and partly because my social life had improved and even expanded. I spent a lot of my spare time with Latin American expatriates, many of whom I met through Joanne Pottlizer and her Theater of Latin America (TOLA) organization. Long before getting my shop set up, I started to put together a tentative publishing program. When writers such as Nicanor Parra and Alejandro Jodorowsky were visiting New York, we would get together and discuss possible projects. TOLA also attracted poets like W. S. Merwin who were interested in Latin American writers. He wanted to translate Parra's poems into English for a Plain Wrapper Press edition to be illustrated by the Chilean painter Nemesio Antúnez. I had in hand the text and rights for Pablo Neruda's *Fulgor y muerte de Joaquín Murieta*, which another Chilean artist, Juan Gómez-Quiroz, wanted to illustrate with multicolor etchings. Carlos Slienger, a Mexican publisher living in New York, was eager to collaborate on a series of books for the Mexican market.

In another vein, already straying from my avowed publishing philosophy, I was negotiating with Caresse Crosby, who with her husband Harry had established the Black Sun Press in Paris in the twenties, for the rights to publish a new edition of Raymond Radiguet's homoerotic poems. Lyon Phelps, with whom I was having an affair, would translate them. Lyon had a lion's mane of blond hair and a smooth thin body. He was a curious kind of lover, believing in lots of foreplay and very slow but intense lovemaking.

Harrison Rivera

One of my boyfriends, Harrison Rivera, who had been passed along to me by Tony Strilko, thought I should print books illustrated by established artists. He suggested several of his Pop artist friends, such as Andy Warhol, Tom

Harrison Rivera, Philadelphia, PA, 1965. (Photo by RPR, courtesy of PWP Archives.)

New York, New York

Wesselmann, Allan D'Archangelo, and Larry Zox, as potential collaborators. He gave me their telephone numbers, saying that he had talked to them and that they were interested in hearing more about what I had in mind. Regrettably none of these projects was ever realized, but the idea of using well-known artists to illustrate my books had its inception with Harrison.

Another friend, Rolf Nelson, introduced me to Robert Indiana, hoping that we would collaborate on a book. Little did I know at the time that the international acclaim the PWP was to receive years later would be based on this premise.

Looking for a Studio

Bret's Rohmer's wife, Harriet Reisman, had wanted to sell the press mainly to free up the space it occupied in their apartment, but it stayed there for at least another five months while I combed the city looking for an affordable studio space. Harriet constantly badgered me at work with telephone calls, insisting that I remove the press from their apartment. Believe me, I wanted nothing more desperately than to find a studio and get Harriet off my back. I followed up every lead I got. John Challis, the harpsichord maker, offered me the ground floor of the clinic on Lafayette Street that he had converted into his home and workshop. But it was in an awkward part of town for me to get to. Later I found a tiny space closer to my home in a brownstone basement on East 75th Street that Jobe Forté used for lining drawers with decorated paper. He offered me the front half, which I was tempted to take. In a burst of enthusiasm and impracticality, I considered using my half as a combination print shop and bookstore, alternating between two equally pretentious names – "Bibliophia" and "Bibliophilia" – for the latter activity. Realistically the space wasn't even large enough for the press, let alone sharing it with a bookstore.

On July 9, 1968, I wrote to Paul Secon and Berta Moltke, "I am so discouraged these days. Each place I find for the press falls through at the last minute. . . . I hate the press and do not want to print on it. It has caused me so much anxiety and frustration."

Around the middle of July, I finally found a studio in an old office building at 32 Union Square East for $55 a month and moved the disassembled Vandercook press into the new studio on August 3. I didn't put it back together again until September.

My new studio was across the park from Andy Warhol's Factory. Even though Warhol and I had been casual friends in the fifties, when he was still making his humorous drawings of shoes for I. Miller ads that frequently appeared in *The New York Times*, I never made any effort to renew our friendship after he became a famous Pop artist. I lacked the confidence to hold my own in his stellar milieu.

Setting Up Shop

John Newbauer, an old Berkeley friend, helped me set up shop. In October I bought a Thompson single-tier metal type cabinet from a trade school that was changing over from hot metal to film type and a wooden type cabinet. I don't remember where it came from or where it ended up after I left New York. At last I was "in business," spending most of my time working on *The Dog Bite: A Dream Narrative*.

By being thrifty I managed little by little to assemble the equipment I needed for the Press. Bret had promised to break me in on the Vandercook, but once the press was out of his apartment, I was never able to get him to come by my studio, even though his Brownstone Press was only a few blocks away. In fact I never saw him again. Either he would call the night before to let me know that he wasn't coming or he just didn't show up.

Berta Moltke and Paul Secon, place and date unknown. (Photographer unknown, courtesy of Berta Moltke.)

New York, New York

A year after my arrival in New York, I was just starting to print my third book. By the mid-November 1968 I was so discouraged by the performance of my primitive Vandercook press that I began looking for a more modern version of it. As I became more proficient on the Vandercook, I realized that it was not the best press for the precise type of work I had in mind.

James Laughlin

James Laughlin, the publisher of New Directions, and I had been brought together by our mutual admiration of Latin American writing. He introduced me to Nicanor Parra at a reading of the poet's work at the Poetry Center on East 92nd Street on June 26, 1968, hoping that Parra and I would collaborate on a book. Laughlin even drew up a writer/publisher contract for us.

On one of my visits to his office, he showed me several books printed by Giovanni Mardersteig, the German/Italian handpress printer whose Officina Bodoni in Verona was one of the preeminent private presses of the twentieth century. Laughlin considered him to be the world's greatest living handpress printer.

Giovanni Mardersteig

In November Laughlin invited me to accompany him to a lecture given by Giovanni Mardersteig at the Pierpont Morgan Library. During his talk Mardersteig casually mentioned that he was the last of the great handpress printers. When he said that the tradition of handpress printing would die with him, I had to restrain myself. I was ready to leap up and say, "Let me study with you. I'll carry on your legacy!" I would have gladly been his disciple. The irony is that even though Mardersteig virtually ignored me when I moved to Verona, I was one of the few printers after his death who promoted the tradition of the handpress that he best exemplified for over fifty years.

The next night I accompanied Robert Halsband, the eighteenth-century literary scholar with whom I was having an affair, to a reception at Columbia University for Mardersteig hosted by Helen Macy, the widow of the founder of The Limited Editions Club. Mardersteig was very gracious. He even invited me to come to Verona.

I spent most of the evening engaged in a very intense conversation with Mardersteig's son Martino, a charming young man who was obviously terrified of his father. Even though Martino managed his father's commercial printing plant, the Stamperia Valdonega, he had an affinity for the handpress, referring to it as "an instrument of perfection." I was immediately won over to his point of view as he enthusiastically proclaimed the superiority of the handpress over the manually operated cylinder proof press. He concluded by saying

Giovanni Mardersteig, place and date unknown. (Photographer unknown, courtesy of Martino Mardersteig.)

that if I were really serious about fine printing, I would have to use a handpress. I was smitten. Martino gave me Reynolds Stone's address in England, believing that Stone, a wood engraver and active in British private press circles, would be a good contact in my search for a handpress. He also mentioned that Verona was a small center of handpress printers and that he would help me if I were to relocate there.

Looking for a Handpress

I had already started printing on my Vandercook with reasonably good results, but after my talk with Martino, I knew I wouldn't be completely satisfied until I had a handpress. So I used a bit of logic. There was one person who would know the whereabouts of handpresses on the East Coast, and that person was Jack Robinson, a sales representative for the paper merchants Andrews/Nelson/Whitehead. After all, most handpress printers

Martino Mardersteig, Verona, Italy, 1972. (Photo by James Weil, courtesy of Martino Mardersteig.)

would be using, or would have used at one time, handmade paper. In those days most of the fine European handmade papers sold in America came from A/N/W. I asked Jack if he knew of any dormant handpresses.

Ram Press
Jack located two or three presses for me, including a small R. Hoe Washington press at Robert Haas's Ram Press at 48 West 25th Street. Haas was always in need of money, so when Jack suggested to him that I was interested in renting a small corner of his printing loft in which to set up my own shop, he was immediately amenable to the idea. Aside from my helping

him defray some of his expenses, he was also eager to have me there for another reason. For many years he had hoped to find someone he could train on the handpress, someone who might carry on the tradition he had brought with him from Vienna but had been forced to abandon for commercial printing. The move filled me with excitement and anticipation. I was going to get to print on a handpress, and at last I would be working with a master handpress printer.

Haas was semiretired and quite a character. He was an exceptionally talented – but bitter – old man. Hundreds of students at Cooper Union had been inspired by him to look at letterforms as works of art, yet he felt that he had not received the recognition he deserved as a typographer or printer. He was particularly resentful about the printing of *The Catalogue of the Frick Collection,* because he was seldom identified with this project. It was a monumental handpress endeavor started in 1928 and not completed until 1955. The project required two handpresses so they could immediately back

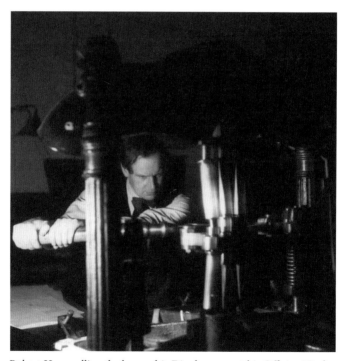

Robert Haas pulling the bar on his Dingler press at his Officina Vindobonensis, Vienna, Austria, ca. 1936, from Gabriel's book *Printing on the Iron Handpress* (1998). (Photo by Pftzner, courtesy of James Fraser.)

New York, New York 133

up the sheet on the second press as it came off the first press. The first 168 pages of Volume I were printed under Porter Garnett's direction at the Laboratory Press at Carnegie Institute of Technology. This portion of the catalog was completed in 1932. The rest of Volume I (pages 169 through 276) and Volumes II and III were printed in Pittsburgh in 1948–1949 under David J. Way's direction. Later, David and Bert Clarke printed the remaining nine volumes on a Vandercook proof press at their Thistle Press in New York, completing the project in 1955.

The Move to Haas's Loft

The move from the Union Square studio to Haas's loft was delayed a couple of times by crippling snowstorms, but eventually on February 12, 1969, I got my meager assortment of equipment installed in a well-lighted corner of Haas's huge loft. I was asking $300 for Bret's Vandercook press, but I ended up selling it for $125. I still had the Thompson type cabinet and a small assortment of type.

In April, with a birthday check from my parents, I bought a stainless-steel restaurant bus tray and a two-handled gelatine roller. In addition I had access to Haas's Chandler & Price clamshell platen presses and his foundry type, most of which was pied and could not be used until it was sorted. But most important Haas said I could use his handpress. He would even show me how to print on it.

However, although Haas had shown me several beautiful books that he had printed at his Officina Vindobonensis in Vienna in the 1930s, when he tried to reconstruct the procedures, he could no longer remember even the rudiments of the press's operation. He had spent so many years printing exquisite photographic books from halftone plates on his large automatic flat-bed presses that he was now at a loss as to where to begin on the Washington press. Even though I was disappointed not to have him as a teacher, I was happy just to have a real handpress at my disposal and was sure I could teach myself how to print on it in no time at all.

I ended up coming away from his shop empty-handed. I felt cheated at the time, realizing he was probably my only hope of ever finding a teacher in New York City. These were not the best of times for Haas. When he did arrive, he was anxiety-ridden and would go off to another part of the loft and putter.

Philomena Houlihan

After our long ago carefree days together at Gordon Fraser's, my old friend Philip Baker had gone on to become a librarian in the Conservation Division at The New York Public Library on Fifth Avenue at 42nd Street. One evening in 1969 he introduced me to Philomena Houlihan, who worked in the Rare Books Room at the same library. Philomena lived near me, and we often got together for supper at my place or at her book-filled apartment on East 83rd Street. She enjoyed showing me her collection of private press books and always had an interesting story to go with each. Among her favorites were those printed by her friends Harry Duncan and Wightman Williams at their Cummington Press in Cummington, Massachusetts. She used to say that I had a lot in common with them.

Many years later, in October 1989, I attended a conference at the University of Nebraska at Omaha to celebrate the fiftieth anniversary of The Cummington Press. Jack Hagstrom, one of the speakers and an avid collector of The Cummington Press, showed a slide of a photograph of a youthful Harry and Wightman. On seeing that intimate image from the distant past on the screen, I was reminded of Philomena, and tears welled up in my eyes: I knew then what she had really meant to say to me.

Rare Books and Manuscripts Division

Like so many other enthusiasts of handpress printing before and after me, I systematically began to read all the old printers' manuals, beginning with Joseph Moxon's *Mechanick Exercises* (1683), in hopes that they would reveal the secrets necessary to operate a handpress. They are interesting reading, but not very helpful from a practical point of view. My book *Nineteenth-Century Printing Practices and the Iron Handpress* was published in 2004. Its two volumes are filled with information I had garnered from the library's collection of early printers' manuals.

During my frequent visits to the Rare Books Room, Philomena showed me what other contemporary printers as well as their predecessors were doing, beginning with William Morris's Kelmscott Press, which was active in the late nineteenth century. I already knew that what I wanted to do was neither new nor original. With that in mind I began to study the work of those who had attempted what I was about to attempt, in hopes of finding my own niche.

I also discovered, with Philomena's help, the two private presses that would remain my favorites and an important source of inspiration: Emery Walker and Thomas James Cobden-Sanderson's Doves Press and Willy Wiegang and Ludwig Wolde's Bremer Presse. Even though PWP books were for the most part illustrated, I continued to strive to emulate the pure typography of these two exceptional presses throughout my career as a printer. For many years I belittled my own work. I wanted to print perfect books like Kelmscott, Doves, Bremer, and the Officina Bodoni.

The use of calligraphy by Edward Johnston at the Doves and Anna Simons at the Bremer also had a major impact on my work, which later prompted me to engage Golda Fishbein, whose distinctive calligraphy helped define the visual character of PWP books. Like Armando Braun Menéndez's private library in Buenos Aires, The New York Public Library provided me with a standard of excellence toward which to strive. Lewis M. Stark, then head of the rare books collection, took me under his wing, and I began to meet and correspond with other handpress printers. Lewis M. Allen was among the first, and he continued to lend moral support and advice until I stopped printing in 1988.

Dorothy and Lewis Allen working at their Smith Acorn press at the Allen Press, Kentfield, CA, 1959, from Gabriel's book *Printing on the Iron Handpress* (1998). (Photo by Stephen M. Allen, courtesy of Muir Dawson.)

Once ensconced in Haas's loft, I worked almost exclusively on the Washington press. It is a sad reflection, but when I first took up the handpress in 1969, there were only five handpress printers in the States producing books on a regular basis: Lewis and Dorothy Allen, Harry Duncan, William Everson, Carolyn Reading Hammer, and Kim Merker. Almost twenty years later, when I abandoned the handpress, neither the status quo nor the names had changed.

Printing on the Handpress

Before moving into Haas's loft, I had finished printing all the text for *The Dog Bite*. I spent the remaining time at Haas's pulling proofs on his Washington press, using a variety of handmade papers. I knew that sized handmade paper needed to be dampened. When I asked Haas how to dampen paper, he said that he had used wool felts, but couldn't remember the exact procedure; so I got in touch with David J. Way. Haas, who was not on speaking terms with David and still bore a grudge against him over the Frick catalogue, would not permit David in his shop. I had to sneak him in late one night to show me how he had dampened paper at the Carnegie Institute of Technology.

David quickly passed a quire of paper (about twenty-four sheets) through a trough of water and then placed each quire between dampened felts. I don't remember what we used for felts that night but I did acquire some etchers' felts soon after. What a mess we had on our hands! David probably did dampen paper that way for the catalog, but it was obvious that I would have to find my own method, one that was less haphazard and more precise. After all, it had been more than twenty years since he had last dampened paper.

I wrote to Martino Mardersteig on April 11, 1969, asking how to dampen paper. He replied they dampened the paper between dampened blotters. I immediately purchased a bundle of white cotton blotters from A/N/W. It wasn't until I moved to Verona in August 1970 that I realized Martino was referring to pulpboards, not blotters. Pulpboards are made from wood pulp, blotters from cotton fibers.

I had ordered five hundred sheets of Umbria paper, which arrived in October. I started a new series of tests for dampening paper using the white blotters – albeit the wrong type – which only compounded my earlier problems. I tried soaking each sheet in a tray of water before spreading it on the refrigerator door until it was ready to handle and stack. My apartment was always a shambles, as well as flooded. It never occurred to me "damp" meant barely moist, not soaking wet. The resulting paper was also badly wrinkled, and therefore useless. The real problem was too much water in the paper and not enough pressure on the pile.

Search for Love

Aside from a few proofs, the only thing I managed to print on Haas's Washington press was a small birthday keepsake, which was accordion-bound with pre-war Chinese tea chest paper over boards in April. The text was a short poem by D.H. Lawrence, illustrated with one of my own rather amateurish linocuts.

> Search For Love
>
> Those that go searching for love
> only make manifest their own lovelessness,
> and the loveless never find love,
> only the loving find love,
> and they never have to seek for it.

Birthday keepsake (1969). (Courtesy of The New York Public Library.)

Barbara Knight

I also printed a few things on one of Haas's Chandler & Price presses, including stationery and a calling card – "Miss Mattie's Trucking Service: A Final Solution for Old Queens since 1929" – for Charles McNab, as well as the following poem, in an edition of one, for Barbara Knight. We had attended Theatre Works, a performance art event, at Hunter College; later that night I wrote "The Patient Lover" for her.

> *The Patient Lover*
> for B.K. on a melancholy night, 9-V-69
>
> He sat quietly, very close to her.
> And as she breathed, she expanded his world.
> Hesitatingly, he touched her shoulder.
> She did not even know that it was he
> For she was with someone else in a silence
> Of her own which never mingled with his.
> Still he went on breaking out of himself,
> Waiting for the moment that she'd be there.

Barbara, a fellow worker at Random House with whom I was having an affair, was on the rebound after separating from a married Greek artist. Later she married Charles Haseloff, the poet and publisher of *Penumbra*.

Leon was always lusting after her, and I wanted to shout out to him, "Eat your heart out, Leon. She's sleeping with me"

Barbara and I had a lot of fun together. We spent a day at the Philadelphia Museum of Art and visited art galleries in New York. One night we

Barbara Knight, New York, NY, 1969. (Photo taken in a public photo booth, courtesy of Barbara Knight.)

went to a happening for the movie *Head* with the Monkees. Philomena had a friend whose son was in the band. I had never seen anything like it. Huge TV screens were set up everywhere projecting the movie, and of course there was a lot of delicious food and drink.

We also went to parties. I recall one in particular on New Year's Eve at the apartment of Fred Blesse, an old friend from Berkeley. I was in the kitchen with a group of women, including a couple of senator's wives. They were discussing a recently divorced friend's new boyfriend. They could find nothing nice to say about him. Too young, too poor. A bit drunk, I piped up and said, "Maybe he has a big dick." That cleared the kitchen. Fred came in and told me he thought it was time for me to leave. Barbara and I headed out into the snow and took a cab back to her warm and cozy place. She was the patient one.

I was intensely in love with her, so when the affair ended nine months later, I was heartbroken.

The printing of this poem taught me a serious lesson about using other printers' equipment and maintaining my own. Haas already had a form in the press – a woodcut by Judith Scholder – that he was getting ready to edition for her. When I replaced his form with mine, I moved the paper grippers closer together to accommodate my smaller format, but I failed to return them to their original position when I had finished my project. When Haas inked up the press the next day, the grippers smashed the woodcut to pieces. Needless to say, I was devastated. After this experience, I became a fanatic about always checking to see if everything was in its proper place before I started to print, even when working alone.

Haas and I never did carry on long conversations, but as time went by the strain of sharing a space with him began to have an adverse effect on me. New York itself was such a constant confrontation that I didn't need one more in "my" studio. Haas used to come to his shop only a few mornings a week. He would find me scurrying cheerfully around the loft. The first thing he would say in his heavy Viennese accent when he greeted me was, "Vat disaster avaits us today?" I had once asked him about buying his Washington press, and he had said if I learned how to print on it, he would give it to me because he wanted to see it used again for printing books. His gesture was well meaning, but if I were to become the legitimate owner of the press, I wanted to pay him for it. When he later mentioned that he was thinking about closing his shop and selling off all his equipment, I offered him $500 – more than I could afford. He replied, "Vat you trying to do, kill me?" Evidently he had forgotten that in a moment of generosity he had offered to "give" the press to me. Now he wanted $1,500 for it. I knew then that it was time to move on.

Return to Alfred A. Knopf

In the early summer of 1969, broke and despondent, I went to work at Alfred A. Knopf as senior book designer. The following year I designed three of my favorite books: *Single File* by Norman Fruchter and *A Pagan Place* by Edna O'Brien for Knopf, and *The Bluest Eye* by Toni Morrison for Holt, Rinehart and Winston. *Single File* was the first book published by Knopf to use the new Fotosetter composition. The text was set in Biretta by Westcott & Thomson in Philadelphia.

Being employed full-time again meant that I would have to conserve my free time as much as possible. Many precious hours were lost each week just getting to and from the studio. About the same time, I decided I could no longer afford both a studio and an apartment. On August 1 I moved out of the tenement on East 82nd Street and into a modest, sixth-floor studio

Chapter opening from *Single File*
(1970) by Norman Fruchter.
(Courtesy of PWP Archives.)

apartment at 444 East 84th Street in Yorkville, determined to use part of the space as a studio for my press. The rent was reasonable, $220.80 per month. I left Haas's loft in mid-August 1969.

Joseph Low's Washington Press

One of the other handpresses Jack Robinson told me about earlier was an 1844 R. Hoe Washington press that had been used to print a weekly newspaper in a West Virginia village as recently as the early forties. It belonged to Joseph Low, the illustrator, who wanted to trade it for a smaller and more manageable proof press. I had not considered his press originally because I thought it would be too big for me, but now that I no longer had access to Haas's Washington press, Jo's offer became more attractive.

Jo and I first discussed my acquiring his press in late November 1968. He was asking $500, less the cost of a suitable proof press that I would also have to find for the exchange. It took me more than eight months to find one, but with Bill Henry's help, I located an old Potter proof press that Jo liked. I paid $200 for it. Jo's invoice was for $509 (including two 16-foot planks for moving the Washington press out of his studio) less the $200 for the Potter. Jo let me pay the balance in four installments.

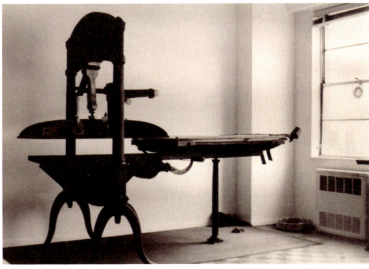

Joseph Low's 1844 R. Hoe Washington press set up at 444 East 84th Street, New York, NY, 1970. This was the third New York location of the PWP. (Photo by RGR, courtesy of PWP Archives.)

Bill was the only letterpress job printer I knew in New York. I referred to him as my surrogate mentor because he was always there for me with moral support and miscellaneous advice about materials and the whereabouts of equipment. Unfortunately he knew nothing about handpresses or how they worked, but he did like to talk about every aspect of printing, so it was always a pleasure to visit him in his cluttered shop on East 13th Street.

For $150, a sum I considered exorbitant at the time, Fred Wickelman and his son – another of Bill's finds – drove me up to Jo's studio in South Norwalk, Connecticut, with the proof press fastened down on a flat-bed truck. With a block and tackle we managed to get the Potter off the truck and Jo's disassembled Washington press onto it. Speeding back to New York I felt the elation of someone who has just pulled off a Brink's armored car robbery. It was a Sunday afternoon, and there wasn't much traffic on the road. We got the truck backed into the basement garage and were unloading the press when the off-duty superintendent walked in unexpectedly. "What's that?" he asked, pointing to the massive frame of the press. "I don't exactly know, maybe a wine press," I replied. "I found it in an antique shop in Connecticut. I'm going to use it for a planter." I didn't dare tell him it was a printing press. He said that it looked kind of heavy and went away not at all convinced. Somehow we managed to get the press, piecemeal, onto the elevator and into my apartment.

After it was set up in the sleeping alcove, the floor always trembled a little whenever the bar was pulled, although I basically felt it was safe where it was. I had put a black rubber mat under the press to keep it from "dancing." My friends liked to refer to the mat as "The Black Death," because it would be the mat, they assured me, not the press, that would kill the unsuspecting nurse who slept in the alcove below. When I wasn't using the press, I kept a few potted plants on the bed just in case the superintendent ever came in to fix something when I wasn't at home.

The Apartment/Print Shop
The apartment had 589 square feet, including an entry with a small coat closet and a living room with a large walk-in closet, in which the Thompson type cabinet, as well as my stock of printing paper was put. It also served as my composing room. There was a small bath, a kitchen, a dressing room with two more small closets, and the sleeping alcove where the press was

New York, New York

set up. A Poco proof press sat on a table between the two front windows, and finally, there was also a small rocker galley press with a flatbed and rails along the sides over which ran a rolling-pin platen about ten inches in diameter.

Between the entry and the living room, I set up a room divider that consisted of a six-foot metal storage cabinet, flanked by two-foot-wide bookshelves. The backs of these were covered with pieces of plywood and draped with floor-length curtains. I slept in the living room on a single bed pushed up against the room divider.

Lure of Spain

My self-imposed one-year stay in New York had already been extended into a second year, and I wasn't any closer to getting away. I realized that I would never get any books printed if my situation didn't change radically. I made a new timetable: I would finish only the two projects for which I already had the type set, and then pack up and take off for Spain.

Some friends owned a small farm on the island of Ibiza that they wanted to sell – their son had overdosed on drugs there and the place was full of unhappy memories for them. I made inquiries about immigrating to Spain, only to find that I would not be able to bring my handpress with me because of the strict censorship laws in Spain under Franco. My parents had already promised to buy the farm for me. The asking price was $5,000.

Amedeo de Franchis

One evening in September 1969, Beni Montresor, an Italian author and illustrator of children's books, brought his friend Amedeo de Franchis to dinner. I was recounting my troubles with the Spanish government when Amedeo asked me why I didn't consider going to Italy. He was the vice consul at the Italian Consulate in New York and would personally help me with the paperwork. After all, hadn't Mardersteig promised to help me if I came to Verona? In truth it seemed much more logical to go to Verona than to an isolated farm in Ibiza, especially since I still didn't know how to print and my chances of finding someone in Spain who might be able to help me were quite remote. Once again, just as my life had taken an abrupt and unforeseen turn when I met Ricardo Palou at the monastery, my destiny had again been placed in the hands of a chance acquaintance.

A Visit to Verona

I may have had a new plan, but I wasn't ready to move yet. First I had to resolve some of the technical difficulties I was having with my printing. So in December 1969 I went to Italy, where I rendezvoused with Paul and Berta for New Year's Eve in Venice. One of their friends, the Austrian painter Manina, gave a New Year's Eve party.

Manina asked me to write down three questions, which she would answer using the *I Ching* method of divination. Here are my questions, with her answers in italic below each question.

1. Do I have the latent talent to achieve what I believe at the moment to be my quest as an artist/craftsman?
Return, turning point.

2. Is a relationship with a Carlos [Cárdenas] or a Barbara [Knight] destructive?
Stagnation.

3. What can I expect in the way of physical love that will help me in my work and sustain me emotionally?
The family (clan).

I am not sure what the answers meant, but I decided they indicated that I should move to Verona and pursue a career in printing.

While in Venice Domingo De La Cueva, a Cuban jeweler with whom I was staying, sent Berta and me to visit two of his friends in Verona, the "Dutch Boys," Ger van Dijck, a Pop artist, and his lover Theo van der Aa. They lived in the Palazzo Guarienti, a wonderful Renaissance palace only a block away from the Duomo, the cathedral in the historic center of Verona. I fell in love with the city at first sight. In addition, Ger and Theo very generously told me that if I came to Verona, I could stay with them until I found a place of my own.

Bruno Bettini

While in Verona Berta introduced me to Bruno Bettini, an engineer and frustrated artist. She must have met him at Luciano Cristini's atelier while having some of her plates editioned. Bruno took us for a long drive in in the surrounding hills. An instant and mutual attraction developed between

New York, New York 145

Bruno and me. Berta even noticed it, saying, "It looks like you have already found yourself a boyfriend here."

The next evening Bruno and I took another drive. At the top of a hill overlooking the lights of Verona, he pulled over, and we began to neck and kiss, but stopped short of sex, knowing we would have plenty of time to consummate our desires once I moved to Verona. However, it didn't happen that way. Bruno, who years before had been hurt in a relationship with an American soldier, couldn't commit to a relationship. We saw each other occasionally in the following years, but our initial intimacy was never rekindled.

Then and there I decided to join the ranks of the Veronese printers. I visited Martino Mardersteig and showed him the proofs I had pulled on the Fabriano Umbria paper in New York. He said that one reason the printing was not sharp was that the paper had no size in it, so naturally it absorbed water like a sponge.

On January 8, 1970, I took the train to Fabriano , and went directly to the Cartiere Miliani-Fabriano mill, where they agreed to replace the paper I had already purchased with sized Umbria paper. By a stroke of luck, Andrews/Nelson/Whitehead had sold the balance of my paper to another client. This meant that in all probability I would have had two different papers in the book because handmade papers differ slightly from batch to batch. They very generously acknowledged this problem and let me return the paper I still had on hand to A/N/W. While at Fabriano I inquired about dampening paper, but no one was able to help me.

Getting Ready to Leave New York

I saw my move to Verona as a panacea. I would have new and supportive friends there who wanted to see me succeed as a printer, and perhaps most important of all, I had been led to believe that I was going to have access to the Mardersteigs for technical guidance, albeit limited, since both had made it clear that an apprenticeship at the Officina Bodoni was out of the question. I could hardly wait to get out of New York. Amedeo arranged for his uncle, il principe Luigi de Giovanni, in Switzerland to take care of all the paperwork for my visa. I was going as an "artist" to Italy, a country where skilled artisans were still looked upon with some respect and even affection. But before I could leave New York, there was some unpleasant unfinished business I couldn't ignore. It was the printing of *The Dog Bite*.

.

Fillet of Sole Stuffed with Crabmeat

Serves 4

In the 1950s, Gladys E. Hares, who edited *1945–1965: An Evaluation of Two Decades of Self-Deception*, took me to brunch at the Tavern on the Green in Central Park. We had the sole dish described below. I recreated the recipe and continued to make it until I moved to Verona. It was one of my standard dinner party entrées. I remember serving it one evening at my apartment on East 82nd Street to Betty Anderson, my boss at Alfred A. Knopf, Hedda Sterne, Philomena Houlihan, and Eyre De Lanux, a quartet of fascinating women.

In July 1971, Eyre came to visit me in Verona, bringing with her a marvelous-looking Greek named Starvos, who ending up bunking with me.

For the fish
   8 small sole filets about 2 inches wide, approximately 1 pound
   1 lemon
      Salt and freshly ground black pepper to taste

For the stuffing
   3 tablespoons unsalted butter, divided
   ½ pound mushrooms, chopped
   2 tablespoons shallots, finely chopped
   1 small garlic clove, minced
   ½ pound fresh crabmeat
   1 teaspoon fresh thyme
   2 tablespoons flat-leaf parsley, finely chopped

For the sauce
   1 can (10¾-ounce) shrimp bisque
   4 drops Worcestershire sauce
   ⅓ cup sherry or cognac

The fish: Rinse filets in cold water and pat dry with paper towels. Rub each side with lemon juice, salt, and pepper.

New York, New York

The stuffing: Melt 2 tablespoons of the butter in a 3-quart sauté pan and sauté mushrooms, shallots, garlic, and herbs until shallots are soft. Blend in crabmeat and cook over low heat, about 2 minutes. Roll a filet around your cupped fingers, leaving a 2-inch opening at the top, and spoon ¼ of the stuffing in the opening of each filet. Melt the remaining butter in the pan and add filets with seam side down. Toothpicks may be necessary to hold them together.

The sauce: Whisk all the ingredients together and pour over filets. Cover and cook over low heat for 7 to 10 minutes. Do not let the sauce boil. Serve over rice or toast points or rounds.

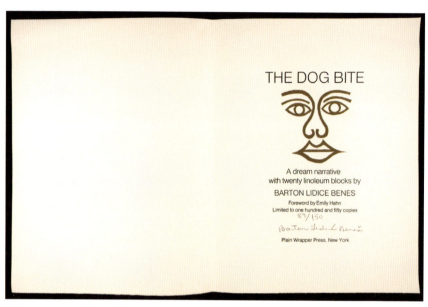

Title-page spread from *The Dog Bite: A Dream Narrative*. (Courtesy of the University of Oregon Libraries.)

Item 3. *The Dog Bite: A Dream Narrative*

A dream narrative and twenty linocuts by Barton Lidicé Beneš;
with a foreword by Emily Hahn. 21 french-folded sheets.
33.5 x 25.5 cm. 150 copies. 1970.

Getting Sidetracked

Before I moved into the Union Square studio in August 1968, I got side-tracked, digressing from the original list of books I had intended to print before leaving New York. Barton Lidicé Beneš, a friend who was just begin-ning to attract attention as a book artist, talked me into postponing all my projects in order to collaborate with him on a small illustrated book he was eager to have published. Barton was sure he could sell at least fifty copies to one of his patrons, Phyllis Lambert *née* Bronfman, a Canadian whiskey heiress who was in the habit of giving unusual gifts, such as gold-plated tool kits, to her friends at Christmas.

He thought we would be able to sell the remaining copies for $75 each. I really wasn't interested in his project, but he kept pleading with me, assur-ing me that it wouldn't take more than a couple of weeks, plenty of time to have the project ready for Christmas. He also stressed that it would be a quick way for me to raise some needed capital to launch my new publishing program. This was the argument, irrational as it was, that finally convinced me. The initial estimates I had received for materials for *Images & Footsteps* and outside labor to edition the etchings were way beyond my means.

Barton Lidicé Beneš

Barton was so creative. His fantasy world may have been alien to me, but it was magical just to be in his presence. I was very conservative, not politically, but certainly artistically.

Barton's book started off in a burst of enthusiasm, although it would be another two years before it was completed in haste and a little begrudgingly. I had shown Barton a copy of *Eros • Thanatos* (1968) with woodcuts by Richard Upton, which I had received as a gift from Interlaken Mills. Barton loved the format, a drop-spine box of french-folded loose signatures printed on one side of the sheet only.

We started talking about the project in June 1968, and he gave me an early draft of the text on July 1. Barton began to cut the linocuts to illustrate a loose narrative he had written based on an erotic dream, not much more than a series of captions for the illustrations. Knowing Barton's work habits and his short attention span, I didn't want to start printing the text until he had cut all the blocks.

Barton Lidicé Beneš, place and date unknown. (Photographer unknown, courtesy of Barton Lidicé Beneš.)

Premature Invitation

Once Barton finished the cuts, I printed an invitation to a party to celebrate the commencement of the project. Somehow, I forgot to include the date, November 9.

Invitation to the commencement party for *The Dog Bite: A Dream Narrative* (1968). The date was added in longhand as a printer's error. (Courtesy of PWP Archives.)

Item 3. The Dog Bite: A Dream Narrative 151

Mounting Frustrations

I had been in New York for almost a full year and was just getting started on my first project on the Vandercook press. To make matters worse, it wasn't even one of my own. On December 19 I wrote to Berta Moltke, a friend in Copenhagen who later illustrated *Images & Footsteps*:

> These are dark days for me. I did not realize how dark they were until I was on my way home tonight. It suddenly occurred [to me] that my short "year stay" was over and I am not leaving New York. I am staying because I am caught and this time without a way out. My job pays just enough to keep me going, barely. I work so hard at my job that when I go to the press in the evenings, I am usually too tired to do anything except shuffle a few papers and then wander home. I do get a lot accomplished on the weekends, but then I am exhausted on Mondays . . . and if I take a morning off to visit a friend, I feel guilty the rest of the weekend. I realize that I shall never be able to print books this way. Like painting or any other art, one must work at it with a steady regularity and rest from it, so one can return to it refreshed. I turn to it more and more as an old, tired man.

I sent Barton a copy of the final manuscript on December 21. Obviously we had long since lost our fifty-copy order, but we were going ahead with the project anyway.

Setting the Type and Printing

I handset Barton's text in Helvetica, although Emily Hahn's foreword was set in Linotype Helvetica at Haber Typographers. Six hundred sheets of Strathmore Chroma paper, which was considerably cheaper than hand-made paper, were machine-folded and trimmed at the Fisher Bookbinding Company and delivered to the studio the last week in October 1968 just before our party. I used Lewis Roberts Frost Black ink, one of Bret Rohmer's recommendations, but I disliked its high gloss and never used it again. I have always preferred matte black inks. Originally I had planned to print each of the eighteen full-page linocuts in a different shade of olive green, progressively getting brighter, like coming out of a dark dream into the daylight. Lewis Roberts sent me four shades of olive green, but, they were transparent offset inks, which I couldn't use. Barton had used Shiva inks for his proofs. I tried to get the same ink from the manufacturer, but they never answered my letters.

Helpers at the Press

I spent most of my weekends printing, and fortunately I had John Newbauer's help almost every Saturday morning. He would bring two of his children, Dana and Miranda, to the studio and we would print for three or four hours and then go around the corner on 14th Street for Chinese food. Sometimes Charles McNab or Fred Blesse would stop by to give me a hand. Even with all this manpower, the printing of the text dragged on until the end of January 1969.

Production Problems

I often stayed at Carlos Cárdenas's apartment on East 24th Street on weekends to avoid the long subway ride home. He was now working for Pan Am in San Francisco. Barton, who lived on East 18th Street only a couple of blocks from the studio, had promised to help me print, but he never showed up, not even once. I would stop by his place on my way to work and find him at the bottom of a heap of naked guys covered in dried cum, sleeping off an all-night orgy. I was always tempted to forget about printing and strip down and crawl in bed with them, but instead I'd disentangle Barton with a slight pang of envy and drag him by his little pecker and balls down the hall and into the shower, his rosy butt glowing from a night of pleasure and pain. Going back into the living room where the German bikers were slowly awakening, I approached the bed, and one of them took my hand and placed it on his cock, and said, *"Was wilst du?"* What did I want? I wanted to get on with the printing. I wanted to be finished with Barton's book. But once Barton had showered, he either went back to bed with his friends or just forgot about coming to help me. During the months that I was printing the text, Barton never stopped by the studio to see how the project was progressing.

In a letter, dated January 26, to Paul Secon and Berta Moltke, I expressed my concern for the project:

Barton's book has turned out to be a terrible disappointment. I will be finished with the text this week. He went to Paris for three weeks. He has been back now for more than a week and has not called me to

Item 3. The Dog Bite: A Dream Narrative 153

even see how the book is coming. He has not been to the press once since actual printing was started. . . . I have paid out in cash over $2,000 so far on this book. . . . I have also worked more than eight full working weeks printing, setting type, and unfolding paper and inserting tissues etc. . . . Of course my intensions were immoral to begin with, I suppose. I thought this would be a snap and fast, easy money.

When I finally got around to printing the linocuts in the summer of 1970, I just wanted to be finished with the project, and so I gave up on the idea of using multiple shades of olive green. I eventually settled on one shade of olive green mixed for me at the Superior Printing Ink Company in New York. It, too, had a gloss, but at least it was compatible with the Frost Black ink.

Before I would start to edition the prints, I had to decide how to handle the rubber-stamp embellishments on them. Barton's original idea was to rubber-stamp words around some of the contours of the images, a device he often used to embellish his drawings, but he quickly changed his mind once he realized how much work was involved. He would have had to make more than thirty-four thousand individual rubber-stamp impressions, something not even Barton was willing to do for his art. Now he wanted to eliminate them altogether

Barton had talked with a psychiatrist friend who told him the words were all wrong because they were just "crutches" to the psychological interpretation of the prints. On the other hand, I felt they should be there because they would graphically enhance the prints. I threatened to abandon the project if he didn't add the rubber stamps. We came to a stalemate over this point. As a last resort, I sought the opinion of two friends who were quite knowledgeable about the current art market. Much to my surprise they sided with Barton. They felt the rubber stamps were merely cheap gimmicks to bolster the artist's basically weak images. I had decided beforehand to abide by their decision.

A Big Compromise
When I told Barton that I was going ahead with the project, he was elated and came by the studio for first time in almost a year. Looking at the piles of printed signatures, he was surprised to see how much space the book actually took up. His enthusiasm returned immediately, and he suggested re-cutting

Left: Text page from *The Dog Bite: A Dream Narrative.* (Courtesy of the University of Oregon Libraries.)

Right: The accompanying illustration.

several of the blocks – although he never did. It looked as if the book might get finished after all, and I might at least recuperate some of the expenses.

Somehow I managed to finish printing all of the text with the exception of the title page, which presented last minute problems and had to be set aside before I moved into Haas's loft. I tried printing the blocks on his Washington press, but couldn't get the results I wanted, so in April I gave up altogether, devoting all my energy to setting type for *Images & Footsteps*, the project I had postponed to print Barton's book. I also spent a lot of time pulling proofs for *Siete Poemas Sajones / Seven Saxon Poems*, which wouldn't be completed until December 1974.

In truth I lost interest in Barton's book as my circumstances and priorities changed. The move to Haas's helped me focus on my original goals and objectives, as did the move into the apartment at 444 East 84th Street. But one thing was very clear to me: I had to finish *The Dog Bite* – if it were to be finished at all – before I left New York for Europe. I had not heard from Barton for more than a year, so early in the summer of 1970, I got in touch with him, saying that unless he helped me finish printing the book, that is, the title page and illustrations, I would dump the whole project into the East

Item 3. The Dog Bite: A Dream Narrative

River. I had no intention of taking the partially printed sheets with me to Italy. Barton said he would help me, and to no one's surprise, he didn't. But at least he did the next best thing: he sent his lover, Howard Meyer, who turned out to be a very capable printer. He came almost every day for several weeks, and thanks to to Howard's energy and determination we were able to get the project finished.

However, before I could edition the blocks, I spent a lot of time trying to get my Washington press in working order. I discovered that the pressure wedge, which adjusts the amount of pressure applied to the type, was "frozen" in the platen cup. Robert Daugherty, a friend from Random House, and Tony Aiello, a printmaker and my last New York lover, helped me get it loose. The threads were completely worn out. I took it to a machine shop, and it was soon reinstalled and working like new.

Tony Aiello in Central Park, New York, NY, 1970. (Photo by RGR, courtesy of PWP Archives.)

Tony Aiello

Tony Aiello also helped me edition the blocks when Howard wasn't able to come. Between Howard and Tony I was able to finish the printing on my Washington press just days before the movers came to haul it away.

One day as I was printing alone in the August heat, I noticed the sun reflecting off a pair of binoculars across the street. Someone was watching me. I was tempted to strip down, but inking the forms and pulling the bar naked would not have been very comfortable.

Final Disaster

Before I left New York, Barton and I worked out a design for the binding of the book. The loose, french-folded signatures were to go first in a black chemise, and then in a slipcase. Poor as I was, I gave him my half of the money

Gabriel in Central Park, New York, NY, 1970. (Photo by Tony Aiello, courtesy of PWP Archives.)

Item 3. The Dog Bite: A Dream Narrative 157

needed to pay the binder and turned the sheets over to him. Months later, when the book was ready to distribute, I discovered that Barton had put each copy into a cheap candy box covered with flimsy black paper. My copies had been stored in a damp place, and so most of the boxes had stuck together. The ugliness of the completed project mirrored the unpleasantness of the collaboration.

I did not want the book to be associated with the Press, so I gave a few copies away, mostly to friends who had helped me produce it, but I never offered individual copies for sale. A copy was included in each of the three sets of PWP items sold in 1975. And it was included in the *Center for Book Arts: The First Decade* exhibition at The New York Public Library in 1984. Richard Minsky, who was later to play a minor role in the binding of another PWP book, bound the exhibition copy of *The Dog Bite* in a "skin of unknown origin," according to the catalog – roadkill, I suspect.

In a letter, dated December 7, 1970, to my parents, I summed up the situation:

> One of the real problems with the book is that I do not want to approach my future customers for sales because it is basically not the kind of book I am printing now, nor do I want it to be associated with the Press. The artist is a friend, and we both mistakenly thought we could make a fast buck with the book. The book has a pseudo-pornographic look, and I am not interested in printing pornography.

Chicken Liver Pâté

Yields 1½ pounds (about 5 ramekins)

Philip Baker and I used to give elaborate dinner parties in Gordon Fraser's apartment. We'd start off with a nice pâté and end with a baked Alaska. Both were easy to prepare and always got raves. I often served them when I lived on East 82nd and East 84th Streets.

    1 tablespoon olive oil
 1¼ ounces shallots, finely chopped
    1 garlic clove, chopped
    1 pound chicken livers, trimmed
    8 ounces salted butter, cut into 8 pieces
    2 ounces cognac
  ½ teaspoon ground white pepper

Rinse livers under cold water. Pat dry with paper towels. Heat olive oil in a large skillet. Add shallots and garlic and sauté on medium-high heat until shallots are translucent, about 30 seconds. Add livers to the skillet and cook on high heat for two minutes. Livers should be barely cooked through, still pink in the centers. Remove from the heat and cool for 10 minutes. Transfer the contents to a food processor. Add butter and emulsify until smooth, then add cognac and pepper. Process until well blended. Pack the pâté into individual ramekins, cover tightly with plastic wrap, and refrigerate overnight. Serve with rounds of crusty French bread and cornichons.

Item 3. The Dog Bite: A Dream Narrative 159

Baked Alaska

Serves 4

Here is my version of Baked Alaska.

½-inch slices pound cake, enough to cover the bottom of a 7-inch
diameter ceramic tart dish
1 ounce cognac
2 egg whites at room temperature
⅛ teaspoon salt
¼ teaspoon cream of tartar
⅛ teaspoon vanilla
¼ ounce confectioner's sugar
1 pint ice cream

Preheat oven to 475 degrees. Trim pound cake to fit snugly on the bottom
of the tart dish. Sprinkle pound cake with cognac. Beat egg whites until
foamy. Add salt, cream of tartar, and vanilla and beat until soft peaks appear.
Gradually beat in sugar until meringue is stiff with shiny peaks. Using a
knife, remove ice cream from the carton in one piece. Place it topside down
in the center of the pound cake slices. Cover ice cream with meringue. Bake
3 to 4 minutes or until meringue peaks are browned.

A corner of the courtyard at via Duomo, 15, with the living room and studio windows visible on the ground floor, Verona, Italy, 1970. This was the first location of the PWP in Verona. (Photo by RGR, courtesy of PWP Archives.)

Verona, Italy: Via Duomo, 15

> In spite of every attempt at honesty, once you describe your own life,
> you can only utter half-truths.
>   – Thomas Mann, "Gide's Unending Search for Harmony"

Before Verona

I had spent almost a quarter of a century looking for some meaning in my life, usually in segments of less than two years each. Part of this was because I was torn emotionally and physically by opposing forces or conflicting interests that kept me in a continual state of flux. Nor was I prepared to cope with the world as it was competitively structured. My inflexible attitudes frequently led to frustration, and just as frequently to unhappiness, because in most cases I wasn't technically capable of achieving the impossible level of perfection I demanded of myself. I continually found myself paralyzed in the middle and instead of taking a stand or compromising, I would flee, usually at a moment when I was on the verge of success, not wanting to accept the reward for my efforts or the responsibilities of the future.

The same was true regarding people and my involvement and contact with them. In a letter dated May 13, 1957, to my mother from Japan, I confessed that I was ready to compete for love, which at that time meant that I felt I had something concrete to offer or exchange.

> All my friends think that I am very happy, all my friends say that they wish they could be as happy as I am because I always appear gay and carefree . . . If those same people could read our letters they would know quite [to the] contrary that I am very unhappy because I cannot compete in the world outside of the family. I have never wanted to because I was afraid I would be defeated [i.e., I have nothing of value to offer, therefore I would not be accepted], but now I want to. As you know I have never experienced love outside of the family, that all of my relationships aside from being perverted have been in search of physical pleasure, only not necessarily sex itself, but the physical pleasure of just lying with someone.

161

My fear of defeat and of love became confused with competing, which in turn became synonymous with and linked to whatever project I was working on at the time because I sought acceptance and love through my accomplishments. For a time it was designing dinnerware, an undertaking that brought me considerable recognition, but which I never felt adequately prepared for and never enjoyed. The hundreds of letters from Japan to Gordon Fraser, who sponsored the project, are full of frustration and self-deprecation. I was also involved in various other design projects for Gordon between 1956 and 1959, including stainless steel tablewares, packaging, promotional pieces, and trade show booths.

I doubt I ever seriously thought printing would be a stabilizing factor in my life, and even though I was never able to eliminate frustration from my work or my life, I learned to handle it by trying to minimize it and even learn from it. I came to know that with each book I printed, even before I started, I would fail to reach the unobtainable perfection that lay somewhere in my mind's obscured eye. I didn't need to be concerned about competing, because success or failure couldn't influence what I was doing. Once I started to print, I couldn't give up, because it was the only thing that reflected my complexities, both positive and negative, and gave me an indefinable pleasure.

The decision to leave New York for Verona soon became a matter of life and death for me. In June 1970, I was fired from Alfred A. Knopf for "rocking the boat." I had been told by the production department to overlook certain shoddy practices that were beginning to erode the quality of the books we produced. It was a very demoralizing experience to be dismissed for trying to maintain the high standard of book production that Knopf himself had instigated. Robert Gottlieb, the publisher of Knopf, and his wife Maria Tucci, an actress, came to a dinner party I gave in my apartment at 444 East 84th Street. When he heard I had been fired, he said that he would intervene to have me reinstated, but I saw no point in fighting to regain a job I would be quitting in a few months.

Like so many unexpected reversals in my life, this one proved to work in my favor. I elected to get by on unemployment and didn't even attempt to find a new position, using my newly gained freedom to prepare for the move to Italy, and in the last few weeks, to finish the printing of *The Dog Bite: A Dream Narrative*. Perhaps being fired was fate's way of making sure that I actually got

Verona, Italy: Via Duomo, 15

off to Verona as planned. I wrote to Paul Secon and Berta Moltke in Copenhagen on July 21, "I am very relieved, although somewhat stunned by my decision [to move to Verona] . . . If I start to worry about surviving even before I get there, think of the mess I will be in there. I have decided; there was no other choice. My life [in Verona] or my slow disintegration here in N.Y."

Moving the Washington Press

Between 1969 and 1988, I moved the Washington press four times, and each time I swore I would not move it again. With each move I felt as if I had lost a year of my life. It had been difficult enough to get the press from Connecticut and into my apartment in New York, but in 1970 it was going on a really long trip to Verona, Italy. The truckers from Overseas Moving Specialists arrived at my apartment on August 24. I wandered around in a daze, pointing out to them what was to go and what was to stay. I asked them to be especially attentive with the Washington press, which I had already taken apart. I pleaded with them to lower the frame gently to the ground, since the legs, which were made of cast iron, could easily snap off if they got an unexpected jolt. I suspect that all truckers are deaf, because later, down on the street, I saw the frame take a little bounce when it hit the ground too fast. I warned one of the truckers to tie the cylinder to the bed of the Poco proof press before picking the press up, but he didn't listen and almost lost a finger when the bed of the press came flying down toward his hand, causing him to drop his end of it. Before they started to load the truck, they brought everything in the apartment down to the sidewalk. The superintendent and the assembled neighbors looked on in amazement as the presses, type cases and cabinets, as well as boxes of paper, appeared from the secret print shop on the sixth floor.

Getting Settled in Verona. A New Life and New Friends

I arrived in Verona on August 27, 1970, with an Olivetti portable typewriter, a few clothes, and a Burmese cat named Burma. She wasn't happy in Verona and was only content when she sat on the wide window ledge instead of roaming the enclosed courtyard. She would only eat imported Purina Cat Chow.

One day in July 1971, Burma "eloped." A few days later, walking home late one night, I heard her hoarse meow. She was wearing me out. In December she went to live with Bryan, a South African boy who changed her

Left: Via Duomo looking toward the side entrance to the Duomo, Verona, Italy, 1980. (Photo by RGR, courtesy of PWP Archives.)

Right: Via Duomo looking toward via Pigna. The portal in the foreground is the entrance to via Duomo, 15, Verona, Italy, 1980. (Photo by RGR, courtesy of PWP Archives.)

Theo van der Aa and Ger van Dijck in the courtyard at via Duomo, 15, Verona, Italy, 1970. (Photo by RGR, courtesy of PWP Archives.)

Verona, Italy: Via Duomo, 15

name to Harry, after Harry's Bar in Venice. Myth has it that Bryan eventually cooked Burma and that we ate her, although I can't say for sure that we actually did.

My printing equipment and a few bare essentials would follow in a few months. In the meantime I temporarily moved in with Ger and Theo.

On September 21, 1970, I went to Lugano, Switzerland, to fetch my papers and visa from il principe Luigi de Giovanni. With the move to Verona, a fantasy had become a reality and a hectic hobby had become my profession, stimulating my entire psyche.

Venetian Friends

I first met Domingo De La Cueva in Venice during the 1969 Christmas holidays. Once in Verona I frequently visited him in Venice. One of my favorite places in Venice was the Casa Frollo, a pensione on the Giudecca facing San Marco. It was a few doors down the quay from Domingo's apartment where I often stayed. I always put my friends up in the Casa Frollo just so I could visit it.

On one visit to Domingo's, I met Pietro Ferrari, a high school teacher in the town of Brescia, where his father was the mayor. Pietro, who wanted to be an artist, had rented a tiny apartment below Domingo's as a weekend retreat from Brescia and the double life he was living there. I usually stayed

Domingo De La Cueva, Venice, Italy, 1966. (Photographer unknown, courtesy of Berta Moltke.)

Pietro Ferrari, Brescia, Italy, 1971. (Photo by Emilio Veclani, courtesy of Pietro Ferrari.)

in Pietro's apartment when he wasn't there; however, late one night in the middle of the week, he appeared unannounced. When he saw me in his bed, he turned off the light, stripped, and slipped into bed with me. He was the sweetest, most tender lover I ever had. Unfortunately the pressures of Brescia became too much for him, and he committed suicide.

The Apartment in Via Duomo

Shortly after my arrival Ger decided that he wanted a larger live-in studio. I spent a lot of time following leads for him, but nothing suited him. Then by a great stroke of luck, in mid-October 1970 Ger and Theo unexpectedly decided to move into a smaller apartment on the top floor of the Palazzo Guarienti at via Duomo, 15, leaving the old apartment to me. It was ideal for my needs because it was on the ground floor and fairly spacious. Considering the weight of my press, around two thousand pounds, this apartment was a dream come true, and the rent was only 32,000 lire a month, (about $54). There were two huge rooms with sixteen-foot ceilings, each with tall windows that faced an enclosed but sunny cobblestone courtyard. The courtyard would soon become an extension of my apartment, because most of the vine-covered Renaissance palace was abandoned. In the meantime I was busy making new friends and learning Italian, since my Spanish was of little use in Italy.

Verona, Italy: Via Duomo, 15

Redecorating the Apartment

While I waited for my belongings to arrive, I redecorated my new living room. The Dutch Boys had whitewashed the apartment when they first moved in, but now the paint was flaking off the walls and ceiling. There were layers of centuries-old paint underneath, so I decided to do the job right by stripping off all the prior coats. The floor was tile so it didn't matter how wet it got. I didn't have any scaffolding, so I built an ordinary ladder out of scraps of wood I found in the rear courtyard. Since the tiles of the floor were naturally slick, I cut planks to brace the feet of the ladder from the opposite wall to keep it from slipping out from under me. Painting the center of the ceiling sixteen feet above the floor presented a unique problem. I tied empty wooden fruit crates to the top of the ladder, which moved me closer and closer to the center of the room with each extension. I was so scared going up and down the shaky ladder that I didn't dare carry the bucket of paint with me; I climbed down for each brushful of paint. I was a terrified painter, but one with the patience of Job.

The walls were now a deep Venetian red with a mauve stripe about two feet below the ceiling. The ceiling and the space above the stripe were painted a shade of blue-gray. My original plan had been to stencil the ceiling with gold stars, the mauve stripe with a floral spray, and the walls with geometric patterns. By the time the press arrived, I was so thankful to have gotten the base colors on the walls that I decided the room was finished. Visitors to the studio used to comment that it was like walking into a three-dimensional Kenneth Noland painting. Even though I divided the space into living and working areas, it seems like most of the time the whole apartment, including the kitchen, was used for work, especially when I was in the middle of a large project.

Setting Up My Equipment

My belongings left New York on October 8, 1970, and arrived in Genoa around November 12. Unknown to me, they were being held in a warehouse in Verona by the forwarders, who were asking an additional, and unexpected, $1,000 to bring them to my studio, claiming the freight had been paid only as far as the port of Genoa. I didn't realize until I started working on this memoir that the forwarders were actually right. I came across a copy of the original contract, and it clearly states "from port New York up to arrival port Genoa" for $1,160. But I was so adamant – and stubbornly believed – I had contracted for door-to-door service that I would not give in. I even managed to convince several of my Italian friends that I was being victimized by unscrupulous forwarders. I was all the more desperate because I had no money left in my budget for more transportation fees. As I sat around moping, my immediate thought was to give up and return to the States. If I couldn't become a printer, then I would become an anarchist, with my first target the movers' headquarters in the Bronx.

Max D'Arpini

Among the new friends I met through the Dutch Boys was a young man with the aura of a Mafia kid. His name was Paolo D'Arpini, but everyone called him Max. A bohemian at heart, Max knew how to throw enormous parties without ever spending a lira of his own money, parties where everyone ate and drank until the sun came up. Indeed, Max had great organizational talents. When I told Max about my predicament, he said, "Don't worry." He enlisted the help of a young lawyer from the south, Antonio Salamone, who remained a staunch supporter of the PWP as long as I lived in Verona. We didn't realize that the press had been sitting in the warehouse for more than a week. Later on November 23 Max and his brother-in-law, Ettore, showed up at my door. Somehow, with his soft Roman double talk and charm, he had convinced the trucking company to loan him one of their

Max D'Arpini in the courtyard at via Duomo, 15, Verona, Italy, 1970. (Photo by RGR, courtesy of PWP Archives.)

Verona, Italy: Via Duomo, 15

trucks together with its driver, a Steve Reeves type, to deliver my belongings. The driver even gave us a hand unloading the truck. It wasn't until early December, however, that Max and Ettore helped me put the press together. How much did it cost? Who knows? Max had made all the arrangements.

By early December the press was in working order. The jolt the frame had suffered in New York left one leg permanently bent, which caused the press to rock unless extra packing was put under that foot to stabilize it. I sometimes affectionately referred to the Washington press as my little club-footed press. Before I left New York I had emptied all of my type cases into small plastic baggies, sorted by typeface and size. I had more than fifty thousand characters to distribute – which took about two weeks – before I could start printing. It wasn't until after the first of the year before I was actually ready to start to work on my first book in Verona.

Camus Christmas Card

As soon as I had the studio set up, I printed a Christmas card for the Dutch Boys on the Poco proof press. Then I printed a rather bizarre greeting card for myself on the Washington press. Set in Horizon Bold Condensed, it was printed on tan Fabriano Murillo cover stock in black and vermilion. It is one of the few pieces of ephemera I printed at the press. I have no idea where I

Gabriel on Ponte Pietra during his first winter in Verona, Italy, 1970.
The first PWP bindery was later opened at the other end of the bridge.
(Photographer unknown, courtesy of PWP Archives.)

> A question put to Camus by DEMAIN.
>
> **One cannot avoid tackling certain subjects today.**
> **The most serious one is a problem for all men:**
> **in the struggles dividing the world today,**
> **must we really be willing to forget**
> **all that is bad on one side**
> **to fight what is worse on the other?**
>
> **Greetings from Richard-Gabriel Rummonds**
> **at the Plain Wrapper Press**

Camus Christmas card (1970). (Courtesy of PWP Archives.)

found the text – it also appears in Camus's *Resistance, Rebellion, and Death* (1961) – but the most puzzling thing about this little card is its message.

What, if anything, did this signify to me at the time? And what did it have to do with printing? I can't answer these questions now. Perhaps it had something obscurely to do with the fact that three years, almost to the day, had passed since I had left Rome, and now I was back in Italy. Certainly, my desire to print had intensified in the interim, even though none of the books I had intended to print had yet been realized. Ready or not, I was about to launch the new PWP.

The Art Scene

It seemed to me that the Dutch Boys knew everyone even remotely connected with the arts in northern Italy. We frequently traveled to cities as far away as Brescia and Padua for gallery openings. Ger was especially social, and they were both provocative conversationalists. That December 1970 they took me to a New Year's Eve party at Olga Gibroni's. Olga, the daughter of a greengrocer in Piazza delle Erbe, painted fantastic canvases of gigantic lettuce, fennel, and squash. She was married to a successful dentist and loved to give big parties at their hillside villa in Parona, just outside Verona. Many of the people I met at her parties remained my friends throughout my stay in Italy, and over the years some of them would also collaborate on PWP projects.

Ger exhibited at the Galleria Ferrari, where Theo made frames. Enzo Ferrari, the owner, had turned his gallery into an important artistic and intellectual hub, attracting visitors from all over Europe. His *salotto* was a gathering place for artists and writers who engaged in lively discussions about art and politics. Enzo also actively promoted the Italian version of the *livre d'artiste*, which was very popular among Italian art collectors. I immediately saw a potential for my own work in this environment.

The exchange was about six hundred lire to the dollar, which meant if I lived modestly, I could get by on $150 per month. Fortunately, my parents had agreed to help me financially for the first year by sending me $200 a month, with the first check arriving on December 29, 1970. With a little luck I might be able to succeed in making the PWP self-sufficient by the second year – a familiar but necessary self-delusion.

A New Piece of Equipment

Early in my discussions with Martino Mardersteig about dampening paper, he mentioned that I would have to apply more pressure on my piles of paper if I wanted the paper to be evenly dampened. By a stroke of luck, in late January 1971, I found an enormous cast-iron standing press at Impresa Veneta Artigiana Tipografica (I.V.A.T.), a printers' secondhand supply company. The owner, Cristiano Cabianca, was fascinated by the idea of an American coming to live and work in Italy at a time when so many Italians dreamed of emigrating to America. I always looked forward to my visits to I.V.A.T., because Cabianca inevitably suggested that we retire to his *cantina* to sample a bottle of his fine wine before I returned to my studio. I paid $250 for the press, which included taking it apart, moving it to my studio, and reassembling it. This press became an essential piece of equipment at the PWP for dampening paper when I used Mardersteig's method – as well as for pressing paper and binding. Weighing around 3,000 pounds, it had a platen that measured 37 x 25 inches. It dominated the entry to my apartment on via Duomo until March 1978, when it was moved to the pressroom of the new studio at via Carlo Cattaneo, 6. I used it last in Cottondale, Alabama, in the 1980s.

A New Lifestyle

I didn't meet all my new friends through the Dutch Boys, who left Verona in the spring of 1971. I began venturing out a little more on my own, and one night in May on one of my nocturnal prowls, I met Giorgio "Hat Shop" Zanolli. We had a brief affair, and when it ended amicably, we remained close friends. Giorgio worked in a hat shop – hence his nickname – across the street from the Casa di Giulietta, where tourists flocked to see a modern re-creation of Juliet's balcony. The hat shop was a convenient meeting place for friends and a jumping off point for the evening's activities. At seven, the hour when Italian shops close, we would stroll the couple of blocks up the cobblestone pedestrian thoroughfare to Caffè Filippini in Piazza delle Erbe, where we would sit out by the fountain and drink our *aperitivi* while making supper plans or concurring on some late-night *divertimento* that usually included sex. We were guided only by our whims and would often go as far away as Venice to satisfy them. We would meet up with Arrigo Mozzo, a flamboyant actor originally from Verona. Usually inebriated, we often spent the night sprawled on the floor of his apartment.

Giorgio Zanolli in the port-cochère at via Duomo, 15, with the entrance to the studio on the right, Verona, Italy, 1971. (Photo by RGR, courtesy of PWP Archives.)

Verona, Italy: Via Duomo, 15 173

That summer we frequently went to La Palma, a restaurant where we could eat *al fresco* and flirt with the waiters. Or we would drive up the Sirmione peninsula on the Brescia side of Lake Garda to swim and cruise for some action on the rocky beach in our skimpy bathing suits no larger than Band-Aids.

Like most single Italian men, Giorgio lived at home but yearned for his own place. When a small apartment – on via Pigna, just around the corner from my studio on via Duomo – became available, he rented it. Giorgio's move into town was an adventure I'll never forget. I accompanied some of his buddies to help him pack his belongings. His mother, who was crying, wove in and out among the young men as they carried Giorgio's possessions out of the house to the caravan of waiting cars. She thought it was a disgrace. "Everyone will think I have been a bad mother," she wailed. After everything was loaded and we started to pull out of the driveway, I noticed that his mother was holding on to the bumper of one of the cars. The driver wanted to know if he should stop, but Giorgio shouted, "No, no, go on. She'll let go." Once he settled in his new place, his mother did the next best thing to having him at home with her: she came every week to clean his apartment, do the laundry, and stock his pantry.

Prowling

Since things were not going smoothly at the Press, I consoled myself by prowling the streets at night. Late in January 1971, I was sitting on a bench in the park in front of the Ufficio Postale when a very old man sat down very close to me. We avoided making eye contact. Then I felt his hesitant hand on my upper thigh. I nonchalantly got up and walked down the path. I heard him shuffling along behind me, trying to catch up with me. He called after me, "Please, I only wanted to touch it." How insensitive young men can be.

Later that winter, I picked up a very low-life fellow along the river promenade. I didn't want to take him home, and he didn't want to do it *al fresco*. Just as we were about to part, a familiar figure came along. It was the junk dealer who collected flattened cardboard boxes in the center of town. He had two young fellows with him and suggested that we join him and his friends at his place.

His place was a hole in the wall on the ground floor, part apartment, part warehouse for the cardboard boxes. Before long the three young fellows and

I had stripped and were engaged in a little orgy. I didn't realize it at first, but the young fellows kept pushing the fully dressed junk dealer away whenever he tried to stick his hand in the action. All at once he started yelling at us, "You know, this is my place. If I can't join in, then you can all get out." They decided to leave. In the shuffle to get dressed, I noticed that my fellow's bright orange Speedo briefs were lying under the bed. I snapped them up and stuffed them into my pocket. When he couldn't find his underwear after having torn the bed apart, he accused the junk dealer of stealing them. I walked the briefless fellow back toward town. He grumbled all the way. We parted near the Ponte Pietra where we had first met. As I crossed over the bridge, I pulled his briefs out of my pocket and dropped them into the rushing water of the Adige below. The junk dealer got his revenge, even though he didn't know it.

The Bricklayer and Joël

In 1971 I saw two young men on a regular basis. The first was a bricklayer who rode around on a rickety old bicycle. He was small but strong and very tanned from his work. He would push his bike and I would follow. When we came to the top of a hill, I got on the crossbar and we coasted down into town. We often went to the reservoir, where we made love on the grass, or went back to my place.

Many years later Golda Fishbein and I were walking down via Seminario when I spotted him coming out of the Trattoria al Cacciatore. We crossed the street, and I gave him a hug. Golda, who has a great nose for food, smelled something she liked and wanted to know more about the trattoria. It became our favorite place to go out to dinner.

The other young man was a frail Frenchman, whom I knew only as Joël. A Veronese artist had shown Joël how to make simple rings and bracelets, which he sold on the street. He didn't seem to have a permanent place to live, so on occasion he would show up at my place late at night. For a bath, meal, and bed, he'd let you have your way with him. I always felt very guilty about this, but he insisted that he needed the release. He would cry, nothing dramatic, just tears. I would wrap him in my arms and hold tight until he fell asleep. For many years I wore a little brass ring with a simple stone in it that he had given me. One day, it just wasn't there anymore. I don't remember what happened to it or Joël.

Verona, Italy: Via Duomo, 15

A Picnic at Pasetto's

In August I took Stephanie Wald, an editor with whom I had worked at Alfred A. Knopf/Random House, to Giorgio "Trota" Pasetto's family trout farm, where we sat out under the summer sun and ate grilled pink trout and drank local wine. For the occasion I made an Ecuadorean hot-air balloon that crashed in a nearby field, igniting the dry cornstalks. We were all so drunk that we didn't see the fire at first. Then someone starting yelling "Fuoco, fuoco!" We sobered up sufficiently to put out the fire. I was reprimanded and told not to bring any more hot-air balloons to the farm.

That afternoon I gave Stephanie a copy of Jurij Moskvitin's manuscript of *The Diamond Stylus: An Essay on the Combat between Rational Thought and Inner-Vision* to take with her, with the intention of hiring her to edit it. Jurij, a friend of Berta's, had brought it to me in the summer of 1971, hoping I would print it. Once Stephanie had read it, she wrote back that she didn't think I should publish it – not that it wasn't interesting, but that it would need a lot of editorial work to put it into proper English.

Giorgio Zanoli and Giorgio Pasetto in the forground, launching a hot-air balloon near Verona, Italy, 1971. (Photographer unknown, courtesy of PWP Archives.)

Uccellini allo Spiedo con Polenta
Spit-Roasted Songbirds with Polenta

Serves 6

In the fall when Giorgio Zanolli was still living at home, we went to his family's house in the village of S. Giovanni Lupatoto – which I always pronounced *lupi-topi* (wolves-mice), to gales of laughter from my Italian friends – where his mother made *speo de osei*, Veronese dialect for *Uccellini allo Spiedo*.

This was a popular dish in Verona when I first moved there. During the October hunting season, there were always several stalls in the market in Piazza delle Erbe that offered songbirds. Already plucked, they were displayed in huge baskets. Today most songbirds, such as sparrows, larks, thrushes, and finches are protected by law. However, in 1971 these birds were still being consumed in large quantities. They are very tender, and the whole bird, including the head, body, innards, and feet is eaten. The bones are crunchy. This is not a recipe for the squeamish. I was first introduced to eating small birds in Japan in the fifties.

For the polenta
  6 servings Polenta

For the birds
  2 or 3 birds per person depending on size
  1 or 2 leaves fresh sage per bird
  1 or 2 pieces lard or fat bacon per bird, about an inch square
      and ¼-inch thick
  1 3-inch sprig of rosemary
  Salt

The polenta: Follow directions on the package. Polenta is sold in both slow- and fast-cooking varieties. When polenta is ready, pour onto a wooden board. Leave a well in middle into which birds will be placed. Cover polenta to keep it warm.

The birds: If birds do not come plucked, pluck them now. Wash in cold water and pat dry with paper towels. Leave innards intact. Some cooks remove

Verona, Italy: Via Duomo, 15 177

eyes and feet. Impale birds through the breast on long skewers, alternating birds with pieces of lard or bacon and sage leaves. Roast quickly, rotating the skewer slowly and basting birds with a sprig of rosemary dipped in melted lard. On the last turn, sprinkle a little salt on birds. Remove birds, bacon, and sage leaves from skewers and arrange in the "nest" of steaming polenta.

NOTE: If the birds are roasted on a rotisserie, a dripping pan may be placed under them to catch the fat. Sometimes polenta is poured into the dripping pan to catch the fat and to flavor the polenta.

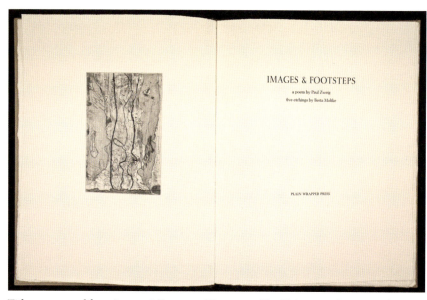

Title-page spread from *Images & Footsteps*. (Courtesy of the University of Oregon Libraries.)

Item 4. *Images & Footsteps*

A poem in nine stanzas by Paul Zweig.
With five etchings by Berta Moltke. 1971.
28 pages. 33 x 26 cm. 200 copies. 1971.

Producing Books at the PWP

Producing an illustrated book has one thing in common with the ancient profession of matchmaking: both try to bring together two disparate but hopefully harmonious elements. In the case of the illustrated book, it is the coupling of an author with an artist. While I didn't follow any specific selection patterns at the PWP, I filed away in the back of my mind or made lists of people whose work I admired. When I had what I thought would be a compatible pair, I set about trying to bring them together. Several PWP books, beginning with this one, started out with an artist, waiting for an appropriate text to come along.

Berta Moltke

Berta Moltke is a fascinating artist whose work is most often described as surrealist. We discussed the possibility of my printing a book using her etchings, and I worked on this book on and off for the next four years. The real meaning in her imagery is hidden beneath the surface, so whenever I see her paintings or prints, I imagine I am standing behind her, looking at coded symbols reflected in a mirror she holds up to her face. We didn't talk much about making a book together during my first visit in Copenhagen, because I was still planning to go back to the monastery in Argentina in the near future. In spite of that, before long we began to discuss a project that Berta would illustrate.

I have found several mentions in letters to her from the late sixties that I was investigating the possibility of printing a book in Rome. In one of these I described a visit to the Rome offices of the Società Nebiolo type foundry, located in Turin. I inquired about buying some Magister type. Perhaps I thought I could work out an arrangement in Rome similar to the one I had in Buenos Aires with the Paulinos. In another letter toward the end

Berta Moltke in Piazza delle Erbe, Verona, Italy, 1980. (Photo by RGR, courtesy of PWP Archives.)

of the year, I wrote, "I am afraid I will have to postpone our book project until there is a little more money in the purse." I don't know how I thought I was going to finance a project of this magnitude, certainly not with the paltry alms I was receiving from IDO-C. This was the first in a whole series of "postponements" that would plague this project.

Once I was in New York, and printing had become the dominant drive in my life, I wanted more than ever to make a book with Berta. However, as much as I tried, I couldn't print the book in New York. There were too many technical problems I couldn't resolve. Again I let sentimental ties, albeit worthy ones this time, divert me from my primary publishing goal: printing bilingual texts by Latin American authors.

Paul Zweig's Manuscript

In the spring of 1968, Paul Secon and Berta came to New York on a visit, and we seriously began to put this project together, realizing at the time that it was a bit premature, because I had yet to find a studio or a printing press. We decided to ask Paul Zweig for a manuscript. He and Berta were close friends, and their work, though in different media, contained many of the same elements. I especially liked the poem he had written for the catalog of one of Berta's exhibitions in Venice. Zweig lived in New York, so the four of

Item 4. Images & Footsteps

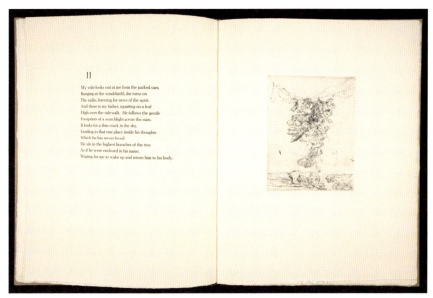

Double-page spread from *Images & Footsteps*. (Courtesy of the University of Oregon Libraries.)

us met one evening at Max's Kansas City, where we decided his long poem, "The Bicycle Odyssey," would be an ideal text to couple with Berta's etchings. It later appeared in the Summer 1968 issue of *The Hudson Review* – I wasn't yet committed to publishing only original texts. The poem is filled with many surreal images, such as the following in stanza VIII:

> A thousand green mouths swam near me in the water.
> When they spoke leaves fell from their teeth.
> Then the bicycle rusted and I had to swim.
> My skin fell off and I had to walk.
> My legs melted and stretched,
> My eyes wandered on a green thread
>
> That I could lengthen or pull in, like radar.
> I saw a woman buried in the sand;
> She wore the ocean like a body.
> Mother, I cried, crawling with eight strong arms
> Over the sand, arms like bodily hair,
> The shape of desire.

Paul Zweig, New York, NY, 1980. (Photo by Robert Mahon, with permission of the photographer.)

Upon her return to Copenhagen, Berta sent me a batch of proofs, which arrived early in May 1968. So far none of the images had been editioned separately as prints; I could select as many as I wanted to use exclusively for the book. Each time I looked at the prints, I felt they would make a great first book. (She also sent a large print, which I also liked, but felt it was wrong for the book. It wasn't in the same scale as the others, making the whole concept suddenly heavy and unbalanced.)

Berta sent the plates a few weeks later along with a proof of one of them in sepia. We all agreed that these images would be perfect for the book. I no longer remember why we didn't edition the etchings in sepia. This is the only major PWP book containing graphics not specifically commissioned for the edition.

Item 4. Images & Footsteps   183

Soon after the proofs arrived, Paul Zweig and his wife Francine, who was a painter, came to dinner at my apartment at 506 East 82nd Street. While Paul and I discussed the text, Francine, like a subdued muse half listening to us, studied Berta's proofs. At one point she turned to us and said, "This book is all about images and footsteps, isn't it?" She was right, and so that's what we decided to call it.

Looking for an Edition Printer in New York

With the plates in hand, I immediately ordered a small sampling of handmade and moldmade papers from Andrews/Nelson/Whitehead. I started looking for someone to pull proofs of the etchings, even though I was still without a studio – I wouldn't find one until August. On May 20 I went to Bob Blackburn's Printmaking Workshop on West 17th Street. He told me about a young Brazilian printmaker named Roberto, who was part of a printmaker's co-op that used Bob's equipment. Bob set up an appointment for us to meet the following week at which time Roberto and I discussed how the prints should be editioned. For one thing, he wanted to use the same French ink that had been used for Berta's proofs, but unfortunately I couldn't find it in the States. Because Berta's images were so delicate, he also suggested having the plates steel-faced. Regrettably he returned to Brazil before I was ready to edition the prints.

1968: A Year of Frustration

The year 1968 ended with the Zweig/Moltke book no closer to being printed than it had been the previous year. After a year in New York I had accomplished nothing. Frustrated but determined, I wrote to Berta on January 11, 1969:

> I MUST print three books – the one I am working on now [*The Dog Bite*], Zweig's [*Images & Footsteps*] and Borges's [*Siete Poemas Sajones / Seven Saxon Poems*] before I can leave. I could never do it there [in Spain]. I must gain the experience I need here first. I do not like the press I have now. It would be foolish to take it. Yet I have not tried out the new one I want. I have not yet printed on paper I have dampened myself. These things I must learn and adjust to first. I want to be able to take all of the equipment I will need with me and until I face the problems as they arise in printing I will never know what equipment I will need.

Continuing the Search for an Edition Printer

In March 1969 I sent Berta a few newsprint proofs of the title page and the first poem, and on April 5 I sent her a proof of the title page printed dry on Umbria paper. Both sets of proofs were printed on Haas's Washington press. In May I visited Bob again. At that time he had a young printmaker named Mohammed Omer Khalil working for him. Mohammed pulled the first proofs of Berta's plates on both Magnani Como moldmade paper and Fabriano Umbria handmade paper, using a variety of black and sepia inks. I eventually found Berta's sepia ink in New York. Even though we all preferred the results on the moldmade paper, I opted for the handmade and placed an order for one hundred sheets so I could continue proofing the etchings and text on it. Mohammed thought the Umbria paper was too soft and its texture would compete with the fine tones of the etchings.

Mohammed, who was a perfectionist, pulled more proofs in the summer of 1969. He was later to open his own atelier, and I was sorry I wasn't able to have him edition the prints for this book. There were five etchings in each copy, which amounted to 1,250 prints, including 250 extras for proofing and spoilage. His first estimate came to $2,187.50 ($1.75 per print), which, of course, I didn't have. I foolishly thought I could raise it by printing *The Dog Bite: A Dream Narrative*, and once the press was set up on Union Square, I became involved with that project full time. With the exception of the few proofs I printed at Haas's, I didn't return to *Images & Footsteps* until the press moved to 444 East 84th Street in August.

In the twenty-two-year existence of the PWP, I never once asked any of my collaborators for financial assistance in producing their books. I have always believed in the old adage, The person who controls the purse strings calls the shots. Over the years, however, I would find out the hard way that this isn't always true.

Selecting the Type

By early 1968 I already had a definite concept of how I wanted the book to look: it would be a large quarto. I originally thought of using a light typeface such as Walbaum for the text, one that would be more harmonious with the feathery lines of Berta's etchings, since they were the impetus for printing this particular book. However, I kept returning to Horizon Light, a modified

Item 4. Images & Footsteps

Bodoni. I sensed on first sight that it would prove to be a workhorse with character, and it did not fail me. It would be six years before I was able to purchase a second typeface.

Initially I dismissed all the typefaces designed by Frederic W. Goudy as too dated, and summarily rejected those designed by Hermann Zapf, whose typefaces I have always admired, simply because of their over-exposure in the marketplace. Ultimately I selected Horizon Light because I wanted a letter that would print dark on the page without being a true boldface. Whether I like to admit it or not, I was probably influenced as well by William Morris's heavy typefaces. In particular I was attracted to certain narrow roman capital letters in the Horizon Light font – such as the E, R, S, and T. I have never regretted this choice. Each time I used this typeface, I did so with fresh enthusiasm.

I ordered the first fonts of Horizon Light type from Bauer Alphabets in July 1968, but for some reason they didn't arrive until the following February, after I had already moved into Robert Haas's loft.

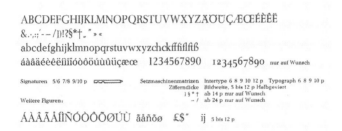

Specimen of Horizon Light type. (Courtesy of PWP Archives.)

As soon as the type had been distributed, I immediately began setting the text for *Images & Footsteps*. Haas, who had an excellent eye for typography, helped me with the optical letterspacing of the display type, as well as with the wordspacing of the text. By mid-November all the text for the book had been set. It was later shipped to Italy tied up in pages.

It wasn't until I started working on the book again in Verona that I began to letterspace the text itself, having been shown how to do this by Renzo Sommaruga, another Veronese handpress printer. We had been introduced by Ger van Dijck, whose book of stunning etchings, *Paesaggi arcaici*, Renzo was about to print.

Horizon Light letterspacing chart. (Courtesy of The New York Public Library.)

Once I understood the basic concept of letterspacing, I devised a complex chart (above) that showed the appropriate amount of spacing material to be inserted between various combinations of letters. I used three different thicknesses of thin paper in addition to the traditional copper (half point) and brass (one point) spaces. By the time I printed *Didascalie*, I had pretty much perfected the letterspacing scheme. The text proofs at the PWP were always covered with hundreds of small pencil marks in a variety of colors to indicate where the adjustments were to be made. Type was set in the composing stick without justifying it. Once the optical letterspacing was finished, the lines could be justified and ready to print.

I had to rely on a steady supply line from New York for additional type and spacing materials because my Horizon Light type was cast in pica, (4.21 mm high) which made it incompatible with most European types, which were cast in Didot (4.51 mm high). Shipping metal type to Italy from the States was prohibitively expensive. Well into the mid-seventies, most visitors from the States were pressed into service as couriers. Hardly anyone arrived at the Press without a little package of type in hand.

Search for the Perfect Ink

My search for the perfect ink also began in New York. I didn't like the Frost Black I had used for *The Dog Bite* and definitely wanted a matte black ink

Item 4. Images & Footsteps   187

for *Images & Footsteps*. I had read in several accounts – in particular, Henry
Halliday Sparling's *The Kelmscott Press and William Morris, Master-Craftsman* (1924) – that William Morris had commissioned Jänecke-Schneemann
in Hanover, Germany, to make his ink. David J. Way had also mentioned
Morris's ink. I wrote to the factory to inquire if it was still available, but I
was told the formula had been lost during the bombing of the factory during
World War II. They recommended another of their inks, and I placed an
order for twenty cans of black and ten of red – probably the minimum order.
It turned out to be a horrible ink because it contained a dryer that made it
unsatisfactory for hand inking. I still had unopened cans of it on my shelves
when I closed the PWP in 1988.

In the late spring of 1968, Lewis M. and Dorothy Allen passed through
New York, and we met for lunch in a motel coffee shop near Madison Square
Garden. When Lewis told me about his forthcoming book, *Printing with the
Handpress* (1969), I ordered a copy on the spot. In his book he recommends
Special Black 42625 L'press ink, especially developed for dampened paper.
It was made by Hostmann-Steinberg in Celle, Germany, and distributed in
the States by John E. Mandlik (which is why I have always referred to it simply as Mandlik ink). It was a marvelous rich black. The ink problem was
resolved, at least for the next several years. I should have profited from
Giovanni Mardersteig's unfortunate experience when he outlived his hoard
of French-made Lorilleux Lefranc ink. When it was no longer available, he
sent Martino to inquire about the ink I was using. Naturally I recommended
the Mandlik ink, although I don't know if he ever ordered any of it. I should
have stocked up on it when I had a chance. I never found another ink to
replace it after the factory stopped making it in the mid-seventies.

Abandoning the Vandercook Proof Press
Of the two presses I had previously used, the flatbed proofing press offered
the greatest possibility for printing large-sized deluxe editions. Even though
I had purchased the Vandercook proof press explicitly to print *Images & Footsteps*, I never used it for that purpose because I sold it before the project went
to press. I was now determined to print this project only on a handpress, but
until I had Joseph Low's Washington press operative, I never made any serious
progress. By then I had switched to the Mandlik ink, and on Bob Blackburn's
recommendation, I replaced my hard rubber brayers with a gelatine roller.

Robert Scudellari apparently changed his mind about not "setting a precedent," because I started taking Fridays and Mondays off from work so I would have an uninterrupted stretch of time in which to print. Even so, I managed to print fewer than twenty-five sheets per day, and I was dissatisfied with all of them. In October 1969 the first stock of Umbria paper for the edition arrived, but I was no closer to printing the book than I had been six months earlier. On November 25 I wrote to my parents, "The press is so slow, and it is so painful not to be able to print the way I want. Last Saturday I spent the entire day solving one small problem. One favorable thing is that after I solve the problem, I can at least go on to the next step toward perfect printing." I was clearly obsessed with perfection long before I had learned the fundamentals of printing.

Hedda Sterne

When Paul and Berta first visited me in New York, they took me to supper one evening at Hedda Sterne's, an old friend of Berta's. They had met in Venice. Hedda was often grouped with the abstract expressionists, who had revolutionized American art in the fifties, although in an interview she claimed that she was not one of them. At one time she had been married to Saul Steinberg, with whom I worked on another project, *Dal Vero,* many years later. When I first met Hedda, she lived in a brownstone on East 71st Street. We would often get together for light suppers and hours of conversation. We talked about everything: art, books, politics, movies, and, of course, my addiction to printing. Hedda was my sole source of strength in those days. She insisted that I be true to my ambitions, that I not compromise myself for "fast money." She was the first to reprimand me – and rightly so – for printing *The Dog Bite.*

Throughout my life I have had strong emotional ties to specific pieces of music, which conjure up vivid memories of the people associated with them. Seeing the Swedish film *Elvira Madigan* (1967) with Hedda was one of these. I can't hold back the tears whenever I hear the andante from Mozart's Piano Concerto no. 21 in C. Hedda also gave me one of my most treasured possessions: a pen and ink drawing on silk depicting a double portrait of Emma Bovary and Gustave Flaubert

Through Hedda Sterne I met Betty Parsons, in whose gallery Hedda showed her work, as well as Jock Truman, Betty's right-hand man. Even

Item 4. Images & Footsteps

Double portrait of Emma Bovary and Gustave Flaubert by Hedda Sterne. (Photo by Weldon DeBusk, courtesy of PWP Archives.

though I had yet to print something of value intellectually and artistically, they liked my enthusiasm and thought that I had the potential to produce fine limited editions, perhaps even work with some of Betty's artists.

Attempts to Print in New York

On May 25, 1970, I started to print the text. Robert Daugherty, a friend from the Random House production department, and Tony Aiello, a printmaker, often came by to help me pull press proofs. We averaged about twenty-five sheets per day. The backup (the alignment of the text blocks on both sides of the sheet) was still off. Eventually I realized that the chase was the problem, so I ordered a new one with a fixed cross in the middle. That way, I was able to lock each of the four pages into its own space independent of the other three pages. I knew that I had to have the letterpress part of the book technically under control before I could give Mohammed the go-ahead to edition the plates.

Resuming Work on the Book in Verona

Aside from pulling numerous proofs, I accomplished very little on *Images & Footsteps* until the PWP relocated in Verona. I had the type standing for this and another book for more than two years. Even though I was tempted to inaugurate my new publishing program with the second, *Siete Poemas Sajones / Seven Saxon Poems*, I decided to go ahead and issue Paul and Berta's book first, as originally planned. It was also the only project for which I had both the text and illustrations in hand. Like all beginners I started off with a project that was too immense for my capabilities and resources. I don't know why I decided to print two hundred copies. Only a starry-eyed dilettante would have attempted such a large edition for a first book.

Gabriel printing *Images & Footsteps* in the via Duomo studio, Verona, Italy, 1971. (Photographer unknown, courtesy of PWP Archives.)

Item 4. Images & Footsteps 191

(The last books I printed in Alabama were all in editions of less than one hundred copies – one hundred and twenty impressions representing for me a full day's work on the handpress.) I decided to print this book as a large quarto since the bed of the press had ample room for that format, and also because I believed I would be reducing some of the press time.

I arrived in Verona without having resolved any of the major technical problems I had with the press in New York. Both Lewis M. Allen and Harry Duncan were giving me a lot of encouragement and a few tips, although there is a limit to what can be conveyed by mail. But no one was able to help me with the quality of the impression of the type on the paper. Haas had mentioned using type-high bearers under the corners of the platen, but he couldn't offer an explanation of how to systematically adjust them.

Nor were the impressions as sharp as I thought they should be. One day when I went up to the Officina Bodoni to talk to Giovanni Mardersteig about my printing, I showed him my press proofs and asked him what I was doing wrong. His reply was that it took him twenty-five years to learn the secrets of the handpress, and I would have to do the same. Stunned, I said, "But, Dr. Mardersteig, if you felt that way, why did you say you would help me if I came to Verona?" He replied in his firm Germanic way, "I didn't think you would come." I swore I would never ask him for help again.

I'd show him: it wasn't going to take me twenty-five years to learn how to print. Ironically, he also withheld many of his trade secrets from his son, Martino, who had come by my studio a few times to see how I was getting along. I gradually realized that Martino wasn't really that familiar with the mechanical functions of the handpress, although he did give me some useful advice on how to position the points on the tympan. He had first mentioned using points for registration when we talked in New York. (The points are sharp pins or tacks that hold the paper in position during the impression.)

Old Mardersteig was not only a bully but also a dreadful misanthrope. He even took the labels off the ink cans in his shop so no one would know what kind of ink he used. I hated this outdated European attitude, typical of craft guilds and their "trade secrets." It seemed unbecoming in a man with such great knowledge, and I vowed that if I ever became skilled on the handpress, I would eagerly teach others all that I had learned about its operation. And I did. In 1998 my book *Printing on the Iron Handpress* was published by Oak Knoll Press and The British Library.

More Tests on Dampening Paper

I still had problems dampening paper, but once the standing press was functional, I replaced the white blotters with Veronese pulpboards. Little by little, with the help of other handpress printers in Verona, I learned how to dampen paper.

Why was it so important for me to be able to dampen the paper correctly? Properly dampened hard-sized handmade paper receives the inked image considerably more sharply than the same paper does when printed dry. There are two reasons for this: one, the type requires less ink, avoiding the squeeze around the edges of the letters caused by the accumulation of ink on the type itself; and two, the printed image shrinks and tightens up as the paper contracts during the drying process.

Renzo Sommaruga as Mentor

I continued to struggle along on my own with occasional advice from Renzo Sommaruga, who started helping me on a regular basis in February 1971. Among other things he directed me to a source for quality rollers in Milan, where I found a large hand roll-up roller made of a synthetic resin. It was perfect for my needs, and Renzo showed me how to avoid over-inking by adding small pieces of masking tape to the roller bearers in order to lift the roller slightly off the outer edges of the type blocks. But even Renzo wasn't able to assist me in determining the right amount of pressure. From the start, pressure had been my nemesis. I would get it right by accident and then print a set of sheets, only to find that when I was ready to print the

Renzo Sommaruga, Verona, Italy, ca. 2005. (Photo by Alessandro Corubolo, courtesy of the photographer.)

Item 4. Images & Footsteps 193

next form, the pressure had changed. (Little did I know then that these fluctuations are inherent in the operation of the handpress.) I spent several weeks making tests, hoping to hit on the right pressure again. I had piles of annotated proofs, but I never was able to find a clue or a pattern that resulted in a formula I could use to obtain the same results each time.

Since most of the forms contained etchings, I was able to print only two forms work-and-turn, an imposition David J. Way had shown me. This meant that I could print the same text on both sides of the sheet without having to change the form or the pressure. Once printed, the sheet was torn in half, resulting in two identical four-page gatherings.

I had almost finished printing the two forms without etchings when Renzo pointed out that I had imposed the book incorrectly. He said that I should be gathering in eights instead of twelves because the paper was so thick. He also recommended leaving two blank leaves at the beginning and the end of the book to help bulk it out. I knew he was right, so I scrapped all the sheets I had already printed. The colophon page was the first to be reprinted using the new imposition.

Taking the Colophon Pages to Denmark

In March even though I had not completed any of the other forms, I got on a train and took the freshly printed colophon pages to Berta in Copenhagen. After she signed them we sent them on to Paul Zweig – who was temporarily in Boston – and on April 21 I retrieved them from the customs house in Milan.

As the train approached Denmark, customs officials came aboard. They wanted to know what was in my wooden box. When I told them the box contained pages from a book, they asked to see for themselves. A screwdriver had to be found before they could remove the lid. I think they were disappointed not to find any drugs. The only other occupant of the compartment was a young Turk, Tony Bakin, on his way to Copenhagen to star in porno movies. I was amazed anyone with such skinny legs would even consider such an idea. I said, "You must have a pretty big cock." He stood up and dropped his trousers and said, "Judge for yourself."

We talked at great length after he revealed that he was a printer, as well as a budding porn star. The customs officials also tore his baggage all apart, again disappointed not to find any drugs. After they left, Tony casually opened the bottom of his suitcase, which was filled, not with drugs, but with airline and train tickets he had printed himself. In fact, he had printed the ticket he was using at the moment. If I really wanted to make money as a printer, he said that I should come to Istanbul, and he would show me how to print counterfeit tickets. I never took him up on his invitation, but in September 1973 I did print some press cards for the bogus Private Press Association, issued by the Institute of Printing History & Graphic Arts. These very authentic-looking press cards usually got my friends and me into the opera and exhibitions for free as members of the international press corps.

Having Luciano Cristini Edition the Etchings

Another advantage of starting with this particular book was that Luciano Cristini's rates were very reasonable: he pulled the etchings for fifty cents per print. His printmaking atelier was within walking distance of my studio, and Berta had often used him to edition her plates. In retrospect one of the things that still amazes me is how I managed to communicate with people like Luciano. After all I didn't know any Italian when I first arrived in Verona, and none of the people who were helping me – with the exception of Martino Mardersteig – spoke any English. Berta's plates were still at Bob Blackburn's when I left New York, but a friend brought them to me in January 1971.

Luciano had recently inherited the Calcografia Artistica Cristini from his father. It was a wonderful place to visit, filled with mementos of the elder Cristini's contemporaries, including Gabriele D'Annunzio. On the wall in Luciano's office, there was a framed letter from D'Annunzio that always fascinated me, and I usually paused to read it. In his dynamic bold script, D'Annunzio commended Luciano's father for his contribution to one of the author's books. Seeing that letter always reminded me that I wanted to *be* D'Annunzio – we shared the same first name, and I envied his flamboyant lifestyle – but at the same time I would have been happy to have been Luciano's father and to receive such a glowing compliment from such an illustrious author. (One of the recurring disappointments I experienced at the PWP was a lack of feedback from collaborators after a book was published. Often they never even wrote to thank me for sending them a copy of the book.) The walls in Luciano's atelier were covered with press proofs of etchings by many of the most famous European printmakers.

Item 4. Images & Footsteps 195

I once mentioned to Luciano that Roberto, the Brazilian printmaker, had suggested that I have the plates steel-faced because Berta's images were so delicate. Luciano concurred, adding that he always steel-faced the plates for large editions. I think he recognized in me someone who would become more than just another client. I would soon exhibit the zeal of an acolyte in my desire to learn everything about the technique of printmaking, always looking for an opportunity to gain hands-on experience.

Printing the Text with the Etchings

In mid-February I started printing the text on the same sheets with the etchings, which presented another set of problems. Etchings should always be pulled before the text is printed, otherwise the bite of the type will disappear when the dampened paper passes under the heavy rollers of the etching press. Luciano wanted to pull the etchings two up, because it would be more economical; there were more than sixteen hundred prints. I should have opted to spend more money and print the book in folio, two pages at a time. Luciano could not pull enough etchings in one day to allow the paper to stay damp during the entire run, so after they were pulled he dried them in a forced-air tunnel. It took several weeks to print all the etchings for the edition. Luciano had dampened the paper by immersion instead of filtration, so some of the size was lost in the process. He finished the first batch in mid-May. Out of the 220 sheets, we had to reprint sixty-five, including twenty-five I had inadvertently destroyed trying to take a short cut in re-dampening the paper.

One of the basic problems of dampening paper is that each time the paper is dampened, it is further removed from its original pristine state. When etchings are pulled, a depression is left in the paper by the plate. If the paper is re-dampened under pressure, the plate mark will disappear, or if it is particularly deep, it might cause wrinkling along the edges of the print. Luciano tried to minimize the depth of the plate mark by using thin plates dropped into wells cut in a mask on the press bed. Even so, in re-dampening the paper I not only pressed out most of the plates, but also created several wrinkles in the prints. As I beat my chest, Renzo would tell me over and over again, referring to the books of Giovanni Mardersteig, "We want to see the fallibility of the hand in all that we do." We certainly see it in this book.

As the printing progressed I became more tense about the book. Cristini assured me that the ink smudges and dirt the sheets had acquired in Luciano's atelier could be easily washed off, so I washed each sheet before dampening it, a process that often roughened up the surface of the paper. If I rubbed too hard, I removed some of the size (the glue that stiffens the paper), which in turn left the sheet streaked. No matter what I did, I had the feeling the pages would look worn out from so much handling. Eventually I re-dampened each sheet individually by immersion, so as not to flatten the plate mark of the etchings, then dried it down successively until just the right amount of moisture remained: first with slightly damp pulpboards and then later with completely dry ones.

It took four days to print each set of forty-five sheets with etchings. I still wasn't aware of the difference between dry and damp measurements, and so my margin calculations were always off, perhaps less than an eighth of an inch away from the gutter margin. Renzo showed me how to use a template to prick the paper before putting it on the points. This guaranteed that the type and the print would always be in the same relative position on all the sheets. I kept finding little errors of judgment, nothing anyone else would have noticed, but they annoyed me.

One day at Cristini's, while inspecting some prints he was editioning for me, I noticed that one of Berta's plates was about an eighth of an inch out of square. I wasn't aware of it on the proof, but on the squared-off page it was obvious that the etching plate was irregular. It was too late, however, because Cristini had finished printing most of them. Thereafter, each time I printed sheets with text and images together, I looked at them with a critical eye, always finding little adjustments I had not made. I knew no one else would notice, but as long as I knew they were there, I was upset. Even with all the frustration of producing this book, the manual labor of printing it remained sensual, erotic.

Documenting My Frustration

A wealth of information in the letters I wrote to friends throughout the spring and summer of 1971 documents the frustration I felt trying to produce this book. I include a few paragraphs from some of them to illustrate how close I came to abandoning printing even before I had finished my first book project.

The first letter, dated November 8, 1967, was to Paul and Berta from Rome:

Item 4. Images & Footsteps 197

I will probably go into hiding somewhere. The sad thing is of course I
have nothing or no one to hide from. . . . But at least in hiding I can do
what I want within my financial limitations. . . . In a way when I went
into the monastery, I committed suicide. If one is terribly attached to
things as I was like my books and paintings and records and 'treasures' and then one suddenly gives it all away, you kill the possessor as
if you had struck him down with a knife, but his body refuses to die, it
goes on stripped of all intelligence, of all direction, of all drive and
eventually it too will die. But the wait is madness.

Later when I was living in Verona Berta wrote to say that she could no longer
take any more of these maudlin letters and that I should stop writing them.

On April 10, 1971, when I thought I was making some positive headway,
I wrote to Hedda, "The problems were really all solved so simply it seems.
The paper was too dry, the ink too much, the roller too pitted, the pressure
too little, the printer too confused."

Later in April, in another letter to Paul and Berta, I wrote:

Yesterday I thought I was going to kill myself. My balance of sanity is
so slight that I do not know what to expect from day to day. It is not a
desire to die; it is simply a desire to be finished with the endless little
aggravations that have plagued me from the very beginning of this
book and my whole wish to print. I set up the press to print the pages
with the etchings and found that all of the pages were dirty with ink
spots and dirt and paste and who knows what else. I just broke down
and cried. . . . Yesterday I was ready to close up the studio and just find
a job and forget about printing until this fall. There is no one to really
talk to here and I just can't take any more reversals. I have dampened
the paper tonight to make another test on the etchings and if it goes
well I will finish the printing as planned around the first of May. If it
does not go well, you must again have patience and understanding,
but I cannot go on. I am finished. The book has completely destroyed
me. When I feel like this I want to throw the whole thing in the courtyard and light a fire to it. . . . Why has life always been so easy for me?
Why has the pain always been real? Why couldn't it have been a
dream? Looking at the etchings yesterday and crying was like looking

at an empty spot where Carlos once sat or where something else precious in life disappeared. You know me. I'll be okay tomorrow, I hope.

And finally in a letter dated June 6, 1971, to Paul and Berta, I wrote:

> You both refer to this book as a *baby*, as my *child*, and that I must suffer through its creation and then I will find the happiness I have always looked for. How contrary all that is. I now openly hate this book. I only hope I finish it and get rid of it before I end up hating the people involved in it . . . both of you encouraged me or made me feel guilty about this book until I had to plunge into it without any experience. . . . One day last week I became hysterical when I discovered that Cristini had made an error of three-eighths of an inch when he reprinted thirty-five of one print. I was crying so convulsively that I picked up a big stick I have here and brought it down on my shoulders and arm with a ferocious whack to bring me back to my senses. I continue to print almost every day although I must force myself to enter the studio. My "child" is a demon, and I am trying to exorcise it. You cannot imagine [my despair while I am trying to] clean up the pages, to iron out wrinkles, and wash off the smudges, knowing that even before the book is finished, it is worn out. Cristini was upset when I came the first time to tell him about the dirty pages and so HE cleans them first but they are still not usable when I get them, actually in many cases they are worse since he is not as careful as I am when he cleans them and sometimes in removing the ink he takes too much paper and leaves a thin spot or a HOLE and then the page is lost. . . . I have lost all interest in printing another book. I may some day print another of those little keepsakes, but I do not want to make another commercial book. I am postponing the Borges book indefinitely. . . . My personal or private life is so entwined with the book that there is nothing additional to say about it.

When reviewing my correspondence from this period I discovered that they had sent me several large checks to help finance the project.

Getting the Books Ready for the Binder

With the printing finished I started to get the pages ready for the binder. I spent most of the summer with a magnifying glass, checking the quality

Item 4. Images & Footsteps

of each leaf, folding, and then collating the books. Brooks and Bonnie Walker helped with this tedious task.

I first met Brooks and Bonnie at a gallery opening early in 1971. They were on their honeymoon, living in a seedy hotel near the post office. Bonnie, a former starlet who had appeared in the Elvis Presley movie *Girls! Girls! Girls!* assumed that their stay in Verona would be temporary, but Brooks, a sculptor, had come to Italy to take advantage of the nearby foundries. As he became more involved in his work, it became obvious they were going to be in Verona for a long, long time, so they began to inquire about apartments. Coincidentally Ger van Dijck and Theo van der Aa had decided to move to Maastricht in the Netherlands, where they opened Agora Studio, an art gallery, but they didn't want to abandon Verona altogether. When Brooks and Bonnie saw the Dutch Boys' apartment, they fell in love with it immediately and worked out an arrangement so the boys could use it whenever they were in Italy. By April the Walkers were living upstairs. One of the perks of having them close by was that Brooks had a car.

Binding the Books

Martino and Renzo suggested that I take the book to their binder, Alessandro Galvagni, whose Legatoria A. Galvagni was located in San Martino Buon Albergo, a village on the road to Venice. I was still very much influenced by the Officina Bodoni style of binding, so I asked Galvagni to bind the book in quarter oasis morocco – a few copies were bound in an uniden-

Brooks and Bonnie Walker, Verona, Italy, 1971. (Photo by Thomas Rummonds, courtesy of Elfie Rummonds.)

tified leather after Galvagni ran out of the oasis – and Fabriano Ingres paper over boards. I even retained the gilt rules at the juncture of leather and paper so common in Officina Bodoni books. After all I had been through with Renzo about the imposition and the two blank leaves at the beginning and the end, Galvagni thought we should cut one of the blank leaves out, but I remained adamant: we kept all the blanks. Printing *Ten Poems & Ten Reflections* also took time away from getting the books ready for Galvagni. I delivered the first fifty copies on July 12, and another fifty on the 19th. It would be several more months before I had the finished books to send out.

I had asked Galvagni to sew the books by hand, but without telling me and "to save money," he decided to machine-sew them. He had also been careless covering the boards. The cover papers on several copies were wrinkled or stained with glue. In November I had to return a number of copies for rebinding. I estimated that out of an edition of two hundred copies only fifty were really acceptable so I decided to withhold about one hundred copies from circulation. Due to carelessness on Galvagni's part, about half of these latter copies had wrinkled cover papers and pastedowns (the leaf of paper pasted to the inside covers of a book). Perhaps it was to be expected, but I felt I had unwittingly been compromised on my very first serious effort. It was a great lesson. I would be more watchful in the future.

Selling the Book

Once the book was bound, I had to sell it. Lewis M. Stark, at The New York Public Library, sent me my first standing order on March 25, 1971. Fortunately, his successors, Maud D. Cole, Laurence Parke Murphy, and Francis O. Mattson, also championed the PWP. I sent out letters and prospectuses to collectors and libraries, and little by little orders began to trickle in. Alexander Lawson at Rochester Institute of Technology placed another of the early standing orders.

Very little ephemera was printed at the PWP. This is the only PWP book for which I personally printed a prospectus on the handpress. All the others were printed commercially.

Presentation of the Book at the Studio La Città

Hélène Sutton, Amedeo de Franchis's sister, managed the most prestigious contemporary art gallery in Verona, Studio La Città. In conjunction with

Item 4. Images & Footsteps

an exhibition of Berta's etchings on October 16, she presented the first exhibition of my work as a printer. As part of the opening-night festivities, I had agreed to print a small keepsake on the gallery's Albion press. Renzo helped me get the press set up, but being unfamiliar with this type of press – and with the distractions of the guests as they crowded around the press and asked questions – I wasn't able to do very much. I have never been very comfortable printing before an audience and ended up finishing the project on the Washington press in the peace and quiet of my own studio. The keepsake was "Saluto all'alba," by the fifth-century Indian poet Kalidasa, a text suggested by Renzo, embellished with a linocut of a rose that Berta made expressly for it. The edition of 150 copies were later sent out by the gallery to the visitors who had attended the opening.

That same night, Vincenzo Fagiuoli, a distinguished Italian collector, bought a copy of *Images & Footsteps*. I was in heaven! Although Fagiuoli was certainly the most influential of my private collectors, he wasn't my first Italian collector. That distinction belonged to Lina Boner Grosselli, who bought a copy of *Images & Footsteps* in the summer of 1971. I met Lina through Max D'Arpini shortly after I arrived in Verona. She owned an insurance agency and was the patron saint of Max's circle of artists, writers, and drifters, often bailing them out of financial scrapes. Little did I realize at the time how dependent I would become on these Italians who loved beautiful books in languages they often could not read. How different they were from the stuffy French bibliophiles who bought only books in French. The *only* French collector of PWP books that I knew of was le comte Tony de Vibraye, an Italophile.

The Aftermath

When it was all over, I wrote to Hedda, "When one considers that I had virtually no previous experience and no one to advise me, the book – especially a first book, even with all its defects, was a remarkable achievement." I seem to have forgotten about all the help I got from Renzo. I have since seen the first books of many young printers, and technically the Zweig/Moltke book pales beside them. The real miracle of my first Veronese printing experience is that I even entertained the idea of continuing to print after having produced such a fiasco.

Printing *Images & Footsteps* was even more involved than *The Dog Bite*. I worked intermittently on the former for more than five years. It took five geographic moves, three changes of printing presses, two premature starts with edition printers, three changes of paper and rollers, two changes of ink, and considerable, but inestimable, frustration.

During the first years in Verona, I kept logbooks in which I recorded my progress on the handpress along with a few personal observations. The entry for June 30 reads:

> Finished printing the last pages at 7:30 [p.m.]today for *Images & Footsteps*. The only real achievement gained was that I still have many more things to learn. I cannot blame anyone – not even myself – that the book is not as I had envisioned it – not as I had hoped and expected it would be. The concept was wrong to begin with. I never should have attempted an illustrated book. The paper was bad, full of iron and fuzz. Cristini only added to my frustration. I'll try to salvage as much as I can.

I guess I am just an optimistic survivor. Distance was already beginning to heal my wounds. By September 1971 I could even write to Paul and Berta with a slight hint of nostalgia, "Yesterday I finished putting all the type for your book back into the typecases. It was a strange feeling breaking up the type . . . It had been standing for almost two years." Actually it had been more than two and a half years.

Item 4. Images & Footsteps   203

Steak Tartare

Serves 4

This is Hedda Sterne's recipe.

   1 pound filet mignon, freshly ground on medium twice
      Watercress for plates
   2 radishes
   1 small lemon
   4 raw egg yolks
      Salt and freshly ground pepper to taste
   3 ounces shallots, very finely chopped
   4 sprigs flat-leaf parsley

Optional seasonings served on the side in small bowls.
      Dijon mustard
      Capers
      Anchovies
      Horseradish

Optional seasonings served in cruets.
      Worcestershire sauce
      Tabasco sauce
      Cognac

Divide ground meat into four patties. Place patties on a bed of watercress on chilled plates. Garnish with half a radish and a lemon quarter. Make a small indentation in patties and place an egg yolk in each. Place one-quarter of the shallots, parsley, salt, and pepper on each patty and mix together with yolk. Some guests prefer to combine the meat with the seasoned egg yolk mixture, others prefer to place a mouthful of meat on a fork and dip it into the egg yolk mixture. Serve with thinly sliced French bread, toasted and buttered.

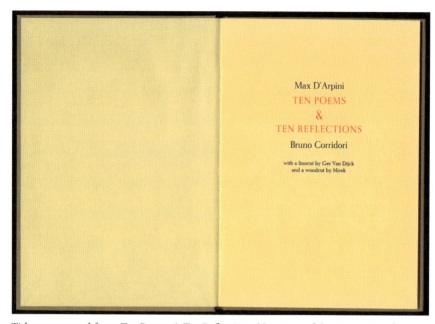

Title-page spread from *Ten Poems & Ten Reflections*. (Courtesy of the University of Oregon Libraries.)

Item 5. *Ten Poems & Ten Reflections*

Ten poems in Italian, French, English,
and Latin by Max (Paolo) D'Arpini and
ten aphorisms in Italian by Bruno Corridori.
With a linocut by Ger van Dijck and a woodcut
by Mirek (Miroslav Zahradka).
52 pages. 24 x 17 cm. 80 copies. 1971.

Another Distraction

In July 1971, feeling "postpartum" blues, I wrote to Berta Moltke, "[Your] book has changed everything. All my values have been warped. I no longer know what I want. I want to sleep. I want it all to go away." What I really should have wanted and been thinking about was getting on with the printing of *Siete Poemas Sajones / Seven Saxon Poems*. However, I was afraid to resume work on it again, even though most of the text had been set for more than a year. I emerged from the Zweig/Moltke book never wanting to print another book, yet within three weeks I had started work on this project for Max D'Arpini.

Ten Poems & Ten Reflections

Max had literally rescued me when he arranged for the delivery of my equipment and belongings that were being held by the freight forwarders in Verona. Every favor is an opening for one in return, and Max had indeed done me a favor. He had performed a Mafia-type miracle, the kind that counts even in present-day Italy. So when he presented himself at my door and asked if he could print a little book of his poems on my Poco proof press, I was naturally eager to repay him. Like the printing of *The Dog Bite* for Barton Lidicé Beneš, the printing of this book for Max was just another digression, one in a long string of projects based on romantic or sentimental attachments or financial need rather than literary merit. These two projects also helped to establish a pattern of destructive and masochistic relationships that I had with some of the authors I published.

Max D'Arpini and Gabriel in the courtyard at via Duomo, 15, Verona, Italy, 1970. (Photo by Reggie Gay, courtesy PWP Archives.)

Max D'Arpini

Max, who had pretensions of being a poet, had seen my first book, *Eight Parting Poems*, and envisioned a book of his own concrete poetry printed in a similar format on my Poco proof press. It was originally going to be a sixteen-page pamphlet, but as work progressed, it grew into a fifty-two-page book. The kindest thing I can say about his poetry is that it has a naive charm. Max wanted to do all the work himself. He assured me that he could set the type, but he was soon having trouble with the process. Would I mind helping him? That is, would I set the type for him?

From the beginning I had second thoughts about letting Max use my equipment because he was unfamiliar with both setting type and the operation of the press. Furthermore I was afraid he would damage the type – type that was essential to my livelihood as a printer – so I reluctantly offered to set the type myself.

Expanding the Project

As the pamphlet began to take shape, Max thought that the project would be enhanced if he included the aphorisms of his guru friend, Bruno Corridori. "It would just be a few more pages," he cajoled in his soft Roman voice.

Item 5. Ten Poems & Ten Reflections

Left: Part title from *"Ten Poems"* with a linocut by Ger Van Dijck from *Ten Poems & Ten Reflections*. (Courtesy of the University of Oregon Libraries.)

Right: Part title from *"Ten Reflections"* with a woodcut by Mirek from *Ten Poems & Ten Reflections*. (Courtesy of the University of Oregon Libraries.)

Bruno's reflections were badly written and very pretentious. By then, because of the book's expanded format, we decided to print it together on the Washington press. The only problem was that by this time Max had found a job, so he no longer had any free time during the day.

Printing the Book

Early on we had decided to use a cheap commercial Vergata Camoscio paper for the text. I set the text in Horizon Light and printed it in quarto, four pages at once. Since there were so few lines on each page, the makeready was fairly easy. His estimate of a couple of days "under foot" had turned into four weeks of solitary labor for me while he was on the road selling toilet paper to factories in industrial lots. I finished printing the last pages on August 6, 1971.

As bad as the situation was, this project offered me an opportunity to work with two artists I admired. Ger van Dijck and Mirek, a Czech artist, belonged to Max's coterie of international friends. They both happily contributed an illustration, a linocut and a woodcut, respectively. Although Ger and I had known each other since my first trip to Verona, I didn't meet

Mirek until October 1970, at the opening of his one-man show at the galleria d'arte moderna "a-dieci" in Padua. We became fast friends. We were the same age and both *émigrés* who shared the intention of staying in Italy. I adored Mirek, and like Paul Secon before him, I looked to him as an anchor in the heterosexual world. We were to collaborate on two more projects at the press, but regrettably we never worked on a major book together.

Binding the Book

Somewhere along the line Max convinced Alessandro Galvagni to bind the book. I doubt that any cash ever changed hands. Those who basked in Max's light were satisfied with just a smile or a caress now and then. The real motive behind this project was to help Max raise a few lire to renovate his house, which he had turned into a private club known simply as EX, an "intellectual" cabaret of sorts, featuring poetry readings and Irish protest singers. I was easily roped into turning out handset posters and programs for the club each week on the Poco proof press.

Helping Max Paint the Galleria "La Meridiana"

A new art gallery run by a Mafioso-type, Umberto Tommasi of the wine-producing family, opened in the spring of 1971. It was called Galleria "La Meridiana" in via Oberdan, just around the corner from the Palazzo Da Lisca, where the PWP would one day move. Umberto had contracted with Max (who, like me, was always short of cash) to paint the small gallery space of less than five hundred square feet. Max suggested that we do it together and share the profits. I was paid about $30 for the whole job. I ended up earning less than a dollar an hour for four twelve-hour days of painting. After the first day Max was always away "on business," occasionally stopping by to check on my progress. I did most of the painting alone. The work went slowly because the walls were covered with burlap that immediately soaked up the paint. It took at least four coats of the cheap white paint to completely cover it. I am not sure why – given my scene-painting experience – it didn't occur to me to seal the burlap first with a glue sizing.

As the day for the grand opening drew near, Max rounded up two volunteers to help me finish the job. One of these was Giancarlo Ferro, a sexy wild man. Exhausted from painting all day, we would drive in his Jeep out to his place in the country to drink wine, smoke some pot, and fool around.

Item 5. Ten Poems & Ten Reflections 209

Since he was always horny, we jerked each other off. Somehow we still managed to get the gallery painted in time for the opening.

One night sometime later Golda Fishbein, her son Mark, and I went out to Giancarlo's for a big raucous party of eating and drinking. As the festivities were winding down, someone offered us a ride back into town, having forgotten that Mark had crawled into an empty bed. It was not until the next morning that Golda realized that Mark hadn't come home with us. She became mildly hysterical. A friend drove us out to Giancarlo's, where we found Giancarlo and Mark coming back from shooting rabbits. Mark wasn't the least bit concerned; he had had a lot of fun hanging out with Giancarlo.

Printing Commissions for Cristini

Once Max's book was off the press, I put the Borges book back on it, only to take it off again in order to print three commissions for Luciano Cristini. I printed the letterpress sections, usually the title and colophon pages and perhaps a short introduction, for several of the suites of prints he editioned for his artists. The completed suites were placed in a handsome portfolio. Fortunately Bonnie Walker pitched in to help me print several of these projects.

A particularly intriguing set of prints, printed in early September 1971, was *Pacci doni* by Gigi Bragantini, a Veronese surrealist whose work I liked very much. As part of my payment, I received one of the prints from the suite. In this way I was able to accumulate an impressive collection of contemporary Italian graphics over the years.

Presentation of the Book at Galleria "La Meridiana"

The final insult connected with the publication of Max's book was the "happening" Umberto staged at the gallery on September 6 with both Max and Bruno reading selections of their texts from the book. I never liked Bruno, who had been in jail for two years for pushing drugs to teenagers. Although small posters announcing the happening were plastered all over town, I only heard about the event through friends. I think Max was embarrassed to tell me what he was going to do. The book was presented as a finely printed, limited edition by "the famous international printer Gabriel Rummonds." When we had first talked about the project, we thought the book would sell for around $5 a copy; I was horrified to find that the gallery was asking twelve times that price. I felt, and justly so, that I had been taken, since in addition to contributing my time and equipment to the project gratis, I was being asked at the opening to authenticate that the book was worth $60. I protested that I couldn't, but fearing Max's disfavor, I compromised: I said if he didn't call on me to sanction the gallery's price, I wouldn't reveal the book's true value. I knew intuitively that something like this might occur, so I omitted the PWP imprint from the title page of the book. I viewed it as just another commission, albeit one without any compensation. I did receive, however, twelve copies of the book in appreciation for my help.

End of My Affair with Max

My first year of happy discovery in Italy was coming to an end. Max and I could talk for hours without my really being able to speak Italian or Max, English. He seemed to know what I wanted to say, and on those nights when we slept together in front of the open fire at his place with the heavy fragrance of wine still on our breath, I felt I had found my vocation – albeit not the religious one I had once hoped for – and sensed that I was, at that very moment, on the verge of living out my fantasies.

After the presentation of his book at Galleria "La Meridiana," and as my circle of friends expanded, I seldom saw Max. He got in touch with me again in August and September 1972 to print a few broadsides on the Poco proof press for one of his social/political clubs. Soon after, he returned to Rome. Once he was gone, I complained of always being sick – aches and pains, stomach problems, probably psychosomatic.

Item 5. Ten Poems & Ten Reflections

Spezzatini di Vitello in Agrodolce
Sweet and Spicy Veal

Serves 12

During that first winter in Verona I made a variety of stews. They were fast, economical, and fed a lot of people. This one is one of my own concoctions for a veal stew.

    4 ounces salt pork, cut into small pieces
    6 tablespoons butter
   12 veal scaloppini steaks, cut into thin strips
      Salt and freshly ground black pepper to taste
   ¼ cup soy sauce
    1 teaspoon ground ginger
    1 teaspoon medium-hot chili powder
   10 slices canned pineapple with juice
   18 prunes, pitted
    1 orange, sliced with rind

Cook salt pork in a 3-quart sauté pan over medium-high heat. Transfer to a bowl and set aside. Add 2 tablespoons of the butter to the pan. Brown one-third of the meat at a time. Lightly salt and pepper the meat before transferring it to the bowl. Repeat the process until the remainder of the meat has been browned. Deglaze the pan with soy sauce. Add ginger, chili powder, and pineapple juice and bring to a boil. Add pineapple, prunes, orange slices, and meats to the pan and mix. Cover and simmer for 1 hour. Serve on rice.

Portfolio and title page from *Le Streghette*. (Courtesy of the University of Oregon Libraries.)

Item 6. *Le Streghette*

Five short prose pieces in Italian and five
multicolor linocuts by Mirek (Miroslav
Zahradka); with an English version by
Gabriel Rummonds. 7 loose sheets in folio.
20 x 22 cm. 81 copies. 1972.

One More Distraction

Even though I was still weary after Max D'Arpini's project, I knew that I
had to reorganize my priorities and commit myself wholeheartedly to *Siete
Poemas Sajones / Seven Saxon Poems* before too much more time elapsed.
Although I did begin to pull press proofs of it, I discovered that the alignment of the text on the backup was being thrown off by the leads and slugs,
the spaces between the lines of type. Having come from different sources,
they varied slightly in thickness. The obvious solution was to scrap all of
the old line spacing material and start over again. While waiting for the new
leads and slugs to arrive, Mirek and I decided to print a small book that we
hoped to have ready to sell to our friends around Christmas 1971. We
wanted it to be something bright and witty. Originally, it was to be illustrated
with dry points, but Renzo Sommaruga thought we should use linocuts.
The book grew in complexity, but not in size like Max's had.

Tinting the Paper

Le streghette means "the little witches" in Italian, and with this theme in
mind, we thought it would be appropriate to print Mirek's humorous text
and multicolor linocuts of scantily dressed young women on a paper that
suggested a cloudy night sky. Once we decided to use linocuts, we needed a
heavy paper that could be folded in half and inserted loose in a portfolio.
We were not able to find a colored paper that exactly suited us, so we ended
up tinting the paper ourselves. The cloudy effect we wanted came quite naturally since the aniline dyes never completely dissolved in the denatured
alcohol bath. Early every evening for more than a week, Mirek would come
by my studio, and we spent a couple of hours alternately dipping the

pre-cut C.M. Fabriano moldmade paper in a shallow tray filled with a solution of 30 grams of blue aniline dye and a pinch of black in 5.5 liters of alcohol, followed by a rinse in a second tray of clear water. The paper was then placed between pulpboards.

Half-intoxicated by the fumes of the alcohol – more than thirty liters in all were needed for the edition – we would interrupt our work to go around the corner for a quick pizza, returning to my studio to dye another batch of paper before calling it a night. Before Mirek left we put the pile in the standing press overnight. Under pressure, most of the moisture in the paper was extracted and the sheets came out nice and flat. My kitchen walls were spattered with blue dye for the remaining ten years I lived in Verona – I never found the time to repaint the walls.

Le Streghette

Mirek was not only an imaginative painter, but an illustrator of children's books. This item was conceived as a children's book for adults, and all the illustrations were somewhat saucy. Since the book was intended for more than just our immediate circle of Italian friends – I was anticipating the sale of a few copies abroad – we decided at the outset to make it bilingual.

I gave Mirek's Italian text a slightly racy English twist. This is what I said about the little witch called Delia:

> She stood around looking like a praying mantis, but that didn't keep her from turning a trick or two now and then.

Double-page spread from *Le Streghette*. (Courtesy of the University of Oregon Libraries.)

Item 6. Le Streghette

Poor Mirek only discovered my little ruse after the book was finished, when one of his English-speaking friends translated my version back into Italian for him.

Even though we worked diligently on this project from the start, we didn't finish the printing until January 17, 1972, too late for Christmas. All the same, we were quite pleased with our efforts. We printed the text and illustrations on dampened paper. The only real problem had been a technical one: getting the colored inks to cover the Horizon Light type properly. At the time, I wasn't aware of the various properties of printing inks, and so out of ignorance I used etching instead of letterpress or lithographic inks. The soft etching inks gave us little trouble on the linocuts, but the same inks weren't stiff enough for the text. I didn't know then that there were ways of "doctoring" these inks. We devised a complex but workable system for registering the text and the multiple blocks for the illustrations.

Brooks and Bonnie Walker

The Walkers, Brooks and Bonnie, were by now comfortably ensconced upstairs. Brooks, who was very gregarious, never let his lack of Italian prevent him from making friends. His Italian consisted solely of pronouns, infinitives, and adverbs of time. For example, to say, "I went to Milan," Brooks

Bonnie Walker near Verona, Italy, 1972. (Photo by RGR, courtesy of PWP Archives.)

would say, "*Io andare Milano ieri.*" In English this would be translated as, "I – to go – Milan – yesterday." Italians adored his energy and enthusiasm, and he soon developed a huge circle of friends. Bonnie, who had never expected (or desired) to stay in Verona long, spoke even less Italian than Brooks and was not always amused by his friends.

I was working downstairs one evening as the sun was setting. It was hot and all the windows were open, so when I heard Bonnie screaming upstairs. "Stay away from me. Help!" I figured Brooks was in one of his horny moods. I rushed up the stairs two at a time, only to find him sitting calmly in his underwear at the table in the entry, working on one of his clay statuettes. Bonnie was in the bedroom still screaming, fighting off some bats that were circling the room.

Bonnie Takes Up Marbling

Although Brooks's work schedule was erratic, he usually spent the mornings sketching or modeling. Bonnie often kept him company, but soon became restless for lack of something specific to do. A guest at the Press had left behind a copy of an American supermarket magazine in which there was an article on how to marble paper. Ever since I had watched the binder in Buenos Aires marble paper, I had wanted to try my own hand at it. I started to experiment with the technique and was soon joined by Bonnie, whose curiosity had also been whetted.

Since the publication of this portfolio, I have done a lot of marbling in Italy and Alabama; however, my experience has for the most part been limited to preparing samples rather than actual production. Bonnie, on the other hand, enthusiastically took up edition-marbling and before long she was turning out quantities of very attractive decorated papers. One of the unique features of *Le Streghette* is the paper Bonnie marbled to cover the portfolios. Marbling quickly became a driving force in her life; even after her divorce from Brooks and relocation to Florida a few years later, she continued to pursue the craft professionally.

Getting Lots of Help from Guerrino Bertaso

The portfolios were made by Guerrino Bertaso. As a young man he had been apprenticed to one of Giovanni Mardersteig's early binders, Peter Demeter, who in turn had been trained by T. J. Cobden-Sanderson at the Doves

Item 6. Le Streghette 217

Bindery in Hammersmith, London. Bertaso no longer did fine bindings – in fact, he now had a large trade bindery. However, he very much enjoyed showing examples of his early work to visitors. He loved to reflect on his accomplishments and reminisce about the old days when he was an apprentice. I never tired of looking at the things he had worked on as a young man. One of the skills he had learned during his apprenticeship was how to make exquisite decorated papers using oil-based inks, rather than the tempera colors used in the more familiar Turkish marbling. I especially liked his papers because the patterns were less rigid than those associated with the French-English papers, and his colors weren't as garish.

I will always be indebted to Bertaso because he introduced me to *sodio alginato* (sodium alginate) – a chemical used to thicken food, among other things. This chemical, mixed with water, constituted the medium on which he suspended his colors, instead of the more traditional carrageen moss bath. Bonnie had started out following the instructions in the magazine article, simply sprinkling oil-based inks on tap water. This method worked fine, except that it gave her very little control over her patterns. Soon after our visit to Bertaso's, she started thickening the bath with *sodio alginato*. She made all the papers for the edition in a marathon session, pulling the last sheet at dawn. Beginning with this item decorative papers played a prominent role in the production of PWP books.

I had originally thought about printing a label for the front of the portfolios, but Bonnie's papers were so beautiful I didn't want to mar them. Instead, I asked Bertaso to add a small gold-stamped dot to the top ribbon tie of each portfolio to indicate the front cover.

The Publication Party

On March 4, 1972, Mirek and I gave a little publication party for *Le Streghette*, for which we also printed about eighty-five invitations on the Poco proof press. We used the butterfly image from the title page. (Sometime later I used one of the illustrations from the book – a naked girl toe-dancing on a ball – for the invitation to another party.) We were quite pleased by the turnout, and we sold most of the portfolios that evening.

The afternoon of the party, I met a cute boy on via Mazzini – a favorite promenade in Verona – and invited him to the party, hoping he might want to stay over because he was from out of town. Sad to say, he tucked one of the portfolios into his belt, pulled his sweater down to hide it, and walked away, never to be seen again. One of the other guests later mentioned that he had seen this guy "pretending" to steal the book, but he didn't think the guy was serious about it or he would have told me.

That spring Mirek and I drove around northern Italy in his rattletrap car, a Citroën 2CV, peddling the remainder of the portfolios. One of the delights of these excursions was stopping off to eat and drink at the little wayside inns along the road. One of our favorite destinations was Lake

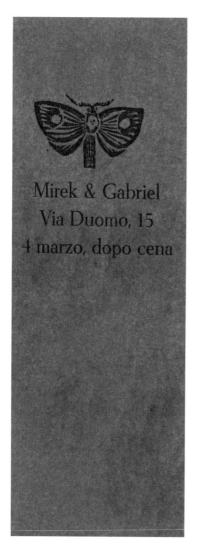

Invitation to the publication party for *Le Streghette* (1972). (Courtesy of PWP Archives.)

Item 6. Le Streghette 219

Garda. *Le Streghette* is filled with pleasant memories; it was the result of a close collaboration of friends working together in perfect harmony. Since most of Mirek's friends were Italians, as were mine, and Mirek spoke no English, the two of us were forced to use and expand our Italian. During my first year in Verona, I didn't know any Americans except Brooks and Bonnie, and even though we lived in the same building and got together occasionally, we had very separate lives and friends.

One evening a couple of months after Mirek and I had finished *Le Streghette*, I joined him and some of his friends from Padua for a glass of wine at the Bottega del Vino, a favorite meeting place for artists and writers. Among the people sitting around one of the heavy wooden tables was a young man named Nino Toninello, who instantly charmed me. He said he would like to see me again, and so I promised to pay him a visit.

Nino lived in Galzignano, a small village near Padua 90 kilometers (about 55 miles) from Verona. In May 1972 I drove there on my Vespa, and after many false starts, I finally found his house. He had told me just to ask any villager where he lived, but when I arrived there, the streets were deserted;

Mirek at Lake Garda, Italy, 1972. (Photo by RGR, courtesy of PWP Archives.)

it was lunchtime. Then I heard the strains of a Mozart piano sonata being played on a slightly out-of-tune piano drifting over the orchards. I followed the music to Nino. We had an *aperitivo* under the fruit trees, and lunch was served *al fresco* by an elderly maiden aunt with whom Nino lived. After eating we took a walk through the fields, and then I got back on my Vespa and returned to Verona.

What has all this to do with printing? Not much, really, except that it was printing that brought me together socially with so many Italians; and it was being with them that made me *feel* that I, too, was now a native, that I belonged in the landscape, that I was no longer just another expatriate.

Gabriel at Lake Garda, Italy, 1972. (Photo by Mirek, courtesy of PWP Archives

Item 6. Le Streghette   221

Pastissada de Caval (Spezzatini di Cavalo)
Veronese Horsemeat Stew

Serves 6

Occasionally Mirek would invite me for a one-pot supper at his studio in
Parona. Being frugal, he would make a stew of horsemeat. He introduced
me to both horsemeat and arugula. Since then I haven't eaten much horsemeat, but arugula has become a salad staple for me. Some recipes call for
the addition of vegetables and spices.

       3 tablespoons olive oil
       4 tablespoons butter
    1½ pounds yellow onions, coarsely chopped
   18½ ounces fresh tomatoes with their juice, strained
               through a coarse sieve
         Salt and freshly ground black pepper
       1 teaspoon paprika
       2 pounds tender horsemeat, cut into bite-sized pieces
       1 bottle red Valpolicella wine

Put olive oil and butter in a 3-quart sauté pan on medium high heat. When
fats begin to bubble, add onions and sauté until golden. Add tomatoes, salt,
pepper, paprika and meat. Cook for about 20 minutes. Add wine and cover.
Cook for 3 hours on medium-low heat. This dish is often served on polenta
or potato gnocchi.

Title-page spread from *Ballata delle Madri*. (Courtesy of the University of Oregon Libraries.)

Item 7. *Ballata delle Madri*

A ballad in Italian by Pier Paolo Pasolini.
With nine etchings, one each by Giuseppe Banchieri,
Giovanni Cappelli, Agenore Fabbri, Quinto
Ghermandi, Walter Piacesi, Mario Rossello, Ernesto
Treccani, Ada Zanon, and Giuseppe Zigaina.
12 loose sheets in folio. 45.5 x 32.5 cm. 172 copies. 1972.

A Commission from Renzo Sommaruga

Nineteen seventy-two was a particularly difficult year for me. I had to accept several commissions in order to keep the press and myself together financially. *Ballata delle Madri* was the first of these.

In late January 1972 Renzo Sommaruga asked me to print the text for a book he was publishing with his Edizioni Verona imprint. It consisted of a long ballad by Pier Paolo Pasolini and nine etchings, each by a distinguished Italian artist. It was to be in the style of the French *livre d'artiste*. Renzo had come to me because his 1842 tabletop Hopkinson & Cope Albion press was too small for the format he had selected. Even though I printed the letterpress for this item in my studio, it would not be fair to claim it as one of my own books, because Renzo was entirely responsible for its contents and design. He also set the text for it, using his beautiful Garaldus type.

Renzo versus Mirek

The experience was not a completely pleasant one. Renzo had said that we could print the book in a week, but the work dragged on for almost three. One reason the printing took longer than anticipated was that Renzo always arrived an hour or two late. Another was that the makeready on my Washington was more involved than it was on Renzo's Albion. On the other hand the printing sessions themselves were usually fun. I came to appreciate Renzo's cynical sense of humor, but the warmth and personal exchange that I had experienced while printing with Mirek was lacking.

When we broke for lunch, he insisted on eating only the sandwich and drinking the wine he brought with him each day, even though I offered to cook us a hot lunch. Unlike Mirek, who always stayed behind to help me tidy up the studio and usually lingered on to relax over a glass of wine while discussing the day's accomplishments, Renzo dashed out the door as soon as he removed the last sheet from the press. His attitude was that he had hired me to print the job, which included cleaning up afterwards.

From the start he had been eager for us to collaborate on several more projects and had even mentioned some of them to me, hoping that our association would open up more foreign markets for his own publications. However, I could already foresee some major problems developing in our working relationship if, indeed, he was going to treat me merely as a hired hand instead of as an equal partner. Printing this item made it evident to me that because of our different temperaments and ages – Renzo was fourteen years my senior – we would never be able to work harmoniously for very long.

Keeping the Paper Damp

Renzo and I kept the sheets damp by storing them overnight in humidors that Renzo Oliboni, a neighborhood cabinetmaker, had made for me following the diagrams in Lewis M. Allen's *Printing with the Handpress*. The synthetic sponge lining was saturated with water to which I added benzoic acid to prevent mildew.

I found Oliboni through Paolo Legnaghi, a sculptor, whose studio was located on the street side of the Palazzo Guarienti. Paolo had had an affair with an American soldier, who had promised to return to Italy after his tour of duty, but he never showed up. Because Paolo always wore black, his friends referred to him as "the widow Legnaghi." He was the most talented of the three artist Legnaghi siblings. He worked in wood, and Oliboni transformed Paolo's small working models into six- or seven-foot-high wooden sculptures. In addition to the humidors, Oliboni made the finely crafted wooden containers for the deluxe editions of *Siete Poemas Sajones / Seven Saxon Poems* and *Will and Testament: A Fragment of Biography*.

Learning from Renzo

Despite our differences I must admit I probably learned more about the craft of printing from Renzo than anyone else during those first years in Verona. While printing – I inked and pulled, and Renzo placed and removed the paper – we talked about the aesthetics of printing. As we worked I picked

Item 7. Ballata delle Madri

up an Italian printer's vocabulary that I continued to use long after I left Verona.

Renzo also taught me how to print a small cut in a second color simultaneously with the text in black. While I was still printing *Images & Footsteps,* Renzo gave me several tips on how to refine my inking technique. I was very fortunate to have had his guidance early on, since his method of inking was to become, with little modification, the one I used thereafter. As we worked on this project, I had an opportunity to see firsthand these refinements in practice. Before I met Renzo I had tried the inking technique Lewis describes in his book, but it didn't work for me. I even tried, unsuccessfully, to imitate what I believed to be Victor Hammer's method, gleaned from photographs of him working at his press. (Curiously, Hammer used a roller with a diameter that was far too small for the amount of type he was inking, and his crisscrossing technique was better suited for woodcuts and wood engravings than metal type.) Renzo introduced me to brass roller bearers, which permitted the roller to pass evenly over the type.

Because the colophon pages were numbered in the press, I also learned how to lock up the numbers and the names for the *ad personam* copies so

Double-page spread from *Ballata delle Madri.* (Courtesy of the University of Oregon Libraries.)

they could be changed without disturbing the whole form. Italian collectors were particularly eager to have copies with low numbers, so Renzo accommodated them by printing several colophon pages with the same low numbers. This was so well known that there was a standing joke among collectors in Verona: "Do you have the *first* copy numbered 1, or the *second*, or the *third*?"

After printing *Ballata delle Madri*, I made two important decisions: I vowed that I would always be scrupulously correct in numbering my own editions and that I wouldn't take on any more commissions that interfered with my publishing schedule. The first vow I was able to keep, but the second was never possible at the PWP. We finished printing the book on February 18 at 4:45 p.m. The $165 that Renzo paid me may have kept my body together a while longer, but I was still having to rely on anonymous encounters to keep my soul from dying.

Reggie Gay was in the studio when Renzo showed us the mockup for the binding. Reggie, who opposed using animal skins for anything, including belts and shoes, started haranguing Renzo about a narrow strip of vellum on the spine of the chemise that held the portfolio. Renzo promptly put him in his place by declaring, "I have given immortality to this beast."

Etching by Giuseppe Zigaina from *Ballata delle Madri*. (Courtesy of the University of Oregon Libraries.)

Item 7. Ballata delle Madri 227

Exchanging Mailing Lists

Renzo and I also exchanged mailing lists. Mine consisted primarily of private collectors culled from the lists Lewis had sent me soon after my arrival in Verona, plus the names of a few libraries with fine-printing collections that I had found in Lee Ash's *Subject Collections* (1967). The nucleus of my list of Italian collectors came from Renzo. I augmented Renzo's list with another from Giorgio Bertani, a leftist publisher in Verona who loved fine books. Before I met Giorgio he had commissioned several limited editions, which he sold through his trade book catalog. Even though he was no longer publishing deluxe editions, he never lost his interest in fine books. Always eager to help me, he would occasionally buy a PWP book. These two lists were later enhanced by others, culminating several years later with the membership list of the bibliophile association I Cento Amici del Libro.

Renzo Sommaruga, the Artist

Renzo had always been a womanizer, and this led to his downfall. When Giovanna, one of his students at the art school where he taught became pregnant, his wife locked him out of the house, banishing him to his second-floor studio on the hilltop side of the house. Guests approaching from the street side had to climb up a ladder and crawl through a window to visit him. I loved to go there with the Dutch Boys and browse through his books. Renzo always provided a lively commentary to accompany each. Once his girlfriend's condition made it impossible for her to use the ladder, his wife relented, a little, and let them use the entrance that opened onto the upper yard. One evening after the baby was born, they invited me to dinner, but there was only one egg, which they offered to me. Renzo was very proud of his little boy and would strip him so he could show off the baby's *pistolino*.

His temperament was very Latin. He would virtually explode one minute and the next he would laugh heartily about something foolish he had done. Having first become intrigued with books while working on the woodcut illustrations for one of Giovanni Mardersteig's editions, he continued to pursue printing as a secondary interest; he still spoke of himself as an artist – primarily a sculptor. I had talked Enzo Ferrari into giving Renzo a one-man show, which opened late in December 1971 at the Galleria Ferrari. At first Enzo was reluctant because everyone said Renzo was under a social curse. Even though his sculpture and books were unquestionably beautiful and he was a very accomplished artist, many people were hesitant about including his work in their collections. Collecting Renzo was compared with bringing the bad luck of a hitchhiker caught in the rain into your car.

Pier Paolo Pasolini

Renzo had promised to take me along with him when he went to Rome to get Pasolini's signature for the book, but for some reason he didn't. Late in September I saw Pasolini in a restaurant in the Campo de' Fiori in Rome. He was dining *al fresco* with one of his favorite actresses, Laura Betti. I joined them for a drink, and we talked about the possibility of his letting me print a small book of his homoerotic poems. I always regretted not going back to his place that night as he had suggested to fetch the text, because Pasolini was murdered before he had a chance to send the manuscript to me.

Pier Paolo Pasolini, place and date unknown.
(Photo by Carlo Bavagnoli, courtesy of Time Inc.
Picture Collection.)

Item 7. Ballata delle Madri

Saltimbocca alla Romana
Veal with Prosciutto and Sage

Serves 4

Ballata delle Madri always conjures up pleasant thoughts of Rome, where one of my favorite dishes has its origins: Saltimbocca alla Romana. It is simple and fast.

For the scaloppini
  2 tablespoons unsalted butter
  8 veal scaloppini, each weighing 3 ounces
  4 slices prosciutto, cut in half
  8 leaves fresh sage
    Salt and freshly ground black pepper to taste

For the sauce
  4 tablespoons Marsala wine
  4 tablespoons chicken broth
  4 tablespoons unsalted butter

The scaloppini: Flatten veal with a meat pounder. Place a piece of prosciutto on each piece of veal and top with a sage leaf secured with a toothpick. Place a 3-quart sauté pan on the burner over medium heat. When the pan is hot, add butter. When butter begins to bubble, add veal, with prosciutto side down. Sauté for 2 minutes, then turn them over and sauté for another minute. Remove them from pan and keep them warm on a serving platter.

The sauce: Over medium-high heat, deglaze the pan with the wine. Add broth and cook for about 3 minutes, then whisk in butter. Return saltimbocca with its juices to the pan for about 1 minute. Plate saltimbocca, prosciutto side up and spoon sauce over the top. Be sure to remove the toothpicks before serving.

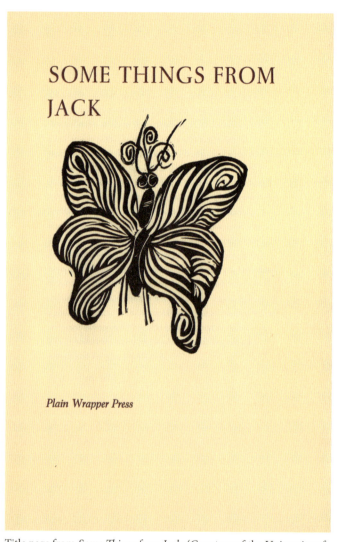

Title page from *Some Things from Jack*. (Courtesy of the University of Oregon Libraries.).)

Item 8. *Some Things from Jack*

A letter and three poems by Jack Spicer; with an introduction by R.R. [Richard Rummonds]. With a linocut by Mirek (Miroslav Zahradka). 12 pages. 26 x 16.5 cm. 91 copies. 1972.

Reconnecting with My Feelings

Having just finished a book for which I felt no personal commitment, I needed to immerse myself immediately in something that would recharge me emotionally and get me back in touch with my own feelings. Knowing that I should have been working on one of my income-producing projects, I chose instead to print a gratis keepsake to send to friends and collectors. Suddenly the euphoria that had motivated me to print my first two books returned. I described this feeling in the introduction to *Some Things from Jack*:

> One of the advantages of having my own printing press is that I can share with my friends certain intimacies, which perhaps take on more importance and somehow become more real in print. Recently I came

Gabriel around the time *Some Things from Jack* was printed, Verona, Italy, 1972. (Photo by Pucci De Rossi, courtesy of PWP Archives.)

across this letter and these poems from Jack, which I had tucked away in a box almost twenty years ago. What distressed me most about finding them once more was that in all this time that they have been in my possession (having carted them around the world), I may have looked at them only twice. Reading them now, I realize that I too have written this *same* letter, these *same* poems, under similar stress with equally sad results. I, too, was not able to break the pattern once it had been established. So in fact these things from Jack have been in me ever since I first received them, from the very moment I desired another's body or hoped for the love of a specific person – who inevitably was also unattainable. I do not want to suppress these things again, and so with a little trepidation I have prepared this small keepsake for myself and for you, my friends.

Returning to my past always filled me with awe, so I emerged from the experience cleansed and charged with new energy. Working with this text conjured up pleasant memories of a very creative period in my life, when I was a student at Berkeley in the spring of 1953, writing my "tinytinytiny" stories and poems. Jack Spicer was a teaching assistant in the second writing course I took from Thomas Parkinson. Even though Tom was the teacher of record, Jack read and criticized almost all of the assignments I wrote for Tom's class. At this point in his life, he was regarded as a poet's guru, having reached the height of his popularity both as an author and as a lecturer. I spent many hours with him, usually talking about my writing, which he criticized relentlessly, but encouraged at the same time. On other occasions Jack would read me some of his own poems or a page or two from someone else's work that he thought I ought to know. I could listen to him read for hours. Our discussions also helped me to keep a physical distance that I sensed he wanted to bridge.

Jack had a perverse sense of humor. For instance, the North Reading room in the Doe Library was very proud of its security system, defying anyone to steal a book from its shelves. One day, Jack arrived there with a book cart and loaded most of the volumes of the *Oxford English Dictionary* (1933) on it. Then he rolled the cart into the men's room, after leaving a note on the empty shelf to let the staff know where to find the missing books.

As the following letter reveals, he was very much in love with me.

Item 8. Some Things from Jack

Jack Spicer, place unknown, 1950s. (Photo by Helen Adam, courtesy of the Helen Adam Collection, State University of New York at Buffalo.)

Dear Richard,

I would like to explain my rather violent attitude toward you and show you why I react in a manner which (since you obviously don't understand it) must seem to you nothing short of idiocy. May I add that if you did understand it (even in part), you are a bastard.

There has been a pattern in my life (one which I must obviously have some part in constructing) of falling in love with a person who has not had homosexual experience, having him use me to find homosexual experience with another person – and then persons. This happened with the first male I fell in love with (some five years ago) in a manner which almost rendered me useless as a person, and has happened twice since then. I am tired of it. Never once was I allowed to go to bed with them. They wanted to be friends.

So it is that I, when I see damnable history repeating itself, buck and kick and try to break the pattern. I kept telling myself if one thing happened differently this time, the pattern would be broken and I would be free, free from the chain of loved unlovers. But everything is the same; no one thing has happened differently.

It is true that we could become good friends. We enjoy many of the same things and I like to laugh with you. But it is also true that friendship with you would be impossible as long as the pattern is in operation. At the moment I can't see a solution which would be acceptable to both of us.

Perhaps we could write letters.

Jack

P.S.: In spite of this I feel an appalling amount of tenderness for you.

J.

Because of my sexual inhibitions, I wasn't able to respond in the way he had hoped, although years later, after we had both left Berkeley, we briefly became lovers. I'll never forget Jack bursting into tears after we made love the first time, blurting out, "You don't know how close I came to killing you after you started seeing Bruce [Boyd, another of Jack's students in the spring of 1953]." The poems in this keepsake were not written specifically for me. I only happened to have copies of them because he wrote them out in longhand one afternoon for me to use as part of a presentation I was making in an oral interpretation of literature course.

Marius Dean

My very first sexual experience was with Marius Dean in October 1950. At the time I was living in Mrs. Hayes's boarding house on Dwight Way in Berkeley, where I worked as a breakfast cook in exchange for room and board. Marius and I had met on several occasions at parties given by Gene McGeorge at his house out in the country. With his Swedish carpenter's build Marius fascinated me. One night we were both out in the persimmon orchard. I was relieving myself when he walked up to me and without saying a word, kissed me on the mouth and then walked away. Marius wasn't a student, but he had a room with a group of students connected with *Occident* in an apartment above the Bosn' Locker in Oakland just outside the Berkeley city limits. Marius usually worked nights, and when I was too drunk to walk home, I would get into his bed fully clothed, thinking he wouldn't come home, but also hoping he would. And one night he did come home early. Seeing me asleep on his bed, he started ripping my clothes off. I was horrified; after all I was still a virgin. He got undressed, and for the

Item 8. Some Things from Jack 235

first time in my life I saw another man's erect penis. He was extremely well-endowed. At first I was frightened, and then I grew ashamed of my own body. My penis seemed so small compared to his, and I assumed incorrectly that all men were built like him. Years later, I realized that I was closer in size to him than I was to most of my subsequent lovers.

Bruce Boyd

It would be more than two and a half years before I could get into bed with another man, in this case, Bruce Boyd. I was a terrible prickteaser in those days, and even though Bruce and I had never even exchanged so much as a glance in class, we were both aware of the tension that was building up between us. One Wednesday I overtook Bruce as he was leaving the class, and without so much as a greeting, I blurted out, "I'm coming to your place for dinner on Friday." Before he could respond, I was off in another direction.

Although I got trapped in my own scheming, I let Bruce seduce me. One of his attractions was that his penis was smaller than mine, so I could allow him a certain leeway in our love-making that I had withheld from Marius.

It really wasn't love, more of an infatuation, but I enjoyed having sex with him even though he had smelly feet. Until I started this memoir, I had forgotten how handsome Bruce was. There was even a slight physical resemblance and an intensity in our temperaments that my narcissism found attractive. He lived in a bohemian apartment on Bancroft Way, with lots of candles and very little furniture. He cooked a vegetarian stew – more a matter of economics than a political statement. After eating we made love on his sleeping mat.

Toward the end of Schorer's English 106A class, I wrote a story for Bruce. Like all S.S.R.S. stories it had a long, convoluted title, "The First William Story *or* What Happens to Animals Once They Have Been Animals and Found They Are No Longer Interested in Being Animals? They Go Right on Being Animals *or* The Bruce Boyd Story." We kept in touch for a few years, although I doubt that I ever sent him a copy of the story.

Bruce was also a poet. During our affair he wrote the following poem for me:

Protreptics to a Portable Apollo

1.

Reminiscences like shadows
Conceal what they're about.
But when the shadow of its own ideal
Finally falls across the ego, Lysis,
Look up and smile and say "Hello,
Hippothales, you're late."

Instead, Hippothales has got to wait.
And you, at night when everything's a shadow,
Regard the mocking bird that sings
Some nightbird song it's learnt from Orpheus,
To teach you indirections.

"The evenings, I recall, were cool.
We took long walks, but in the end
Lacked guidance."
There were no gods, we said,
No charms we could pronounce:
The brief real bird was dead
And we, unschooled in auspices,
Could only call the strung-out entrails guts,
And hasten to the public streets
And hope to find familiar things.

2.

But it wasn't at all simple,
Just as one ought to have known.
Familiar things looked changed, perhaps,
And living seems a little disarranged just now
(Or is anyone who talks
About confusion ever in it)?

I think you shouldn't only talk.
I really think you should begin it.

Item 8. Some Things from Jack 237

But just suppose you don't.
You'll have your household things, of course;
You'll play the role they'll have you play
And people seeing you on the street will ask
"Who's that?" and say
"That's Mr. Lysis,
Oddly enough a family man,
The father of a family."
But really in the inner rooms already
Your household gods avert their faces
Murmur and desert their places
With a nugatory gesture.
They see there's nothing they can gain.
You'd try, but couldn't do it really well.
So what the hell?
Come on in out of the pain.

3.
Or again, suppose you do.

I think we should begin
With prayers to Eros and Anteros
To prepare us to be wiser
Than we've been.

There's nothing more one ought to say,
No words in haste.
I am afraid that all
The little birds would screech
And fly away
And say that Lysias's speech
Is less offensive to their taste.

After Bruce left Berkeley in the summer of 1953, he moved to San Francisco and was active in the circle of poets known as the San Francisco Renaissance, which included Jack Spicer. A few years later three of his poems were published in *The New American Poetry* (1960), edited by Donald M. Allen. Little is known about his life after 1970.

A Poem for Richard by Jack Spicer

I never had an opportunity to publish any of the poems Jack wrote for me, but here is one he dedicated to me (with my last name misspelled) in *After Lorca* (1957):

> *Narcissus*
> A Translation for Richard Rummond[s]
>
> Child,
> How you keep falling into rivers.
>
> At the bottom there's a rose
> And in the rose there's another river.
>
> Look at that bird. Look[,]
> That yellow bird.
>
> My eyes have fallen down
> Into the water.
>
> My God,
> How they're slipping! Youngster!
>
> – And I'm in the rose myself.
>
> When I was lost in water I
> Understood but won't tell you.

Printing the Keepsake

I loved printing *Some Things from Jack*. I started work on it early in March 1972 and finished printing it on April 16. One of the major frustrations I had in printing *Images & Footsteps* was getting the makeready right, compounded by the necessity of keeping the paper damp until all the forms in each set of sheets were printed on both sides. One solution was to set the press up for half-sheet imposition (work-and-turn). This meant that as long as I was printing in one color, I only had to prepare one makeready for each set of sheets. Even though this item was printed in two colors, the makeready for the second color, which was used for the book title, poem titles, and the page numbers, wasn't complicated. The inking of the linocut was still a bit gray, even though I used two inking plates and rollers for the black so I could give extra ink to the linocut. I should have printed it separately.

Item 8. Some Things from Jack

Gabriel printing *Some Things from Jack*, Verona, Italy, 1972, (Photo by Guido Trevisani, courtesy of PWP Archives.)

After the pressure was correct for the text, I would dampen the Fabriano Umbria handmade paper, needing only half the total number of sheets required for the edition, because each printed sheet consisted of two identical four-page gatherings. I dampened the paper using the pulpboard method.

I printed all the sheets in a form on one side the first day, then the next day, I turned them over and printed the other side. Leaving the sheets overnight in a humidor gave the ink an additional chance to set, thus reducing the amount of setoff the second time they went through the press. I was still using only Horizon Light for all my work.

I was working with Mirek again, so all I had to do was make a few suggestions about subject and size, and he would appear a couple of days later with a linocut illustration in hand. During this period I also designed and printed personalized wine labels for some of Angelo Gavioli's preferred clients. Angelo headed the export department of the Tenuta Villa Girardi, a distinguished winery just outside of Verona. I also helped him with his business letters in English. As a token of his appreciation, he frequently dropped off a case or two of his fine wines. Mirek also made individual linocuts for these personalized labels, including one for me. I loved arriving at a party and presenting the host with two bottles of my "Vino Gabrielis – Private Stock."

Two Visits to Martino Mardersteig

Even though I was printing smaller and lighter forms, I still had trouble getting the right amount of pressure for the impression. In mid-March 1972 I took some proofs to Martino in hopes of finding out what I was doing wrong. Martino said the pressure should be controlled only by the wedge, not by the corner blocks. He also recommended using as little packing as possible. Once the arm reaches the "bite" (the moment of first resistance), no more pressure should be applied.

Nothing Martino said seemed to help, so I returned to him again in May. I asked if it would be possible for the two printers at the Officina Bodoni to come and look at my press, but Martino said no. It was the old Mardersteig mantra about "secrets." He did make one more suggestion about the packing, however. I needed to get the outer edges of all four blocks of type uniformly heavy, and then correct the middle area with thin sheets of packing. I continued to incorporate some of his suggestions until I devised my own methods of pressure and packing.

A Poem by Laure Vernière

Laure Vernière, a French poet, moved to Verona in 1971. I published a selection of her poems in *Géographie du Regard* in 1976. After reading *Some Things from Jack* and being inspired by a phrase in Jack's letter to me, she wrote the following poem:

Item 8. Some Things from Jack   241

A Song for Gabriel

> Buck and kick and try to break the pattern

Repeating words that don't mean much
But somehow split hearts like almonds
Gathered between male and female trees

Caring for objects that are useless
But somehow burn the belly as a last
Rum drink between night and dawn

Walking with those clownish crutches
That somehow may help standing up
Between a lover and another

Smiling with pained and twisted lips
But somehow the laughter will rise
Between a sharp scream and pleasure

Double-page spread from *Some Things from Jack*. (Courtesy of the University of Oregon Libraries.)

A Visit to Fernanda Pivano

On one of my frequent trips to Milan, I gave a copy of this keepsake to Fernanda Pivano, an Italian critic best known for her essays on Jack Kerouac and the Beat poets. Even though Jack Spicer was not part of the Beat movement, Nanda was particularly fond of his work. We talked about doing a bilingual edition of Beat poetry, but nothing ever came of it. We both got caught up in other obligations. There were always many more ideas for projects than time to execute them. A surprisingly large number of these projects were sufficiently developed that I announced them as forthcoming publications in my brochures, only later to set them aside for good.

Drinks with Robin Blaser in Seattle

Prior to his visit to Seattle in 1998, the last time I had seen Robin Blaser was in Boston in 1966. I had written a review of *Poet Be Like God: Jack Spicer and the San Francisco Renaissance* (1998) by Lewis Ellingham and Kevin Killian, and Robin wanted to "catch up." Knowing I had been one of Jack's lovers, he asked me if it were true that Jack had a tiny penis. I was so shocked that what had been a delightful conversation about Berkeley and old friends was suddenly reduced to faggoty gossip that I replied, "Well, if you never saw it when you were friends, I guess you'll never know for sure." I never heard from Robin again.

Item 8. Some Things from Jack

Coniglio alla Reggiana
Rabbit with Herbs

Serves 4

Having fine wine on hand was always an excuse to put together a tasty dinner for a few friends. The recipe below is easy. Everyone enjoys a well-cooked rabbit. I chose this recipe in part because one of Jack's publishers was the White Rabbit Press.

  1 rabbit, about 2½ pounds, cleaned and cut into 8 pieces
  ½ cup olive oil
  1 garlic clove, peeled and crushed
  2 sprigs (3 inches long) rosemary, leaves only
  4 fresh sage leaves
  8 juniper berries, whole
  3 tablespoons vinegar
  ½ cup white wine
    Salt and freshly ground black pepper to taste

Soak rabbit, covered with cold water overnight in the refrigerator. Rinse several times in cold water and pat dry with paper towels. Put oil, garlic, herbs, vinegar, and rabbit in a large, 3-quart sauté pan over low heat. Cover and simmer for 1½ hours, occasionally turning the rabbit pieces. Add wine, salt, and pepper. Increase the heat to medium and cook uncovered for an additional 30 minutes.

Gabriel's smashed-up Vespa, Verona, Italy, 1972. (Photographer unknown, courtesy of PWP Archives.)

Verona: The Vespa

The truth is rarely pure and never simple.
– Oscar Wilde, *The Importance of Being Earnest*

Acquiring the Vespa

The Vespa, as is well known, is a popular Italian motor scooter. Its name means "wasp," and one literally buzzes around on it. Mine played an important role in my early years in Italy.

One of the first Italian friends I made on my own was Franco Casati. He came up to my table one day at Caffè Filippini and introduced himself. He was a university student looking for someone with whom he could practice his English. Since my Italian, weak as it was, was stronger than his English, we ended up speaking in Italian and continued to do so even after he became quite fluent in English. Franco was also a budding author. (His first novel, *Tema astrologico* (1980), was published while I was still living in Verona.)

Franco had a 1959 Vespa, and when he upgraded to a more powerful model, he sold me his old one for 15,000 lire (about $25) on April Fools' Day 1972. I must have been feeling flush at the time; I was earning $100 a month teaching English.

The Marble-Topped Table

Besides the Vespa, Franco was responsible for an earlier contribution to my lifestyle in Verona: a seven-foot-long marble-topped table. One Saturday in December 1971, we took a ride out into the country on his Vespa, retracing his summer postal route. We stopped for a glass of wine at an inn, sitting outside under the bare trees and winter sun at the only marble-topped table in the graveled side yard. All the other tables were new and had shiny Formica tops.

As we drank our wine, I told Franco I wished I could find such a beautiful table for my studio. He thought the innkeeper might want to sell this table because he had replaced the other marble-topped tables in the side yard with Formica ones earlier that summer. He would ask the innkeeper's wife. She wasn't sure, but she thought her husband did indeed

245

want to get rid of it. If we were serious about the table, we could have it for 12,000 lire (about $20). Franco and I rushed back to town, found a friend with a truck, and returned to fetch the table. In my imagination, I held my hands over my ears all night long because I didn't want to hear the screams of the innkeeper's wife as he beat her for asking so little for such a grand table.

In February 1973 I printed a small broadside for Franco on the Poco proof press – one of the few pieces of ephemera printed at the PWP – consisting of one of his poems and an etching by Brooks Walker. Franco gave it to a cousin on the occasion of the cousin's marriage.

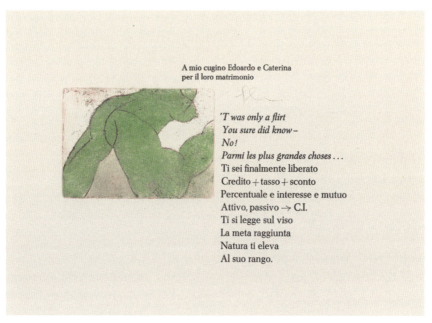

Franco Casati's broadside (1973) (Courtesy of The New York Public Library)

Nocturnal Prowling

How I loved that Vespa. It not only provided me with transportation, but was also an intrinsic part of my erotic life. With wheels I was able to extend the bounds of my nocturnal prowling. One of my favorite places was the open-air movie theater near the Basilica of San Zeno, a short distance from the center of town. I picked up Italian soldiers and took them to my place for a glass of wine and a good time.

Verona: The Vespa

The train station was another favorite haunt. One night I turned a trick for money in park in fornt of the station. With my ill-gotten earnings in my pocket, I rushed back to Verona and invited Brooks and Bonnie Walker for a late-night drink at Caffè Filippini.

One of the after-dark fixtures at the train station was Irma, an old prostitute who hung out against one of the high walls supporting the railroad tracks. Half-hidden by bushes she would service Italian soldiers who patiently waited in line for their turn. Between each client Irma would rip a page out of a photo-romance magazine to tidy up. One night I was standing behind a cute drunk soldier from Sicily. He was having trouble finding his way in. I grabbed hold of his little cock, positioned him in the right direction, and gave him a bump on the rear end. He let out a little squeal, so I knew he had achieved his goal.

My First Sales Trip

I had had the Vespa only a couple of weeks when I decided to take my first sales trip. I buzzed down to Reggio nell'Emilia, 105 kilometers (about 65 miles) south of Verona, to see Dino Prandi, an antiquarian bookseller who also carried a large stock of contemporary illustrated books. He bought a couple copies each of *Images & Footsteps* and *Le Streghette*. With ready cash in my pocket, I felt particularly elated, so on the trip home I stopped and treated myself to a nice lunch at a country inn. Afterward, in a grassy field on the banks of the Po River, I slept off the wine I had consumed with the meal. I got back on the Vespa and continued my journey through the flat countryside, with rice fields on either side of the road as far as the eye could see. The Vespa provided me with an opportunity to indulge my fantasies. I now had the means to travel the byways with the same wanderlust that had driven Goethe and Berlioz to explore Italy more than a century before.

Isabel Freud Hanson

Isabel Freud, my old friend from Berkeley and San Francisco, stopped by with her husband Lou Hanson and their three sons in May 1973. I had not seen her since my visit to her family late in the 1950s in San Andreas, California, where Lou taught music in the local high school. They were only passing through Verona, so our visit was short, but it was great to see her. She looked wonderful and so happy.

Lou and Isabel Hanson and their three sons in the courtyard at via Duomo, 15, Verona, Italy, 1972. (Photo by RGR, courtesy of PWP Archives.)

Whenever I hear Domenico Scarlatti's Sonata in E major, K.380, on the radio, it transports me back to those happy days in San Francisco with Isabel, who often played this piece for me on her upright piano.

Golda Fishbein

In the spring of 1972, Golda Fishbein, who had worked with me at Alfred A. Knopf/Random House in 1968, wrote to ask if she could visit me that summer. Naturally I wrote back that I would be delighted to see her; I would even come to Milan – the location of the closest airport to Verona – to fetch her. On the July day that she was scheduled to arrive, I was returning from a prior engagement before heading to the train station on the Vespa when a car driven by a man from Milan hit my tail, tipping me over and sending me skidding on my stomach and elbows against the curb. Fortunately it was early in the morning when there was little traffic. All the shopkeepers rushed out of their shops and surrounded the culprit. As I was rushed off to the hospital, they gave me his license plate number, hastily jotted on a scrap of paper. They were ready to testify on my behalf.

At the emergency room I was quickly bandaged in gauze – nothing serious, just a few minor scratches – and released. I took a bus to the train station, managing to arrive just as the train was pulling in. When I didn't

Gabriel after the Vespa accident, Verona, Italy, 1972. (Photographer unknown, courtesy of PWP Archives.)

show up at the air terminal in Milan, Golda had taken the first train to Verona, hoping I would be waiting for her on the platform. I looked like an extra from a World War I movie, blood oozing from my bandages as I hobbled down the platform to welcome her. Not exactly a propitious start for a visit that would be a turning point in both our lives. A deep and loving relationship blossomed between us that summer.

Golda swore she would not go anywhere with me on the Vespa, but within a few days I had the damage repaired, and we went off to Lake Garda. In the late afternoon on our return trip we ran into an impromptu summer storm, with lightning flashing at our heels. It was raining so hard I couldn't see the road. I asked Golda, who was seated behind me, to wipe off my glasses. Terrified, she was sure we would be killed or maimed for life. She reminded me that she had two small children to support.

I gave up the Vespa in April 1974, after hearing of the death of my friend John Alcorn's teenage son, Tommy, from head injuries in a Vespa accident in Florence in March 1974.

Golda Fishbein in Venice, Italy, 1972. (Photo by RGR, courtesy of PWP Archives.)

We also went to Venice by train for the day, and I introduced her to my Italian friends there. Later in the week Mirek drove us in his Citroën out into the countryside near Verona to visit the Roman ruins.

A Stream of Visitors

The summer of 1972 saw a steady influx of visitors from the States and Europe. In addition to Golda and Robert Daugherty, three co-workers from Alfred A, Knopf/Random House spent a couple of days in Verona, each arriving with a small, heavy packet of printing materials or type.

Paul Secon and Berta Moltke came with their son Lucas in late summer. They were frequent visitors, and their company always cheered me up. Over the years I often visited them in Copenhagen. On June 21 I wrote to Berta in my melodramatic way that I had a tumor and couldn't print anymore. I was probably just constipated.

In January 1972 Carolyn Reading Hammer, a handpress printer and head of Special Collections at the University of Kentucky, wrote to ask for more information about my Press and its publications. When she visited me in the fall, we became close friends. Later she became instrumental in my going to the University of Alabama in the late seventies to start the MFA in the Book Arts Program.

Verona: The Vespa

Pasta e Fasioi (Pasta e Fagioli)
Pasta and Bean Soup

Serves 4

This is a favorite soup in the Veneto.

- 1 pound dried cranberry *or* red kidney beans
- 5 ounces boneless pork ribs
- 1 onion (about 6 ounces), finely chopped
- 1 carrot, diced
- 1 stalk celery with leaves, diced
- 2 garlic cloves, minced
- 3 tablespoons olive oil
- 3 quarts water
- Salt and freshly ground black pepper to taste
- 10 ounces ditalini pasta *or* any small tubular dry pasta
- 1 tablespoon butter
- 2 tablespoons Parmigiano-Reggiano cheese, freshly grated
- 2 sprigs flat-leaf parsley, chopped
- A drizzle of extra-virgin olive oil for each serving

Soak dried beans overnight in enough water to cover. Put ribs in a large pot of water and bring to a boil for 5 minutes. Drain, cut into small pieces, and set aside. In a large soup pot, heat oil, then add onion, carrot, celery, and garlic. Cook for 5 minutes over medium heat. Add ribs and stir together with vegetables. Cook for an additional 5 minutes. Add water and deglaze pot. Add beans. Cover and simmer for 30 minutes. Add salt and simmer for 40 minutes more. Stir from time to time. Remove the pot from the heat. With a slotted spoon, remove half the beans, vegetables, and all the meat and set aside. Put the remaining beans and vegetables in a blender and purée before returning to the pot. The soup should be slightly grainy, not smooth. Add pepper and bring to a moderate boil. Stir in pasta and cook until tender, about 10 minutes. Turn off the heat and stir in butter, cheese and parsley. Pour soup into individual bowls and cool until a thin film forms on surface, about 10 minutes. Drizzle a thin stream of olive oil in the form of a cross or a swirl across the top of the soup. *Pasta e fasioi* is served warm, not piping hot.

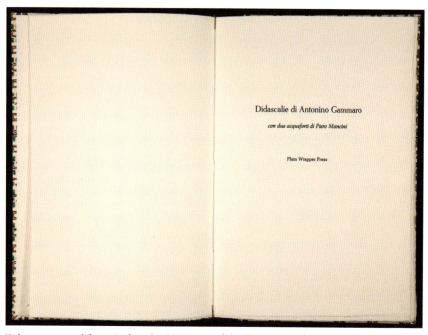

Title-page spread from *Didascalie*. (Courtesy of the University of Oregon Libraries.)

Item 9. *Didascalie*

Ten poems in Italian by Antonino Gammaro.
With two etchings by Piero Mancini.
29 pages. 28 x 19 cm. 99 copies. 1972.

My First Real Commission

One of the things that made it pleasant – and possible – to work in Verona was the widespread Italian tradition of individuals and bibliophile organizations commissioning private presses to print books for them. Both Giovanni Mardersteig and Renzo Sommaruga relied heavily on such commissions to keep their presses viable. Some of these commissions, such as this book that I printed in 1972 for Antonino Gammaro, a Veronese cosmetics salesman, were nothing more than vanity press editions.

Gammaro had a manuscript of his own poetry that he wanted Renzo to print, but Renzo was too busy to meet the projected publication date.

Antonino Gammaro with his daughter Linda, Verona, Italy, 1977. (Photographer unknown, courtesy of Antonino Gammaro.)

253

I also suspect that Renzo disliked the text. Even when he was desperate for money, he would never print anything he didn't believe in completely. In order to get himself out of an awkward situation with a friend, Renzo suggested to Gammaro that I – who should have had Renzo's scruples but didn't – might be able to squeeze his book into my tight schedule. Gammaro would pay for all the materials, which included the Fabriano handmade Imperiale paper from his private stock. I would again use my Horizon Light type. He also paid me the princely sum of $165 for my labor, and I could keep twenty copies to sell to my collectors.

At the time I was still trying to solve some of the technical problems I was having with the press. Even though I had not yet found an artist for the Borges book, I put the project back on the press in May 1971 and pulled more proofs, all of which were unsatisfactory. By the middle of June, the frustration was such that I gave up on pursuing my own projects, and in September I accepted Gammaro's commission, though I didn't finish it for another year.

Changing projects wasn't going to alleviate the difficulties or resolve the technical problems I was having, but I chose to delude myself about this.

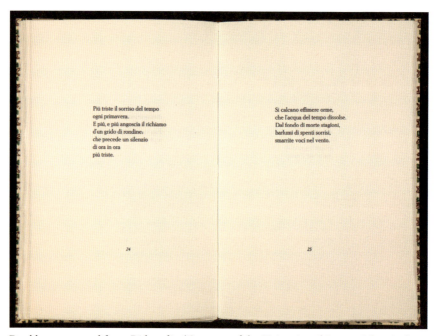

Double-page spread from *Didascalie*. (Courtesy of the University of Oregon Libraries.)

Item 9. Didascalie 255

After several false starts I put the first pages of the Gammaro book in the bed of the press on June 8, 1972, but I didn't begin to print these pages until July 26. Again I set the press up for half-sheet imposition (work-and-turn), the method I had earlier found to be the most efficient for me. I managed to get an even impression on newsprint, but when I changed to dampened paper, the impression was off again.

As patient as Gammaro was, he tended to hound me. My studio was along the route where he walked his dog, so he would frequently just pop in to see how I was doing. In addition to the anxiety I felt at not being able to get the results I wanted, I began to feel the pressure to meet an impossible deadline. The situation was literally making me sick. I had to escape from Gammaro, his dog, and his book for a while, so early in August I took a train to Munich to visit my brother Tom and his family. They always provided a refreshing change of venue when I was feeling frustrated or unhappy with my printing.

A Breakthrough on Getting the Pressure

One afternoon at Dietrich Leube's in Munich, I met a young physics student named Michael Nedo. Michael listened carefully as I explained the technical problems I was having on the handpress. Even though he had never even seen a handpress before, he said it was simply a matter of leverage and wrote out a formula that he thought would solve the problem.

It amounted to a two-step process. Before any type was put in the bed, the outer corners of the platen had to press firmly against all four of the corner blocks (the platen bearers) and completely immobilize them with each pull of the bar. Then, with the type locked into the chase, the blocks must be adjusted to compensate for the placement of the type in the bed. They must remain tight, otherwise the impression would be uneven from one type-block to another. I used different thicknesses of Mylar to pack the corner blocks to achieve the proper contact with the platen. Using Michael's formula I resumed printing on the last day of August. I had already printed one set of pages before I left for Munich, and there was a visible difference in the quality of the weak pages I printed before the trip and those I printed after.

Even though there were still some minor details to resolve, at least I now knew what was happening each time I pulled the bar, and most important

I was able to repeat my experiments with consistent results. Except for the two part titles and the etchings, I completed Gammaro's book pretty much to my satisfaction at 4:00 a.m. on September 1.

Harry Duncan, the noted handpress printer, confessed to me at a workshop I gave at the Rochester Institute of Technology in 1992 that he had always found the pressure through trial and error, continually making changes until it was right. He regretted he had not known about this formula early in his career.

Piero Mancini

Gammaro's book is illustrated with two etchings by his friend the painter Piero Mancini. Gammaro was always very cost-conscious; so when I suggested having Luciano Cristini pull the etchings, Gammaro balked, saying

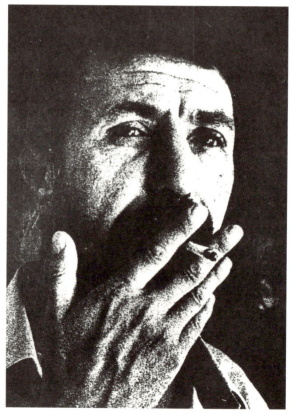

Piero Mancini, place and date unknown. (Photographer unknown, courtesy of Antonino Gammaro.)

Item 9. Didascalie

that Luciano's price of fifty cents per print – which was what I had paid for Berta Moltke's etchings – was too high. Quite by chance I ran into Giuseppe (Beppe) Bussola, one of Luciano's printers, who had helped edition Berta's plates. Since I had last seen him, Beppe had left the Cristini atelier to continue his education. In our conversation, he mentioned that he had an etching press at home and would be willing to pull the etchings for less than Luciano was asking. We had intended to print the etchings on Brooks Walker's press, but Beppe decided that he wanted to use his own. The etchings were printed between late September and early November. There were a few difficulties printing them. The plates were of different thicknesses, requiring a special makeready for each plate. Beppe and I were to collaborate on three more projects, including another commission for Gammaro.

Illustration from *Didascalie*. (Courtesy of the University of Oregon Libraries.)

The Binding

This is probably the best bound of all the books produced at the PWP in Verona. Gammaro arranged for the binding personally, and for some perverse reason he would never reveal the binder's name, no matter how much I implored him.

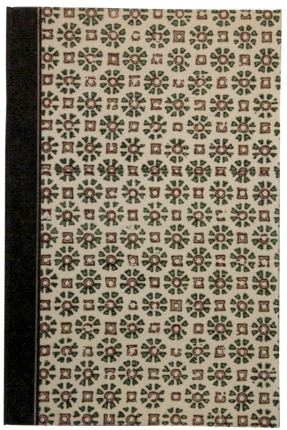

Cover for *Didascalie*. (Courtesy of the University of Oregon Libraries

Socializing with the Upper Middle Class

Being a printer in Verona opened many doors for me socially. My friends were not limited to artists and authors. I was able to develop many warm and lasting relationships with the collectors of my books, most of whom were professionals or business people. Their interest in my work gave me

Item 9. Didascalie   259

an opportunity to see a side of Italian society that wouldn't have been accessible to a person of my limited means. For instance, Ninì, Gammaro's wife, was very fond of me and frequently invited me to have supper with them – under the pretense of having to discuss the book – because she was afraid I wasn't getting the nourishment I needed, living alone as I did.

Granetto Family

Gammaro also enjoyed "showing me off" at the frequent *soirées* he gave, or taking me along – he always left Ninì at home – as his guest to meet his friends at their houses. It was through Gammaro that I met the Granetto family. The mother, Margherita, was my age, but she treated me more the way she treated her three sons. The oldest, Enrico, was away attending university in Milan. Gigetto, the middle son, was a poet and publisher; he and his wife Enrica lived in a separate apartment in his parents' house. The youngest, Paolo, was still in high school and also lived at home. I spent a great deal of time with them.

In November 1972 Margherita noticed that my wardrobe was lacking anything that could be thought of as stylish, so she told Gigetto to give me some of his old clothes. He brought out heaps of designer clothes, which I gladly accepted and frequently wore.

Margherita served wonderful lunches, and I was often invited *in famiglia*. Having lunch with the Granettos was like suddenly finding oneself thrust into a scene in a Fellini movie. At one end of the table, the father constantly petted Paolo, and at the other Margherita shamelessly flirted with Gigetto. The two ends of the table clashed when Gigetto, an extreme leftist, argued with his father, an industrialist, about the inequities of life as white-gloved servants passed trays of savory pastas and succulent meats.

Margherita was always very sensitive about her weight. I remember one lunch when she made one of my favorite chocolate mousses topped with lots of whipped cream. The mousse came out on a large round silver platter. She gave all of us a generous serving, refusing to take any for herself, saying that she was on a diet. "Gabriel, how is it? Is it the way you like it?" I assured her that it was perfect. "Well, then, I'll just have a tiny taste to see for myself." By the end of the meal, she had slyly finished off all that remained on the platter. Such contradictions became everyday occurrences of my life in *bella Verona*.

Double exposure of Gabriel pulling the bar of the Washington press around the time he printed *Didascalie* in the via Duomo studio, Verona, Italy, 1971. (Photo by Luca Steffenoni, courtesy of the photographer.)

A Bit of Low-Life on the Side

I still found time to indulge in escapades with less intellectual company. Once I met a young high school student at a pot party and invited him to the movies. A few nights later we drove out into the countryside on the Vespa to a parochial movie venue. We were on our way to see an Italian pirate movie called *Il Corsaro Nero (Blackie the Pirate)* with Terence Hill and Bud Spencer. The boy had told me earlier that he didn't want to see anything that was *troppo impegnato*. This simple action film turned out to be too intellectually demanding for him. Fortunately, he was more flexible in bed.

Item 9. Didascalie

Indonesian Spicy Eggs

Serves 8

During my visit to Dietrich Leube's, his companion, Anita Albus, cooked a dish with spicy eggs that I made frequently in Verona. One of the ingredients is an Indonesian spice called laos. I always referred to this dish as Eggs Anita.

16 hard-boiled eggs, halved and set aside
3 tablespoons peanut oil
1 white onion (about 15 ounces)
2 large garlic cloves
2 tablespoons fresh ginger, finely chopped
2 tablespoons laos powder
1 tablespoon Sambal Oelek
¼ teaspoon sugar
   Salt and freshly ground black pepper to taste
1 can (28 ounces) Italian peeled tomatoes without basil
½ cup milk

Put peanut oil in a 3-quart sauté pan. Quarter onion and pass it through an onion press directly into the pan, including the juice. Sauté until golden and translucent, about 5 minutes. Pass the garlic cloves through a garlic press directly into the pan. Add ginger, laos powder, Sambal Oelek, sugar, salt, and pepper to the pan. Cook uncovered over low heat for about 20 minutes. Add tomatoes, breaking them up with a wooden spoon or spatula. Lay eggs, yolks up, on top of the mixture. Slowly pour milk over the top of the mixture. Press eggs just below the surface of milk. Do not stir. Cook uncovered over medium-low heat until the mixture begins to simmer, then reduce the heat to low. The mixture should cook until it has been reduced to the consistency of a sauce, about 20 minutes. Serve over couscous.

Title page from *Poesie dal Tappeto Volante*. (Courtesy of the University of Oregon Libraries.)

Item 10. *Poesie dal Tappeto Volante*

Four poems in Italian by Alessandro Mozzambani.
With a multicolor screenprint by Rodolfo Aricò
and a lithograph by Bernard Cohen. Six sheets in folio.
51 x 35 cm. 50 copies. 1972.

Another Commission

Hélène de Franchis Sutton, the publisher of this portfolio, opened Studio La Città in the early seventies in partnership with a group of prominent Veronese citizens, who hoped it would become an artistic and intellectual center. The original plan, in addition to the usual gallery space, included a printmaking atelier where graduates of the local Liceo Artistico Statale (high school of fine art) could continue to work and study under a master printmaker. It was in this environment that I met two young artists with whom I would later work: Pucci De Rossi and Fulvio Testa.

Hélène had lived for many years in London, where her father had been the Italian ambassador to the Court of St. James. She was married to an Englishman, Oliver Sutton, although they no longer lived together. Oliver had been a pilot in the Royal Air Force and for a while taught flying. After one of his students hijacked an airplane, he moved to Switzerland, where he tried his hand at selling planes instead of flying them.

Alessandro Mozzambani

Hélène brought her passion for English pop artists to Verona and to her gallery, which was held in high esteem throughout Europe. As a result of an influx of British art, juxtaposed with kindred works by contemporary Italian artists, the gallery thrived. Alessandro Mozzambani was influential in establishing the gallery's reputation in his capacity as an art critic for *L'Arena di Verona*, the local daily newspaper. (His chief occupation was in the civil service.) In appreciation for his support, Hélène decided to publish a portfolio of Sandro's poems, together with original graphics by two artists whose work she exhibited in the gallery: Rodolfo Aricò, an Italian, and Bernard Cohen, an Englishman. She commissioned me to print the text and coordinate the production of the portfolios.

This project had one of the largest formats I ever printed – the sheets of the Magnani moldmade paper measured 51 x 70 cm. (about 20 x 28 inches) – although the text blocks themselves ended up being no bigger than those in *Images & Footsteps*. Before I saw the text, I assumed the poems would be similar to Sandro's others, which all had unusually long lines. I hoped to set the text in Horizon Light, the only possibility I had to put my personal mark on the project. When Sandro gave me the manuscript, I was stunned to find that not only were his poems brief, but they all had extremely short lines. I didn't have enough characters in any of my fonts of Horizon Light type to set even one of the poems, and it would have been impractical and expensive to order enough display fonts just for this job. My only option was to have the text set in Monotype. I selected a large size of Monotype Garamond italic that I thought would read well even when surrounded by so much white space on the large pages. On Martino Mardersteig's recommendation, I had the text set by Ruggero Olivieri in Milan. (All of the Monotype composition I used in Italy was supplied by this old and reliable company.)

The original plan called for an edition of sixty-five copies of four sheets folded in folio, so I ordered the paper accordingly. Earlier Sandro had told me that the poems didn't need to appear in any specific order, but after the paper arrived, he decided he did want them to be in a particular sequence, which increased the length of the text and added two extra sheets to each

Alessandro Mozzambani, Verona, Italy, date unknown. (Photographer unknown, courtesy of Alessandro Mozzambani.)

Item 10. Poesie dal Tappeto Volante 265

portfolio. Thus we were obliged to reduce the edition from sixty-five copies to fifty, because there was not enough time to order more paper if we were to have the project ready for the gallery show Hélène had already scheduled. I started printing the text on October 23, 1972. Fortunately the sheets, which were printed dry, had previously been scored and folded.

Hélène had selected Luigi (Gino) Berardinelli to edition the Aricò design, which I picked up in Milan on October 16. Gino converted it to a screenprint, and on November 5 I started helping Gino edition the print, but my presence made him nervous, so he ended up printing it alone.

An artist himself, Gino had recently returned from Paris to open his own atelier. When I first met him, he was busy editioning, with great precision, a suite of large screenprints by David Leverett, another of the English pop artists in Hélène's stable. Sandro's project was Gino's first book collaboration and the beginning of a long relationship between his atelier and the PWP.

Cohen's lithograph was editioned by Bud Shark in London. When the prints arrived around the middle of October, I discovered that Shark had sent me exactly fifty prints, all numbered and signed by Cohen. No allowance had been made for proofing or printing errors. Fortunately I didn't need more, because I had prudently set aside a few sheets of the Magnani paper for proofing.

As my frustration increased with each commission, I regretted more and more not going to Ibiza as originally planned. Aside from the fact that I couldn't have brought my press to Spain, where would I have found even the most modest of professional help there?

I finished printing the text on November 14 at 3:10 in the afternoon; it had taken nearly twenty-three days. I barely managed to assemble a proof copy of the portfolio in time for its presentation at a gala opening at Studio La Città the next day. Sandro read his poems, and a number of works by the two artists were on display. But in its own way, this item was a fiasco. Sandro, at best, could be considered no more than a minor poet, and his slight text, including the three poems inspired by the work of three very diverse contemporary artists, was inflated into an enormous and pretentious format. Two of the artists, Aricò and Cohen, provided prints to accompany the poems dedicated to them. The third poem was for Barnett Newman. Since Newman was dead, his name was printed in small type centered in the middle of an otherwise blank page facing the poem dedicated to him. It looked

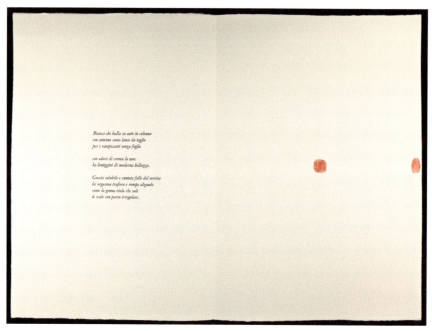

Double-page spread with Bernard Cohen's illustration from *Poesie dal Tappeto Volante*. (Courtesy of the University of Oregon Libraries.)

very much like an *in memoriam* notice in the local newspaper. If Newman had been alive at the time, it was a conceit to assume that he would have even entertained the idea of contributing a print to this portfolio.

Charles McNab arrived from New York in time for the opening at the gallery. He helped me assemble the remainder of the portfolios. With the pressure off me, I was able to show him around Verona. I also found time to print some stationery for him on the Washington press.

Despite its weakness, in one sense it was an important project. Both artists were well-known in international art circles and their works demanded high prices. Their contributions to the portfolio were no doubt tokens of appreciation for Hélène's exhibitions of their works in her gallery. This was also Aricò's first excursion into screenprints, a medium he would later use with great success.

Ennio Caloi

One of the few positive aspects of this project was working with Ennio Caloi, the binder. He had a large industrial bindery located on the edge of town near

Item 10. Poesie dal Tappeto Volante　　　　　　　　　　　　　　267

the Arnoldo Mondadori Editore printing plant. (To some extent Mondadori was responsible for the wealth of book workers in the area, since it jobbed out a considerable amount of its work. Giovanni Mardersteig's first handpress in Italy had been set up in the Mondadori plant between 1927 and 1937.) I don't remember whose idea it was to use Ennio – probably Luciano Cristini, who needed portfolios for the suites of prints he pulled for his artists – but Ennio turned out to be an excellent artisan. My neighbor, Fabio Ambrosi, made the bronze plate that Ennio used to gilt-stamp the cover of the portfolios.

My only regret is that Ennio and I never had a chance to work together again, because his bindery wasn't set up to handle limited editions. However, long after the project was completed, I often called him for advice regarding materials or dropped by to see him, and he always stopped whatever he was doing to help me. I will always be grateful to him for having introduced me to the Van Heek-Scholco cloths, which were used for many subsequent PWP editions.

Paltry Remuneration

I still wasn't charging enough for printing commissions. The $1,000 I was expecting from this commission was greatly reduced. Hélène paid me about $100 for my labor, plus six copies, valued at $150 each. As a printed book it was overpriced even at $85, the price I would have to charge my American collectors. As a *livre d'artiste*, however, it was a great bargain, especially for collectors of the artists' major works. This meant I had three copies I could sell, because in those days, I was trying to hold onto at least three copies of everything I printed: a copy for myself, one for my parents, and another for my brother Tom. Even though I could have used the money at the time, I never regretted setting aside the three copies.

Several years later, in Alabama, I was able to draw from my parents' and Tom's collections when I was putting together two complete sets of PWP books to sell to the University of Georgia and the University of Texas at Austin. The sale of these two sets provided me with the much-needed capital to build a studio next to my house in Cottondale.

In hopes of finding more commissions, I approached several art galleries, such as Renato Cardazzo's Galleria del Naviglio in Milan, to which Hélène provided letters of introduction. They liked my work, but the visits didn't result in any commissions.

Ossobuco alla Milanese
Braised Veal Shanks

Serves 6

The folks who hung around the Studio la Città were for the most part professionals, such as doctors and lawyers, and internationally acclaimed artists. In addition to modern art, they loved to eat and drink well, especially in Verona's better restaurants. One of the dishes I liked when eating out was ossobuco, a rich, succulent dish that is both expensive and time-consuming to make. I still make it for friends on special occasions. The following recipe is the way it is made in Milan.

4 tablespoons unsalted butter

12 ounces onion, finely chopped

⅔ cup carrot, chopped

⅔ cup celery, chopped

⅓ cup canola oil, divided

    All-purpose flour for dusting

6 veal hind shanks, 1½-inches-thick, with skin tied tightly around the middle

1 cup dry white wine

½ cup beef broth

½ cup water

¾ pound fresh tomatoes, peeled and diced *or* 1½ cups imported canned Italian plum tomatoes, coarsely chopped with their juices

2 bay leaves

2 teaspoons salt

½ teaspoon freshly ground black pepper

¼ teaspoon fresh marjoram *or* thyme, finely chopped

1 teaspoon lemon zest

1 teaspoon orange zest

1 large garlic clove, minced

½ cup flat-leaf parsley, finely chopped

Item 10. Poesie dal Tappeto Volante 269

Heat butter in a Dutch oven large enough to accommodate the shanks without overlapping. When butter begins to bubble, add onion, carrot, and celery and sauté on medium, about 6 minutes. Remove from the heat and set aside. Pour two-thirds of the oil into a large skillet and heat on medium-high. Dust two shanks, shaking off excess flour. When oil is hot, place shanks in the skillet and brown for 1 minute on each side. Transfer to the Dutch oven. Repeat procedure for the remaining shanks. Sprinkle salt and pepper over browned shanks. Add wine to skillet and let it simmer on medium heat while deglazing the skillet and reducing wine. Pour juices in the skillet over shanks. Add broth, water, tomatoes, and bay leaves to the Dutch oven and bring to a simmer on low heat. The liquid should come two-thirds up the sides of shanks. Add more broth if necessary. Cover the pot tightly and cook for 2 hours on simmer. Turn and baste shanks every 20 minutes. Sprinkle thyme, lemon zest, orange zest, and garlic over shanks. Cook for another 2 minutes. Remove bay leaves. Place on individual plates and sprinkle with parsley. Traditionally, ossobuco is served with risotto alla milanese.

Double-page spread from *The Ill-Timed Lover*. (Courtesy of the University of Oregon Libraries.)

Item 11. *The Ill-Timed Lover*

A poem by Gabriel Rummonds.
With an etching by Brooks Walker.
8 pages. 20.5 x 14 cm. 6 copies. 1972.

A Trip to Umbria by Vespa with Federico Rossi

Around the middle of September 1972, having finished the Antonino Gammaro commission, I took a trip by Vespa to Umbria with my friend Federico Rossi, a young man from Brescia who sold large photocopies of pop icons in front of Standa, a department store facing the Biblioteca Civica di Verona. He frequently came to Verona, and whenever he did, he would spend a few days with me. He was so beautiful, with a body that was both delicate and discretely formed.

Federico Rossi, Verona, Italy, 1972. (Photo by RGR, courtesy of PWP Archives.)

Franco Casati loaned me his Vespa, which was more powerful than mine, so we could use the freeways whenever we wanted to venture off country roads. With no more than a general direction in mind, Federico and I headed south, passing our days leisurely wandering around the beautiful old hilltop towns in Umbria, such as Todi, Gubbio, and Assisi, and then going farther south to Orvieto. At night we sought out a secluded field or orchard, where we would sleep peacefully, undisturbed by the preoccupations of the world around us.

Gabriel, Spoleto, Italy, 1972. (Photo by Federico Rossi, courtesy of PWP Archives.)

While in Spoleto, I wrote the following poem for Federico. And later, as a very personal memento of that trip, I printed it as a keepsake for him. It is without a doubt the rarest PWP item because it was printed in an edition of only six copies, although a few proof copies were sent to public institutions with standing orders.

The Ill-Timed Lover

Without even knowing of you
I had waited for you to come –
unaware of when it would be.

But then, after we met, I knew
that I would have to wait some more
for our bodies' rhythms to agree.

Item 11. The Ill-Timed Lover

The Last Leg of the Trip

Traveling from Bologna to Verona was somewhat harrowing. An unexpected cold rain beat down on us most of the way, and to make things worse, we were not dressed for such weather and got soaked through and through. I had to slow down because the rain clouded my glasses and I couldn't see the road clearly. In addition we were almost out of money. These were the days before ATM machines, but even if there had been such machines, I had practically nothing left in my bank account. We calculated how much to set aside for the last fuel stop, hoping we could fill the tank with enough gas to get home. It was still raining when the sun set, and we had not eaten since breakfast. Around Isola della Scala, near Verona, we pulled into the empty parking lot of a roadside restaurant/cafe. We counted our loose change and had just enough for one caffè latte. The dining room was deserted. I ordered one caffè latte, paying for it with an assortment of small coins. When the owner brought the caffè latte to the table, she gave us a sympathetic glance. We looked like two kittens that had been tossed into a river. She returned moments later with two brioches on a plate. As she set the plate down, she apologized that they were left over from that morning.

Brooks Walker, place and date unknown. (Photographer unknown, courtesy of Brooks Walker.)

Printing the Keepsake

It is hard to believe, as minimal as the text was, that a typographic error managed to creep into the colophon: "Federico suppied [*sic*] the motive." Over the years I have prided myself on producing error-free texts. When errors have occurred they have usually been in the colophon or the expository material that I wrote.

I produced this keepsake in a joyous atmosphere. Everyone wanted to help. Brooks Walker illustrated it with an etching, which Giuseppe (Beppe) Bussola editioned on Brooks's press; Bonnie Walker marbled the Kraft paper wrappers. Jacques Vernière and I printed the slight text, which was set in Horizon Light, on Amatruda moldmade wove paper. We printed it in one day, December 2, working from nine in the morning until eight that night.

Jacques Vernière

Jacques, who worked as an editor for a publisher in Paris, had a sister in Verona from whom he had heard about the PWP. He had become intrigued by the idea of printing and publishing on the handpress and had come to Verona on a visit in November 1972, hoping I would take him on as an ap-

Cover for *The Ill-Timed Lover*. (Courtesy of the University of Oregon Libraries.)

Item 11. The Ill-Timed Lover 275

prentice. Helping with this project was his introduction to handpress printing. I certainly could have used the extra help, but it was still premature for me to consider accepting apprentices. My schedule was much too erratic, and I was in no position to teach anyone how to use the handpress because I had not yet satisfactorily resolved many of the problems I myself was having with it.

In January 1973 Jacques moved to Verona with his wife Christine. Soon after, he acquired a beautiful Italian Albion press from Cristiano Cabianca, setting up his own shop in via Filippini. Like me he was determined to print even if it meant that he was going to have to teach himself. After issuing his first book, Jacques used the handpress primarily to edition relief prints. A few years later he returned to Paris with his Albion press, leading the French government to believe that it was part of a larger purchase of printing equipment that he had made on behalf of a government-sponsored printmaking atelier in Paris. Fortunately, I had given Jacques a letter for French customs declaring that he was the rightful owner of the press, which gave his son Julien a claim to the press after his father died.

Hélène Sutton's Etching Press

When Hélène Sutton decided to disband the printmaking facility at Studio La Città, she gave her etching press to me. I didn't have enough space to set it up, so for a long time it sat in pieces in one of the small anterooms in my apartment. Brooks had started making etchings, so he asked if he could move the press upstairs to his apartment, where there was plenty of room. I was happy to let him borrow it, knowing that once Brooks had the press operative, I would find many uses for it. Even though Beppe had editioned the Mancini plates for Gammaro's book on his press at home, we decided to use mine for *The Ill-Timed Lover* so Brooks and I could see how it worked.

Through a series of misunderstandings, Brooks eventually became its acknowledged owner when Hélène offered him the press in lieu of a commission payment she owed him, forgetting she had already given the press to me.

Once the etching press was moved upstairs to Brooks's aprtment, I built a loft in the anteroom where it had been stored. This tiny space, accessed by a ship ladder, had a low ceiling and one small window that looked down into the kitchen. It was where many of the PWP apprentices slept and stored their belongings and came to be known as the "Black Hole of Calcutta."

I always found projects like *The Ill-Timed Lover* the most gratifying, partly because I was completely involved in every aspect of their production. Each finished keepsake represented much more than just a pamphlet; it became an object that couldn't be severed from the sentimental source of its inspiration.

That December 1972 Federico and I went to Copenhagen for the holidays with Paul Secon and Berta Moltke. We were scheduled to arrive the day before Christmas Eve, but Federico missed his train. When he arrived in Verona, there were no more trains to Denmark until the next day. I called Paul and Berta and explained the delay. The customs officials at the Danish border wouldn't let Federico proceed; he didn't have a passport, which he didn't realize he would need because one usually traveled over most of Europe with nothing more than an identity card.

I gave him all the money I had, and he went back to Hamburg until we could send him a visa. When Berta, who was very well connected diplomatically, called an acquaintance in the consulate and guaranteed to vouch for Federico, they gave him a temporary visa, and he arrived in time for Christmas Eve dinner. This little escapade threw a dark shadow over the holiday festivities. By the time we got back to Verona, my feelings for Federico had cooled considerably. I seldom saw him after that.

Edward Melcarth

Another pleasant memory around this time was visiting Edward Melcarth in Venice. He was a figurative painter and sculptor, primarily of young men. Brooks Walker, also a figurative sculpltor, had introduced us. In November of 1971, one of his students, Richard Taddei, had come to see me in Verona. I had a big crush on him and had always hoped he would illustrate a book for me. Even though Edward was twenty-seven years older than me, I felt a real kinship with him. He died in 1973.

Item 11. The Ill-Timed Lover

Spaghetti con Vongole e Cetrioli
Spaghetti with Clams and Cucumbers

Serves 2

When Federico and I got home from our Vespa trip, I put water on for spaghetti. We dried off and changed into fresh clothes, then I made a clam and cucumber sauce for the pasta. The apartment was so cold that we huddled together under a blanket as we ate the steaming dish before crawling into bed, exhausted.

 2 tablespoons unsalted butter
 1 garlic clove, minced
 1 tablespoon flour
 1 cup clam juice
    Salt and freshly ground black pepper to taste
 1 teaspoon fresh thyme
 1 cup bottled clams
 2 servings dried spaghett
    Freshly chopped flat-leaf parsley to garnish

In a small saucepan, let butter come to a bubble. Add garlic and sauté for 1 minute. Stir in flour. When it begins to thicken, add clam juice, salt, pepper, and thyme and cook over medium heat for 10 minutes. Add clams to the pan and cook for 2 minutes. In the meantime, cook spaghetti according to the instructions on the package. Transfer spaghetti to a large serving dish and pour the sauce over it. Garnish with parsley.

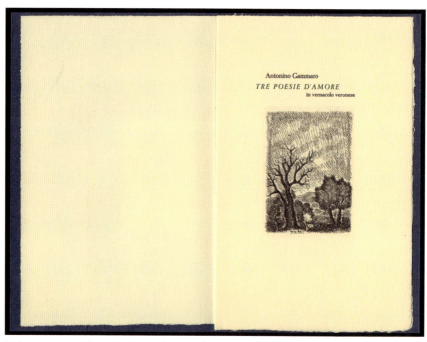

Title-page spread from *Tre Poesie d'Amore*. (Courtesy of the University of Oregon Libraries.)

Item 12. *Tre Poesie d'Amore*

Three poems in Veronese dialect
and a glossary by Antonino Gammaro.
With an etching by Giordano Zorzi.
8 pages. 26 x 16.5 cm. 140 copies. 1972.

A Christmas Keepsake for Gammaro

I had no more than finished printing *Didascalie* for Antonino Gammaro in September 1972, when he came to me with another commission: a Christmas keepsake he planned to give to his friends. He would pay for all the materials, and I would supply the printing. He was again the author of the text. I suggested to Gammaro that he consider Brooks Walker to illustrate it, but he had already enlisted Giordano Zorzi, a local artist and teacher, to make the frontispiece etching. Giuseppe Bussola editioned the prints at his studio early in November, after which the sheets, still damp, were brought back to my studio. I printed the text by myself, although on the last day of printing I was joined by Jacques Vernière, who was still in Verona. I used some of my left-over Fabriano handmade Umbria paper and set the text in Horizon Light.

Jacques and I finished printing the remainder of the text on December 1, and two days later we spent most of the day folding and tearing the sheets into signatures. One of my fondest memories associated with this project was the time I spent at Gammaro's apartment the following week. After supper, Ninì and I would sew the edition into wrappers, spreading the work over two evenings so I would have to come back for another delicious supper. The project must have gone fairly smoothly, because the keepsake was ready to send out before Christmas.

It was a long and difficult job. The Veronese dialect required so many accents that I ended up printing each poem as a separate form. This meant three times through the press instead of one. In the end, I received about twenty-five cents per hour for my labor, but I learned a valuable lesson: I never wanted to print another commission, neither for Gammaro, nor for anyone else. It wasn't in my character to print for hire; it seemed to go against my grain and values. I can't complain too much about these commissions;

after all, they helped to keep the Press viable during its first two years in Verona, and with each project I learned how to print with more finesse.

Giordano Zorzi

On the downside Zorzi behaved like a real bastard. When he heard that Gammaro had offered me $25 plus twenty copies from the edition of 140 copies to print the keepsake, he was livid. He wanted seventy copies instead of the sixty he originally agreed upon in exchange for his etching, saying that when Gammaro had promised him sixty copies, he thought that he was getting half the edition. He wanted to know why the printer, who was being paid for his work, should get any part of the edition. At this point Gammaro and I could not increase the size of the edition because I had already finished printing some of the forms and was not about to start over again. Gammaro had no choice but to give Zorzi what he wanted. My number of copies was reduced to ten, the most Gammaro could spare.

I was less upset about not getting my fair share of the edition than I was about Zorzi's attitude toward the project. Producing books in limited edi-

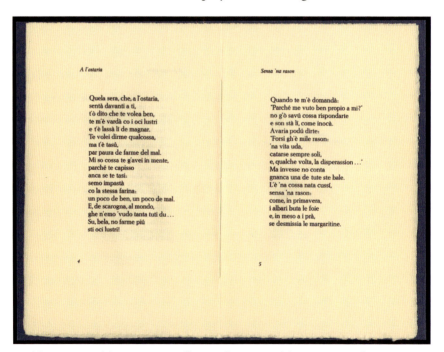

Double-page spread from *Tre Poesie d'Amore*. (Courtesy of the University of Oregon Libraries.)

Item 12. Tre Poesie d'Amore 281

tions should be a true collaboration among all the participants, built on the common desire to produce a work of beauty and permanence, whether a deluxe book or a keepsake. I always paid my collaborators, perhaps not at the market value of their work, but with fees in proportion to the total budget and the intent of the project. Artists such as Zorzi, whose only concerns are monetary, always rubbed me the wrong way. And in many cases such artists are not even particularly talented. By contrast Gammaro had given Piero Mancini only six copies of their book as payment.

Kurt Vonnegut Jr.

Several years later I found myself in a similar situation, this time with an author with an inflated sense of entitlement. I had a conversation at the Algonquin Hotel in New York with Kurt Vonnegut Jr. about a possible collaboration. As we talked I was reminded of a passage in his book *Palm Sunday* (1981) in which he mentions that he always grades his own work with an A, B, C, or D. So when I said in a lighthearted way that I hoped he would be sending me one of his A pieces. He was miffed. I certainly didn't mean it as a put-down, and so I was not prepared for his reaction. I wasn't surprised when nothing ever came of our discussion. In my mind's eye I will always see Vonnegut as a tired old woman with a goatee.

Failed Expectations

Vonnegut's reaction reinforced something I have long suspected, however: authors, like artists, instead of sending their very best to a printer of fine editions, often send what no one else wants, which is not the same as sending something good that may have been rejected by a commercial publisher because of its limited appeal. What a distortion of values!

I tried to avoid working on projects with people who were not completely committed to producing a fine edition and to seeing a project through to completion despite delays and setbacks. The printer needs the moral support and continued enthusiasm of his collaborators right up to the very end. The hardest book to complete is one written by a lover who leaves you before the printing is finished.

Bollito Misto
Mixed Boiled Meats

Serves 10

At times, when everything appears to go wrong, I need some good old-fashioned comfort food. On cold, foggy nights, some of my Italian friends and I would drive the short distance from Verona to the village of Madonna di Dossobuono for *bollito misto* at the Trattoria Ciccarelli. My friend Giorgio Zanolli also prepared it for a dinner party at his apartment when I visited Verona in 1999. It is another of those expensive, time-consuming, but greatly satisfying dishes. I continued to make it on special occasions in foggy Seattle, always with the traditional *salsa verde* and *pearà,* a peppery sauce made of bone marrow and breadcrumbs.

> 6 quarts water
> 1 ounce coarse salt
> 1 bouquet garni (flat-leaf parsley, bay leaf, smashed garlic clove, tied in a cheesecloth bag)
> 2 yellow onions (about 6 ounces each), one studded with 6 whole cloves, the other quartered
> 3 carrots, cut into 2-inch pieces
> 3 celery stalks with leaves, cut into 2-inch pieces
> 1 beef bone with marrow, about 4 inches long
> 2½ pounds boneless beef, eye-round *or* chuck
> 1 beef tongue, 2 pounds
> 1 whole chicken, about 3 pounds
> 2½ pounds veal shanks
> 1 pork sausage in one piece, such as cotechino *or* zampone, about 1 pound, cooked separately
> 1 teaspoon black peppercorns

Put water and salt in a large stockpot. Add the bouquet garni and the onions, carrots, celery stalks, bone with marrow. When water begins to boil, add beef and tongue. Turn heat down to a gentle boil. Skim off foam throughout the cooking. Turn the heat down to low and cook, covered, for 1 hour.

Item 12. Tre Poesie d'Amore

Remove tongue, peel and return to pot. Add chicken and tomatoes and raise heat to a gentle boil, then reduce to a simmer for 2 hours with pot lid slightly askew. The liquid should at all times cover meats. Prick surface of sausage and place in a large saucepan and cover with water. When water begins to boil, reduce heat to low and cook for 2½ hours. Leave it in the hot water until ready to serve. Remove various meats from the stockpot one at a time and slice as needed, leaving the rest of meat in the hot broth. Place on a large, deep platter. Pour a small amount of broth over the meats as they are served. Be sure to return sausage to its own pot after slicing what you need. The host serves each guest according to his request. Bollito misto is served with two condiments, Salsa Verde and Pearà. Boiled potatoes, dressed with olive oil, salt, pepper, and chopped Italian parsley, are generally served on the side. A special treat is to serve the broth with a little cooked pasta, such as anellini, as a first course.

Salsa Verde
Green Sauce

> 1½ cups flat-leaf parsley leaves
> 5 tablespoons capers
> 12 anchovies
> 1 teaspoon white wine vinegar
> 1 cup extra-virgin olive oil
> Salt to taste

Put all the ingredients in a food processor and blend to a smooth, uniform consistency.

Item 12. Tre Poesie d'Amore

Pearà

Pepper Sauce

> 8 ounces beef marrow, finely chopped
> 2 tablespoons butter
> 1 pound dry breadcrumbs, unflavored and finely chopped
> 6 cups hot beef broth from the bollito misto
> 3 pinches salt
> A liberal quantity of freshly ground black pepper
> 3 tablespoons freshly grated Parmigiano-Reggiano cheese

Place marrow and butter in a saucepan and mash together. Cook over medium heat until the mixture begins to bubble. Add breadcrumbs and cook for a minute or two. Add broth a little at a time, always letting it be smoothly absorbed into the breadcrumb mixture. Repeat until all the broth is used. The sauce should be thick and creamy without any lumps. Add salt, pepper, and cheese and stir. If too thick, the sauce can be thinned with more broth.

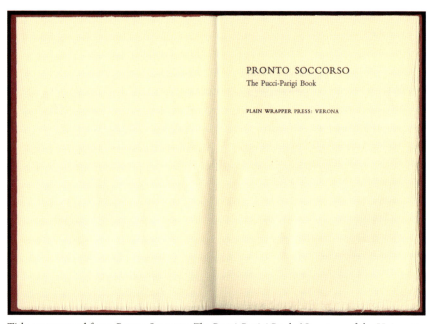

Title-page spread from *Pronto Soccorso: The Pucci-Parigi Book*. (Courtesy of the University of Oregon Libraries.)

Item 13. *Pronto Soccorso: The Pucci-Parigi Book*

A miscellany consisting of a preface in English by Gabriel Rummonds; a prose poem in French by Jacques Vernière; a poem in French by Alitché (Laure Vernière), together with an Italian translation by Isa Covre; and a tribute in Italian by Maurizio Bergamini. With an etching by Pucci De Rossi and a tipped-in photogravure reproduction of a photograph of De Rossi by Guido Trevisani. 16 pages. 29 x 20.5 cm. 120 copies. 1973.

Pucci De Rossi

Pucci De Rossi was one of the many students I met at Studio La Città before its printmaking facility was disbanded. Pucci was certainly one of the most talented, and in fact he has since gained an international reputation as an innovative sculptor. He was also in that circle of friends who gravitated around and partied with Max D'Arpini. When Max moved to Rome, Pucci's studio in via Filippini became the gathering place for the group. Like most of his contemporaries in the arts in Verona, Pucci lived a financially marginal but socially and artistically rich and energetic life.

Pucci De Rossi in the red room at via Duomo, 15, Verona, Italy, 1973. (Photo by RGR, courtesy of PWP Archives.)

In the summer of 1971 he went to the States on a visit, and when he returned in the fall he brought with him a French wife, Laure Vernière. Laure was an accomplished author, and at the time of her marriage to Pucci she was on the faculty of Sarah Lawrence College. They were later joined by her three children from a previous marriage – Eva Plank and the twins, Tania and Cybèle.

Pucci was very resourceful, and not having the means to buy marble or have his work cast at the foundries, he relied on found objects such as wood and ornaments from discarded furniture and inexpensive copper and brass sheeting for his sculpture. He was also industrious, and within a short time he had assembled an impressive number of pieces.

Knowing that Pucci could not interest any of the local galleries in showing his work and that many of my collectors enjoyed an occasional taste of the bohemian life, I suggested he hold an open house in his studio to exhibit his sculptures. In late March 1972 I printed the invitations on the Poco proof press, as well as the title page for a souvenir pamphlet titled *Concerto per ottone e rame di Pucci De Rossi* (1972) on the Washington press. It was illustrated by Pucci and mimeographed in ninety copies by Gigetto and Enrica Granetto. It included short pieces by Gigetto, Roberto Ossolengo, and Laure. It was the precursor to *Pronto Soccorso: The Pucci-Parigi Book*, which I printed and published the following year. The open house was widely attended, and Pucci sold all of his pieces. With his new-found wealth Pucci and Laure went off to Paris to find a gallery for his work.

Invitation to the presentation of Pucci De Rossi's sculpture at his studio (1972). (Courtesy of PWP Archives.)

Item 13. Pronto Soccorso   289

As a thank-you gesture for my help in putting together the open house, Pucci made me a brass and copper bracelet that had the same rough quality of his hammered and riveted sculptures. I often likened it to Eleanor of Aquitaine's glass-studded crown, which I had seen in the fifties at one of the Dahlem Museums in Berlin. My bracelet later inspired Pucci to make a whole series of "jewels" – mostly rings and pendants – fashioned out of copper and brass wires that held irregularly formed semi-precious stones.

Coming to Pucci's Aid

When the De Rossi returned to Verona from Paris – broke but successful in their quest for a gallery – Pucci began to work on the pieces for his forthcoming show. As the date for the opening drew near, he realized he wasn't going to have enough money for the train fare to Paris. Again his friends rushed in to help, this time providing a type of "first aid" – hence the title: *Pronto Soccorso*. The idea was to give Pucci something tangible he could easily sell to some of his local collectors for a few dollars, thereby raising the necessary money for the trip. Like the earlier pamphlet this one included

Gabriel in the via Duomo studio around the time he printed *Pronto Soccorso: The Pucci-Parigi Book,* Verona, Italy, 1973. (Photo by Guido Trevisani, courtesy of PWP Archives.)

contributions by a number of Pucci's friends. Laure (under the *nom de plume* Alitché) contributed the following poem in French, which was accompanied by an Italian translation by Isa Covre:

L'Évidence

Ta main-oiseau ta main ailée
Main trop vivante contre ma nuque nue
Main-regard devenue l'odeur même de l'ombre
Cri-oiseau
Main savante main présente
Cri-oiseau
Nous brisons joyeux l'éclat de la mémoire
Force lucide
Force précise et légère
Force indécise de la vie même
d'où va jaillir dans sa plus simple forme
la vie-oiseau

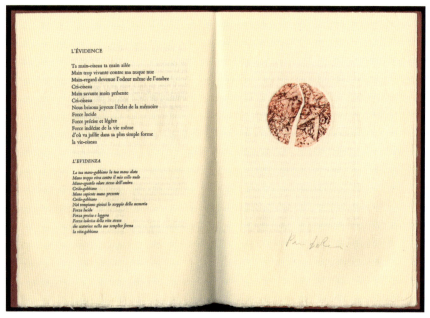

Double-page spread from *Pronto Soccorso: The Pucci-Parigi Book* with Pucci De Rossi's etching on the right. (Courtesy of the University of Oregon Libraries.)

Item 13. Pronto Soccorso

The only out-of-pocket expenses I had were for the typesetting and the printing of the tipped-in photogravure of a photograph showing Pucci at work. The photograph was taken by Guido Trevisani and printed at the Istituto Salesiano San Zeno.

Guido was one of my students at Glaxo, a pharmaceutical company where I taught English four evenings a week. He is the subject of "The Photographer," a poem I wrote and printed for him as a birthday greeting on February 6, 1973, and later reprinted in *Seven Aspects of Solitude*.

During the second week of April, employing the familiar half-sheet (work-and-turn) imposition, Jacques Vernière and I printed the text – which was set in Monotype Bembo at Ruggero Olivieri in Milan. We used the

Pucci De Rossi at work in his studio, Verona, Italy, 1973. (Photo by Guido Trevisani, courtesy of PWP Archives.)

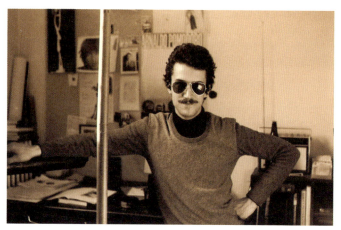

Guido Trevisani in the via Duomo studio, Verona, Italy, 1973. (Photo by RGR, courtesy of PWP Archives.)

Amatruda moldmade wove paper that I already had on hand. Mark Fishbein also helped us.

Pucci made the plate for the illustration by crumpling up a sheet of copper and then smashing it with a hammer before cutting it in half with a pair of tin snips. It has always amazed me that Olaf Idalie, who pulled the prints upstairs on Brooks Walker's etching press, was able to get such vibrant results from an otherwise unconventional printing surface. Golda Fishbein also helped Olaf pull the etchings.

Olaf Idalie

Olaf Idalie was a mysterious young Frenchman who worked around the corner in the printmaking sweatshop run by Nereo Tedeschi. He never spoke of his family, and it wasn't until years later that I discovered that his mother was the historical novelist Zoé Oldenbourg and his father a noted Parisian antiquarian bookseller. Olaf quickly became a regular member of the PWP extended family.

As a Frenchman he was an anomaly. He couldn't cook – his idea of a culinary treat was a fried egg with a squashed banana over spaghetti with Jell-O for dessert; he was oblivious to fashion – everything in his wardrobe was covered with makeshift patches; and he adored obese women – while vehemently denying it. He was always cheerful and a joy to be around, in addition to being an exceptionally talented engraver.

Item 13. Pronto Soccorso

Olaf Idalie standing at the entrance to Tedeschi's studio in via Pigna, Verona, Italy, 1973. (Photo by RGR, courtesy of PWP Archives.)

Binding the Pamphlets

Once the printing of *Pronto Soccorso* was finished, I rounded up a crew to fold, collate, and sew the pamphlets. Mark Fishbein, then eleven, and Tania and Cybèle Plank, seven, were all pressed into service. (Throughout their stay in Verona, Golda and her two children would often pitch in at the PWP in moments of crisis.) I set aside enough copies from the edition for my few standing-order collectors and turned the rest over to Pucci. On May 5, 1973, there was a lively presentation of the pamphlet at Le Terre, another of the local "culture clubs" – this one financed by Max D'Arpini's former patron, Lina Boner Grosselli. As I recall, Pucci did raise enough money to buy the train tickets. However, on the way home from the club – with the remaining unsold copies wrapped in a packet – he and Laure stopped off at an unfamiliar bar to have a nightcap. In the excitement of the evening and the anticipation of leaving for Paris the next day, they forgot to take the packet with them. Several years later Pucci wandered into the same bar. The bartender recognized him and returned the forgotten packet to him. The lost copies of *Pronto Soccorso* were miraculously recovered.

Another attempt to raise money for Pucci took place in June 1974. Jacques printed the first batch of invitations on his Albion press from old wood type. Pucci and Laure quickly ran out of these, so Mark screenprinted Jacques's Art Market lettering and rubber-stamped the place, days, and hours of the event. It was another great success: Pucci sold most of the pieces he had on display.

A Sad Observation

In retrospect even my closest friends – no matter how much they admired my work or how well-meaning they were – had no concept of how time-consuming it was to produce these gratis pamphlets. Strictly speaking they may not have been job printing, but neither were they fine printing by any stretch of the imagination. With the items produced so far, I was straddling the proverbial fence, waiting for the push that was soon to come, the push that would forever define my direction as a printer.

Invitation to the Art Market in Pucci De Rossi's studio (1974). (Courtesy of PWP Archives.)

Item 13. Pronto Soccorso

Tacchino con Funghi in Panna
Turkey with Mushrooms in Cream

Serves 12

One of the great treats when we felt flush was to serve Phyllis Liparini's turkey with mushrooms in cream. Phyllis was a young American woman married to an Italian art restorer. She loved to cook and welcomed one and all to her abundant table.

  4 ounces dried porcini mushrooms
  3 pounds turkey breast, cut across the grain into small strips
        and pounded
    Flour for dusting
 12 tablespoons unsalted butter, divided
    Salt and freshly ground black pepper to taste
  1 cup dry white wine
  3 garlic cloves
  2 cups strained mushroom water
  4 cups crème fraîche

Soak mushrooms in 1 quart of warm water. Add 4 tablespoons of the butter to a large skillet. When the butter begins to foam, dust one-third of the turkey strips and add them to the skillet. Quickly brown on both sides. Lightly salt and pepper strips on the second side. Transfer to a Dutch oven. Repeat process with the remaining strips. Pass garlic through a garlic press directly into the skillet. Sauté quickly. Deglaze the skillet with wine and transfer garlic and wine to the Dutch oven. Drain mushrooms and pat dry with paper towels. Strain liquid. Add mushrooms to the Dutch oven along with 2 cups of the mushroom water. Cover and simmer for 20 minutes. Add crème fraîche and simmer uncovered for an additional 20 minutes.

Group photograph in the courtyard at via Duomo, 15, Verona, Italy, 1973. *Front:* Golda Fishbein, Gabriel, and Pucci De Rossi. *Back:* The "New" Dutch Boys, Mark Fishbein, Tania (above), Cybèle (below), and Eva Plank. (Photographer unknown, courtesy of PWP Archives.)

Verona: The Lull before the Storm

> There is, it seems, no mechanism in the mind or the brain for ensuring
> the truth, or at least the veridical character, of our reflections.
> – Oliver Sacks, "Speak, Memory"

It would be more than a year and a half before the next PWP book, *Siete Poemas Sajones / Seven Saxon Poems*, would be issued. Its publication was to change the course of my life and catapult the press into international fame. *Pronto Soccorso* was the only PWP item printed in 1973.

Although the year was also spent on several small printing commissions and projects, it was a year full of other events, including many new friends, as well as the arrival of Golda Fishbein and her ten-year-old son Mark.

In 1969, when Golda and I were working at Alfred A. Knopf/Random House, she invited me to a dinner party at her suburban home in Ardsley, New York, where I met her two children, Lauren and Mark, for the first time.

Golda Fishbein's Move to Verona

In the summer of 1969, I invited Golda to a cocktail party in my small tenement apartment at 506 East 82nd Street in New York. As it turned out Golda was the only woman at the party. I seem to have neglected to invite any others, but it really didn't matter to Golda. She was soon immersed in conversation with Paul Secon and his American friend Mark, both of whom were visiting from Copenhagen, where they were living. They were apparently quite eloquent regarding the joys of the expatriate life, because Golda became interested in living abroad after talking with them.

After visiting me in the summer of 1972, Golda decided that Verona was just the place for her. In November she wrote that she had decided to move to Verona and asked me to find an apartment for her that didn't cost more than $50 a month.

Looking for the Ideal Apartment

Golda wanted an apartment close to my studio, if possible. In those days, before the historic center became fashionable, the only way to find an apartment in that section of town was through a *mediatore*, one of those neighborhood old cronies who hung out in the bars and cafés reading the obituaries. I started with the cafés in my neighborhood. Fortunately gossip had it that I had come to Italy alone to set up my print shop, and once I was settled I would send for my little family. This belief made me a much more sympathetic figure, one worthy of an inexpensive place to raise my family.

Ideally Golda needed a three-bedroom apartment, but everything I looked at was beyond her budget. All the mediators thought "we" could get by with a one-bedroom apartment. After all I was an artisan not a tradesman. The parents could have the bedroom; the daughter, the living room, and the son, the kitchen, where many Italian boys slept.

I was still looking for this dream apartment when Golda and Mark arrived in early February 1973, so they were temporarily installed in Brooks and Bonnie Walker's apartment upstairs until a suitable place could be found. Jacques Vernière was also staying there. With Golda behind me on the Vespa, we went off to check out each new address provided by one of the mediators, but they were all too expensive.

As luck would have it, we finally found a place at via Duomo, 6, just one block from my studio, without the help of the mediators. It was perfect and affordable. Franco, "the Fascist," who owned the milk bar down the street, told me one day that Milena, a skinny whore – and her pet monkey – had been evicted. Milena had used the apartment to entertain tricks before her pimp beat her up, putting her out of business. The landlord was looking for a respectable family. By late February Golda and Mark had moved in. Golda decided that she would sleep in the living room, and within a year Pucci De Rossi built a bookcase wall in the former dining room, dividing it in half so Mark and Lauren could both have their own rooms.

Getting Settled

Golda had been able to get to Verona with the help of a letter I wrote to the court, in which I offered her a job at the PWP, employment being one of the terms of her divorce that would allow her to remove the children from the New York City area. At one point during the hearing, the judge became quite concerned. He feared that because of bureaucratic delays, the PWP's offer might be withdrawn. Golda assured him that "the PWP was very flexible."

Verona: The Lull before the Storm

Golda Fishbein and her son Mark on the Adige River esplanade with Ponte Pietra in the background, Verona, Italy, 1973. (Photo by RGR, courtesy of PWP Archives.)

A few weeks after Golda's arrival, the three of us went out for a pizza one evening with Olaf Idalie – at the time Golda was helping Olaf edition Pucci's plate for *Pronto Soccorso*. Mark, always inquisitive, was beginning to wonder when his mother was going to start working, when Olaf, who spoke English, mentioned the PWP in passing. Mark's eyes nearly popped out of his head. He pointed his finger at me accusingly and said, "*You're* the Plain Wrapper Press!"

The children had been divided about the move to Italy. Mark was looking forward to the change, but Lauren, a talented softball player, didn't want to miss her final year of Little League. However, they both agreed they wanted even less to stay behind with their father. I may not have been an ideal parent, but I was around, and I have always cared a great deal for them. On July 3 Lauren, who was thirteen, accompanied by Golda's mother, Sophie Goldblatt, joined us in Verona. Several days before leaving the States, Lauren had pitched her team to a Little League championship.

One of Mark's classmates was very Veronese when it came to eating. He disliked any dish that had more than three or four ingredients. When Golda served him a Russian salad made with diced vegetables and mayonnaise, he sat there picking out the peas. When asked why, he replied, "*Troppo confusione.*" My own cooking to a large extent was based on this preference: avoiding too much confusion.

Teaching English

Even though I was spending more time at the press working on commissions and job printing – to the detriment of getting on with my own publications – I was always short of money. Soon after I met Franco Casati, he asked if I would print some small cards for him to let people know that he was available for private tutoring. He was sure I would find some good-paying students if I printed some for myself offering lessons in English. It wasn't a bad idea. I had had some prior experience in Buenos Aires, where I found that I not only enjoyed teaching English, but that I also had a natural aptitude for it. His suggestion turned out to be a panacea for me as well as for a whole coterie of expatriates who were looking for ways to survive financially in Verona while trying to circumvent the restrictions on working without a permit. Beginning in the summer of 1971, there appeared a cluster of small cards – tacked up in numerous cafés around town – that I had printed announcing various tutoring services provided by native speakers of English, French, and German. I was still printing these as late as 1973.

As a result of my little announcement, I found a few private students, foremost among them Angelo Gavioli and Paolo Holland, a skinny teenager who was very unhappy at home. His father was a well-known antiquarian dealer. Paolo was very tactile, always petting my arms and thighs. He begged

An example of the small cards advertising language lessons (1972). (Courtesy of PWP Archives.)

Verona: The Lull before the Storm   301

me to let him come and live with me in via Duomo. His father would be happy to be rid of him, he said. But I had enough trouble keeping my own body and soul together, let alone having to look after an emotionally needy schoolboy.

As my confidence grew I decided to tackle the "big time": the private language schools. The Oxford and Cambridge schools – which were franchised by the English universities of the same names – were the two most competitive. Since both schools advertised that they taught British English, they were reluctant to hire anyone with an American accent. The Cambridge School of English started using me first as a substitute, and then occasionally as a private tutor. It was an ideal arrangement because all classes met in the evening, leaving my days free to work at the Press.

Through the Cambridge School I met a group of young people from Australia and New Zealand, all teachers at the school. One night I got high at a party given by Jan Sterling and the English journalist Dalbert Hallenstein. Unknown to me the birthday cake had been laced with hashish. I was not in the habit of taking hard drugs. It was a terrible experience. I just couldn't come down and spent two days just lying on my bed, unable to get up and go back to work. In those days I did drink a lot of wine, but at least I was able to get up the next morning and work, seldom suffering a hangover. Wine always gave me the same high that I got from hashish, so why bother with the after-effects?

My first regularly scheduled classes were given four nights a week in the library at Glaxo, a pharmaceutical company on the edge of town. I went on the Vespa, beginning in November 1971. I earned about $50.00 a week, working ten hours but getting paid for fourteen to compensate for the long commute. I was also earning a little more from my private students, plus an occasional translation.

It didn't take me long to realize that most students were not really interested in learning English. The classes were just another excuse to socialize, so I tried to make them entertaining as well as instructive. I once asked the students, "What are we doing now?" They responsed in unison, "Teaching you Italian."

One of the things that made my classes popular was the year-end party I always threw for the students from my combined classes. I usually printed an eye-catching invitation – most of the ephemera printed at the PWP consisted of invitations. Golda, Mark, Lauren, and I prepared lots of American-style comfort food to supplement the Italian wine that flowed so freely at these events. The most memorable feast was when we served two seven-foot-long sandwiches. A neighborhood baker accepted the challenge to

Invitation to a party for Gabriel's and Golda Fishbein's combined English classes (1973). (Courtesy of PWP Archives.)

Verona: The Lull before the Storm

make the unusually long loaves needed for the sandwiches. Golda, who also taught English privately, was able to get all the fillings for the sandwiches from one of her former students, who put his thumb *under* the scale at the *salumeria* instead of on top of it, enabling us to walk out of the shop with four heavy bags of cold cuts and cheeses for little more than a song.

Robert Cornfield

I first met Robert Cornfield through Karen Kennerly at The Dial Press in New York in 1970. I had designed a couple of books for her, as well as one for Bob. He had been touring Italy in March 1973 and was travel-weary. He decided to visit me in Verona so he could relax and unwind. Everyone loved Bob. Mark gave him a guided tour of Verona, which Bob later said was the best tour he had ever taken.

Golda, Mark, and I also joined Bob in Bologna for La Fiera del Libro per Ragazzi (the Children's Book Fair). The highlight of the trip, however, was the lunch Bob offered us at the famous Il Pappagallo restaurant. "It's on me," he said. "Order anything you want." With so many succulent dishes to choose from Mark's head was spinning, but he settled on half a boneless roast chicken. That meal was the beginning of his fondness for Italian food. He's had a discerning palate for it ever since.

Left to right: Mark Fishbein, Golda Fishbein, Olaf Idalie, and Robert Cornfield in Piazza delle Erbe, Verona, Italy, 1973. (Photo by RGR, courtesy of PWP Archives.)

Printing Commissions

On March 4 and 5, Jacques Vernière and I printed the letterpress portions of a large-format portfolio, *Zand*, for Ger van Dijck and Theo van der Aa, issued with the imprint of their Agora Studio in Maastricht, the Netherlands. The text, in Dutch, was set in all caps, giving me an opportunity to practice my optical letterspacing. I didn't receive an advance, so I had to pay out of my own pocket all the costs of the materials. The paper only cost about $8.00, but the type, 24-point Didot Garamond, which was set by Ruggero Olivieri in Milan, cost about $44.00. Guido Trevisani and Jacques helped set the text, and Golda and I letterspaced it. The project was complicated by the fact that the Dutch Boys wanted half the edition in a vertical format and the other half in a horizontal format.

In March and April I editioned a few woodcuts and linocuts for a couple of local artists. I charged them about $1.00 per print. They each complained that I was asking too much, but I was just doing what was necessary to survive.

Harvey Simmonds

That May another and very unexpected helper, Harvey Simmonds, arrived at the PWP. A former Grolier Club librarian, he was in Verona that spring with Leslie Katz, working on Lincoln Kirstein's *Elie Nadelman* (1973) for the Eakins Press. The book was being printed by Martino Mardersteig at the Stamperia Valdonega. After Leslie left Harvey stayed on for another month, spending most of his free time at the PWP. Harvey deserves much of the credit for the survival of the PWP in those days because he guided me to many new American private collectors and strengthened my list of libraries that purchased private press books. He also brought me out of my isolation and into contact with the resurgent world of fine printing in America. From this point on, the story of the PWP is full of people who can be traced back, directly or indirectly, to Harvey Simmonds.

He wanted to be my lover but after one try, I knew it wouldn't work. So he chased after Fulvio Testa, another of his unrequited crushes.

In May Harvey helped me print some stationery for an Italian friend's sister on the Poco proof press. We used the new Post Mediaeval type, which I purchased as a second typeface for the PWP. The first use of it in a book was for *A Lost Poem*. He also helped print the party invitation for my English classes. During the last week of his stay, we printed the first half of a promotional piece for Angelo Gavioli on the Poco proof press. I ended up printing the last fifty copies after Harvey left Verona.

In late June I put together a very limited edition of a suite of Olaf's copperplate engravings, *Éclairs ou lacunes de raison: Trois gravures au burin* (1973), enclosed in a simple printed folder, which Ennio Caloi had die-cut and scored and Olaf and I had printed on the Washington press.

Early in July Olaf and I spent three days printing approximately one hundred invitations for the reception to inaugurate the publication of his suite of prints. We drove around town on the Vespa, delivering as many as we could on such short notice. Some said it was just another excuse for a big party, and perhaps it was, but Olaf sold most of the suites that evening.

Arthur Dixon, a professor at the University of North Carolina at Greensboro, showed up that summer and continued to return to Verona on a regular basis. He gave both moral and financial support to the Press. Arthur thought there should be dancing at Olaf's reception. I didn't have a phonograph, but that didn't stop Arthur. He went out and bought a half dozen

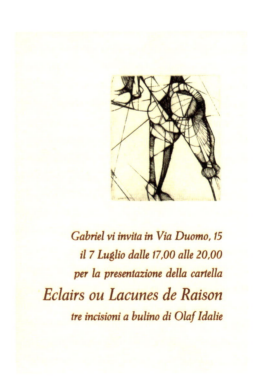

Invitation to the reception for Olaf Idalie (1973). Courtesy of PWP Archives.)

dance records, including LPs by James Brown and Tina Turner, as well as Norman Greenbaum's "Spirit in the Sky." Fulvio Testa loaned me his small portable phonograph. Arthur danced in the cobblestone *porte-cochère* well into the night and was among the last to leave.

José Noe

Also in July of that summer, I met a young man of Italian descent from Argentina named José Noe, who was hitchhiking around Italy. He was a Mormon; that is to say, he didn't smoke, drink, or have sex. I respected his dedication to his church and located a Mormon temple near my apartment where he went every Sunday. José, who stayed with me for several months, was very domestic, spending most of the day cleaning, washing, and ironing. I still did the cooking. I liked having him around, having his warm body next to mine in bed. He would let me enter him, but he didn't want to come. On the rare occasions when he did, he would be sullen for the next couple of days. Even though I wasn't in love with José, I was very fond of him, perhaps more than I realized.

Toward the end of the summer, I found myself caught in the middle of a tacky affair he was having with Michael Haggerty, an Englishman who worked at Studio La Città. I was emotionally distraught and wounded by his unfaithfulness. Later that winter I would occasionally see him in bars drinking wine and smoking cigarettes with Michael, who was a chainsmoker. Eventually, completely dissipated, José went back to Argentina.

Mirek's Departure from Verona

In September 1973 Mirek married Phyllis Maiorana, an Italian-American from Monterey, California, who worked in Rome. Thus I lost the companionship of my best and most stable friend in Verona. We seldom saw each other after Pucci and I helped him move to Bracciano, a small town northwest of Rome.

Fulvio Testa

As it had happened so often in the past, when one important person in my life left, another soon stepped in to fill the void. In this case it was Fulvio Testa, who had been living abroad and only recently returned to Verona. Fulvio had been the protégé of Štěpán Zavřel, a Czech artist who directed

Verona: The Lull before the Storm

Fulvio Testa, Verona, 1973. (Photo by RGR, courtesy of PWP Archives.)

the printmaking workshop at Studio La Città. It was Štěpán who had helped launch Fulvio's career as a successful illustrator of children's books.

For several years in a row, Fulvio had won prizes for his drawings at the Joan Miró competition in Barcelona, and we both lamented the fact that most art galleries seldom mounted major exhibitions of drawings. Fulvio and I decided to do something about this by opening a small gallery exclusively for drawings, which we were planning to call Studio Immagini. In November 1973 I located a small studio facing the old Roman bridge, Ponte Pietra. I signed a lease for it in April 1974. The rent was about $37.00 a month and it even had running water. However, before we were able to open the gallery, Fulvio went off again on one of his many extended trips. I kept the studio until the fall of 1981, and in those eight years it served many purposes.

Old Pals and New Chums

There always seemed to be a group of guys who hung out at my place. We did a lot of partying together. Two of the fellows, Giorgio Zanolli and Giorgio Pasetto, were old friends from my first year in Verona. Mario Lencia and Marco Sorgetti lived in Turin but frequently visited Verona. They became lifelong friends. Mario eventually moved to Verona. He loved cooking, entertaining, and carousing.

Misbehaving, as Usual

Left mostly on my own that winter, I returned to my old habit of nocturnal prowling. Pucci and his friends smoked a lot of pot. I wasn't much into pot, but occasionally indulged myself if it meant getting into a guy's pants. Roberto Bianchet, who was a high school teacher and one of Pucci's friends, and I would meet by the Garibaldi Bridge and sit in his car and smoke. We inevitably ended up at my place, and after a couple of glasses of wine we

Group photograph in the courtyard at via Duomo, 15, Verona, Italy, 1973. *Old pals:* Giorgio Zanolli *(back, second from right)* and Giorgio Pasetto *(front, second from right); New Chums:* Mario Lencia *(front, first from right)* and Marco Sorgetti *(front, seated).* (Photo by RGR, courtesy of PWP Archives.)

screwed. Roberto was very sensuous. Just kissing him or touching his cock would cause him to shudder. His ejaculations seemed painful. He would lie in my arms like a small child and whimper. Then he would get dressed and go home. He never stayed the night.

One of Mario's friends, Corrado, who lived around the corner from me, gave big parties with lots to drink and smoke. There were always a dozen or more attractive and available young men. In the winter it was wonderful to be able to make out on a bed with a genuine mink coverlet. Best of all, it was away from the damp banks of the river.

A Couple of Pleasant Memories

Around Easter of 1974 Mario Lencia and his lover, Marco Sorgetti, came from Turin to Verona for a visit. Marco cooked a wonderful Easter Monday lunch, which we lazily enjoyed in the hills above Verona. The photo below was taken during their visit.

Left to right: Mark, Golda, and Lauren Fishbein in Piazza delle Erbe, Verona, Italy, 1974. (Photo by RGR, courtesy of PWP Archives.)

Carlos Cárdenas's Last Visit to Verona

Also in the spring of 1974, Carlos Cárdenas made his last visit to Verona. The weather was fantastic, so we wandered around the Veneto, visiting Padua and Vicenza. The tenderness we shared was similar to our first days together in New York, minus the sex, which didn't seem important any more.

Carlos Cárdenas being playful, Verona, Italy, 1974. (Photo by RGR, courtesy of PWP Archives.)

Golda and Lauren Go to Perugia

In August 1974 Mark was shipped off to Boy Scout camp, and Golda and Lauren went to Perugia for an intensive course in Italian at the Università per Stranieri. There they met Jerry Bingold and Todd Hara, students in a program sponsored by the University of Oregon. They drove Golda and Lauren to Verona over the Ferragosto holiday (August 15) to pick up Mark, because Golda was afraid to let him travel alone on the train after a recent bombing at the Bologna train station.

They also met two medical students, Roger Ruggiero and Bob DaRossa, who were headed to the Università di Padova that fall. They visited Verona that September and returned in April 1975 with their friend Jack Drescher, with whom *la piccola famiglia* is still in touch. Later that spring, Jack gave a party in Padua and invited us. We had such a good time that we returned again and again to his parties. Jack stayed in my apartment in Verona while I spent the spring semester at the University of Alabama in 1977.

Pasta Piccante
Penne with Spicy Tomato Cream Sauce

Serves 4

One of my private students, Alberto Piras, was a banker. He and his wife Susi were from Sardinia. The three of us became good friends, and she taught me how to make this pasta.

⅓ cup olive oil
1 garlic clove, minced
2 ounces pancetta *or* thick-cut bacon
2 cups canned whole, peeled tomatoes with their juice, coarsely chopped
¼ teaspoon red pepper flakes
2 tablespoons Sambal Oelek
Salt to taste
1 cup crème fraîche
1 tablespoon coarse salt
1 pound dried penne
12 medium basil leaves, torn into small pieces
1 tablespoon extra-virgin olive oil
2 tablespoons pecorino cheese, freshly grated

Put oil and garlic in a 3-quart sauté pan over medium-high heat and cook until garlic begins to sizzle. Add pancetta and cook until well-browned, but not crisp. Add tomatoes, red pepper flakes, Sambal Oelek, and salt if necessary. Reduce the heat and simmer, about 30 minutes. Add crème fraîche and simmer for an additional 10 minutes. Bring 4 quarts of water to a boil. Add the coarse salt and penne. Return the sauté pan to medium heat and add basil. When pasta is ready, drain and pour into a large serving bowl. Add the sauce and toss. Add extra-virgin olive oil and cheese and toss again.

Box and cover for *Siete Poemas Sajones / Seven Saxon Poems.* (Courtesy of the University of Oregon Libraries.)

Item 14. *Siete Poemas Sajones / Seven Saxon Poems*

Seven poems in Spanish and a foreword and notes in
English by Jorge Luis Borges; with English
translations of the poems by Alastair Reid and
Norman Thomas di Giovanni; with a printer's note
and acknowledgments in English by
Richard-Gabriel Rummonds. With eight
blind-embossed impressions in the text and three
gold-plated bronze bas reliefs on the cover by
Arnaldo Pomodoro. Enclosed in a wooden box with a
relief-etched brass plate by the artist on the lid.
40 pages. 39 x 29 cm. 120 copies.1974.

Getting Serious about Borges

My limited amount of practical printing experience certainly didn't qualify
me to undertake such an elaborate and costly project. Since arriving in
Verona I had in fact printed only two items that could truly be called books:
Images & Footsteps and *Didascalie*. Everything else had been ephemeral.
Siete Poemas Sajones / Seven Saxon Poems went through more metamor-
phoses before becoming a book than any other PWP edition.

Writing about this book in *Plain Wrapper Press Newsletter: One*
(December 1974), I noted, "It started out as a relatively simple book, but by
the time it was finished, it had become an artistic synthesis requiring the
collaboration of a team of artists and artisans with highly individual temperaments. Each gave to the book not only his skill, but his personal enthusiasm and interest. Even the tiniest detail, such as the color and weight of
the headbands, involved extended research and effort.... Beholding the finished book, I can only marvel at the results. The poems and the impressions
brought together one of the most profound poets and one of the most imaginative sculptors of our time."

First Encounter with Borges

While I was still living in New York in the sixties, Armando Braun Menéndez made good on his promise to introduce me to Jorge Luis Borges by

sending me a letter of introduction, which I gave to Borges backstage after his reading at the Poetry Center of the 92nd Street YM-YWHA on April 8, 1968. Borges was very fragile and his eyesight was failing.

We met the following day for breakfast with Norman Thomas di Giovanni, Borges's traveling companion and later his preferred translator.

Jorge Luis Borges, Buenos Aires, Argentina, 1970s. (Photo by Amanda Ortega, with permission of the photographer.)

Norman's influence over Borges was eventually usurped by Franco Maria Ricci, publisher of the Italian-based magazine *FMR*. Ricci had the means to deify Borges.

Item 14. Siete Poemas Sajones / Seven Saxon Poems   315

Borges was noticeably excited about the possibility of a collaboration, and at that first meeting he proposed that we use a selection of his poems with Anglo-Saxon themes as the text, believing it to be an appropriate choice for a work destined for an English-speaking audience. The poems had been published only in Spanish and had never been collectively issued as a single work. Norman Thomas di Giovanni and Alastair Reid had already begun to translate them for a forthcoming edition of Borges's *Selected Poems, 1923–1967* to be published by the Delacorte Press in 1972. At the time of our talks, none of the translations had yet appeared in print; it was Borges's intention that their first publication would be in this PWP edition. Regrettably, the project experienced so many delays that all seven poems were published in magazines before the book was finished. The book does, however, contain some unique material written especially for this edition by Borges: a foreword in which he expands on his love of Anglo-Saxon literature – dating back to his boyhood – and notes on each of the poems. Borges's inspiration can clearly be seen in this poem translated by Alastair Reid:

> *Poem Written in a Copy of Beowulf*
>
> At various times I have asked myself what reasons
> Moved me to study while my night came down,
> Without particular hope of satisfaction,
> The language of the blunt-tongued Anglo-Saxons.
> Used up by the years my memory
> Loses its grip on words that I have vainly
> Repeated and repeated. My life in the same way
> Weaves and unweaves its weary history.
> Then I tell myself: it must be that the soul
> Has some secret sufficient way of knowing
> That it is immortal, that its vast encompassing
> Circle can take in all, can accomplish all.
> Beyond my anxiety and beyond this writing
> The universe waits, inexhaustible, inviting.

My only disappointment regarding the translations is that both poets relied heavily on the Latin roots of English words rather than their Anglo-Saxon roots.

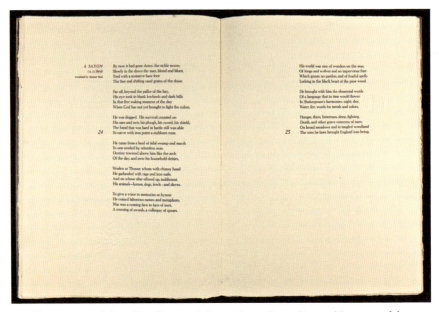

Double-page spread from *Siete Poemas Sajones / Seven Saxon Poems*. (Courtesy of the University of Oregon Libraries.)

Designing the Book

Within a short time Borges sent me the manuscript, and I began to design the book. The original format was quite modest. It was going to be a small quarto printed on Barcham Green Charter Oak handmade paper with woodcuts by Don Bolognese, a well-known book illustrator and brother of my former art director at Random House. However, with my future plans still up in the air – in addition to being on the verge of leaving New York – I was hesitant to commit myself wholly to any artist until I was actually ready to proceed with the production of the book; Don was put on hold. As things turned out I had second thoughts about the suitability of his work for this project, and so even before Don had an opportunity to cut any of the blocks, I decided not to pursue the collaboration any further.

I had selected the Horizon Light type in part for this project. Even though a large portion of it was already committed to *Images & Footsteps*, I began to set the Borges text in March 1969. By the time the book was completed, the type had been standing for more than six years. I had been buying small job fonts, which I supplemented with Spanish accents fonts; I was continually running out of letters, forced to put the typesetting aside until more type arrived. It was several more years before I discovered that the practical way for me to order type was in book fonts or by the line.

My archives at The New York Public Library contain a few proofs of the title page and foreword printed on Barcham Green paper that I pulled on Robert Haas's Washington press in 1969. The design was not very inspired, especially for a limited edition press book. It looked much more like the trade books I had been working on as a book designer at Alfred A. Knopf.

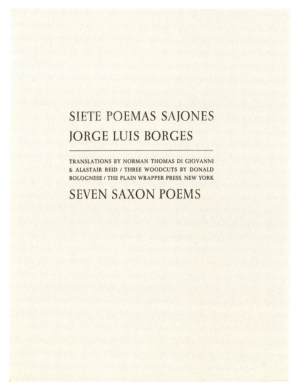

Proof of the title page from *Siete Poemas Sajones / Seven Saxon Poems* on Barcham Green paper, New York, NY, 1969. (Courtesy of The New York Public Library.)

Second Encounter with Borges

When Borges and I met again on December 8, 1969, after another of his readings at the Poetry Center, I apologized for the delay. He said, "Don't worry, take your time. I know it will be a beautiful book." Norman, always at Borges's side, merely snarled. Two years later, I was still trying to explain or justify the delays to him.

On Again, Off Again

From the fall of 1970 until the book was finished four years later, I continued to resuscitate and then withdraw the project. The only two artistic elements that remained constant were the large format and the typographic design, both of which I worked out shortly after I arrived in Verona. Friends continued to bring fonts of type and other printing supplies from the States, because my type was calibrated in pica points, which are smaller than Didot points, the European standard. By February 22, 1970, all of the Spanish text was set. For some reason now forgotten I didn't send the proofs to Norman until August.

First Attempts to Find the Right Artist

Once I decided not to use Don Bolognese – the logistics of working long distance with someone I hardly knew were daunting – I renewed my search for an artist. In April 1971 I approached Joseph Low, whose woodcuts I had always admired. Also, the idea of a collaboration between the past and present owners of my Washington press appealed to my sense of continuity, tinged with a touch of sentimentality. I wrote to him again in November, explaining how urgent it was for me to hear from him, but he didn't respond to either of my letters until February 1972. He apologized for the delay, explaining that he was not well and could not take on any new commissions.

The next artist to become involved with the project was Renzo Sommaruga, whose forte was linocuts. While we were printing *La Ballata delle Madri* in February 1972, we talked about my future plans. He knew that I had not yet settled on an artist for the Borges text and begged me to let him try his hand at it. "No obligations," he assured me. Having no other immediate prospects, I gave in to his pleas. When I saw the results later that March, I was less than enthusiastic about them. He had designed several Kelmscott-like borders, well delineated, but too derivative and heavy-handed for the book I had in mind. He had already used something quite similar for one of his own publications, which diminished their appeal for me even more. When I told him they were not what I was looking for, he dramatically tore up the sketches instead of trying to find a solution that would satisfy both of us. In a hysterical rage he threw me out of his studio, tossing the shredded scraps of paper after me. Renzo lived out

Item 14. Siete Poemas Sajones / Seven Saxon Poems   319

in the country – he usually drove me to and from his studio – so I found myself stranded in the middle of the night on a hilltop from which I could see the bright lights of the city in the distance. I had no choice but to walk home. Fortunately, it was mostly downhill. Renzo and I were never reconciled.

Giuseppe Capogrossi

By the spring of 1972, the Veronese approach to printing, or perhaps more accurately, its aesthetic sensibility, was beginning to influence me personally and shape my work. Italian press books – of which I had seen many – seemed to combine the best of two diverse traditions: the English typographic book and the French illustrated book. Accordingly I came to the realization that a text by an internationally known author such as Borges deserved illustrations by an artist of the same stature.

One afternoon I was at the Granetto's for lunch, eating chocolate mousse and lamenting my failure to find an appropriate artist for the Borges text, when Gigetto suggested that I might want to consider using Giuseppe Capogrossi, an artist whose work he very much admired. After lunch Gigetto showed me one of the books in his library that Capogrossi had illustrated. I immediately saw the potential for an exciting marriage of the diverse talents of Borges and Capogrossi. Capogrossi's work involved symbols and language, exactly what the Borges poems are about. I went to see Paolo Cardazzo at his Galleria del Cavallino in Venice, because Paolo was a close friend of Capogrossi, and under his imprint, Edizioni del Cavallino, he had published several trade books illustrated by Capogrossi. He thought the artist would be interested in the project and arranged for me to meet him in Rome in mid-March.

Although quite ill at the time, Capogrossi was very gracious, and with his daughter's help we selected from his numerous portfolios three brush and ink designs that he thought could be successfully screenprinted for the book. Capogrossi wanted Franz Larese, his representative in Switzerland, to negotiate the contract for him. This made a lot of sense because Capogrossi was sick, and in addition to showing his work in Larese's Erker-Galerie, Larese also published several livres d'artiste with Capogrossi's work at his Erker-Presse. Early in April I went to St. Gallen in Switzerland to discuss the project with Franz Larese. In June Capogrossi entered a clinic.

Unfortunately, he died that October before an agreement with Larese could be completed. I continued to discuss the project with Larese and Capogrossi's widow, but after his death the price of his work skyrocketed far beyond my means, and our negotiations ended in an impasse. I had apparently made Larese an offer, which he subsequently turned down. I am sure it was too low.

In January 1973 Hélène Sutton called Capogrossi's widow. She was still interested in the project, but by then there was no way that I could proceed with it. At about the same time, Cardazzo suggested Horst Antes as a possible illustrator for the book.

Arnaldo Pomodoro

The Borges project was delayed again. However, later that month Hélène and her Studio La Città once again came to the rescue of the PWP. In the fall of 1970 she had mounted an impressive exhibition of Arnaldo Pomodoro's work in collaboration with two of the most prestigious art galleries in Italy: Studio Marconi in Milan and Marlborough Galleria d'Arte in Rome. Together these two galleries became a prime source for PWP artists. Hélène talked with Arnaldo, who unlike many of his contemporaries had yet to "do"

Arnaldo Pomodoro, Milan, Italy, date unknown. (Photo by Mario Carrieri, courtesy of Arnaldo Pomodoro.)

Item 14. Siete Poemas Sajones / Seven Saxon Poems

a book. When she told him that Borges had written the text, there was no stopping him – he was a great admirer of Borges's work. He wanted to get together with me as soon as possible.

We hit it off from our very first meeting in late January 30, and by April he had the preliminary sketches ready to show me. Arnaldo's major contribution to the book – three gold-plated bronzes embedded in the cover of the book and a relief-etched brass plate on the lid of the box – resembled tablets from a long-forgotten language, a language that could no longer be deciphered. They mirrored Borges's poems, which often spoke of the symbols of language, their evolution, and the difficulty of knowing their primal meanings. Arnaldo and I frequently met to discuss the project. He not only prepared sketches and models quickly but also was sensitive to the fact that his enthusiasm for the book was getting me into a situation that was plummeting out of financial control.

Arnaldo often came to Verona because he was having some of his work cast at one of the foundries there. Our meetings usually took place at a café in the train station, and we could frequently be seen running down the platform still discussing the book, as he jumped on the already moving train bound for Milan. Golda Fishbein likened our meetings to *The New Yorker* cartoon with the caption: "We can't go on meeting like this."

Arnaldo's ideas were not always practical. For example he proposed putting a thin sheet of embossed copper in the middle of the book to divide the Spanish text from the English. Without expressing my reservations about its impracticality, I made a mock-up of the book exactly the way he wanted it. The moment he opened the mock-up, he discarded the idea as being forced and clumsy.

On another occasion he was so eager to have the book produced that he prematurely had the brass plates made for the box lids. Unfortunately they were the wrong size, because he had used the dimensions for the book instead of those for the box. My despair – how was I ever going to absorb the cost of this error? – didn't daunt him in the least. He simply had the smaller plates mounted on wooden panels and numbered and signed them, giving them to me as a consolation present. Their sale helped keep the PWP afloat until the book was published in December 1974. (The patina on the brass plates, which were used for both the mounted wall panels and the box lids, was achieved by burying the plates in the ground for three months.)

Finding the Right Paper

I now had an artist but I wasn't any closer to finding a suitable paper, because I had decided not to use the Barcham Green Charter Oak paper. It had originally been selected for its gray-green color, a color that vividly suggested to me the cold, dark Anglo-Saxon world.

I was now leaning toward heavier Italian handmade papers. In February 1971, while Renzo Sommaruga and I were still friends, we took a night train to Rome and then on to Salerno the next day for a short visit with Edoardo Sanguineti, a constructivist poet who was also one of Renzo's authors. I was also interested in publishing Sanguineti, so I was looking forward to meeting him in person.

The trip started off on a high. Luca Steffenoni and I drove through the hills around Verona on his Moto Guzzi, stopping off for a few glasses of wine before he dropped me off at the train station shortly before midnight. Hanging onto Luca as we raced along narrow country paths always gave me an erotic thrill.

Cartiera Fernando Amatruda fu Luigi

The next day Renzo and I went on to the Cartiera Fernando Amatruda fu Luigi high in the hills above Amalfi. The paper mill had changed little since the early nineteenth century. The workers were still using a manually operated sheet-forming machine built around 1810 to make moldmade paper. They called their paper "handmade" because the crank was turned by hand. The paper was hung up, air dried, and then finished under a primitive log stamper. Even though the paper was thinner than I preferred, I ordered 2,400 sheets, more than enough for the Borges book. I had read a short piece called *Carta a mano di Amalfi* (1970) by Margaret McCord, published as a twelve-page pamphlet by the Crannog Press, which led me to believe that the Amalfi paper was handmade. There is a confusion in Italian regarding the terms for fine papers. *Carta a tino*, meaning paper made by hand-dipping it into a vat of pulp, is the correct term for handmade paper. *Carta manomacchina* is the Italian term for moldmade paper, which is made on a machine. Both are sometimes referred to as *carta a mano*.

I spent two weeks in April getting the first form ready to print, so that when the paper arrived in May, I could begin testing it on the press. Gener-

Item 14. Siete Poemas Sajones / Seven Saxon Poems　　　323

ally speaking, it printed well, but when dampened it had a tendency to stretch irregularly – a known characteristic of machine-made papers – and dry out too quickly. I immediately realized I was going to have too many production problems with it, since I was planning to print the book in two colors, which meant four forms and four makereadies for each set of sheets. Despite all these problems, I continued to test the Amatruda paper between May 1971 and October 1973.

Cartiere Miliani-Fabriano

Having rejected the Amatruda paper, I began to look for another paper. I heard that the Cartiere Miliani-Fabriano still had a stash of its pre-war Esportazione "GF" handmade paper in its Padua warehouse. I ordered a sample; it was the right format, a brilliant white – almost like parchment – and heavily sized.

On January 22, 1974, Brooks and Bonnie Walker drove me to Padua where we picked up their remaining stock of the Esportazione "GF" paper, about 4,000 sheets. I immediately started testing it for dampness, and it proved to be an excellent printing paper. It, too, was eventually rejected for the Borges book, although I later used it for three subsequent PWP editions.

Moulin Richard de Bas

In October 1973, prior to purchasing the Fabriano paper, Jacques Vernière showed me samples of a French handmade paper he was planning to use for his first book. It was soft and supple, yet had enough size in it to meet my requirements for dampening. I wrote to the mill asking for samples and prices.

On January 3, 1974, I took the night train to Paris, and the first thing the next morning I placed an order for 1,500 sheets of the Richard de Bas paper at Arjomari-Prioux, the mill's sales office in Paris. On my way back to Verona, I stopped off at the fourteenth-century Moulin Richard de Bas in Ambert, where the paper was made. It has always amazed me that this beautiful paper was actually the product of such antiquated technology.

While in Paris, I stayed with Gerardo Yávar in his sister's apartment. Gerardo and I had met in Verona the year before. The French Connection – the De Rossi and the Vernière – had picked him up in a café; however, once they found out that his father was a member of Augusto Pinochet's govern-ment at the Chilean Embassy in Paris, they brought Gerardo to my place, thinking I might have more in common with him than they did. Indeed we did. He stayed on for a few days of sightseeing and sex.

While I was in the tourist office at the train station, I met Tony Favro, an American living in Florence. He was looking for a *pensione*, I for direc-tions to Gerardo's sister's. I was very attracted to Tony, but the subject was never broached, and we continued to see each other from time to time in Florence and later after he moved to Rochester, New York.

Over the next few weeks, I ordered, canceled, reinstated, and again can-celed my order, due to the fact that the Moulin Richard de Bas had not even started to make my paper. On January 14 I took another night train to Paris. That was the second time I canceled the order. I was so frustrated that I took the train back to Verona the same day. Jacques was losing pa-tience with me.

Even though I thought the order had been canceled, out of the blue, in mid-February the sales office sent a telegram saying that my order was ready. Fulvio Testa and I drove to Ambert in his Citroën to retrieve the paper. It was the dead of winter, but we had a wonderful, lazy trip through this iso-lated, rustic part of France. We picked up the paper on schedule and planned our return trip so we would pass through the tunnel into Italy in the early hours of the morning. I was concerned that we would be stopped at the bor-der and asked to pay duty on the paper, which was in the back of the car with a blanket thrown over the cartons. All through the tunnel I rehearsed various scenarios with Fulvio. As we approached the Italian border, we could see the small, brightly lighted guardhouse in the distance. Coming alongside it, we found a sleepy guard inside, flipping through a photo-romance mag-azine. He opened the window and stuck his head out, wanting to know our nationalities. We held up our passports, and he waved us on. The paper smugglers had succeeded.

Once I had the Fabriano and Richard de Bas papers in my studio, I made some tests of Arnaldo's blind impressions that were to embellish the text. I showed the results to Arnaldo in late February, and we both thought the Fabriano paper was too stiff to emboss effectively and should not be used for the book. On the other hand we were both enthusiastic about the results on the Richard de Bas paper.

Item 14. Siete Poemas Sajones / Seven Saxon Poems

Printing the Book

Between June 1971 and October 1974, I recorded more than 130 pages of notes in my logbook concerning the problems I had making this book: dampening the paper, positioning the type in the bed of the press, and finding the right pressure, to name the most obvious.

It was obvious that I was going to need some help if I were ever going to finish the printing. I had always been on friendly terms with the art students who worked in the printmaking atelier around the corner. That was where I had found Olaf Idalie. He had since left for Paris and wouldn't be returning to Verona until October, but one of his co-workers, Gianni Psallidi, said he

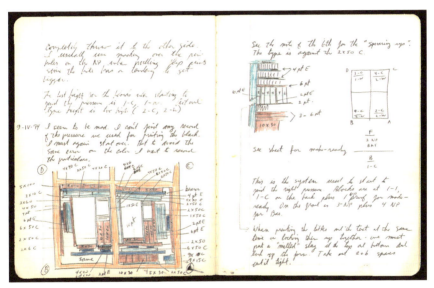

Double-page spread from Gabriel's logbook related to finding the pressure. (Courtesy of The New York Public Library.)

would like to work for me. He started on February 20, 1974, coming in three days a week. By spring, however, despite Gianni's help, the work was still progressing very slowly. The people at Marconi and Marlborough were pressuring me for books.

In the meantime, I was still having problems dampening the paper. On June 18, 1974, Rino Grazioli and Mario Facincani eventually took pity on me. Knowing that old Mardersteig didn't want me (or, for that matter, anyone) to visit the Officina Bodoni when they were working, they sneaked Gianni and me in when the old man was away and showed me some of the master's trade secrets. The most valuable thing I learned from them was how to dampen paper. They placed a few sheets of dry paper, depending on the thickness of the paper, between pulpboards – not blotters. The pulpboards were first immersed in a vertical trough and stacked by rotating every other board. The pile

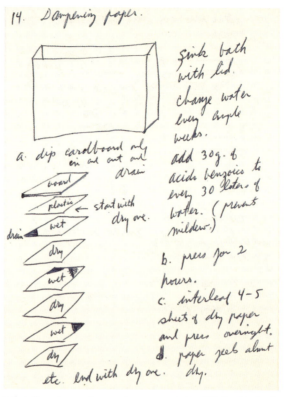

Gabriel's notes on dampening paper at the Officina Bodoni. (Courtesy of PWP Archives.)

was left in the standing press for a few hours to distribute the moisture under tremendous pressure. Sets of four or five sheets of dry paper were then alternated with the dampened pulpboards, and the reconstituted pile was returned to the standing press, where it remained under pressure overnight. The next day the paper was ready to use. At the Officina Bodoni, they never let the pulpboards dry out completely. Sodium benzoate, a mildew retardant, was added to the water, and the boards were kept damp indefinitely. Once dampened, only every other board was passed through the water a second time. This system is fine as long as a new batch of paper is being dampened every day. Since I wasn't printing as fast as Rino and Mario, who printed between sixty or sev-

Item 14. Siete Poemas Sajones / Seven Saxon Poems 327

enty sheets an *hour*, I dried out my pulpboards after each dampening session. By now I was printing around 120 sheets per day, a lot less than the 125 sheets per hour that Benjamin Franklin printed on his wooden common press in the eighteenth century. With a few modifications of my own, this is basically the method of dampening I always used at the PWP and later at EXO in Alabama.

Perhaps it was due to my lack of fluency in Italian, but the only thing I didn't learn from Rino and Mario was how to gauge the correct amount of moisture in the paper. This I picked up from Renzo Sommaruga, who explained the cheek test to me. A piece of dampened paper is held for a second or two against the tester's cheek. The paper should feel cool, while the cheek remains dry.

During another visit to the Officina Bodoni I also mentioned the problems with the pressure. Rino said they couldn't help me with that. Perhaps I should ask the bishop to come and bless the press. Yes, yes, whatever works, I supposed.

Gianni and I started printing the text in early April. It progressed slowly but relatively smoothly. In early May the first big breakthrough in perfecting the makeready was the introduction of thin sheets of Mylar fastened to the tympan. One particularly memorable makeready took the better part of a month. I had leads and slugs from several different sources, which caused problems with the backup, mostly on pages with many lines of text. First I tried numbering each lead and replacing it – after reversing it from left to right – in the same order in the backup composition. Another attempt involved filing down damaged type and using it at the ends of the lines. Even though both of these methods worked, they were tedious and time consuming. Finally I resorted to scrapping all the old spacing materials. I splurged on some very expensive leads and slugs that were made of a hard aluminum alloy. They had been precision machined and were wonderful to use. I never had any more trouble with backup after that.

In August 1972 Michael Nedo had resolved the pressure problems. Two years later, an American soldier named Ed, whom I had picked up in Piazza Brà and taken back to my place, was fascinated by the Washington press. When I told him about the pressure problem, he confirmed Michael's theory. The blocks must be tight even when the weight of the platen shifted. Both Franco Riva and Martino Mardersteig came by the Press and made contradictory suggestions about how to get the pressure right. In the end, I decided to stick with Michael's method.

But my inking was still uneven. I eventually discovered that this uneven-ness was caused by a "well" in the bed of the press. Since I had already printed more than half the book, I decided to wait until I had finished all of the letterpress before I had the bed and platen of the press rectified.

I tried printing this book in every conceivable format. Some of the forms were printed in quarto, some in folio, and some with half-sheet imposition. Only toward the end of my career did I come to realize that no matter how large the bed of the press may be, printing in folio is the simplest and most practical format for the handpress.

We were lucky that Sommaruga had suggested having my roller re-covered back in November 1971, because we had no problems with inking after that.

Gianni and I finished printing the last form on September 26, 1974. The boys from Tedeschi's brought a bottle of wine to the studio to celebrate. Soon after, Gianni went off to do his obligatory service in the Italian Army.

The Costs

A rough estimate of the costs I made in June 1973 put the retail price of the book at $1,000 a copy. In November I sent Arnaldo a revised estimate in which the projected price of the book had risen to $1,500 ($2,000 in the galleries). He talked Giorgio Marconi at Studio Marconi and Carla Panicali and Bruno Herlitzka at Marlborough Galleria d'Arte into putting up almost $14,000 to support the project.

Out of an edition of 120 copies, forty were to go to Arnaldo, forty-six to be divided between Marconi and Marlborough at $300 a copy to repay the advances they had given me, and twelve copies to the collaborators. This left me with twenty-two copies to sell. Standing order collectors got the book for $1,000. In December 1974 I noted in a newsletter to collectors that there were twelve copies left. The price had gone up to $1,800, but a special price of $1,250 was offered to collectors who placed their orders before May 7, 1975. In his Winter 2008 Catalogue 22, Item 239, the San Francisco book-seller Thomas A. Goldwasser offered a copy of the book for $25,000.

Getting Books Ready for the Binder

Ariel Parkinson, who was in Verona working on the etchings for *A Lost Poem* and helping with quality control, noticed a misspelled word in the last sen-tence of my "Printer's Note." She sought Golda's advice on whether or not to

Item 14. Siete Poemas Sajones / Seven Saxon Poems

tell me. Together they read over the text, discovering that not just one word, but three were misspelled in the last sentence. Knowing that such a disclosure would have incapacitated me, they decided not to say anything to me until later. How well they knew my state of mind. I am not sure that I would have reprinted the sheets, although I did whenever such an error occurred in later books. I was told about the misspelled words only long after the first batch of books had been bound, too late to do anything rash, and by then I was strong enough to begrudgingly accept my shortcomings.

Fantasies of a Proprietary Typeface

Fabio Ambrosi's engraving workshop at via Duomo, 13, was next to my studio. I seldom used linecuts in those days because Fabio could make type-high bronze engravings of almost everything I needed, including binders' dies. Fabio respected my ambition to print books on a handpress. It took guts, he thought, for a foreigner to settle in a city well known for its printers and hope to compete with them. I would often run to him in desperation, and he would interrupt his own work to help me resolve some small technical problem that was plaguing me at the moment, or he would rush through a cut or die that was holding me up.

Fabio often worked late, and sometimes if I saw a light on in his workshop, I would stop by to watch him work. I was fascinated by the pantographic engraving tool. Watching him handle the engraving tool also suggested a way that we could give the dies for Arnaldo's blind impressions a third dimension. They are quite unusual because they are embossed both above and below the surface of the paper. Fabio accomplished this by manually raising and lowering the engraving tool following enlarged, coded diagrams that I had made of Arnaldo's sketches. After the printing was completed, I took the sheets to Renzo Pavanello's box factory on the edge of town near Ennio Caloi's bindery. Together we blind embossed the sheets on one of his enormous die-cutting presses.

I envisioned the pantographic tool as a means to engrave matrices for a PWP proprietary typeface. Like Mardersteig, I thought of myself as a type stylist. I had "designed" several typefaces for my graphic design work in the 1960s. Paul Hayden Duensing, knowing of my interest in a proprietary typeface, had earlier suggested that I contact a Japanese matrix cutting company – one more impractical project that I never realized.

Even though Mark Fishbein may have thought that my getting his mother to Italy to work at the PWP was a trick, Golda made a major contribution to the aesthetic appearance of many of the books I printed. To begin with, she designed the distinctive pressmark – one of the best known among contemporary private presses. She also lettered the title page of the Borges book, the first of many title pages she did in the years that followed. It was Golda's lettering that helped form the visual character that separates PWP books from the majority of press books produced at the time. I had designed the first pressmark, not a particularly distinguished one, which was used on several early items printed in Verona. I also used it on the first PWP stationary and promotional pieces.

Binding the Book

As early as January 1974, I had contacted Marcello Fornaro about binding books for the PWP. He was recommended to me by Francesco Ariani, who had a small trade bindery two blocks from my studio. Marcello was an excellent binder, having been trained at the Istituto Salesiano Don Bosco at Castelnuovo in the province of Asti. Unknown to me at the time, he had been

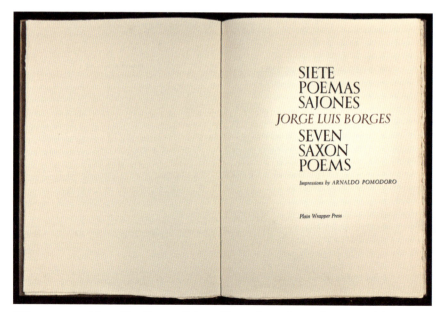

Title-page spread from *Siete Poemas Sajones / Seven Saxon Poems*. (courtesy of the University of Oregon Libraries.)

Item 14. Siete Poemas Sajones / Seven Saxon Poems

binding books for many Veronese printers for a number of years. We had a good working relationship until 1976, when he tried to pull off a scam that ended in a legal battle. I wasn't entirely surprised by his desperate action, because I had defaulted on the balance I still owed him for binding this book.

There was a vellum and parchment tannery across the Adige River from Verona called La Pergamena, which was owned by Lanfranco Lui. It took Lanfranco more than two years from the time I placed my order to accumulate the number of Sardinian black sheepskins needed for the whole edition.

It was also necessary to place the book in a box in order to protect the gold-plated bronzes embedded in the cover. The box was made by Renzo Oliboni, but covered and finished by Marcello. Arnaldo's original concept had been to offer the book enclosed in a protective box, with the box lid doubling as a decorative panel that could be hung on the wall.

Getting Borges's Signature on the Colophon Page

Printing books in Italy by authors and artists who lived scattered throughout the world often presented unique challenges above and beyond the normal difficulties involving the return of proofs and answers to editorial queries. There was always the problem of how I was going to get the colophon pages signed and safely returned to me.

In the case of this book, by a fantastic stroke of luck in the summer of 1974, Sherry Rosenstein, Harvey Simmonds's sister-in-law, introduced me

Sherry Rosenstein and Mario Lencia in the red room at via Duomo, 15, Verona, Italy, 1974. (Photo by RGR, courtesy of PWP Archives.)

to Mirko Franceschin, a young man with whom she worked at a tourist agency in Milan. He was going to lead a tour to Buenos Aires, Argentina, in a few days. In July I called Borges to arrange a meeting between him and Mirko. I also told him that I had finished the printing, although in truth it wouldn't be finished until September. I barely managed to get the colophon pages to Mirko on August 11, the day before his flight. He went to see Borges, who by now was almost completely blind. Mirko helped him sign the pages by placing his hand in the right place on each leaf. And *voilà*! I had the pages back – all signed – within a week.

Getting Pomodoro's Signature on the Colophon Page

When it was time for Arnaldo to sign the colophon page, the books were already bound. Brooks Walker drove me to Marcello's workshop in the village of Roncà. I wanted the books signed in ink. Arnaldo, who was used to signing prints in pencil, had not thought to bring a fountain pen with him. We spent most of the morning hunting one down. I was always extremely nervous when bound books were being signed, but fortunately the signing went without incident, and we were finished in time to lunch at Marcello's brother-in-law's superb country restaurant. I was truly elated that afternoon and drank a great deal of wine. At last I had a few copies of the book to sell!

Getting Books to Pomodoro, Marlborough, and Marconi

Now that I had bound copies of the book, I needed to deliver them to Pomodoro and the two backers, Marlborough Galleria d'Arte and Studio Marconi. Each book weighed over nine pounds. In early May 1975 I took several copies to Giorgio Marconi for an exhibition on the making of the book in his gallery. Fortunately John and Nancy Richardson were in Verona that spring, so they took copies of the book to Pomodoro. Around the same time, I took ten copies to Marlborough in Rome.

The Italian Version of the Text

I commissioned Jacques to print *Sette poesie sassoni* (1975), a small pamphlet of Italian translations of the seven poems in Spanish, which I intended to give to Italian collectors who bought *Siete Poemas Sajones / Seven Saxon Poems*. The translations were done by Paolo Serra, a Veronese pub-

Item 14. Siete Poemas Sajones / Seven Saxon Poems 333

lisher who specialized in Italian editions of Spanish-language authors. Jacques also made a rustic woodcut which he printed blind on the title page. Arnaldo was not at all happy with the pamphlet, believing that Jacques had deliberately imitated the blind-embossed impressions in our book in order to mislead collectors. Arnaldo and I had been through a lot together, and I owed him too much to let something like this come between us. Even though I could justify Jacques's woodcut – conceptually it was very different from Arnaldo's subtle designs – I ended up not distributing the pamphlet to my Italian collectors.

Closure

Almost seven years after our first breakfast in New York, Borges was finally able to savor the richness of our collaboration. Mario Aguirre Mac-Kay let me know that the author had received his *ad personam* copy of the book. Later, Ricci told me that Borges was greatly moved by the book's sensuousness and the tactile qualities of Arnaldo's blind-embossed impressions and sculptures. Armando Braun Menéndez also wrote me that Borges was very pleased with the results, but I never heard directly from Borges himself.

The Aftermath

From the moment of its publication, *Siete Poemas Sajones / Seven Saxon Poems* caused a considerable stir. It was featured in several international exhibitions of Arnaldo's work, and in April 1976 it won the prestigious Premio Internazionale Diano Marina. Copies of it went into the collections of several heads of state. Without a doubt, it is *the* book that established the PWP's reputation around the world. Dealers of fine printing and contemporary art were taking notice of a new type of press book.

Not all collectors thought of this book as a press book. One of them, Stuart B. Schimmel, commented in his review of The New York Public Library's exhibition "Seventy from the Seventies" in the *American Book Collector* (March/April 1980): "This is quite a beautiful book, but perhaps be more suited to an exhibition of illustrated books in which the artist completely dominates the end result." I have always avoided getting into discussions about pigeonholing my books. I let the books speak for themselves. As far as I am concerned, the Plain Wrapper Press was a literary fine press that used original artwork to enhance the author's words.

Some Collectors

I would like to pass along several stories connected with this book – some amusing, some sad. While it was nice to be able to say that the shah of Iran and the president of Venezuela had a copy of the Borges/Pomodoro book in their libraries, perhaps my favorite collector was a scoundrel named Richard Jeakins, who loved the book so much that he stole a copy from Bertram Rota's bookstore in London in January 1978, boldly writing his name on one of the front leaves. Much later, when the thief was caught, the headline in one of the local dailies read: "A Fairy Grotto of Stolen Goods." It seems that Jeakins lifted whatever he liked, including a Picasso print and a William Blake painting, as well as a large oriental rug that had earlier in the day been nailed to the floor of Harrods department store. This sort of passionate collecting has always fascinated me, even though I would be the last to condone it. Jeakins was eventually arrested for stealing a can of furniture wax. The newspaper article went on to say, "It took the clerk 12 minutes to read the charges and Jeakins laughed quietly as the list mounted. . . . His bizarre get-away vehicle was a bicycle." The Jeakins copy was eventually returned to Rota in October 1978.

Selling the Book

Because of the book's value, I wanted to avoid sending copies through the mails, so Golda and I took advantage of a trip to London in early October 1975 to deliver a copy – the one Jeakins was later to steal – to Rota. I was carrying it under my arm as we went through the Italian checkpoint when the guard asked me what I had in the box. I told him it was a book, but he was determined to see it for himself. Once the box was open, he said, "Hey, now, that looks pretty expensive. What's it worth?" And I replied without flinching, "About $50." "You mean someone would actually pay that much for a book?" he asked. At that moment a Milanese industrialist behind us turned to his wife and pointing to the book, said, "Look, a Pomodoro!" Golda gave him a gentle nudge to quiet him down. As I nonchalantly replaced the book in its box and passed through the gate, I said to the guard, "Occasionally."

Perhaps the saddest comment on this book – which is really an indictment of sorts on how illustrated books are sometimes marketed – came from an unexpected source. Margit Chanin, director of the art gallery at Rizzoli

Item 14. Siete Poemas Sajones / Seven Saxon Poems   335

International Publications on Fifth Avenue in New York and a former print curator at the Museum of Modern Art, once said, "I can't sell this book. It doesn't have a single illustration that a collector can tear out and frame."

A Final Thought on the Book

Producing this book nearly killed me by calling attention to all my weaknesses and inadequacies, but I learned that if I persisted I could solve many of the technical problems that tormented me. Its reception by the public also demonstrated that there was a market for expensive, finely crafted books, and soon after its publication other private presses began to offer their own versions. And last but not least, the Borges/Pomodoro book gave me a new perspective on my work and set the standard for all future PWP books.

Spezzatini di Maiale e Pollo

Pork and Chicken Stew

Serves 8

I may have been frustrated trying to find an artist, the right paper, or the correct amount of pressure for the Borges book, but a good antidote for low spirits and debilitating frustration is always to cook a big dinner and invite over a lot of friends. This is one of the dishes I liked to serve especially during the foggy winter months in Verona.

    6 tablespoons unsalted butter, divided
    3 tablespoons olive oil, divided
  18 ounces yellow onions, coarsely chopped
    4 small green peppers, seeded and sliced into thin strips
  24 small cremini mushrooms, sliced
    1 teaspoon red pepper flakes
1½ pounds boneless pork ribs, cut into nuggets
     Salt and freshly ground black pepper to taste
1½ pounds boneless chicken breast, cut into nuggets
  ½ cup dry white wine, divided
  ½ cup sour cream

In a 3-quart sauté pan, add 2 tablespoons of the butter and 1 tablespoon of the oil over medium heat. When they begin to bubble, add onions, green peppers, mushrooms, and red pepper flakes and sauté until onions are translucent. Transfer to a Dutch oven. Add 2 more tablespoons of the butter and 1 more tablespoon of the oil to the sauté pan. When they begin to bubble, add pork nuggets and brown on all sides. Lightly salt and pepper them and transfer to the Dutch oven. Deglaze the pan with ¼ cup of the wine and pour it over pork. Add the remaining butter and oil to the pan. When they begin to bubble, add chicken nuggets and brown on all sides. Lightly salt and pepper them and transfer to the Dutch oven. Deglaze the pan with the remaining wine and add to the Dutch oven. Cover and simmer over low heat for 40 minutes. Add sour cream and simmer for an additional 20 minutes.

Radicchio di Verona al Forno
Roasted Radicchio

Serves 8

Radicchio is a member of the chicory family. There are two types: radicchio di Verona and radicchio di Treviso. Both are red and slightly bitter. The one from Verona is round and plump; the one from Treviso is elongated and slim. This is an excellent side dish to serve with stews.

    4 pounds radicchio di Verona, quartered lengthwise
    ½ cup olive oil
        Salt and freshly ground black pepper to taste

Preheat the oven broiler. Place radicchio wedges on a rimmed baking sheet. Drizzle oil over radicchio and sprinkle with salt and pepper. Toss gently leaving the wedges on a cut side. Roast, turning once, until the leaves begin to wilt and the edges are slightly charred, about 10 minutes. Transfer to a warm platter.

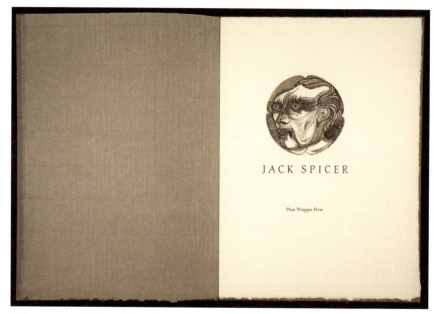

Title-page spread from *A Lost Poem*. (Courtesy of the University of Oregon Libraries.)

Item 15. *A Lost Poem*
A poem by Jack Spicer; with a postscript
by Richard-Gabriel Rummonds.
With two etchings by Ariel [Parkinson].
8 pages. 33.5 x 24.5 cm. 114 copies. 1974.

Ariel Parkinson

Another project in production for many years was a proposed edition of *Forgeries*, a book of poems by Thomas Parkinson, to be illustrated with several etchings by his wife, Ariel, who wanted to work on the plates in Luciano Cristini's atelier. I had given her a projected date for the completion of the Borges/Pomodoro book so she could plan her trip accordingly. I should have realized by this time that it was impossible to keep a schedule at the PWP. After waiting for more than a year, Ariel and her nine-year-old daughter Chrysa arrived on September 27, 1974, the day after I finished printing the last sheet of the Borges text. I found them a room in the attic of one of Golda Fishbein's widowed neighbors, down the street from my studio.

Ariel Parkinson on the University of California at Berkeley campus, 2003.
(Photo by RGR, courtesy of PWP Archives.)

The room came without kitchen privileges, but that really didn't matter because they would be taking most of their meals with me.

There were now two women in my life, both with children. The locals, who loved to gossip, concocted their own scenario, which went as follows: Golda was being usurped by Ariel, who probably had a prior claim on me – perhaps she was my legal wife. The matronly women in the pastry shops and the clerks in the neighborhood markets, who had always been civil but somewhat reserved toward Golda, suddenly went out of their way to be sympathetic and kind to her. Golda's domestic situation was being threatened. I actually rather enjoyed this new role that had been thrust upon me.

I still had the enormous task of quality control, sifting through huge piles of printed sheets from the Borges book, before I could take the collated gatherings to the binder. Ariel helped me – in fact, it was Ariel who discovered the misspelled word in the "Printer's Note."

Refurbishing the Washington Press

After having been involved for so many years with the Borges/Pomodoro book, I shouldn't have been surprised that just finishing it left me completely exhausted and depressed. On September 15, taking advantage of my inertia, I dismantled the press, and sent the bed and platen to Ugo Falconi's machine shop to be rectified (planed to get rid of the concave wells in both pieces). The previous year I had taken the steel parts to a specialist to be nickel-plated because they were beginning to rust in the Veronese dampness. While the press was dismantled, I scrubbed it with turpentine and painted the cast-iron pieces with a fresh coat of black paint mixed with a touch of forest green. On November 15 I reassembled the press.

A Manuscript from Thomas Parkinson

I was so dejected that I couldn't face the prospect of immediately starting to print another large book. Tom had sent the *Forgeries* manuscript to me in November 1971. It contained twenty-five poems, and as originally laid out, it would have come to forty pages – a few more than the Borges/Pomodoro book – plus four large etchings and three or four smaller ones. Ariel had already begun the sketches for the illustrations. We converted the space at Ponte Pietra into a studio where she could work when she wasn't at Luciano's transferring her images to copper disks. We envisioned the illustra-

Item 15. A Lost Poem 341

tions as large medallions to be printed back to back, suggesting Roman coins. I wanted to avoid blank verso pages, which I have always detested and tried – not always successfully – to eliminate in my books.

Forgeries was announced in *Plain Wrapper Press Newsletter: One* (December 1974) as the first of two projects in preparation for the new Berkeley Poets Series. Later it was listed in the brochure for the Arte Fiera '76 as one of six projects in preparation. Of these six projects only three were actually published. By the time *Forgeries* was abandoned, Ariel had completed and proofed all the plates for the illustrations, and I had finished setting all the type for it. Undoubtedly, this would have been a stunning book, but for some reason it seemed doomed from the start, and I never could muster the necessary determination to finish it. Here is one of the poems as it was set for the PWP edition:

> Imperial friend, I'm writing to resign.
> Prefect, consul, I've been those two, and more.
> And all through your affectionate piety.
> More than an emperor, more than a son,
> You have the right to keep me from my ease,
> But do not exercise it. I've gone dry.
> The nights lack length to let me rest. The days
> Are shorter than my work. Let me return
> To poetry and wine. Do not keep me
> From my aging pleasures. Burdigala
> Calls me, city of my birth, and my death.

I had known Tom and Ariel Parkinson since the early fifties, when I was a student at Berkeley. Tom was one of my teachers, and Ariel was an accomplished artist. At the time I had a crush on her. I often saw them socially, and I occasionally baby-sat their older daughter, Kathy. Ariel and I had also collaborated on set and costume designs for university theater productions. Even though I abandoned the theater early on, she continued to work in it with great success. For many years after I left the university, we continued to correspond, following each other's careers with considerable interest. Two of Ariel's oil paintings have long been among my prized possessions.

Tom enjoyed fraternizing with his students and frequently showed up at their parties. He had a commanding voice and an infectious laugh that both terrorized his students and made them adore him. Perhaps he was compensating for the breakup of the Berkeley Renaissance – or Poetry Renaissance, as it was sometimes called. In addition to Tom the poets included Robert Duncan and Jack Spicer. They had all been students at Berkeley between 1946 and 1950 – before the migration to the West Coast of the better-known Beat movement, which was dominated by Allen Ginsberg and Lawrence Ferlinghetti. I met many of the Berkeley Renaissance poets at the frequent parties held in and around the Bay Area, parties that often took the form of poetry readings or theatrical presentations. I liked their work and later published four of them in the Spring 1954 issue of *Occident*.

A Lost Poem

Ariel empathized with my reluctance to begin our collaboration with *Forgeries*, so we discussed the possibility of printing something much more modest. Of all the Berkeley Renaissance poets, Jack Spicer was the one I most admired. Ariel also adored him and knew many of his poems by heart. Because of our mutual high regard for Jack's work, we decided to print a poem that he had written out for her in 1946. The original manuscript had

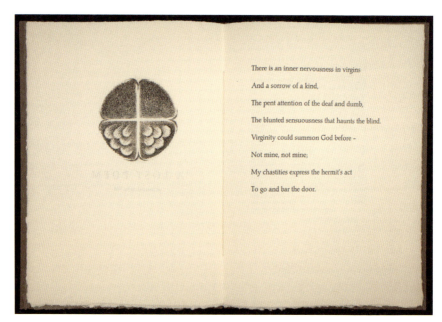

Double-page spread from *A Lost Poem*. (Courtesy of the University of Oregon Libraries.)

Item 15. A Lost Poem   343

long ago been lost, but Ariel transcribed it from memory. Here is the poem
as it appears in this edition:

> There is an inner nervousness in virgins
> And a sorrow of a kind,
> The pent attention of the deaf and dumb,
> The blunted sensuousness that haunts the blind.
> Virginity could summon God before –
> Not mine, not mine;
> My chastities express the hermit's act
> To go and bar the door.

I described my strong feelings about Jack's work in a short postscript to
the poem:

> Jack's poetry appears to have been written for each individual reader,
> giving to the inarticulate the words which he feels must be hidden
> somewhere inside himself. More precisely, reading the poetry draws
> one out of one's own life and affixes it to Jack's like a bandage. When
> the poet says, "Not mine, not mine," the reader's inner voice drowns
> out Jack's. Jack is too strong, however, to be covered up. His simplicity,
> naturalness, and inexorable logic are common to us all, but he speaks
> first for himself, for the torment, the rejection, the self-destruction. It
> is from this very personal substance that the final order and clarity of
> his poetry evolve.

After such a long hiatus, it was nice to go back to Luciano's well-organized
atelier, at the back of which was a secluded space with natural light, where
artists could work on their plates under his critical eye. Temporarily setting
aside Tom's book, Ariel made two new medallions: a portrait of Jack and an
abstraction that suggested the balance and symmetry of his poetry. We
wanted to use these plates to test the feasibility of pulling prints back to
back for *Forgeries*.

For Tom's book I ordered the Post Mediaeval type from the H. Berthold
Type Foundry in Berlin. It was a lighter, more delicate typeface than the
Horizon Light. The first fonts started arriving in late February 1973, but it
came in strange assortments – predominantly German – that I couldn't use.
It was at this time that I compiled the PWP book-font schemes, taking into

account that in addition to English I would be setting type in Spanish, Italian, French, and German. Another advantage of printing *A Lost Poem* first was that its shorter text would give me an opportunity to get the feel of the new type before I started to set Tom's much longer text.

Printing the Book
Luciano finished printing the etchings on November 30, 1974, and Ariel and I printed the last form of text the following week. The book was printed in quarto – four pages at once – on Fabriano Michelangelo Roma handmade paper, even though the half-sheet imposition I had favored in the past would have presented fewer problems.

This was the first publication issued in the new Quartus Series. The idea behind this series was that the whole book would be printed on a single sheet of paper, making eight pages when folded and trimmed. Even though our experiment of pulling etchings back to back could not be realized – the intricate details of the first etching were diminished during the backing-up process – we had them optically "backing up" on consecutive leaves.

The Binding
The binding had an innovative feature that I continued to use for many years. In its original form a single eight-page signature with an outside wrap-

Gabriel in the via Duomo studio around the time he and Ariel Parkinson printed *A Lost Poem*, Verona, Italy, 1975. (Photo by Giorgio Vigna, courtesy of PWP Archives.)

around was sewn into the fold of the continuous pastedown that connected the hard covers, giving the appearance of a book with traditional endpapers. Marcello Fornaro made the cases. The primary reason for putting this item into hard covers was financial. I wanted to sell it as a book, and I knew that I would end up giving it away as a keepsake if I bound it as a pamphlet. It was, nevertheless, eventually given gratis to standing order collectors.

La Terra Guasta

During Ariel's stay we decided to put on a play, an ecological fairy tale that she had written in a strange mixture of English and Italian. It was called *La terra guasta (The Wasted Land)*, a play for children, but in reality a children's play for adults. The living room of my apartment was turned into a theater, and my double bed – which I had made from large sheets of pressed wood and mounted on a low platform – was converted into a stage. We built a proscenium arch in front of it and strung up a curtain and canopy.

One night at a local experimental theater, Ariel met a skinny teenage boy named Giorgio (Giorgiolino – Georgie Boy as he was known at the PWP) Vigna. Still in high school, he was extremely interested in all aspects of theater. She mentioned to him in conversation that I had at one time also been involved in the theater. He was eager to meet me so she invited him to have supper with us. Knowing that Ariel had written a play we were about to put on, he was hoping we would include him in our production plans.

Giorgio Vigna, Padua, Italy, 1975. (Photo by RGR, courtesy of PWP Archives.)

After that first supper, the three of us frequently got together in the evening to discuss the play. We all enthusiastically assumed various responsibilities for the production. Ariel looked after the script, I was to design the sets and costumes, and Giorgiolino was to direct the play. In addition to Ariel the adult cast included Pucci De Rossi, Golda Fishbein, and Giorgio "Hat Shop" Zanolli in a witch's pointed hat. Giorgio, who had a natural flair for the theater, sat perched atop my massive forty-drawer oak filing cabinet narrating the story. We also enlisted several of the expatriate children, all of whom attended Italian schools and spoke fluent Italian. Mark Fishbein played the Prince to Chrysa's dancing Princess. (She went on to become a professional ballet dancer.) The twins, Tania and Cybèle Plank, and one of

A curtain call from *La Terra Guasta* in the red room at via Duomo, 15, Verona, Italy, 1975. *Front:* Tania Plank, an Italian classmate of Chrysa's, and Cybèle Plank. *Back:* Chrysa Parkinson, Mark Fishbein, and Giorgio Zanolli. (Photographer unknown, courtesy of PWP Archives.)

Chrysa's Italian classmates rounded out the cast. To complete the ensemble, the musical accompaniment was provided by Jacques Vernière on flute and Lauren Fishbein, who played a bass drum up-ended like a kettle drum, which had been given to me by Giuseppe Zambonini, the director of an avant-garde theater company in Verona. He claimed that the drum had crossed the Alps with Napoleon's army.

Item 15. A Lost Poem

There was a lot of tension during the rehearsals. Pucci and Ariel were not getting along. At one point he gave her a whack with a plastic club, and she stood up and reminded him that it was just make-believe – he wasn't supposed to hurt her. Golda was miffed because she had no lines – her primary task was to open and close the curtain – a role not too far removed from Vanna White's letter-turning role on a popular American TV show. Giorgiolino kept changing his directorial mind every few minutes, only to be contradicted by Ariel. The actors became very confused.

The play's finale included the release of a live dove that was suppose to fly out the open window. During the first performance on Saturday night, however, it got away. The person stationed in the courtyard to catch it couldn't hold on to it, so it escaped into the twilight sky. At the same moment when the dove was let out of its cage, the front edge of the black canopy that hung over the stage was "magically" lowered, revealing a backdrop of simulated green foliage. Wow! One Italian friend commented after the performance, "Is this what would be called modern theater?" After an affirmative nod in response to his question, he said, "Good, now I know why I didn't understand it."

The plan was to present the play at a special performance for grownups early Saturday evening followed by an early performance on Sunday,

Invitation to the play (1975). (Courtesy of PWP Archives.)

February 2, for our friends with young children. Just after the Friday night rehearsal I received a telegram to call my brother Tom in Munich. When we spoke, he told me that our father had died earlier that day. Giorgiolino had accompanied me to the phone office at the train station since I didn't have a telephone in my apartment. As we walked back to my place, I talked about everything except the news I had just received. I didn't want to upset the plans for the production by telling my friends, but I felt I had to communicate my loss to someone that night – I would tell Golda and Ariel the next day. Back in the familiar security of my own apartment, I confided in Giorgiolino. He stayed with me that night, and we became lovers. He is the subject of the poem "The Dedication" in *Seven Aspects of Solitude.*

Ariel and Chrysa left on February 5, 1975, a few days after the presentation of the play. It was amazing how much stuff, including large tuna tins, that Ariel had accumulated in three months. Fulvio Testa and I barely managed to squeeze all her things, plus the two of them, into his car. Golda observed that the car's rear-end was only inches off the ground as we drove over the Ponte Pietra on our way to Genoa, from where they would sail back to the States. Ariel and I may not have accomplished our main objective – to print *Forgeries* – but in those few months together we did create one of the most popular of all PWP publications.

Once back in Berkeley Ariel sent me a manuscript copy of Michael McClure's play *The Derby*, which she hoped I would be interested in publishing with her illustrations. She had designed the sets and costumes for his *Minnie Mouse and the Tap-Dancing Buddha.* Nothing ever came of this project either, but it certainly would have been a challenge and would have given me a great deal of pleasure. I doubt that there has ever been a printer who procrastinated as much as I did or one who lost so many opportunities to print extraordinary books.

Item 15. A Lost Poem   349

Shirred Eggs

Serves 1

This is a dish that Jack Pooler frequently made during our affair. I will always associate it with him and my happier times there.

½ tablespoon unsalted butter
1 small slice of spiral ham, julienned
1 medium mushroom, sliced
1 scallion, white part only and thinly sliced
2 eggs
  Salt and freshly ground pepper to taste
1 heaping tablespoon sour cream, stirred to soften
1 heaping tablespoon Gouda cheese, grated

Adjust rack to the top third of the oven and preheat to 500 degrees. Heat butter in a small saucepan. When it begins to bubble, add ham, mushrooms, and scallions and sauté. Transfer to a 5-inch gratin dish. Crack eggs on top of mixture, being careful to keep yolks from touching the rim of dish. Season to taste with salt and pepper. Gently spread sour cream over eggs and top with cheese. Bake until egg whites are set, about 4 to 5 minutes.

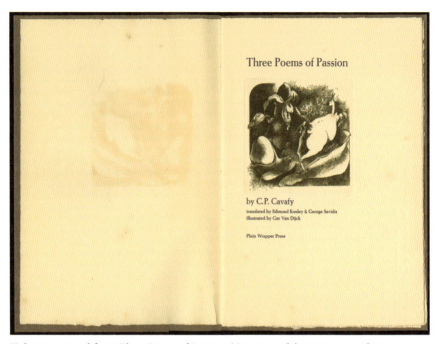

Title-page spread from *Three Poems of Passion*. (Courtesy of the University of Oregon Libraries.)

Item 16. *Three Poems of Passion*

Three poems by C.P. Cavafy [Konstantinos Petrou Kabaphes] translated from the Greek into English by Edmund Keeley and George Savidis; with a foreword in English by Richard-Gabriel Rummonds. With two intaglio reproductions of pen and ink drawings by Ger van Dijck. 12 pages. 29 x 19.5 cm. 97 copies. 1975.

Ger van Dijck

I had been fascinated by Ger van Dijck's work ever since I first saw it. I often regretted that *Ten Poems & Ten Reflections*, our only joint effort, had been so trivial. As early as 1970 we had talked about collaborating on a Flemish and English edition of the fifteenth-century Everyman play *Den spyeghel der salicheyt van Elckerlijc* (1965), but nothing ever came of it. Then in the summer of 1974 I was given another and quite unexpected opportunity that would reunite us for a project of special interest for me. Ger had stopped in Verona for a few days en route from Greece to Holland. During this visit he showed me a portfolio of mysterious erotic pen and ink drawings he had made while on vacation, some of which Luciano Cristini was transferring photographically to intaglio plates. The moment I saw his

Ger van Dijck in the courtyard at via Duomo, 15, Verona, Italy, 1970. (Photo by RGR, courtesy of PWP Archives.)

drawings, I knew that they would make perfect illustrations for a book of C. P. Cavafy's poems that I longed to publish.

C. P. Cavafy

One of the last trade books I designed before leaving New York was Cavafy's *Passions and Ancient Days* (1971), with translations by Edmund (Mike) Keeley and George Savidis, which was published by The Dial Press. Karen Kennerly, the editor, had given me complete freedom regarding design and production, and I have always considered it to be one of my best trade book designs. (I received $550 for the design, the most I was ever paid.) I selected three poems from the book for my PWP edition.

My Identification with Cavafy

Cavafy's sentiments always seem to reflect my own. If I could choose to write like any poet, I would surely choose him. His suppressed eroticism,

C.P. Cavafy, place and date unknown. (Photographer unknown, courtesy of PWP Archives.)

Item 16. Three Poems of Passion 353

always on the brink of boiling over, reminded me poignantly of my own. In the foreword to this keepsake dated January 1975, I wrote:

> I felt in such harmony with Cavafy through his poems; it was as if he had written down my thoughts and feelings years before I was born. . . . I found myself completely immersed in this poetry, and my heart and mind became flooded with similar experiences and memories as their simple narratives conjured up my own forgotten passions.

In July 1974 I wrote to Mike asking his permission to reprint the three poems I had selected in a keepsake that I wanted to distribute gratis to friends. He never responded to any of my letters, so I pirated the poems, which included the following one:

> *The Photograph*
>
> In this obscene photograph secretly sold
> (the policeman mustn't see) around the corner,
> in this whorish photograph,
> how did such a dream-like face
> make its way? How did you get in here?
>
> Who knows what a degrading, vulgar life you lead;
> how horrible the surroundings must have been
> when you posed to have the picture taken;
> what a cheap soul you must have.
> But in spite of all this, and even more, you remain for me
> the dream-like face, the figure
> shaped for and dedicated to Hellenic love –
> that's how you remain for me
> and how my poetry speaks of you.

In 1991 Mike wrote to me that he had revised the first three lines of the first stanza:

> In this obscene photograph sold secretly
> in the street (so the policeman won't see),
> in this lewd photograph,

And the seventh line in the second stanza:

> shaped for and dedicated to the Greek kind of sexual pleasure.

I preferred the earlier version.

Early Layouts for Cavafy

I must have been thinking for some time about printing Cavafy's poetry, because I have two mockups of a Cavafy project, made in 1971. Both were for a sixteen-page pamphlet consisting only of "The Photograph," although the illustrations were going to be different for each project. One of the mockups used a nineteenth-century postcard of a man in a "Greek" pose, and the other, segments of a photograph taken from a contemporary male erotica magazine that would have been cropped and blown up so that the dot pattern almost obscured the subject. The first would have included the eye, with other segments progressively showing more of the body. Both concepts were dropped once I decided to use Ger's drawings. In 1976 Harvey Simmonds carried a packet with Mike's share of the keepsakes to him in the States.

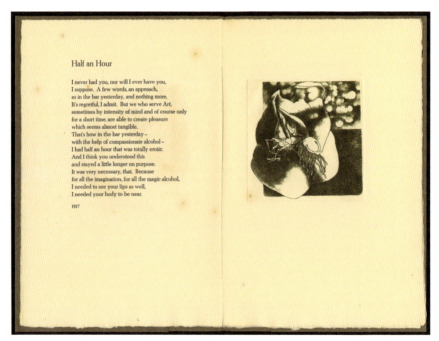

Double-page spread from *Three Poems of Passion*. (Courtesy of the University of Oregon Libraries.)

Item 16. Three Poems of Passion   355

Seeing Mike at the PWP Retrospective

At the PWP retrospective at The New York Public Library in January 1981, Mike apologized for never having answered my letters or acknowledged that he had received the keepsakes. We joked about the anxiety I felt at the time, knowing that I was doing something illegal. Before we parted – having gotten along so well that evening – we decided to collaborate on a book of poems by Yannis Ritsos, a contemporary Greek poet and political activist. Mike sent me a manuscript, *Poems from "The Wall Inside the Mirror,"* but unfortunately the PWP was closed before I had a chance to publish it, although a selection from that manuscript was eventually printed by some of my students at the University of Alabama.

Arrival of John V. Richardson Jr.

John V. Richardson Jr., a student in the library school at the University of Kentucky, wrote to me in January 1975 asking if he could come to Verona to work as an apprentice at the PWP. By then I thought I knew enough about the handpress to demonstrate some of the things I had taught myself. John's interest in fine printing had been nurtured by Carolyn Reading Hammer, head of Special Collections at the University of Kentucky.

When John and his wife Nancy arrived on April 12, 1975, I wasn't at home; I was in a nearby hospital. One of my doctor friends, Renato Da Pian, had put me in his ward so I could get some proper rest and perhaps shake off the tension and anxiety, as well as the back problems, which were still plaguing me after printing the Borges/Pomodoro book. Later I was transferred to another ward so the medical students could examine an honest-to-goodness American liver. Italians are obsessed with liver ailments – not altogether unrelated to the amount of wine they consume. The interns spent days running dyes in one of my arms and out the other, as well as poking and X-raying me.

Golda Fishbein and Giorgio (Giorgiolino) Vigna brought the Richardsons to the hospital, where they found me sitting out in the garden in pajamas and slippers, enjoying the sunshine like the other ambulatory patients. As we walked about, John immediately started asking questions about printing: "Gabriel, how did Gutenberg make his ink?" and so on. Golda recalls the scene with delight: the prophet with his disciples trailing at a discreet distance.

When John and Nancy came to the hospital, they were wearing jogging suits, their only possessions after their bicycles and knapsacks were stolen in

Florence. I remember loaning John a T-shirt and a pair of gym shorts so he could wash his jogging suit at Golda's. While there he confided to her his concern that I might "pounce" on him. Golda took one look at John's ankles and said, "I don't think you have anything to worry about."

Printing the Keepsake

After I was released from the hospital on April 30, 1975, John and I started to ready the press to print the Cavafy. We began by re-covering the tympan. But first we had to take the dampened sheets to Luigi Pradella's so he could edition the plates before we could print the text.

Tagging along with me gave John an unusual opportunity to see the day-to-day operation of the PWP. We took a bus – the Vespa was now permanently out of commission – to deliver the paper to Pradella, whose atelier was in his garage near I.V.A.T., where I had purchased my standing press. He editioned all the prints in two days. The Lorilleux sepia ink he used printed a grayish green. Back in my studio we had to dry down the sheets with newsprint before we could print the text. Printing limited editions at the PWP – even keepsakes –continued to be a collaborative effort, often requiring the skills of many diverse artisans.

John V. Richardson Jr. and Gabriel printing *Three Poems of Passion* in the via Duomo studio, Verona, Italy, 1975. (Photo by Nancy Richardson, courtesy of the photographer.)

Item 16. Three Poems of Passion   357

We finished printing the text on May 23, with none of the hair-raising experiences associated with past projects during the printing. Even the makeready seemed less complicated; by now I had solved most of the problems that had frustrated and perplexed me. It was difficult not to get beautiful results from the Horizon Light type on the Richard de Bas paper, which always took the ink so easily. I think John enjoyed the work, and I hope he gained something useful from the experience.

Even though all the copies of this keepsake are deteriorating because of bleeding caused by the dryer in the intaglio ink, it remains my personal favorite of all PWP publications. I have looked at it countless times, each time finding it hard to believe that I can still be so moved by its contents.

Richardson's Article

John later wrote a rather informative article about me and the PWP – one of the first to be published on my work. When I read his article, "Richard-Gabriel Rummonds: A Veronese Printer" in the spring 1980 issue of the Book Club of California's *Quarterly News-Letter*, I was amazed at how much research had gone into it. John wrote:

> Rummonds is part of this twentieth-century revolution combining elements of traditionalism and experimentation. . . . In terms of technique, he has mastered the same hard-learned principles of an Emery Walker and is more than a careful printer; he is a fine printer.

It has always puzzled me why John avoided mentioning his apprenticeship at the PWP in his article. He did note the custom-made type cabinet I had acquired shortly before his arrival. Its imposing presence in the studio caught the eye and fancy of practically every writer who visited the Press.

The First Custom-Made Type Cabinet

I had gone to a printing-equipment trade show in Milan in November 1974, where I saw an extensive display of type cabinets. I had shipped from the States a twenty-two-drawer Thompson school type cabinet that barely held all my Horizon Light type, let alone the new Post Mediaeval type. Believing I would soon be rich from the sale of the Borges/Pomodoro book, I ordered the first of two cabinets made by the Xilografia Italiana in January 1975. It had two rows of California job cases flanked on the outside by two rows of smaller drawers for accents and sorts. I modified the California job case by adding an extra row of compartments inside the cap side for brasses and coppers and additional sorts. My only regret is that I didn't remember enough from my early reading on printing history to order separate cases for lowercase and uppercase type since I was primarily printing books, not job work.

Just before this cabinet was finished, the company manager notified me that the next payment on my order was about to come due. Since the factory was only a few hours away by car in Badia Polesine, I talked Brooks and Bonnie Walker into going on a country excursion in their Fiat 700 so I could make the payment in person and see for myself the progress the factory had made. The cabinet was indeed magnificent, lacking only the lacquer finish and brass handles before it would be ready to deliver. Because all the cabinets at the trade show were sprayed with a metallic gray lacquer, I was surprised to find that the unfinished cabinets were made of a fine Romanian oak. Struck by the cabinet's natural beauty, I asked the manager to have mine sprayed with nothing more than a clear lacquer. In May I ordered a matching storage unit graduated for leads and metal furniture, one half for pica and the other half for Didot, to sit on top of the type cabinet. Early in 1978 the same company made me a second cabinet.

Little by little the studio in via Duomo began to look like a real print shop. I now had all the basic equipment I needed to print books: the Washington press, the Poco proof press, the standing press, two type cabinets full of type, two humidors, and plenty of work space. A few years later I added a bindery in the hope that it would make me completely autonomous, a long-standing but never-to-be-achieved desire.

Some Social Notes

In June 1975 Nancy Foosaner Long, my high-school sweetheart, came to Venice with her husband, Don, and their children, along with another couple with their children. Both couples were returning from an extended stay in Hong Kong. Nancy invited me to join them for lunch at a Chinese restaurant in Venice because they didn't have time to come to Verona.

Giorgiolino and I took a morning train and rendezvoused with them at the restaurant. We were too large a group to be seated at one table, so the adults sat together, and the children, including a miffed Giorgiolino, sat at a second table. The other couple assumed that he was my son, rather than my lover.

In October Hadassah Brooks, a New York psychiatrist, was sent to visit Golda by a mutual friend. Hadassah and I became fast friends. She invited me to travel with her to Pompeii and the Amalfi coast. I needed some time away from Giorgiolino. In Pompeii, we sat on a curb in the hot sun surrounded by tourists as we speculated on the imagined sex lives of our parents. Hadassah played a very important part in my life after I started teaching at the University of Alabama in 1977.

Ben Meiselman

An importer of Italian ceramics, Ben Meiselman often came to Italy to visit with his suppliers. He was also related to Golda by marriage. One time Golda and I met up with him in Bassano del Grappa for lunch. It was a glorious summer day and we had taken a rickety old train with wooden seats that stopped at every village along the way. I was wearing one of my favorite straw hats.

Golda Fishbein, Ben Meiselman, and Gabriel at the approach to the Ponte degli Alpini, Bassano del Grappa, Italy, 1974. (Photographer unknown, courtesy of PWP archives.)

Prosciutto e Melone o Fichi

Prosciutto and Melon or Figs

Serves 4

In the summertime I liked to serve cold lunches in the side courtyard, featuring dishes like this one and the next:

1 small melon, such as cantaloupe or honeydew or 12 fresh figs
¼ teaspoon salt
⅛ teaspoon freshly ground black pepper
¼ pound prosciutto di Parma, thinly sliced

Cut melon into narrow wedges, about three per person. Remove seeds and rinds. Lightly salt and pepper. If using figs, quarter fruit, but leave pieces attached at the stem. Serve on individual salad plates with slices of prosciutto.

Item 16. Three Poems of Passion   361

Pomodori con Mozzarella e Basilico
Tomatoes with Mozzarella Cheese and Fresh Basil

Serves 4

The tomatoes and the mozzarella must be very fresh.

    Bibb lettuce, a few leaves per serving
  4 ripe tomatoes, sliced
  1 pound mozzarella cheese, sliced
16 fresh basil leaves
    Dressing of extra-virgin olive oil, balsamic vinegar, capers, salt, and freshly ground black pepper

Spread a thin layer of lettuce on a platter. Alternate tomato and mozzarella slices, tucking 2 basil leaves between each slice. Drizzle dressing over the salad.

Title page from *Géographie du Regard*. (Courtsey of the Oregon Libraries.)

Item 17. *Géographie du Regard*

Six poems in French and three in English by Laure Vernière; with an afterword in English by Richard-Gabriel Rummonds. With a two-color wood engraving by Jacques Vernière.
48 pages. 19.5 x 29 cm. 71 copies. 1976.

Laure Vernière

I first met Laure Vernière in October 1971 in Lina Boner Grosselli's kitchen, where Pucci De Rossi had gathered his closest friends to meet his new wife. We sat around the table drinking wine and talking about many things – art, life in Verona, but mostly about poetry. A couple of volumes of Laure's poetry had already been published in Paris, and that evening she read a selection from *Poemes* (1971), a book published earlier that year by Caracters. She later translated Sylvia Plath's *Ariel* (1978) into French. Even though my French was rusty, I felt that I understood the poems by dint of their force and magnetism. That night we agreed that I would print a book of her new poems. She had been actively writing in both French and English while teaching French literature at Sarah Lawrence College – a tenured position she eventually gave up to live permanently in Verona.

Laure Vernière, at "Bora Bora," Pucci De Rossi's country place near Verona, Italy, 1970. (Photo by Luciano Luise, courtesy of Laure Vernière.)

Selecting the Poems

Laure and I began talking seriously about a PWP edition of her poems in October 1972. In the weeks that followed, she showed me her voluminous manuscripts, and together we selected nine poems. Here is "Stop Motion," one of the poems from our book:

> Passion: I shall answer your call in the growing
> lightness; filled with strange games and lives; there to be felt
> and tightly, softly possessed, once; but always
> terrified to be, once;
> but always tender at the thought. So sure
> of the object (be it real birds, facing cranes,
> bricks, or plastic fruit) or maybe, so sure
> of that which is no daring secret, that which
> is waiting and shouting within: compassion. And we
> said it was a day like any other day, but voices
> from elsewhere and memories were blurring that very
> day in a way that a man alone could not stand it; so that this
> very day, the only one we should have been interested in,
>
> took the nostalgic shape of our restated deaths. Everything
> I said or did was doomed to be false: facing
> the day, running away, shaking another real sloppy
> day (the previous one just as idiotic as this one, just as
> useless, just as pretentious, just as incomplete). The waiting
> becomes unbearable: the paper, the machine,
> and the gin 'n tonic as well. A miserable joke indeed
> is the outside world, playing the puppy, the fat
> doll, the docile object between voices, weeks, and incomplete
> years. Words. Their secret order, as usual, escapes me. I
> would have preferred touching your silence in the utmost
> darkness with mine; then we could
> have indeed recovered the fragility
>
> of this in-between terror. Can you – can you
> understand the purpose of such a movement? the lightness

Item 17. Géographie du Regard 365

of such a daring step where castles and sidewalks
meet? An exact calculation is a poor and tired
attempt toward a still deeper silence. We are almost
there, but not quite; the day has turned
fragile and totally unprepared. Our awareness
is childlike; our seriousness, pregnant; our
loneliness, total. Compassion: to avoid traps, gaps, and
terrors. The void devours itself (can we still kneel
here where any number may shout itself between a museum
and an arch?) to avoid a direction – very much set – a diabolic
series of closed doors and tightened certainties. A film
is shown, not so funny, but rich in old fantasies: a broken
body, broken solely by a mirror; the chairs are
alive and I fight the motion. We are between a
beginning and an end, just here,
closed and very insensitive to the next shot. We
have invented thousands of fights which didn't
happen, couldn't happen as we were, just then, strangled and
kept sane with little care and few sobs. Here
singled in the darkness, so dear, so terrifying, so
soft, white, black, and complete. We are waiting
for nothing now, being *waiting* itself in the blue
sharpness of the other side, where the fight is just a fight
and *sleeping* has the sweetness of death.

There is a wonderful energy in these lines, as there is in all Laure's poems.

This was another project that started off in a burst of enthusiasm only to lie dormant for several years. It really wasn't fair to Laure – or to any other author – to have gotten her excited about a project before I was ready to proceed with it. Circumstances often beyond my control frequently halted a project in midstream, as was the case with Laure's book. Once I had her manuscript, I designed the book with the Amatruda paper in mind. I selected an album format because I didn't like the idea of having to accept an unusually large number of turnover lines. Part of the impact of Laure's poetry is the way it appears on the page, and breaking the long lines so typical of her style seemed wrong. The album format also meant that since

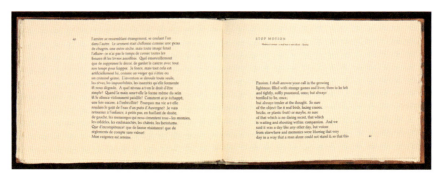

Double-page spread from *Géographie du Regard*. (Courtesy of the University of Oregon Libraries.)

the poems were quite long, each would occupy more than one page, which added to the narrative flow of her work. The only other format possible would have resulted in a book the size of the Borges/Pomodoro, which was financially out of the question.

Engaging Manina to Illustrate the Book

In April 1972 I introduced Laure to Manina, an Austrian-born painter who lived in Venice, part of that group of expatriates I had met through Berta Moltke in 1969. Manina was a great beauty as well as a fascinating and multitalented artist. Her father, Victor Tischler, had been an artist, and her mother, Matilde Ehrlich, had sung with the Vienna State Opera. She had been married to the Czech screenwriter Robert Thoeren, and later married the French poet Alain Jouffroy. The talented and eccentric gravitated from the world over to Manina's salon, One never knew what or whom to expect there. She was quite taken with Laure's poetry and eager to illustrate the book.

My original plan was to use etchings, in part because of the proximity of Luciano Cristini's atelier, and because intaglio prints were becoming a characteristic of PWP publications. Luciano prepared a set of plates coated with an acid-resistant resin, which I took to Manina in October 1972.

The book was announced as "in preparation" in *Plain Wrapper Press Newsletter: One* (1974), mentioning three etchings by Manina. I later revised the printing schedule and the number of etchings, noting that the printing would begin in November 1975 with only one etching.

Item 17. Géographie du Regard

Part-title spread from *Géographie du Regard*. (Courtesy of the University of Oregon Libraries.)

I had seen many of Manina's etchings before, and I wasn't prepared for the lackluster images she returned to me. I discussed them with her, but she was inflexible so soon after a successful retrospective show of her work at the Galleria Borgonuovo in Milan. At this point I didn't want to scrap the project altogether, so I wrote to Manina in November that I had decided to use only one of her plates, citing the cost of editioning so many prints as my excuse. Of course she saw through my ruse and was offended, writing back "All or none." And so it was to be none. Manina was fond of saying, "We live from shock to shock." How true this was for this book, in fact for most PWP books.

Taking Up the Book Again

Because of this setback it would be two years before I put Laure's book back into production. By then, I had decided to use the Post Mediaeval type instead of the Horizon Light and had switched to the Richard de Bas paper, using part of what was left over from the Borges/Pomodoro book. It was the same size as the Amatruda paper, so the album format could still be used. I began setting the text in the winter of 1974, and was grateful to have Ariel Parkinson's help in editing the poems.

Jacques Vernière

The book was eventually illustrated with a two-color wood engraving cut by Laure's brother, Jacques, who by December 1975 was editioning woodcuts on his own press. During the proofing I accidentally damaged the brown

Jacques Vernière, Verona, Italy, 1970s. (Photo by Luciano Luise, courtesy of Julien Vernière.)

block, and a linecut had to be substituted for it, although the black image was printed from the original block. Jacques's blocks were editioned in January 1976. Commenting on his wood engraving, I wrote in the afterword:

> [The artist sees the poet] as terrain – mapped and charted; and as a cartographer, he spreads her out to look for the geographic center of her real existence hidden somewhere between rationality and sensuality.

Printing the Book

On August 21, 1975, Kenneth Pettitt, my old buddy from Berkeley, arrived for an extended visit. We began to ready the press to print the book. I continued making tests through November. Around this time, I also started using a lithographic rolling pin roller, which made the inking more consistent. I used these rollers for all subsequent editions at the PWP and EXO.

Item 17. Géographie du Regard

Since this was a two-color project, it meant the paper had to be kept damp for several nights in the humidors between runs. I didn't finish printing the book until April 22, 1976.

Gabriel placing the paper on the points in the via Duomo studio, Verona, Italy, 1975. (Photo by Giorgio Vigna, courtesy of PWP archives.)

The Binding

This was the last book Bonnie Walker worked on for the PWP. She had become tired of living in Verona and especially tired of Brooks's antics. Bonnie had been led to believe that after their honeymoon they would return to the attractive "society" life she had left behind in Palm Beach, Florida, where her mother lived and where Brooks had courted her. She spent the entire night before she left for the States in the fall of 1975 marbling the papers for this book.

In May 1976 I talked with Mario Rigoldi, a binder whose atelier was in Monza. All the collaborators had selected their favorite papers and written their names on the backsides. I asked Mario to match the names on the papers with the names or numbers on the colophon pages. When he covered the cases, however, he forgot to make note of the numbers, and so none of us got the papers we had selected. He also added a gilt rule at the juncture of the parchment and paper, even though I had specifically asked him not to. He thought the books looked "unfinished" without the rules. Binders always have a way of adding things the publisher didn't ask for.

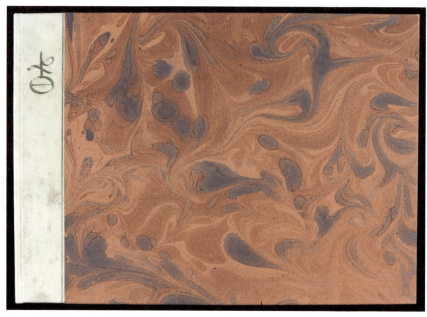

Cover for *Géographie du Regard*. (Courtesy of the University of Oregon Libraries.)

Eating and Drinking

The Vernière-De Rossi clans and *la piccola famiglia* frequently got together to celebrate on the slightest pretext, or just to eat and drink. Laure insisted that I had the best "sense of the feast" of anyone she had ever known, and I boasted that she was a miracle-worker when it came to preparing and serving dinners.

Postscript

On April 11, 1981, at "The Art of the Printed Book" conference at the University of Nebraska, Omaha, I mentioned Laure in my talk "Author and Publisher: A Love Story, of Sorts":

> As the years accumulated between our meeting and the printing of this book, her mood changed. Verona was not the intellectual challenge she had imagined it would be, and as a consequence, she became slightly bitter, cynical, and tired.

Item 17. Géographie du Regard   371

Pollo al Forno con Patate
Roast Chicken with Potatoes

Serves 6

Often a dozen or more people would gather around the table at the De Rossi's – some invited, others who just happened to be hanging out downstairs in Pucci's studio. Art and politics were the predominant subjects of discussion. The De Rossi and their circle were avid leftists.

One of Laure's friends, Alexandra, was the wife of the chief of one of the leftist parties. She owned the most exclusive boutique in Verona. When asked if she would be happy wearing one of Mao's drab uniforms, she said, "Certainly not; I'll bring them up to my level."

Everyone was careful not to take a large helping, so at the end of the meal there would still be morsels of meat on the one small roasted chicken she had served as the main course. Here is Laure's recipe:

    1 roasting chicken, about 3 pounds
    2 pounds medium-sized yellow waxy potatoes, peeled and quartered
    12 ounces onion, coarsely chopped
    2 sprigs fresh rosemary
    ¾ cup olive oil
       Salt and freshly ground black pepper to taste
    1 pound unpeeled garlic cloves

Preheat the oven to 425 degrees. Clean chicken and cut into 12 or more pieces. Put chicken, potatoes, onions, and rosemary in a flat roasting pan. Pour olive oil over the mixture. Season with salt and pepper and toss. Scatter garlic cloves on top of the chicken and potatoes. Place the pan in the oven. After 20 minutes, turn the heat down to 375 degrees. Roast for another hour, occasionally turning contents.

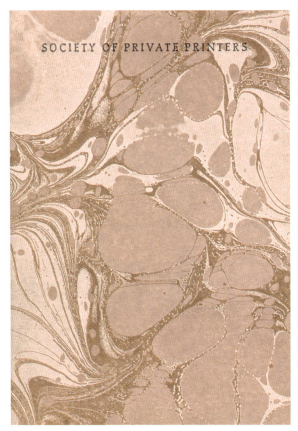

Cover for *Society of Private Printers: Third Exchange*.
(Courtesy of the University of Oregon Libraries.)

Item 18. *Society of Private Printers: Third Exchange: A Display of Presses*

Notes on the Washington press and the PWP pressmark
by Richard-Gabriel Rummonds. With two halftone
reproductions of photographs by Lauren Fishbein
and Richard-Gabriel Rummonds.
12 pages. 13 x 9 cm. 84 copies. 1976.

Society of Private Printers

Shortly after arriving in Verona, I joined the Private Libraries Association. From its membership directory I garnered many of the names of English-speaking collectors who were later to form the nucleus of the PWP mailing list, considerably augmenting the lists I had received from Renzo Sommaruga, Lewis M. Allen, and Harvey Simmonds.

In 1974 David Chambers, the editor of the association's quarterly journal, *The Private Library*, and coordinator of the Society of Private Printers, invited me to participate in the *Third Exchange: A Display of Presses*. Even though I have never considered myself a hobby printer and frequently ranted against many of them for their lack of interest in the technical aspects of the craft, I accepted his invitation. The theme of this international exchange was printers and their equipment, which piqued my curiosity. I was anxious to see what sort of equipment these hobby printers were using, hoping I might uncover at least one with a handpress, and if I did perhaps the owner would be interested in exchanging some technical information with me.

Printing the Keepsake

I set the text for this miniature pamphlet in 9-point Post Mediaeval type, the only time I ever used such a small size for text, and I printed it on offcuts of the Richard de Bas paper. The brief text contains a short explanation of the origin of the PWP pressmark that Golda Fishbein designed:

> It is a calligraphic stylization of the Washington Press's famous figure-4 toggle coupled with a cross section of the platen and the bed.

I finished the printing on May 8, 1976. In June of the previous year, Giorgio Vigna had marbled the papers for the wrappers at the Ponte Pietra studio. My contribution to the *Third Exchange* was distributed along with the other twenty-five by the association as a nicely boxed set. Lauren Fishbein and I took the photographs, one of which shows me incorrectly pulling the bar of the press with bent elbows.

Double-page spread from *Society of Private Printers: Third Exchange.* (Courtesy of the University of Oregon Libraries.)

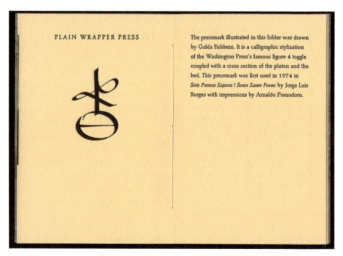

Double-page spread from *Society of Private Printers: Third Exchange.* (Courtesy of the University of Oregon Libraries.)

Item 18. Society of Private Printers: Third Exchange 375

The Washington press as it appears in *Society of Private Printers: Third Exchange*. (Photo by RGR, courtesy of PWP Archives.)

Gabriel pulling the bar of the Washington press in the via Duomo studio, Verona, Italy, 1976. (Photo by Lauren Fishbein, courtesy of PWP Archives.)

Roderick Cave versus the PWP

Roderick Cave, the self-appointed authority on private presses, wrote an article for The Australian Printing Historical Society's *Wayzgoose II*. I have seen only the galley proofs of the article sent to me by James Taylor, the editor in 1987. Cave says that Gabriel Rummonds "has born a grudge ever since we decided in 1970 that ... his Plain Wrapper Press was *not* the private press he claimed it to be." Actually, Cave had decided in 1970, when the PWP was still in New York and under his geographic jurisdiction as an editor of the organization, that my work should not be recorded in *Private Press Books*, the annual checklist issued by the Private Libraries Association. He alluded to a PWP letterhead which indicated that the Press was incorporated – heaven forbid that a private press should ever be incorporated. In 1970 only nonprofit entities could apply for certain types of grants, the types of grants I thought could help me raise seed money for a worthy endeavor: publishing bilingual texts of Latin American authors in fine limited editions. By the time I got around to applying for a grant from the National Endowment for the Arts, however, I was living in Verona, and the regulations had changed. There are some examples of The Plain Wrapper Press, Inc. stationery Cave found so objectionable in the PWP Archives at The New York Public Library. In all my research I have yet to come across any document showing that the Press was actually incorporated. I seem to have acted prematurely when I printed the letterheads.

What Cave apparently found more odious than the Press being incorporated was that I had also listed a board of directors on the stationery. I did this for two reasons: first, to demonstrate that the PWP was more than just a one-man hobby press; and second, to acknowledge the people who were intellectually sustaining me. John Newbauer and Kenneth Pettitt, who were both school friends from Berkeley and had worked with me on *Occident*, were associate editors; Lee Epstein, who had been my lawyer and business manager, was the secretary; Paul Secon, who lived in Copenhagen and knew many authors and artists throughout Europe, was the European consultant; and Mario Aguirre Mac-Kay, who lived in Buenos Aires and was actively helping me locate Latin American authors, was the Latin American consultant. These five continued to lend their support to the PWP long after their names had been dropped from the letterhead.

Item 18. Society of Private Printers: Third Exchange 377

Veronese Fine Press Printers

Once I was in Verona and reporting directly to Anthony Baker, who was responsible for the checklists of publications for European presses, I became the continental correspondent for *Private Press Books* between 1970 and 1977. The Officina Bodoni was the first press I listed in 1970, with updates issued in the following years. In the 1971 issue I included a retrospective checklist of my prior work and a retrospective checklist of the publications of the Officina Chimèrea. The 1972 issue contained a retrospective checklist of Sommaruga's work and another of Editiones Domenicae. These were followed in the 1974 issue by a current listing of the Belacqua Presse. These presses were updated each year in subsequent issues. I am sorry to say that I wasn't able to include Mark Fishbein's work in *Private Press Books*, because I stopped contributing to the publication in 1977, the year that Mark's Stamperia Ponte Pietra issued its first book.

In the introduction to the 1971 issue, the editors (of which Cave was one at the time) acknowledged my contributions on Italian printers.

Giovanni Mardersteig

Giovanni Mardersteig's Officina Bodoni was the only Veronese press listed in *Private Press Books* when I was originally contacted by Anthony Baker in 1971 to keep the bibliographical information on Mardersteig's work current. In addition to Mardersteig and myself, there were six other printers – four Italians, a Frenchman, and an American – actively producing books in Verona in the mid-seventies, all but one using the handpress. I really enjoyed this journalistic assignment, because it gave me an opportunity not only to meet the other printers who lived and worked in Verona, but also to examine their books in detail.

Renzo Sommaruga

When I first took the assignment, Renzo Sommaruga and I were still friends. I had seen his work on many occasions, so I began by compiling a checklist of the sixteen items he had issued through 1970. Renzo's books were characterized by their rich darkness.

He preferred heavier typefaces and often used relief prints, usually linocuts, to illustrate his books. My favorite of his publications was a handsome edition of Gérard Blanchard's *Pellegrini di terraferma* (1964), translated into Italian by Lionello Fiumi, with nineteen linocuts by the author.

Rino Grazioli pulling the bar on Giovanni Mardersteig's Dingler press at the Officina Bodoni, Verona, Italy, 1960s. (Photographer unknown, courtesy of Martino Mardersteig.)

Gino Castiglioni and Alessandro Corubolo at work on their Albion press at the Officina Chimèrea, Verona, Italy, 1987. (Photo by Enzo Bassotto, courtesy of Officina Chimèrea.)

Item 18. Society of Private Printers: Third Exchange 379

Gino Castiglioni and Alessandro Corubolo

When I first moved to Verona, many of the bookstores and art galleries had special sections devoted to private press and illustrated books, making the work of fine printers known to the general public as well as to the specialized collector. While browsing these shelves, I frequently saw the work of two young Veronese men who printed in their spare time, having begun when they were both around eighteen years old. They were Gino Castiglioni, a banker, and Alessandro (Sandro) Corubolo, an IBM executive. Their Officina Chimèrea was the second checklist I compiled. They had been encouraged to print by Franco Riva. Even though their printing didn't have their mentor's technical perfection, it was fresh and exciting. They were particularly fond of English authors and had already published books by W. H. Auden, Stephen Spender, Ezra Pound, and T. S. Eliot. They frequently worked with well-known Italian artists, and their books were noted for their multicolor illustrations, such as the charming edition of Aesop's *La cicala e la formica* (1966) with five linocuts by Alberto Manfredi.

Franco Riva

The most distinguished of the Veronese printers, and by far the most intellectual and skilled, was Franco Riva, who printed and published under the imprint Editiones Dominicae (Sunday Editions). I first met him shortly after my falling out with Renzo early in 1972. Franco, who had gotten in touch with me through Gino and Sandro, had also quarreled with Renzo in the past, and they were no longer on speaking terms. We quickly became close friends, and I would often visit him in his office at the Biblioteca Civica di Verona, where he was the acting director. Franco and I spent hours talking about printing, cataloging, and descriptive bibliography, a subject I would later teach at the University of Alabama. He gave me unrestricted access to the library stacks where the fifteenth- and sixteenth-century books were shelved, as well as to the small reading room that housed the private press collection.

Under Italian law publishers must deposit one copy of each book they issue with the public library in the city in which the book was printed. This accounts for the abundance of fine printing to be found in the Biblioteca Civica di Verona. Franco assumed the position in my life that I had hoped Robert Haas or Giovanni Mardersteig would. He was always available to look at my work and criticize it constructively, but above all he was a man of great taste and culture. The selection of the perfect text was paramount for him. I introduced Franco to Mirek, who made three etchings for Franco's *Inni di Goethe* (1974), a bilingual edition in German and Italian of three hymns by Goethe. Franco favored lighter typefaces, and his books had a warm delicacy that made them very accessible to the eye and touch.

Franco Riva pulling the bar of his Albion press at the Editiones Domenicae, Verona, Italy, 1950s. (Photographer unknown, courtesy of Officina Chimèrea.)

Jacques Vernière

As I mentioned earlier Jacques Vernière came to Verona from Paris in January 1973 with the intention of working as an apprentice at the PWP. Even though I wasn't able to offer him an apprenticeship, he was not discouraged, being single-minded in his quest to become a handpress printer. Shortly after he established his Belacqua Presse – for which Golda also designed a pressmark – he printed a very striking book, *Le Soulèvement de la vie* (1974) by Maurice Clavel, which Jacques and Olaf Idalie lavishly illustrated with full-page prints. In spite of the book's beauty, he had a difficult time selling it because of the text, an ultra-left political tract advocating the elimination of the bourgeoisie, the very people who would be interested in collecting fine printing.

Mark Fishbein

The last of these six printers, Mark Fishbein, my surrogate son, was the only one not using a handpress. He began by screenprinting ephemera and later printing books on a Poco proof press. Mark deserves to be mentioned here despite the fact that he was only fifteen when he printed his first book. He produced four very attractive books illustrated with a variety of graphic techniques in the few years before he went off to Harvard University for his undergraduate education. His first book, commissioned by Harvey Simmonds, was *Marsh Marigolds* (1977) by Gene Baro and illustrated with wood engravings by Clare Leighton. Mark set up shop in the studio at Ponte Pietra, calling his press the Stamperia Ponte Pietra. He modified my Poco proof press by adding a tympan and frisket unit so he could print on dampened paper with perfect registration. His last and most ambitious project was an impressive edition of Horace's *Est modus in rebus* (1980) in Latin with two etchings by Fulvio Testa. Mark's interest in printing continued at Harvard, where he helped resurrect Philip Hofer's press in the basement of the Houghton Library.

I have mentioned only the printers who were actually producing books on a regular basis during this period. Several others had given up printing before I moved to Verona, though I still saw their work on display.

Mark Fishbein demonstrating the screen-printing process to a fellow scout at an Italian Boy Scout camp near Negrar, Italy, 1976. (Photographer unknown, courtesy of Golda Laurens.)

Mark Fishbein in Florence, Italy, 1980, around the time he printed *Est modus in rebus*. (Photo by RGR, courtesy of PWP Archives.)

All of these Veronese printers were consummate artisans with distinct styles of their own, hidden in the shadows and obscured by the fame of "the last of the great handpress printers." In his essay "Un' eredità di Mardersteig: i torchi tipografici a Verona" ("Mardersteig's Heritage: the Handpresses of Verona"), written for an exhibition catalog of Mardersteig's work, Gino Castiglioni points out that all these printers are undeniably linked to Mardersteig by their preference for the handpress – or in Mark Fishbein's case the manually operated proof press – and their steadfastness to his unfaltering devotion to the craft of printing. Castiglioni, recognizing the circumspect world of fine printing even in Italy, goes on to credit my presence in Verona with helping to bring international recognition to these "heirs" when he says, "[Gabriel Rummonds became] a point of reference for private press printers, booksellers, graphic arts students ... and for the American academic world interested in typography" (my translation). I continued to promote their work long after I left Verona.

Item 18. Society of Private Printers: Third Exchange 383

Early in 1972 having met all of the Veronese printers I tried unsuccessfully to convince them to issue a collective monograph commemorating the five-hundredth anniversary of the first book printed in Verona: Robertus Valturius's *De re militari* (Johannes Nicolai de Verona, 1472). Much to my chagrin, I discovered that few of them were on friendly terms with one another, and in most cases their grievances went back many years, making it impossible for us to do anything as a group.

On Being Self-Taught

None of the above, including Mardersteig and myself, had had any formal training; we were all self-taught. For the most part our prior interests had been intellectual or artistic. None of us had been as fortunate as T.J. Cobden-Sanderson, who through Mardersteig had indirectly influenced the Veronese printers. At least Cobden-Sanderson had the benefit of skilled craftsmen trained by Emery Walker to print his books, and the help of William Morris, who presumably taught him how to bind books. It must have been Morris's influence that gave Cobden-Sanderson the confidence to think of himself as a bona fide bookbinder, because in *The Journals of Thomas James Cobden-Sanderson, 1879–1922* (1926) he quotes a comment from Lady Russell about his work as a bookbinder. (Marianne Tidcombe speculates in her book, *The Bookbindings of T. J. Cobden-Sanderson*, that she was the wife of Lord Arthur Russell, one of Cobden-Sanderson's clients.) Lady Russell's remark is widely known:

> I heard of your bookbinding, but I own with regret. With an education such as yours I should like better to hear that you were employing your mind on something which others of less cultivated intellects could not do. I can, however, well understand the interest of being brought into contact with a class of human beings of whom we know little except by the articles they produce.

Without fear of further "rummondizing" Roderick Cave – a term he coined – I should like to point out that he has misquoted the above passage from Cobden-Sanderson's journals in both editions of *The Private Press* (1971) and (1983), substituting "interests" for "intellects." Cave made the same error in an earlier article "Cobden-Sanderson: Bookbinder," which appeared in the Winter 1968 issue of *The Private Library*.

Enrico Tallone

One of the few non-Veronese presses – and there weren't many – I came to know well was run by the Tallone family, Bianca and her sons, Aldo and Enrico. Although not a handpress it embodies all of the virtues of one. I described my visit to the Press, located in Alpignano near Turin, in "A Visit to Bianca Tallone," an article that appeared in the January 1980 issue of *Fine Print*. Enrico, the younger son, and I remained in touch after my visit, and I have followed his career with considerable interest. Having inherited an enthusiasm for printing from his late father, Alberto Tallone, he is following in the tradition of fine press books his father championed. Part of a new generation of Italian fine printers, he has since acquired a Stanhope press and occasionally uses it to print small editions and ephemera.

Enrico Tallone inking a form on his Stanhope press in Alpignano, Italy, 1999. (Photo by RGR, courtesy of PWP Archives.)

Item 18. Society of Private Printers: Third Exchange

Carpaccio (Foccio)
Raw Beef

Serves 6

Carpaccio, also known as *Foccio*, is a nice summer dish of raw beef served cold. It was first served at Harry's Bar in Venice in 1950. Variations on the original recipe are served in most up-scale restaurants in Italy. The following is my version:

For the carpaccio
- 1½ pounds of shell steak, boned and trimmed of all fat, sinew, and gristle
- 6 mushrooms, thinly sliced
- 2 stalks celery, cut into ¼-inch pieces
- Arugula, a few leaves for serving

For the dressing
- ⅓ cup extra-virgin olive oil
- Salt and freshly ground black pepper to taste
- 2 tablespoons lemon juice
- 2 dashes of Worcestershire sauce

Have the butcher cut the meat into the thinnest possible slices without letting it fall apart. The meat should be served chilled. Place a bed of arugula on each salad plate. Arrange slices on top of arugula. Sprinkle mushrooms and celery over the meat. Drizzle the dressing sparingly over the meat.

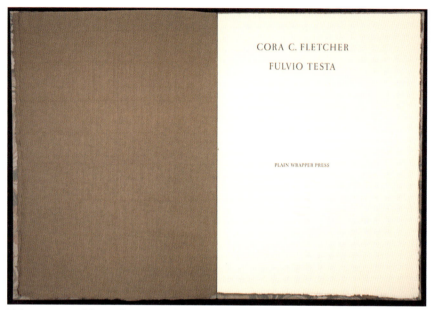

Title-page spread from *The Emperor's Lion*. (Courtesy of the University of Oregon Libraries.)

Item 19. *The Emperor's Lion*

A short story by Cora C. Fletcher [Richard Rummonds]; with a postscript by Richard-Gabriel Rummonds. With an etching by Fulvio Testa.
8 pages. 33.5 x 24.5 cm. 71 copies. 1976.

Back to School

I returned to Berkeley in the spring of 1953, moving into a rooming house at 2415 Haste Street. On the outside I appeared to be more or less conforming, but I was still a rebel on the inside. I became involved with *Occident* and was subsequently named editor of the Spring 1954 issue, which featured a contribution by Cora C. Fletcher.

Cora C. Fletcher

To begin with, who was Cora C. Fletcher? She is not exactly a familiar or popular literary figure. And why did her appearance in *Occident* cause such a scandal?

Constance Fletcher. (Photo by Weldon DeBusk, courtesy of PWP Archives.)

Miss Fletcher came from an illustrious nouveau riche, although fashionably bohemian family. The portrait of her grandmother, Constance Fletcher was acquired in an antique store on lower Shattuck Avenue in Berkeley in the early 1950s and has hung in all of my apartments and houses ever since.

According to the short biographical note that accompanied the publication of her story, "The Emperor's Lion," we know that Cora C. Fletcher was born in San Francisco in 1891. She was connected with the "Exiles," a group of avant-garde writers in Paris in the twenties. Several small volumes of her stories were printed privately by S. T. Comberback's White Albatross Press (think Coleridge). She is best known for her collection of lusty stories of Greek and Byzantine life grouped under the title *The Then and Now Stories*. In 1954 she was living in Mexico.

Miss Fletcher's contribution to the magazine consisted of a letter, an article, and a short story. In her letter of March 1954 to me, she gossiped about many of her acquaintances, some real, some fictional: Isabel Comfort,

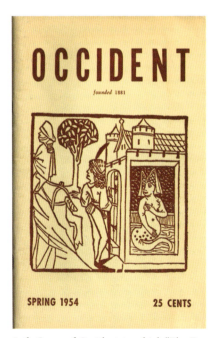 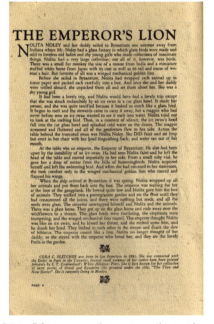

Left: Cover of *Occident*, in which "The Emperor's Lion" first appeared. A note on the inside of the front cover reads, "The cover in no way reflects the contents of the magazine, but is merely a whim of the editor." (Courtesy of PWP Archives.)

Right: The full text of Miss Fletcher's short story in *Occident*. (Courtesy of PWP Archives.)

Item 19. The Emperor's Lion 389

Margaret Shedd, Edward Cox, Djuna Barnes, Gertrude Stein, Elena Gruber, Mary Mary Murphy, Laura Riding, Jackson Allen, Elizabeth Demarest, Frieda Lawrence, Witter Bynner, Isadora Duncan, Mable Dodge, Matilda Broom, Martin DeQuincy, Hillary Hiler, S.T. Comerback, and Kenneth Rexroth.

Her article was on the "tinytinytiny" story. We know from this article that she is not talking about the traditional short story. The "tinytinytiny" story, sometimes compared to the flowery and ornate language of purple prose, is a genre that was predominantly used by female writers such as Cora C. Fletcher, Djuna Barnes, Laura Riding, and Mary Butts, to name a few. Miss Fletcher's story is a prime example of this genre.

Here is the page with the story as it appeared in *Occident*:

Nolita Noley and her daddy sailed to Byzantium one summer away from Indiana where Mr. Noley had a glass factory in which glass birds were made and sold to loveless old ladies and shy young girls who made collections of inanimate things. Nolita had a very large collection; not all of it, however, was birds. There was a small fur monkey the size of a mouse from India and a miniature stuffed white horse from Japan with its coat as well as its tail and mane of woman's hair. But her favorite of all was a winged mechanical golden lion.

Before she sailed to Byzantium, Nolita had wrapped each animal up in tissue paper and packed each carefully into a box. And once she and her daddy were settled aboard, she unpacked them all and set them about her. She was a shy young girl.

It had been a lovely trip, and Nolita would have had a lovely trip except that she was struck melancholy by an ice swan in a cut glass bowl. It made her swoon, and she was quite terrified because it looked so much like a glass bird. It began to melt, and the stewards came to carry it away, but a magpie, who had never before seen an ice swan, wanted to see it melt into water. Nolita tried not to look at the melting bird. Then, in a moment of silence, the ice swan's head fell into the cut glass bowl and splashed cold water on the diners. The magpie screamed and fluttered, and all of the gentlemen flew to her side. Across the table, behind the truncated swan, was Nolita Noley. She DID faint and sat limp but erect in her chair with her head languishing back; and water ran out of her mouth.

At the table was an emperor, the Emperor of Byzantium. He also had been upset by the instability of an ice swan. He had seen Nolita faint, and he left the head of the table and moved imperially to her side. From a small ruby vial, he gave her a drop of nectar from the bills of hummingbirds. Nolita acquired herself and left the swimming bird. And when she had returned to her stateroom, she took comfort only in the winged mechanical golden lion who roared and flapped his wings.

When the ship arrived at Byzantium it was spring. Nolita wrapped up all her animals and put them back into the box. The emperor was waiting for her at the foot of the gangplank. He bowed quite low, and Nolita gave him the box of animals. They walked into a pomegranate garden and ate the fruit until they had consumed all the juices, and there were nothing but seeds, and all the seeds were glass. The emperor unwrapped himself and Nolita and the animals. There was a glass horse. They got up on the glass horse and rode away over the wildflowers to a stream. The glass birds were tintilating, the elephants were trumpeting, and the winged mechanical lion roared. The emperor thought Nolita was like an ice swan and he kissed her throat, and she melted upon him, and he drank her head. They bathed in each other in the stream and drank the dew of hibiscus. The emperor roared like a lion. Nolita no longer thought of her daddy; so she stayed with the emperor, who loved her, and they ate the lovely fruits in the garden.

I was also responsible for the outrageous typographical design of the magazine, in which all the defects of an inexperienced designer were evident in its design. Like so many beginners I went to extremes and nearly destroyed the legibility of the text, for example by setting the poetry in all caps. When Robert Duncan complained, I set his poem in a smaller size of upper- and lowercase type. I also took a special interest in the typography, paper, and printing. This issue was printed by George McClusky at the Professional Press in Berkeley. I insisted that he print the magazine on colored papers. I suppose I was trying to produce an avant-garde magazine like *The Tiger's Eye*. Fortunately, by the time I moved to Verona and started printing on the iron handpress, I had refined my typographic skills.

While editor of the Spring 1954 *Occident*, I met a young aspiring poet named George Ingraham at a rowdy drinking and pot-smoking party. He was

Item 19. The Emperor's Lion 391

already on the junior staff of the magazine but was eager to be part of the *Occident* clique. He asked me to come to his apartment. He was skinny and a little homely in a sexy Midwestern way, but that was part of my attraction to him. The room was sparsely furnished with a twin bed mattress on the floor, a couple of chairs, and a desk. A naked light blub hung from the ceiling. He gave me a small brightly colored plastic ukulele and kissed me on the lips. Even though I desired him, I nearly fainted. With nothing more to say, we went back to the party. I held onto that ukulele for several decades before it was lost in a move.

Similar Writing Styles

Miss Fletcher and I shared an uncanny similarity in writing styles, as exemplified in the next two short excerpts from my own stories. Both were published in earlier issues of *Occident*, misrepresenting their value since I was on the staff of both issues.

The first one, "The Little Boy in the Bell Glass," was published in the Spring 1951 issue:

> There was once a lady. A very prim and proper lady who succumbed to a Victorian young man's desires; so he married her because he was a Victorian young man and she was a prim and proper lady. He took her away to his Victorian house which was covered and choked and cooled by a cream-colored rose brier.

The second one, "Mrs. Bebe Bear and the Announcing Angel's Egg," was published in the Winter 1953 issue:

> Bebe Bear wanted a baby. It wasn't necessary for it to be a boy, for a girl would do if she could not have a boy. Mr. Bear would not hear of boy or girl and so each morning before they got out of their warm bed, he would brush his hand over her forehead and kiss her very gently very and she would know that this was his indication that he loved her and that he had the desire to desire her.

Documenting Cora C. Fletcher

I have always been obsessive, both at work and in life. Not only did I fabricate Cora C. Fletcher, I wrote the letters attributed to her that began arriving for me at the *Occident* office. My friend Alcyone O'Hanrahan, who lived in Mexico City, sent them to me.

Never one to do things halfway, I thoroughly documented her literary career by inserting forged entries for her works, as well as cross-references to them, into the card catalog, to which I had easy access because I worked part time in the library. Library pages were frantically searching the shelves for her missing books. One English professor remembered having read her books in college and was planning to add *The Then and Now Stories* to his reading list.

In the Morrison Room I found a copy of an oversized book of original photographs called something like *The One Hundred Most Beautiful Women in the World,* limited to one hundred copies. I was able to "borrow" one of the photos, which I claimed was Miss Fletcher.

The fate of that photograph is uncertain, although it was restored to the book before I left Berkeley. It was very similar to this one of Djuna Barnes.

Djuna Barnes, place unknown, about 1921. (Photographer unknown.)

Drumming Up Interest in the Spring 1954 *Occident*

Securing Miss Fletcher for *Occident* was considered a great literary coup. She would certainly add prestige to the magazine and broaden the scope of its readership. I also thought it would increase the circulation.

On April 16, 1954, the *Daily Californian* ran an article describing some of the highlights in the forthcoming issue of *Occident,* including a mention of the "Tinytinytiny Story" and an evaluation of it written by Cora C. Fletcher.

Item 19. The Emperor's Lion

Trouble Brewing

By early May 1954 things were getting out of hand at the *Occident* office, and they eventually imploded just a few days before the magazine went on sale. On May 5, at a noon meeting of the publications board, Edwin Cohen, the manager of *Occident*, revealed that Cora C. Fletcher was a hoax, and furthermore that I had fabricated her. There was pandemonium throughout the room. I upended the conference table and stormed out of the room. Again, the nagging question was raised: who is this person called Cora C. Fletcher? I could only respond as Flaubert did to Amélie Bosquet when she questioned him about the origin of Madame Bovary: *"C'est moi!"*

Edwin Cohen

But more important: Who was this dastardly Edwin Cohen? He was a business major with theatrical aspirations. I first met him in November 1953 during rehearsals for a campus production of *The Affected Ladies* by Molière, for which I had designed the sets and costumes. He played one of the valets who is pressed into impersonating his master in order to teach the affected young ladies a lesson in decorum. While discussing costumes Edwin said, "Any color but pink." I must not have been listening.

During the run of the play, we both served on the editorial board of the Winter 1953 issue of *Occident*. Even though I wasn't in love with Edwin, we became sexually involved, getting together at my place to fool around.

Edwin Cohen in costume for *The Affected Ladies*. (Photo by Richard Capp, courtesy of PWP Archives.)

On one of these occasions Miss Fletcher unexpectedly materialized. I was stewing; I had failed to put together a symposium on the "tinytinytiny story." I still had my heart set on having one in the Spring 1954 issue. All of a sudden, a solution came to me. I said to Edwin as I pointed a finger at Constance Fletcher's portrait, "Her granddaughter, Cora C. Fletcher, is going to send me a story and an article." "But she doesn't exist," Edwin reminded me. "Then I'll invent her!" We never discussed Miss Fletcher again. Only two other people, Jack Spicer and Kenneth Pettitt, knew the truth about her origin. They became conspirators. Jack even helped edit her article and volunteered to impersonate her if an occasion arose requiring her physical presence in the Bay Area.

All during the spring semester, Edwin and I quarreled over editorial policy. At one point I was so angry with him that I removed his name from the magazine's masthead. The situation escalated, culminating in that unfortunate publications board meeting.

Several hours later I was still fuming at Edwin's effrontery and betrayal. Even though I was on my way to San Francisco to attend a semi-formal dinner party given by one of my high-school girlfriends, I stopped by his apartment. We got into a terrible fight. He was actually better at fighting than I was. I ended up with a black eye and a bloodied lip. At one point he put his hands around my throat and was choking me. I bit one of his fingers almost to the bone. I left him screaming and hurried off to San Francisco. Among the guests at the dinner was a journalist from the *San Francisco Chronicle*. When he saw my black eye and bloodied lip, he asked me jokingly if it was something that might make the papers. I chuckled and said, "No, no, just a personal misunderstanding."

The next day the *Oakland Tribune* ran a short article headlined: "U.C. Editor Bites Aide's Finger in Literary Spat." The article mentioned that "a long-brewing clash of artistic temperaments in the top echelon of the University of California's literary magazine ended in a fight last night in which the editor bit the manager on the finger, police reported." Doctors repaired the damaged digit with a Band-Aid.

A few days later I was fixing lunch for Kenneth and myself at the Purple Place when the phone rang. Kenneth answered it. It was Officer Sam Chapman at the Berkeley Police Station. I lowered my voice and said, "Hello." He wanted to hear my side of the story. I told him that Edwin had made a pass at me, and that's when I hit him. Chapman said, "No need to come down to the station. That sort of thing happens all the time around here."

A Mysterious Poem by S. T. Comberback

When reviewing the Spring 1954 issue for this memoir, I discovered a poem by S. T. Comberback in a section of short poems titled "Sombras."

> Coleridge adenoidal
> Kubla snuffle
> wheeze the Kahn
> tore at himself
> with the good brain,
> left his shapeless
> face outside the dream
> took the soft way
> out of the flesh.

I don't recall who wrote it, but I certainly didn't. Stylistically, I would guess that it was probably written by Kenneth.

Kenneth Pettitt, Seattle, WA, 1953. (Photographer unknown, courtesy of Clara Pettitt.)

The Ensuing Scandal

Why was the appearance of this story so scandalous? I certainly didn't set out to perpetrate such a hoax. I had only wanted to publish a symposium of avant-garde women writers from the twenties and had written to at least a dozen of them. Only one, Laura Riding, responded, and she was retired – living in a trailer in Florida. She did not want to get involved in any more literary controversies. I had only asked them to defend the genre I termed the "tinytinytiny story." Discouraged, I sought out my friend Witter Bynner, a chronicler of the avant-garde writers of that period, who happened to be visiting Berkeley in the winter of 1953. Seeing my disappointment, he tried to cheer me up by telling me stories about each of the women I had invited to participate in the symposium. He had known all of them personally and loved to talk about them. His anecdotes became the stimuli that spawned Cora C. Fletcher.

It was Witter who supplied me with most of the gossip in her letter. There is a mixture of real and fictional people mentioned in it. Of course, Djuna Barnes, Mable Dodge, Laura Riding, and Gertrude Stein were real and famous authors. Others in this august company sounded like real people – Jackson Allen, Elizabeth Demarest, Martin DeQuincy. And then there are the clues that something is not quite right in bohemia. S.T. Comberback was the name Samuel Taylor Coleridge assumed when he enlisted in the Fifteenth Regiment in 1793. Does the White Albatross ring a bell? In the "Rime of the Ancient Mariner," Coleridge wrote, "Water, water, every where, / Nor any drop to drink."

However, in the end, after all the brouhaha surrounding Miss Fletcher had died down, I was expelled from the university and eventually went on to become a private press printer.

Richard, the summer after he was expelled from the University of California at Berkeley, Cazadero Lodge, CA, 1954. (Photographer unknown, courtesy of PWP Archives.)

Item 19. The Emperor's Lion 397

The PWP Edition of *The Emperor's Lion*

This edition of T*he Emperor's Lion* included the story and the biographical note that had been used in *Occident*, as well as a new postscript, which best sums up the consequences of my foolhardy actions:

> The story you have just read caused a small clamor when it was first published in 1954 in the student literary magazine "Occident" (of which I was then the editor) because the fabled *Exile* from San Francisco Cora C. Fletcher had been found alive, living in bohemian clutter and seclusion in Mexico. She was immediately in great demand by the San Francisco and Berkeley literati who added her hard-to-come-by books to their reading lists of twentieth-century authors and by museums which wanted her to give readings of her precious, little stories and to *gossip*; however, she never appeared. She never appeared simply because she never really existed except in the mind of her creator, the printer of this Quartus. The eventual discovery of the "hoax" was sufficient for the Dean of Men to ask for the perpetrator's withdrawal from the university, whereupon I found myself without a college degree. In the twenty-two years since, I have done many things which never seemed to require one. Probably the most decisive of these was to start the Plain Wrapper Press, which I did just ten years ago [1966] in Quito, Ecuador. This Quartus is to celebrate the Press's anniversary by commemorating the incident that committed me to a life dedicated to art and eventually to hand printing: my expulsion from the University of California at Berkeley.

The printing of this project was rife with hysteria and melodrama. There was a lot of tension festering between Giorgio (Giorgiolino) Vigna and me.

Giorgiolino moved in with me shortly after Ariel Parkinson's departure in February 1975. His mother and father, who were quite close in age to me, were traditional Italian parents and not particularly pleased with the arrangement. It was only after the second time Giorgiolino dramatically tried to commit suicide that they consented to let him live with me – on the condition that we have Sunday dinner with them every week. Once his family got to know me, I think they actually came to like me.

Giorgiolino graduated from high school that spring, leaving him with a lot of time on his hands. In an effort to keep him occupied – since he wasn't interested in printing or, as José Noe had been, in housework – I introduced

Giorgio Vigna and Gabriel, Pesaro, Italy, 1975. (Photographer unknown, courtesy of PWP Archives.)

him to the pleasures of marbling paper, with the idea that he might be useful around the press and possibly take Bonnie Walker's place as a source of decorated papers for PWP editions. He turned out to be one of those rare geniuses whose talents, once unleashed, surprise even the most indifferent observer. Quickly mastering the techniques of marbling, he began to elaborate on them. His intrinsic good sense of color made even the most mundane patterns come alive. He began marbling paper in the kitchen, adding his vibrant spatters to those that Mirek and I had left on the walls a few years earlier. As his production increased it became more difficult to prepare meals. Since the studio at Ponte Pietra was empty, we decided to move his marbling activity there – where it remained until we parted company the following year.

Giorgiolino produced papers faster than I could think of uses for them; so to provide him with a bit of pocket money and a sense of independence, I showed him how to make desk accessories incorporating his papers. These

Item 19. The Emperor's Lion

items were a great success, and he was soon selling them in boutiques and fine stores throughout Europe and the United States.

A Trip to Turkey

It was impossible in those days to separate my professional life from my private one. With the studio just inside the front door and its contents spreading into every nook and cranny of the apartment, we were, in effect, living in a print shop. During the time I was with Giorgiolino, I had sex only with him; I had given up my nocturnal prowling.

I was distracted by the proximity of the studio. Whenever Giorgiolino and I returned home after an evening out I couldn't walk past the open doors to the studio without automatically gravitating toward the press, despite the late hour. Invariably, I would find some little task that needed my immediate attention. I would say to him, "You go ahead, I'll join you in a minute. I just need to check on. . . ." Hours later when I crawled into bed, my amorous overtures would be coldly received. I realized the solution was to have a separate location for my work, which at the time was out of the question financially. An immediate but temporary solution was to go off somewhere together, far, far away from Verona and the studio.

As early as March 1975, I mentioned the possibility of going to Turkey that summer, but the trip was postponed until September. My friend Dietrich Leube in Munich, a political journalist for a leftist publication, had traveled extensively in Turkey on assignment for his magazine, and during one of his visits he had taken a long-term lease on a two-room house a miller had constructed at the edge of his millpond. Dietrich was never able to use it because shortly thereafter, he was declared *persona non grata* by the Turkish government. The little house was unoccupied most of the time, so Dietrich offered it to me. I eagerly accepted his invitation, because I had done little traveling outside Northern Italy and had never had a real vacation. I was also writing a book on the unique problems of compiling bibliographies of private press books, and I looked upon this as an ideal opportunity to finish my manuscript, as well as to spend some carefree time with Giorgiolino.

Dietrich Leube's House in Turkey

I invited Fulvio Testa, a seasoned traveler, to join us. On August 30, 1975, we sailed from Venice to Izmir, where we took a bus to the village nearest the house, then completed the final leg of the trip by taxi. Like all good Italians traveling abroad, our suitcases were stuffed with pasta, rice, cheese, olive oil, and cans of tomatoes and tuna – all the things we thought we would need for our meals. In addition to the foodstuffs, I brought my Olivetti portable typewriter and a small reference library. From Dietrich's description of the house I didn't realize how isolated it was.

The setting was idyllic but primitive. Water buffalo and camels frequently came to cool off in the millpond. The house itself was absolutely devoid of amenities. It had no running water, but it did have some semblance of illumination emanating from naked electric bulbs at the end of ratty wires. We cooked on a portable camp stove and used the millpond as our cooler. The isolation of the house would not have presented any problems to Dietrich, who had a luxurious Volvo, but for three poor travelers like us, the 30 kilometers (about 18 miles) to the nearest village often seemed insurmountable. With no vehicle, just supplementing our daily food supply became a major chore.

Tensions soon began to mount between Giorgiolino and Fulvio. At every turn Giorgiolino felt compelled to test my indulgence like a naughty child, and I humored him like a permissive parent – much to Fulvio's exasperation. Eventually, Fulvio took off on his own, leaving Giorgiolino and me alone to resolve our personal drama. Every few days we would walk up to the highway and either hitchhike or flag down a careening taxi to go into Marmaris, where we could buy provisions.

Gabriel, worn out and looking like a refugee from a concentration camp, in Dietrich Leube's house near Marmaris, Turkey, 1975. (Photo by Giorgio Vigna, courtesy of PWP Archives.)

Item 19. The Emperor's Lion

Carlo Nanni and Paula Geldenhuys

One day while browsing in a rug shop, we overheard a couple speaking Italian and were drawn into their conversation. As it turned out Carlo Nanni, one of those smartly uniformed policemen – a Florentine *vigile urbano* who directed traffic near the Ponte Vecchio – and Paula Geldenhuys, his South African girlfriend, were traveling through Turkey on a motorcycle. They were as surprised as we were to find Italians in this isolated seaside resort.

Giorgiolino and I invited them to come back to our place for a real Italian lunch. We flagged down a taxi, and with our groceries in the front seat and Paula between Giorgiolino and me in the back, we tore out of town, with Carlo trying to keep up with us on his black and yellow Ducati motorcycle. We were so engaged in conversation that we forgot to keep an eye on Carlo. When finally we turned around to check on him, we were horrified not to see him behind us.

Poor Carlo had been delayed when he ran into a swarm of bees from some beehives that had fallen off a flatbed truck as it crashed over an embankment. He eventually caught up with us, smarting from bee stings and annoyed that he had lost Paula's helmet. At last we arrived at the house, and I prepared lunch while Giorgiolino and the guests took a dip in the cool water of the millpond. By a remarkable coincidence we had reservations on the same ship for the return trip to Italy, so we would be seeing each other again soon.

Paula Geldenhuys in the millpond at Dietrich Leube's house near Marmaris, Turkey, 1975. (Photo by Carlo Nanni, courtesy of the photographer.)

Exploring Turkey

There was no reason to stay any longer at the mill. I wasn't getting any work done, and Giorgiolino was even more restless than he had been in Verona, so we decided to tour Turkey. We traveled by bus, eventually meeting up with Fulvio at Pamukkale, the site of an ancient thermal spa. From there we went on to Konya and Kayseri, where we bought kilims and other handicrafts. We stayed in off-the-beaten-path hotels and inns. In one of them the sheets were changed only once a month, and we arrived toward the end of the month. Fortunately we had our own blankets, so we were able to strip the beds and curl up in relative comfort for the night. One of the highlights of the trip was a visit to the ruins at Ephesus, where one of the stones in the pavement bears an inscription that directs men down the road to a prostitute.

Carlo and Paula met up with Giorgiolino, Fulvio, and me at the dock a week later, and the five of us departed for Italy. Our projected two months in Turkey had been trimmed to three weeks. The voyage back to Italy was probably the most memorable part of the trip because I established a deep and lasting friendship with Carlo and Paula, who married the following year, and whose son Giordano is my godchild.

Printing the Book

Going to Turkey really didn't accomplish much. I didn't get any work done on my manuscript, and Giorgiolino was still sulking. Once home I had to make up for the time lost at the press, even though a lot of the work on the project had been completed before our trip. The text had been set in Horizon Light, corrected, and ready to print.

Fulvio had finished the illustration, an etching, which has always been a favorite of mine. Fulvio perfectly captured the Byzantine spirit of the story in his depiction of the winged mechanical lion. This was the first of three projects we worked on together.

In May 1976, before the trip to Turkey, I helped Loris pull the etchings at Luciano Cristini's. I was very disappointed in the results. Luciano had not steel-plated the plates, so the image gradually grew lighter with each succeeding print. Loris also mixed the colored ink from scratch each day, so the color was inconsistent from one set of sheets to the next. Luciano really had a significant negative impact on the project. I never used him again.

Item 19. The Emperor's Lion 403

Fulvio Testa, Pesaro, Italy, 1975. (Photo by RGR, courtesy of PWP Archives.)

Gabriel inking a form in the via Duomo studio, Verona, Italy, 1975. (Photo by Giorgio Vigna, courtesy of PWP archives.)

Though I continually tried to print this book, I wasn't able to achieve the desired results with the Fabriano Roma paper until much later. It was difficult to concentrate on this project. I kept setting it aside because at the same time I was frantically trying to finalize plans for the next three titles, without much success. I'm not sure why I decided to use the Fabriano Roma paper for this Quartus, considering all the trouble I had had printing *A Lost Poem* on it. Being a heavily sized laid paper, it had to be extra damp to pick up the intricate details on the plate when the etchings were pulled. After that I had to redampen the sheets and then dry them down, leaving just the right amount of moisture in the paper. If they were too damp the black ink would bleed through the paper; if too dry it wouldn't print with the razor-sharp precision I wanted. The printing was finally completed on August 26, 1976.

Here is the first page of the story with Fulvio's etching. As you can see, the typography of the *Occident* and the PWP editions of the story varied greatly. In the latter edition, the typography is understated, refined. It reflects the influence of my mentor, Jack Werner Stauffacher.

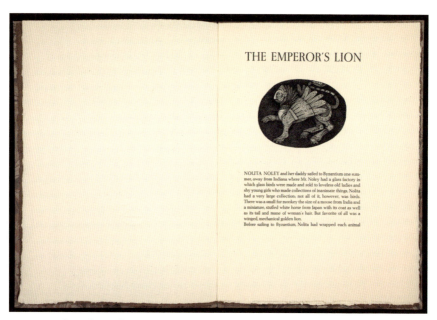

First page of text from *The Emperor's Lion*. (Courtesy of the University of Oregon Libraries.)

Item 19. The Emperor's Lion

Trip to England

Giorgiolino and I went to England for a week in mid-June 1976 to attend Hoyt Rogers's graduation from Magdalen College at the University of Oxford. The festivities included a private performance of Gluck's *Orfeo ed Euridice*. Hoyt had stayed with us in Verona the summer before, along with Nicholas Callaway, the photographer and publisher. They had been sent to us by Harvey Simmonds, who had commissioned Nicholas to take photographs of the fourteenth-century Virgin of Verona statue in the fountain in Piazza delle Erbe. While Giorgiolino and I were in Oxford, an incident took place that precipitated the end of my relationship with him. He fell in love with another of the guests, a dashing young man from Cambridge University. I have always been an over-possessive and jealous lover and couldn't bear the thought of Giorgiolino being in love with anyone else, even though he chose at the time to postpone consummating his flirtation until he could visit the lad alone in Cambridge – which he never did.

Hoyt Rogers and Gabriel at Magdalen College, Oxford University, England, 1976. (Photo by Giorgio Vigna, courtesy of PWP Archives.)

The Bitter End

As in all affairs that involve the maturation of a younger partner, Giorgiolino eventually outgrew his need for me. On the night of July 16, shortly after our return from England, we exchanged heated words and got into a fistfight, which left Giorgiolino's frail body bruised and bloody. I was so angry that I threw him out of the apartment. Of course, my rash decision caused me a lot of pain. I was depressed and despondent for the next three or four weeks, unable to concentrate on the printing of *The Emperor's Lion*. It is curious that the only physical fights I can remember were related to this text. First, there was the fight with Edwin Cohen in 1954, and then this one with Giorgiolino.

Later that night, reflecting on what I had done – I had completely lost my temper – I decided that it was time to break off our relationship. For a long time afterwards, I harbored such bitter feelings toward him that I wasn't even sure I would use the beautiful papers he had made for the book. In my dictatorial way, reminiscent of the Turkish government's ban on Dietrich, I declared Giorgiolino *persona non grata* at the PWP. In the end, however, I did use his papers.

Cover for *The Emperor's Lion*. (Courtesy of the University of Oregon Libraries.)

Item 19. The Emperor's Lion 407

While preparing this episode for my memoir, I realized what a dreadful, rather nasty, self-centered, and arrogant person I was in the two periods covered by these events. I hope that in the succeeding years I have mellowed.

Years later, when I was in the habit of stopping at unfamiliar bars for a glass of wine, I ran into Giorgiolino's sister, Laura, who was with her husband, Gianni Signorini. They were with friends and asked me to join them. Laura introduced me as her ex-brother-in-law.

What Went Wrong?

In a way, it is fitting that this particular book should be enmeshed in all the melodrama recounted in this chapter. Where had I gone wrong? What made the circumstances surrounding the publication of this story so unsavory that my expulsion in June 1954 was the administration's only alternative? Any future enrollment was subject to administrative approval; my petition for readmission was denied in 1955.

Life After Giorgiolino

Below is the last photograph of me with Giorgiolino. From then on I was on my own. Luckily by the summer of 1976 the PWP had become a popular stopping-off place for bibliophiles visiting Italy. The Press was beginning to acquire some of the ambiance I had admired so much at the Greenwood Press. I had

Gabriel and Giorgio Vigna at Lake Garda, Italy, 1976. (Photo by Mario Lencia, courtesy of PWP Archives.)

an excellent reference library, authors and artists often dropped by for a chat and a glass of wine, and I was even getting a few books printed.

In mid-September 1976 Harvey Simmonds guided the participants of Dr. Robert L. Leslie and Abe Lerner's Typophiles World Printing Museum Tour around Verona. Abe, who had given Golda Fishbein her first book jacket assignments, became an avid PWP collector and a tireless champion of the Press, often defending it in print against its detractors. There were about thirty-eight in the group, including several friends from the publishing world such as Mary Ahern, Warren Chappell, Antonie Eichenberg, Alice Koeth, Bert Waggott, and Lili Wronker, as well as a few librarians and publishers, including Catherine Brody from Queen's College, Dale Roylance from Yale University, and the Peter Pauper Press publisher Edna Beilenson. Golda and I decided to fix an impromptu buffet lunch for them, which everyone seemed to enjoy, because it was frequently mentioned in many of the later published accounts of their trip. It wasn't unusual in those days to find sixteen to twenty people sitting around the marble-topped table for meals. Commenting on these get-togethers, Mark Fishbein once said, "You can always tell when Gabriel is miffed with you – he puts you between two people whose languages you don't speak."

With The Typophiles was a young man named Donald Sigovich. We had been corresponding since he was a student in the early seventies at Rochester Institute of Technology. Meeting Donald in person was an unexpected pleasure for me, and his unabashed enthusiasm for my work later led to my association with the new Limited Editions Club, where he was the art director.

On the day The Typophiles departed, I arranged for them to see a display of books printed by the Veronese printers. Individual tables were set up in one of the reception rooms at the Albergo Due Torri, where The Typophiles were staying. Though it wasn't really a cooperative event, at least all the presses were represented and most of the printers were in attendance. Among the PWP books on view was *The Emperor's Lion*, a simple eight-page book that after more than a year's work was finally completed. Though I didn't realize it at the time, I was on the verge of emerging from the quagmire of inertia that had prevented me from being more productive.

Item 19. The Emperor's Lion   409

Risotto alla Pilota
Risotto with Sausage

Serves 8

Fulvio Testa was very fond of driving into the countryside for a light supper. One of his favorite meals was risotto alla pilota, a specialty from one of the rice-producing areas around Verona. Each year after the final harvest, the owners would prepare this dish as a "thank you" for the workers.

For the rice
- 11 ounces water
- ¼ teaspoon salt
- ½ tablespoon butter
- 8 ounces Vialone Nano rice

For the risotto
- 5 tablespoons butter, divided
- 1 ounce shallots, finely chopped
- 6½ ounces pork sausage meat
- 2 dashes of nutmeg
- Salt and freshly ground black pepper to taste
- 2 ounces Parmigiano Reggiano cheese

The rice: Put water, salt, and butter in a saucepan, cover and bring to a boil. Spread rice evenly over the bottom of the pan and cover. When water comes to a boil, turn the heat down to medium low. Cook for 8 minutes. Remove from the heat. Place a couple of paper towels between the rim of the pan and the cover and let sit for 15 minutes.

The risotto: Melt 1 tablespoon of the butter in a large saucepan. When butter starts to bubble, add shallots and stir until clear. Add sausage meat, browning it like hamburger. Add the remaining butter, nutmeg, salt, and pepper. When rice is ready, add half of it to the sausage mixture. Stir in half the cheese. Add the rest of rice to the sausage mixture. Stir in the remainder of the cheese and mix until well blended. Serve with additional cheese sprinkled on top.

Title-page spread from *Will and Testament: A Fragment of Biography.* (Courtesy of the University of Oregon Libraries.)

Item 20. *Will and Testament: A Fragment of Biography*

A short story by Anthony Burgess.
With eight multicolor screenprints and a
letterpress ornament on the title page by Joe Tilson.
Enclosed in an oak box with five decorative
panels by the artist on the lid.
44 pages. 38.5 x 28.5 cm. 1977.

Another Deluxe Book

Bruno Herlitzka at the Marlborough Galleria d'Arte in Rome contacted me in February 1975 about the possibility of collaborating on another deluxe book. The Borges/Pomodoro project had been such an enormous artistic and financial success for the gallery thlo-res.at he was hoping we could put together something similar that would be equally rewarding. Remembering that I had once mentioned in passing that Anthony Burgess had offered to send me an original manuscript, Bruno thought I should pursue him for a text. Carla Panicali, the director of the gallery, and he would concentrate on getting one of their artists – Francis Bacon was their first choice – to illustrate it. Both Burgess and Bacon were very marketable in Italy. I wrote to Bacon in March 1976, suggesting a collaboration.

Anthony Burgess

I met Anthony in New York in the late 1960s, having been introduced to him by Robert Gottlieb, who at that time was the head of Alfred A. Knopf. Even though we had not kept in touch, I wrote to him in May 1975, not hesitating to remind him of his earlier offer to send me a manuscript. He responded by inviting me to visit him in Bracciano, a small town northwest of Rome, where he was living. He was already familiar with my design work. He had seen *Passions and Ancient Days* (1971) by C.P. Cavafy that I had designed for The Dial Press at Edmund Keeley's house in 1971. The book's design had inspired him to review it for *The New York Times*.

In August I went by train to see him, taking along a copy of the Borges/Pomodoro book to illustrate the type of project I had in mind. Anthony was immediately excited about the collaboration, so we started tossing ideas for the text back and forth. I had read his biography of Shakespeare, as well as his Shakespearean fantasy, *Nothing Like the Sun* (1975), and assumed he probably had a lot of unused research material left over from these two works. I wasn't necessarily looking for another story about Shakespeare, although I did like the idea of having it set in that period, perhaps with Christopher Marlowe as the principal character. Anthony later wrote *A Dead Man in Deptford* (1995), a novel with Marlowe as the protagonist. Before leaving, I reiterated that my suggestions were intended only as springboards; the final choice, of course, would be his. As it turned out Anthony did write another story about Shakespeare. Even though Marlowe is mentioned in the story, his role is quite negligible. *Will and Testament: A Fragment of Biography* became the first text commissioned from a major author to be published at the PWP.

Will and Testament

One of my favorite parts of the story tells how Shakespeare, despondent because he had not been asked to help translate the King James Bible of

Double-page spread with the 46th Psalm as it appears in *Will and Testament: A Fragment of Biography*. (Courtesy of the University of Oregon Libraries.)

Item 20. Will and Testament 413

1611, contrived to insert a cryptogram of his name in the 46th Psalm, one of the few that Ben Jonson had secretly given him to versify. In the story, Shakespeare – who was forty-six years old at the time – changed "tremble," the forty-sixth word from the beginning, to "shake," and "sword," the forty-sixth word from the end, to "spear."

> *God is our refuge and strength: a very present helpe in, trouble.*
> *Therefore will not we feare, though the earth be removed:*
> *and though the mountaines be caried into the midst of the sea.*
> *Though the waters thereof roare and be troubled,*
> *though the mountaines ~~tremble~~ with the swelling thereof.* **shake/**
> *Selah.*

>   . . .

> *He maketh warres to cease unto the end of the earth:*
> *hee breaketh the bow, and cutteth the ~~sword~~ in sunder,* **spear/**
> *he burneth the chariot in the fire.*
> *Be stil, and know that I am God: I will bee exalted among the heathen,*
> *I will be exalted in the earth. The Lord of hosts is with us;*
> *the God of Jacob is our refuge.*
> *Selah.*

I had a difficult time finding a copy of the Bible in English. All of mine were in Spanish. Then I thought, who in Verona would have an English Bible? Who else but those pesky Mormon missionaries? I went to where they lived and knocked on the door. One of them responded from behind the closed door. I explained in English that I was looking for a copy of the King James Bible. They told me to go away. Eventually The British Library sent me a photo print of the page I needed.

Anthony worked incredibly fast. The manuscript needed practically no editing at all, and most of the words I queried had either been invented by the author or were archaic. There was enough Post Mediaeval type to set only sixteen pages at a time. I sent him the page proofs in installments. Golda Fishbein installed a telephone in her apartment in the spring of 1977, so Anthony could reach me there with any last-minute corrections. It was only after the whole story had been printed that Anthony – despite what we thought had been careful editing on our part – found a textual error. He had inadvertently switched Francis Beaumont's and John Fletcher's surnames, and, to make matters worse, the type for these pages had already been redistributed. We could reset and reprint the four-page signature, but Anthony said it wasn't worth the trouble. Inventive as always, and taking the problem completely in his stride, he composed an erratum in the form of a seventeenth-century riddle/epigraph.

> Confounde *Fayrhill & Arrowman* (as they be
> oft confounded); let *Iohn Benson* lay brickes
> & *Ianglespurre* lay egges on his *Warwickshire*
> dungheape. There is more honest bawdrie
> in the Word of God.
>> *Giue You Good Den My Maisters*
>>> 1612, 31.2.

The mix-up in surnames can be found in the second line on page 31 of the PWP edition. Fortunately there was a blank leaf in the front matter I could use for the errata. I had reserved two pages for a rather byzantine introductory note I had written, the tone of which was somewhat reminiscent of Walter Hamady's rambling Perishable Press colophons. When I replaced my introductory note with Anthony's errata, I definitively put an end to my self-indulgent practice of tacking my own words onto another author's text.

Looking for the Right Artist

From the beginning the quest for an artist did not progress smoothly. Carla and Bruno had not been able to convince Bacon to illustrate the book. He claimed, not untruthfully, that he was a painter, not a printmaker. I started following other leads. My association with Arnaldo Pomodoro had brought me into contact with the directors of many prestigious art galleries throughout the world. One of these was Brigitte de Almeida Lopes, director of the Swiss affiliate of the Marlborough conglomerate of galleries. Carla Panicali had introduced us at an art fair in Basel, and I occasionally visited Brigitte in Zurich. She, too, had had great success selling the Borges/Pomodoro book, so she was now anxious to help me find an artist for the Burgess text, hoping I would select one she represented. In particular, she championed Fernando Botero, a Colombian artist whose work I greatly admired, but I felt that only an English artist could really do justice to this text. I had an

Item 20. Will and Testament   415

ulterior motive for not wanting to use Botero for this project: I was saving
him, hoping some day to bring him together with Julio Cortázar, another
Argentine author I wanted to publish.

Getting Away from Giorgio Vigna

I needed a little time away from Giorgio (Giorgiolino) Vigna, so early in
October 1975, just a few months after returning from Turkey, Golda and I
went to England for a few days – the first of several trips I would take before
this project was completed. Golda and I set aside one day to call on John
and Rosalind Randle at the Whittington Press in Andoversford. I had seen
a notice somewhere that John was offering printing workshops, and I
wanted to see firsthand what they were about, since I was seriously considering signing up for one. While I enjoyed the visit immensely, I was disappointed to find that John didn't have much to offer me in the way of
expertise on the handpress. He had a young apprentice named Tim Jollands,
whom I lusted after and tried to entice to come to Verona. I also visited the
St. Bride Printing Library, where I met Peter VanWingen, who much later
would help me get started on my book *Nineteenth-Century Printing Practices
and the Iron Handpress*.

Joe Tilson

My main mission in England, however, was to talk to Anthony Reichardt at
Marlborough Fine Art in London. Even though he had not been able to
change Bacon's mind, Tony remained enthusiastic about a collaboration and
suggested several other artists the gallery represented, including Graham
Sutherland and Victor Pasmore. Another of their artists was Joe Tilson,
whose work very much appealed to me.

   I didn't meet Joe until the following June, but after I returned to Verona,
we were frequently in touch by phone, which was a source of amazement
to Joe, because I didn't install a telephone at the PWP until 1980. Normally,
long-distance calls had to be placed through the switchboard at either the
phone company's downtown office or the train station, but that was before
I found a way to make free calls. Golda was employed by the Italian telephone company to teach English to its international operators. When she
had her appendix removed in December 1975, I substituted for her. I had
the operators practice placing overseas calls from the "live" phones on their

desks. Later, when I was no longer teaching, all I had to do was go to a public phone, dial the operator, and ask for one of my former students, who would then connect me anywhere in the world. The first call I made to Joe was in March 1976. Just before settling on him, I was making calls around the globe trying to track down David Hockney, who had once said he would be interested in collaborating with me on a project. Even with all the help from the phone company, I never did get through to Hockney.

Joe frequently came to central Italy to work at his country home. Long after this book was finished, the Tilson family continued to stop off for a few days in Verona on their way to and from Cortona. At the time Joe was probably a better choice in terms of the book's commercial success than either Bacon or Hockney, because he was represented by Studio Marconi in Milan and the Marlborough Galleria d'Arte in Rome, and his work sold just as well in Italy as it did in England. Ironically, however, I ended up publishing this book without any financial support from either of these galleries.

Financing the Project Myself

Instead of arranging to give the galleries a very low price on the books in exchange for payment in advance, as I had done with the Borges/Pomodoro book (on which I ultimately lost money), I decided to forego the advance payment and sell the books upon publication at the regular gallery discount. This was perfectly acceptable to the galleries, but no one foresaw the changes that would occur before publication. Joe left Marconi soon after the printing started, and the Marlborough galleries were involved in a huge international art scandal. Neither gallery ordered a single copy. Having gone into the project believing that I would again have their support, I wasn't prepared to finance it alone. I got deeper and deeper into debt, some of which I was still paying off long after the Press closed. I swore I would never publish another deluxe book. I could neither afford the costs nor manage the stress associated with producing such expensive books.

PWP Fabriano Paper

Hoping to avoid the problems I experienced with the paper on the Borges/Pomodoro book, I decided to commission Fabriano to make a paper appropriate for handpress printing. The sheet was based on a pre-war paper I had seen at the mill on my first trip to Fabriano in 1970. At the end of November

Item 20. Will and Testament   417

1975, and at a cost of $7,000, I ordered two thousand sheets watermarked with
the PWP pressmark in one corner, more than enough paper for several PWP
editions. I always referred to it as Fabriano PWP paper. Even though it was a
beautiful sheet, it required a little extra handling. Before the paper could be
dampened, it had to be candled for embedded pieces of iron, grit, and undis-
solved granules of sizing in to prevent damaging the type during printing.

The first thing I did on my next trip to England in mid-June 1976 with
Giorgiolino, was to visit Joe in London. Together we delivered enough sheets
of the paper for proofing to Christopher Prater, Joe's screenprinter at Kelpra
Studio, where the prints were going to be editioned.

Later that week we stayed a few days with Joe and his wife Jos at their
home in Wiltshire, where Joe and I discussed the project in more detail. I
gave him a small mock-up of the book. Like Anthony, Joe used my suggestions only as a point of departure. Neither had interpreted my ideas literally,
but both respected the essence of my suggestions. Whenever I commissioned a text or illustrations, I tried to be as explicit as possible about what
I envisioned without making the author or artist feel unduly constrained.
Joe's illustrations were perfect for this book. They had all the intrigue of the
early seventeenth century and his own modern word games complemented
the playful spirit of Anthony's text.

A Visit to the Burgesses in Monte Carlo

In February 1976 I travelled by train to Monte Carlo to deliver three post-
dated $200 checks still due Anthony for his story. He lost the second and
third checks, but eventually found them buried in the clutter of his living
room/studio. Anthony was away during my visit, and Liana didn't know
how to cook. Their son, Andrea, who worked in a local restaurant, did all
the cooking for them, but unfortunately he was at work. I looked through
the cupboards and found enough foodstuffs to put together a pasta. I always
felt sorry for Andrea. Poor boy, he had to be the adult in his dysfunctional
family. He eventually committed suicide.

Editioning the Illustrations

Back in London a third time in November 1976 to pick up the finished
prints, I discovered that Chris had misinterpreted Joe's layouts and imposed
the six images in such a way that the two blanks on the sheet were out of

sequence. Like Pomodoro, Joe came up with a solution to turn a potential problem into an asset. Rather than reprint the whole job, Joe offered to fill these blanks with two new illustrations. Even though this meant I would have to modify the layout slightly, it solved the immediate problem and salvaged the paper that would have been lost if Chris had had to start over again from scratch.

Printing this book was a long, drawn-out ordeal. After Giorgiolino and I broke up early in the summer of 1976, we rarely saw each other. In a somewhat depressed mood I continued to work alone at the press the rest of that summer and fall, setting the type for the new book and finishing up the printing of *The Emperor's Lion*.

There was a slight possibility that Roberto (Robertino) Gatti, a friend from Venice who had some printing and binding experience, would come to work with me at the Press that October. We had been friends for several years, and I liked him very much. He and Bob Frontier, an American, had been partners in the Legatoria Piazzesi, a stationery boutique and bindery in Venice. Bob had recently been killed in an automobile accident in which Robertino had been the driver. He wanted to leave Venice to get away from the accusations of Bob's friends.

Roberto Gatti

In September Robertino joined me for a few weeks in Belgium, where we worked at the Centrum Frans Masereel, a state-run printmaking facility in the village of Kasterlee near Antwerp. Remi de Cnodder, an art critic I had met in Diano Marina, thought the Centrum might be interested in adding a typographic module to its program. It turned out to be a rather impractical idea, but I did learn a lot about pulling etchings and printing lithographs. Though I had a formula for author's fees, I hadn't yet established one for artists. Remi made many suggestions that turned out to be impractical for private press books. He thought in terms of editions of prints, which demanded higher prices than books illustrated with original graphics. In June 1976 I offered Joe £2,500 (British pounds), but Remi said that was not enough. To this day I am not sure now how much I paid Joe for the prints.

Robertino and I got along very well – so well that I began fantasizing about our future together. However he wasn't quite ready to take such a big

Item 20. Will and Testament   419

step. He needed a little more time before committing himself to a move to Verona. In the interim an event took place that completely changed the course of the PWP: the arrival on the scene of another young man.

Alessandro Zanella

Shortly after my return from Belgium, I began to notice a new young man wandering around the neighborhood, usually pushing a bicycle. He had a wild mop of hair and piercing blue eyes. I was often tempted to engage him in a conversation, but the moment never seemed appropriate. Then one day in mid-October, there was a knock at my door, and the same young man, Alessandro Zanella, introduced himself. He had recently been discharged from the army and was interested in printing books. He had applied to the Istituto Superiore Industrie Artistiche at Urbino, which included a School for the Book in its curriculum, but he had been rejected. Since it was now too late to take the entrance examinations for another school, he had sought out Jacques Vernière in hopes of finding an apprenticeship in his studio. Jacques was no longer printing books, so he sent Alessandro to me.

Alessandro's eagerness to learn and his dedication to the craft were evident from the beginning, but his arrival didn't mesh well with my own schedule, since I would be leaving for the States in late December. I had been invited to be a guest lecturer in the Graduate School of Library Service at the University of Alabama for the 1977 spring semester.

The Decision to Take Alessandro with Me to Alabama

Even though it would be for only a couple of months, I agreed to take Alessandro on until the end of December. The more we worked together, however, the more convinced I was that he might just be the catalyst needed to get the Press operating on a more professional level. Working alone I spent far too much time sitting around in cafés procrastinating, or committing to projects that could never be realized. I didn't want to run the risk of losing Alessandro during my absence. Even though we had only worked together for such a short time, I suggested that he accompany me to Alabama, where he would have an opportunity to expand his printing skills in the university's typographic laboratory. There was another motive, a selfish one: I had developed a terrible crush on him the moment I first laid eyes on him in the street. We left for New York a few days after Christmas.

Extra Help at the Press

In October Mark Fishbein also helped set the Burgess text, but the only steady helper I had had before Alessandro's arrival was Fausto Daolio, the son of the porter at via Duomo, 15. Beginning in November Fausto worked half days at the Press setting the text. He had been trained as a typesetter and was therefore very helpful around the studio. Luckily for the PWP Fausto had recently been inducted into the army and was awaiting his travel orders, so no one wanted to hire him. Fausto stayed on until Alessandro and I left for the States.

Overextending Myself

During this period I was even more overextended than usual, which complicated not only projects but personal relationships. One of the worst messes I got myself into involved Marcello Fornaro. Even though Marcello was an excellent binder and we had always gotten along well, I couldn't take any more work to him because I still owed him a lot of money for the Borges/Pomodoro binding. A couple of days before Alessandro and I were to leave for the States, Marcello came by my studio with a "dealer" who wanted to buy more than a dozen copies of the book as an investment. We worked out a favorable price, and they took the books away. Marcello was to bring a certified check the next day, less the amount that he felt was still due him. Hopefully there would be enough left over to pay my debt with my other major creditor, Fabriano. The mill was pressing me for the balance I still owed. I was so anxious to settle these debts that I didn't see Marcello's action for what it was, a scam. When he didn't show up with the check at the appointed hour, I called him. He told me he was going to hold the books ransom until I paid him. What could I do on such short notice? I was leaving the next day. I immediately rushed to Sandro Sartori, one of my lawyer friends, who called Marcello and threatened him with a lawsuit if he didn't return the books that very day. Sandro worked out a deal with Marcello, who got to keep a certain number of the books at cost to cancel my debt; then Sandro convinced Fabriano to wait for its money until I got back from the States. Thus, I lost two valuable resources – a binder and a paper mill – because of my own mismanagement.

In addition to Sartori I had several mentors who were continually bailing me out whenever I got into trouble. They included my dentist, Alessandro Megighian; my radiologist, Antonio Squassabia; and my neurologist, Renato Da Pian.

Item 20. Will and Testament

My First Visit to Alabama

My first visit to Alabama in 1977 was an enormous success and resulted in the school offering me an adjunct faculty position. I would be expected to teach every other spring in Alabama and offer workshops in Europe during the alternate summers. My proposal for a full-fledged book arts program was approved by the faculty in May 1979 during my second visit. This program was eventually developed into the first Master of Fine Arts in the Book Arts Program in the States.

Printing the Book

Back in Verona in May I realized that because of Alessandro's precise nature and his ability to quickly apply what he learned, he would soon be an invaluable asset to the Press. At the same time, as he became more involved in the production of the Burgess/Tilson book, he saw a potential career in printing evolving for himself. Perhaps there was after all a future for us together as printers. For the time being, however, we set everything else aside and concentrated on getting the book printed. Because none of the illustrations were printed together on the same sheets

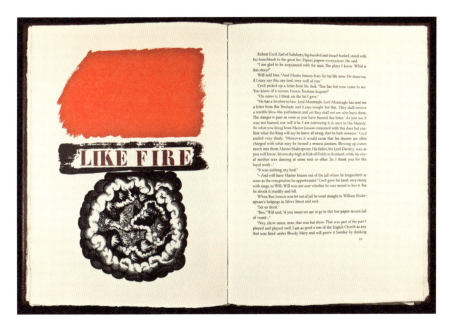

Double-page spread from *Will and Testament: A Fragment of Biography.* (Courtesy of the University of Oregon Libraries.)

with the text, we could print the text without having the illustrations on hand.

The book was printed in quarto, and because of the full pages of type, it required, I am sure, some of the most devilish and complicated makereadies in the entire history of printing. I often forgot that cast-iron handpresses were never intended for fine printing, and they have a way of constantly frustrating anyone who is a perfectionist.

Again Golda beautifully lettered the title, which was printed in a rich brown ink. In April 1976 we discovered the Lefranc & Bourgeois letterpress inks, which were available in a wide range of colors. We used one of them for the second color. These inks were sold in two-inch tubes in most art supply stores. One of the benefits of hand inking is that it consumes a relatively small amount of ink, and there is practically no waste. Perhaps my only real misgiving with this book was the black ink. I had exhausted my supply of Mandlik's Special Black 42625 L'press ink, which I had used for the PWP editions already printed in Verona. The new Mandlik ink, which was made in Canada, was not as heavily pigmented, which accounts for the grayness of the text pages. I tried other inks without much success, and at one point I made several suggestions to Daniel Smith, the inkmaker, to help him in his effort to develop a new ink for the handpress. The result, however, was disappointing; his ink was too grainy and insufficiently stiff for hand-inking.

Syndi Beth Master

One of the godsends in those hectic days was the presence of Syndi Beth Master, who as a student had worked with William Everson at the Lime Kiln Press at the University of California at Santa Cruz. She first wrote to me in April 1976 about an apprenticeship at the Press. Unfortunately, by the time she arrived in September 1977, we were between projects. Even though she didn't have an opportunity to do any printing, she put her organizational skills to work to restructure the Press financially. She also saw us through the difficult chore of filling out progress reports for the National Endowment for the Arts grant that I had been awarded in June 1977.

The Arrival of the Burgesses

We finished the printing early in the fall, and by the beginning of October 1977, we were ready for Anthony Burgess and Joe Tilson to converge on

Item 20. Will and Testament

Verona to sign the colophon pages. On the appointed day Golda, Alessandro, and I were waiting around for the Burgesses to arrive. We had put them up at the Albergo Due Torri, Verona's most luxurious hotel, which was established in 1694 and hosted many luminaries, including Mozart and Goethe. It was just a few blocks from the studio. When they didn't show up, we walked down the street toward the hotel, talking about the influx of gypsies in Verona. Instead of gypsies, I realized that it was the Burgess family approaching. I said, "There they are." Coming toward us was a disheveled trio, Anthony, Liana, and their son Andrea. Liana was wearing what looked like house slippers and a sateen bathrobe. They all had wind-tossed hair. Later I observed that she had the dirtiest fingernails I had ever seen on a civilized woman.

Joe Tilson in the red room at via Duomo, 15, Verona, Italy, 1977. (Photo by RGR, courtesy of PWP Archives.)

Anthony Burgess and Syndi Beth Master at an *al fresco* lunch, Verona, Italy, 1977. (Photo by RGR, courtesy of PWP Archives.)

We met up with Joe Tilson and Caroline Michahelles, a collector friend who had come to Verona from Florence for the signing. We all went to lunch, including the children and Syndi Beth, and then back to the studio to sign the colophon pages.

Signing the Colophon Pages

The signing went without incident, although Anthony did threaten to draw a gun with his name coming out of the barrel on the colophon page intended for the Dallas Public Library. That library later canceled its tentative order, but Anthony must have only talked about drawing the gun because there is no "smoking gun" on the Dallas colophon that ended up in the PWP Archives. Lauren Fishbein reminded me that Anthony also signed a colo-

Anthony Burgess signing the colophon pages, accompanied by Liana and Andrea, in the red room at via Duomo, 15, Verona, Italy, 1977. (Photo by RGR, courtesy of PWP Archives.)

Item 20. Will and Testament 425

phon for The New York Public Library with a lion, and two others with calligraphic flourishes, one with A and B music notations and another in Arabic.

Once the book was finished, Anthony presented a copy to Princess Grace of Monaco on behalf of us both. He mentioned having breakfasted with the Princess, during which corn flakes were served from the box. I was disillusioned to learn that the royal breakfast had not been more elegant.

Searching for a New Binder

Since it was no longer possible to work with Marcello, I needed to find another binder for this book. It was not going to be easy. I knew of no one else in Verona with Marcello's skills. From the start I had dreamed of adding a bindery as an integral part of the Press. It was the only sure way to assure that PWP books would be bound according to my exacting specifications.

I had heard of the binding workshops at the Center for Book Arts in New York, so on our way back to Verona from Alabama in May, Alessandro and I sought out Richard Minsky, the center's director. We told him of our desire to operate our own bindery. He had been training young people in edition binding for several years and thought a binder-in-residence program at the PWP would be an excellent opportunity for binders who wanted to develop their edition-binding skills. He offered to personally help us set up

Left to right: Ernie Lehmann, Golda Fishbein, and Richard Minsky at a restaurant in Sirmione, Italy, 1977. (Photo by RGR, courtesy of PWP Archives.)

a bindery in Verona if we would pay his expenses, which we agreed to do. Some people might say that Minsky had simply scammed us into giving him a free trip to Italy. Minsky wrote in June that he could come in September.

Meanwhile, in preparation for Minsky's visit, Alessandro and I decided to turn the former marbling studio at Ponte Pietra into a bindery. The first pieces of equipment we bought were a large standing press, which came from the printmaking studio around the corner, and a board cutter. When Minsky, in his threadbare green velvet trousers, flew into Rome instead of Milan, and drove a rental car non-stop to Verona (518 kilometers, about 322 miles), we should have known then that we were dealing with a mad man. His visit consisted of nothing more than a series of very expensive wild-goose chases. Our relationship with Minsky and company was one of the most regrettable of all PWP collaborations.

A personal regret in my relationship with Minsky was that we were sleeping together in the loft of my apartment because Frank and Barbara Alweis, American friends visiting from Le Barroux in the south of France, were staying in the red room. Horny as always, I was drawn into having mediocre sex with him.

NEA Grant

We had hired Minsky's students on the strength of my NEA grant, which was awarded in June 1977, even though I had yet to receive any funds from it. In my application I proposed to continue and expand my activities as a handpress printer. I would also use the funds to buy additional equipment and foundry type and handmade paper. Many of my projects had been delayed as much as a year for lack of them.

Fortunately Ben Meiselman, a very supportive patron of the Press who lived in New York, advanced the money to the binders so they could buy their tickets and depart on schedule. Minsky's students, Randolph Hunt and Mary Jane Etherington, arrived in Verona by train on a sunny fall day in late November 1977, laden with so many heavy suitcases – filled with adhesives, tools, etc. – and enormous rolls of leather, cloth, and paper that Alessandro, Lauren, Mark, and I had a hard time getting all of their belongings off the train before it departed for Venice.

Randy and Mary Jane immediately began to put the Ponta Pietra bindery in order. They stayed temporarily in a locanda near the Arena, the Roman

Item 20. Will and Testament 427

amphitheater, and then in the Hotel Alla Posta before we found an apartment for them on via Cappello.

Selecting the Leather for the Binding

Early in January 1978 Randy and I made a trip to the Conceria Cecchi in Pescia to select the hides for the binding. The tannery, which had once been a nunnery, looked like something out of a Frankenstein movie: there seemed to be miles of eerie underground vaults and passageways. On the day of our visit, the tannery appeared to be abandoned – there weren't any workers around except Sergio Bartolini, the manager, who didn't give the impression that he belonged there. As we circled the huge vats where the hides were being cured, hidden under a scum of Argentine bark, we expected at any moment to see a partially decomposed hand float to the surface. The rustic hides we ordered, however, added a great deal of "period" charm to the book.

Randy and I stayed at Caroline Michahelles's villa in Florence. We slept in a freezing cold attic room. Our bodies were touching most of the night, and while Randy was deep in sleep, I put my hand on his limp cock. David Hockney had made a beautiful nude drawing of Randy – a protégé of Henry Geldzahler's – which had roused my curiosity. Before we climbed the stairs to the attic, Caroline took me aside and said, "Stay away from that boy; he's bad news."

Binding the Book

Alessandro and I had developed a very good relationship with Francesco Graziani, the book restorer at Verona's Biblioteca Capitolare, the oldest continuously operating library in the world. Francesco was able to help Randy and Mary Jane with the basic construction of the book. Even though we were extremely patient and didn't want to rush them, by early February 1978 we were beginning to get a little concerned about their lack of progress. By then they had been working in the bindery for three months, and we had yet to see a prototype. Once we did we had to wait another month for the first bound copy. The grant money was running out. If we didn't have some books to deliver soon, we would go broke. It finally became clear that we had made a mistake, and in May, Randy and Mary Jane parted company with the PWP. They had completed only about twenty of the eighty-six copies in seven months. One of the problems was that they were moon-lighting instead of working full time on our project. We learned that they were taking on private commissions and making blank books for Giorgi-olino, often with our materials, to earn extra money. Another problem was their tortured relationship with each other.

Changing Binders

In September I asked Carol Joyce if she would be interested in coming to Verona to finish binding the edition. She arrived in October 1978 and stayed on through January 1979. I had met Carol in September 1977, when she had dropped by unexpectedly at the via Duomo studio. I liked her enthusi-asm and straightforwardness, but unfortunately we were already committed to Randy and Mary Jane, so we weren't able to offer her anything at the PWP. Carol was an extremely conscientious and diligent worker, eager to make all of the books she bound structurally sound – sometimes too sound for my taste. If we disagreed on anything, it would be the aesthetics of binding structures. I think if we had worked together a little longer, I could have brought her around to my more "fragile" concept of binding.

By the time Carol arrived in Verona, both the studio and the bindery had been relocated catty-corner from each other in the side courtyard. The stand-ing press we had purchased for the bindery at Ponte Pietra was left behind. Carol had to run back and forth between the bindery and the pressroom every time she needed to use our standing press. Under these taxing conditions she managed to bind several more copies, taking the balance back with her to New York, where she eventually finished the edition.

The Box

The box for this book created another set of problems. Renzo Oliboni had made the boxes with a cabinetmaker's precision out of Romanian oak. We overlooked the fact that his work was more exact than Randy's, and so a few adjustments had to be made to some of the boxes to accommodate the books. We finished the boxes in our studio, where we oiled and lined them.

Embellishing the Boxes and Covers

Five small wooden panels had to be inset in each lid, but first Joe needed to wood burn them with decorative elements. In the dead of winter in Decem-

Item 20. Will and Testament

ber 1977, I decided to take the more than six hundred panels to Joe in Wiltshire. I was already having a lot of trouble with my back, and handling the two suitcases full of panels was a real ordeal. When the train pulled into Verona, the PWP crew got me settled into a compartment, which I was sharing with a young Scotswoman named Jennifer Gray, who was on her way home for the holidays. Jennifer came to my rescue at the next station. I couldn't lift the suitcases, so she carried them for me. Thank God for strong women.

Once I arrived in Wiltshire, the enormity of the project became apparent, and Joe, as had Barton Lidicé Beneš years before, realized that he was not up to the task. He wasn't about to wood burn five hundred panels and stencil two names – letter by letter – on another hundred. I ended up bringing the panels back to Verona – *plus* the electric branding iron, the brands, and a stencil kit. Alessandro and I eventually branded the panels ourselves, and Christopher Borden, the last PWP apprentice, finished what was left of the coloring and stenciling just before the PWP closed in 1982. Alessandro and I also had to fire-brand the labyrinth on the book cover because none of the binders dared to do it for fear of ruining the book. Mark Fishbein screenprinted the same labyrinth on the prospectus, which was printed commercially.

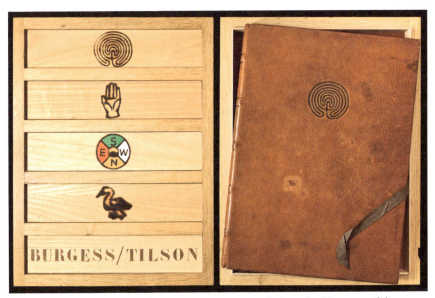

The box and cover for *Will and Testament: A Fragment of Biography*. (Courtesy of the University of Oregon Libraries.)

A Much-Deserved Getaway

Even though we had not finished the printing by August, Alessandro went to Sardinia for two weeks with his girlfriend Antonia, and I kept the studio open while he was away. After he returned, I went to Naples, Panarea, and Sicily with Golda Fishbein and Hadassah Brooks for the first two weeks in September. In Panarea we stayed with Hadassah's friend Cristina Zucca in a primitive native house, where we feasted on freshly caught fish every day. From there we travelled to Sicily, and Hadassah and I climbed to the top of Mount Etna.

Left to right: Hadassah Brooks, Gabriel, and Cristina Zucca at Cristina's summer house, Panarea, Italy, 1977. (Photo by Golda Fishbein, courtesy of PWP Archives.)

One time we got lost and I went into a roadside bar for directions. I was wearing a large straw hat and a gauze kaftan. They gave me directions in the Sicilian dialect, which I barely understood. On my way out one of the patrons turned to me and asked, "Where you from?" With a flip of my head I replied, "Hollywood."

A Fancy Dinner in Florence

Caroline Michahelles gave a party for Anthony Burgess at her villa in Florence in January 1978. I was invited to co-host because she had originally met Anthony through me. Caroline redecorated her dining room in orange, and there were marvelous bouquets of bright orange calendulas everywhere

Item 20. Will and Testament

Gabriel in Sicily, 1977. (Photographer unknown, courtesy of PWP Archives.)

–intimations of *A Clockwork Orange* (1962). In Verona Anthony had told her explicitly that it was his least favorite novel. I don't know why she ignored his request. The party was very elegant. There were two tables of special guests for dinner, followed by more people invited for coffee and drinks. I'll never forget watching Anthony as he talked to the curious guests, switching effortlessly between English and Italian. He had a way of moving forward while answering their questions, gradually herding the huddled crowd of listeners into a corner. Then turning abruptly he would abandon them, leaving them speechless.

Mark Livingston's Review of the Book in *Fine Print*

Possibly the single most unpleasant memory associated with this book was Mark Livingston's negative review in the July 1979 issue of *Fine Print*. Aside from the fact that the price quoted in the review was $300 more than the actual price of $1,300, Livingston made the following observation:

> Born into the Imperial Easter Egg succession of the book world – neither much advancing nor injuring the common generations of printers and readers – it stands off, as point of reference, marking one extreme of the scale. Seen in their least flattering light, such books, howsoever handsome and graced with original work, are mere totems of luxury; their high prices seem unethical and ostentatious. Viewed more indulgently, they may be prized as grand gestures of the printer's artifice, wholly freed, for a rarity, from constraints of the marketplace.

Even though Abe Lerner took the opportunity in the January 1980 issue of *Fine Print* to reply to Livingston's review: "All we can ask from [Rummonds] is beautiful books, well made, in whatever style he chooses as a framework"– the damage had been done. Other critics of the PWP would eagerly apply the "Imperial Easter Egg" epithet to put down the Press's publishing program. The Burgess/Tilson book did not sell well after the Livingston review.

Martin Ackerman

Because neither Marlborough nor Marconi had ordered any copies and our standing-order collectors were not obliged to buy any of the books in the Deluxe Series, we were left with a larger number of these books in stock. In October 1980 in an effort to reduce this inventory, I approached Martin S. Ackerman, head of a New York-based foundation that was buying art books to donate to libraries. I first became aware of his foundation through its gifts to the library at the University of Alabama. The aim of the program was admirable, but in practice Ackerman was buying whole editions at a fraction of their true value and offering them to potential donors at inflated prices for which the donors then received a full charitable tax credit. Our markup at the PWP was only twenty percent, so the large discount Ackerman wanted would have meant too great a loss. Even though his cash offer was tempting, I opted to keep the books, eventually selling the last copy in 1988.

Item 20. Will and Testament 433

Mussels in White Wine and Herbs

Serves 4

One of the pleasures of Antwerp was the mussels. I still prepare them the way they were served in the dockside taverns there.

    4 pounds live mussels
    2 cups dry white wine
    6 ounces shallots, finely chopped
    1 ounce garlic cloves, finely chopped
    ½ teaspoon coarse salt
    ⅓ cup herbs, finely chopped (flat-leaf parsley, chervil, basil, thyme,
        winter savory)
    6 tablespoons unsalted butter

Rinse and scrub mussels under cold running water. Remove the beards. In a large stockpot over medium heat, combine wine, shallots, garlic, and salt. Simmer for 5 minutes. Add mussels. Cover and raise the heat to high. Cook until mussels open, about 5 minutes. Stir in the herbs and butter. Remove from the heat. Discard any mussels that do not open. Divide mussels and broth into four bowls. Serve with a thinly sliced baguette.

Title-page spread from *Le Stagioni*. (Courtesy of the University of Oregon Libraries.)

Item 21. *Le Stagioni*

A poem in Italian by Antonino Gammaro. With
four linecut reproductions of three woodcuts by Hans
Holbein, the Younger, and a composite ornament
assembled from elements in his woodcuts.

4 pages. 19 x 14.5 cm. 140 copies. 1977.

The Last Commission for Gammaro

Shortly before Christmas 1977 we had a visit from the perennial Antonino
Gammaro, who wanted me to print one of his poems for another Christmas
keepsake. Naturally I was a bit reluctant to accept any more commissions
from him, but he persisted. I finally gave in when he offered me three copies
of *Didascalie* in exchange for printing the new keepsake, plus a generous
share of the edition. I had been after him for several years to let me buy back
a few copies of that early work, since I occasionally had requests from collectors for it. Even though I had received twenty copies, I only had two left:
a personal copy and one for the PWP Library.

Just a month earlier Alessandro and I had started to assemble two additional complete sets of PWP publications – one for the PWP Archives and
the other for Alessandro. Our chances of locating copies of all the missing
items were slim. However over the years we did manage to find most of
them. With these developing collections in mind, Gammaro's offer was a
godsend in disguise. Beginning with the Burgess/Tilson book, in addition
to the *ad personam* copies for myself and the PWP Library, we began printing an *ad personam* copy for Alessandro and another for the PWP Archives.

The Illustrations

After Gammaro's unfortunate experience the year before with Giordano
Zorzi, we talked him out of using original graphics. I suspect it was also a
matter of cost, as well as his natural aversion to sharing part of the edition
with a third collaborator. The choice of illustrations – anything in the public
domain – was left to us. We found the Holbein woodcuts in a Dover Publications reprint of *Alphabets and Ornaments* (1968) by Ernst Lehner, and
had linecuts made of them. They had originally been used in *The Pastyme*

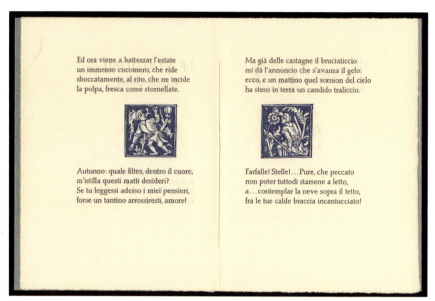

Double-page spread from *Le Stagioni*. (Courtesy of the University of Oregon Libraries.)

of People printed by John Rastell in London in 1529. The ornament on the wrapper and colophon page is a linecut of a collage made from various elements found in Holbein's work that Alessandro reassembled à la W.A. Dwiggins.

Printing the Keepsake

Once we settled on the illustrations, we were able to print this little pamphlet relatively quickly, using the Fabriano Imperiale paper left over from Gammaro's first book. Regrettably, we were still using the Mandlik Canadian black ink, not yet having found a suitable replacement for it, so the Post Mediaeval type looked rather washed out. Gammaro was very pleased with the results, however, and for once I came out ahead in my dealings with him.

Item 21. Le Stagioni 437

Involtini coi Carciofi
Beef Rolls with Artichokes

Serves 4

Winter in Verona, with its dense fog, provided the perfect atmosphere for gatherings of friends for dinner, wine, and conversation at home. Here is one of my favorite recipes for a large group, although the following recipe serves only four persons.

  8 pieces beef top round, each weighing 3 ounces, thinly sliced
  4 ounces prosciutto, finely chopped
  3 tablespoons butter, divided
 16 frozen artichoke heart sections
  2 tablespoons olive oil
  6 ounces onion, coarsely chopped
    Flour for dusting
  5 tablespoons dry white wine
    Juice of 1 lemon
    Salt and freshly ground black pepper to taste
  8 tablespoons hot beef stock

Beat the meat slices with a meat pounder to flatten. Mix prosciutto with 3 tablespoons of the butter and spread over the meat. Top each with two artichoke heart sections. Roll the meat around stuffing and tie securely with string. Heat the olive oil in a 3-quart sauté pan over medium high. Add onion and sauté for 5 minutes. Dust rolls with flour and add to the pan. Sauté until brown on all sides. Add wine, lemon juice, and salt, and pepper. Lower the heat, cover the pan, and cook gently for 45 minutes. Occasionally turn the rolls during cooking. Add stock as necessary to keep them from sticking. Arrange rolls on a platter and pour juices over the meat.

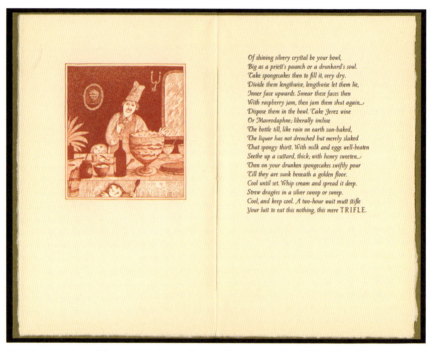

Double-page spread from *A Christmas Recipe*. (Courtesy of the University of Oregon Libraries.)

Item 22. *A Christmas Recipe*

A recipe for a raspberry trifle versified
by Anthony Burgess. With a linecut
reproduction of a pen and ink drawing by
Fulvio Testa. 4 pages (1 french-folded sheet).
24 x 15.5 cm. 180 copies. 1977.

A Christmas Keepsake for the PWP

Inspired by the ease with which we had been able to produce Antonino
Gammaro's Christmas keepsake, Alessandro and I decided to print one
for ourselves. Our greeting would take the form of a Christmas recipe,
something I had wanted to do for a long time. In fact, I had discussed
using a recipe for this purpose with Julia Child as far back as May 1974,
when she was in Verona with her husband, Paul. Golda Fishbein and I had
run into them walking down Corso Sant'Anastasia. Of course we recognized her immediately and invited them to join us for an impromptu coffee
in Piazza delle Erbe. Unfortunately the project never materialized for lack
of a manuscript.

Anthony Burgess Writes a Recipe

One evening during Anthony Burgess's colophon-signing visit, I told him
about my idea for a Christmas keepsake and how disappointed I was that
Julia had never sent me a recipe. As I sorted through my recipes, trying to
decide which of them might be suitable, Anthony volunteered to write one.
With drink in hand and my old Olivetti portable typewriter in front of him,
he sat down at the marble-topped table, and after one false start banged out
this recipe in verse for a raspberry trifle. Andrea Burgess, who had accompanied his parents to Verona, helped set the poem later that night.

> *English Trifle*
>
> Of shining silvery crystal be your bowl,
> Big as a priest's paunch or a drunkard's soul.
> Take spongecakes then to fill it, very dry.
> Divide them lengthwise, lengthwise let them lie,

Inner face upwards. Smear these faces then
With raspberry jam, then jam them shut again.
Dispose them in the bowl. Take Jerez wine
Or Mavrodaphne; liberally incline
The bottle till, like rain on earth sun-baked,
The liquor has not drenched but merely slaked
That spongy thirst. With milk and eggs well-beaten
Seethe up a custard, thick; with honey sweeten.
Then on your drunken spongecakes swiftly pour
Till they are sunk beneath a golden floor.
Cool until set. Whip cream and spread it deep.
Strew dragées in a silver swoop or sweep.
Cool, and keep cool. A two-hour wait must stifle
Your lust to eat this nothing, this mere TRIFLE.

Golda Fishbein Makes Burgess's Trifle

A few days after the Burgesses left, Golda made the trifle, following Anthony's recipe so that Fulvio Testa, who had never seen one, could make a pen and ink drawing for the keepsake. Once Fulvio had finished his drawing, the assembled guests eagerly devoured Golda's trifle.

The last photograph of the studio in via Duomo, Verona, Italy, 1977. (Photo by RGR, courtesy of PWP Archives.)

Item 22. A Christmas Recipe 441

Printing the Keepsake

We had great expectations for the coming year, so this keepsake was produced in an atmosphere of camaraderie and merriment, reflecting those aspirations. It was printed in quarto on Fabriano Esportazione "GF" paper, on one side of the sheet only, in two colors. The black form was locked into one half of the bed and the red in the other. The two forms were inked separately and then printed together. Half the copies went to the Burgesses, and the other half to the PWP. *A Christmas Recipe* was the last item to be printed at the via Duomo studio.

The Last Photograph of the Studio in via Duomo

There is a feeling of mystery and melancholy in this photo on the opposite page, almost as if the printers had slipped away, never to return again.

Gabriel and Alessandro Zanella at the Washington press in the via Carlo Cattaneo studio, Verona, Italy, 1980. (Photo by Studio Gulliver, courtesy of PWP Archives.)

Verona: Via Cattaneo, 6

> I don't tell truths. I tell what ought to be true.
> – Blanche DuBois in Tennessee Williams's *A Streetcar Named Desire*

Searching for a New Studio

For many years I fantasized about buying a dilapidated old farm above Montorio, east of Verona, for living quarters and studio. I referred to it as the Phantom Farm. It had been abandoned for many years. How I thought I could finance such a project is inconceivable now.

The Phantom Farm, Montorio, Italy, 1975. (Photo by RGR, courtesy of PWP Archives.)

This was not a new idea. There was the farm in Ibiza my parents had offered to buy for me, and Guillermo Ramos's non-existent farm in Ecuador, and more recently Max D'Arpini had shown me a primitive farm house in the country near Parona that I could have purchased for $5,000.

I didn't start looking seriously for a separate studio until early August 1976; however, it wasn't until the fall of 1977 that the search began in earnest. As the activities of the PWP expanded and I continued to accumulate more equipment, the press began to infringe more and more on my personal life, making it imperative to find a studio away from my living quarters. In October 1977 Alessandro Zanella and I were having our customary morning *cappuccini* at Bar Gar, a nearby café – so named by Kenneth Pettitt, a friend visiting from Berkeley, because of its proximity to the Ponte Garibaldi – when we saw an ad in the local newspaper offering what appeared to be a fantastic studio for rent.

Alessandro and I immediately went to see the space and fell in love with it at first sight. It was in a beautiful old palace only a block away from Piazza Brà, Verona's principal square and the site of the Arena, a first-century Roman amphitheater, famous for its open-air performances of operas in the summer.

The place consisted of two spacious rooms, but the real attraction was

Front courtyard at via Carlo Cattaneo, 6, Verona, Italy, 1996. (Photo by Diana Thomas, courtesy of the photographer.)

Verona: Via Cattaneo, 6

its large, sunny, private side courtyard. The rent was modest, and so we entered into negotiations with the owner, la marchesa Maria Da Lisca. She must have found our references satisfactory because we won out over several other applicants. I wasn't surprised, because the PWP was quite well known in art circles in Verona, and once I started teaching graduate students at the University of Alabama, I was regarded by the Veronese as a *dottore* (university professor), in their eyes a respected member of the community. Bruna Da Re, a former English student of Golda Fishbein's and ardent supporter of the PWP, helped us negotiate the rental contract in February 1978.

Side courtyard at via Carlo Cattaneo, 6, Verona, Italy, 1981. (Photo by Jürgen Reuter, courtesy of the photographer.)

Renovating the Space

The space was not in particularly good shape, but it had great potential. One of my architect friends, Renato Marchesini, drew up the plans and got the work permits and construction crew for us. Once it was ours, we set to work cleaning it up. The passageway between the two rooms was only four and a half feet high; so the first thing we had to do was get a crew of bricklayers to come in and enlarge the opening in the two-foot-thick wall. Before long, one thing led to another, and we were soon wiring and plastering the whole studio. The ceiling in the smaller of the two rooms also had to be replaced once we decided to expand into an adjacent storeroom. After all the alterations were completed, Lauren Fishbein, who had started to paint the studio when we first moved in, finished the job.

Originally we had planned to put the Washington and standing presses in the larger of the two rooms, but our architect told us the old wooden flooring wouldn't carry the weight. Luckily, the floor of the smaller room was solid. The vaults under it were filled with rubble from the bombing of Verona during World War II, so the floor was sturdy enough to hold both presses.

A "ghost" image of Gabriel walking away from the Washington press in the pressroom in the via Carlo Cattaneo studio, Verona, Italy, 1981. (Photo by Irwin Dermer, courtesy of the photographer.)

Moving the Studio from via Duomo to via Carlo Cattaneo

Moving the short distance across town in March 1978 was a major operation. I had accumulated a considerable amount of extremely heavy equipment, as well as what seemed like tons of paper and type. A friend who had a specialty butcher shop in Porta Borsari found a flatbed truck and rounded up a couple of strong fellows to help us move. Fortunately Cabianca had moved the Washington and standing presses into the new studio the day before.

Verona's labyrinth of one-way streets from via Duomo to via Carlo Cattaneo compounded the problem by making the shortest distance to our destination *against* the flow of traffic. Once again, the perks of having taught English came to my rescue. Some of the *vigili urbani*, the policemen, who had been my students, simply halted all the traffic to permit us quick and free passage – the wrong way – down one-way streets to the new studio. During the final run they invited Alessandro and me into a bar for a refreshing glass of wine, leaving the truck in the middle of a narrow road blocking the street in both directions. The *vigili* toasted our success, oblivious to the honking of the irate motorists outside.

Type cabinets in the composing room in the via Carlo Cattaneo studio, Verona, Italy, 1981. (Photo by RGR, courtesy of PWP Archives.)

Laying Out the Studio

The presses were set up in the smaller of the two rooms, and the larger was used as a composing room, office, and library. In early 1978 the company that had constructed my first type cabinet made a second one for me, this one with two rows of drawers for lowercase type flanked by galley racks and a sloped metal work surface.

Going Legit

One of the first things I did after we signed the lease with la marchesa was to apply for a commercial printer's license from the Comune di Verona (City Hall). Soon after the fire department checked out the new studio, the license arrived on August 8, 1978; then I joined the artisans' union. I had not really been too concerned about a license earlier, because I had an artist's visa and worked at home, as did many Italian artisans; however, after so many years of printing on the sly, I was now acknowledged as a legitimate printer, as well as a card-carrying member of the union. Until then I had merely been an eccentric American artist tinkering with his antiquated toys. Once the PWP was licensed to operate as a print shop, I opened a bank account in the name of the press. The Cassa di Risparmio di Verona Vicenza e Belluno even gave me a line of credit. By May 1978 I had made the final payment to Fabriano for the PWP paper, so I was reasonably debt free.

There were no orderly lines in the banks in those days. Everyone just crowded around the window. Once Phyllis Liparini, our American friend from Chicago, was trying to secure her spot when a Veronese woman in a fur coat pushed her aside saying, "I am in a hurry, I have a taxi waiting." The other women around the window simply moved aside.

Often I was as ill-mannered as that woman. Since I knew several of the clerks personally, I would give them a little wave, and they would move to a closed window to help me.

Before we even had a chance to settle into the new studio, the first students from the University of Alabama descended upon us early in June for a five-week printing workshop. Three months after their departure, we were still trying to find things and get on with the business of printing books.

Verona: Via Cattaneo, 6

Sliced Chicken with Tuna Sauce

Serves 8

One of the pleasures of summer was *al fresco* luncheons in the side court-yard. This is my variation on the traditional *Vitello Tonnato* that I make with thinly sliced roasted chicken breast and a creamy tuna sauce.

12½ ounces canned solid white tuna, discarding water or oil
2 ounces canned anchovies, discarding oil and patted dry
3 tablespoons capers
3 tablespoons lemon juice
⅓ cup chopped flat-leaf parsley
2 cups mayonnaise
16 pieces of thinly sliced roasted chicken breast
Extra-virgin olive oil for drizzling
Salt and freshly ground black pepper to taste
Salad greens to line the plates
Sprigs of flat-leaf parsley for garnish

Put tuna, anchovies, capers, lemon juice, parsley, and mayonnaise in a food processor and blend until the sauce has a creamy consistency. Spread a generous line of the sauce across the width of each slice of chicken before rolling it toward the narrow end. Place them, seam side down, on a platter and cover with plastic wrap. Refrigerate for 24 hours. Before serving, arrange the rolls on a bed of greens, such as endive, watercress, and arugula. Drizzle a thin stream of olive oil over them and lightly season with salt and pepper. Garnish with sprigs of Italian parsley.

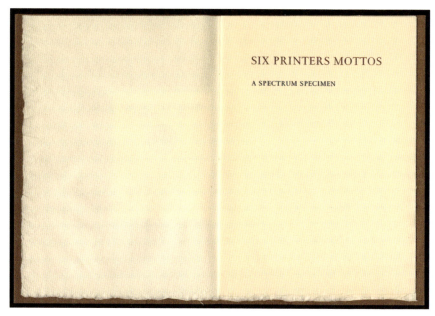

Title-page spread from *Six Printers Mottos: A Spectrum Specimen*. (Courtesy of the University of Oregon Libraries.)

Item 23. *Six Printers Mottos: A Spectrum Specimen*

Mottos from Sebastian Gryphius (Latin), Christopher Plantin (Latin), Geofroy Tory (French), Mark Flynn (English), Theodore Martens (Latin), and Aldus Manutius (Latin), printed together with specimens of Spectrum type. 4 pages (1 french-folded sheet). 20.5 x 14.5 cm. 70 copies. 1978.

Verona Workshop

Almost five years after I had first mentioned to Carolyn Reading Hammer the idea of offering a printing workshop in Verona, the University of Alabama sponsored "Printing and Publishing on the Iron Handpress," from June 6 through July 7, 1978.

It was a stimulating but exhausting experience for Alessandro Zanella and me. There were twelve participants plus a few spouses. Once our equip-

Brochure for the "Printing and Publishing on the Iron Handpress" workshop (1978). (Courtesy of PWP Archives.)

Workshop students in the Private Press Room at the Biblioteca Civica di Verona, Verona, Italy, 1978. Mark Flynn is second from the left bending over the table. (Photo by James D. Birchfield, courtesy of the photographer.)

Brochure for the Villa Emo di Fanzolo (1978). (Courtesy of PWP Archives.)

ment was in place, the new studio didn't seem as ample as we had thought it would be, nor did we have all the presses and materials we had anticipated having on hand. The logistics of the workshop were very demanding. Aside from teaching the students about printing and publishing on the handpress, we had to act as their bankers, interpreters, tour guides, and hosts, as well as cope with a few temper tantrums. Once a week for each of the five weeks we took the students on an out-of-town excursion by bus or train.

One of the most memorable trips was a Fourth of July picnic given by la contessa Barbara Emo at her Villa Emo di Fanzolo, a stupendous Palladian villa near Vicenza, where American fried chicken and my potato salad were the fare for the day. We also visited the lofts in the out buildings where silkworms were voraciously munching on mulberry leaves. Once the worms matured, they enclosed themselves in cocoons.

The day after the final session, we went to the Re Teodorico restaurant next to the Castel San Pietro on a hill above Verona for a superb dinner with lots of wine and promises to stay in touch.

Golda Fishbein and Gabriel outside the Re Teodorico restaurant above Verona, Italy, 1978. (Photo by Lauren Fishbein, courtesy of the photographer.)

Bradley Hutchinson

After the workshop Bradley Hutchinson, one of the participants, stayed on in Verona. Even though Brad was still an undergraduate, he had been allowed to take my graduate courses on printing at the University of Alabama in the spring of 1977. I consider him the first *real* PWP apprentice, even though a few others had worked at the press before him. We had promised him room and board in via Duomo, all the wine he could drink, and $240 a month, of which he received a camp bed in the Black Hole of Calcutta and ample wine, but no cash.

The workshop had completely devastated the studio. Many of the student projects remained unfinished, so Alessandro and Brad completed them and made portfolios to enclose the collected examples of the work done by the students. It is actually a handsome record of a very intense five weeks.

Brad had no more than settled in when we went to lunch at the Corticella Paradiso, a nearby restaurant run by my friend Pino Bendinelli, who was an excellent chef. Pino was an ardent leftist who thought the proletariat should also eat venison and pheasant. The *haute cuisine* in his restaurant was in sharp contrast to the family-style seating arrangement and the ridicu-

Brad Hutchinson in the via Carlo Cattaneo studio, Verona, Italy, 1978. (Photo by Hoke Perkins, courtesy of the photographer.)

Item 23. Six Printers Mottos: A Spectrum Specimen 455

lously low prices. On this particular day Pino was nervously pacing the floor. He was expecting two hundred guests for a banquet that night and his waiters had walked out on him. "Pino," I said, "don't worry. Brad and I will come back and help you."

We got there early to set up. The place was decked out with banners celebrating both the contribution of the Resistance in World War II and proclaiming the glories of the Communist Party. Only then did I realize what we were in for. The old-timers – the resistance fighters – were in the large, central dining room. Off of this were three smaller private rooms: one for the radical students, another for the affluent professionals, and another for the artists and intellectuals. Confusion reigned from the moment we got there. The old-timers wouldn't stay put and kept wandering around the room, reminiscing with old comrades. The students were loudly singing political songs and impatient for dinner to be served; they were going somewhere else afterwards. There was no place for the wives of the professionals to hang their fur coats. Most of the artists and intellectuals had yet to arrive. I told Brad, who didn't know more than a handful of Italian words, to just say *subito* (immediately) to everything he was asked. He would come running into the kitchen asking, "What does *forchetta* mean?" I'd hand him a fork, and he'd dash off again into the rowdy throng. By the end of the evening, the place was in wild disorder.

Abe Lerner

That fall Abe Lerner, a long-standing collector of PWP books, came back to Verona with his new wife, Kit Currie. I had known Kit for many years from my dealings with Dawson's Book Shop in Los Angeles, where she had worked before marrying Abe.

Even though I didn't always agree with Abe's assessment of the PWP's place in the scheme of private presses, he was one of the most vocal supporters of my work. I have always thought of the PWP as an Italian press, but Abe preferred to group it with the American presses, as he did in his talk, "Assault on the Book," delivered at the Double Crown Club in London in 1978. The text of this lecture was later published in a pamphlet of the same name. In it he said, "I feel [Rummonds] belongs in this survey [of American presses]. He is an American, and his impulses and motivations are from an American background in bookmaking." He went on to give me

Mark Fishbein, Abe Lerner, Golda Fishbein, Brad Hutchinson, and Gabriel in the via Carlo Cattaneo studio, Verona, Italy, 1978. (Photo by Kit Currie, courtesy of the photographer.)

the sort of compliment I rarely received but always cherished: "His presswork is extraordinary, some of the finest that is being done in the world today." I read into his encouraging words an acknowledgement of the struggles I had endured trying to perfect my craft.

A Keepsake for Abe Lerner's Seventieth Birthday

In appreciation of Abe's support as collector and critic, we decided to print a small keepsake to celebrate his seventieth birthday in the form of a Spectrum specimen, set from type we had recently received from Joh. Enschedé en Zonen in The Netherlands for our next project, *Stella Variabile*. Five of the mottos are well known, but the sixth came from Mark Flynn, another of my students from Alabama who took the summer workshop. Mark was often heard saying, "The large type giveth and the small type taketh away." He did not aspire to be another Aldus Manutius, but his motto certainly seemed to echo the sentiments of many of the student printers, who could frequently be heard repeating it. I often puzzled over exactly what it meant.

Item 23. Six Printers Mottos: A Spectrum Specimen   457

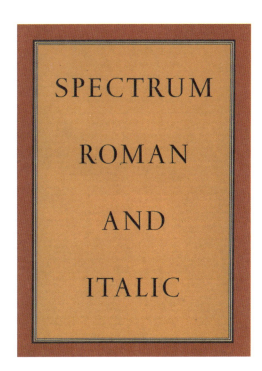

Cover for the Spectrum type specimen brochure from the Joh. Enschedé Type Foundry in The Netherlands. (Courtesy of The New York Public Library.)

Double-page spread from *Six Printers Mottos: A Spectrum Specimen*. (Courtesy of the University of Oregon Libraries.)

This keepsake was printed work-and-twist on one side of the sheet only. The paper was dampened, but as always the Amatruda paper didn't remain very stable during the printing.

A Birthday Dinner for Abe Lerner

Golda Fishbein cooked one of her fabulous beef-in-Burgundy dinners, which we consumed *al fresco* in the courtyard at via Duomo. Martino and Gabriella Mardersteig were among the guests to help us honor Abe on his birthday. After dinner I nearly started another fire when I launched one of my Ecuadorean tissue-paper hot-air balloons in the courtyard. On its ascent it toppled over and crashed into a wall, bursting into flames.

Abe's party marked the end of another era at the PWP, as it was the last time I was able to use the via Duomo courtyard to entertain guests. Soon afterwards the upper floors of the palace were renovated, and il conte Francesco Guarienti – the "Humping Medic," whose bedroom was directly above mine – moved his family in along with two vicious schnauzers that roamed the courtyard, terrorizing everyone who came to see me. I kept a camel whip and a large bucket of water just inside my front door. I would attack them with the whip or drench them with water when they got too close. They always ran off whimpering. When il conte eventually moved the dogs to his villa on Lake Garda, everyone was happy.

The Ill-Fate of the Wall

The wall into which the hot-air balloon crashed was the victim of a later, more violent attack. "Count Dracula" – my landlord and Francesco's older brother, il conte Luigi Guarienti, whose long, somber face was the source of his nickname – decided to renovate an adjacent palace with a common wall on the courtyard. A huge crane was set up, and before long, the dilapidated palace was completely gutted. The plan had been to retain the historic exterior wall that faced the courtyard. One day I saw il conte in front of the crane wildly gesturing and incoherently stuttering. I knew what he was trying to say, but the wrecker didn't. What he was trying to say was, "Not the wall!" But before he could get the words out, the wall came tumbling down. I managed to salvage some handmade nine-inch spikes out of the rubble, which I was prone to refer to as "nails from the True Cross." After all, if Constantine's mother could find some of these nails more than three hundred

Item 23. Six Printers Mottos: A Spectrum Specimen   459

years after the Crucifixion, there was no reason why I couldn't uncover a few in Verona. In any event when the façade was reconstructed, no one could tell the difference.

Postscript

Five years later in Alabama, I participated in another birthday celebration for Abe – his seventy-fifth. I was one of thirteen printers who contributed to a portfolio of keepsakes organized by Kit Currie and Jerry Kelly, the calligrapher and book designer.

Potato Salad

Serves 12

This is my mother's recipe. I have made it for years, especially for Fourth of July picnics. My mother used a boiled dressing, but the one given below is just as tasty.

For the salad
- 3 pounds Yukon gold potatoes
- 4 to 6 scallions, save the green parts for the garnish
- 6 stalks celery
- 8 hard-boiled eggs, quartered

For the dressing
- 1 cup mayonnaise
- 1 teaspoon hot mustard
- ½ teaspoon curry
- ½ teaspoon salt
- ½ teaspoon freshly ground black pepper
- Sprigs of flat-leaf parsley for garnish

Wash potatoes and boil with the skins on, about 30 minutes. Remove the skins while still hot. Cut in half, length-wise, and then into ¼-inch slices. Spread slices over the bottom of a large flat bowl and let cool for at least 30 minutes. Cut celery and scallions into ⅛-inch slices and spread over potatoes. Mix dressing and pour it over potatoes, celery, and scallions, folding it in with care. Lay hard-boiled eggs on top of the salad, and lightly salt and pepper them. Garnish with a few springs of flat-leaf parsley and sliced greens from the scallions.

Item 23. Six Printers Mottos: A Spectrum Specimen   461

Boeuf Bourguignon
Beef Stew in Red Wine

Serves 6

This is Golda's variation of Julia Child's recipe. It is very time consuming, but worth the effort. It can be made the day before and reheated before serving.

For the marinade
- 3 cups red wine
- 1 carrot, diced
- 6 ounces onion, diced
- 1 bay leaf
- 1 large garlic clove, crushed

For the meat
- 3 pounds chuck pot roast, cut unto 2-inch cubes
- 6 ounce slab bacon with rind
- 1 tablespoon olive oil
- 1 carrot, sliced
- 6 ounces onion, sliced
- 1 teaspoon salt
- ¼ teaspoon freshly ground black pepper
- 2 tablespoons flour
- 2 to 3 cups brown beef stock
- 1 tablespoon tomato paste
- 2 large garlic cloves, mashed
- ½ teaspoon fresh thyme
- 1 bay leaf, crumbled

For the small onions
- 18 to 24 small white onions about 1-inch in diameter, peeled
- 1½ tablespoons butter
- 1½ tablespoons olive oil
- ½ cup beef stock
  Salt and freshly ground black pepper to taste

1 herb bouquet (4 springs flat-leaf parsley, ½ half bay leaf, ¼ teaspoon fresh thyme tied in cheesecloth)

For the mushrooms

4 tablespoons butter

2 tablespoons olive oil

1 pound mushrooms, left whole if small, or sliced or quartered if large

Salt and freshly ground black pepper to taste

4 tablespoons shallots, minced

The marinade: The meat should marinate overnight in the red wine with carrot, onion, bay leaf, and crushed garlic clove.

The meat: The next day, remove the meat and set aside marinade. Pat the meat dry with paper towels. Preheat the oven to 450 degrees. Remove rind and cut bacon into 1½-inch long strips by ¼-inch thick. Simmer rind and bacon in 1½ quarts of water for 10 minutes. Drain and dry. In a Dutch oven, sauté bacon in oil over moderate heat for 2 to 3 minutes. Remove with a slotted spoon to a large bowl and set aside. Brown the meat, a few pieces at a time, in the hot oil and bacon fat in the Dutch oven. Transfer browned meat to the bowl with bacon. Brown vegetables and transfer to a separate bowl. Pour out remaining fat in the Dutch oven. Return the meat and bacon to the Dutch oven and toss with salt and pepper. Then sprinkle flour over meat and toss again to lightly coat beef. Set the Dutch oven, uncovered, in the middle position of the preheated oven for 4 minutes. Remove the Dutch oven and toss meat and return it to the oven for another 4 minutes. Remove the Dutch oven. Turn the oven down to 325 degrees. Remove carrot, onion, bay leaf, and garlic clove from the reserved marinade and discard. Measure the marinade before adding it to the Dutch oven, adding more wine to make a total of 3 cups and enough beef stock to barely cover the meat. Add browned vegetables, tomato paste, garlic cloves, thyme, bay leaf, and bacon rind. Bring to a simmer on top of the stove. Turn the oven down to 325 degrees. Cover and return the Dutch oven to the lower third of oven. Let the meat simmer slowly for 3 to 4 hours.

The small onions: The onions are braised separately from the meat. Add butter and oil to a skillet. When butter and oil begin to bubble, add onions and sauté

Item 23. Six Printers Mottos: A Spectrum Specimen

over moderate heat for 10 minutes, rolling onions about so they will brown as evenly as possible. Do not break their skins. Pour in stock, season to taste, add herb bouquet. Cover and simmer slowly for 40 to 50 minutes, until most of liquid has evaporated. Discard herb bouquet and set onions aside in a bowl.

The mushrooms: The mushrooms are cooked separately from the meat and onions. Add butter and oil to a skillet. When butter and oil begin to bubble, add mushrooms and sauté over high heat, tossing and shaking skillet for 4 to 5 minutes. Reduce the heat to medium and add shallots and sauté for 2 minutes. Set mushrooms and shallots aside in a bowl. When the meat is tender, pour contents of the Dutch oven into a sieve set over a stockpot. Wash out Dutch oven and return meat and vegetables in the sieve to it. Distribute onions and mushrooms over meat. Skim fat from the sauce and simmer it in a saucepan for 2 minutes, skimming off additional fat as it rises. There should be about 2½ cups of sauce. Pour the sauce over the meat and vegetables. Cover and simmer for 3 minutes. Serve with boiled potatoes and chopped parsley.

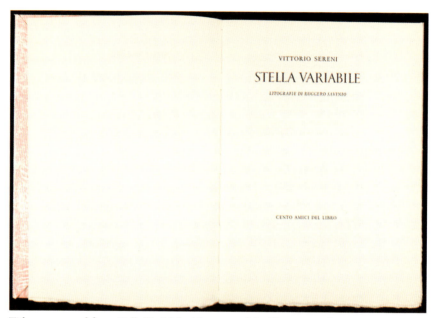

Title-page spread from *Stella Variabile*. (Courtesy of the University of Oregon Libraries.)

Item 24. *Stella Variabile*

A preface, thirty poems, a prose piece, and
notes in Italian by Vittorio Sereni. With seven
multicolor lithographs by Ruggero Savinio.
90 pages. 30.5 x 22 cm. 130 copies.1979.

Commission from I Cento Amici del Libro

Between 1939 and 1974 Giovanni Mardersteig printed twenty-one limited
editions for the Italian bibliophilic society, I Cento Amici del Libro (The
Hundred Friends of the Book), based in Milan. During the last couple of
years before his death in December 1977, however, he had been unable to
print any books because of ill health. Several members of the society, in particular Alberto Falck of the Italian steel-manufacturing family and president
of the society, were anxious to keep the Cento Amici intact and wanted to
see its illustrious publishing program continue.

The bylaws of the society made it difficult but not impossible to find another printer: the book had to be printed on a handpress in Italy – but not
necessarily by an Italian. On the other hand both text and illustrations had
to be by Italians. Even though there were a number of qualified printers, the
main obstacle in selecting one was Mardersteig's contention that if he couldn't
print the book, the society should disband. Falck had approached Franco
Riva, but Franco never accepted commissions. Franco, in turn, recommended that the society engage me to print their next book. Since I used a
handpress, he thought I would be an acceptable choice, reminding Falck
that many of the society's members were PWP collectors and already familiar with my work. Nevertheless, Mardersteig remained adamant about not
relinquishing his prerogative, and the society didn't want to offend an old
and revered friend.

As despicable as Mardersteig's behavior was, he remained our role model.
He had made it as a handpress printer and received worldwide recognition
for his achievements.

On the day of Mardersteig's funeral, Franco Riva and a number of Milanese industrialists, including Falck, surrounded me on the steps of the
Chiesa di S. Stefano in what must have appeared to the casual observer a

466 FANTASIES & HARD KNOCKS

rather bizarre scene. As the hearse conveying Mardersteig's remains went in one direction, this group of distinguished mourners whisked me off in the other. At lunch they officially offered me the commission to print the next book for the society. The restaurant was called the Torcolo, another word for torchio, which means "handpress" in Italian, an especially appropriate place to negotiate this particular printing contract. The Torcolo was across the street from our studio, and we often took guests there for lunch or dinner.

Preliminary Preparations for the Book

More than any other PWP book, *Stella Variabile* required extraordinary preparation prior to printing. Since every step had to be approved in advance, Alessandro Zanella and I often went to Milan to discuss the project with Falck and the editorial committee. Just deciding on the typeface took several months.

Once the Spectrum type arrived, we began setting the text. Even though the Spectrum roman by itself is quite beautiful, I don't find its narrow companion italic particularly compatible with it. The text contained large segments of italic, which complicated our work. To begin with we had to expand *all* the italic with paper letterspacing, hoping to make it more harmonious with the roman. In addition the long descenders of the italic were kerned – they extended unprotected beyond the type body – and were prone to snap off during printing. The type had apparently been cast in a particularly brittle alloy. For each form we had to stop after every tenth impression to check for broken italic descenders, using a mask that blocked out all the type except the kerned letters. Needless to say these complications slowed our progress considerably.

We were eager to use the pre-war Fabriano Esportazione "GF" paper that I had purchased in Padua several years before for the Borges/Pomodoro project because we already had it on hand. When folded it made a very pleasing quarto. Even though this paper was used for the mock-up of the book, the actual sample pages – with our proposed typographic design – were printed on a fine, polished newsprint. When we first showed them to the editorial committee in Milan, one of its members, Carlo Chiesa, a noted antiquarian bookseller whose shop was full of books printed by Aldus Manutius and Giambattista Bodoni, fingered the newsprint proofs and ex-

Item 24. Stella Variabile

claimed, "*Com'è bella questa carta!*" (What beautiful paper!) He wanted to know why we didn't print the whole book on it.

This was the society's first attempt to publish a book with a decidedly contemporary look – a move, I suspect, on Falck's part to bring younger blood into the society. Both the author and the artist were well-known intellectual nonconformists.

Vittorio Sereni

One of the biggest frustrations we had with this book was Vittorio Sereni's propensity for continually rewriting his work. He frequently changed his poems from edition to edition and in our case, from proof to proof. Our patience may have been taxed, but in the long run it was worth it because

Vittorio Sereni, Milan, Italy, no date. (Photo by Luca Carrà, courtesy of Parvum Photo.)

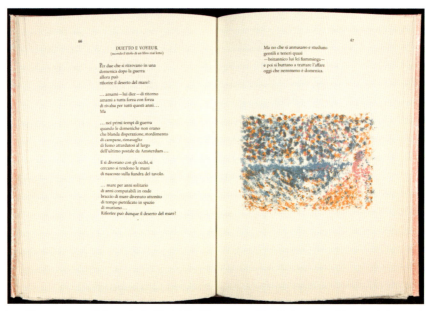

Double-page spread from *Stella Variabile*. (Courtesy of the University of Oregon Libraries.)

we liked his poetry. It wasn't every day that we were given an opportunity to publish one of Italy's major living poets. Vittorio dedicated this book to his friend, Dante Isella. After the publication of *Stella Variabile*, we stayed in touch with him, and he continued to be a supportive friend of the press until he died in 1983.

Here is one of Vittorio's shorter poems from the book:

Altro Posto di Lavoro

Non vorrai dirmi che tu
sei tu o che io sono io.
Siamo passati come passano gli anni.
Altro di noi non c'è qui che lo specimen
anzi l'imago perpetuantesi
a vuoto –
e acque ci contemplano e vetrate,
ci pensano al futuro: capofitti nel poi,
postille sempre più fioche
multipli vaghi di noi quali saremo stati.

Item 24. Stella Variabile

Ruggero Savino

Ruggero Savinio, the illustrator, worked in colored pastels, using a drawing technique closely akin to lithography. His vibrant multicolor abstractions subtly reflected the moods of the poems. Like Vittorio he also persisted in making last-minute changes. He kept adding illustrations, which disrupted the pagination and complicated the imposition. Several were on double-page spreads and had to be tipped onto the adjoining signatures so the sewing wouldn't cut through the images. Ruggero's lithographs were printed by Giorgio Upiglio in Milan. I had met Giorgio at an awards ceremony in Diano Marina in 1976 and was looking forward to someday working with him. His shop was considered the premiere printmaking atelier in Italy. This was the first of our three collaborations.

Ruggero Savinio, Rome, Italy, 2008. (Photo by Ruggero Passeri, with permission of the photographer.)

Printing the Book

Stella Variabile, the longest text printed at the PWP, took a full year to produce. This was due in part to my five-month absence from the press while I was teaching at the University of Alabama in the spring of 1979. Since Alessandro and I had legalized our partnership before I left – insuring the smooth operation of the press whenever I was away – he and Bradley Hutchinson were able to continue without me, completing most of the printing before I returned. Golda Fishbein's lettering beautifully complemented the Spectrum type, adding a quiet dignity to the kaleidoscopic brilliance of Ruggero's lithographs.

The studio with its three-foot-thick walls was a pleasant place to work in during the spring and fall, but a bit humid in the summer and an icebox in winter. During that first winter we had no heating in the studio, not even a little electric space heater; Alessandro and Brad would step outdoors into the courtyard to warm up. They liked to joke that this was the first book to be printed on frozen paper instead of dampened paper. Brad particularly suffered with his lightweight Alabama wardrobe. A group of his Italian friends took pity on him – he was, in their eyes, practically an indentured servant – and invited him to go on a weeklong ski trip in the Dolomites. His friends, in their designer ski outfits, were incredulous that he wasn't chilled to the bone in his flannel shirt and blue jeans, but he explained that the cold, dry mountain air was a welcome break from the penetrating, humid chill of the studio. I missed all the cold weather, not returning from the States until July.

That fall Brad returned to Alabama, where he continued his undergraduate studies at Spring Hill College in Mobile. Luckily for me, he was back at

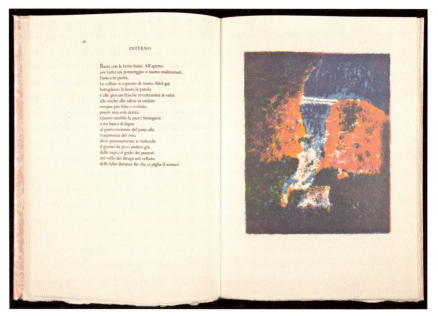

Full-page illustration from *Stella Variabile*. (Courtesy of the University of Oregon Libraries.)

Item 24. Stella Variabile

the University of Alabama working on his Master of Library Service degree when I returned to the States after the PWP closed in 1982.

The Cento Amici included several royal patrons among its members. One day while we were printing, our landlady, la marchesa Da Lisca, dropped by – as she was inclined to do – to show the Press to one of her out-of-town friends. When she asked what we were doing, I explained that we were printing the collectors' names on the colophon pages and showed her the one that I had just finished printing. This fortuitous *ad personam* read: *"Questo esemplare è stato stampato per S.R.A. Duchessa Anna d'Aosta"* (This copy was printed for Her Royal Highness Anna, Duchess of Aosta). "I see, I see," gasped la marchesa.

Binding the Books

We took the collated books to Alessandro Galvagni, who had been binding editions for the society for many years. It was a particularly tedious task because practically every signature required special handling. Galvagni was phasing out his edition-binding operation, so he kept setting our work aside for more lucrative jobs. Despite our pleas we had to wait several months before the books were finally ready to deliver to the Cento Amici.

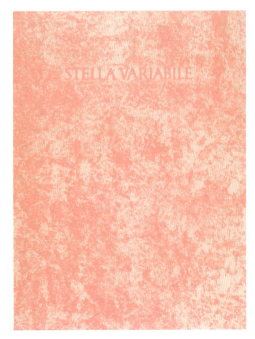

Cover for *Stella Variabile*. (Courtesy of the University of Oregon Libraries.)

PWP Bindery

Ever since moving into the new studio, we had had an eye focused on another smaller building that also opened onto our side courtyard. We thought it would be an ideal place to put our bindery. It was separated from our studio by an arched passageway leading to the rear courtyard. At first we thought it was empty, but then we noticed that about every other week a shadowy figure puffing on a cigarette – we later learned he was an accountant – would disappear into the little office. After a couple of hours he would lock up and leave, never responding to our greetings. One day we realized that we hadn't seen him for several weeks, so we approached la marchesa about also renting this space, if indeed it was vacant. Even if we gave up the studio at via Ponte Pietra, the new combined rent would be more than we could manage alone. In an effort to minimize our expenses, we offered half of the new space to Ernest Lehmann, president of The Overseas Federation of Teachers (a union for teachers who taught on U.S. military installations), convincing la marchesa that Ernie was our business manager. For Ernie, whom I had met during the summer of 1972 through Brooks Walker, the real appeal of the studio, aside from being near his friends, was the private parking space that came with it. In the historic center of Verona, parking was always at a premium. As soon as the rental contract was signed, we consolidated the PWP's activities at via Carlo Cattaneo.

Item 24. Stella Variabile 473

Gnocchi di Patate
Potato Gnocchi

Serves 6 to 8

One of the specialties at the Torcolo was *gnocchi di patate*. Gnocchi can be found throughout northern Italy. This is the classic recipe for potato gnocchi as it is made in the Veneto, usually without eggs. The absence of eggs gives these gnocchi their light and fluffy texture and delicate potato flavor.

A basil pesto sauce is one of the most popular for potato gnocchi. Purists will want to make the pesto using a mortar and pestle; however, most cooks today prefer to use a food processor. The sequence of steps is the same for both.

For the gnocchi
- 2 pounds of mature boiling potatoes
- 5½ ounces of "oo" flour *or* all-purpose flour, plus flour for dusting
- 1 teaspoon salt for the dough
- 1 tablespoon coarse salt for the gnocchi water

For the basil pesto sauce
- 1 large garlic clove, crushed
- ½ teaspoon coarse salt
- 2 ounces fresh green basil leaves, preferably small
- 1 ounce freshly grated pecorino sardo cheese
- 2 ounces freshly grated Parmigiano Reggiano cheese
- 1½ ounces pine nuts, lightly toasted
- ½ cup extra-virgin olive oil
  Additional freshly grated Parmigiano-Reggiano cheese for the topping
  6 to 8 slivers of cold butter for the garnish

The gnocchi: Select potatoes close in size and put them, unpeeled, in a large pot of unsalted cold water. The water should extend about half an inch above potatoes. When water begins to boil, reduce heat to a gentle simmer. Cover and cook until tender, about 20 to 30 minutes depending on their size. Do not prick potatoes while they are cooking. If the skins are broken, the potato pulp will absorb unwanted water and lose some of its starch. Drain potatoes and cut in half. Pass potatoes through a potato ricer onto an unfloured wooden board. Discard skins after each pressing. Ricing potatoes while still hot will keep them from becoming gluey. With your fingers, gently spread the mound of riced potatoes out until it forms a disk about an inch thick. Sprinkle salt evenly over potatoes. Let riced potatoes cool for about an hour. Cold potatoes will absorb considerably less flour than hot ones, thus producing lighter gnocchi. Shake about a third of the flour evenly over riced potatoes. Gently toss potatoes and flour together with your fingers as you spread the mixture out again. Do not apply any pressure; at this point the mixture should still be light and crumbly. Repeat the procedure for a second and third time. Gather the mixture into a large ball for kneading. Do not dust the working surface, the dough, or your hands with flour while kneading the dough. If you work fast, you should be able to knead the dough in 3 to 5 minutes. As soon as the dough starts to hold its shape, it is ready. Do not over-knead the dough. It should be soft and smooth on the outside and slightly moist on the inside.

Roll the dough into a log about eight inches long. Then cut off a two-inch piece and squeeze it into a thick coil about 6 inches long. With your fingers spread wide apart and using a gentle back-and-forth motion, roll the dough into a long thin coil, about 12 inches in length by ¾ of an inch in diameter. Begin in the middle and gradually work toward the ends, I personally like to roll the coil toward me, lifting and repositioning it at the top of the working surface each time. If the dough will not stay together or is stringy, it needs to be kneaded a bit more before you can roll it into coils. Lightly dust the working surface and roll the coil, one more time, from the top of the board to the bottom. With a paring knife, cut the coil into ½-inch lengths. Keep pieces small; potato gnocchi should be bite-size. Repeat procedure until all the coils have been cut into small pieces. Form the gnocchi on the back of a dinner fork and place them on a cookie sheet lined with paper towels. The ridges and indentations in the gnocchi will hold the sauce better. Select a large pot with a wide mouth, minimum 9-inch diameter. The number of gnocchi cooked at one time should never exceed the number that can float comfortably on the surface without crowding or overlapping. Bring 3 quarts of water to a rapid boil and add the coarse salt. Reduce the heat to a lively simmer and drop gnocchi into the water. They will fall to the

Item 24. Stella Variabile 475

bottom of the pot. With a long-handled wooden spoon, gently stir the water for a second or two to be sure none of the gnocchi are sticking to the bottom of the pot or to each other. Beware: vigorous boiling could cause the gnocchi to break apart or disintegrate. When the gnocchi are cooked, about 3 to 5 minutes, they will float up to the surface. Let them simmer on the surface for only a second or two before removing them from the pot with a large slotted skimmer, tapping the bottom of the skimmer on a paper towel before transferring them to a warm serving dish. Do not overcook gnocchi; if you do, they will be soggy. Try to remove them in the same order that they rose to the surface. Repeat procedure until all the gnocchi are cooked.

The basil pesto sauce: Crush garlic and salt. Tear basil leaves into small pieces and combine with garlic and salt. Add grated cheeses and pine nuts. Mash until the mixture is a coarse paste. Add oil in a steady trickle, stirring continually, until the mixture is well blended. Serve on individual plates or in a large bowl with extra grated cheese on the side. Top with a rounded teaspoon of pesto per serving and a sliver of butter.

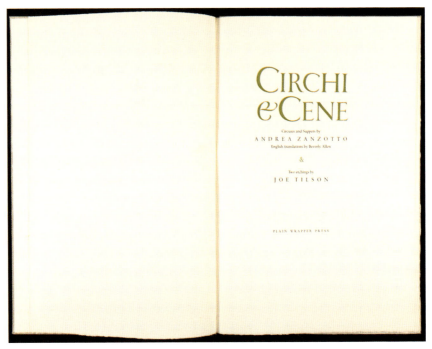

Title-page spread from *Circhi e Cene / Circuses and Suppers*. (Courtesy of the University of Oregon Libraries.)

Item 25. *Circhi e Cene / Circuses and Suppers*

Two poems in Italian by Andrea Zanzotto; with
English translations and a postscript by Beverly Allen.
With two multicolor etchings by Joe Tilson.
20 pages. 38.5 x 25.5 cm. 150 copies. 1979.

Re-evaluating the PWP Publishing Program

The move of the studio from via Duomo to via Carlo Cattaneo radically changed my life. I was more determined than ever to make a success of the Press. After *Stella Variabile* the publishing program at the PWP began to place more emphasis on texts in Italian. Italian collectors already accounted for more than one-third of the sales, and I saw an excellent potential for increasing this number through the Cento Amici del Libro. As far as I was concerned, the PWP – like the Officina Bodoni before it – was a *bona fide* Italian press, having lost its expatriate image several years earlier.

After finishing the commission for the Cento Amici, Alessandro Zanella and I looked forward to getting on with our own projects. We decided to start with another Quartus, which we hoped would lift our sagging spirits and bring in some badly needed income. Because of its simple format the average Quartus book – printed in one color throughout – could be produced with a minimum of two forms in less than two weeks.

Andrea Zanzotto

Jacques Vernière once showed me a text by Andrea Zanzotto that he had been planning to publish but never did. We contacted Zanzotto, the foremost poet in the Veneto, in January 1978. I liked Zanzotto's poetry very much, so Alessandro and I approached him about a PWP collaboration. A few months later he sent us a manuscript. In April, through Zanzotto we made contact with one of his translators, Beverly Allen, who taught at the University of California. In her note "On Translating Zanzotto," Beverly wrote:

> Translating Zanzotto's poetry is like wrestling with a myriad of minuscule angels. The translation process – always inevitably interpretive – here encounters a splendid play of arbitrariness, a constantly multi-faceted motivation in the original signs.

Andrea Zanzotto on the Lido, Venice, Italy, 1998. (Photo by Joe Oppedisano, with permission of the photographer.)

Zanzotto was well known in literary circles as a hypochondriac, and his preoccupation with medicines and their side effects often surfaces in his poetry, as seen here in these lines from "Circus-Cocò":

> Latches, latchesses in ready supply.
> Key of circus-colors-coach circus. Banners.
> In the toyed with fresh town, toy circus.
> Tiny little circus. Tonguelings that lick. Inguens. Bifed,
> trifed banners, battles. Billiards. Bottles.
> Oh that like a stream of streams banners bounces all the circus-cocò.

I started working on the layouts while still in New York in the spring of 1979, having been detained by extremely debilitating back problems, which continued to plague me until I left Alabama in 1988.

I was bedridden in the home of Hadassah Brooks, who looked after me while I was convalescing. Hadassah had first come to Verona on a visit in October 1975, and in spirit she never left. She quickly became a dear friend, and whenever she returned I took time off to travel around Italy with her. On these trips I was always able to put the cares of the PWP momentarily behind me.

Item 25. Circhi e Cene / Circuses and Suppers

Gabriel, sick in bed at Hadassah Brooks's apartment, New York, NY, 1979. (Photographer unknown, courtesy of PWP Archives.)

Designing the Book

Being incapacitated, I had plenty of time to study my layouts. In July 1979 I realized that the text was too long – even without illustrations – for an eight-page book. I redesigned it as a double Quartus: one in Italian and the other in English, with an original graphic in each, but this didn't make much sense, because the binding usually represented the major cost of a PWP book. On top of everything else, I could foresee certain marketing problems. We would be issuing two separate titles – unless we boxed them together – and the likelihood of our Italian collectors buying both was not particularly promising. I redesigned the project again, this time as a single bilingual volume. Like many other PWP projects, on the surface this one appeared to be trouble-free, but a number of unanticipated problems arose throughout its production.

Joe Tilson

Alessandro and I decided to ask Joe Tilson to illustrate the text because we had been very pleased with his work on the Burgess book. From the outset our relationship with him had been amicable and stress free. Joe wanted to use two multicolor etchings for this book. He would be in Milan toward the end of the summer having some of his giant etchings editioned at Giorgio Upiglio's atelier and could work on ours while he was there. This would minimize some of the logistical problems we experienced with the Burgess

Joe Tilson in the side courtyard at via Carlo Cattaneo, 6, Verona, Italy, 1980. (Photo by RGR, courtesy of PWP Archives.)

book. Giorgio, however, couldn't schedule our project until later that fall because of the impending August vacations that close everything down in Europe and his previous commitments. This meant not only that the book would be delayed for several more months, but even more critical, it would also leave us idle at the Press because we didn't have another project ready to put on the press in its place. Contrary to our preferred practice, we went ahead and printed the text first, and when Giorgio reopened in September, we took the printed sheets to him.

Giorgio, who was normally a precise and careful printer, had failed to notice that the trough in which the paper was being dampened was dirty. Most of the prints arrived covered with tiny ink spots that had to be removed with erasers and sandpaper. He offered to reprint the illustrations, but if he did, we would have to reprint the text as well, delaying the book even more. In retrospect we probably should have opted to reprint the text, even though none of the collectors seemed to be aware of the intensive cleanup job we had done.

Double-page spread from *Circhi e Cene / Circuses and Suppers*. (Courtesy of the University of Oregon Libraries.)

Alessandro Prints a Keepsake

In April 1979, while I was away in Alabama, Alessandro printed a small keepsake consisting of two poems by Zanzotto to commemorate the twenty-fifth wedding anniversary of his parents. The poems were originally written for Fellini's 1976 movie *Il Casanova di Fellini* and published in a book called *Filò* the same year.

Binding the Book

In December 1979 Roberto Gatti discussed the possibility of working in our bindery part time, but later changed his mind because he didn't feel that he was quite ready to tackle an expensive fine edition. After our trip to Belgium, he opened his own small trade bindery in Mestre near Venice. However, we did eventually convince him to make the slipcases for the book.

Through one of the paper salesmen who called on us we heard about another binder in Verona, Giuseppe Rossi, and went to see him. He showed us some work he was doing for Franco Riva, so we naturally assumed that

Left to right: Golda Fishbein, Roberto Gatti, Alessandro Zanella, and Roberto's girl friend in the rear courtyard at via Carlo Cattaneo, 6, Verona, Italy, 1980. (Photo by RGR, courtesy of PWP Archives.)

he was a qualified edition binder. What we didn't know was that Franco later withdrew the project because he was dissatisfied with the quality of Rossi's work. Rossi's wife sewed the books by hand, using a hit-and-miss technique that left unsightly holes in the book's gutter. Her clumsiness led me to devise a jig for pre-punching the holes in the signatures, which we used for all subsequent editions. She didn't know how to make endbands, so we took the sewn books to Francesco Graziani at the Biblioteca Capitolare, who added them. Once he was finished the books were brought back to Rossi to have the covers attached. He had a great deal of trouble with the pastedowns, which were self-ends, and many of the copies ended up with unsightly wrinkles. Alessandro was so frustrated by the experience that he suggested we put all future editions in European-style wrappers, which we could do ourselves in our studio.

A Financial Misunderstanding

The biggest blow of all was completely our fault. We had not discussed payment schedules with Rossi prior to leaving the job with him, and he de-

Item 25. Circhi e Cene / Circuses and Suppers

manded full payment before he would release any of the books – money we didn't have. One of the advantages of having a large number of Italian collectors was our ability to raise sizable sums of money within a few weeks *after* books were bound and delivered. None of the binders we had worked with before had asked for cash on delivery. In most cases the payment schedules had been rather vague, as in the unfortunate experience I had with Marcello Fornaro. Rossi's demand put one more crimp in our already tight cash flow. Somehow we managed to beg and borrow enough money to bail ourselves out. Printing was definitely ceasing to be pleasurable. Alessandro and I worked long, hard hours, often from 8 a.m. to 7 p.m. Even so, we never had enough money to pay ourselves anything close to a halfway decent wage.

Contractual agreements should be well defined. It would take many more years of blundering around in the dark before I realized the need for having a written understanding with my suppliers and sub-contractors that clearly specified each party's obligations.

In a letter, dated December 17, 1979, to Harvey Simmonds, I vented my misgivings about the Zanzotto book:

> There are things I don't like about it – as with all our books, I still haven't printed a book I really like – but on the whole it came out okay. One thing that upsets me terribly is to find errors in the printed text. This is inexcuseable for hand printed books. I was a little careless with the proofs for the English text. Brad set the text and Alessandro and I proof read it. The proof corresponded to the manuscript we had, but it was a Xerox and two punctuation marks got lost. I discovered this after the English text had been printed and I was comparing the Italian to the English. By then it was impossible to reprint the English – besides I would have had a revolution on my hands. Things were very tense, in fact, as soon as the text was printed my back went out again and I was confined to bed for two weeks.

Selling Books to the Cassa di Risparmio di Verona Vicenza e Belluno

For many years prior to my arrival in Italy, the banks were one of the chief sources of patronage for handpress printers in Verona. Each bank gave expensive limited editions as Christmas gifts to their most valued clients, many of whom – because of the bank's initiative – continued to expand their own collections directly through the printers. The crunch for money became more evident as the Italian economy slowed down in the mid-1970s. Although the banks started to cut back on their *noblesse oblige*, they still continued sporadically to buy a few books.

The officer in charge of public relations at the Cassa di Risparmio di Verona Vicenza e Belluno, the largest bank in the Veneto and holder of the PWP account, was dott. Giovanni Padovani, a bespectacled young man who stuttered. One day in February 1980 Alessandro and I had an appointment with him. Upon our arrival, we were ushered into his office – a grandiose relic of Fascist architecture – including exotic wood paneling and a twenty-foot-high ceiling. He indicated that we be seated. We showed him our books. He thought they were very attractive, but the bank could no longer afford such extravagances. Alessandro squirmed. Padovani twitched. There was a silence.

Padovani stood, as did Alessandro. The interview was over, but I remained seated. After a moment Padovani sat down again and leaning across the desk said, "What do you want from me?" "I want you to buy a few books," I replied. He murmured nervously, "Okay, okay, this time, but let's not make a habit of it." We all stood and bowed slightly to each other, shaking hands all around. Business Italian style.

Item 25. Circhi e Cene / Circuses and Suppers
485

Za'leti
Veneto Cornmeal Cookies

Yields about two dozen cookies

Zanzotto, who wrote most of his poetry in a combination of Italian and Solighese dialect, always conjures up memories of the traditional dishes of the Veneto region. Many a lazy afternoon in winter was spent drinking hot coffee and eating warm Za'leti cookies. Here is the recipe I prefer.

    3 cups yellow cornmeal
    2 cups all-purpose flour
    ¼ teaspoon salt
    1 teaspoon baking powder
    ¾ cup dark raisins
    ¾ cup grappa
    3 large eggs
    ½ cup sugar
    2½ ounces pine nuts
    Zest of 1 lemon
    2 teaspoons vanilla extract
    8 tablespoons unsalted butter, melted
    Flour for dusting the work surface
    Powdered sugar for dusting the cookies

Preheat the oven to 350 degrees. Sift cornmeal, flour, salt, and baking powder together and mix. Soak raisins in grappa until swollen. In a bowl, beat eggs, then add sugar and beat until blended. Add the cornmeal mixture a little at a time to the egg mixture. Add raisins along with grappa to the mixture along with pine nuts, lemon zest, vanilla, and butter. If dough is too stiff, add a little milk. On a dusted surface, roll out the dough to about ⅜-inch thick. Cut cookies into diamonds. Put za'leti on a cookie sheet lined with parchment paper. Place in the middle of the oven and bake for 25 to 30 minutes. Serve warm sprinkled with powdered sugar.

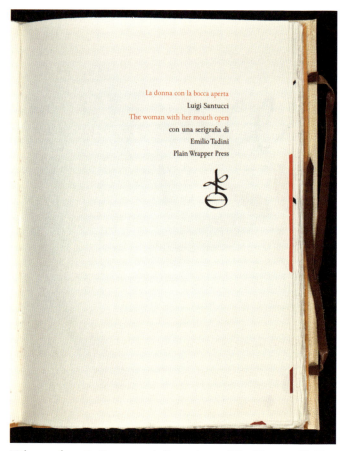

Title page from *La Donna con la Bocca Aperta / The Woman with Her Mouth Open.* (Courtesy of the University of Oregon Libraries.)

Item 26. *La Donna con la Bocca Aperta / The Woman with Her Mouth Open*

A story in Italian by Luigi Santucci; with an
English translation by Richard-Gabriel Rummonds.
With a three-page multicolor screenprint by Emilio Tadini.
48 pages. 31 x 22.5 cm. 110 copies. 1980.

Luigi Santucci

While I was designing books at Alfred A. Knopf in the late sixties, I came across a novel that completely captivated me. *Orfeo in Paradise* by Luigi Santucci (curiously enough designed by Golda Fishbein) is an account of a despondent young man who is mourning the death of his mother. In flashbacks Santucci unfolds an unusual story regarding their relationship. (In the nineties Robert Randall and I adapted this novel for a screenplay that was never produced.)

Luigi Santucci in his garden, Milan, Italy, 1998. (Photo by RGR, courtesy of PWP Archives.)

Shortly after I arrived in Verona I went to Milan to meet Santucci. His house was exactly like the one in the novel, and I expected at any moment to encounter his fictional characters roaming the halls or descending the stairs. I immediately let him know how much I admired *Orfeo*, rambling on and on in my faltering Italian. I finally mustered the courage to ask him if he would write a short story for my newly relocated Press. Not content that he graciously accepted my offer, I boldly went on to suggest that he use the relationship between mother and child again as the central theme. He responded favorably to the idea, and I left believing that I would soon have a text from him – the first manuscript to be commissioned by the PWP.

Over the next seven years Santucci and I were often in touch, although I had to wait until May 1978 before he gave me a manuscript. Alessandro Zanella and I personally went to Milan to pick it up from Santucci, who served us tea. I explained to him that jointly with the author we often presented a copy of our collaboration to a distinguished person, and asked him to recommend an appropriate recipient. He suggested his close friend Pope Paul VI, Giovanni Battista Montini, the former cardinal of Milan. Alessandro nearly fell off the sofa. His leftist friends would never let him live it down if word got out we had given the pope a PWP book. Alessandro didn't have to worry, because the pope died in August of that year – two years before the book was ready for distribution. Santucci received 400,000 lire (about $665) for his story.

Santucci's Manuscript

Set in the Middle Ages, *La Donna con la Bocca Aperta* / *The Woman with Her Mouth Open* is a gothic tale of an unborn child who speaks through the open mouth of its mother. I was extremely pleased with the story; so much so that I decided to translate it myself. By then my Italian had improved to the point that I felt confident I could undertake such a daunting task. Alessandro is credited in the colophon as co-translator; however, I did this more as a gesture of our solidarity than an indication of his actual collaboration. Both Alessandro and Golda did make invaluable suggestions as they read through my drafts, helping me find the exact word or refining a phrase. It was a slow endeavor; writing has never come easily for me. I worked sporadically on the translation after receiving the manuscript, but by the fall of 1979 the urgency to get it on the press after the holidays forced me to concentrate more diligently on it.

Item 26. La Donna con la Bocca Aperta 489

    Olga Gibroni, an old friend from my first year in Verona, loaned me her apartment on Lake Garda for October and November. I could write there without being disturbed. I would get up early and after my morning *cappuccino* stake out a bench on the promenade facing the lake. Surrounded by notebooks and dictionaries, I tried to be faithful to Santucci's unique voice while painstakingly rendering his story into English. After having already revised the text many times, even as Alessandro was making last-minute adjustments on the press, I was still editing the proofs for the pages we were about to print. Once the press was ready, Alessandro would call out, "Gabriel, last chance for changes!" And I would reluctantly join him at the press, accepting the finality implicit in the act of printing.

    These few lines toward the end of my translation illustrate the richness of Santucci's prose:

> Geneviève felt that someone was setting himself in motion inside her body, someone who was doing her violence. She felt limp, then her blood began to flow from her, spilling onto the floor.
>
>   The Child was now struggling all by himself like a beast determined to escape; doing less and less to save her life, concerned only with his own.

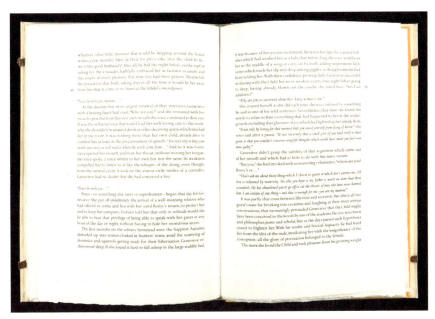

Double-page spread from *La Donna con la Bocca Aperta / The Woman with Her Mouth Open.* (Courtesy of the University of Oregon Libraries.)

And as he approached the outlines and images of the world, his knowledge dissolved. Now, above all, he was abandoned by his true mother, Memory: that prophetic remembrance of everything that had come to him from his ancestors and even from the oldest animals before them.

In December 1979, using the Spectrum type which had been redistributed after the Sereni and Zanzotto books were bound, we began setting the text. It was very time consuming because there were a lot of long passages in italic, which again had to be letterspaced with paper. It was my idea to set the child's speeches from the womb in italic. Later when the story was reprinted by Arnoldo Mondadori Editore, these were set in roman.

Printing the Book

Alessandro and I had been pleased with how well the Spectrum type had printed on the Fabriano Esportazione "GF" paper, so we decided to use it for this book. Another reason for selecting this paper was economic. We had a large supply of it in our storeroom, which helped minimize our cash outlay.

Alessandro Zanella and Gabriel at the Washington press in the via Carlo Cattaneo studio, Verona, Italy, 1980. (Photo by Robert Mahon, with permission of the photographer.)

Item 26. La Donna con la Bocca Aperta 491

Looking for the Right Artist

I often thought of Santucci's work as verbally related to Marc Chagall's paintings, so I was looking for a contemporary artist whose style would resemble that element of fantasy found in Chagall's work. As early as 1975 – before I had a manuscript – I had discussed this project with John Alcorn, hoping he would want to illustrate it. In a brochure distributed at the Arte Fiera '76 in Bologna, this collaboration was listed as a "book in preparation." John, a talented American artist who lived in Florence – and one of Golda's former classmates at Cooper Union in New York – was best known in Italy for his lively and figurative book jacket illustrations, primarily for Rizzoli Editore. Unfortunately John returned to the States before I finished translating Santucci's manuscript, and I was reluctant to get into a long-distance collaboration on this particular item. (John later illustrated a book for me that was printed by my students at the University of Alabama.)

Emilio Tadini

The next artist to become involved with the project was Emilio Tadini, whose work Alessandro and I had seen at an impressive exhibition at Studio Marconi in Milan. Tadini was really arrogant, not the least bit amenable to suggestions about the illustrations. Though stylistically quite different, Tadini captured Chagall's spirit with his hard-edge, collage-like paintings of floating figures. It seemed a perfect match, all the more so since Tadini and Santucci were contemporaries. They had even been school friends.

Tadini oviously didn't take the challenge very seriously, because what he gave us was a minimal graphic statement comprised of a few obvious symbols from the text: candles and mushrooms, for example. The big mistake we made was not expressing our disappointment with his sketch right away. It wasn't until many months later, when we were ready to print the book, that we admitted to ourselves that his multipage illustration wasn't appropriate for the text, but by then it was too late to remedy the situation.

Difference between Working with Authors and Artists

There is a complicated schedule involved in printing illustrated books that does not apply when printing texts alone. Authors are used to the long hiatuses that occur between editing, proofing, printing, binding, and marketing. Artists, on the other hand, are used to instant gratification. What they

Triple-page illustration from *La Donna con la Bocca Aperta / The Woman with Her Mouth Open*. (Courtesy of the University of Oregon Libraries.)

produce is immediately before them. When there is a delay in the publication of an illustrated book, the artist tends to lose interest and doesn't like to be asked to make modifications long after the illustrations have been accepted and approved. We waited too long to reopen any kind of a meaningful dialog with Tadini, so we had to use his sketch as it was. It was, however, beautifully screenprinted by Luigi Berardinelli.

Carol Joyce and the Binding of the Book

Taking advantage again of the proximity of Lanfranco Lui's La Pergamena parchment tannery, we decided to elaborate on the medieval setting of the story by putting the book in a limp parchment binding. Each skin, enough for one copy, cost 21,000 lire (about $35). Carol Joyce came back to Verona for six weeks in May and June 1980. During her stay, with careful planning, she was able to bind most of the edition of one hundred ten copies and still catch her scheduled flight home.

She wrote about her detail-intensive experience in the *Guild of Book Workers Journal* (volume 19, numbers 1 and 2, 1980–81):

> There were 2200 precise slits to be made in the vellum and 2200 lacings to be fitted through them, 880 holes, 440 slots, 880 folds, 220 headbands, 880 corners to cut out, 440 thongs to pare, 220 endsheets to make.

Item 26. La Donna con la Bocca Aperta

Cover for *La Donna con la Bocca Aperta / The Woman with Her Mouth Open*. (Courtesy of the University of Oregon Libraries.)

Robert Mahon and Carol Joyce standing in front of the PWP bindery in the side courtyard at via Carlo Cattaneo, 6, Verona, Italy, 1980. (Photo by RGR, courtesy of PWP Archives.)

Fortunately she had the help of Mauro Rubin, a young Italian interested in the book arts, with some of the cutting and folding. Golda also helped Carol assemble the books. After Carol returned to the States, Mauro, who had been meticulously trained by Carol, was able to finish binding the last ten or twelve copies on his own.

Even though we had decided not to bring our second standing press from Ponte Pietra to via Carlo Cattaneo – there was no room for it in the new studio – Carol had the use of a small press that we had borrowed from Gino Castiglioni and Sandro Corubolo, two young printers who were very supportive of the PWP. This made her work a little less hectic compared to the Burgess/Tilson book. My biggest regret is that we didn't put the book in a drop-spine box; the chemise and slipcase, which were made elsewhere, were somewhat clumsy and distracted from Carol's elegant and refined binding.

During Carol's visit Santucci came to Verona to sign the colophon pages, which she documented in a photo-essay.

Postscript

My translation of "The Woman with Her Mouth Open" appeared in the Fall 1987 issue of *Boulevard*.

Gabriel, Luigi Santucci, and Alessandro Zanella in the via Carlo Cattaneo studio, Verona, Italy, 1980. Santucci is signing the colophon page. (Photo by Carol Joyce, courtesy of the photographer.)

Risotto con Zafferano alla Milanese

Milanese-Style Saffron Risotto

Serves 6 to 8

Santucci was the epitome of the Milanese gentleman, so pairing him with one of the great culinary treats of the region seems a natural choice. Milan is famous for its saffron rice, which is also popular throughout the Veneto. I prefer the recipe below.

6 cups beef stock, divided
3 pinches saffron strands
3 tablespoons butter, divided
2 tablespoons olive oil
3 tablespoons beef marrow, diced
1 teaspoon freshly ground white pepper
6 ounces yellow onion, peeled and finely chopped
2 cups Arborio risotto rice
½ cup dry white wine
1 teaspoon salt
½ cup freshly grated Parmigiano-Reggiano cheese, plus additional for the table

Bring 5 cups of the beef stock to a boil in a medium saucepan over high heat. Reduce the heat to keep warm. Warm the remaining cup of stock in a small saucepan over medium heat. Add saffron. Reduce the heat to keep warm. Put 1 tablespoon of the butter, oil, marrow, pepper, and onions in a large saucepan and cook over medium-high heat until onions are pale gold, about 7 minutes. Add rice, stirring to coat it with the butter and oil mixture. Add wine and salt and cook for 1 minute. Add 1 cup of the simmering stock at a time, stirring constantly. Wait until almost all the stock has been absorbed before adding more. Add the remaining cup of stock with saffron and cook until rice is tender, about 35 minutes. Remove from the heat and vigorously stir in cheese and the remaining butter.

Title page from *Lo Stemma Cittadino*. (Courtesy of the University of Oregon Libraries.)

Item 27. *Lo Stemma Cittadino*

A very short story by Franz Kafka
translated from the German into
Italian by Ervino Pocar.
8 pages. 25.5 x 18 cm. 160 copies. 1980.

Another Misunderstanding

I Cento Amici del Libro was based in Milan, so we often went there to discuss projects with Alberto Falck and members of the editorial committee. Though *Stella Variabile*, our previous commission for them, was generally pleasing to the membership, Falck was unhappy that it had taken so long to produce. There was also a misunderstanding as to whether the copies for the PWP were to be included in the edition. Our contract with the society stated that we would receive a specific number of copies in addition to our

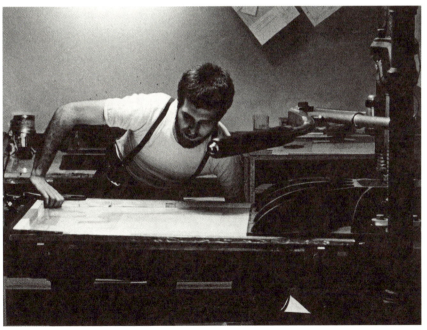

Alessandro Zanella rolling the bed under the platen of the Washington press around the time *Lo Stemma Cittadino* was printed in the via Carlo Cattaneo studio, Verona, Italy, 1980. (Photo by Robert Mahon, with permission of the photographer.)

fee, and I assumed these would come from the thirty extra copies printed for the collaborators. One cannot always rely on the veracity of the information found in the colophons of some Italian press books; the stated number of copies of an edition may be misleading. Falck thought that we would print extra copies for ourselves – as Giovanni Mardersteig had always done – but this had never been my practice, nor had we been asked to do so by him. In the end we took part of our copies from the edition and the balance in bound proofs.

I usually tried to schedule a short piece, something like a keepsake or a Quartus, immediately after completing a major book. So in June 1980 – still exhausted from printing the Santucci book – Alessandro Zanella and I offered to print a small keepsake for the society in order to get back into their good graces before starting on their next book, *Epistole* by Felice Feliciano.

We selected a text by Franz Kafka, *Das Stadtwappen* in German and *The City Coat of Arms* in English. Our text, pirated from a popular Italian edition of Kafka's short fiction, describes the building of the Tower of Babel. For us it was a private joke on a situation that had inadvertently been rife

Franz Kafka, place and date unknown. (Photographer unknown.)

Item 27. Lo Stemma Cittadino

with misunderstandings about the number of copies from the edition that we were entitled to. The keepsake, which required only three forms plus a fourth for the wrapper, was quickly produced, using materials on hand. Mauro Rubin also helped at the press. The keepsake was sent out gratis to the Cento Amici and PWP collectors.

The Payoff

Ironically we ended up not doing any more work for the Cento Amici. A few of the members objected to Vittorio Sereni's text for *Stella Variabile* and most of them to the "modernity" of Ruggero Savinio's illustrations. They lobbied for a return to classic texts and figurative graphics, as well as a more traditional approach to the typography. In the end the printing of the annual book for I Cento Amici del Libro reverted to the Officina Bodoni – run by Martino Mardersteig's wife Gabriella – where the society's members could be assured of receiving Giovanni Mardersteig clones, books that would offend no one. More than a decade later, however, Alessandro printed the annual book for the Cento Amici in 1993, 1999, 2000, 2005, and 2007 at his Ampersand studio.

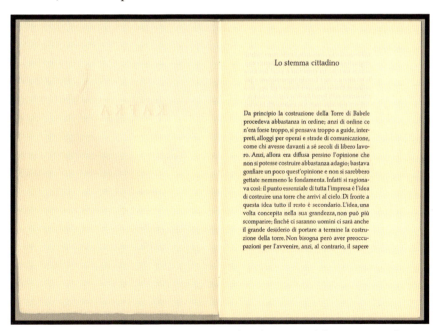

The first page of the story from *Lo Stemma Cittadino*. (Courtesy of the University of Oregon Libraries.)

Perhaps I got my just reward, because my motives in seeking the commission had not been entirely honorable. On the one hand, I pursued it in order to spite Mardersteig, who was still alive when the negotiations began, and to prove to him that I had become a printer to be reckoned with; on the other, I anticipated finding new PWP collectors through the society's mailing list. In the end I lost on both counts. I had given Falck what he asked for, meanwhile losing more than a year of press time on PWP projects. Few of the Cento Amici who were not already PWP collectors bought our subsequent editions.

A Project for Fulvio Testa

Around this time we also printed the text for fifty copies of *Bestiario vegetale*, a portfolio of four etchings by Fulvio Testa. Luciano Cristini pulled the etchings, and Mauro made all of the handsome portfolios. We always liked being involved in projects with friends. In June 1982 Fulvio, Alessandro, and I went to Washington, DC, to see Ruth Fine, curator of Prints and Drawings at the National Gallery. The three of us slept on the floor at Judith Sillari's, whom I first met when she accompanied Brendan Gill to Verona in the summer of 1979.

Agnello alle Olive
Lamb with Black Olives

Serves 6

Italians are very fond of lamb dishes. They are easy to prepare, and any left-overs make delicious sandwiches.

     3 sprigs fresh rosemary, 4 inches long
     1 large garlic clove
     1 (5-pound) leg of lamb, trimmed of fat with the sirloin end
          removed, the shank bone cracked and tucked under the thick
          part of the leg
       Freshly ground black pepper to taste
     2 tablespoons extra-virgin olive oil
       Salt to taste
    12 ounces red onion, coarsely chopped
    ⅔ cup dry red wine, plus 3 tablespoons, divided
    ½ cup drained canned tomatoes
    ½ cup Niçoise olives, pitted
    ½ cup meat stock, if needed

Remove leaves from rosemary sprigs and put them in a mortar. Add garlic and crush to a paste with a pestle. Using a paring knife, cut small slits in the meat. Fill them with the crushed rosemary mixture. Sprinkle the meat with pepper. Cover and refrigerate 8 to 24 hours. Select a Dutch oven large enough to hold the meat snugly. Heat oil over medium heat. Add the meat and lightly salt. Slowly brown the meat for 1 hour, turning it every 20 minutes. Lower heat if necessary. Add onions. Add wine and bring to a simmer. Cover with the lid askew over low heat for 2 hours. Turn frequently as it cooks, basting it with its juices. Stir in the remaining 3 tablespoons of wine and olives. Slowly simmer, uncovered, for 35 minutes. The lamb is done when an instant-reading thermometer reaches 140 degrees. Add a little more stock if juices have evaporated. Transfer meat to a cutting board and cut into ¼-inch thick slices. Arrange slices on a warm platter. Pour the juices over the sliced meat.

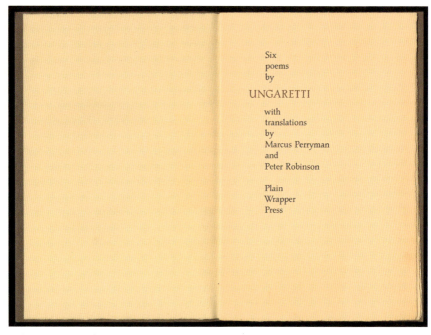

Title-page spread from *Six Poems*. (Courtesy of the University of Oregon Libraries.)

Item 28. *Six Poems*

Six poems in Italian by Giuseppe Ungaretti; with English translations of the poems by Marcus Perryman and Peter Robinson, and a note in English on printing bilingual editions by Richard-Gabriel Rummonds and Alessandro Zanella.
12 pages. 29 x 19.5 cm. 120 copies. 1980.

Giuseppe Ungaretti

In the summer of 1980 Marcus Perryman and Peter Robinson, having heard of the PWP, came by to ask Alessandro Zanella and me if we would be interested in printing a short selection of Giuseppe Ungaretti's poems in Italian with their translations in English. Marcus, who taught English in Verona, and Peter, an editor in London, were trying to persuade an English publisher to commission them to translate a more comprehensive collection of Ungaretti's work.

Printing Bilingual Editions

We enthusiastically accepted their proposal because it coincided with a project we had considered for some time: a small keepsake in which we could

Giuseppe Ungaretti as a soldier in World War I, Vallone, Italy, 1917. (Photographer unknown.)

demonstrate a variety of ways to present bilingual editions of poetry. The Borges text had established a pattern for PWP bilingual editions. The complete text in the original language came first, followed by the translation. This was done primarily to keep the flow of each text intact.

In this book the presentation of each poem and its translation was deliberately styled in a different way. In our note we said:

> We hope this exercise will inspire others to look more closely at the typographic challenges which are inherent in bilingual editions.

Printing the Keepsake

We were able to secure the rights to print the poems in Italian from our friend Vittorio Sereni, an editor at Arnoldo Mondadori Editore. We printed it in July, giving the translators half of the edition.

We didn't have enough Richard de Bas paper left in stock for the entire edition, so half of the copies had to be printed on Fabriano PWP paper. Since both papers were the same size, this didn't present any problems. *Six Poems*

Double-page spread from *Six Poems*. (Courtesy of the University of Oregon Libraries.)

is the only PWP publication issued in a variant edition. All others were uniform in materials and bindings.

Example of Ungaretti's Poetry

Ungaretti's poems were considered quite avant-garde for their time. This one from 1916 uses no punctuation, which is typical of Ungaretti's work:

> *Sleepiness*
>
> These ridges of hills
> have stretched out for the night
> in the dark of the valleys
>
> Nothing's left
> but the grating of crickets
> which reaches me
>
> And matches
> my forebodings

Marcus Perryman, Vittorio Sereni, and Peter Robinson in the side courtyard at via Carlo Cattaneo, 6, Verona, Italy, 1981. (Photo by RGR, courtesy of PWP Archives.)

Postscript

The following summer when Vittorio was visiting in Verona, we introduced him to Marcus and Peter, who were interested in translating his work as well as Ungaretti's.

In one sense this was another thankless task. After we printed the keepsake and introduced the translators to Vittorio, we never heard from them again. Who knows if our keepsake helped them get the Ungaretti commission they sought, or if they went on to translate Vittorio's poetry into English? I believe Vittorio died before Marcus and Peter were able to conclude any formal agreement. On the positive side our typographic design for this project inspired Alessandro's design for *Il Cinque Maggio / Der Fünfte Mai*, the last commission printed at the PWP.

Item 28. Six Poems

Zabaglione
Marsala Custard

Serves 4

In one sense *Six Poems* was not much more than a bit of fluff, a promotion piece for the translators and the printers. Fluff always reminds me of zabaglione, a light Italian dessert served in the summer with fresh berries. It is also quick to make.

4 large egg yolks
¼ cup sugar
½ cup Marsala wine
    Pinch of cinnamon, optional

Put egg yokes and sugar into the top of a double boiler and, using a large whisk, beat until they are thick and pale yellow, about 5 minutes. Add water to the bottom of the double boiler and bring to a simmer. Set the top half of the double boiler into the bottom half. Gradually drizzle Marsala, whisking continuously. Continue whisking until the mixture is light and foamy and holding soft peaks, about 15 minutes. Top with a pinch of cinnamon and serve warm or chilled.

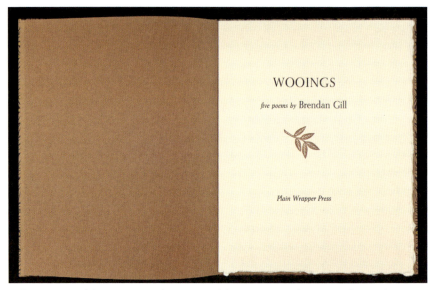

Title-page spread from *Wooings*. (Courtesy of the University of Oregon Libraries.)

Item 29. *Wooings*

Five poems by Brendan Gill.
With a linocut ornament by Fulvio Testa.
8 pages. 28 x 22.5 cm. 155 copies. 1980.

Incapacitated

During the winter of 1978–79, the problems with my back that I had been having intermittently since I moved to Verona became more intense. I had no sooner arrived in the States in December – en route to Alabama for my second teaching stint – when I became incapacitated. I couldn't even sit up in bed. Fortunately, I was again the guest of Hadassah Brooks, in whose home I usually stayed when I was in New York. Before long she had me on my feet again and safely on my way to Alabama. Luckily, I didn't miss many classes, but discomfort continued throughout the semester, and on my return to New York from Alabama in May I had a relapse that forced me to stay in bed for a couple of weeks, this time with a herniated disc. By early June, however, I was well enough to hobble around with a cane and even ventured out to visit a few friends.

Brendan Gill

One day in June 1979, Herbert Mitgang at *The New York Times* casually mentioned that Brendan Gill had filled in at the last moment for their mutual friend Anthony Burgess, who had been scheduled to give a reading at Sarah Lawrence College the previous fall. Herb said he thought Brendan would be interested in seeing the Burgess/Tilson book.

Soon after, I called Brendan and made an appointment to visit him at the "Hideaway," his private refuge on West 43rd Street, a few floors below his office at *The New Yorker*. Since I could just barely manage to carry my own weight around, let alone a bag of heavy books, I asked Frank Alweis, a close friend of Hadassah's, if he would like to come along with me – be my porter. Frank lived in the south of France but was in New York on a visit. Being an avid reader of Brendan's work in *The New Yorker*, he eagerly accepted my offer.

Feeling a bit like a wandering gypsy peddler, I spread my wares – the Borges/Pomodoro and the Burgess/Tilson books – out on Gill's coffee table.

509

Brendan Gill, place and date unknown. (Photographer unknown, courtesy of Brendan Gill.)

He was fascinated by them, turning the leaves and pausing here and there to read a bit of the text. What really intrigued him that afternoon was that an antiquated technology was being employed to produce these very contemporary-looking books. As we talked we were both surprised to discover how much we had in common. I immediately responded to his humor and catholic tastes. He talked passionately about books, the theater, movies, architecture, photography – all the things I enjoyed in Verona and missed during my brief sojourns in the culturally arid climate of Tuscaloosa, where the university was located.

I got back to Verona in July 1979, and Brendan came to visit in August with his friend Judith Sillari. Hadassah and Fulvio Testa joined us for *aperitivi* in an outdoor café. As Brendan and I chatted, a plan for this book emerged.

Item 29. Wooings 511

He had several poems that had already appeared in magazines, as well as a couple of unpublished ones he thought would make an enjoyable little book. When the manuscript arrived in December, I was delighted with it. In addition to everything else, it was the perfect length for a Quartus.

"Norfolk" is one of the poems Brendan wrote specially for this edition:

> *Norfolk*
>
> High in an attic room, on a bed
> Unsheeted, with rusty springs, they made love
> As if among green treetops. In her eyes,
> He saw the sun falter. Hard or soft,
> Whatever they touched tasted
> Not only of themselves but of good fortune.
> In the garden below, their friends drank
> And talked, not yet missing them.
> Nothing had readied them for this encounter.
> "How lucky we are!" he said. From the taut
> Cage of her ribs, a pizzicato of heartbeats:
> "Hush! Not a word!" Only the bed
> Sang on, and speech was not its language.

By the end of the summer of 1980, we had already printed one long book and two keepsakes. So, for a well-deserved rest Alessandro went to Sardinia for the month of August, and I stayed behind in Verona, keeping the studio open with the help of Mauro Rubin. I was especially anxious to print this item before the end of the year because I wanted to include it in the two PWP retrospectives that were coming up in 1981.

Printing the Book

Mauro and I had many problems printing this Quartus. When damp, the British Hand Made Parchment Substitute paper we were using did not want to absorb the brown ink. I didn't realize this until after we had already printed the text in black on both sides of the sheet and the titles in brown on one side. As we were backing up the titles, which had been printed only a few days earlier, I discovered that they were setting off onto the slipsheets, leaving nothing more than mottled ghosts where they had been.

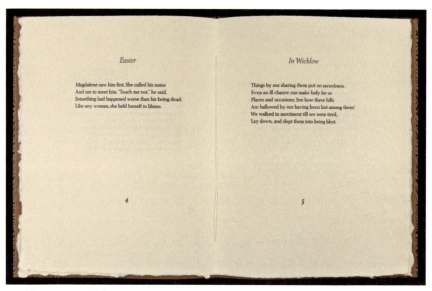

Double-page spread from *Wooings*. (Courtesy of the University of Oregon Libraries.)

Since *Wooings* was being printed like any other quarto in two colors, this is probably a good place to explain the printing sequence at the PWP. Following the practices of printers of the handpress period, we began with the inner form – the one that included the next-to-the-lowest-page number. Printing the inner form first was done to prevent the pages on the reverse side of the sheet from being marred by the deep impression of the type during the backing-up process, although with hard packing, we were usually able to minimize the bite of the type into the paper. After the second form of text was printed, we would start to print the titles in the second color, reversing the order of the forms, because it was easier to put the paper back on the points exactly as it had come off during the printing of the previous form.

In retrospect, I don't think it was the fault of the paper – the black ink did not set off when we backed up the text. There was probably something in the brown ink that prevented it from adhering properly to the dampened paper. Even so, I continued to blame the paper. I was under a great deal of pressure to finish this book, so I wasn't thinking logically. Logic would have dictated changing the brown ink, but instead I scrapped the whole edition, and we started over again – this time without dampening the paper. For many years

Item 29. Wooings 513

I had taken it for granted that any western handmade paper, especially a heavily sized one, could be printed damp. After this experience I vowed to test each new paper before ordering it.

On the basis of a 2 x 3-inch sample, I had ordered two thousand sheets when the Inveresk Paper Company ran a special on it. The paper, which was made at the Wookey Hole Mill, was reasonably opaque and looked handmade, with very irregular feathery deckles. I don't know why I didn't ask for a few test sheets. It was not ordered for any specific project, just for stock. I never tried to use it again for bookwork, and the balance of the stock was eventually sold to W. Thomas Taylor, a bookseller and publisher in Austin, Texas.

Although my prolonged visits to Alabama were increasing the sales of PWP books as well as the visibility of the Press in the States, combined with the pressure to complete projects before my departure they also had a noticeably negative effect on the quality of the work at the PWP. With only eight pages of text, a typographical error crept into the colophon, which Brendan immediately spotted as he was about to sign the page. Having already printed the book twice, I couldn't face reprinting it a third time – even though it would have required only four forms – so Brendan and I devised an evasive errata sheet, never specifically mentioning the error.

> *By Way of Errata*
>
> To our chagrin, an error was discovered on the colophon page as Brendan Gill was about to sign it. Since we are unable to reprint these pages, we ask the indulgence of both the author and our collectors.

Handling Paper with Full Deckled Edges

The exaggerated feathery deckles on this paper remind me of another minor technical point. Many PWP collectors have commented on the presence of small pencil marks on the upper, outside edges of the leaves, and asked why these pencil marks were not erased. We did not erase them because they were an intrinsic part of the printing process. Since handmade paper has an irregular deckle on all four sides, it is impossible to use traditional guides to position it for printing. In order to guarantee perfect registration, the paper is placed on points attached to the tympan.

Most handpress printers simply put the paper on the points by eyeballing it and then applying a little pressure. I devised a system I considered to be more precise. First the sheet was folded in half by bringing the two narrow ends together, keeping the long sides as parallel as possible. Any irregularities in the dimensions of the paper were equalized along the narrow ends. A small tick mark was made with the side of a soft pencil along the outer edge of the crease at both ends. Then the paper was unfolded and dampened. The next day the paper was taken out of the humidor, and a Mylar template with holes pricked in it to correspond to the position of the points on the tympan was aligned on the sheet, using the tick marks as guides. The paper was then pricked with a pushpin. After the sheets were printed and pressed, these same point holes, which in quarto were centered vertically and horizontally between the upper and lower text blocks, could be used as guides when folding the signatures.

Fulvio Testa

Fulvio Testa cut the leaf ornament for the title page. The original idea was to have a stem with five leaves to accompany the first of the five poems, the stem reappearing and progressively losing a leaf with each of the following poems. Fulvio, a master of the fine line, was never completely at ease with the bold, rough-hewn strokes of relief prints. Since I was not particularly

Fulvio Testa, Paris, France, 1980. (Photo by Henryk Wieniewski, courtesy of Fulvio Testa.)

Item 29. Wooings   515

enthusiastic about the ornaments he had cut, I decided to use only the five-leaf stem on the title page. I suppose the symbolism was a little trite to begin with. Even though I was a little disappointed with Fulvio's ornament, I found his decorated papers, screenprinted by Luigi Berardinelli, very effective. Screenprinting continued to offer many alternatives to letterpress printing at the PWP, although we never carried it to the heights of sophistication Frances Butler and Alastair Johnston did at their Poltroon Press.

Brendan Gill's Support

After the publication of *Wooings*, Brendan continued to be an enthusiastic supporter of my work. He brought John Cheever and me together for a project that was originally scheduled as the last PWP book; however, the press was closed before the manuscript arrived. (I later decided to print it as the premier work issued in Alabama by Ex Ophidia, the successor to the PWP.) As the president of The Library Fellows of the Whitney Museum

Cover for *Wooings*. (Courtesy of the University of Oregon Libraries.)

of American Art, Brendan was also instrumental in my being commissioned by that group to print their first two limited-edition gift books in 1983 and 1984.

In the spring of 1981, during my third teaching stint in Alabama, Brendan suggested that I get in touch with Gray Boone, publisher of *Horizon* magazine, believing she might be able to expand my social life and broaden my cultural contacts in the South. Gray lived in Tuscaloosa and was very fond of Brendan, having published several of his articles in her magazine. She came to dinner one night with Mary Mathews, wife of the president of the university. I served squid and shrimps with artichoke hearts sautéed in garlic and olive oil as the first course. Mary was squeamish about eating the squid. "I can't eat testicles," she kept saying, and Gray would respond, "Mary, they're not *testicles*; they're tentacles." And Mary would squeal again, "That's what I said. I can't eat testicles."

Through no fault of Brendan's, my lifestyle in Alabama did not improve; but meeting Gray did have an indirect effect on the Press. She put me in touch with Ray Bradbury, who had written an article for the July 1979 issue of *Horizon* in which he reflected on his friendship with Bernard Berenson, the art connoisseur. In it Bradbury reported that Berenson always drank Burgundy wines. I found this rather puzzling since Berenson lived in the heart of Chianti country near Florence, where some of the best Italian red wines are produced. Incredulous, I wrote Bradbury, who replied that it was indeed true. He is the author of one of my two all-time favorite short stories: "The Cold Wind and the Warm" (the other being "Paul's Case" by Willa Cather). I had hoped that someday Bradbury and I would work together on a project. At the time, he appeared to be interested but nothing ever came of it, perhaps because I was not sufficiently persistent.

In the same article Bradbury described how Berenson handled the hordes of visitors to the Villa I Tatti, his home. He would send them off on a sightseeing jaunt and meet them later for lunch to hear about what they had seen. At the PWP we had nowhere near Berenson's volume of visitors, but one or two inquisitive people underfoot in the studio was enough to interrupt our printing rhythm for the whole day. So like Berenson we solved the problem by sending them off sightseeing. Then on their return we would set up a large table in one of our two courtyards, depending on the sun's position in the sky, for an *al fresco* lunch.

Item 29. Wooings

William Weaver

William Weaver, who later translated the Italo Calvino text for us, wrote an article called "Two Gentlemen of Verona" for the March 1982 issue of *Attenzione*, in which he described what seemed to him an endless stream of visitors to the PWP during his visit in August 1981:

> As I hung around the courtyard of the Palazzo Da Lisca for a few days, I occasionally wondered how Rummonds and Zanella ever managed to finish any work at all. True, they are both early risers and usually start their day at the press around eight, working on until eight at night … But the premises at Via Carlo Cattaneo 6 resemble a club. One morning, while I was talking with Rummonds, a highly varied and colorful series of people dropped by: a German glass blower [Jürgen Reuter], an Indian printer [Zahid Sardar], a local sculptor [Brooks Walker]. Joe Tilson, his wife, and daughter came by to say goodbye (they had been staying with Rummonds for a few days). The next day an American writer [Mary Doris] from Paris was expected, and a photographer [Irwin Dermer] from Zurich. Zanella assured me that Verona in winter attracts fewer visitors.

In one sense it was this "endless stream of visitors" that made printing in Verona so special for me. Visits from fine-printing enthusiasts and creative

William Weaver in the side courtyard at via Carlo Cattaneo, 6, Verona, Italy, 1981. (Photo by RGR, courtesy of PWP Archives.)

people such as Brendan gave the press a special and unique imprimatur. Thus, that often-dreamed-of ambiance – always synonymous in my mind with Jack Werner Stauffacher's Greenwood Press – had become a reality.

It was always a pleasure to meet young people interested in printing and publishing, such as the members of the Society of Young Publishers who visited the press in the summer of 1980. Even though they all worked for trade publishers, they were very curious about how books were produced on the handpress.

Society of Young Publishers from England in Piazza delle Erbe, Verona, Italy, 1980. (Photo by Stephen Kigsley, courtesy of the Society.)

Item 29. Wooings

Antipasto of Squid and Shrimp with Artichoke Hearts

Serves 4

This is the antipasto I served Gray Boone and Mary Mathews.

- 12 defrosted artichoke hearts, cut in halves
- ¾ pound whole jumbo shrimp, peeled and deveined
- ¾ pound squid, cleaned, retaining the tentacles and cutting the body into ¼-inch rings
- 2 tablespoons butter
- 2 tablespoons olive oil
- 3 garlic cloves, finely chopped
- Salt and freshly ground white pepper to taste
- 1 tablespoon flat-leaf parsley, finely chopped, plus 4 sprigs to garnish
- 1 sprig fresh thyme
- ¼ cup dry white wine
- 4 toast rounds

Cook artichoke hearts, following the directions on the package. Pat dry with paper towels and set aside. Pat shrimp and squid dry with paper towels. In a 3-quart sauté pan over medium heat, heat butter and oil. When they begin to bubble, add garlic and sauté for 2 minutes. Add shrimp and squid and sauté until shrimp turn pink, about 3 minutes. Season with salt, pepper, parsley, and thyme. Remove from the pan and set aside. Add wine and artichokes to skillet. Bring to a boil for 1 minute. Turn off heat and stir in the shrimp and squid mixture. Remove the thyme stem. Serve on 2-inch toast rounds. Garnish with sprigs of parsley.

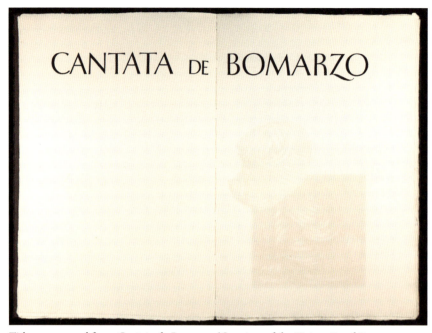

Title-page spread from *Cantata de Bomarzo*. (Courtesy of the University of Oregon Libraries.)

Item 30. *Cantata de Bomarzo*

An introduction in English and a libretto consisting
of three narratives and three cantos in
Spanish by Manuel Mujica Láinez; with English
translations by Gabriel Rummonds.
With seven etchings by Luciano De Vita.
40 pages. 40.5 x 27.5 cm. 83 copies. 1981.

Cantata de Bomarzo

There was hardly a PWP book that was not postponed or delayed at some
point in its production. The seemingly endless postponements and delays
associated with the making of the Borges/Pomodoro book have already
been described. Even though no other project took as long to produce, *Cantata de Bomarzo* certainly comes in a close second. It was issued six years
after it was first conceived.

While still living in New York in the late sixties, I attended the New
York City Opera's production of Alberto Ginastera's *Bomarzo* with Salvador
Novoa in the title role, at the New York State Theater at Lincoln Center. I
had heard Ginastera's music in Ecuador and Argentina, and even though
it was clearly derivative of Igor Stravinsky, it had an exuberance that appealed to me. It was the first opera I had seen that was staged like a movie,
including many cinematic devices such as the use of flashbacks. The libretto
was written by Manuel Mujica Láinez, one of Argentina's most prolific novelists. I saved the program with the intention of someday getting in touch
with him.

I looked forward to when I would be able to combine my printing skills
with my past enthusiasm for the theater by printing a dramatic work at the
PWP. It would also be an interesting typographic challenge.

A Prospective Artist for the Book

In June 1975 I went to the first Arte Fiera in Bologna. Next to the fairgrounds
was a new museum, the Galleria d'Arte Moderna. The main attraction at the
opening was a huge retrospective exhibition of the work of Luciano De Vita,
a was a painter, sculptor, scenic designer, and stage director. I was particularly

fascinated by his works for the theater so I sent Ariel Parkinson, who also designed sets and costumes, a note about his work. His sets and costumes were so finely integrated with the mood of the operas that I could easily imagine the effect they had on spectators. Singers did not necessarily like his costumes, as they were often bulky and confining; in fact, in a few productions some of the singers had to be wheeled on and off the stage on dollies because they could not walk in their costumes.

As soon as I saw his work, I remembered the *Bomarzo* production in New York. Some day I would bring Mujica Láinez and De Vita together for a book, but at the moment it was premature to think about such an elaborate project. I had just gotten started on the Burgess/Tilson book.

Manuel Mujica Láinez

In February 1976 I asked José María Martín Triana to put me in touch with Manuel Mujica Láinez. José María, a childhood friend of Carlos Cárdenas, was Mujica Láinez's editor at Ediciones Felmar in Madrid. That March I wrote to Mujica Láinez of my interest in publishing his libretto for *Bomarzo*.

Manuel Mujica Láinez and Gabriel at Caffè Filippini, Verona, Italy, 1977. (Photographer unknown, courtesy of PWP Archives.)

Item 30. Cantata de Bomarzo

In his reply he outlined the evolution of the work. Originally it had been a novel, then he transformed it into a cantata with music by Ginastera and later into a full-length opera with music by the same composer. Knowing that I was primarily interested in previously unpublished texts, he informed me the text of the opera had already been published with the recording. He suggested that if I wanted an original text, I could have the unpublished cantata, which he enclosed. Since it was not long – and a subject to which I felt emotionally drawn – I decided to translate it myself. Mujica Láinez was paid $600 for the publication rights.

Golda Fishbein was designing book jackets for Felmar, including one for a recent Mujica Láinez book. She was having trouble cashing the checks that Felmar sent her in pesetas. One day I went with her to the bank. The clerk said, "But where does this money come from?" I looked him straight in the eye and said, "She's a kept woman." A bit shaken, he said, "Oh, yes, yes, of course." She never had any more problems cashing her checks.

Manucho – as Mujica Láinez was known to his friends – and his young Argentine companion, Oscar, an architecture student, arrived in Verona

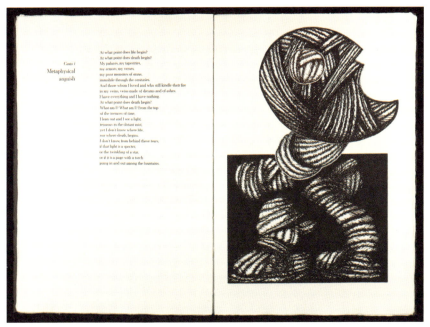

Double-page spread from *Cantata de Bomarzo*. (Courtesy of the University of Oregon Libraries.)

on August 5, 1977. They stayed with me at via Duomo. Before his arrival I had made a rough draft of my translation, and we spent many hours going over it, clarifying nuances and metaphors. Manucho's flair for the dramatic comes through in my translation in this final scene from one of his narratives :

> Here among my monsters, I decided to banish myself forever from Bomarzo, in the very heart of Bomarzo itself, in the cave known as the Mouth of Hell. There I slowly lifted up the chalice and drank the milky liquid which would procure for me the eternity announced in Benedetto's horoscope. Time no longer existed. Various terrible images began to ascend from the arcana. But time did not exist. From far away some desperate cries reached me, and only then did I understand that I was about to die.

An Indiscretion

One day, while Manucho was away with Golda on a visit to Il Vittoriale, Gabriele D'Annunzio's art nouveau kitsch villa on Lake Garda, I foolishly allowed myself to be seduced by Oscar, who had stayed behind. He said he was in love with me, but I knew the difference between real love and pas-

Park of Monsters in the Sacred Woods of Bomarzo, Viterbo, Italy.

sionate declarations of it in the throes of sex. My giving in to the thrill of the moment was unforgiveable. Afterward I wrote in my logbook, "I will make Manucho's book great," as a compensation for my bad judgment. Oscar was nonplused about the incident, because he didn't feel that having sex with me was a betrayal. He didn't have sex with Manucho; he only masturbated while Manucho watched.

On Manucho's return from his outing with Golda, the naive young man confessed our transgression. Needless to say this breach of conduct put a slight strain on my relationship with Manucho for the rest of the visit. For a while I was afraid he might withdraw the manuscript, but shortly after his return to Argentina he wrote, "Lovers come and go, but works of art endure forever." He could afford to be magnanimous, because he had already taken his revenge: my favorite straw hat mysteriously disappeared the morning he left Verona.

Luciano De Vita

I first made contact with Luciano De Vita early in February 1976, a few weeks before writing to Manucho. (The PWP listing in the Arte Fiera '76 catalog mentions an untitled book in preparation to be illustrated by Luciano De Vita.)

Luciano De Vita in front of his studio, Bologna, Italy, 1980. (Photo by RGR, courtesy of PWP Archives.)

Luciano didn't begin working on the project until January 1978, soon after Alessandro Zanella and I went to see him in Bologna, leaving him a copy of the text in Spanish. He was immediately excited by Manucho's retelling of this true story of a hunchbacked Italian Renaissance duke who poisoned himself in his garden surrounded by grotesque stone monsters.

Luciano didn't want to depict the monsters literally – they can still be seen in Bomarzo's garden just outside Rome – but rather to invent his own, which would be just as frightening. It is this approach that makes the illustrations so effective and vibrant.

The Prints

The prints were pulled by Cataldo Serafini, one of Luciano's printmaking students. Cataldo's impeccable work ensured the fidelity of the most minute detail in Luciano's menacing dark images.

Cataldo Serafini in his studio, Bologna, Italy, 1980. (Photo by RGR, courtesy of PWP Archives.)

Item 30. Cantata de Bomarzo

Printing the Book

I decided to use the Horizon Light type for the text, because it was strong enough to hold its own when juxtaposed with Luciano's enormous etchings. Golda's title lettering was again simple and elegant: a single line of capitals alone at the top of a double-page spread.

We had ordered the Wookey Hole paper especially for this book. Even though it is an attractive sheet, we had technical problems with it. The surface of the paper was covered with small red fibers, probably from the felts, which kept springing up at the most inopportune moments, usually after we had finished printing the text on the sheet. It was also a very soft paper. Because of the large format, the point holes in the paper had a tendency to stretch.

We began printing the text in folio in September 1980, just in time to have a few loose signatures to display at the forthcoming PWP retrospectives in Rome, New York, and San Francisco. Alessandro and Mauro Rubin finished printing the text while I was in Alabama.

One of the perks of having my own Press was that I could still indulge myself in little whims. I chose my fiftieth birthday – April 26, 1981 – as the publication date.

Cantata de Bomarzo had been conceived as the third title in our series of boxed deluxe editions; but after the recent financial setback with *Will and Testament: A Fragment of Biography*, we decided to issue it in our regular Press Book Series. To do this we had to scale down the design of the book, but this was not particularly difficult. The projected wooden box with a sculptured lid and a printed velvet cloth for the binding were eliminated. It had to be priced below $550, the maximum price our standing-order collectors were obliged to pay for a single volume. Even though we lost money, at least we were able to sell eighty percent of the edition upon publication. The price was increased to a more realistic $650 later that fall at the Frankfurt Book Fair.

Binding the Book

In the end we used a decorated paper for the cover and slipcase, the design of which was taken from a piece of screenprinted burlap Luciano had used as a backdrop in one of his productions. I am not sure why we didn't also have it screenprinted. Instead, we did it the hard way. Alessandro, with

Cover for *Cantata de Bomarzo*. (Courtesy of the University of Oregon Libraries.)

Mauro's help, painstakingly printed it from a linecut on the handpress. The book itself was bound and enclosed in a matching slipcase by Mario Rigoldi in Monza.

Jürgen Reuter

In the summer of 1981 I met a young German glassblower named Jürgen Reuter at a small *tavola calda* with a sunny deck near Piazza delle Erbe. I took an instant and lustful interest in him, and since he had no specific itinerary, I invited him to stay with me. We were very compatible sexually. During the weeks he was in Verona he spent a lot of time in the studio taking photos, many of which appear in this memoir.

A Misguided Project

As early as October 1976, *Cantata de Bomarzo* was being considered as a possible commission for the Hilliard Collection in Munich, a division of VGM Gesellschaft für Münzeditionen – a high-end operation similar to the Franklin Mint in the States. Ortwin Berghammer, the director, had

Item 30. Cantata de Bomarzo

Jürgen Reuter in the side courtyard at via Carlo Cattaneo, 6, Verona, Italy, 1981. (Photo by RGR, courtesy of PWP Archives.)

offered me half a million dollars to produce two titles for his company. Each edition was to consist of two hundred fifty copies at $2,400 per copy. Once I started to calculate the logistics of the project, I had to turn down his tempting offer. The time frame was such that we would have needed a minimum of forty hand bookbinders to get the five hundred copies bound and delivered on time. We had enough problems finding one good binder, let alone forty.

The second book projected for the Hilliard Collection was a new edition of *The Moor of Venice*, taken from a tale by Giovanbattista Giraldi Cinthio in his *De gli hecatommithi*, which was published in 1565. Berghammer wanted Jim Dine to illustrate it. Before Berghammer's involvement in the project, it was going to be a collaboration between the PWP and Franca Mancini's prestigious Galleria Il Segnapassi in Pesaro on the Adriatic Sea. I had met Franca at Arnaldo Pomodoro's atelier in Milan one afternoon, and she invited me to come to Pesaro. During that visit in June 1975, she proposed that we co-publish the Cinthio text with illustrations by Mario Ceroli, who was one of her artists.

I went to see Ceroli at his studio in Rome and again in Venice, where he had assembled a large wooden crate in Piazza San Marco. Luca Steffenoni had gone to Venice to photograph it, and I went along as his camera carrier. As my negotiations with him progressed, Ceroli continued to ask for more and more concessions. Finally I just backed away from the project, letting it slide into oblivion, where it remained even after Berghammer unsuccessfully tried to resurrect it.

Gabriel in Piazza San Marco, Venice, Italy, 1975. (Photo by Luca Steffenoni, with permission of the photographer.)

Item 30. Cantata de Bomarzo 531

Luca Steffenoni

During this period, Luca Steffenoni would frequently take me along on some of his photo assignments in the Veneto. We would stop for lunch at an out-of-the-way *osteria* and have such local dishes as ass-meat stew or horsemeat tartare, washed down with plenty of the local wine.

I adored Luca, whom I met soon after I moved to Verona. I would often end up at his apartment across the street from Castelvecchio on those late nights when I had been out drinking alone, trying to pick up soldiers near San Zeno. He would always welcome me into his warm bed to sleep off my stupor and folly.

Baked Macaroni and Cheese

Serves 6

At moments when I felt under a lot of pressure, I liked to indulge in my favorite comfort foods. When I was a kid, my brothers and I could request anything we wanted for dinner on our birthdays. They always ordered steak and potatoes. I, on the other hand, asked for macaroni and cheese with pineapple upside-down cake for dessert. Here are my mother's recipes for these two dishes.

2½ cups milk
2 bay leaves
1 pound elbow pasta
2 tablespoons coarse salt for the pasta water
4 tablespoons butter, plus extra to grease the baking dish
3 tablespoons flour
12 ounces sharp Cheddar cheese, grated
3 ounces Parmigiano-Reggiano cheese, freshly grated, plus 1 ounce to sprinkle on top of the dish
Salt and freshly ground black pepper to taste

Preheat the oven to 400 degrees. Bring a large pot of water to a boil. Warm milk and bay leaves in a small saucepan over medium-low heat. When small bubbles appear along the sides of the pan, about five minutes, turn off the heat and set the pan aside. Add coarse salt to boiling water. Add pasta and cook for about 7 minutes. Drain and rinse pasta to stop cooking and transfer to a large bowl. In a second saucepan over medium-low heat, melt butter. When it begins to bubble, stir in all the flour at once until it thickens, about 5 minutes. Remove bay leaves. Add all the milk at once to the flour and butter mixture, continually stirring with a wire whisk. The sauce should be thick and smooth. Add Cheddar cheese and blend with the sauce. Pour the sauce over pasta, toss in Parmigiano-Reggiano cheese, and season with salt and pepper. Grease a 9 x 13-inch baking dish, and turn the pasta mixture into it. Top with remaining Parmigiano-Reggiano cheese. Bake until cheese browns, about 15 minutes.

Item 30. Cantata de Bomarzo

Pineapple Upside-Down Cake

Serves 12

This is my mother's recipe for an upside-down cake, which was made in a rectangular cake pan instead of the traditional cast-iron frying pan. Another difference is separating the eggs. This results in a much lighter cake. My mother, always concerned about germs, would cover the cake with a piece of wax paper before inserting the birthday candles.

    3 large eggs, separated
    1½ cups cake flour
    1 tablespoon baking powder
    1½ cups sugar
    ½ teaspoon salt
    ¾ teaspoon vanilla extract
    ½ cup boiling water
    8 ounces canned crushed pineapple, drained
    8 tablespoons butter
    4 ounces brown sugar

Preheat the oven to 375 degrees. Separate eggs and beat whites until stiff. Beat yolks until light, then fold into whites. Shift flour, baking powder, sugar, and salt together. Mix vanilla with water. Fold the flour mixture into the egg mixture, alternating flour with water. Melt butter and brown sugar in a saucepan, stirring until it becomes a thick syrup. Add pineapple. Pour the pineapple mixture into a greased 9 x 13- inch cake pan, then pour the cake batter on top of it. Bake for 30 minutes. Let the cake cool for about 15 minutes before reversing it onto a serving plate.

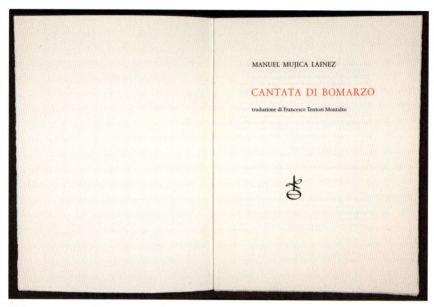

Title-page spread from *Cantata de Bomarzo*. (Courtesy of the University of Oregon Libraries.)

Item 31. *Cantata di Bomarzo*

A libretto consisting of three narratives
and three cantos by Manuel Mujica Láinez
translated from the Spanish into Italian
by Francesco Tentori Montalto.
12 pages. 27 x 20 cm. 130 copies. 1981.

Italian Version of *Cantata de Bomarzo*

Our Italian collectors expressed a great deal of interest in the *Cantata de Bomarzo*, so Alessandro Zanella and I felt it was necessary to provide them with an Italian version. The idea of putting the original text and two translations in the same volume seemed excessive, although that is exactly what I would have done it if we had accepted the Hilliard Collection commission. A PWP trilingual edition would have considerably increased the production costs and taken the book out of the Press Book Series price range. I am sure the visual impact of the book also would have suffered.

This keepsake was designed by Alessandro and printed by him with Mauro Rubin's help in the spring of 1981. Alessandro had even negotiated with Francesco Tentori Montalto for the translation. I was very pleased with the result when I saw it. Alessandro was never afraid to let his own tastes emerge when working on projects he designed. Under Alessandro's guidance the Press could function without me, as the printing of this keepsake proved, but the publication of this item also marked a change in my lifestyle. The PWP was no longer mine alone. Alessandro and I worked together during the day, but we didn't socialize much outside the studio. He had his own life, which began to put more personal demands and responsibilities on him.

Alone in Verona

When I returned to Verona in May 1981, I was for all intents and purposes alone for the first time since I moved to Italy. Early in the seventies the Dutch Boys moved to Maastricht in The Netherlands, Max D'Arpini returned to Rome, and Mirek settled in Bracciano. By early 1977 the De Rossi and Vernière clans had decamped to Paris. Over the years I had grown accustomed to life with my surrogate family, the Fishbeins. First Lauren

Fishbein went back to the States to attend Sarah Lawrence College in 1978, then Mark left for Harvard University in 1980, and finally Golda followed them in December 1980. She eventually moved to New York after a brief sojourn in Cambridge, Massachusetts. *La piccola famiglia* had gone their separate ways.

Life without *la Piccola Famiglia*

Life at via Duomo was never the same after Lauren, Mark, and Golda departed. In fact it became downright depressing. The apartment on via Duomo now seemed cold and unwelcoming. I almost dreaded going there after an invigorating day at the Press. In addition I was ashamed of the shabbiness of the apartment and hesitated to take friends there.

The red room, which had been the hub of so many social activities and glorious parties, was showing its age. It hadn't been repainted in ten years. The old paint was peeling, and large areas of mildew were spreading in the corners of the ceiling and under the window. Most of the furniture and all the equipment had migrated to the studio at via Carlo Cattaneo. Only the bare essentials were left behind: the platform bed, an antique dresser, and a

Double-page spread from *Cantata di Bomarzo*. (Courtesy of the University of Oregon Libraries.)

Item 31. Cantata di Bomarzo   537

lopsided Noguchi floor lamp. There was no radio or television to break the silence. The huge marble-topped table, along with the Italian chairs I had brought with me from the States, and the Italian-style forty-drawer filing cabinet that Lauren had so lovingly refinished one summer were all gone. For a while a small, wobbly, Formica-topped table and four beat-up, mismatched chairs – remnants of Bonnie Walker's days in Verona – were moved back and forth from the red room to what had been the pressroom.

The few dinner parties I had after the studio was relocated were limited to no more than a handful of old friends. Alessandro and I started entertaining visitors for lunch in the side or back courtyards of the new studio or at a nearby *trattoria*. Bruna Da Re, an old friend, would frequently help out with the cooking on those rare occasions when I had company. The days of huge dinner parties were a thing of the past – no more roasts cooked in wine with grilled vegetables. More than anyone else Bruna kept me from retreating into seclusion.

Old Pressroom

The old pressroom, which had once been dominated by the majestic Washington press, had been turned into a dormitory with a couple of camp beds. Since the walls hadn't been repainted in that room either, one could still see where the type cabinets and other pieces of equipment had once stood. Two more apprentices came to Verona in the summers of 1981 and 1982 before the PWP closed. They both lived in the former pressroom, which offered little privacy – an old sheet hung at the window as a makeshift curtain. The interior French doors had long since been taken off their hinges and stored in the palace dungeon.

Stefano Massetta

My days of intimacies had all but come to an end. With the exception of Stefano Massetta – a young married friend – I lived the last years of my life in Verona without any real affection or meaningful physical contact. There is a poem for Stefano in *Seven Aspects of Solitude*. As the activities of the Press wound down, I became bitter and somewhat frightened, feeling like an old man, even though I was only fifty at the time.

Luca Steffenoni introduced me to Stefano, an orphan from Venice who did occasional carpentry work and made architectural models. He was married to a very tiny woman named Giovanna from Sardinia. I drove around town with him and his little mongrel dog Bricioli (Crumbs), helping him square up a door, hang a shutter, or repair a broken chair. We laughed a lot, drank wine in taverns, and slept together when his wife was in Sardinia.

One time the three of us went to visit my friends Carlo and Paula Nanni in Florence. The sleeping arrangements were such that I was to sleep on the sofa with Stefano and Giovanna on a futon in front of it. Giovanna, who was significantly shorter and smaller than me, said there was no need for me to be cramped up on the narrow sofa. She would sleep on the sofa, and Stefano and I could share the futon. I loved sleeping spoon style with Stefano with my arm across his hip and my hand embracing his crotch.

I frequently had dinner with them, and Giovanna always prepared Sardinian dishes. One night her father, Pietro, sang some folksongs in the Sardo dialect which I recorded. He couldn't believe his ears, not recognizing his own voice. "What a marvelous machine; it even knows Sardo songs." Pietro also gave me a beautiful wool "printer's" cap, which I wore until I gave up printing.

In March 1981 Stefano, Giovanna, and I went to a Mardi Gras party in the hills above Verona at a bar that was popular among the gay crowd, called Bella Verona. Earlier in the day I had picked up two cute guys, one Italian and the other Australian, at Bar Ponte Pietra and asked them to join us. I made skimpy angel costumes for the five of us. The costumes consisted of short white tunics with a sash around the waist and a pair of wings that I made out of silver paper feathers. The guys didn't wear any underwear. We were a great hit and won first prize for the best group of merrymakers. After the party the two boys and I went back to my apartment for a threesome.

A Trip to Rome with Stefano

In September 1981, after having helped Alessandro and me print *Verona e i Suoi Fiumi,* Stefano took me on a leisurely trip to Rome. On our way into Rome we passed through a grass fire blazing out of control on either side of the highway. The heat was intense and the smoke stifling. Stefano had friends in Rome, and we were able to crash on their living room floor.

A Disastrous Outing at Lake Garda

Four of us, Stefano and I along with Selwyn Jones, who had exchanged his apartment in San Francisco for Fulvio Testa's in Verona, and an English girl,

Item 31. Cantata di Bomarzo

Stefano Massetta and Gabriel arriving in the outer courtyard at via Carlo Cattaneo, 6, after a trip to Rome on Stefano's Moto Guzzi, Verona, Italy, 1981. (Photo by Alessandro Zanella, courtesy of PWP Archives.)

drove out to Lake Garda to a beach near Punto Virgilio on the east coast of the lake. We settled ourselves on a blanket and drank wine and ate snacks.

I had my hand on Stefano's crotch, aware that he was aroused more than usual. He whispered in my ear, "I have my finger in her pussy." I was stunned, as if struck by lightening, but I managed to calmly stand up, feeling betrayed. I was jealous and angry with myself, and left without saying goodbye to any of them. I hitchhiked back to Verona. I did not see Stefano again until I was living in Los Angeles.

When Stefano came to the States in the early 1990s, he took a bus from San Francisco to Los Angeles to visit me. I met him at the Greyhound bus station; we hugged each other and started to cry. Neither of us mentioned the incident on the beach, but I am sure we both were thinking about it.

During the week he was in Los Angeles, we renewed the loving relationship we had had in Verona. Since I was in between jobs, we went sightseeing: the La Brea Tar Pits, Watts Towers, an exhibition on Japanese kimonos at the Los Angeles County Museum of Art, and the Santa Monica pier. We also drove up the coast on Highway 1 to a place near Malibu, where we walked in the surf, arm-in-arm.

A few months later Giovanna called me in the middle of the night to let me know that Stefano had hanged himself in a tree in an isolated field near Verona. By the time they found his body, it had been desecrated by birds. Like the ghost of Carlos Cárdenas, the ghost of Stefano will haunt me to the end of my life.

After the Breakup with Stefano

Alone in Verona I returned to my nocturnal prowling, mostly anonymous, but it had ceased to be exciting. Now it was just demoralizing. I no longer remembered their names, faces, or bodies.

Item 31. Cantata di Bomarzo 541

Brasato di Bue al Barolo
Braised Beef in Barolo Wine

Serves 6

Here's a recipe reminiscent of earlier dinner parties at via Duomo, 15.

4 tablespoons olive oil
2 pounds top-round beef roast
2 garlic cloves, crushed
4 ounces shallots, sliced
1 teaspoon fresh rosemary leaves
1 teaspoon fresh oregano, finely chopped
2 celery stalks, sliced
1 large carrot, diced
2 whole cloves
1 bottle Barolo wine
  Hot beef broth, if necessary
  Freshly grated nutmeg
  Salt and freshly ground black pepper to taste

Heat oil in a flameproof casserole and brown the meat. Remove it from the casserole. Add garlic, shallots, herbs, celery, carrot, and cloves and sauté for 5 minutes. Place the meat on top of the vegetables. Pour in wine. Cover and simmer for about 2 hours. Remove the meat. Put cooking juices and vegetables in a blender. Add a little beef broth if necessary to thin. Season with nutmeg, salt, and pepper. Pour the sauce over the sliced meat.

Montserrat Lehmann, Verona, Italy, 1980s. (Photo by Ernest Lehmann, courtesy of Montserrat Lehmann.)

Verona: Getting the Word Out

> If one waits long enough, the truth becomes a lie
> and a lie becomes the truth.
> – José Saramago, *The Gospel According to Jesus Christ*

Administrative Duties

Operating a private press in Italy presented many unique problems, not the least of which was letting collectors in the rest of the world know about the PWP and its multilingual editions. In one sense it was a lot easier to produce the books than it was to sell them. I started getting the word out shortly after I arrived in Verona, before I had even printed my first book. Despite my spelling, which always left much to be desired, and my not being particularly agile at the keyboard, I nevertheless laboriously banged out scores of letters to libraries and private collectors on the little Olivetti portable typewriter I had brought with me from New York. Letter writing soon became a wearisome and time-consuming part of my role as a printer/publisher.

In 1972, my second year in Verona, I wrote just over 130 letters; less than a decade later the annual volume had increased to almost nine hundred. I was flooded with requests for information about PWP editions, questions concerning printing, and inquiries regarding visits to Verona. The correspondence nearly killed me, but I still felt obliged to answer each letter personally. Gabriella Monferdin, a secretary at Hélène Sutton's Studio La Città, typed many of the letters to prospective collectors of *Images & Footsteps*. She later married Carlos Strápico, an Argentine, who proofread my Mujica Láinez translation.

Oh what I would have done for a computer in those days. By the time the Press moved to via Carlo Cattaneo, 6, in 1977, the PWP mailing list contained more than five thousand names, and it kept growing. Even though we were more than 80 percent subscribed, we continued to send out thousands of prospectuses, simple leaflets or brochures. Graphically they were not very distinctive, because they were set in Linotype and printed commercially by local job printers.

In order to keep track of mailings and purchases, the name of each collector was entered on a separate 5 x 7-inch index card, which I designed especially for that purpose. Names and addresses were typed onto master lists, three across, and later photocopied onto sheets of mailing labels.

A Series of Part-time Secretaries

Alessandro Zanella and I eventually had to hire a part-time secretary. The first was Susan Franks, wife of an American serviceman stationed in Verona. I wrote all of the letters out in longhand, and Susan would type them. She also took care of invoicing and bulk mailings.

When Susan's husband was transferred back to the States, Sydna Mersereau took her place, but within a short time her husband, too, was transferred, leaving us temporarily without a secretary. In the interim we shared Ernie Lehmann's administrative assistant, Sheila Sutherland, until Ernie's wife, Montserrat, came to work for us. Montsie, who had a wonderful, cheerful disposition, loved her job at the PWP. For her it was a cross between an extended family and a social club. I have recollections of how flustered she would get when she was asked to type a letter to Anthony Burgess or Ray Bradbury. Most of all I think she enjoyed serving as the ex officio hostess to the stream of visitors who came to the press.

I can't say for sure how many sales our mailings actually generated, but I do know that they greatly contributed to making the PWP one of the best-known presses in the world of fine printing. I was often approached by collectors at meetings or conferences who had never seen any of our books but seemed to know all about the press and its publishing program.

Someone once asked me, "How come you know so many rich people?" "They have money to buy expensive books," I answered.

Booksellers

It was also necessary to develop a coterie of foreign booksellers who could represent the press outside Italy. Many collectors abroad were hesitant to purchase such expensive books sight unseen, and having the books listed in a reputable bookseller's catalog always helped legitimize our selling price. By 1975 I had negotiated special standing orders with four international bookstores: Monk Bretton Books in Toronto; Herb Kaplan's Argus Books in Sacramento; Rizzoli International Publications (later replaced successively by

Verona: Getting the Word Out   545

Brentano's and James Cummins, Bookseller) in New York; and Bertram Rota in London. These booksellers agreed to take three copies of every regular edition and one copy of every deluxe edition we issued. They received a 30 percent discount. Even though we often referred collectors to these booksellers, the real inducement for the booksellers was a listing in our promotional materials.

They were soon joined by Deighton, Bell in Cambridge and Robert Krauthammer Buchhandlung in Zurich, who placed standing orders for one copy of every regular edition at the normal booksellers' discount of 20 percent.

Roderick Brinckman of Monk Bretton Books was the first bookseller in the English-speaking world to buy PWP books. We had corresponded in the summer of 1975, but did not meet until October at the London Book Fair, where I also met John Beech from Deighton, Bell – another bookseller I knew only through correspondence. When I saw them in London, I was in a terrible state of mind, suffering from recurring doubts about my prowess as a printer, but Roderick and John were so encouraging in their praise of my work that I decided I would try to persevere a while longer in Verona. A few months earlier, I had given serious thought to closing the press and returning to the States. These two booksellers continued to support the PWP throughout its most difficult years in Italy.

Golda Fishbein went with me to London for the book fair, and we took along with us a few examples of my work to show Anthony Rota. He responded enthusiastically to the books, and before long he was one of the Press's most ardent advocates. His critique in the January 1977 issue of *Fine Print* was the first major review of my work, and because of it a large segment of collectors from the English-speaking world became aware of my printing. Anthony and his assistant, John Byrne, were instrumental in placing many PWP books in important public collections worldwide.

The 1974 Fiera del Libro per Ragazzi

In April 1974, *la piccola famiglia*, along with Riccardo Stevanoni, took a day trip to Bologna to visit the Fiera del Libro per Ragazzi (Children's Book Fair). Fulvio Testa, who shared a huge apartment in an old palace with Riccardo, had a couple of his children's books on display. Fulvio introduced us to several of his publishers as well as Tim and Susan Benn, who because of Tim's interest in practical printing and printing history, stayed in touch with me after the fair.

Gabriel, Bologna, Italy, 1974. (Photographer unknown, courtesy of PWP Archives.)

Riccardo Stevanoni, Golda Fishbein, and her children, Mark and Lauren, Bologna, Italy, 1974. (Photo by RGR, courtesy of PWP Archives.)

Arte Fiera '76

At the end of May 1975, the city of Bologna launched an annual art fair called Arte Fiera. To inaugurate the event, the city threw an extravagant party that Golda and I attended. I decided then and there that the PWP must participate in the show the following year. Taking a stand at Arte Fiera '76 marked the beginning of a program to market the PWP more aggressively in Europe. The stand was small, around 179 square feet. Here my experience as an industrial designer proved to be quite beneficial, enabling me to design a simple but effective display for the books. I used a series of lightweight folding screens with sloping shelves across the back. Information panels were set up at both aisle corners of the stand. Each of the sloping shelves featured an eight-page signature – pamphlet-sewn and permanently attached to the shelf by stubs. That way the casual browser could examine the printing without actually handling the bound books, which were kept under cover and brought out of hiding only on request.

The panels were embellished with transfer-letter graphics that described each of the books in print and listed the works in preparation. An enlarged photograph by Luca Steffenoni of me working at the Washington press was mounted on the center panel along the back wall.

PWP stand at Arte Fiera '76. Giorgio Vigna is second from the left and Gabriel is on his right, Bologna, Italy, 1976. (Photographer unknown, courtesy of PWP Archives.)

Giorgio Vigna and I manned the stand in Bologna for all but a couple of days in June when we went to Diano Marina to accept the international prize I had won for the Borges/Pomodoro book. During our absence Golda and Jacques Vernière took over.

Several projects publicized at the fair that year never materialized, among them two books that would have been the first in the Berkeley Poets Series: Thomas Parkinson's *Forgeries*, to be illustrated by Ariel Parkinson (Ariel later self-published this book as *September Elegy* in 1991), and Ken-

This photo of Gabriel was used for the center panel of the display, Bologna, Italy, 1976. (Photo by Luca Steffenoni, with permission of the photographer.)

Verona: Getting the Word Out   549

neth Pettitt's *A Lamentation Over the Destruction of the World*, to be illustrated by Chris Orr (Kenneth later self-published this book as *Destruction of the World* (1994). These books both reached varying stages of production before they were abandoned.

A third project was Luigi Santucci's text, which was eventually published at the PWP, but illustrated by Emilio Tadini instead of John Alcorn, as announced in our brochure. John did, however, create the PWP tenth-anniversary poster – screenprinted on plain brown paper and very much in demand by visitors to our stand.

The Burgess/Tilson book was the only one listed "in preparation" that actually got published, although there was also a mention of a book illustrated by Luciano De Vita with "text to come." This was eventually published as *Cantata de Bomarzo*.

The Frankfurt Book Fairs in 1980 and 1981

By the time Alessandro started working at the PWP, my efforts to make the PWP more visible were beginning to pay off. A few years later we decided to try the big time: the Frankfurt Book Fair. Our presence there in October 1980 and 1981 substantially increased our circle of collectors, which by the late seventies could be divided equally into three geographic areas: Italy, America, and the rest of the world. However, despite the fact that we were constantly augmenting our number of guaranteed subscribers, we still could not produce enough books with our imprint in a year to make even a modest living.

The Frankfurt Book Fair always reminded me of the housewares trade shows I used to attend when I was an industrial designer – they were not only places to sell merchandise, but also occasions to meet one's competition and make deals. Alessandro and I always looked forward to attending the book fairs because they permitted us to leave the cares of the Press behind in Verona and enjoy ourselves with old and new friends alike.

One of the most helpful people at the fair was Mario Vigiak, a close friend and publisher from Conegliano, a small town northeast of Verona. He had published some of Fulvio's children's books under his imprint, Quadragono Libri. Mario took us under his wing and introduced us to many of his colleagues, including the London publisher Klaus Flugge. As a result of the rapport we established with Klaus, he became a steadfast PWP collector and an enthusiastic supporter of the press.

Gabriel manning the PWP stand at the 1980 Frankfurt Book Fair, Frankfurt, Germany. (Photo by Alessandro Zanella, courtesy of PWP Archives.)

Also on our first trip to Frankfurt, we met a young man from Zurich, Theodor von Oppersdorff, who was still in his early twenties. I can't explain why, but Theo fell madly in love with our books and would frequently drop by our stand just to leaf through them or pause to read a bit of text. It was obviously some sort of symbiotic passion, which we didn't question. Shortly after the fair closed he arrived in Verona with two empty suitcases and bought as many books as he could stuff into them, including a copy of the Borges/Pomodoro and Burgess/Tilson books. I have often wondered whatever became of Theo and all the PWP editions he purchased so impulsively that fall.

Our stand was on the same floor with other publishers of art books and small literary presses, so it gave us an excellent opportunity to meet other printers. Roswitha Quadflieg was there from Hamburg with her Raamin-Presse. I got to know her a little better on the second trip, and of course took time to study her magnificent editions. Like her books, she was very articulate and precise.

At the 1981 fair we made many more contacts. John Christie, an artist/printer who worked with Ron King at the Circle Press in Guildford, Surrey, showed me the beautiful pamphlets of new English poetry he was printing and illustrating with his own screenprints of colorful and provocative

Verona: Getting the Word Out

Alessandro Zanella manning the PWP stand at the 1981 Frankfurt Book Fair, Frankfurt, Germany. (Photo by RGR, courtesy of PWP Archives.)

images. I was especially eager for a collaboration with him. Among others, Alessandro and I talked to the writer Günter Grass, who was also an accomplished printmaker, about a future project that he would write and illustrate. Stephan Keller, the exhibitor in the adjacent stand, had stimulated our enthusiasm for Grass's work when he showed us a recent portfolio of Grass's intricate etchings. Another author/artist of exceptional talent was Judy Ling Wong, whose work I first came to know at the fair. Judy had her own press in London, and I was very impressed with a book of her own poetry that she had recently printed and illustrated with lithographs of calligraphic abstractions of dancers. She proposed working together on a similar project, which very much appealed to me. Alas, so many tantalizing contacts that added up to so many unrealized dreams.

Across the aisle from our stand was a young American couple, Susan Hostetler and her boyfriend, the writer Patrick Pfister. Susan made paper at her Jinn Handmade Paper, which was located in the remote German village of Friedberg. Coming out of the tradition of papermaking that can be traced back to Robert Serpa's Imago Hand Paper Mill in Oakland, California, Susan had also studied with Kathryn Clark in Brookston, Indiana. I liked Susan's papers very much and wanted to try them, but they were simply too expensive for bookwork. Handmade papers in general are very costly, without enough size, too translucent, and either too light or too heavy.

We intended to print prospectuses for the Gill and Mujica books, but the advance sales left us with so few copies that it didn't seem worth the effort. We had also planned to issue another newsletter for the Frankfurt Fair, although that project never materialized.

Visits to the University of Alabama in 1977, 1979, and 1981

One of the things that helped to increase the visibility of the PWP was my teaching at the University of Alabama in Tuscaloosa. In March 1976 James D. Ramer, the dean of the Graduate School of Library Service, had invited me to teach two courses, "History of Books and Printing" and "Descriptive Bibliography," in the spring of 1977, as well as to print a small book, *A Child's View of Secession* by James Stanford Barret (1977), with help from students in the Typographic Laboratory. But Ramer's real purpose in asking me to come to the university was to evaluate the Typographic Laboratory and lay the groundwork for an MFA in the Book Arts Program in the library school.

Since his student days at Columbia, Ramer had had a keen interest in fine printing. He had been encouraged by Carolyn Reading Hammer and Raymond Francis McLain, who had been a friend of the Hammers when he was president of Transylvania University in Kentucky. In 1977 McLain was vice-president for academic affairs at the University of Alabama. He had been instrumental in setting up the existing Typographic Laboratory on the fifth floor of the main library with Glenn House as instructor.

1977

On my first visit to Tuscaloosa in 1977, Alessandro and I were met at the airport with a big banner that said, "Welcome pizza breath." I knew we were in trouble. We lived in Rose Towers, a high-rise apartment building for students on campus.

Since we didn't have a car, I bought a second-hand Honda scooter. We dashed around town on it, as well as speeding through the campus. I wore the black shepherd's cape that Mirek had given me to ward off the fogs in Verona. We were often stopped by the campus police for driving too fast. I would say to the officer, "No speak English," and with a wave of my hand add, "Thank you very much." Toward the end of our stay, the same officer stopped us again and said, "I know you don't speak English, but next time I catch you speeding on campus, I'm gonna to give you a ticket."

Ramer went out of his way to make us feel welcome, and Jewel Morris, his administrative assistant, was kept busy ordering materials and equipment for the Typographic Laboratory. Frances Wilson, Ramer's secretary, helped with my correspondence. And as I had hoped, Alessandro had an opportunity to develop his skills on the handpress.

Jewel Morris, Frances Wilson, and James D. Ramer, Tuscaloosa, AL, 1979. (Photographer unknown, courtesy of PWP Archives.)

Alessandro Prints a Baudelaire Keepsake

Because I had faculty privileges, Alessandro was able to enroll in Richard Zoellner's printmaking class. Because of his eagerness to learn, Richard took him under his wing. Alessandro editioned an etching portrait of Charles Baudelaire, later printing three poems from *Les Fleurs du mal* on the handpress in the Typographic Laboratory. It was a lovely piece, and I could see that Alessandro had a proclivity for fine printing.

Spring Break

During spring break we drove north to spend some time with Carolyn Reading Hammer and her nephew, W. Gay Reading, in Lexington Kentucky. Aside from the pleasure of getting to visit with Carolyn, I had an opportunity to see Victor Hammer's old studio and study his books in depth. Gay was a wonderful host and wined and dined us as only an accomplished gourmet could.

A long-standing rapport was established that spring between the University of Kentucky and myself. David Farrell, who had recently replaced Carolyn as head of Special Collections and Archives, indulged me by letting me wander unrestricted through the stacks. On successive trips to Lexington I would set aside copies of Victor Hammer's books or those printed at the Doves and Kelmscott presses, and David would have slides made of them for my illustrated lectures. Both David and Gay travelled to Verona in the summer of 1978 for the "Printing and Publishing on the Handpress" workshop.

On the way to Lexington, Alessandro and I stopped off in Nashville for a performance at the Grand Ole Opry – a uniquely American experience neither of us would forget. On the way home, we swung around through North Carolina so we could visit with Arthur Dixon in Greensboro and see the private press collection in the Jackson Library, curated by Emilie Mills, an aspiring handpress printer. We stayed with Arthur, who lived out in the country where he had a stream filled with watercress that we picked for sandwiches.

Papermaking

Later that spring I received a call from Charles Morgan, a painting instructor at the University of Georgia, where a paper mill had recently been set up on campus. Charles had invited Howard Clark, Kathryn's husband and partner at Twinrocker Handmade Paper, to give a papermaking demonstration to his students. He called to see if I would be interested in having Howie stop in Tuscaloosa on his way back to Indiana. Because I thought this would be an excellent opportunity to get to know more about American handmade papers, I immediately said yes. From visits to the Fabriano and Richard de Bas mills, I was already familiar with the process, but it was a real treat to see how paper was being made in the States by this new breed of young papermakers. In April 1977 Howie gave a fascinating slide show in the Art Department illustrating how he and Kathy – in collaboration with Claire Van Vliet and her Janus Press – had formed the paperwork landscape on which Claire had printed Hayden Carruth's *Aura* (1977). This was followed the next day by a wonderful demonstration on how paper was made at their mill.

Verona: Getting the Word Out 555

Gabriel and Alessandro Zanella at the handpress in the Typographic Laboratory at the University of Alabama Library, Tuscaloosa, AL, 1977. (Photographer unknown, courtesy of PWP Archives.)

Left: Carolyn Reading Hammer at home, Lexington, KY, 1970s. (Photo by Bekir Arpag, courtesy of the Margaret I. King Library at the University of Kentucky.)

Right: Alessandro Zanella and Arthur Dixon at the University of North Carolina, Greensboro, NC, 1977. (Photo by RGR, courtesy of PWP Archives.)

1979

In January 1979 I was back in Tuscaloosa, alone this time. I again stayed at Rose Towers. Shortly after I arrived Glenn House, who taught with me in the Typographic Laboratory, invited me and two of my students, Mark Flynn and Phil Teague, to his mother Ma 'Cille's house in the small rural town of Gordo for a possum dinner. The local newspaper ran an article about the event, accompanied by a photograph and describing me as a friend of the shah of Iran.

Keith Thrash

One cold March night at a party in the country, I was trying to make out with a young man sitting on my left when I felt a tap-tap-tap on my right knee. Once he had my attention, he said, "Ya wanna go some place and kiss?" I did, and soon after that night Keith Thrash moved in with me.

Keith was a typesetter by trade. I hoped he would join me later in Verona, where his skills could certainly be put to good use at the press – and perhaps I might even find a little domestic stability in the bargain, because our sex was very good. However, he chickened out, getting only as far as New York before he turned around and went home to the things I could never offer him in Italy: chitlins and rutabaga.

In June even though I was still suffering horribly debilitating pains in my back, I ventured a trip to New York, where I met with Frank Mattson to

Keith Thrash in the Gorgas Oak pressroom at the University of Alabama Library, Tuscaloosa, AL, 1979. (Photo by RGR, courtesy of PWP Archives.)

discuss the forthcoming PWP retrospective at The New York Public Library. While in New York, I accepted an invitation from Dr. Robert L. Leslie to join him at a Typophiles luncheon where Monroe Wheeler would be discussing his private press, Harrison of Paris. I was horrified by the recklessness that Wheeler exhibited by permitting his beautiful books to be passed around the table so the guests could examine them at their leisure. I could see spaghetti sauce and veal parmigiano potentially disfiguring the pristine pages of the books. I did, however, enjoy talking with Glenway Wescott, Wheeler's partner. Wescott was the first gay novelist I was to meet.

Gabriel with Glenway Wescott at a Typophiles luncheon, New York, NY, 1979. (Photographer unknown, courtesy of PWP Archives.)

1981

On my third visit to Tuscaloosa, I took a small apartment in the Prince Apartments, halfway between my two favorite bars, The Chukker and Egan's. With each successive stay in Tuscaloosa, I became more incorrigible. When one of the faculty members hosted a Valentine's party that year I decided to liven it up by bringing a naked Cupid to the party. I posted notices all over campus and in a few local bars advertising for a small but muscular fellow. Much to my surprise I got quite a few responses and interviewed most of them. I chose Phillip Vaughn, who was perfect in every way. He also wrote poetry. The winged Cupid was dressed only in a narrow sash that tied diagonally across his chest and a quiver to hold his arrows. Cupid made his entrance into the party accompanied by David McClure in full Mae West drag.

I instructed Phillip to go up to the guests and give each a little pinch or a kiss and then present them with a small card on which was typed: "You've been hit by Cupid," followed by some silly little thing he gave them permission to do, such as "Good for one night with Gabriel." I always knew where Cupid was by the screams and shrieks that resounded throughout the house. During the evening, as people consumed more alcohol, I saw one of the professors from the English Department talking with Cupid. The professor asked, "Aren't you afraid of getting a hard-on?" To which I replied, "Well, if you don't stop fondling his pecker, he just might." Poor Cupid! He kept ending up in a closet with one or more of the graduate students from the English Department. There must have been something in the water in their drinking fountains.

Poster announcing the search for a cupid (1981). (Courtesy of PWP Archives.)

Verona: Getting the Word Out 559

I often wish I had the strength of my convictions regarding the PWP. As I became older and weaker, and more insecure about my abilities as a printer and publisher, I was afraid to take a chance and stay put in Verona. Most likely I could have weathered the bad times and survived as a printer. Instead I took the coward's way out and retreated to Alabama. In truth I left Italy primarily for selfish reasons that had little to do with printing, such as financial security, a health plan, and retirement benefits. However, I did believe that if anyone could teach the craft of fine printing in a systematic way, I was that person. There were already a number of highly qualified people teaching it as an artistic expression, but few were teaching it with an emphasis on the technical aspects of the craft that I would later describe in detail in *Printing on the Iron Handpress* (1998).

Interaction with Art Students

Because of my work with international artists, Chris Kakas, who replaced Richard Zoellner in the printmaking department, once invited me to a critique of his students' work, which was tacked up on the walls around the room. He began by saying to each student, "You are a lovely person, very sensitive," and without giving any constructive criticism, he moved on to the next. Once he was finished, he asked me if I would critique their work. I realized the predicament I was in and bowed out, pleading that I was just a guest. After the class adjourned several students came up to me and said, "That's what he always says, no real criticism. But at least he didn't throw the work on the floor and stomp on it before tossing it out the window like the painting instructor did." They had my attention. "Come on," they said, "you can tell us the truth about our work." So we went to a restaurant bar nearby, and I spent a couple of hours over several glasses of wine telling them what was good and bad about their work. Many of us became fast friends.

Trips to New York

One of the advantages of teaching at the University of Alabama was that it afforded me an opportunity to spend a considerable amount of time in New York, thanks to the generosity of my incredibly patient hostess, Hadassah Brooks. I was able to do a lot of work for the press during these visits, such as meeting with prospective authors and artists, selling books, and giving three or four talks a year in which I discussed my work in minute detail.

I gave a talk at the Heritage of the Graphic Arts in New York in March 1977. Following my introductory remarks I launched into my prepared text:

> I must admit that I have never really identified my activities as a printer with those of the Arts and Crafts Movement, although my work most likely reflects many of the ideals embodied in this movement. . . .
> I did not like the Kelmscott Press books when I first saw them, nor do I now; however, I have come to appreciate them within their historical context. What I sought from Morris and his followers was not their sense of aesthetics, but their insights into their experience with the craft of printing. Like Morris I realized that if I wanted to produce fine limited editions that would have lasting, and therefore, intrinsic value beyond the age in which they were produced, I would have to return to the instruments, materials, and techniques of the handpress period.

A Talk in Monza, Italy

I was still giddy with the euphoria of my initial oratorical success two years before at the Heritage of the Graphic Arts when I accepted my most unusual speaking engagement. The sculptor Pietro Coletta, who with his wife Assunta often stayed over in Verona on their way to and from Milan to visit Assunta's family in northern Italy, taught at a noted design school in Monza that was housed in the former royal stables. When he asked me to be the Honor's Day speaker at his school in June 1979, I was at first reluctant, but eventually he sweet-talked me into it. This was the first time I addressed a large audience in Italian. Perhaps the students were just being polite, but the talk was well received, and many stayed on afterward to ask questions.

The second and last time I discussed my work in Italian was when I spoke about my book *Printing on the Iron Handpress* at the inauguration of "Stampatori, Torchi, Libri," an exhibition of photographs from the book at the Biblioteca Civica di Verona in April 1999. I apologized in advance for my rusty Italian. After all I had been away from Italy for more than sixteen years by that time. At one point my old friend Giorgio Zanolli blurted out, "But you *never* spoke good Italian!"

The Omaha Conference

By 1981 I had begun to take more interest in getting the word out through lectures. In January I gave a talk, "From Dilettante to Professional: A Meta-

Verona: Getting the Word Out 561

morphosis," at a Typophiles luncheon in New York. It was followed by "The Plain Wrapper Press: A Retrospective Survey" at Dawson's Book Shop in Los Angeles. Brendan Gill once told me if I ever felt at a loss for words at a lecture I should just gossip, and I often followed his advice.

My first important talk about printing was delivered at the "Art of the Printed Book" conference at the University of Nebraska at Omaha in April 1981. The conference presented me with a forum in which to express some of my ideas related to printing and publishing, as well as an opportunity to meet private press printers from all around the country. Looking at their books – many for the first time – I was surprised to discover that there were so many skilled and talented printers out there, having believed that craft printers like myself were a rapidly vanishing species. (In retrospect, I probably left the States for Europe prematurely. If I had only investigated the contemporary scene, especially in the San Francisco Bay Area, I might have stayed. In fact I almost did stay. In the fall of 1969 when I was in California visiting my parents, they had unsuccessfully tried to convince me to set up my Press in Inverness, a small town north of San Francisco.)

For me the highlight of the conference was finally meeting Harry Duncan, with whom I began corresponding soon after I arrived in Verona. He had helped me solve many of the most devastating problems I was having with my press. After corresponding for so many years, it was a thrill to sit down with him and just chat like two old buddies catching up on the latest gossip.

One of the topics I had written about to Harry was how we determined the fees we paid to authors and artists. This became the subject of my talk "Author and Publisher: A Love Story, of Sorts." I began, "Friends, competition, and women" – an allusion to what I often dubbed the "feminist Mafia printers" – and then activated a double-screen slide show: "Guess the Author," which went too fast and only added to the confusion. After the first few slides Joyce Lancaster Wilson stood up and said, "Gabriel, please turn off the slide projector." She was right; it only distracted from my talk, so I turned it off.

I tried to clarify many of the problems that confronted small literary presses when they worked with living authors. Once when I asked Giovanni Mardersteig why he so seldom published living authors, he replied, "Dead authors don't talk back, and you don't have to pay them." I distributed copies of the "Plain Wrapper Press Guidelines for Authors," which Brendan Gill had helped me formulate the summer before in Verona.

Harry Duncan inking a form during the Rochester Institute of Technology workshop "Problem-Solving on the Cast-Iron Handpress," Rochester, NY, 1992. (Photo by Diana Thomas, courtesy of the photographer.)

Before getting down to the topic at hand, I said:

> As you all know by now, I approach printing from the horny end. My talk is comprised of a core and gossip. I was very tempted to dispense with the core and just gossip, but I truly feel that this conference has been a learning experience for all of us, and so I don't want to discredit our intentions, and will speak seriously about author-publisher relations.

My talk ended on a rather maudlin note. I projected a slide of Alessandro and me standing next to the Washington press.

> In the future, recollecting the Plain Wrapper Press, the one image that will always be foremost in my mind is this one frozen in time; there

Verona: Getting the Word Out 563

was already a sadness, a melancholy upon our brows. Bureaucracy had won.

This image belies the tremendous effort that was required just to produce these few plain volumes *and* it also belies those moments of elation when we would present the author with his *ad personam* copy.

I recall standing with Anthony Burgess and Alessandro, none of us saying a word, with silly grins on our faces and tears of joy streaming down our cheeks.

Adrian Wilson was also at the conference, and this gave us a chance to renew our friendship. Except for his and Joyce's brief visit to Verona in April 1976, I had not seen them since the early fifties, when Adrian had his print shop set up in the lobby of The Interplayers, the highly esteemed avant-garde theater company in San Francisco they had helped found. He printed all the playbills on a Colts Armory press. Many of my friends from Berkeley were involved in the productions, so I got to see most of the plays. I'll never forget Joyce's fine performance in T. S. Eliot's *The Family Reunion*. I was always fascinated by the work Adrian did in his theater print shop. He was combining the same crafts – printing and theater – that would also ultimately consume me, although in my case not simultaneously. Who knows where I would have ended up if I had offered to help him print the playbills?

I met many printers during the conference, most of whom I continued to see for years afterwards; however, on the last night I decided to get away from them. That afternoon the conference participants had visited a bookstore in Omaha that specialized in fine printing. There was an attractive young clerk, David Littrell, working there so I invited him to have supper that night. He agreed, but when I called back later to let him know where to meet me, Dan Gleason, the owner of the bookstore, told me that David had already left. Years later in Seattle Dan told me the teenager told him about my call: "Dan, a man asked me to have dinner with him. I'm hungry, but I think he wants more than just dinner." Little did David know that I was just tired of talking about the book arts, and all I wanted was an attractive face and a little harmless conversation to pass a few hours before wandering off to bed. He missed a good dinner. I went out of my way to be particularly nice to myself, treating myself to a couple of martinis, an Omaha filet mignon with all the trimmings, and an excellent bottle of red wine.

The Columbia Conference

One of my greatest opportunities as a representative of the handpress community came when Alessandro and I were invited to participate in "The Fine Printing Conference at Columbia University" in May 1982, a conference of peers that brought together many of the printers I had gotten to know over the past few years. I consider the transcript of the Proceedings published in 1983 to be the single most important document on private presses and literary publishing up to that date. All the participants had something important to contribute, and most wanted to share their experiences and discoveries. Claire Van Vliet best expressed our common goal as printers when she said, "I don't want to wear my type. I want to put the least amount of ink, getting the maximum cover, using the minimum impression." This may sound simplistic, but in my opinion that *is* the essence of the mechanics of fine printing and – typography aside – she described exactly how it can be achieved.

Golda Fishbein's Cross-Country Sales Trip

Golda was in the States in the late fall of 1978 on business for the Overseas Federation of Teachers, the union Ernest Lehmann headed. Once she finished her work for Ernie, she set off on a coast-to-coast sales trip for the PWP. Golda was single-handedly responsible for the international fame and fortune of the PWP. She visited libraries in New York, Washington, DC, San Antonio, Detroit, Chicago, San Francisco, and Ann Arbor, which resulted in standing orders from the University of San Francisco and the University of Michigan at Ann Arbor, to name two of her major successes. Our mass mailings from Verona had paid off: everywhere she went people wanted to see PWP books – in particular, the Borges/Pomodoro book. After placing a standing order, D. Steven Corey, the curator of rare books at the Richard A. Gleeson Library at the University of San Francisco, gave Golda a photograph of himself to bring back to me – so I would know what the newest PWP acolyte looked like.

While on the West Coast Golda was guided by Judith Hoffberg, a friend of Harvey Simmonds. She was the publisher of *Umbrella*, a journal dedicated to artists' books, and knew everyone even remotely connected with fine printing and artists' books. Judith took Golda around Los Angeles, introducing her to numerous librarians and booksellers. Judith often visited

Verona: Getting the Word Out 565

D. Steven Corey, place and date unknown. (Photographer unknown, courtesy of D. Steven Corey.)

the Press in later years, and it was through her that I slowly came to understand the *raison d'être* of artists' books and was better able to temper my bias against the visual artists who made them.

San Francisco 1979

In May I went to San Francisco on my own sales trip and stayed with Steve. On the third evening he organized a reception for me in the Gleeson Library. Surrounded by display cases filled with forty years of graphic designs by Albert Sperisen, I got to meet many California printers for the first time. Kenneth Pettitt, Betsy Davids, and Jim Petrillo came over from Berkeley for the reception. Afterward we went with Steve to an Italian restaurant, where we ate, drank, and talked shop until the wee hours.

Toward the end of my stay with Steve, I was still smarting from the thirteen stitches in my foreskin required to correct a congenital problem. The doctor in Alabama had told me the stitches would work their way out in a few days. It was now over a month and I was getting worried. I woke up one morning and turned to Steve, asking him if he would mind pulling them out, because I was afraid to do it myself. He let out a little squeal, "Not on your life!" We called a nearby hospital and their advice was to wait one more day and soak in a tub of hot water. To everyone's relief, the stitches were gone the next morning.

In addition to my other health problems, I was plagued by the onset of Peyronie's Disease, a buildup of plaque in the urethra, which some doctors believe is genetic. Two of my brothers also suffered from it. The cure often involves invasive surgery. When I returned to Verona, I went to see my friend Dr. Renato Da Pian, who had looked after me when I was suffering from back pain in the mid-seventies. He had heard of a new oral treatment that he wanted me to try. Whatever the medicine was, it dissolved the plaque, and I never had any trouble again.

Visiting Printers

Jonathan Clark of The Artichoke Press and his wife Barbara were among the first American printers to visit the PWP in Verona, arriving sometime in June 1976 – the Wilsons had stopped by earlier in April with Martino Mardersteig. Jonathan had just finished printing *The Photograph As Symbol* by Wynn Bullock and had brought along one of the few bound copies to show me. I was very impressed with the book and was sure he would do well as a fine printer.

I didn't, however, see Jonathan again until the Gleeson Library reception in May 1979, which he had missed, but joined Steve and me a few days later for supper at one of Steve's favorite Japanese restaurants. Stoically, Jonathan told me he still had copies of the Bullock book in sheets; it had not sold well. I was really sorry to hear this, because it was a beautiful book and embodied so many expectations for its young printer.

Bayerische Staatsbibliothek

My sister-in-law Elfie Rummonds had seen an article in a Munich newspaper about the fine printing collection at the Bayerische Staatsbibliothek. Since Tom and Elfie had a copy of everything I had printed to date, she volunteered to show their collection of PWP books to the appropriate curators at the library. Much to Elfie's surprise, she was welcomed with open arms by Drs.

Verona: Getting the Word Out 567

Karl Dachs and Elmar Hertrich. They had heard about the Press and had even made inquiries in Verona, but no one seemed to know the whereabouts of the PWP. Giovanni Mardersteig told them that he didn't know anything about a press by that name. They ordered a copy of everything still in print and gave Elfie a standing order for all future editions.

On my frequent visits to Munich I often visited the library. Dr. Hertrich would get me settled somewhere in the stacks and then have one of his assistants bring out a parade of treasures that he knew would interest me. He and I shared a particular fondness for the Bremer Presse, and later he put me in touch with Herbert Post, who designed the Post Mediaeval type that we used at the PWP. Post offered me the last typeface he had designed for the Berthold type foundry as a proprietary typeface for the PWP, but unfortunately he died before we could make the final arrangements.

I also discovered from Dr. Hertrich that Joseph Blumenthal had been at the Bremer Presse for a few weeks in the summer of 1930. Later, when I asked Joe about his experience there, he sent me a copy of his pamphlet *The Dampening of Hand-Made Paper* (1978), printed by August Hechscher at his Printing Office at High Loft, which included a note on how paper had been dampened at the Bremer Presse. Surprisingly enough it was quite similar to the way Giovanni Mardersteig's staff at the Officina Bodoni had shown me. I was pleased to think of this as a thread, superficial as it might be, that linked the PWP to the Bremer Presse.

More Visitors to the PWP

A continuous stream of visitors to the Press also helped get the word out. Irwin Dermer, an American photographer living in Switzerland, arrived one day in the summer of 1978 in the entourage of Count Geoffrey Potocki de Montalk, an eccentric Polish/English hobby printer. I was away, but they somehow managed to track down Golda. Irwin returned to Verona often, and during one visit he made a beautiful photographic essay of the Press that I have always cherished. He and I spent many hours talking about photography as an art and exploring non-traditional techniques for reproducing photographs.

Betsy Davids and Jim Petrillo were among the printers who visited the PWP in the summer of 1979. When not entertaining in the side courtyard, we often took guests to the Trattoria La Fontana. One evening when we were there with Betsy and Jim, I overheard a cute Italian girl translating the menu for her companions, a group of handsome English boys. "One of the specialties of the house is braised language" she explained confidently.

In the summer of 1980 Jack Werner Stauffacher sent two of his friends who were in Italy on their honeymoon, William Turnbull, the publisher of North Point Press, and Paule Anglim, the director of a prestigious art gallery in San Francisco. I really enjoyed having them in Verona, because it gave me an opportunity to discuss one of my favorite subjects: literary publishing. Bill reminded me of my old friend James Laughlin at New Directions. They were both doing the kind of publishing I admired, excellent texts in fine trade editions.

In conversation Bill said that he would like to be on our mailing list, so I gave him one of our packets of information. At dinner on their last night in Verona, Bill slipped me the mailing list form, adding that he would come by to see me before he left. The next day, as I started to enter his name on a mailing list card, I found that he had checked the box for a standing order and ordered a copy of every book we had in stock. When Bill arrived later that morning with a check in hand, my head was still whirling. There were often hard times at the Press, but occasionally they were lightened when an unexpected angel like Bill passed through the doors.

Thwarted Projects

Tommaso Landolfi was one of the Italian authors I wanted to publish. I had read *Cancerqueen,* translated by Raymond Rosenthal and published by The Dial Press. In the fall of 1970 Robert Cornfield had commissioned me to design the book; however, unexpected delays were further complicated by my move to Verona. In January 1971 he gave the manuscript to another designer, although he did put me in touch with Rosenthal. I wrote to him in March, but if he responded, I can't locate any correspondence from him.

If the PWP had published all the books that I had envisioned, it would have been the premier private press of the second half of the twentieth century. Alas, my actual accomplishments fell far short of my grandiose aspirations. Many of these projects never progressed beyond talk, while others were carried to slightly more advanced stages before fading away.

Verona: Getting the Word Out 569

For example, when we were still looking for an artist for the Anthony Burgess book in 1976, Bruno Herlitzka at the Marlborough Galleria d'Arte in Rome suggested R.B. Kitaj, an American artist who spent much of his time in England. Kitaj put me in touch with his compatriot, the novelist and social satirist Frederic Tuten. I met with Kitaj in New York in January 1979 to discuss the project. We offered him $4,000 plus five copies of the book. He declined the offer, asking for one-third of the edition, which was what I had paid Pomodoro for his work for the Borges/Pomodoro book. After thinking it over I capitulated and accepted his terms. The Tuten/Kitaj project was well along when it came to an abrupt halt. Kitaj had made three screenprints, which Chris Prater was to edition for the book; however, Chris refused to proof them on our paper, and we did not want to commit ourselves to $5,000 worth of prints without seeing proofs first. After all, it was Chris who had messed up the printing on the Burgess/Tilson book. Even though Kitaj believed we were right, he withdrew from the project rather than confront Chris.

In one attempt to shore up the press financially, we decided that one viable direction might be to publish more medium-priced books – those selling for $150 to $250 – with more emphasis on text and less on costly graphics. With this in mind I stepped up my quest for authors and got in

Proof of one of R.B. Kitaj's illustrations for *Tallien: A Brief Romance* (1979). (Courtesy of the University of Utah.)

touch with Elizabeth Hardwick, James Purdy, Muriel Spark, Mary Renault, and Tennessee Williams, to name a few. During a phone conversation in January 1979, Williams said to get back to him when I was ready to talk seriously about a project, adding that he could probably find something.

I had already received a manuscript from Purdy in November 1976. I had met him through John Carlis in June. John and I had known each other since our days as industrial designers. He had also worked as the art director for *Opera News*, and it was there that I first met Andy Warhol. Years later John worked in the art gallery at Rizzoli's.

Around the same time Renault sent me a piece called "History In Fiction," which had been previously printed in a periodical. She thought it might make a nice little book. But this and the above mentioned projects eventually had to be set aside in favor of printing commissions.

Harold Acton is another author I had hoped to publish. We met at a party given by la contessa Barbara Emo and discovered we shared many

Harold Acton at La Pietra, Florence, Italy, 1981. (Photo by RGR, courtesy of PWP Archives.)

Verona: Getting the Word Out   571

interests, including printing and private presses. We got into a discussion about his friend Nancy Cunard who had published some of his work at her Hours Press. Harold wrote the kind of fantasy story I have always liked, but even though I frequently cajoled him to send me a manuscript, he kept procrastinating. The last time I saw him was in 1981 at his magnificent villa in Florence, La Pietra, which was sumptuously adorned with rare Chinese art objects. I had brought my godson, Giordano Nanni, still a toddler, along with me. As Giordano stuffed cookies and chocolates into his mouth, Harold looked at me out of the corner of his eye and asked in a stage whisper, "Is he housebroken?"

Lawrence Durrell contacted me in February 1978 about collaborating on a book, when I had suggested he might like to write a short story about the early life of Scobie, the old homosexual/transvestite policeman who is kicked to death by British sailors in *The Alexandria Quartet* (1957–60). He was intrigued by the idea, but in January 1980 he turned the negotiations over to Anthea Morton-Saner, his agent in London. She thought she was dealing with Random House, and was looking for megabucks. In February 1980 we offered Durrell through his agent $2,000 for a sixteen-page story. She replied that it was an absurd offer. I was put off by her abrasive vulgarity.

In one of my failed attempts to reach Durrell in person, I met one of his neighbors in the south of France, Mai Zetterling, the multitalented actress turned writer and director. Her infamous film *Night Games* was at the center of a censorship battle spearheaded by Shirley Temple Black in San Francisco in the late sixties. I had eagerly followed the controversy in the newspapers. In a letter to Mai on June 10, 1981, I wrote:

> I think you are absolutely right when you suggest that we should meet if we decide to pursue this venture. Our type of publishing is very intimate; it almost becomes a love affair. Alessandro and I live with the manuscript for months, pore over it daily, set it letter by letter, almost know it by heart, give it shape on the page, and finally dress it in a binding to send it out on its own. But the love doesn't end there. It goes on and on with each re-reading of the text, with each re-examination of the book."

Mai came to Verona on July 4, 1981, and we discussed a possible collaboration. Soon after she returned to her home in Le Mazel, she sent the manuscript of *Requirements for a Goddess*, another project I regret never having published.

Another author whose work fascinated me was Donald Barthelme. He had published a short story in the August 22, 1977 issue of *The New Yorker* called "Cortes and Montezuma." I adored this story; it also inspired Alessandro and me to attempt to write the libretto for a grand opera called *The Conquest of Mexico*. We could visualize it – horses and all – on the stage of the Arena, the Roman amphitheater in Verona where operas were performed in the summer. I wrote to him in March 1980, but it was senseless to talk about developing new projects when we knew the PWP would soon be closing.

August 1981 was full of visitors to the Press, including John Tagliabue and his wife Grace. John left a manuscript of his poems, and I seriously considered printing a selection of them. Beni Montresor, who had been instrumental in my coming to Verona, had built a wonderful house nearby in Bussolengo and frequently stopped by for a glass of wine.

Hans Magnus Enzensberger, a German poet, whose name kept coming up in conversations with other poets, appeared at the studio unannounced one day in the summer of 1982. I had read several of his poems and liked them very much, but he had arrived too late. Any potential collaboration with Hans got lost in my move to Alabama.

A Danish artist, Pia Schutzmann, visited the Press while I was coordinating a workshop in Alabama that summer. She left a few examples of her etchings with Alessandro, and we were very impressed with her work. When I first saw it, I immediately wanted to ask her to illustrate a book for the PWP, forgetting that there weren't going to be any new projects from the Press. The final list had already been drawn up. So many of these rare opportunities to work with talented artists like Pia never had a chance to come to fruition.

One reason we failed to complete so many projects is that finding authors was much easier than dealing with the day-to-day production problems at the Press. Hardcover bindings would always be the single most expensive item in the production budget, and finding a local binder whose work we liked was next to impossible. Then came the type and the paper. We could reuse the type, as we often did, but we usually ordered the paper specifically for each edition. It was not practical to order it until the manuscript had been received, and preferably not until both the manuscript and illustrations were in hand. We usually had to wait three to four months – sometimes as many as six or eight months – for the paper to be delivered. Not being in a position to order paper for more than one book at a time, we often found ourselves

Verona: Getting the Word Out 573

doing busy work in the studio during these down periods, because we weren't equipped for job printing.

PWP Retrospective Exhibitions in 1980 and 1981

In my extensive travels I have seen many presentations on fine printing, but none made a more lasting impression than the two concurrent exhibitions I saw at the Victoria and Albert Museum in London in the late seventies. The first was devoted to books printed at the Stanbrook Abbey Press. The display cases were filled with numerous proofs, correspondence – including letters from Emery Walker (William Morris's mentor and co-founder of the Doves Press with T. J. Cobden-Sanderson) and many books from the Stanbrook Abbey Press. The second exhibition documented the step-by-step making of a facsimile of *The Book of Job* illustrated by William Blake. Arnold Fawcus was on hand from the Trianon Press in Paris to explain the different techniques used to produce this remarkable facsimile. Fawcus combined pochoir with collotype, two graphic techniques that have fascinated me ever since. I never had an opportunity to use either in any of my books, but I did teach them to my students at the University of Alabama, having enlisted the expertise of Barry Spann, an artist who once worked at the Trianon Press and came to Tuscaloosa to help develop the collotype module for my class. Golda's nephew Jim Lefkowitz, who had studied printmaking at SUNY at Purchase, taught the class.

I wanted to duplicate for the visitors who came to the PWP retrospectives the excitement I felt at the Victoria and Albert exhibitions. It was rewarding to hear from so many collectors that the very thing that made these PWP retrospectives so intriguing was the wealth of ancillary materials. There were original manuscripts, corrected proofs, sketches, mock-ups, binding models, original plates and blocks for the illustrations, notebooks, as well as selected correspondence. Two copies of each book – one open and the other closed – were displayed, along with loose leaves to show additional text pages. The photographer Robert Mahon who had accompanied Carol Joyce to Verona the year she bound the Santucci/Tadini book assembled a beautiful photographic essay showing the Washington press in operation, and some of these photographs were featured in the exhibitions. All together these varied artifacts gave the viewer a true insight into how a fine press book was conceived and produced.

We started planning the PWP retrospective exhibitions early in 1979, and the first of them opened in November 1980 at the Libreria Galleria Giulia in Rome. Walter Cantatore, whom I had known when he was at the Marlborough Galleria d'Arte, was the new director of the Giulia. He was interested in a possible collaboration between the PWP and the Giulia – perhaps something along the lines of the one I had had with the Marlborough. Like so many galleries in Italy, the Giulia was a combination art gallery and bookstore. The bookstore, which had its own entrance on the street, primarily sold books on art and architecture, artists' books, and prints. It was run by Mario Quesada, a well-known poet who liked our work and on Walter's recommendation offered us a retrospective exhibition in the bookstore's own gallery space. It proved to be a dress rehearsal for the New York retrospective.

Because we were already in the process of preparing *A Checklist of Books Printed by Richard-Gabriel Rummonds and Alessandro Zanella at the Plain Wrapper Press, 1966–1980*, a catalog for the New York and San Francisco retrospectives, we decided to issue it also in Italian for the exhibition in Rome. Kenneth Pettitt, who had been associated with the Press for many years, wrote an introductory note for the catalog during one of his visits to Verona. While students at Berkeley, Kenneth and I had flirted, but it was not until several years after we had both left Berkeley that I willingly let him seduce me first in a seedy hotel room in San Francisco, and later when I was living in New York.

An earlier PWP retrospective had been scheduled for April 1978 at Mario Vigiak's Galleria Quadrangolo in Conegliano. I don't remember now why the exhibition was canceled. When Mario and I met in Milan in 1999 at the last PWP retrospective, he said he always regretted not being able to show our books in his gallery.

The second retrospective exhibition opened at The New York Public Library on January 9, 1981, and ran through April 30. I had worked closely with Francis O. Mattson in the Rare Books and Manuscripts Division. He did a marvelous job of coordinating the exhibition by sifting through all the boxes of collaborative materials I had brought with me from Italy. I could easily have been one of the Collyer brothers: it appeared that nothing, not even a scrap of paper, was ever thrown away. Frank also got a lot of support from David H. Stam, the Andrew W. Mellon Director of the Research Libraries.

Golda Fishbein at the entrance to The New York Public Library, 1981. (Photo by Robert Mahon, with permission of the photographer.)

Francis O. Mattson and Gabriel at the opening of the PWP retrospective at The New York Public Library, New York, NY, 1981. (Photo by Robert Mahon, with permission of the photographer.)

Golda Fishbein and Ben Meiselman at the opening of the PWP retrospective at The New York Public Library, New York, NY, 1981. (Photo by Robert Mahon, with permission of the photographer.)

Abe Lerner, Ben Meiselman, and John Newbauer, three PWP collectors, as well as my brother Tom Rummonds loaned books from their collections to supplement the library's holdings. I had brought all the supplementary materials, such as proofs, letters and photographs for the show with me on my third visit to Alabama. (Thanks to Bernard McTigue, the PWP Archives were later acquired by The New York Public Library, which already had a complete run of PWP publications.)

A reception was held in the Trustees Room to inaugurate the exhibition, at which Brendan Gill said a few words about the Press. Elizabeth Hardwick, Robert Penn Warren, and Edmund Keeley were among the authors who attended. The fine printing enthusiasts present included Joseph Blumenthal, Leslie Katz, August Hechscher, and Harvey Simmonds, as well as Abe Lerner, Kit Currie, and Ben Meiselman, who were all enthusiastic collectors. At one point we ran out of wine, and Brendan went over to his office at *The New Yorker* to fetch a few more bottles.

Edwin McDowell wrote in the March 20, 1981 issue of *The New York Times* about the retrospective:

> [NYPL] is featuring what is considered to be one of its most beautiful exhibitions ever: the 29 limited edition volumes published by the Plain Wrapper Press, together with original manuscripts, artists' renderings and authors' correspondence.

Brendan Gill, Gabriel, and David H. Stam at the opening of the PWP retrospective at The New York Public Library, New York, NY, 1981. (Photo by Robert Mahon, with permission of the photographer.)

Reviewing the same exhibition in the July 1981 issue of *Fine Print*, David Becker wrote:

> This show was a model of what such a show should be in both its form and content, affording an unusually complete portrait of the process and personalities of the press, in addition to successfully revealing the strengths and beauties of the books produced.

These were encouraging words for two very dejected printers.

At the same reception Robert Penn Warren told me that he wanted us to publish his long poem "Chief Joseph of the Nez Perce Indians" in a limited edition before Random House brought out the trade edition. During the 1981 spring break I went to see Albert Erskine, Warren's editor at Random House, who was also in favor of the idea. I had worked closely with Erskine in the late sixties on the design of Karl Shapiro's *White-Haired Lover* (1968), which was selected for The Fifty Books of the Year exhibition, sponsored by The American Institute of Graphic Art. Later in 1981 Tony Wimpheimer, also from Random House, came to Verona to discuss the project in more detail, but nothing ever came of it.

A third retrospective exhibition, which also opened in January and ran through February 1981, was put together by Kenneth Pettitt, who had a near-complete collection of PWP items through *The Emperor's Lion*, which he loaned to the Book Club of California in San Francisco for a show, giving

View of the PWP retrospective at The New York Public Library, New York, NY, 1981. (Photo by Robert Mahon, with permission of the photographer.)

many local collectors the first glimpse of my work. In a sense it was a preview of the next exhibition.

The fourth retrospective opened at the Richard A. Gleeson Library at the University of San Francisco in May and ran through June 1981, with a reception for the printer on May 7. A selection of materials from the New York retrospective were loaned to the University of San Francisco by The New York Public Library. The night before the opening, I gave an illustrated talk, "The Return of This Native," at the Colophon Club of San Francisco.

Adrian and Joyce Wilson very kindly let Fulvio and me stay in their house above the Press in Tuscany Alley for a few days while they were away. It was truly awesome for me to be so completely surrounded by the artifacts of a printer's life – Adrian's books and equipment – and to feel the evidence of his intellectual pursuits on every floor. Staying at the Wilson's also propelled me on an unexpected sentimental journey, because Isabel Freud and I had lived directly across the street from Tuscany Alley in the early 1950s. More than thirty years later, I found myself wandering the old neighborhood, ferreting out forgotten haunts, looking for signs of recognition. I even met Isabel for lunch one day in a nearby restaurant to chat about our present

Verona: Getting the Word Out

lives. So much had happened in the intervening years that there was little left to remember of the happy life we once had together. In addition I always looked forward to visiting San Francisco and seeing my early mentor Jack Werner Stauffacher.

During this trip to the West Coast, I also had a chance to visit with friends in Berkeley, first spending some time with Betsy Davids at her Rebis Press, and later with Wesley Tanner at his Arif Press. I had met Wesley in April at the Omaha conference. He took me to lunch at Chez Panisse. As we climbed the stairs, I paused to look at many of the commemorative menus he had printed for the restaurant. He later sent me a sampling of them. Even though Wesley and I seldom wrote or called each other, when we did I always felt a special bond between us. I concluded my trip to Berkeley with a visit to Thomas and Ariel Parkinson. Once I had been Tom's mischievous and rebellious student, but now I was a fifty-year-old man, and Tom had become the personification of the grizzly old bard.

Promoting the Image of the PWP

PWP books have been included in major exhibitions in museums throughout the world, including the Victoria and Albert Museum in London, the Rijksmuseum Meermanne-Westreenianum in The Hague, the Klingspor-Museum in Offenbach/Main, and the Biblioteca di Milano. Wherever PWP books have been shown, they have always attracted a lot of attention – once in quite an unexpected way.

During a visit to Tuscaloosa I received a frantic call from Jared Loewenstein at the University of Virginia shortly after their copy of the Borges/Pomodoro book had been brought up from the vault for an exhibition. Apparently the display case in which the book had been placed was not ventilated, and the heat of the spot lights had the book's vellum binding twisted in what he described as "raving contortions." I advised Jared to wrap the book like a mummy in gauze bandages and return it to the cool vault. Every day for several weeks, he was going to have to rewrap the book, each time applying a little more pressure until he had finally tamed the beast.

During the 1979 spring break, I stopped off in Washington, DC, to visit John Y. Cole at the Center for the Book at the Library of Congress. The Center's National Advisory Board had just concluded its first meeting so many of the participants remained for the reception that followed. I had an opportunity to meet several of the board members, including Sandra Kirshenbaum, the publisher of *Fine Print*. Even though her magazine had been in existence for only a couple of years, it was already accepted as the preeminent journal in its field. Our paths were to cross often: in San Francisco, Omaha, and New York. Sandy was the keynote speaker at the Collegiate Press Conference I organized at the University of Alabama.

Starting in January 1980 I became a contributor to the magazine, writing articles as well as reviews of press books. Regrettably, as a critic I acquired the reputation of being a "hatchet man," called in whenever the editors needed someone who wasn't afraid to tackle a difficult or controversial book.

Sandy also published my article, "The Economics of Printing Limited Editions," in the July 1987 issue of *Fine Print*. It contained formulas for arriving at the retail price of a book. To my knowledge, nothing as specific has ever been written on the subject.

William Burton, publisher of *American Book Collector*, engaged me to write a column on press books for his magazine. The first appeared in the September/October 1982 issue, and the column became one of the most widely read features of the magazine. Even though my opinions were often considered heretical and many thought that I was vitriolic, I helped make the collectors of private press books – and some printers – more aware of the craft of fine printing as it relates to literary publishing. I continued to write for *ABC* until it ceased publication in 1987. My last column, "A Difference of Imagination: Guy Davenport in Limited Editions," unfortunately did not make it into print before the magazine's demise; however, I was able to use much of it for a couple of lectures I gave in later years.

The Limited Editions Club

Donald Sigovich was among the visitors to the press when the Typophiles passed through Verona on their World Printing Museum Tour in September 1976. I didn't see him again until the early spring of 1981 by which time he had become the art director at The Limited Editions Club. I had always had a crush on Donald, so I stopped by his office for a chat, but as it so often happens, one thing led to another and before long I was telling Sidney Shiff – whom I had just met – why I thought he was making a mistake to pursue the club's old publishing program. Sidney, who had just recently purchased the LEC, was in the process of restructuring it. I told him that today's younger collec-

Verona: Getting the Word Out 581

tors – especially those who had been educated after the Great Depression –
were no longer interested in the classics as our parents' generation conceived
them. Like their parents many of them wanted to have fine editions in their
libraries, but they wanted twentieth-century classics: books of their own generation that had in some way affected them sentimentally or contained strong
emotional implications. I went on to say that these younger collectors would
eagerly buy authors like F. Scott Fitzgerald and Jorge Luis Borges. Whether
or not they would ever reread the books was less important than the fact that
they *had* once read them and would cherish that memory. I mentioned
two such books, Norman Mailer's *The Naked and the Dead* and Tennessee
Williams's *A Streetcar Named Desire*, which had radically altered my life as a
teenager. Before I realized what I was getting into, Sidney hired me as an editorial consultant and commissioned me to design a series of books for the club.

My first design for the LEC was Tennessee Williams's *A Streetcar Named
Desire* (1982), illustrated by Al Hirschfeld. I saw Al in March 1981. He turned
out to be another of those stubborn, egocentric artists who often made life
at the PWP miserable. He drew an original lithograph for the frontispiece,
and even though I sent him a diagram of the page, explaining that the image
should be vertical, he delivered a horizontal image, which had to be tipped
into the book on its side. Fortunately the image was so bad, so confusing,
that few people realized it was supposed to be viewed horizontally. The book
was superbly printed by Daniel Keleher at his Wild Carrot Letterpress.

One of my chores as the club's consultant was to mend fences with suppliers and collaborators. On my second trip to San Francisco in May 1981,
I went to see Helen Lee at the Mackenzie-Harris typefoundry to convince
her that Sidney was indeed serious and would meet his future obligations.
Helen and I continued to work together until I left Alabama in 1988. Othmar Peters at Mackenzie-Harris did a beautiful job of setting the type for
A Streetcar Named Desire, a factor that I feel contributed immensely to the
book's eloquence.

As it turned out, *A Streetcar Named Desire* was the only book I designed
for The Limited Editions Club. After Donald left, Sidney's son, Ben, took
over the production aspect of the club's operation. In 1983, while I was still
the editorial and design consultant to the LEC, I went with Ben in a stretch
limo to visit Larry Rivers in Southampton on Long Island about illustrating
Isaac Bashevis Singer's *The Magician of Lublin*. Rivers was also a notorious

drug user, so he and Ben got along famously. I spent most of the time wandering around Rivers's studio. By the time the book was published in 1984, I was no longer working for the LEC.

Visits by Schoolchildren to the PWP

It may not have much to do with getting the word out to collectors, but as part of its community service the PWP would occasionally invite classes of schoolchildren to visit the press. After the death of his father, Martino Mardersteig continued to refuse to let visitors into the pressrooms at the Stamperia Valdonega or the Officina Bodoni. Although an exception was made for The Typophiles visit in 1976, I never saw the inside of the Stamperia Valdonega.

Alessandro's girlfriend Antonia Cardini would occasionally bring her elementary school class to the PWP. Alessandro loved children, and so on the days we were expecting "the little ones," I would usually escape out the back door as soon as I heard them pouring into the side courtyard. Alessandro would quickly take them through the history of printing and then pull a few proofs on the Washington press that the children could take back to class. The visits ended with each child getting to pick a piece of type out of the hell box, a receptacle for damaged type. Once I came back just as the children were about to leave. Alessandro always asked them if they had any questions. Usually there were none; however, this day a hesitant little boy, pointing to two file boxes behind the desk, asked, "Who are the dead?" His gaze was focused on the labels of the boxes holding our mailing list. They were marked VIVI (active) and MORTI (inactive).

The private press printer of my day – without the benefit of family backing or a private income – had to be part showman and part hustler to succeed. Knowing I was both, I only hoped that my shenanigans were not too detrimental to the Press's integrity. Don Bruckner, another champion of the PWP, included the Press in his survey of fine printing in "With Art and Craftsmanship, Books Regain Former Glory" in the October 28, 1984, issue of The New York Times Magazine: "[T]he books [Rummonds] and his associate Alessandro Zanella have issued are superb." His words may appear to be an oversimplified summation – and I have my personal doubts – but I sincerely hope that that is how most collectors of PWP editions will remember them.

Verona: Getting the Word Out

Stinci di Agnello
Braised Lamb Shanks

Serves 4

One of the specialties of the Trattoria La Fontana was its braised lamb shanks. While there are many variations on this dish, the recipe below reflects the way I prefer to prepare them.

> 3 tablespoons olive oil
> 4 lamb shanks, about 1 pound each
> 5 garlic cloves, sliced
> 12½ ounces leeks, after trimming and cutting to 5-inch long pieces
> 2 teaspoons fresh rosemary, chopped, plus sprigs for garnish
> Salt and freshly ground black pepper to taste
> ¾ cup of dry white wine

In a flameproof casserole, warm oil over medium heat. When hot, but not smoking, add shanks and brown on all sides, about 12 minutes. Transfer to a plate. Reduce heat to medium low. Add garlic and sauté for 30 seconds. Cut leeks in quarters lengthwise. Add to casserole and sauté until translucent, about 7 minutes. Return shanks to casserole and add rosemary, salt, pepper, and wine. Raise heat to medium high and bring to a boil. Turn heat down to simmer. Cover casserole and braise for 2 hours, turning two or three times. Add water to maintain original level of liquid. Garnish with sprigs of rosemary.

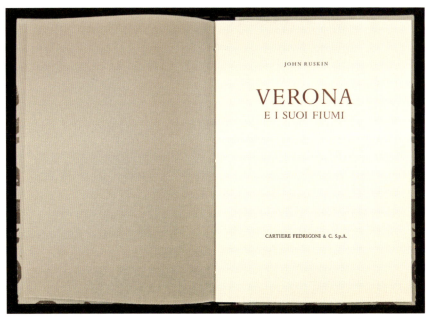

Title-page spread from *Verona e i Suoi Fiumi*. (Courtesy of the University of Oregon Libraries.)

Item 32. *Verona e i Suoi Fiumi*

As essay in twenty-two numbered sections
by John Ruskin translated from the
English into Italian by Amerigo Guadagnin.
With a two-color screenprint
adapted from a sketch by Ruskin.
24 pages. 33 x 23.5 cm. 400 copies. 1981.

Looking for a New Studio

Each year the rent on the studio in via Carlo Cattaneo almost doubled. By the summer of 1981 – a few months before our lease was up for its third renewal – Alessandro Zanella and I had to face the reality that we were paying an exorbitantly high rent for a studio space that even at the outset had been barely affordable. Nor was there any indication the rent would level off in the near future. We were in a real bind since this was an inflationary period in Italy. The government had recently removed rent controls, so if we moved the rent would still be beyond our means. We had three options: first, to stay where we were and accept higher annual increases; second, to look for a less expensive studio elsewhere in the historic center, with little hope of finding one; and third, to move to one of the industrial parks that surrounded Verona. Even though the third option offered much more space at a considerably lower cost, the ambiance wouldn't be conducive to handpress printing. Another argument against this option was the fact that neither Alessandro nor I had a car. We would have to rely on public transportation, which would not always be compatible with our printing schedules. The buses serving the industrial parks stopped running early in the evening and didn't run at all on the weekend.

Roberto (Pat) Pasini, an architect and early Veronese chum, had recently remodeled the top floors of an old palace around the corner from where I still lived in via Duomo. He was hoping to find a friend who would be interested in taking over the ground floor and had already proposed the PWP to the owner as a possible tenant. The space had potential. There were several large rooms with french doors that opened onto a private courtyard, as well as a main entrance with direct access to the street. The interior, however, was a horrid mess, having been unoccupied for several years. Pat assured us that the owner would remodel it to our specifications, including new wiring and plumbing. The rent would be low for the first few years, basically covering only the landlord's renovation costs, but once he had recouped them, he intended to bring the rent in line with the current market rate. No one could even guess what that might be. The real catch – which was not an unreasonable demand – was that if we broke our lease for any reason we would be liable for *all* the initial remodeling costs. In addition to the usual expenses involved in moving a print shop, we were concerned about the amount of lost production time. More than ever, this was a period when we needed to concentrate our efforts on getting books produced. In the end Alessandro and I were too insecure about the future to make this sort of major commitment, so we decided to stay where we were in via Carlo Cattaneo.

Accepting More Commissions

It was imperative that we quickly find some additional income. One solution was to print more commissions such as the annual book for I Cento Amici del Libro. Another was to pursue the specialized bookstores that were still on occasion commissioning limited editions. While these commissions relieved us of most of the production costs and worries, they also required us to relinquish control over the choice of illustrations and text – although we were usually able to maintain control over the design. I sincerely believe that the moment we decided to accept this type of commission as our primary source of income, we sealed the fate of the Press. Perhaps these commissions could have sustained us indefinitely, but by contracting ourselves out in this way, we were compromising the original intent and spirit of the PWP. Ten years earlier the Press had to accept a disproportionate number of commissions in order to survive. Now it appeared that it would be pressured into doing the same thing in its final years in Verona.

For the first time in a decade of printing on the handpress, I was beginning to lose my enthusiasm for the craft, mainly because I was being forced to choose between printing books for others – usually projects for which I had little personal interest – or closing the press altogether. We had a series of books in preparation, with texts by Paul Zweig, José María Martín Triana, and Italo Calvino that I looked forward to printing, but the commissions ultimately took precedence. If we were lucky, the commissions might generate enough profit to buy a few materials for one of our own editions.

Item 32. Verona e i Suoi Fiumi	587

Wade Pettitt

When Kenneth Pettitt's son, Wade, arrived at the Press on July 3, 1981, someone took him to via Duomo and told him, "Put your things anywhere; Gabriel assigns the sleeping spaces." He immediately began working at the press and stayed through most of September. Kenneth and Wade had been present at the inauguration of the PWP retrospective exhibition at the University of San Francisco in May 1981. Later that evening we drove down to North Beach for a nightcap, where Kenneth enticed Wade into going to Verona as an apprentice at the PWP. He felt the experience would help the young man focus his life. Wade was not particularly interested in the craft of printing, but the idea of spending a few carefree months in Europe must have ignited his adventurous spirit. He proved to be an excellent and conscientious worker, quickly picking up the necessary skills to make himself a valuable asset around the shop. He especially enjoyed working in the composing room, where he meticulously set type.

Gabriel and Wade Pettitt in the composing room at the via Carlo Cattaneo studio, Verona, Italy, 1981. (Photo by Jürgen Reuter, courtesy of PWP Archives.)

Wade had a lot of fine qualities: he was good-hearted, he had a wonderful sense of humor, he was dependable and strong and a fast learner. But he wasn't particularly articulate. Perhaps he felt intimidated, surrounded by so many people who did not converse in English. Sebastian Carter, of the Rampant Lions Press, and his family came through Verona on a visit in early August, 1981, and we invited them to join us for one of our *al fresco* lunches in the side courtyard. The guests were bursting forth with conversation in several languages when Wade, atypically, enthusiastically joined the conversation. Sebastian's young son, Benjamin, who could distinguish Italian, French, and German, turned to his father and said, "What language is he speaking?" Perhaps it was Wade's California accent that threw Benjamin off.

Wade and I didn't socialize much. On the weekends he went out to Pino Zanfretta's house in the country, where he was readily accepted by Pino's easy-going friends. He cultivated marijuana, went swimming naked, smoked pot, and who knows what else? He always returned to the studio on Monday mornings, refreshed and ready to come back to work.

Acquiring Another Albion Press

That summer, we also acquired another handpress. Flavio Frattini, a paper-maker and distributor of handmade papers, had approached us several times about exchanging his 1884 Luigi Ghisi Albion press for the large standing press that was still in the studio at Ponte Pietra. Finally we set a date, and early in August he brought the Albion press down from Varese on a flatbed truck. With Wade's muscle and a block and tackle, we managed to get the press, which had already been taken apart, into the studio. Then we helped Flavio load the standing press. The old bindery was now completely empty.

Eventually we relinquished the Ponte Pietra space to a maker of architectural models who had been pestering me for a long time to let him take over the lease. I frequently passed it on my jaunts through the neighborhood or on my nocturnal visits to a favorite nightspot across the river. I could never walk by its bright red doors without feeling pangs of frustration and guilt or being flooded with vivid memories of my anguished days with Giorgio Vigna.

The Albion press came with its last tympan intact. From it we were able to glean a little about its history. At that time in Italy, many handpresses were still being used to print the *annunci funebri* (obituary broadsides) that were pasted up in the neighborhood of the deceased. Our new press had been one of them. The printer usually kept the ornate border standing and just changed the names and dates. We found many of them superimposed on the tympan. With great patience Wade scraped and cleaned the press, then painted it with Rust-Oleum, using three parts black to one part forest green, the preferred color for all the cast-iron equipment in the studio. Before long we had the press reassembled and operative.

Gabriel, Alessandro Zanella, and Wade Pettitt standing beside the new Albion press in the pressroom at the via Carlo Cattaneo studio, Verona, Italy, 1981. (Photo by Jürgen Reuter, courtesy of PWP Archives.)

Luciano Elianti

The first of these new "rent-paying" commissions came to us from Luciano Elianti, the head of public relations at Cartiere Fedrigoni, a large commercial paper mill in Verona. I had known Luciano from my first months in Verona and frequently saw him at the openings at Studio La Città. A few years before I arrived in Italy, he and several other local bibliophiles had co-published, using the Le Rame imprint, a very handsome limited edition of *Anabase* (1967) by Saint-John Perse in French with Italian and English translations by Giuseppe Ungaretti and T. S. Eliot. The book was illustrated by the Spanish artist Miguel Berrocal and printed at the Officina Bodoni.

Luciano had originally taken the Fedrigoni project to Martino Mardersteig, who was unable to print it because he could not fit it into his schedule
at the Stamperia Valdonega before the August holidays. The main problem
that concerned Martino, one that later plagued us as well, was that a text
had not yet been selected. This presented a rather scary situation for all concerned, since the absolute deadline – an already scheduled anniversary banquet for Gianfranco Fedrigoni, the company's honorary president – was
only a few months away.

Initial Preparation for the Project

Luciano was familiar with our Quartus Series of books and thought a quartus
would be the perfect format for this project. We told him having a twelve-
page, Quartus-style pamphlet printed and bound on time for the banquet
depended on his delivering the text by a certain date. He continued to pro-
crastinate, however, and only at the last minute did he bring us the John
Ruskin piece, whose title in English is *Verona, and Its Rivers*. It was the text
of a lecture Ruskin had given at the Royal Institution in February 1870.

We were in for a shock when he gave us the manuscript, because it was
twice the length we had agreed on. In addition he wanted to double the
number of copies, making it an edition of four hundred copies. Naturally,
Fedrigoni would increase our fee for the additional work and copies, but
that was not the point. We were already under a great deal of pressure.
Alessandro and I had serious doubts about whether we were going to be
able to meet the impending deadline.

The Dante Type

From the outset Luciano had wanted the text set in Dante, a typeface designed
by Giovanni Mardersteig. During his negotiations with Martino, he must have
mentioned his preference for Dante to someone at the typesetting firm of
Ruggero Olivieri in Milan. Apparently unaware of the change in printers, they
cast the text using Mardersteig's private matrices – which varied slightly from
the regular Monotype Dante. When Martino heard that we were using the
Stamperia Valdonega's exclusive Dante type, he telephoned to say we couldn't
use the composition, which we had picked up a few days earlier from Olivieri.
Already behind schedule, we would never make up the lost time if we had
to wait until Olivieri reopened in September to recast the text. Thanks to

Item 32. Verona e i Suoi Fiumi 591

Luciano's intervention Martino gave us permission to use the Valdonega Dante type for the Fedrigoni project as well as two projected PWP editions. Martino kindly supplied us with missing sorts for both of the latter books.

Olivieri set the title in 36-point Didot, the largest size he had, but I wanted the word "Verona" to be larger than the other words in the title. We pulled a clean proof, which we then had photographically enlarged and retouched. I don't know why we didn't ask Fabio Ambrosi to make an engraving of it while he was cutting the Fedrigoni trademark for the colophon page. It would have been simple to print the title on the Albion press, but it was eventually screenprinted in sanguine – one of the colors in the two-color illustration printed by Luigi (Gino) Berardinelli. He also screenprinted the papers used to cover the boards.

Finding an Illustration for the Text

Luciano wanted the book to be illustrated, but again he fumbled around, having nothing concrete in mind. As a last resort he suggested we look for something at the Museo di Castelvecchio, which was housed in a medieval castle on the banks of the Adige River. Licisco Magagnato, the director of the museum, had mounted a large show of Ruskin's sketches in the late seventies, but all he could produce from the show's archives were a few bad photographs of the sketches reproduced in the catalog. All of Ruskin's drawings were undeveloped thumbnail sketches, hardly good material for illustrations. In desperation, I finally selected a sketch of an equestrian statue of the Cangrande I della Scala, a medieval ruler of Verona, and Gino helped convert it into a rather successful two-color screenprint, which he editioned while we were waiting for the text to be set.

The Paper

Fedrigoni supplied the paper – Luciano also intended to use the book to inaugurate a new line of machine-made text papers with a heavy laid texture. We used Scaligera white for the text and Castoro gray-brown for the endpapers and covers. When we gave the paper to Gino, we assumed we would be printing the text dry – completely ignoring our earlier resolve always to test the paper before starting to print. Only after we started pulling proofs did we realize the paper had to be printed damp if we were going to get a sharp impression. I am still puzzled why we didn't dampen it in the

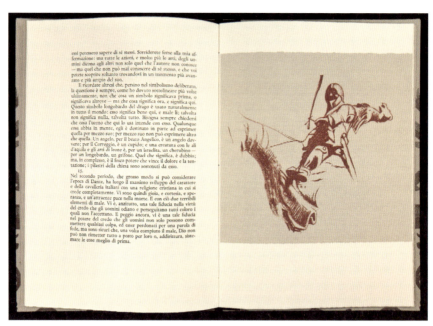

Double-page spread with illustration from *Verona e i Suoi Fiumi*. (Courtesy of the University of Oregon Libraries.)

standing press – the same way we always dampened handmade papers. By the time we were ready to print the text, Gino had finished editioning the illustration and the title, which meant we had to take into consideration the fact that the area of the sheet with the large screenprint would not expand when the paper was dampened because of the dryers in the inks and the density of the image. In addition the paper had to be handled with extreme care to avoid cockling.

Printing the Book

The Ruskin book, which was printed in August and September, was the first book we printed on the Albion press. Even though I initially felt some guilt about it, I came to prefer the Albion press over the Washington press. We had to hire several more hands in addition to Wade to get the book finished on time. Stefano Massetta and his wife Giovanna dropped whatever they were doing to come to our rescue. There was a tremendous amount of work involved. Fifteen hundred sheets of paper had to be folded in half, tick-marked with a pencil on the crease, and then unfolded. We set up an assem-

Item 32. Verona e i Suoi Fiumi

bly line to dampen the paper. The first person drenched the paper, one sheet at a time, in a tray of water, and then sponged off the excess; the second person pressed the sheet between two thick pulpboards to blot up the rest of the surface water; the third person dried the paper down even more between another two pulpboards; and, finally the sheet was passed on to the paper handler, who pricked the holes – using the PWP Mylar guide – before placing the sheet on the points.

Alessandro Zanella and Stefano Massetto printing *Verona e i Suoi Fiumi*, at the via Carlo Cattaneo studio, Verona, Italy, 1981. (Photo by RGR, courtesy of PWP Archives.)

As the printed sheets came off the press the second time, we interleaved them between thin dry pulpboards, leaving the pile overnight with weights on top. During the night the pulpboards drew all the moisture out of the dampened sheets and left them as crisp and flat as they had originally been. This process also eliminated having to hang the sheets up to air dry and then flatten them between thin sheets of index stock in the standing press. We saved so much time and the sheets looked so much better that this method of processing the sheets after printing became a standard procedure at the PWP.

The Cover of the Book

Fedrigoni also supplied the paper for the covers, a soft gray-brown. But it was too bland by itself. To liven the cover papers I thought about using a high-contrast photo of the ironwork around the Cangrande's tomb at the Arche Scaligere near Piazza delle Erbe, but when we proofed it in black, I did not like the results. I was about to give up on using decorated papers on the covers

Cover for *Verona e i Suoi Fiumi*. (Courtesy of the University of Oregon Libraries.)

when I noticed that Gino was working with a brown ink that he had doctored with a copper metallic one. I really liked the effect. When he finished his run, he set up the screen for the cover papers and pulled a proof. It was perfect: it added the necessary dimension to the design that had been missing. We were very much indebted to Gino for his help getting the edition out on time.

Binding the Book

Once the printing was finished, the fifteen hundred sheets had to be cut in two and folded into three thousand four-page signatures. The collated books were trimmed on three sides on the board cutter and pamphlet-sewn into the covers, which had been made elsewhere. Considering how hectic the project had been, the completed book was surprisingly attractive.

We delivered the finished books to Luciano the morning of the banquet, and that night he distributed most of the copies to the guests. A few days later he came by the studio to see if we could print up another hundred copies, but we had already learned our lesson. "Thank you, Luciano, but no thank you!" we told him in no uncertain terms.

Item 32. Verona e i Suoi Fiumi 595

Agnello con Finocchio
Lamb with Fennel

Serves 4

This recipe is from Sardinia, where lamb is the favorite meat. There are dozens of ways to prepare it, but I particularly like cooking the lamb with fennel. Select the smallest bulbs you can find.

 5 tablespoons olive oil
 2 pounds leg of lamb, boned and cut into pieces
 12 ounces onion, chopped
 1¾ cups tomatoes, skinned and mashed
    Salt and freshly ground black pepper
 1½ pounds fennel, quartered
    A couple of the feathery stalks

Heat oil in a Dutch oven. Add lamb and brown over moderate heat. Stir in onions and cook for 5 minutes more. Add tomatoes, salt, and pepper. Cover and simmer for 40 minutes, add a little water if lamb becomes too dry during cooking. Cook fennel in boiling salted water for 20 minutes. Drain and reserve 1 cup of the cooking liquid. Add fennel and reserved cooking liquid to the Dutch oven and cook for an additional 20 minutes. After 15 minutes, add the fennel stalks.

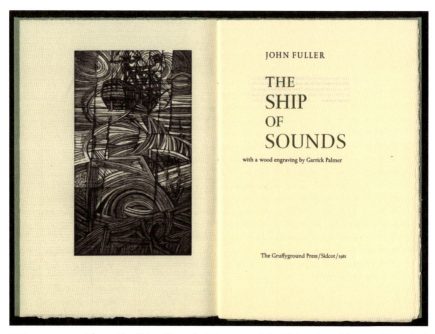

Title-page spread from *The Ship of Sounds*. (Courtesy of the University of Oregon Libraries.)

Item 33. *The Ship of Sounds*

A poem in eight parts by John Fuller.
With a wood engraving by Garrick Palmer.
16 pages. 25 x 17 cm. 130 pages. 1981.

Another Commission

As the continental correspondent for *Private Press Books*, I was engaged in a lively exchange of letters with one of its editors, Anthony Baker. Anthony was not a printer, but a publisher who had commissioned a number of fine printers around the world to produce books for his Gruffyground Press, usually at the rate of one a year. Claire Van Vliet had already printed three titles for him at her Janus Press. One subject Anthony frequently touched on in his letters was his desire to have the PWP print a book for his imprint, an opportunity I had always sidestepped in the past. Now that Alessandro Zanella and I were more actively seeking commissions he was one of the first publishers I contacted.

He was exceedingly pleased with the prospect and soon sent a manuscript by John Fuller. Anthony, who had definite ideas about both the printing and the binding, had already selected two Fabriano Roma papers, Michelangelo white for the text and Veronese green for the wrappers – he wanted the pamphlet to be "very Italian." It wasn't a particularly wise choice, because the strong laid texture of the paper competed fiercely with the fine lines of the Garrick Palmer wood engraving that Anthony had chosen to illustrate the poem. It was like trying to print a delicate mezzotint on coarse, dry paper. In order to minimize the laid lines during the printing of the wood engraving, we had to increase the amount of moisture in the paper – a risky procedure when using Roma, because the ink has a tendency to bleed through the paper if it is too damp.

Dampening the Paper

Since paper – no matter how damp – will only expand so much before it stabilizes, it was possible to vary the amount of moisture in the sheets without altering the paper's dimensions. When printing on papers that required two different degrees of dampness, we started with the damper of the two

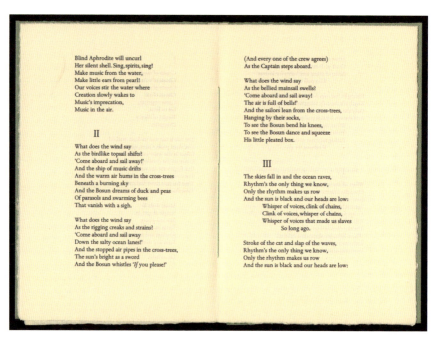

Double-page spread from *The Ship of Sounds*. (Courtesy of the University of Oregon Libraries.)

by adding more water to the pulpboards during the overnight pressing. After it was removed from the standing press, we placed the paper in the airtight humidor overnight to "rest" in order to let it expand.

Printing the Pamphlet

The pamphlet was printed in November 1981. First we editioned the wood engraving, but before printing the letterpress, we had to dry down the paper, taking care not to dry it out completely. The following method, used for the first time on this pamphlet, became a standard procedure at the PWP thereafter. Six stations, each consisting of a pair of pulpboards topped with a plywood pressing board, were set up. We inserted one sheet of paper at a time between the pulpboards at each station, remaining only as long as it took to repeat the process by replacing the dried-down sheets with fresh ones. If the paper was still too damp we repeated the process with another set of dry pulpboards. Sometimes we went through as many as three or four sets before we were able to reduce the moisture to the right amount. The dried-down paper was again left overnight in the humidor to redistribute the

Item 33 The Ship of Sounds

remaining moisture evenly throughout the pile. Each sheet in every edition – whether printed or not – had to be dampened the same way, since dampening and pressing alters the surface of the paper.

Anthony never said that he was displeased with *The Ship of Sounds*, but I can't help but think that he may have been a little disappointed in it. I certainly was. On the whole it seemed to lack vigor. Fortunately for him, and to his credit, he has a distinguished publishing record, so to have missed perfection on one may not have been as upsetting to him as it was to me.

Pollo alla Cacciatora
Hunter's Style Chicken Stew

Serves 6

In November Verona can be very foggy and chilly, perfect weather for chicken stew. The following recipe resembles the various versions served in trattorias throughout Italy.

- 1 chicken (3 to 4 pounds), cut into 8 pieces
- 2 tablespoons olive oil
- Flour for dusting
- Salt and freshly ground black pepper to taste
- 18 ounces yellow onions, thinly sliced
- 1 carrot, cut into thin slices
- ½ celery stalk, thinly sliced crosswise
- 2 garlic cloves, minced
- 1 cup dry white wine
- 1 can (28 ounces) peeled Italian plum tomatoes, chopped with their juices
- 1 bay leaf
- 1 tablespoon fresh rosemary leaves, minced
- 1 cup chicken stock as needed
- ¼ ounce flat-leaf parsley, minced

Wash chicken in cold water and pat dry with paper towels. Heat oil in a large deep skillet over medium-high heat. When oil is hot, dust the chicken pieces with flour. Put into the skillet with the skin side down and brown. Then turn pieces over and brown the other side, about 4 minutes per side. Transfer to a plate, and sprinkle with salt and pepper. Add onions, carrots, and celery to skillet and sauté, occasionally stirring, about 10 minutes. Add garlic and sauté, occasionally stirring, about 2 minutes. Add wine to deglaze skillet and let the mixture simmer for 3 minutes. Return chicken to skillet, reserving breasts for later. Add tomatoes, bay leaf, and rosemary. Season to taste with additional salt and pepper. Reduce heat to low. Cover and simmer for 40 minutes, adding chicken stock as tomato juice evaporates. Add

Item 33. The Ship of Sounds 601

chicken breasts and cook for another 15 minutes. Turn and baste pieces from time to time. Remove bay leaf. Transfer the chicken pieces to a plate. Reduce pan juices to a light sauce and return the chicken pieces to the skillet. Garnish with parsley.

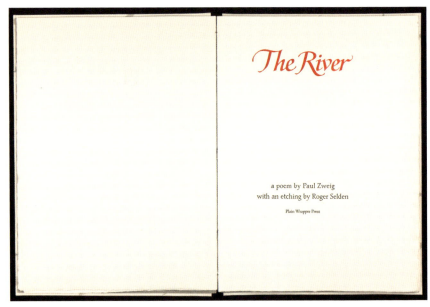

Title-page spread from *The River*. (Courtesy of the University of Oregon Libraries.)

Item 34. *The River*

A poem in seven stanzas by Paul Zweig.
With a multicolor etching by Roger Selden.
20 pages. 27 x 20 cm. 120 copies. 1982.

Thor Wood

One day in July 1979, Thor Wood appeared in Verona, sent to us by D. Steven Corey, Special Collections Librarian at the University of San Francisco, and the San Francisco bibliophile Albert Sperisen. Thor was chief of the Performing Arts Research Center at The New York Public Library and a private press enthusiast. We became fast friends, and I frequently visited Thor and his wife Ann on my trips to the States. Early in 1981 the Woods gave a dinner party at their home in Brooklyn. Among the guests were Paul and Francine Zweig.

Paul Zweig, New York, NY, 1980. (Photo by Robert Mahon, with permission of the photographer.)

604   FANTASIES & HARD KNOCKS

Paul was already very sick with the cancer that killed him at age 49 in 1984, but at the Wood's party he was lively as ever and talked enthusiastically about a new work. He mentioned a poem structured around watching the activity of pleasure boats and freighters on the Hudson River. I was instantly captivated by the subject matter. In the mid-fifties when I was living with Gordon Fraser, I also had a view of the Hudson and was often drawn to the windows, where I would stand and stare down, fascinated by the river traffic below just as he described it in the first lines of stanza 4:

> From my high window,
> I watch the sawed-off shells of freighters,
> Pleasure boats churning white wakes,
> Oil barges washed with rubbery pleats.
> Everywhere, man: cars skirting the river bank;
> Ball fields in the park,
> The swollen pistil of the pitcher's mound,
> The foul lines' beige petals narrowing to water's edge.

I told him that I would like to publish this poem, and he promised to send me a copy. Paul considered it one of his best pieces, and I agreed with him. After the poem arrived we worked closely together editing it, sending comments back and forth until we had it ready for publication.

Anita Karl

This was the only PWP book with hand lettering not done by Golda Fishbein. She was no longer living down the street, and even though we were frequently in touch by mail, I felt unjustifiably sorry for myself, believing for some time that she had abandoned me, which she had not. Golda first tried without success to find work in Italy, so she returned to the States hoping there would be more and better paying opportunities there.

In a feeble attempt to break my dependency on Golda, I asked Anita Karl to do the lettering. Anita and I had been friends since the late sixties. As a staff designer at Alfred A. Knopf, I was frequently asked to be the liaison for her freelance assignments, although we had never met in person. I first encountered her at Bill Henry's print shop. Dressed in a thin cotton minidress, she was standing at the front of the shop before a huge window with the sunlight silhouetting her voluptuous body. Bill was wrapping a stack of

Item 34. The River

Double-page spread from *The River*. (Courtesy of the University of Oregon Libraries.)

invitations to a costume party that she had ordered. The invitations commanded that guests "Come as the GOD that you are." When Bill introduced us we both squealed with delight, and she invited me to her party. Never one to pass up a costume party, I invited Barbara Knight, my girlfriend at the time, to join me. I went dressed as Apollo. My costume was an enormous sunburst made of silver leaves taped to a clear vinyl tunic. Anita, her boyfriend Bruce Kennedy and I continued to see a lot of each other, especially in the months just before I moved to Italy. Anita's lettering added a bright, crisp look to *The River*.

Roger Selden

Alessandro Zanella and I decided to seek Giorgio Upiglio's advice on an artist for this book, because his printmaking atelier, one of the foremost in Europe, attracted many major artists. We described the poem to him, and he brought out some prints by Roger Selden, an American artist living and working in Milan. Roger's work contained the exact flair we wanted for the book, so we made an appointment to visit him in his studio, where he showed us his recent paintings and graphics, which were filled with spontaneous, childlike doodles – whimsical images that would be perfect for the

Roger Selden in his studio, Milan, Italy, 2009. (Photo by Filippo Selden, courtesy of Roger Selden.)

text. Imagine our later surprise and disappointment when two hard-edge, geometric prints arrived.

When we tried to reach Roger, we discovered that he and his family had already left for the summer, so nothing more could be done until he returned in the fall. Once Roger was back in Milan, he called us. We got together again in his studio, pointing out the specific works we had liked on our first visit. This time he produced the two prints we used in the book. Even though they were stylistically what we were looking for, they didn't have very much verve. Later when we met with Roger at Giorgio's atelier to discuss the editioning of the prints, I suggested that a second color be added to the outer edges of the plates that could be printed together with the black. This was a technique I had seen Berta Moltke use with great success. The blue borders framing the prints made all the difference in the world, injecting some life into his otherwise listless prints.

Printing the Book

The colophon states that the printing was completed in September 1981; however, because of the delays in getting Roger's illustrations – and the Fedrigoni commission to fill the gap while waiting for them – we were still printing the text in January and February 1982. (It is somewhat ironic that the completion date of Paul's first PWP book, *Images & Footsteps*, was also

Item 34. The River 607

misstated.) This was the last item we printed on the Washington press before it was shipped to Alabama.

Starting in January 1981 we had the help of Arturo Rinaldi, a sixteen-year-old boy from the Centro per la Formazione Professionale Grafica, a printing trade school at the Istituto Salesiano San Zeno, who worked afternoons at the PWP. Arturo was exceptionally tall for an Italian. He had a head of bushy curly hair that reminded me of those youths in Renaissance paintings. He arrived at the studio on a moped and would occasionally take me with him when he ran errands for the Press. At those moments I was in heaven.

Arturo's mother would sometimes stop by the studio to see how he was doing. I always liked seeing her; she was young and beautiful, and in winter she arrived wrapped in a luxurious fur coat.

Giovanni De Stefanis

We did not have to go looking for a binder this time, because the binder came looking for us in 1982. Giovanni De Stefanis, one of the few members of I Cento Amici del Libro who had liked *Stella variabile*, wrote to ask if we would consider letting him bind one of our future editions. We were

Cover for *The River*. (Courtesy of the University of Oregon Libraries.)

extremely flattered, because De Stefanis was the premier binder of fine editions in Italy. Despite his unwillingness either to sew the books by hand or to make endbands – his staff was not trained in these areas – we commissioned him to bind this and the following edition. After our unpleasant experience with Giuseppe Rossi, we spoke quite frankly with De Stefanis about our financial situation, and he offered us very liberal credit terms. It was a pleasure to work with him, to be drawn into his world of expertise.

We sewed the books ourselves, using the hole-punching jig I had devised to hide the displaced pulp in the gutter caused by the needle entering from the outer fold. We also dyed the sewing thread gray, which added a nice touch to the binding.

Roger made an attractive lithograph that we used as a decorated paper to cover the boards. One of the unique features of the binding is the intaglio print set into a recessed opening in the cover of the book. De Stefanis had been working on something very similar on my first visit to his atelier, and later on I would use a variation on his basic design for a book I printed in Alabama.

I will always be indebted to De Stefanis for introducing me to the drop-spine box. From the beginning, I had an intense dislike of slipcases, mostly

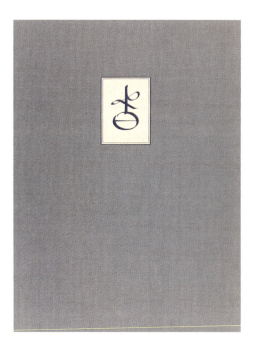

Drop-spine box for *The River*.
(Courtesy of the University of Oregon Libraries.)

Item 34. The River 609

because they tended to damage the books they were supposed to protect. From this point on I put all my books into drop-spine boxes.

Perhaps for the first time in my career, I felt I had a grip on what I was doing. *The River* exemplified the type of edition I most enjoyed and should have been producing all along. Even though printing in two colors doubled the production time, it was worth the extra effort for such an excellent text and the harmonious and playful graphics. The book was well received, being modest in both size and price. As the Italians are fond of saying, "*Fa una bella figura*" (It makes a good impression). Indeed it did.

PWP Cocktails

Per person

Finishing a book always provided an excuse for a big party. When we were flush, which was rarely, we would opt for martinis and negronis as well as wines. And of course lots of finger food. Today I use Broker's London Dry Gin. It is less aromatic than most gins.

For the martini

2½ ounces gin

2 teaspoons extra dry white vermouth (Noilly Prat)

2 small Italian Picholine (*or* French Lucques) green olives with pits

Put six to eight ice cubes in a glass pitcher. Add vermouth. Stir with a chopstick or small wooden spoon. Strain off liquid. Add gin and stir – never shake. Strain into a martini glass and garnish with olives.

For the negroni

1 ounce gin

1 ounce Punt e Mes (bitter red vermouth)

1 ounce Campari

Half-inch twist of orange peel

Pour gin, Punt e Mes, and Campari over cracked ice in a glass pitcher and stir with a chopstick or small wooden spoon. Strain into a cocktail glass and garnish with orange peel.

These cocktails were served with finger food. Two of my favorites are tramezzini and polenta with Gorgonzola cheese.

The tramezzini: Tramezzini are little mayonnaise sandwiches made with dense, but not heavy, white bread. In Italy, the bread comes in square loaves. The filling can be almost anything: tuna, slices of mozzarella cheese, tomatoes, chicken liver pâté, sliced hard-boiled eggs. Once the filling is spread over the bread, the crusts are removed, and the sandwich is cut diagonally twice.

Item 34. The River 611

The polenta with Gorgonzola: Prepare polenta according to instructions on package. When ready, pour it onto a 9 x 13-inch baking sheet, spreading polenta evenly over the surface. Generously sprinkle Gorgonzola cheese over polenta. Put baking sheet in the oven on broil. When cheese melts, it is ready to serve. With a wooden knife, cut polenta into bite-sized squares and place on a warm platter.

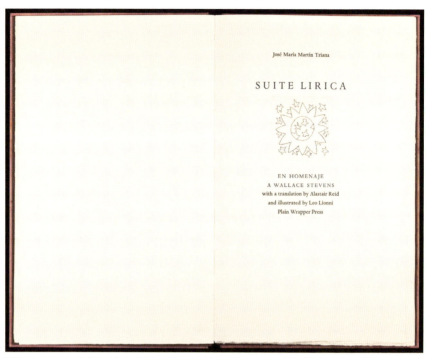

Title-page spread from *Suite Lirica / Lyric Suite*. (Courtesy of the University of Oregon Libraries.)

Item 35. *Suite Lirica / Lyric Suite*

A suite of ten verses in Spanish by José María Martín Triana; with English translations by Alastair Reid; and Wallace Stevens's poem "Final Soliloquy of the Interior Paramour" in English; and the author's note translated from the Spanish into English by Richard-Gabriel Rummonds.
With five etchings by Leo Lionni.
32 pages. 34.5 x 21.5 cm. 90 copies. 1982.

José María Martín Triana

José María Martín Triana, a Cuban writer living in Madrid, was an editor at Ediciones Felmar, where his primary activity was translating English texts into Spanish and preparing them for publication. He had heard a lot about me and the PWP from Carlos Cárdenas, who lived in New York and was a frequent visitor to both Madrid and Verona.

José María Martín Triana in the rear courtyard at via Carlo Cattaneo, 6, Verona, Italy, 1980. (Photo by RGR, courtesy of PWP Archives.)

In June 1976 José María and his partner Joe Smyth visited Verona. José María brought along some books of his own poetry for me to read. He also described a suite of ten verses he was working on that used images and metaphors from Wallace Stevens's "Final Soliloquy of the Interior Paramour" from Stevens's *Collected Poems* (1954) as an homage to the poet. When the suite was finished in 1980, José María sent it to me along with an English translation he had made as well as a second translation by Carlos. Both translations were more literal rather than poetic. Sensing that this was going to be one of the last PWP books printed in Verona, I did not want to delay its publication with one of my own thorough but slow translations. I asked Alastair Reid, who had translated some of the poems in the Borges/Pomodoro book, if he would be interested in working on this project. In the meantime I went ahead and translated José María's text for my own amusement.

I am not sure that Alastair was fully aware of the homoerotic implications in José María's verses. Nevertheless, many of the undertones of sensuality in Stevens's poem are present in Reid's translation, which are exemplified in the following three stanzas:

> There is scarcely light. You are alone,
> the turbulence of flesh by now behind you;
> by now almost forgotten the recent lover
> whose trembling goes trembling on in you.

> A weariness lies darkly on the twilight,
> turning you into someone unencumbered.
> You are no longer clasped in the embrace,
> but left to yourself alone, like someone old.

> A hand lights the first light of evening,
> and despite your languor you would like
> to linger with another in this room –
> difficult target for the solitary.

Poem for Gabriel

In November 1977 José María sent me a poem he wrote inspired by a comment I had made about a young man I had seen in Venice: "Es tan viva su belleza que llegaría a matar por ella."

Item 35. Suite Lirica / Lyric Suite

Quien ha contemplado la belleza, está ya destinado a la muerte
Para Richard-Gabriel Rummonds

Caminábamos. Hacía sol. Era domingo y septiembre.
La Biennale y Riva degli Schiavoni quedaron atrás.
Como agazapada, la Venecia pobre y cancerosa,
de limos y sucios canales empezó a lucir tímidamente
sus opacos joyeles, tras los palacios y los templos.
Como un dandy de otra época ibas, fino bastón
y sombrero más fino, verde chaqueta, pantalones sedosos.

Súbitamente le viste, acompañado de señoras y aburrido.
Si acaso quince años. –Es como Tadzio, exclamaste
y no te prestamos mayor atención. Al bullicio de la plaza,
de las terrazas volvimos. Al embarcadero de góndolas
y la vista del espejeante San Giorgio. La multitud
turística, desaliñada o dominguera pudo con nosotros,
mas entre tantos rostros anodinos, vislumbraste
aquel pelo, la playera de listas azules, el perfil despreciativo
y nuevo, y desmintiendo al elegíaco que suspire comprendiste
que ya no *amarías aquello que nunca veremos dos veces.*

Más tarde le tropezamos de nuevo y hasta se fijó en tí.
–Es tan viva su belleza que llegaría a matar por ella,
o bien moriría en sus manos; no se puede ser tan hermoso
sin ser criminal al mismo tiempo. Y el nombre de Tadzio
resonó como un alejado eco de tu indentificación.
Acababa el estío condenado a muerte por su misma
esbeltez asesina, y ambos teníais las edades del relato
y la película, estábamos en Venecia y todo sonaba
a Mahler, pero aquella noche solo y andando,
ah las huelgas italianas, regresaste a Verona.

Leo Lionni

Leo Lionni was an artist whose work I had been familiar with for many years. He had been an art director at *Fortune* magazine and a noted children's book author and illustrator. He now made his home in Tuscany, and he frequently exhibited in leading galleries throughout Italy. In early 1972

Leo Lionni in the rear courtyard at via Carlo Cattaneo, 6, Verona, Italy, 1981. (Photo by RGR, courtesy of PWP Archives.)

I saw an exhibition of his lithographs of fantasy plants at the Galleria Linea 70, a small but prestigious art gallery in Verona. That very night I suggested the possibility of a collaboration, and we agreed to stay in touch.

José María's manuscript reminded me of Leo's strange, surreal images, which contained a subliminal eroticism similar to that found in José María's text. I sent Leo a copy of the manuscript and the dimensions for each of the illustrations: two full-page and three smaller ones. After the experience Alessandro Zanella and I had with Roger Selden – who had given us something so contrary to what we had discussed with him – we asked Leo to show us sketches before he started transferring his images to the plates.

On one of his frequent trips through Verona, he stopped by the studio to show us his sketches. He had abandoned the idea of lithographs, having decided instead to try his hand at mezzotints, a technique he had never attempted. His sketches were very minimal, with none of the mystery and

Item 35. Suite Lirica / Lyric Suite

Part-title spread from *Suite Lirica / Lyric Suite*. (Courtesy of the University of Oregon Libraries.)

detail I liked so much in the lithographs. When I pointed this out to him, he said that these were just rough sketches. He was sure we would be pleased with the final prints.

While in New York, Leo had a commercial printmaking atelier prepare the plates, which he sent to us along with the proofs. His accompanying note explained that the proofs were not very good, but he was sure our printer could bring out the images he had put on the plates. Luigi (Gino) Berardinelli looked at the proofs and then examined the plates through a magnifying lens. He told us what we already suspected: it would be impossible to print from Leo's plates. The person who proofed them in New York had almost completely erased the already faint images during the proofing. The plates were made of soft zinc instead of hard copper. Gino even tried retouching the original proofs, using them to make a new set of plates photographically, but the resulting prints, though better in quality, were still dull and artistically uninteresting. Leo maintained it was *our* printer who had destroyed his plates. How arrogant he was!

Double-page spread from *Suite Lirica / Lyric Suite*. (Courtesy of the University of Oregon Libraries.)

After further discussions and a little diplomacy – not something for which I am well known – I managed with Fulvio Testa's help to convince Leo to let us bring him another set of copper plates. Alessandro borrowed a car and we drove to Tuscany. After a delicious lunch prepared by Leo's wife Nora, Leo worked on the plates while we browsed his library. Back in Verona Gino etched the plates and proofed them. They were technically fine, but regrettably these new images were even more removed from the lithographs of fantasy plants that had initially prompted this collaboration. Again the circumstances of a demanding schedule required us to push on even though we were disappointed with Lionni's etchings. We paid Leo $1,500 for his illustrations. Note the great discrepancy between his fee and the $600 paid to the author, José María, and the $225 paid to Alastair, the translator.

When the book was finally issued, Walter Bareiss, a PWP collector and an old friend of Leo's, disliked it and of course blamed us for Leo's weak illustrations. Perhaps he was right. If an artist can't judge weakness in his own work, then I suppose it is the publisher's duty to suppress it.

Printing the Book

The text was set in the same Dante that had been used for the Fedrigoni commission. Martino Mardersteig generously supplied us with missing sorts and the 36-point Didot capitals used for the stickup initials, which were printed in blue throughout. I especially liked the page format of this book, having always favored the tall and narrow proportions of Nicolas Jenson's books to the more square proportions of John Baskerville's deluxe editions. The choice of paper also represents a shift away from my previous preference for heavily sized Italian papers – such as those made by Fabriano – to the softer handmade ones from Cartiere Enrico Magnani in Pescia.

Type in the bed for *Suite Lirica / Lyric Suite*. (Photo by RGR, courtesy of PWP Archives.)

The book was printed on the Albion press in March and April 1982 with the help of Chris Borden, the last of the PWP apprentices to come to Verona. He had attended my "Practical Printing and Typography" demonstration at the Center for Book Arts in New York on May 16, 1981 and had been seduced by the idea of learning how to print on the handpress. Another of the participants was George Laws, who would later illustrate *Printing on the Iron Handpress*, my first book on printing.

Chris Borden

Chris arrived in Verona early in the morning of February 28, 1982, having taken the night train from Paris the same day he arrived in Europe. I met him at the station and brought him back to the studio. He barely had a chance to acclimate himself to the strange new environment of the studio before he was sent out to La Cantina, a bar down the street, to fetch our tray of morning coffee. Even though Chris didn't speak any Italian, Giulio Marchetti, the bar-

Chris Borden in the composing room at the via Carlo Cattaneo studio, Verona, Italy, 1982. (Photographer unknown, courtesy of PWP Archives.)

man, knew exactly where he had come from and what to give him. Once we had finished our coffee, I handed Chris a broom so he could sweep out the studio. Montserrat Lehmann, our part-time secretary, began to cry. Shaking a finger at Alessandro and me, she said, "How can you guys be so heartless? The poor boy must be dead tired." True, but this was our way of letting Chris know that working at the PWP was not going to be an Italian holiday.

After lunch I took Chris to via Duomo so he could settle in. In a conversation I had with him several years later, he told me that I made him sleep on the floor for a week. I do not remember this, but I am sure his memory is better than mine. What reason there was for this I can't imagine, because he could have used either of the camp beds in the old pressroom.

With Chris staying with me in via Duomo, my erotic life stood still. I never felt comfortable bringing someone back to my apartment when I had guests. Besides, my work schedule put many more demands on my time.

Binding the Book

In the Biblioteca Capitolare in Verona there is a wonderful manuscript referred to as the *Evangeliarium purpureum*. The text was written in silver on red vellum that had turned purple with age. From the beginning I had planned to use vellum, which I always considered an extremely sensuous material, to cover the boards of this edition. I thought it would be especially appropriate given

Item 35. Suite Lirica / Lyric Suite

Cover for *Suite Lirica / Lyric Suite*. (Courtesy of the University of Oregon Libraries.)

the book's erotic content. In addition, we had an excellent source of vellum nearby: Lanfranco Lui's La Pergamena tannery. Alessandro and I experimented with different dyes before we finally found one we really liked, a red-violet dye from Bayer A G that complemented the natural mottling of the skin.

By seriously applying ourselves we managed to finish dyeing the last of the vellum on the day before Alessandro and I left for New York to attend the "Fine Printing Conference at Columbia University." We had stretched each piece of vellum out between dry pulpboards, using the same basic technique we used to dry paper. Chris went away to visit friends in Rome until Alessandro returned. We asked an American acquaintance to come into the studio every few days to replace the pulpboards so the vellum would dry flat and not mildew.

Collectors have always been drawn to this book, even with its faults, commenting on its sensuousness and noting the degree of craftsmanship exhibited in its production. For some printers – although not for me – this would be reward enough.

Gnocchi di Spinaci e Ricotta alla Salvia
Spinach and Ricotta Gnocchi with Butter and Sage Sauce

Serves 4

Frustrations like those caused by Leo Lionni always required comfort food, and a plate of gnocchi is one my favorite pacifiers. In Florence this type of gnocchi is called *strozzapreti* (it strangles priests). Its name implies that gluttonous priests would eat them so fast that they choked to death on them. Other greens such as chard, arugula, and watercress, may be used either alone or combined with spinach.

For the gnocchi
- 10 ounces fresh unwashed spinach after large stems have been removed
- 2 large eggs
- 12 ounces fresh, large curd, whole milk ricotta cheese
- 1 ounce freshly grated Parmigiano-Reggiano cheese
- Pinch freshly grated nutmeg
- 1 teaspoon salt
- 2½ ounces all-purpose flour, divided, plus extra for forming the gnocchi
- 1 tablespoon coarse salt for the gnocchi water

For the Sauce
- 6 tablespoons unsalted butter
- 16 large fresh sage leaves, rinsed and patted dry
- Pinch freshly grated nutmeg
- Salt and freshly ground black pepper to taste
- Freshly grated Parmigiano-Reggiano cheese for serving

The gnocchi: Wash spinach in cold water. Place, still dripping, in a large pan without adding more water. Cover and cook over a medium-low heat. As soon as spinach goes limp and starts to give off steam, it is ready, about 2 minutes. Remove spinach from the pan and spread out in a colander. Let cool until you can handle it. Do not rinse with water. Form spinach into a large ball and squeeze dry. Finely chop and set aside. In a large bowl, lightly

Item 35. Suite Lirica / Lyric Suite

beat eggs until yolks and whites are evenly blended. With a spatula, gradually incorporate ricotta with eggs until the mixture is fluffy. Add cheese, nutmeg, and salt. Slowly stir in flour, one-quarter at a time. Do not overbeat the dough. Gently fold in spinach, frequently scrapping the sides of the bowl. Cover and refrigerate for 30 minutes. Remove the bowl from the refrigerator. Cover the bottom of a shallow soup plate with flour. Scoop out a teaspoon of dough, dropping three or four lumps into flour. Gently roll gnocchi in flour, then pinch into small balls. Dust your palms with flour and roll gnocchi into small balls. Remove excess flour by bouncing each ball in a loose fist. The finished gnocchi should be the size of a large grape. Be sure there are no cracks or they may break apart while cooking. Place gnocchi on a lightly floured baking sheet as you form them. They should not touch each other. Refrigerate, uncovered, for at least 20 minutes. Select a large pot with a wide mouth, minimum 9-inch diameter. The number of gnocchi cooked at one time should never exceed the number that can float comfortably on the surface without crowding. Bring 3 quarts of water to a rapid boil. Add coarse salt and reduce heat to a lively simmer. Gently drop gnocchi into water. They will fall to the bottom of the pot. Gently stir water to be sure none are sticking to the bottom of the pot or to each other. Vigorous boiling could cause gnocchi to break apart or disintegrate. When gnocchi are cooked, about 3 to 5 minutes, they will float to the surface. Let them simmer for only a second or two. Using a large slotted skimmer, gather up four or five gnocchi. Touch skimmer down on a paper towel to remove access water before transferring them to a warm serving dish. Do not overcook; if you do, the gnocchi will be soggy. Repeat procedure until all are cooked. Serve with the butter and sage sauce below.

The sauce: Melt butter over medium heat in a small saucepan. When butter begins to bubble, stir in sage leaves. Add, salt, and pepper and sauté until leaves are crispy, about 2 minutes. Do not let butter or sage burn. An attractive way to serve this dish is to blanch 24 small leaves of spinach in the gnocchi water, about 30 seconds. Arrange drained leaves on individual warmed plates. Place gnocchi on the bed of spinach. Spoon the sauce over gnocchi. Serve with grated cheese on the side.

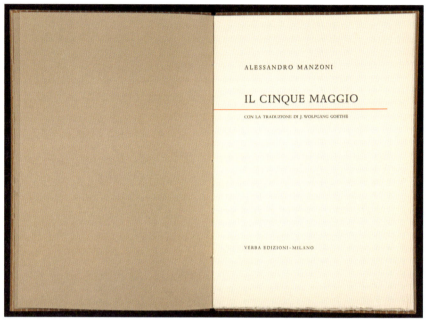

Title-page spread from *Il Cinque Maggio / Der Fünfte Mai*. (Courtesy of the University of Oregon Libraries.)

Item 36. *Il Cinque Maggio / Der Fünfte Mai*

An ode in Italian by Alessandro Manzoni; with a
German translation by Johann Wolfgang von Goethe;
and an introduction in Italian by Giuseppe Fontana.
16 pages. 28 x 19.5 cm. 120 copies. 1982.

Rising Production Costs

By the spring of 1982, I was becoming more and more frustrated and disillusioned trying to print in Verona. Because of the compromises I had to make
each day, I began to dread going to the studio. Contributing to my low spirits
was the fact that the Italian government had introduced a new fiscal system
for every commercial transaction requiring receipts signed by both parties in
an official state-issued account book. The system was so byzantine that if we
took a book out of our studio to show to a bookseller down the street, we had
to fill out a form and have the bookseller sign it, even if he didn't buy the book.
The paperwork was tedious and exasperating, and Alessandro Zanella now
had to spend one full day a week satisfying this obligation. The government
slapped huge fines on artisans, particularly those it believed had been avoiding
the payment of taxes by not reporting their true income. The police frequently
stopped people on the street for spot checks and asked them to show sales slips
for any new merchandise in their possession. At the same time many of the
artisans and salesmen that Alessandro and I had worked with or bought materials from in the past now persisted in doing business as usual – cash under
the table – which meant we had fewer receipts to show for outside labor and
materials. When we insisted on receipts, they would add another twenty or
thirty percent to their estimates to "cover administrative costs." Shortly after
we closed the Press, ironically, the government relaxed some of the regulations.

The Last PWP Book Printed in Verona

One person who had always been *a posto* (above board) with us was
Giuseppe Fontana, a Milanese industrialist and bibliophile. He had published several limited editions under his own imprint, Verba Edizioni, just
for the pleasure of creating beautiful and interesting books. Giovanni
Mardersteig had printed a number of these. Fontana had been a PWP

collector for many years. His own son was not interested in fine books, so Fontana transferred some of his paternal and bibliophilic expectations onto Alessandro, whom he seemed to adore. Even though the three of us usually met together, I stayed in the background and let Alessandro and Fontana do all the planning. Alessandro also designed this book.

Fontana's commission had been prompted by one of the design solutions for setting bilingual texts that we had used in a keepsake of Giuseppe Ungaretti's poems. The poem, "Chiaroscuro," was set in two columns, with the Italian adjacent to the inside gutter and the English translation adjacent to the outer margin.

Alessandro Manzoni's Text

"Il Cinque maggio" ("The Fifth of May") is one of Manzoni's most famous poems; its first lines are known by heart by thousands of Italian schoolchildren. It is an ode to Napoleon, who died on that day in 1821. Goethe, almost forty years Manzoni's senior, was so impressed with the work that he translated it into German.

The Italian text was composed in 16-point Dante and printed in black; the German, in 12-point, was printed in a rust color. Following the typo-

Alessandro Manzoni, Milan, Italy, 1841. (Painted by Francesco Hayez, courtesy of the Pinacoteca di Brera, Milan.)

Item 36. Il Cinque Maggio / Der Fünfte Mai

graphic design of one of the editions of the poem, we capitalized the first word of each line. Here are the first two stanzas in Italian:

> Ei fu. Siccome immobile,
> Dato il mortal sospiro,
> Stette la spoglia immemore
> Orba di tanto spiro,
> Così percossa, attonita
> La terra al nunzio sta,
>
> Muta pensando all'ultima
> Ora dell'uom fatale;
> Né sa quando una simile
> Orma di piè mortale
> La sua cruenta polvere
> A calpestar verrà.

When Alessandro returned from the States in June 1982, he was able – with Chris Borden's help – to finish printing this book before I returned from Alabama the following month.

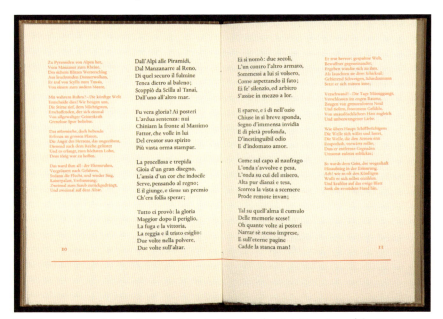

Double-page spread from *Il Cinque Maggio / Der Fünfte Mai*. (Courtesy of the University of Oregon Libraries.)

The Decorated Papers for the Covers

One of my favorite reference works in my library in Verona was *Printing of To-Day* (1928) by Oliver Simon and Julius Rodenberg. I especially liked the woodcut-patterned papers used to cover the boards. Shortly after his visit in the summer of 1981, Sebastian Carter sent us a sample book of the attractive papers he was printing at his Rampant Lions Press, which rekindled our interest in printing our own decorated papers.

We had a large supply of fruitwood blocks, and with screwdrivers, nails, and leather punches we began to cover several of them with incised geometric patterns. By pasting up multiple proofs, we created a master in the form of a large composite, from which a linecut could be made. The binding was a variation on the Quartus Series style, the main difference being that we usually added a strip of cloth to the spine for strength whenever we had to sew through more than an eight-page signature.

This was the last PWP book issued in Italy. With it more than a decade of striving after an impossible dream came to an abrupt end. Had I been tilting at windmills, deluding myself all these years? Even now, I can't say for sure that I was not. There had been too many unfulfilled projects not to feel some remorse.

Cover for *Il Cinque Maggio / De Fünfte Mai*. (Courtesy of the University of Oregon Libraries.)

Item 36. *Il Cinque Maggio / Der Fünfte Mai*

Group photo in the side courtyard at the via Carlo Cattaneo studio, Verona, Italy, 1982. *Front:* Pino Zanfretta, Bruna Da Re, and Alessandro Zanella. *Back:* Chris Borden and Peter Eustace. (Photo by RGR, courtesy of PWP Archives.)

Closing the Press

A group of old friends came by the studio to help us close it up. Pino Zanfretta – one of my former students at SIP, the Italian state telephone company – lived in the country, and we often went mushroom hunting in the mountains around his house. Bruna Da Re was one of Golda Fishbein's former students who also became a close friend. After Golda's departure, Bruna helped me prepare the few dinner parties I gave. Peter Eustace was an Englishman on whom I had a crush. After reading my keepsake *Seven Aspects of Solitude*, he wrote a poem to thank me for it.

For many years a small and unobtrusive oak panel with the names of the Press and the printers lettered by Golda hung over the entrance to the studio from the *porte-cochère*. It was the last thing Alessandro and I removed.

Plain Wrapper Press sign above the main entrance to the via Carlo Cattaneo studio, Verona, Italy, 1981. (Photo by Jürgen Reuter, courtesy PWP of Archives.)

Gabriel and Alessandro Zanella, holding the PWP sign, in the side courtyard at via Carlo Cattaneo, 6, Verona, Italy, 1982. (Photo by Pino Zanfretta, courtesy of PWP Archives.)

I still have a photograph showing the two of us with tears in our eyes standing in the side courtyard holding up the sign. This photograph, which Pino Zanfretta took to commemorate the event, shows two very forlorn men, both with beards – the older slightly paunchy and balding, the younger slim and bushy-haired, a final acknowledgment of their togetherness and the printing that had bound them together for the past six years.

Going Our Separate Ways

When Alessandro first appeared at the PWP in 1976, he brought with him a specific dream: he wanted to print Heinrich von Kleist's *Über das Marionettentheater* in a German and Italian bilingual edition. After working at the PWP he was more than prepared to fulfill that youthful ambition. In 1983 he published von Kleist's text in a handsome edition with four etchings by Neil Moore, as the first book from his Edizioni Ampersand, for which Golda designed a beautiful pressmark. In 1983 I, too, would establish a new press, Ex Ophidia, but I would have to wait until 1986 before issuing my first book.

Item 36. Il Cinque Maggio / Der Fünfte Mai

Arrosto di Maiale al Latte
Pork Loin Braised in Milk

Serves 6

A dish that always brings back fond memories of Verona and my friends there is pork loin roast braised in milk. Pino and Angiolina Zanfretta invited Golda and me to go with them out into the country where friends of theirs were celebrating some event. Angiolina and the hostess kept an eye on the roast while the guys drank wine and talked politics. The roast was ready when all the milk had been absorbed, leaving on the bottom of the pan tiny clusters of curd that are used to make the sauce.

> 2 pounds pork loin roast in one piece, with a little fat, securely tied
> 10 fresh rosemary sprigs, 1 inch long
> 2 large garlic cloves, cut into slivers
> 2 tablespoons butter
> 2 tablespoons canola oil
> 1 teaspoon salt
> 4 twists of freshly ground black pepper
> 2½ cups milk
> 2 tablespoons water

With a paring knife, punch holes in meat just large enough to insert the rosemary sprigs and garlic slices. Heat butter and oil over medium heat in a flameproof casserole large enough to hold the meat snugly. When butter begins to bubble, add meat, fat side down. Brown thoroughly on all sides. If butter begins to burn, turn the heat down. Add salt and pepper. Slowly pour milk over the meat. Bring milk to a boil, then turn heat down to medium and partially cover. Cook slowly for 1½ to 2 hours, turning and basting meat occasionally. If necessary, add more milk. By the time meat is cooked, milk should have coagulated into small brown clusters. If pale, raise heat to a boil until the clusters darken. Remove meat and let it rest on a carving board for a few minutes before removing trussing string. Draw off most of the fat and discard. There could be as much as 1½ cups. Add water and turn up the heat. Deglaze casserole as water evaporates. Put sauce in a small bowl to serve with the sliced meat.

Front of the Canyon Lake house facing the water, Cottondale, AL, 1982. (Photo by RGR, courtesy of PWP Archives.)

Cottondale, Alabama: Settling In

> There comes a time when you realize that everything
> is a dream, and only those things preserved in writing
> have any possibility of being real.
>   – James Salter, *All That Is*

Settling In

Of the many things I have written about the Press, no other single document sums up my emotional involvement with printing as well as "Some News and Bits of Gossip from Gabriel," a newsletter I sent out to friends and collectors in January 1983 from my new home in Cottondale, Alabama, about 15 miles east of the campus at Tuscaloosa. Since it chronicles the events leading up to the closing of the PWP on August 31, 1982, and reflects the optimism I felt for what lay ahead of me, I have included several long excerpts.

Some News and Bits of Gossip from Gabriel

Somehow, maybe the fault of evil spirits, I managed to get through both Christmas and New Year's without getting laid. But that really belongs at the end of my letter, not the beginning; so let me go back a few months.

Even though it was still early in July, for me the summer was over the night [of the] farewell party for the participants who had attended the Book Arts Institute, five intense weeks of total immersion in those ancient crafts. The students, who had come from all over the country, quickly fused into a close-knit family – albeit, not without some of the problems usually inherent in "family" life. I loved them all dearly, and perhaps one of them too dearly; so that when we parted – and no one that night was without tears in his eyes, tears of joy, of sadness, and of sheer exhaustion – I knew that whatever had passed between the two of us that summer, even though never completely or satisfactorily consummated, would have much less of a chance of survival and growth once we were separated. Our last kiss/embrace before taking leave of each other, seemingly no different than that of all the others, was for me as

Eberhardt binding workshop, Book Arts Institute, Typographic Laboratory at the University of Alabama, Tuscaloosa, AL, 1982. Fritz Eberhardt in the front row center; his wife Trudi behind him on the left; and Gabriel in the back row fourth from the left. (Photographer unknown, courtesy of PWP Archives.)

scorching as the infamous kiss of Judas for it could never again be repeated without overtones of betrayal [and without acknowledging publicly that we had been lovers].

. . .

I suppose I never really thought that I would ever have to close the PWP, let alone leave "bella" Verona. By then [1982], I had been living there, as an honorary citizen, for more than twelve years – always in the same, old, run-down Renaissance apartment with its sixteen-foot ceilings in via Duomo with "Count Dracula" and the "Humping Medic" always at my heels. Originally the press was housed in one room, and I in the other with a table, a chair, and a bed – a Spartan or monastic life, to be sure. But in those days my only all-consuming interest really was printing. I was so completely surrounded by good Veronese friends and drinking companions that physical comforts had long since ceased to be important to me....

It was not easy to face the bulk of belongings which I had accumulated in the last twelve years, augmented by those which I had brought from New York.... little by little, the books and photographs and me-

Cottondale, Alabama: Settling In

mentos of more than half a century were either packed or thrown away, many having traveled around the world several times a few decades earlier in their original wrappers – to borrow a phrase from the booksellers – such as the Thanksgiving of '41 place card and the ruptured piece of a silvery defense blimp which had been moored near our house in '42 to prevent the Japanese from dropping bombs on us. I sorted through it all, a little at a time, always with a glass of that wonderful local wine close at hand to console me.

The Black Hole of Calcutta – where Brad Hutchinson had slept and wrestled with numerous hangovers – had already been dismantled. The tongue-and-groove flooring, beams, and posts had gone to Stefano Massetta, and the bookcases had been hauled up five flights of stairs for Alessandro on his birthday last April [1982]. But what terrified me most was the realization that I had less than a month to arrange my decampment since I had to be back in Alabama by the first week in September.

There were still two very difficult and thorny questions to be confronted: the legal separation and the moral separation. Legally most of the equipment, the archives, and a good part of the stock belonged to me since Alessandro officially became my partner in December 1978, even though we had been working together since October 1976. Indeed, we lived marginally those years since our editions were frightfully expensive to produce and any income went back into the press. The one piece of equipment that we had bought together was an Albion press. Its final disposition nearly destroyed the two of us physically and emotionally, as well as any love that had grown between us in those years when we had struggled together so optimistically to gain international recognition for the press. Each considered himself entitled to the Albion press. I felt that I could not return to the States after twelve years with nothing more to show for my effort abroad than the very same equipment which I had brought with me. . . . On the other side, Alessandro, as well, was afraid that he would be left with nothing tangible to show for all his years of work at the press. As the tension continued to build up, each of us felt more threatened, and so it came as a great relief when one day, quite by chance, we went to via Duomo to have lunch, and the subject came up, and, consequently, out into the open, and with excruciatingly painful tears and professions of great affection on both sides, we resolved the disposition of the Albion press. It was decided that we should buy a third press, and that Alessandro should have first choice of the two on the condition that a third press could be found and brought to the studio in time to be packed up before I had to leave. We had had several leads about presses nearby, and soon a beautiful [1854] Stanhope press surfaced which Alessandro liked very much; so we bought it. With that settled, we continued to divide and pack and crate the contents of the studio and delivered them to the shipper's warehouse just a few days before I boarded the plane for Alabama. We never mentioned the other thought that was always foremost in our heads: that we would miss each other terribly once the move was final.

But aside from the problems of closing the press, in general I was in a foul mood that month, and to exacerbate the situation several American friends decided to come to Verona for a final visit. Needless to say, I felt terribly put upon in my final, urgent hours when I was asked to help cash checks, make travel arrangements, or be a gracious host. Consequently, with little effort, I managed to alienate most of my dearest and oldest friends before I left. Stefano [Massetta], who had been like a kid brother to me, and I had a falling out almost immediately upon my return, and remorsefully we never saw or spoke to each other again. Mutual friends were forced to take sides. Since neither Stefano nor I ever told anyone what had happened between us, our friends found it difficult to know which of us to blame. In the end, they all did what most intelligent people would have done, they sided with the friend who was staying behind, and so in those last days, I found myself completely alone, literally abandoned for the first time since I had moved to Verona. Some friends became belligerent; others, like Stefano's wife Giovanna, who loved me dearly, were merely mystified. My last days were sweetened only by the unmitigated maternal love of AnnaMaria Mezzelani [the mother-in-law of a friend] and the seasoned acceptance of Pino and Angiolina Zanfretta who chose to stay close by, although somewhat suspiciously, always hoping to reconcile Stefano and me.

Verona, even though more immediate, is as far away as Mexico or Ecuador or Argentina or Japan for me now. I am only aware, and vaguely sense, that I have once lived in these remote places because I have photographs, today's unquestionable documents, in which I am posing with people whose names I can't even recall today. But Verona, the PWP, and my Veronese lifestyle and friends had been the substance of my existence for many years. I used to measure my comings-and-goings in two-year stints; so these Veronese echoes are things that won't quickly, if ever, become nameless or silent.

...

If I had thought that leaving Verona would be traumatic, I was not prepared for the difficulties of resettling in the States. I had to begin from scratch. First, a car. I hadn't owned a car for more than seventeen years, not since I went bouncing over the roads in Ecuador scraping the bottom of my Triumph Spitfire. Being more practical in my old age, I bought a '74 Dodge Dart. It runs and that's about all that can be said for it, except that it is great in drag races at red lights, always first across the intersection. Second, a place to stay. Last summer [1982] Nina Martin, with whom I teach, had lent me her house on Canyon Lake for the day so the students in the Institute could have a Fourth of July picnic and a swim.... Somehow we managed to find it hidden away off the main road, arriving loaded down with baskets of Southern fried chicken and potato salad. Fritz and Trudi Eberhardt, who were teaching the binding

Canyon Lake in front of Gabriel's house, Cottondale, AL, 1982. (Photo by RGR, courtesy of PWP Archives.)

segment [at the Institute], also came along for the festivities. I fell in love with the house immediately. It is a small, wooden house up on a full basement with a fireplace upstairs and another downstairs – a very unpretentious house. It had been condemned "white trash" housing on campus property before Nina moved it out to the lake. . . . Before going back to Verona, I arranged to rent the house from her with an option to buy it – since it was, at that time, up for sale. I became more and more enamored of the house as I lived in it. It sits about fifty feet from the water's edge and has three hundred feet of shoreline. There is almost an acre of land around the house with pines and oaks, wilderness, and mallard ducks abounding on the site.

When Jim Ramer, the dean of the Library School, heard that I was closing the PWP, he moved my customary alternate spring semester up to the fall so I could teach here while he worked on finding a permanent appointment for me. The task was not an easy one since there had been prorationing and cutbacks here in addition to his having some opposition from the dean of the Graduate School who resisted accepting on a permanent basis a Berkeley [outcast] without a degree on the teaching staff of the Library School.

Expected to do my part in convincing the university to hire me, I was frequently interviewed and often photographed displaying my books. Or I would give talks to small gatherings such as at Alice McLean Stewart's club, where the ladies gathered in the afternoons to drink mint juleps and martinis. Before I addressed the group, Alice took me aside and whispered in my ear, "Be brief; we have short attention spans."

I was getting very anxious, and very nervous, primarily because I did want to stay here at the university, but I felt that I could only do so if certain assurances were forthcoming since I needed to buy a house as soon as possible so I could begin to set up another press. For a while things were looking pretty grim, and so I began to put out feelers at other universities that I knew had an interest in my work.

About that time [September 1982], I went over to Austin to see Decherd Turner at the Harry Ransom Humanities Research Center. He has been a long-standing friend of the PWP and purchased one of the two complete runs of PWP editions from the press's archives.

Gabriel displaying two of his PWP publications in the W.S. Hoole Special Collections Library at the University of Alabama, Tuscaloosa, AL, 1983. (Photo by Chip Cooper for *Dialog*, courtesy of PWP Archives.)

He also indicated that he would find a place for me there if Alabama failed to do so. I had to let him know by the first of November, and so we now had a real cutoff date. To make things even more hectic, I heard that the container with my belongings from Verona would be arriving in New Orleans early in December. Just before zero hour, Jim came through. The University would match the Texas offer. A new position had been created for me: Director of the Institute for the Book

Group photo of the student printers and faculty for the Ritsos/Chafetz book, Parallel Editions, University of Alabama, Tuscaloosa, AL, 1983. *Front:* Bradley Hutchinson, Megan Benton, Susan Hendrie, and Jeffrey Haste; *Middle:* Kathryn Miller, Sue Harris, and Peter Kruty; *Back:* Glenn House, Gabriel, and Barry Neavill. (Photo by J.P. Forsthoffer, courtesy of PWP Archives.)

Arts.... One of my major goals this year will be to get the collegiate press firmly on its feet so that it can eventually be self-supporting. Peter Kruty and Jeff Haste from last summer's Institute have been working with me at the press since last September. Our current project is a book of new poems by Yannis Ritsos in Greek and English, with translations by Edmond Keeley and five woodcuts by Sidney Chafetz....

Fanfare 1

The first week in December, I bought the house from Nina. It is the very first house I have ever owned, and I have to keep reminding myself that it really is mine. With only a day's notice, I was informed that the container had indeed arrived in New Orleans and that it would be at my house the next day at three in the afternoon. I don't know how I managed to do it all on such short notice, but I rounded up seven strong fellas and the always reliable Glenn House to help with the unloading, had some wood delivered so we could build a platform, and arranged for a

The Canyon Lake house facing the water, Cottondale, AL, 1982. In the lower right-hand corner one can barely see one of the presses covered in plastic. (Photo by RGR, courtesy PWP Archives.)

The new studio on the right with nine windows facing the lake, Cottondale, AL, 1984. (Photo by Antony O'Hara, courtesy of the photographer.)

fork lift to get the presses off the truck. It rained or drizzled all afternoon, but we managed to get everything indoors or covered up before anything really got wet. The presses were set on a platform near the lake. A few days later there were flash flood warnings, and the lake started rising, but fortunately it never came up as high as the presses, which to my horror were only about six feet away from the water's edge.

Right away, and masochistically so typical of me, I wanted to build a new studio, a dream studio of enormous proportions, next to the house; so I began to torture myself, and lose many nights of sleep, with plans and designs and minute details which no one . . . would even have noticed. Finally, after much trimming, I settled on about 850 square feet with a flank of windows twenty-four feet wide facing the lake – half the size of my original sketch. Ground was broken on the third of January, so I hope, as ever optimistically, to be printing by March. There are still two more PWP projects to complete, and then I'll start publishing under my own new, although still tentative, imprint: EX OUROBOROS [eventually named Ex Ophidia].

. . .

One of the advantages for me, of unrequited physical love, if one can ever consider such a thing as an advantage, is that this self-imposed state of being keeps me quite docile and calm – and this was certainly a period in my life when it was important not to get involved with anyone – I couldn't even answer simple letters from friends without getting uptight – since my immediate problems were more than I could cope with. I even failed at following through on "something quick and casual" snatched away from me under "The Sistine Chukker."

Fanfare 2

Now that my primary problems have been, for the most part, resolved, I hope I can relax a bit and misbehave on occasion; as you all know, I'm not a saint.

"Sistine Chukker" painted by Tom Bradford for the ceiling of the Chukker bar, Tuscaloosa, Al. (Photographer unknown, courtesy of PWP Archives.)

Cottondale, Alabama: Settling In 643

Fanfare 3 (adagio)

I feel that 1983 will be yet another important crossroads in my life and that I'll encounter and accept the challenges as they are offered, and I expect to act on them successfully. In closing, I hope that 1983 will hold equally stimulating challenges for all of you, dear friends.

P.S. I haven't been laid between New Year's and the writing of this letter, but I'm working on it.

A New Life in Alabama

That first full year in Tuscaloosa and Cottondale was occupied with getting the studio constructed and organizing the Book Arts Program. In the fall of 1984, Peter Kruty and Jeffrey Haste enrolled as the first full-time students in the fledgling program. The MFA in the Book Arts Program wasn't officially inaugurated until the fall of 1985.

After the traumatic parting with Stefano, I became more cautious about committing myself to a serious affair. Needless to say I still occasionally engaged in casual sex with university students and strangers that I picked up in my favorite bars.

From the very beginning there was a problem with beavers on the property. They had a small dam downstream. I had planted more than two-dozen fruit trees around the house and the new studio. These beavers were so aggressive that they would roam my property at night and chew down the fruit trees for their dam. As a last resort, I bought myself a lightweight aluminum baseball bat that I kept handy in the carport. When I heard them gnawing away at the trees, I would grab my highway flashlight and the bat and pursue them. Once I found them, I would shine the light in their eyes and give them a couple of good whacks on the head. A redneck acquaintance of mine would carry off the carcasses. A few weeks later he'd return with beaver hams.

Setting Up the Albion Press

The first PWP book to be printed in Cottondale was delayed two years. In the meantime I had expected to move into the new studio in March 1983; however, due to numerous construction interruptions the studio was not ready until July.

When it came time to set up the Albion press in the new studio in the fall of 1983, I created a photo essay of the procedures. The following two images are from this essay.

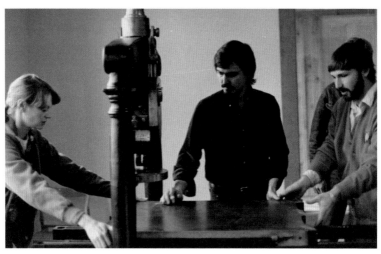

Placing the bed on the rails of the Albion press in the Canyon Lake studio, Cottondale, AL, 1983. Megan Benton, Peter Kruty, and Brad Hutchinson. (Photo by RGR, courtesy PWP Archives.)

Leveling the bed of the Albion press in the Canyon Lake studio, Cottondale, AL, 1983. *Front:* Brad Hutchinson, Gabriel, and Peter Kruty. *Back:* Paul Benton and Jeff Haste. (Photographer unknown, courtesy PWP Archives.)

Cottondale, Alabama: Settling In

Disruptions in the Publishing Chronology

Thus was my state of mind when I began printing in Alabama. I had a large, comfortable, well-equipped studio. Perhaps even more important, for the first time in more than twelve years I had some financial security.

Not only was the move to Cottondale traumatic, it also threw my own printing and publishing program into shambles. Up to this point, the books in this memoir have been arranged by imprint, following a strict chronological order based on the publication date. This order was interrupted by the move to Alabama. Two books were published with the EXO imprint – commissions for the Whitney Museum of American Art – followed by one with the PWP imprint, which was followed by two more with the EXO imprint, and ending with the final publication with the PWP imprint. If the reader wishes to follow the chronological publishing sequence, the order is as follows:

(1983) EXO Item 39. *Dal Vero*

(1984) EXO Item 40. *Could I Ask You Something?*

(1985) PWP Item 37. *Prima Che Tu Dica "Pronto" / Before You Say "Hello"*

(1986) EXO Item 41. *Atlantic Crossing*

(1986) EXO Item 42. *Journeys in Sunlight*

(1988) PWP Item 38. *Seven Aspects of Solitude.*

A Closing Observation

Jack Werner Stauffacher's typography segment at the Book Arts Institute in June 1982 was a high point for me. I had been able to bring my early mentor to Alabama. One of his handouts included a quote from Paul Valéry that sums up my own beliefs about the purpose and use of typography in books:

A fine book is first of all a perfect *reading device*, the properties of which may be defined with some exactitude by means of the laws and methods of optics; at the same time it is a work of art, a *thing*, though one having its own personality, showing the features of a particular way of thinking, suggesting the noble intentions of an arrangement both successful and determined. *Let us not forget, however, that typography excludes improvisation;* it is the result of trails that disappear, the result of an art showing finished works only, an art that rejects outlines and sketches, that knows no stages between existence and non-existence.

Pâté aux Herbes
Herb Pâté

Serves 8

The winter that Federico Rossi and I went to Copenhagen, we had Christmas dinner at the Moltke family estate. The pâté below was the most memorable part of the meal. Berta gave me the recipe, which I occasionally served in Cottondale for special feasts.

      1 pound pork shoulder
      4 ounces boiled ham
      4 ounces salt pork
     12 ounces onion, finely chopped
      2 ounces garlic cloves, finely chopped
      4 large eggs
      1 tablespoon basil, finely chopped
      1 tablespoon flat-leaf parsley, finely chopped
      1 tablespoon fresh rosemary leaves
     ⅛ teaspoon ground nutmeg
     ¼ teaspoon freshly ground black pepper
     ¼ teaspoon cayenne pepper
      4 ounces butter
      7 tablespoons cream
        Larding fat to line the baking dish
      6 slices of lean bacon to cover pâté

Preheat the oven to 325 degrees. Cut the meats into small pieces. Add onions, cloves, and the seasonings. Lightly beat the eggs and mix with the meat mixture. Cut chicken livers into small pieces and sauté them in butter until brown. Add cream and bring to a boil. Combine with the meat mixture. Line a 4 x 11-inch terrine with thin slices of larding fat. Pour the meat mixture into the dish. Press down firmly on the mixture. Top with bacon. Cover and bake in a water bath for 1 hour. Remove from the oven and place a heavy weight on top of the pâté, and let it cool. Reheat at 200 degrees for 10 minutes before serving.

Cottondale, Alabama: Settling In 647

Pickled Okra

Makes 6 pints

One of the great culinary surprises of living in Alabama was okra. I had always avoided it because I detested its slimy texture. However, once I learned to pickle it, I have enjoyed its crisp, crunchy texture when combined with assorted spices and herbs.

- 2 pounds young okra pods, about 4 inches long
- 2 cups cider vinegar (5 percent acidity)
- 2 cups French tarragon vinegar (7 percent acidity)
- 2 cups water
- 2 tablespoons sugar
- 5 tablespoons kosher salt

Pickling spices for each jar
- 1 thin slice of lemon
- 1 garlic clove, quartered
- ⅛ teaspoon dried hot red pepper flakes
- ½ teaspoon mustard seeds
- ¼ teaspoon dill seeds
- ½ teaspoon black peppercorns
- 1 small sprig of flat-leaf parsley

Pack okra in sterilized jars, alternating stem-side up and stem-side down, leaving a ½ inch at the top. Place vinegars, water, sugar, and salt in a stainless steel saucepan and bring to a boil. Reduce the heat to low when the sugar and salt have dissolved. Pour the hot vinegar mixture into the jars. It should come up to ½ inch of the rim of the jar. Run a small wooden spoon around the sides of the jar to release any air bubbles. Clean the rims of the jars and screw the lids down firmly, but not too tight. More air will escape during the processing. Put the jars in a large stockpot of water, allowing 2 inches of water above the lids. Bring the water to a boil and process for 15 minutes. Remove the jars, placing them on kitchen towels. You should here a "pop" which means the jar is properly sealed. You can return the jars that didn't pop back in the boiling water.

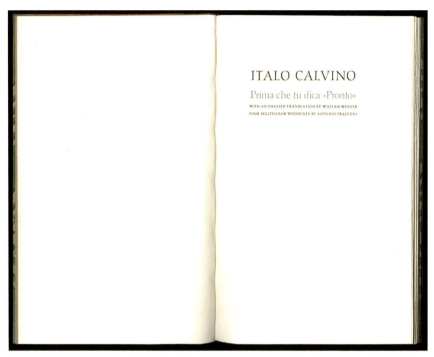

Title-page spread from *Prima Che Tu Dica "Pronto" / Before You Say "Hello."* (Courtesy of the University of Oregon Libraries.)

Item 37. *Prima Che Tu Dica "Pronto" / Before You Say "Hello"*

A short story in Italian by Italo Calvino;
with an English translation by William Weaver.
With four multicolor woodcuts by Antonio Frasconi.
32 pages. 30.5 x 19 cm. 75 copies. 1985.

January 1982 Letter to PWP Collectors

In January 1982 Alessandro Zanella and I sent the following letter to our collectors, which was later reprinted in the March/April 1982 issue of *American Book Collector* under the headline "Plain Wrapper Press to Close." The letter began:

With many regrets, Alessandro and I want to let you know that we will have to close down the Plain Wrapper Press this spring. Hopefully, we will be able to finish printing all of the projects which are now in various stages of preparation before we do so. Allowing ample time for binding, we expect that the actual delivery of these last books will begin in the spring and continue on through the summer.

Curiously enough, this Press, with its odd and often annoying name, started out with no other motive than to fulfill a very simple, but intensely personal, desire of mine: to print and distribute a small booklet of my own poems. From this almost happenstance beginning, the PWP evolved, and within a short time, it came to be regarded as one of the most esteemed handpresses in the world. Over the years, trying always to remain faithful to our original aim which was to produce illustrated first editions in very limited numbers on the handpress, we perfected our technical skills to such a degree that our books were admired for their exacting craftsmanship as well as for their unique contents. More recently, however, skyrocketing production costs combined with the limited production capacity of the handpress, Italian taxes and red tape, compounded by the high cost of living in general, have all contributed to creating a situation for which we no longer have ready resources, nor the moral or physical energy, to continue to confront. A dreadful, but real, sense of defeat has crept into and infected our very spirits. The closing of the Press comes at a time when the PWP is at the height of its fame, when there is a constant and growing demand for its books, when there is an abundance of interesting and stimulating projects ready to be produced, and when there is a list of commissions waiting to be printed. But all of these seemingly positive things came too late. The Press had already expired before any of these transfusions could give it sufficient new life.

The letter went on to describe four projects that we expected to complete before we closed the Press, but as the few remaining months slipped away from us, we were forced to draw up a more tenable schedule, planning to conclude our publishing program with this short story by Italo Calvino.

Italo Calvino

I had first discussed the project with Calvino in a telephone conversation in December 1979 while he was still living in Paris. Early in 1981 Calvino invited Alessandro and me to visit him in Rome. He had a manuscript he thought we might be interested in printing. Calvino was very gracious and

Italo Calvino at his writing desk, Rome, Italy, 1979. (Photographer unknown, courtesy of Mondadori/Getty Images.)

Item 37. Prima Che Tu Dica "Pronto" / Before You Say "Hello" 651

looked forward to the collaboration. It was a pleasure to discuss a project with an author who was so sympathetic to our publishing goals. Within a few months we had Calvino's manuscript in hand.

In May 1981 Calvino put us touch with William Weaver, one of his translators – Bill visited the Press that summer. In the meantime Alessandro set the Italian portion of the text in Post Mediaeval and sent the proofs to Calvino to correct. We had to wait until the Italian text was printed and the type redistributed before we could set Bill's translation. In April 1982 we sent Calvino a check for $375 as a down payment. In July 1983 I sent him the $500 balance from Alabama.

For once the paper – which had held up so many PWP projects in the past – was on hand, having been made specifically for this project by Cartiere Enrico Magnani. However, our only hope of getting this book printed prior to my departure for Alabama depended on our ability to find the right artist without further delay.

Looking for the Right Artist

As with the Borges/Pomodoro book, the search for an illustrator proved extremely frustrating. The first artist – and ironically the last – to be considered was Antonio Frasconi whose work I first saw at an impressive exhibition sponsored by the Republic of Uruguay at the 34th Biennale Internazionale d'Arte in Venice in 1970. We had been corresponding since then, becasue I was trying to convince him to illustrate a PWP book, but we did not meet personally until February 1981 at Abe Lerner's apartment in New York City. Abe and his wife Kit Currie had invited Antonio Frasconi and Joseph Blumenthal to supper, and I joined them afterwards for coffee and dessert. When I mentioned that I was expecting a short story from Italo Calvino, Antonio was overjoyed, seeing this as an opportunity to collaborate on a project at last. He had always wanted to illustrate a book by Calvino, one of his favorite authors.

Shortly after I received Bill's translation in July 1981, I sent a copy to Antonio. Even though he liked the story, he found it difficult to relate graphically to the storyline. Toward the end of the summer, he wrote back, saying he would prefer to pass on this project – but only if I promised to send him another manuscript later on. I understood his feelings and certainly didn't want to pressure him into working on something that didn't inspire him. There would be other texts.

Alan Frederick Sundberg

The next artist to express an interest was Alan Frederick Sundberg, an American living in Berlin, who was listed as the forthcoming book's illustrator in the January 1982 letter to our collectors. Having seen the PWP listing in a 1981 Frankfurt Book Fair catalog, he stopped by our stand to introduce himself. He had been following our publishing program for many years and was eager to illustrate a PWP book. We knew of him and his work through frequent letters beginning as early as February 1978, and he often sent us invitations to his gallery openings. At the Frankfurt Book Fair in 1980, he showed us a number of exhibition catalogs and a copy of a book he had recently illustrated for Wolfgang Tiessen, a German publisher of fine limited editions whose press I greatly admired. We were very impressed with Alan's etchings. There was something bookish – perhaps a better word would be intellectual – about his prints that appealed to us. Also, as if he had been predestined to work with us on this project, many of the intaglio prints he showed us that day had the same unsettled look of crossed and tangled telephone wires. Such motifs were ideal for the story about a man who chaotically telephones women friends all over the world but is never able to get through to any of them. Calvino's story begins:

> I hope you have stayed close to the telephone, and if someone else calls, you will ask him to hang up immediately so the line will remain free: you know a call from me could come at any moment. I've dialed your number three times already, but my appeal has been lost in the jammed circuits, perhaps here still, in the city from which I'm calling you, or else there, in the network of your city: I don't know. The lines are overloaded everywhere. All Europe is telephoning all Europe.

From the beginning Alan showed great enthusiasm for the project, and he was both talented and articulate. When Alessandro and I returned from Frankfurt we made photocopies of a number of pages from his catalogs. In order to give him a clear indication of what we were looking for, we cut four small medallions of different diameters out of the photocopies and pasted them into position on our layouts. At first glance these cropped, abstract details could have been cross-sections of telephone lines. We sent the sketches off to him with specific instructions that we wanted four disks, and we included the exact diameters of each. Before long we received a packet of

Item 37. Prima Che Tu Dica "Pronto" / Before You Say "Hello"   653

proofs. Much to our surprise, all his illustrations were horizontal rectangles, and he had included several extra images he insisted we use in the book because he felt that four etchings by themselves would not adequately show his bravura.

Artists seldom seem to realize that the retail price of an illustrated book is in direct proportion to the number of original graphics it contains. Our collectors were primarily text-oriented people who rarely focused on the illustrations, which was one reason why we tried to minimize the number of prints in each edition.

After facing so many adverse situations together, Alessandro and I were able to communicate without even uttering a word; we both saw the panic button flashing. I called Alan, but he remained adamant in his demands. Thus another misguided, egocentric artist went down the drain, and another several months of precious time was lost.

Sergio Pausig

Though our cutoff date was rapidly approaching, we didn't dare start printing the text until we had all the plates in the studio, a lesson we had learned from our recent experience with Leo Lionni. Not knowing where to turn, we continued to drift until one evening we saw an exhibition of small etchings by Sergio Pausig, a Friulian artist, at Toni De Rossi's Studio della Quaglia. Pausig's work displayed a marvelously original approach to fantasy. His most frequent themes were miniature guillotines and boxes. I could easily see how these images might be transformed into telephone booths. It just so happened that only a few days earlier Sergio had asked Toni and Luigi (Gino) Berardinelli – who had editioned the prints on display in the gallery – to introduce us, becasue he wanted to collaborate on a book. When we met, it was clear the book he had in mind – having heard of our search for an artist from Gino – was this Calvino text.

Having been so thoroughly disillusioned by Alan, we proceeded more cautiously with Sergio. In our discussions we insisted at the outset that the plates be circular, and as an incentive we gave him a cash advance so he could devote his undivided attention to this project. When he delivered the proofs, we were horrified to see that his prints, like Alan's, were also rectangles, except that his were vertical. But even more discouraging, he had done nothing more than make a few minor modifications on a couple of his old plates. I had reached the end of my rope. We shelved the project until I could resume work on it once I was reestablished in Alabama.

Antonio Frasconi, Again

In March 1983 I had a card from Jasper Johns, to whom I had written earlier about the Calvino project, saying he didn't have time at the moment to illustrate this book. Later, in October 1983 Antonio Frasconi invited me to give a talk to a group of art students at the State University of New York at Purchase. During that visit he inquired about the Calvino project and I reluctantly had to admit that I still had not published it – partly because I had been unable to find an artist who would work within my specified parameters. I related the problems I had had working with Alan Sundberg and Sergio Pausig. Antonio, who had always wanted to illustrate at least one PWP book, asked me to send the manuscript to him, saying he would like to give it another try. Knowing of his wonderful landscapes and not wanting to risk disappointment again, I gave up on the idea of having circular illustrations and suggested that he use the geographic locations mentioned in the story as themes for his illustrations. And that is exactly what he did with great success. Antonio received $1,200 for his woodcuts.

Antonio Frasconi in his studio, South Norwalk, CT, 1980s. (Photographer unknown, courtesy of Miguel Frasconi.)

Item 37. Prima Che Tu Dica "Pronto" / Before You Say "Hello"

Even though I now had an artist on whom I could rely, I was not able to put this project into production until the spring of 1985. The first distraction was the new Book Arts Program at the University of Alabama, and the second was two commissions for the Library Fellows of the Whitney Museum of American Art in New York.

The workload at the Press was overwhelming, and it soon became apparent that Bradley Hutchinson, who was working with me in Cottondale, and I needed to hire another person. In August 1984 we were joined by Antony O'Hara, who had been an assistant in the printmaking department at the University of Kansas. Having completed his undergraduate studies, he was looking for an opportunity to broaden his experience as a printer before applying to graduate school. Tony was a godsend: he was an extremely neat and careful worker, and even though his experience with typography was negligible, under Brad's watchful eye he was soon setting type following the PWP style guidelines, dampening paper, and assisting at the handpress. One particularly valuable asset he brought with him was his

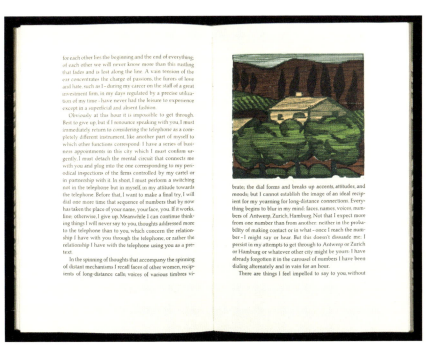

Double-page spread from *Prima Che Tu Dica "Pronto" / Before You Say "Hello."* (Courtesy of the University of Oregon Libraries.)

Antony O'Hara on the porch of the Canyon Lake house, Cottondale, AL, 1985. (Photo by RGR, courtesy of PWP Archives.)

John Coleman in the driveway along the lake at the Canyon Lake house, Cottondale, AL, 1985. (Photo by RGR, courtesy of PWP Archives.)

Item 37. Prima Che Tu Dica "Pronto" / Before You Say "Hello"   657

printmaker's understanding of inks. I had so much confidence in him that when Brad left for Baltimore, Maryland, in mid-December, Tony managed the studio while I taught at the university. The following January Tony and I encouraged another student from the University of Kansas, John Coleman, to come work with us.

John Coleman

John moved into the downstairs room that had been occupied by Brad. He was a very talented artist who spent most of his spare time making watercolor sketches, which were scattered over the entire floor of his room. He had a little red MG, and I had a schoolboy crush on him. Since Tony, when not working at the Press, was occupied with his girlfriend, John and I spent a lot of time together going to the movies and bars.

I took John with me to New York, and on the way back to Tuscaloosa on the night train I put my hand in his crotch. He was a very deep sleeper. What I thought was a hard-on turned out to be his Swiss Army knife, which I still have.

Printing the Book

Tony and John, who both had a keen eye for color, spent a lot of time carefully matching the inks for Antonio's multicolor woodcuts, since those he had used for his progressive proofs were no longer available. The sheets with illustrations were printed two forms up on the Washington press. First the woodcuts were editioned, requiring a separate form for each color. Because of the softness of the Magnani paper new registration holes had to be pricked in the paper for each succeeding form.

As soon as we finished printing the colophon pages, I sent them to Ellen Klein, an American friend in Rome. She contacted Calvino's residence in the city but was informed that he would be at his country house in Pineta di Roccamare for the summer. Instead of waiting for his return to Rome, Ellen arranged to meet him there for the signing. It is fortunate that she was so persistent, because Calvino died a couple of weeks later in Siena, Italy, on September 19, 1985. In fact, this PWP edition was mentioned in Calvino's obituary, which Herbert Mitgang wrote for the September 20, 1985, issue of *The New York Times*, a rare reference for a private press.

The Binding

Having been unhappy with certain aspects of most PWP bindings in the past, it was essential, now that I was located in the boondocks of Cottondale, to find a binder in the States who could put up with my sometimes unorthodox demands, yet provide what I was looking for in a fine binding. One of the most fortuitous professional relationships I ever had was with Craig Jensen, whom I first met in November 1982 at the Harry Ransom Humanities Research Center in Austin, Texas, where I delivered a talk titled "The Plain Wrapper Press: A Bittersweet Recollection." I showed slides, mostly of people and places, and talked about what it had been like to live and print in Verona. The subject was sometimes too emotionally charged even for me and I would crack and shed a few sentimental tears just as one does when suddenly confronted with an image, smell, or sound of a forgotten lover that interrupts a conversation or a dreamy train of thought.

In discussions with Craig later that afternoon and subsequently in Cottondale, I gleaned that there existed between us the potential for a mutual

Cover for *Prima Che Tu Dica "Pronto" / Before You Say "Hello."* (Courtesy of the University of Oregon Libraries.)

Item 37. Prima Che Tu Dica "Pronto" / Before You Say "Hello"   659

understanding regarding edition binding. When it came time to bind this edition, I prepared a mock-up of what I had in mind and sent it to him along with a copy of Harry Duncan's *Doors of Perception* (1983), which had been bound by Sarah Creighton and Carol J. Blinn. As far as I was concerned, this was one of the most perfect edition bindings I had ever seen. I liked everything about it: the book lay flat when open; had thin boards (covers), small squares (the distance between the top of the covers and the text block), and sewn-on endsheets; and perhaps most important, it was cased in so tightly that the book block didn't fall away from the covers when handled.

Craig accepted my mock-up and the Duncan book as starting points. They were rough sketches – indications of the aesthetic statement I wanted my books to make. The book was sewn using an unsupported long stitch instead of sewing it over cords or tapes. He was able to fashion the sort of technically sound binding I have always admired in Carol Joyce's work, augmenting it with a certain something else that I had unconsciously been looking for and regrettably had not known how to express until now: *delicacy* – I wanted my books to have strength, but at the same time I wanted them to appear vulnerable.

This particular book was further complicated – in both the printing and binding – by an unusual collation. Four non-traditional six-page gatherings were sandwiched between two traditional eight-page gatherings. These unusual six-page signatures were formed by folding the sheet in half parallel to the short ends and then folding it again parallel – instead of perpendicular – to the first fold. The tops and bottoms were later trimmed after the printing was completed. This oddly folded configuration, when sewn, resulted in a signature with two single leaves followed by a folded leaf – the one on which the illustration was printed. At first glance, the folded leaf appeared to be bound into the book in the Oriental fashion, since its fore edge was uncut. Craig was binding Calvino's personal copy of the book at the moment the news of Calvino's death was broadcast in Austin.

Making the Paste Papers

During the last months in Verona, Alessandro and I experimented with making paste and Varese-style papers, two types of decorated papers of which I am particularly fond. Influenced by the very effective paste papers Carol J. Blinn had made for the Duncan book, I decided it would be a fitting testimony to the Press's Italian years to use paste papers on the last PWP book, so I showed Tony how we had made them in Italy. With his excellent sense of color and natural dexterity, he produced a series of vibrant and imaginative papers that Craig later used to cover the boards.

Even though the Calvino/Frasconi book was flawed by a repeated line in the English text – the error was not discovered until the books were bound – this item came closest to achieving what I had so long desired to produce in a fine book: an excellent text, provocative but not overpowering illustrations, quality materials, understated typography, sharp, clear printing, and a binding that harmoniously brought it all together. How few times I was able to judge my work with such conviction. This was also the last book I printed on the Washington press.

Doing What I Was Hired to Do

By the fall of 1985, there were eight students in the MFA in the Book Arts Program, four printing majors and four binding majors. Two of them, Linda Samson Talleur and Cary Wilkins, were in their second year. The stacks containing the library's collection of books on the history of printing, typography, and library science were replaced by a dedicated printing studio with a handpress, a bindery, and an exhibition space. By this time the curriculum was also well-established.

I am not going to get into the internal battles I had to weather in the Library School. It is enough to say that I have so many memories of frustration and meanness while I was there that I don't want to spend any more time discussing my life at the university.

A Collaboration with the English Department

Thomas Rabbitt initiated a collaboration between the visiting writers in the English Department and students in the Book Arts Program. The first of these was *Neighborhood: An Early Fragment from Ray* (1981) by Barry Hannah. The second was *The Origin of Sadness* (1984) by Wright Morris.

In 1983 before the MFA in the Book Arts Program was established, I hired trained book arts specialists to help finish some of our projects. Philip Dusel, a binder I had met in San Francisco on one of my trips to the West

Item 37. Prima Che Tu Dica "Pronto" / Before You Say "Hello" 661

Book arts students in the Fifth Floor Gallery at the University of Alabama, Tuscaloosa, AL, 1985. *Kneeling in front:* Susanne Martin; *Standing:* Ann Borman, Rosie Gross-Smith, Linda Samson Talleur, John Balkwill, Sandy Tilcock, Paula Gourley, and Cary Wilkins. (Photo by RGR, courtesy PWP Archives.)

Coast, was one of them. I engaged him to bind the Wright Morris book. The school brought him from San Francisco and put him up in the Prince Apartments. Once he arrived Philip and I had no social contact, not even a drink at Egan's. Perhaps he was afraid I would pounce on him. He need not have worried: he was not my type – too effeminate. But he was a great hit with the orgy boys, Bob and Ernie, across the river in Northport.

The third collaboration was *Just Shades* (1985) by James Tate and illustrated with a five-color frontispiece by John Alcorn. This was the first collegiate press book to be printed in the new space, which had windows along one side so visitors to the fifth floor of the library could watch the students printing. The book was bound by the binding majors. Don Hendrie was the coordinator for the Wright and Tate books. In 1985 the visiting writer, Margaret Atwood, broke the tradition when she refused to give the Book Arts Program a manuscript.

The students, being small in number and united by a singular goal of perfecting their craft skills, worked together in class and socialized as a

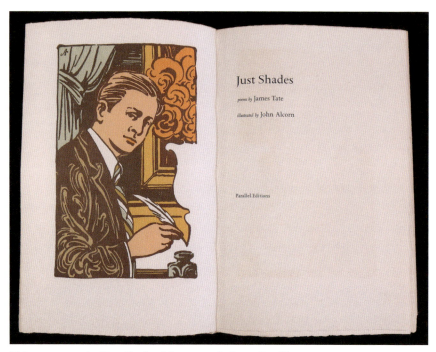

Title-page spread of *Just Shades*. (Courtesy of John Balkwill.)

"family" outside of the academic environment. There were frequent parties at my place in Cottondale as well as socials at students' homes. One Sunday Rosie Gross-Smith had us over for a brunch. The photo of me on the the following page, looking happy and relaxed, was taken there.

The "Green Slug"

In the summer of 1983, Claire Van Vliet taught a workshop on "Printing Illustrated Books" through the Institute for the Book Arts. Since I was laid up with back problems Claire had use of my '74 Dodge Dart, which she christened the "Green Slug." By the spring of 1985 the car had become unreliable. It would stop in the most inconvenient places, usually in the middle of an intersection. One night Tony was driving John and me home from Egan's. I was passed out in the front seat, and John, with his head out the back window, was throwing up. We were a bad influence on that sweet young man. The next day we decided I needed a new car. Tony and I went down to the Mazda dealership, and I ordered a new red Mazda pickup truck. For my

Item 37. Prima Che Tu Dica "Pronto" / Before You Say "Hello" 663

Gabriel at a student picnic given by Michael and Rosie Smith, Tuscaloosa, AL, 1985. (Photographer unknown, courtesy of PWP Archives.)

birthday I was presented with a vanity license plate with the words: Garbage Man. The implication was that I picked up all the trash in town. The "Green Slug" was banished to the far corner of my property next to an unfriendly neighbor's house.

A Fabulous New Year's Eve Dinner

Two students from the English Department, Shelton Waldrep and Jane Kuenz, were regulars at book arts festivities. For a 1985 New Year's Eve party at my place, Shelton prepared an incredible standing rib roast, augmented by other wonderful dishes made by the book arts students, their spouses, and friends. There were close to twenty guests: the men, for the most part, wore tuxedos, and the women, party dresses. At midnight we went out on the deck and launched a display of fireworks.

Shelton was also responsible for *Sextet* (1986), a booklet of short poems by students in the MFA in Creative Writing Program issued with the Parallel Editions imprint. He also helped print it.

Ann Borman was another of the great hostesses among the students. She threw elegant dinner parties with fine linens, candles, and flowers, as well as preparing fantastic food. I assume the guests contributed something for dinner besides wine.

A Much Deserved Trip to Italy

With the Calvino book finished and at the binder's, Tony and I decided to visit Italy in the summer of 1985. We spent time in Verona and Florence, where I had a chance to see my friends Barbara Emo and Harold Acton for the last time. Also in Florence I picked up a set of *bocce* balls, which I still use occasionally.

Item 37. Prima Che Tu Dica "Pronto" / Before You Say "Hello"

Baked Halibut

Serves 6

This is my version of a dish that Rosie Gross-Smith made for one of her Sunday brunches. She used cod, but I prefer halibut.

2 tablespoons olive oil
1½ pounds halibut in one piece
½ cup crème fraîche
½ cup mayonnaise
1 teaspoon fresh thyme leaves
2 sprigs fresh flat-leaf parsley, about 4 inches long
1 tablespoon capers, crushed
1 teaspoon salt
½ teaspoon freshly ground white pepper
Fresh dill for garnish

Preheat the oven to 350 degrees. Cover the bottom of an 8 x 11-inch baking dish with olive oil. Place fish, skin side down. In a small bowl, mix all the remaining ingredients except fresh dill. Spread the sauce over fish. Bake for 30 minutes. Garnish with finely snipped fresh dill and serve.

Title-page spread from *Seven Aspects of Solitude*. (Courtesy of the University of Oregon Libraries.)

Item 38. *Seven Aspects of Solitude*

A miscellany by Gabriel Rummonds.

16 pages. 26.5 x 19. 275 copies.1988.

A Final Keepsake

As early as 1975 I had planned to issue a keepsake of my own work titled *Seven Aspects of Solitude.* It was originally conceived as a thirty-two-page specimen display of the Press's new Post Mediaeval type. The extant layouts indicate that most of the text had already been set. Each of the type specimens is shown with a text in English set in the same size as the specimen with all the Italian translations set in 9-point Didot. These pairings of bilingual texts were placed in various arrangements on double-page spreads. The earlier project included the present "Excerpt from a Letter," "The Photographer," "The Florist," and the ambiguous graffito: "CHI SONO." Three other poems and a note on acquiring the Post Mediaeval type were dropped along the way, and three new poems and an introduction were added.

For the original project I translated all of the poems into Italian with the help of Paola Meroni. Paola and I began by exchanging Italian and English conversation lessons, but as so often happened in Verona, we ended up speaking Italian most of the time. This helped me, but didn't do much to improve Paola's English. One of our tasks was to translate these poems, which gave me a great deal of pleasure, in addition to presenting me with an excellent opportunity to study and understand Italian poetic forms.

At one point it appeared that this project was destined to be shelved indefinitely, because when Alessandro Zanella and I started setting the Burgess manuscript in the fall of 1976, we needed all the Post Mediaeval type we could get our hands on. The original composition for *Seven Aspects of Solitude* was cannibalized, without ever having been printed, and what remained was redistributed over the years. However, I never gave up on the idea of someday printing the text. I resurrected it again and again, rewriting, editing, and ultimately resetting it in Walbaum.

I was determined that this keepsake would be the last item to bear the PWP imprint – just as Alessandro and I had announced in our January 1982

668   FANTASIES & HARD KNOCKS

letter to our collectors – a fitting end to a publishing program that had begun with another keepsake of my own work, *Eight Parting Poems*. I hoped to issue this one immediately following the Calvino/Frasconi book, but its publication was further delayed by the two commissions for the Whitney Museum of American Art.

The Introduction

Here is the Introduction in its entirety:

> Whether consciously or unconsciously my life has been circular, ouroborian. So many of the things that have occupied me over the years have risen up out of the demise of one aspect of my life and led me on to another or returned, years later, full cycle to their beginnings. With the publication of this keepsake I deliberately reverted to the origins of the Plain Wrapper Press and end its publishing program by producing another keepsake of my own writing for friends and collectors. Like *Eight Parting Poems*, the first keepsake, this one is also self-indulgent, and I beg the reader to accept it in the spirit in which it was written and distributed.
>
> *Seven Aspects of Solitude* contains an excerpt from a letter written from Japan in 1957 and six poems written over a period of twenty-two years, plus a line of graffiti of anonymous origin which I first saw sprayed on a Roman bridge, the Ponte Pietra, in Verona in 1973. Each of these contains a similar, but individually poignant, aspect of solitude. In the letter an isolated pantomime is described as it unfolds. Self-engulfed, a young man uses a camera to place himself in a specific moment in time that he wanted to record. Perhaps he succeeded, but the experience left me somewhat shaken since he was forced to acknowledge, in the act of taking his own photograph, the detachment and loneliness of his life.
>
> The poems belong to diverse periods – each seemingly unconnected, but in actuality, loosely joined together by their emotional intensity and mood. It was usually during the depression at the end of an intimacy, when all communication had ceased, that the erstwhile lovers were replaced by poems.
>
> The Italian of the original graffito is ambiguous. Is it CHI SONO [io], Who am I? or CHI SONO [loro], Who are they? [Let me explain

Item 38. Seven Aspects of Solitude

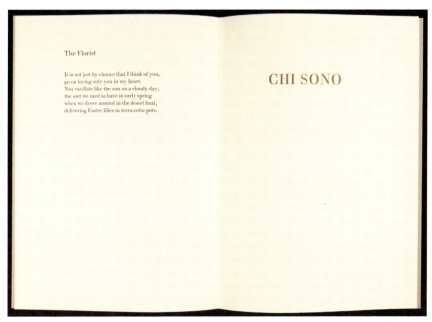

Double-page spread with CHI SONO from *Seven Aspects of Solitude*. (Courtesy of the University of Oregon Libraries.)

the ambiguity of *sono*; it is both the first person singular and the third person plural of the Italian verb *essere* (to be), and used here without the identifying pronoun.] I prefer the first interpretation; I can clearly see the person who stopped for a nervous moment, in the dark of night, to spray these two words in green on this particular bridge – and surely elsewhere – hoping for an answer that probably never came. By printing these selections, as unpolished as they may be, I too am searching for an answer to the same question: Who am I?

Revising the Text
I am as bad as Vittorio Sereni when it comes to rewriting. I persisted in revising the text even after it was on the press. One of the poems, the one I wrote for Stefano Massetta, "Abandoned by a Married Man," was started in 1976 for another married man several years before I knew Stefano, but as I worked on it, it came to be about Stefano and how I reacted to our traumatic falling out:

There is no getting you out of my system.
You're the one who keeps me awake at night.
I can't help but associate you now with my youth,
with those horrid, nocturnal ramblings
through the streets and parks of Sacramento
where I was always falling down, dead drunk,
and waking up – just before dawn –
chilled, still covered with frost.

A Poem for Giorgio Vigna

After my falling out with Giorgio Vigna, I wrote the following poem for him.
Considering the maudlin tone of the keepsake, this poem is particularly apt.

The Dedication

When you gave me your photo
    (the one with a cigarette half out of your mouth),
I was quite charmed and very touched by your simple,
    although somewhat prosaic, dedication.
Then, this afternoon, I saw you with your new lover,
    awkwardly clinging to his arm.
You didn't see me –
    I was half-hidden in a dark shop,
gazing out at nothing until arrested
    by your familiar shape and his self-assured presence.
When I got home, I looked again
    at your photo and reread
the words that you had put there
    with your calligraphic pen:

With all my love for ever and ever, your Giorgio

And for a moment – before I completely went to pieces –
    I could not help but laugh
at how terrible, how ironic, how naive
    first love is,
and what fools we old experienced men are
    to be taken in anew each time.

Printing the Pamphlet

I had a curious habit dating back to my first days in Verona of kissing the bar of the handpress after the final sheet in each form was printed, proclaiming aloud, "*Grazie, bel torchio*" (Thank you, beautiful press). Alessandro and I engaged in this ritual until we closed the studio, and I continued it in States. At the time I printed these words in Italian on the colophon page of this keepsake, I didn't realize they would be so prophetic – my last "thank you." *Seven Aspects of Solitude* was the last item I printed in Cottondale.

When I began printing this item on the Albion press in March 1988, I did not intend it to be my swan song. But after six years at the university, my situation – which had begun with such optimism and good will – had deteriorated to the point that I felt my only recourse was to leave; therefore, I resigned my post in May 1988. Depressed and bitter over the circumstances that had brought on my decision, I wasn't sure if I would ever print again. I was so demoralized I didn't even want to go into my studio, and when I did, the work progressed slowly, dragging on through July. I found it difficult to concentrate on what I was doing. Perhaps my lack of concentration was responsible for printing the line of type on the front wrapper slightly off center.

Double-page spread from *Seven Aspects of Solitude*. (Courtesy of the University of Oregon Libraries.)

Gabriel giving *un gran gesto* after printing the last sheet in a form on the Albion press in the via Carlo Cattaneo studio, Verona, Italy, 1981. (Photo by Robert Mahon, with permission of the photographer.)

In retrospect it is unclear why I printed 275 copies of this item, except that I had drawn up a tentative list of 200 possible recipients. 150 impressions were as many as I could handle in one day, so it meant my time and agony at the press were doubled.

The only real regret I have concerning this keepsake is that I was not able to use the small copperplate engraving Olaf Idalie had made for the original project, but the cost of printing 275 intaglio prints was prohibitive. Even though I had to make a compromise on the selection of paper – machine-made instead of handmade – I was not displeased with how the Mohawk Superfine Text paper printed. Since I did not have a guillotine, Bradley Hutchinson – who by then was working as a printer for W. Thomas Taylor in Austin, Texas – cut all the paper to size and shipped it to me, which saved a considerable amount of pre-press time.

Binding the Edition

Before I had a chance to bind the edition, I left Alabama, resettling in Los Angeles in September 1988. Somehow by the end of the year I managed to finish binding all 275 copies of the edition, using the five-station pamphlet stitch Craig Jensen had taught me. I liked it much more than the simpler three-station one universally used for pamphlet binding.

Item 38. Seven Aspects of Solitude 673

What Next?

At the time I had not yet given any serious thought to abandoning printing altogether or starting a completely new career. About the only thing I knew for sure was that I didn't want to teach the book arts ever again. If I decided to pursue printing, my options included staying on in Cottondale – not a particularly inviting one since I was already beginning to feel a great deal of animosity around me in the community – or relocating elsewhere, perhaps in Texas or Georgia near friends who would give me the moral support I desperately needed. One indication that my future was still linked to printing was that I had already contacted Antonio Frasconi about illustrating *The Waiting Room*, a play by Weldon Kees that Dana Gioia had sent me. But in the end I couldn't muster the enthusiasm to plan another publishing program.

A Couple of Happy Days

One of the few pleasures I had that spring was a visit from Alessandro and his wife Carla Bellini. They spent their honeymoon visiting friends in the States. Their visit coincided with my last semester of teaching and getting ready to leave Alabama for Los Angeles. Having them there was reminiscent of closing the Plain Wrapper Press in Verona. I felt like the present batch of students had betrayed me, so I no longer socialized with them. I remember Mark Flynn and Phil Teague, former students, came by one night, and we drank a lot of wine and played cards.

An Unexpected Comfort

Living in Cottondale that summer offered few opportunities to socialize after I cut myself off from the university. One consolation was a Chinese graduate student named Ting Zheng, who was married to a ballet dancer studying in Paris. He worked long hours in the computer laboratory. We would run into each other in the deserted halls when I came up to the fifth floor to clean out my office. One night I invited him to come out to the lake for supper. He didn't have a car, so he slept over that night and many that followed. He slept in woolen briefs, and I would slip my hand into them, and half asleep, run my fingers through his pubic hair. We both needed a little affection in our lives. He would come over and cook Chinese food, and after dinner we would watch a Chinese movie rented from a Chinese deli. It gave me an additional thrill, knowing that Ting was the protegé of one of my nemeses in the library school.

Peter Eustace

A pleasant response to the keepsake came from Peter Eustace, an Englishman living in Verona, who sent me the following poem he had written:

Distant Friends

Lines, by way of thanks, on receiving a keepsake
book from Gabriel Rummonds, Printer and Publisher

Not many of us are brave enough
To air those innumerable vanities,
The jumble shop of sentiment,
The weaknesses, the frailties
That necessarily represent
The stuff

We are made of. Fewer still
Turn the shambles into something
To admire or even begin to let
The heart speak of its bungling
Attempts at compromise, yet
Life will

Insist on always being like that.
We hide and never ask the question
"Chi sono? Who am I (or who are they)?"
Preferring the mental indigestion
Of rehearsed comfort in the accepted way,
A favorite hat,

The same tie and much the same ideals
As everyone else, delighted to be
Utterly undistinguished, bored and boring.
At least you still ask, amidst the
Pleasantry and the snoring,
"Who still feels?"

Rare Books and Manuscripts Preconference

In New Orleans, on July 7, 1988, I was a panelist with May Castleberry in a discussion on "Collecting Fine Press Printing: Library and Museum Perspectives." I had been asked to define "fine printing." Here are my opening remarks:

Item 38. Seven Aspects of Solitude 675

It is somewhat ironic that I should be here today discussing this subject, since only last month I resigned as director of the MFA in the Book Arts Program at the University of Alabama. Just before leaving for New Orleans, I finished printing what will probably be the last book issued from my personal Press, Ex Ophidia. A series of very unpleasant events during the past year have forced me to abandon printing professionally. Even though I have devoted almost twenty-five years of my life to fine books and their production, I doubt that I will ever print again. However, I hope my personal decision to leave the world of books in order follow a career in film will not diminish the validity of my remarks this afternoon.

The End Comes at Last

I sent out the following letter along with the keepsake from Los Angeles in November 1988:

As many of you may have already heard, I have decided not to print anymore. I have sold all of my equipment and moved to Los Angeles where I am taking courses in screenwriting. The Alabama experience was one of the most frustrating of my life. The complete lack of vision by the school, the university, the administration, the faculty, and the students made me realize that my dream for a book arts program based on high academic standards and historic technical skills would never come to fruition.

I want to thank all of you for your continued support of my presses. Some of you have been collecting my work for more than twenty years. Without your sustained help, I would not have been able to print as long as I did.

The subject matter of this last keepsake may offend some of you, and if it does, I'm truly sorry. I have always been a very personal printer – a private press – in the truest sense of the term, even though that idiot in New Zealand who writes about private presses would not agree with me. The sentiments in this work are universal: loneliness, isolation. I can't believe there isn't one of you who hasn't been touched by these feelings at least once in your life. If you forget the homoerotic overtones, I'm sure you will be able to relate to the intimacy expressed in these pages.

I also want to thank those of you who volunteered opinions regarding the merits and faults of the books. Your comments were always appreciated even when I didn't agree with them. It showed me that you looked at the books, that you read the texts. I have always considered myself a transmitter of texts, and so these remarks served to help mold the publishing program of my presses.

Again, my heartfelt thanks to all of you for your support.

Change of Address Card

Chronologically, it is here that my life as a printer properly ends, because with *Seven Aspects of Solitude*, the PWP ceased to exist, and shortly after, I abandoned printing in favor of screenwriting. Even though I had no illusions about how difficult it was going to be to strike out on my own again, one thing was clear: I definitely knew what I was leaving behind. My change of address card, which was sent out to a larger audience than the keepsake, enumerated some of those things in one long, vitriolic sentence:

* * *

Plain Wrapper Press, 1966–1988
Requiescat in pace

Richard-Gabriel Price Rummonds has forsaken Cottondale, Alabama, wimpish deans, dragonlady paper decorators, ungrateful students, rednecks with their brains in their dicks, southern belles with their panties in a wad, and the general grand malaise of the South for the bright lights of Southern California. Yes, Mr. De Mille, Gabriel is ready for his closeup.

Richard-Gabriel Price Rummonds · 3612 Kalsman Drive · Los Angeles, California 90016 · 213-839-2887

Gabriel's change of address card (1988) printed by Bradley Hutchinson. (Courtesy of PWP Archive.)

Item 38. Seven Aspects of Solitude

Brasato di Agnello al Ginepro
Braised leg of Lamb with Juniper Berries

Serves 4

This recipe is simplicity itself. The meat is not browned first. All of the ingredients are braised together in a Dutch oven on top of the stove.

    2 pounds leg of lamb
    1 carrot, sliced
    1 tablespoon chopped celery
    2 tablespoons chopped onion
    2 garlic cloves, peeled and crushed
        Salt and freshly ground black pepper to taste
    1 sprig fresh rosemary
    1 cup dry white wine
    1½ teaspoons lightly crushed juniper berries

Place all the ingredients in a Dutch oven. Cover and simmer over medium-low heat for 1½ hours, occasionally turning and basting the contents.

EX OPHIDIA

Page 26 from *Anatomia auri* (1628) by Johann Daniel Mylius. (Courtesy of the Department of Special Collections, University of Wisconsin-Madison.)

Cottondale, Alabama: Ex Ophidia

> It's my fucking life. I'll remember it the way
> I want to remember it.
> Ava Gardner – *Ava Gardner: The Secret Conversations*

Setting Up the New Studio

With the usual delays and setbacks, I wasn't able to move into the new studio until July 12, 1983. In designing the space I included a pair of eight-foot-high double-doors to accommodate a small forklift, knowing I would eventually need one to move the presses into the studio and reassemble the standing press. Piece by piece the three cast-iron presses were retrieved from the edge of the lake and hauled up the paved road – zigzagging to avoid the pot holes – then down the steep concrete driveway into the breezeway, up an improvised ramp, and finally into the studio. The type cabinets and work-

Gabriel in the Canyon Lake studio with the Albion press in the foreground and the Washington press behind him, Cottondale, AL, 1987. (Photographer unknown, courtesy of PWP Archives.)

Albion press in the Canyon Lake studio, Cottondale, AL, 1983. (Photo RGR, courtesy of PWP Archives.)

Washington press, with the paper cutter on the counter behind it, in the Canyon Lake studio, Cottondale, AL, 1983. (Photo RGR, courtesy of PWP Archives.)

Cottondale, Alabama: Ex Ophidia

benches – along with the rest of the equipment and materials from Italy, including the type stored downstairs – were brought up to the studio by the brawn of half a dozen students, including Scott Davis, a married student in the library school and my lover for a brief spell. Since his wife worked days, Scott and I would go over to his house for lunch and sex, a nice way to break up the workday.

The Canyon Lake Studio
On the right was an alcove facing the road above the studio. This space was used as a composing room and included the type cabinets, a Poco proof press, and ink and solvent storage.

There was a second alcove to the left of the entrance that had a tiled floor and was outfitted for running water, although during the time I was there it wasn't hooked up. This room was used primarily for handling and dampening paper.

The move caused me a lot of stress, and in May 1983 I had surgery on my lower back. My friend Beth Thompson was concerned that I wouldn't be able to take care of myself, so she sent her boyfriend Henry Compton to

Type cabinet and Poco proof press in the composing corner of the Canyon Lake studio, Cottondale, AL, 1983. (Photo by RGR, courtesy of PWP Archives.)

sleep with me. I knew I was on the road to recovery when I started getting horny as Henry held me in his arms. Even so, I continued to have crippling chronic back pain until I left Alabama, when my back problems disappeared for good.

A New Publishing Venture

The closing of the PWP meant more than just relocating the equipment and starting up another press in the States. It involved a decided shift in my publishing philosophy. The PWP was an international press which relied to a certain extent on its geographic location to attract authors and artists. As much as I always enjoyed publishing bilingual editions, I resolved to forego them in favor of concentrating on American writing. A new publishing program also called for a new imprint. Two considerations propelled me toward this end. First, the PWP had belonged to both Alessandro Zanella and me – although I founded it, I didn't feel right about using the name on my own. Second, the Harry Ransom Humanities Research Center (HRC) at the University of Texas at Austin was negotiating to purchase one of the three complete sets of PWP books, which would supply much of the capital needed to finance the construction of the new studio. Decherd Turner, director of the HRC, had always been an enthusiastic supporter of my work, beginning with his tenure as director of the Bridwell Library at Southern Methodist University in Dallas, Texas. He agreed to buy the collection only if I offered him a definitive set, which would include the last two items – the Calvino/Frasconi book and *Seven Aspects of Solitude* once they were printed.

With the help of items from my parents' and my brother Tom's collections, I managed to assemble two more complete collections. This meant that in addition to The New York Public Library and the HRC collections, the University of Georgia and the University of Oregon would also have complete collections. The University of San Francisco and the University of Utah eventually bought near complete collections as well.

Shortly after I arrived in Alabama, Bernie McTigue, curator of the Arents Collection and Keeper of Rare Books, suggested that the PWP Archives should go to The New York Public Library, where they are today. The library provided funds for a computer and printer so I could catalog the materials.

Cottondale, Alabama: Ex Ophidia

Establishing the Ex Ophidia Imprint

For years I had been fascinated by the ouroboros symbol, a reptile with its tail in its mouth, the eternal circle of disintegration and regeneration. Along with this pressmark, I planned to use a line from T. S. Eliot as my motto: "In my end is my beginning." However, I quickly abandoned this idea before I published the first item with the new imprint. I had an extensive file of these images from a variety of cultures. Quite ironically, while searching through a box of old papers, I found a photocopy of a title page from a book printed by Joseph Low, the former owner of my Washington press. It was from Jo's edition of Aesop's *Selected Fables* (1967), issued by his Eden Hill Press. The pressmark he used was one of his own woodcuts showing a snake with its tail in its mouth.

There was an experimental theater in Piazza Pitti in Florence, Italy, called Ouroboros Centro di Sperimentazione Musica-Teatro, whose eye-catching posters had a screened pattern of crowned ouroboros as a background. I was intrigued by both the name and the image. My first impulse was to call my new press Ex Ouroboros "From the Serpent," but it was too much of a tongue twister, especially since I am prone to dyslexia. Brendan Gill once said, "Gabriel, if you can't pronounce it, don't use it." He suggested instead "The Viper's Tongue Press," perhaps a not so veiled reference to the negative reviews I wrote for *Fine Print* and the *American Book Collector.*

While still looking for a suitable name, I remembered having used the word *ophidian* in my translation of Manuel Mujica Láinez's *Cantata de Bomarzo*. I translated *coda de ofidio* as "ophidian train," an unfamiliar phrase found in a Spanish/English dictionary. *Webster's New World Dictionary of the American Language*, 2nd College Edition (1970) – my primary word authority at the PWP – defined *Ophidian* as "the former name of the suborder Serpentes."

Ex Ouroboros became Ex Ophidia. I liked it and I could pronounce it. Several artists cut serpent pressmarks for me, including Antonio Frasconi and John DePol, but none of these interpretations were as appealing as the gargoylean reptile biting its tail in Johann Daniel Mylius's *Anatomia auri,* issued in Frankfurt in 1628. The symbol directly related to the name of my new imprint. From the beginning I intended to have the image recut by a wood engraver, but Ex Ophidia ceased publishing before this could be done.

During the five years of its existence, only two items were issued with the EXO imprint, and these had to wait until I finished printing four more items: two commissions for the Whitney Museum of American Art, the Calvino/Frasconi book, and *Seven Aspects of Solitude.*

Cottondale, Alabama: Ex Ophidia

Pork Tenderloin

Serves 2

When the crew and I weren't eating stews, I sometimes prepared something special like the following pork tenderloin dish. The recipe is easily doubled, tripled, etc.

    1 small pork tenderloin (about 1 pound)
    2 tablespoons Dijon mustard
    3 tablespoons olive oil, divided
    1 teaspoon dry sage leaves
    1 teaspoon curry
       Salt and freshly ground black pepper
    ⅓ cup dry white wine

The meat must marinate for at least one hour. For the marinade, mix mustard, 1 tablespoon of the oil, sage, curry, salt, and pepper together in a flat bowl. Put meat in the bowl and brush marinade over it. Place bowl in the refrigerator for at least an hour. In a 3-quart sauté pan, heat the remaining oil and cook on medium high for 5 minutes, browning on all sides. Reduce heat to medium and cook for another 3 minutes. Add wine and deglaze the pan and cook for another 2 minutes. Do not overcook. Remove to a cutting board and let sit for about 5 minutes before slicing and serving.

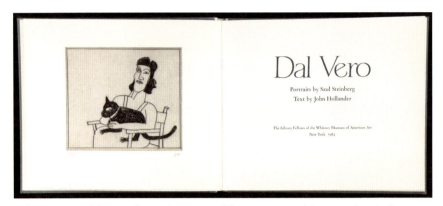

Title-page spread from *Dal Vero*. (Courtesy of the University of Oregon Libraries.)

Item 39. *Dal Vero*

A foreword, sixteen prose pieces, and an
afterword by John Hollander. With a dry point
print and sixteen offset reproductions of multicolor
drawings in various media by Saul Steinberg.
44 pages, plus tipped-in frontispiece.
21.5 x 26 cm. 140 copies. 1983.

The Library Fellows of the Whitney Museum of American Art

On February 1, 1983, I gave a talk titled "Two *New* Gentlemen from Verona"
at a gathering of The Library Fellows of the Whitney Museum of American
Art in New York. Brendan Gill, chairman of the group, was eager for me to
print a gift book for them. He hoped my talk would stimulate interest in
the project among the members. Friends of library organizations are not
rare, but this one was founded on an interesting concept: the membership
was limited to one hundred friends, each contributing $1,000 per year to
the library. As May Castleberry, the librarian, explained to me, it was easy
to find people to make contributions toward the purchase of art works for
a museum, but not toward books for its library. As an incentive Brendan
and May came up with two very attractive gimmicks to hook potential
members: an illustrated annual gift book and special social events held in
the homes of various members. The membership ranged from Lily Auch-
incloss to Tom Wolfe.

I gave my talk in Paul Walter's apartment overlooking the East River.
Even though Walter, a well-known collector of photography, was not a
Library Fellow, he was very supportive of the group. Arriving at his door
brought back a flood of New York memories. In the early sixties I had
occasionally visited the same building – the apartment of Edgar Kaufmann
Jr. – to attend meetings of the Committee for American Participation in the
Triennale for the 1964 Triennale di Milano, the prestigious international industrial design show. Greta Garbo also lived in the same building, and May's
assistant, Tim Nolan, who missed my presentation because someone had to
stay in the lobby to take the guests' coats, was rewarded with seeing Garbo
come home. I would gladly have traded places with him that evening.

689

Saul Steinberg

The genesis of the book was Saul Steinberg's offer to give the Whitney Library reproduction rights to a series of drawings that he called *dal vero* (from life), mostly in colored pencil. They were all delightful, although quite unlike his familiar pen and ink sketches. Without realizing what was involved, the library accepted Steinberg's offer only to find out later that the cost of reproducing the drawings would be more than they had budgeted for the whole project. It was at this point that I became involved. Brendan and May had reached an impasse on how to proceed with the book and didn't know where to turn.

Saul Steinberg. Place and date unknown. (Photographer unknown, courtesy of PWP archives.)

Finding a Printer for the Illustrations

I went back to New York in April to visit various printers who specialized in quality four-color offset lithography, getting from each an astronomical estimate. Eventually, on her own, May found the Village Craftsmen in New Jersey, who were willing to do the work at a more competitive price than the others in hopes of getting catalog work from the museum. I was enlisted to coordinate the production and print the text. I was also able to convince May that the book should contain at least one original print. I went to see Stein-

Item 39. Dal Vero

berg to plead my case. As a result he did a charming dry point of a lady holding a fat cat in her lap for the frontispiece. I had not met Steinberg before, although I had heard a lot about him from his wife, Hedda Sterne. Steinberg and Hedda had long since separated.

Designing the Book

I was initially going to print the text on the right facing the illustrations on the left, but once we heard how expensive the four-color offset lithography was going to be, I redesigned the book. The sixteen drawings were ganged on one large sheet of paper – eight on each side – which cut the reproduction costs by more than half. In order to avoid having two pages of illustrations facing each other in the bound book, the large sheets of illustration had to

Double-page spread from *Dal Vero*. (Courtesy of the University of Oregon Libraries.)

be cut into single leaves with an illustration on each side. It turned out to be a good solution, because it broke the monotony of having all the images on the left-hand side of the double-page spread. I had successfully used the same device of back-to-back illustrations in the Burgess/Tilson book. Printing the drawings on a single sheet also meant that the text of the book would have to be printed on the same paper. We selected a heavy machinemade Mohawk Superfine Text paper, which printed offset and letterpress equally well.

John Hollander's Text

One of the things I liked about this project was the text. John Hollander was asked to look at Steinberg's drawings and to divine – in one page or less – what was happening. Although they were prose pieces, each made a strong poetic

John Hollander signing the colophon pages of *Dal Vero,* New York, NY, 1984. (Photo by Robert Mahon, with permission of the photographer.)

statement. When I started discussing the project with May, I was afraid we were going to end up with nothing more than an art monograph on Steinberg, so I was especially pleased that the book included such a distinguished literary text.

John's conjecture, written to accompany a black and white sketch of two men sitting at opposite ends of a table in a café – there is a third glass, a bottle of wine, and a siphon between them – gives the men a larger dimension:

> Whether a third person had recently left their table or was, indeed, yet to join it; and whether the younger or the older of them had more to learn from their association; and whether what the siphon was rather sharply remarking to the wine bottle had any bearing on either of these matters, one cannot know. Similarly – as a matter of fact – it was just that same early autumn that one only half-knew (and dreaded knowing the rest) that oneself and the other person, who had sat in their characteristic postures together for so long, would not be at the same homely table for too much longer.

Printing the Text

I was no sooner home in Alabama when my back went out again. Fortunately I was able to count on Bradley Hutchinson, now a student in the library school. He came out to the studio several times a week to help me print. Brad and I

Bradley Hutchinson and Gabriel on the porch of the Canyon Lake house, Cottondale, AL, 1984. (Photo by Antony O'Hara, courtesy of the photographer.)

had always worked well together. Like Alessandro Zanella he had a talent for keeping me from getting bogged down with minutiae. "Come on, Gabriel, let's print it" was his familiar rallying call.

The text was set in Monotype Van Dijck at Mackenzie-Harris and later passed through the stick at the press. Golda Laurens (formerly Golda Fishbein) beautifully lettered the title, giving it a unique but compatible flair as a companion to the text type.

Binding the Book

Carol Joyce bound the book and made the drop-spine boxes. It was a complicated binding because so many single leaves had to be guarded with Japanese paper, creating a series of five-leaf signatures. Carol's conservation training served her well here. Few collectors realized how labor-intensive the construction really was. Working on this project with so many people associated with the PWP in the past brought back many memories of the pleasant times we had working together in Verona.

A Great Disparity

A final curious bit of information concerning this book has to do with the world of art versus that of fine printing. I was paid $18 per *copy* to print the letterpress; Maurice Payne, who pulled the dry points, received $35 per *print*. I wasn't bitter, just sorry that my contribution had so little value. In October 1983, there was a presentation of *Dal Vero* at The Grolier Club, but because of my back problems I missed it, and Brad went in my place.

Item 39. Dal Vero

Piccata di Vitello con Limone

Veal Scallops with Lemon

Serves 6

This is a quick dinner entrée. It can also be made with 1 teaspoon of Marsala wine added with the lemon juice to deglazed the pan.

⅔ cup flour
2 teaspoons salt
½ teaspoon freshly ground pepper
6 veal scallops, (about ¼ pound each, pounded to $\frac{1}{16}$-inch thick)
8 tablespoons unsalted butter, divided
¼ cup lemon juice
¼ cup flat-leaf parsley, finely chopped

Mix flour, salt, and pepper together. Dip meat in the seasoned flour mixture. In a 3-quart sauté pan, heat 6 tablespoons of the butter until it bubbles. Add meat and cook, on very low heat, 2 minutes on each side. Remove meat and keep warm. Add lemon juice and deglaze pan. Add the remaining butter and parsley. Stir well and pour over meat.

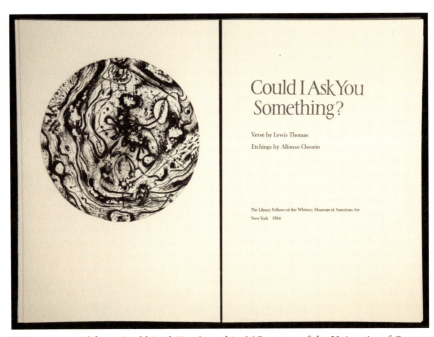

Title-page spread from *Could I Ask You Something?* (Courtesy of the University of Oregon Libraries.)

Item 40. *Could I Ask You Something?*

Fourteen poems by Lewis Thomas.
With eight etchings by Alfonso Ossorio.
36 pages. 37 x 25 cm. 120 copies. 1984.

Another Commission for the Whitney

In one sense I had been called in on the Saul Steinberg project after the fact. This time May Castleberry and Brendan Gill included me in the initial planning stages. Brendan took me along to see Alfonso Ossorio at his home in East Hampton in October 1983.

Alfonso Ossorio

Ossorio lived in a forty-room 1899 Mediterranean villa called "The Creeks" on fifty-seven acres of waterfront. Originally built for the painter Albert Herter, the house was surrounded by a fantastic garden filled with rare conifers and Ossorio's own outrageous sculptures. The interior of the house reminded me of the various apartments in which Barton Lidicé Beneš had lived. Both artists created living spaces constructed out of artifacts of their own making or erotic objects assembled and arranged in such a way that they became totally integrated with their flamboyant lifestyles. A mutual friend once referred to Ossorio's place as "that arboreally transvestite environment." Almost every inch of space was covered with something: paintings, hangings, objects, or baubles. I love to visit houses such as these, although I could never live in one of them for more than a few days because they are so distracting. I find it hard to carry on a conversation in a room filled with objects that are competing for my attention.

Lewis Thomas

Lewis Thomas was not there that afternoon, but he had given Brendan a file folder of his work containing both published and unpublished pieces. Brendan and I sneaked away from the massive rooms and found a bench in a relatively uncluttered passageway in front of a large window where we serenely read Thomas's poems. Before we parted we had selected those that we liked and hoped Thomas would concur with our choices. "Earth-Orbital" was one of them.

Lewis Thomas, Ted Dragon, and Antonio Ossorio at the reception for *Could I Ask You Something?* at the Whitney Museum of American Art, New York, NY, 1984. (Photographer unknown, courtesy of the Whitney Museum of American Art.)

> *Earth-Orbital*
>
> This thermal spectral sensing apparatus
> Stuck on a satellite will read the surface
> Of rivers and the ground, charting the space
> Beneath each orbit, telling the home office
> The lizard population in a field of cactus
> The drift of continents, the chemotaxis
> Enmeshing birds and coral, trees and fishes,
> Predicting time, direction, warmth and force
> Of solar wind upon the solar plexus,
> Recording, from great distances, a voice,
> Counting the tears on any upturned face.

Our efforts were successful: we put together a fine text consisting of fourteen poems. But I later lost the battle with the artist, as I so often I did at the PWP. Ossorio insisted on including nine etchings – eight of which were full-page prints – in the book. Somehow I managed to convince him to let me put the

Item 40. Could I Ask You Something?

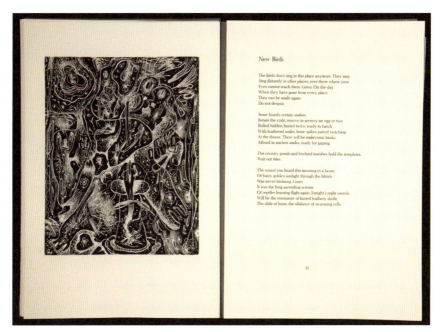

Double-page spread from *Could I Ask You Something?* (Courtesy of the University of Oregon Libraries.)

only small one on the cover of the box. Thankfully, Thomas was more flexible and gave me permission to arrange the poems – several of which were quite short – in the order that best suited the layout. After numerous revisions in the sequence, I still had one etching left over. Ossorio demanded that it be included; so I arbitrarily put it on the leaf preceding the colophon. It faced a blank page and, needless to say, looked very much out of place. Two of the etchings had intense colored backgrounds: one was tomato soup red and the other banana peel yellow. A third etching was printed in cake icing blue. Altogether an unsavory conglomeration. When selecting the ink for the title, I mixed all three colors together, and, surprisingly enough, I came up with a pleasant warm gray.

Printing the Etchings and Text

The printing went slowly because we first had to send the sheets to Sylvia Roth in New York. With Roberto DeLamonica she pulled the etchings two-up on full sheets of PWP handmade paper, to which we had already added the registration marks. Sylvia had never pulled etchings for a book, so the need to adhere to such strict tolerances caused her a great deal of anxiety. When we got the sheets from her, we had to redampen them before adding the letterpress. Not wanting to lose the platemarks as I had done on the Zweig/Moltke book, we dampened each sheet in a tray of water and then gently dried it down, using the same extremely slow and tedious technique we had first used for drying down the paper on the Fedrigoni commission.

Bradley Hutchinson, who had graduated from the library school in May 1984, was now living downstairs. Antony O'Hara arrived later that summer and quickly learned everything he needed to know about printing from Brad. Tony took the spare room upstairs. The three of us printed the text using, for the last time, one of my favorite PWP typefaces, Horizon Light.

The Title-Page Lettering

I asked Ken Williams, who taught calligraphy at the University of Georgia, to teach a summer workshop at the University of Alabama. To show my confidence in his work, I asked him to letter the title page for this book, a difficult assignment due to the length and wording of the title. Ken's work was so perfect that many collectors thought the lettering was actually large type.

Binding the Book

The biggest challenge in producing this book was the binding. If the book had been designed as a traditional codex, we would have ended up with eight blank pages scattered throughout the text, because we did not want to

John Coleman and Tony O'Hara binding *Could I Ask You Something?* Cottondale, AL, 1984. (Photo by RGR, courtesy of PWP Archives.)

print on the back of the full-page etchings. I decided the best solution would be to print the sheets with the fold at the fore edge instead of in the gutter, although at the time I did not envision an accordion binding appropriate for it. Somehow I thought we were going to sew it, perhaps on stubs. Even though Craig Jensen wasn't able to fit the book into his schedule, he came to Cottondale to see what could be done with the binding. Everything we tried seemed forced and ugly. At one point Ossorio wanted to use a glass eye stuck on the cover of the book. Fortunately, he dropped that idea.

Eventually we settled on a double-accordion format, a variation on the Japanese double-leafed album (*nobiru gajo*), which has alternating cut edges and folds. However, instead of stacking each gathering on top of the next, we tucked the cut edges into the folds of the alternating gatherings. Binders still chastise me for using 3-M Photo Mount Spray Adhesive to fasten it all together, but we tried the more traditional adhesives and they cockled the paper. Brad and Tony made a special jig to spray the cut edges and jog the signatures into place before whacking the book in the standing press. The noise was insufferable, and Tony had to wear industrial earmuffs whenever he assembled the books.

Left: Cover for *Could I Ask You Something?* (Courtesy of the University of Oregon Libraries.)
Right: Box cover for *Could I Ask You Something?* (Courtesy of the University of Oregon Libraries.)

The Covers and Drop-Spine Boxes

The covers are thin museum boards covered with silver tea-chest paper onto which a panel of gold tea-chest paper has been added. The original idea was to reverse the colors, but the gold was water soluble and came off on one's fingers in handling. We also made the drop-spine boxes, the design based on the binding I had used for *The River*, which had one of Roger Selden's etchings embedded in the front cover. John Coleman had taken over Brad's old room downstairs after Brad moved to Baltimore. He also helped Tony finish the drop-spine boxes.

Reevaluating The Library Fellows' Publishing Program

The Library Fellows executive committee found that once they had paid the high costs of producing these annual gift books, there was little money left over to purchase books for the library. The executive committee decided they would reap more rewards for the library by issuing finely printed trade books, which would cost considerably less to produce than the books I was printing for them. Even though I enjoyed working with May and Brendan – and of course basking in the accompanying prestige through my association with the museum – I was not particularly unhappy about their decision. Since I couldn't find the time to print more than one edition in a year, their decision freed me to return to my own publishing program.

The Faulkner Project

Between 1984 and 1986 I was involved in an ongoing battle with faculty members over a potential collegiate press edition of a selection of William Faulkner's unpublished poems. I describe the whole mess as it unfolded in Appendix II on page 753.

John Wagner's Parties on West 15th Street

John Wagner, a graduate student in the Creative Writing Program, threw great, uninhibited, drunken, out-of-control parties. He has reminded me that on many a night of drinking at Egan's I was too soused to drive home, so I would crawl into bed with one of my pet students or crash on John's vinyl sofa. He would find me in the morning still fully dressed under a ratty blanket.

John told me another story that I had forgotten all about, which I repeat here with edits. A number of marginal characters of limited mental capability

Item 40. Could I Ask You Something? 703

found themselves wandering the streets of Tuscaloosa with nowhere to go. One of these was a sweet-faced youth named Roger. I liked him and often took him home with me.

One day, after I had spent the night at John's, he noticed that his favorite jean jacket was nowhere to be found. A few days later he saw Roger walking down the street in his jacket. John caught up with me that afternoon in the library and said, "Did you fuck that poor little Roger and give him my jacket?" I replied with no shame for my actions, "He was cold." John angrily said, "You get that jacket back." I just said, "Well, I guess that means I'm going to have to screw Roger again."

A couple of evenings later, I marched into Egan's wearing the jacket, strutting around like I was on a catwalk. John got his jacket back.

A Social Life Away from The Book Arts Students
My two favorite bars, the Chukker and Egan's, provided an important outlet for my raunchy behavior. One night while I was having dinner at my place, I heard a knock at the door. When I opened it I discovered an obviously lost young couple from New Orleans, Leigh McDonald and her husband Bruce. She was a singer, billing herself as Little Queenie, scheduled to perform at the Chukker the following night. I invited them in and gave them something to eat and drink while I called Bruce Hopper, the owner of the Chukker and my neighbor on the lake. He came over and joined us for a drink, after which he took them back to his place. I was a big fan of Little Queenie and loved her singing, a bit reminiscent of the raspy voice of Janis Joplin.

I could also easily be led astray at the Chukker, due to my restlessness I suppose. I once was peeing in the men's room, which had no door, when I noticed the guy behind me hopping from one foot to the other. I said, "Hey, I'm not shy, come on in." After one look at his little pecker I took him home for the night.

Teaching Rhoda Italian
Rhoda was a very good-looking doctoral student in the English Department. We liked each other and joked around while getting drunk at Egan's. She wanted to learn Italian, so I started giving her lessons. First I would kiss her forehead and say, "*Fronte,*" and then she would kiss my forehead and

repeat the word. Next, her eye, "*Occhio*," lips, "*Labbra*," and so on, ending with her hand on my cock, "*Cazzo*." There was no end to our vocabulary.

The Dirty Old Man
Tony O'Hara and John Coleman also helped me keep my sanity during that period in Cottondale. John and I would often go into town to see the latest teenage trash movie, and the three of us played a lot of pool and drank a lot of beer at the Chukker, a popular student hangout. The three of us even performed there one night in 1985 along with John Wagner, billed as the "Dirty Old Man Sings the Blues." Tony and John Wagner were on guitars, and John Coleman played a washtub bass. I handled the vocals and told off-color jokes between numbers. We wrote our own songs, including "Baker Man." The refrain started out: "I need a baker man, someone to knead my buns."

We went to a pre-performance party at David McClure's, who as usual was in Mae West drag. We were already fairly drunk by the time we staggered over to the Chukker. There was a little stage with a black curtain at one end of the bar. With their instruments in hand Tony and the two Johns walked out on the dark stage. When the lights came up someone announced over a loudspeaker, "And now, The Dirty Old Man." David sashayed out, and

Poster for the "Dirty Old Man" concert at the Chukker drawn by Tony O'Hara, Tuscaloosa, AL, 1985. (Courtesy of PWP Archives.)

the crowd went wild. I rushed on stage and grabbed the microphone from him and said, "Wait a minute. *I'm* The Dirty Old Man." David disappeared behind the black curtain, although he did reappear between sets to sing a couple of songs in his own voice. Cheered on by the audience we drank whatever we were offered. I preferred tequila shots, but most of all we just had fun, laughing right through the very last number.

New Orleans

In April 1984, I had a surprise call from Luca Steffenoni, my photographer friend from Verona. He had been hired to drive a luxury car from New York to New Orleans and they had stopped for the night at a motel in Tuscaloosa. Along the way he had picked up a sweet punk English girl named Jenny. After freshening up they came out to the lake. Brad and I decided to meet them in New Orleans for the Jazz Festival. Luca and Jenny stayed with Mark and Leisa Flynn in their house on Ponce De Leon Street –a couple of blocks from the fairgrounds. Mark , a former student of mine, told me that during the week before Brad and I arrived Luca helped him put in a vegetable garden and cooked Italian food as well. Pollo alla Diavola was one of the most memorable dishes Luca prepared. Mark still makes it.

Left to right: Jenny, Gabriel, and Luca Steffenoni at the Old Absinthe House, New Orleans, LA, 1984. (Photo by Mark Flynn, courtesy of PWP Archives.)

One night we went to Tulane University for a concert given by The Roches, one of whom said something about their music not being for old people. I stood up on my chair and shouted, "Speaking as an old fart, some of us do like your music." Of course I was drunk. At Tulane they served alcohol to anyone who wanted a drink.

Mark was a great host. We had café au lait and beignets at Café du Monde, and he also took us around town for crawfish, oyster po'boys, and drinks at bars such as the Old Absinthe House.

The following April I returned to Mark and Leisa's for another Jazz Festival. This time we – Tony O'Hara, John Coleman, Linda Samson Talleur, Cary Wilkins, and Barry Neavill – again crashed on the floor at their house.

A Visit from Brendan Gill and May Castleberry

I stayed in touch with Brendan and May throughout the printing of the Thomas/Ossorio book, and with Brendan until his death in 1997. Handcrafted books, especially mine, had always fascinated Brendan. He and May came down to Cottondale for a Fourth of July picnic and to check on the

Brendan Gill setting up the table for a Fourth of July picnic at the Canyon Lake house, Cottondale, AL, 1984. (Photo by RGR, courtesy of PWP Archives.)

Item 40. Could I Ask You Something?

May Castleberry at the Fourth of July picnic at the Canyon Lake house, Cottondale, AL, 1984. (Photo by RGR, courtesy of PWP Archives.)

progress on the book, which was extremely slow. Golda Laurens, who was also visiting that summer, prepared a lot of the food including her mother's famous coleslaw, which we had enjoyed so often in Verona.

Peter Kruty and John Engels

I had not intended to find a new lover in Alabama, although I did have a few short-term affairs of the heart. One of them was with Peter Kruty, a student in the 1982 summer Book Arts Institute workshop. After I moved to the lake and he was enrolled in the Book Arts Program, we continued to get together for dinners and sleepovers. His future wife would telephone him at my place in the middle of the night to ask if Peter were there. They would exchange a few words, he would hang up, and we would go back to sleep. After Peter got married I pretty much slept alone. As the house filled up with Brad, Tony, John, and Cary, opportunities for sleepovers with boyfriends or tricks were less frequent.

On the heels of Peter came John Engels, a Ph.D. candidate in the English Department, whom I met at one of John Wagner's raucous parties. I was instantly smitten. He was small of stature, reminiscent of Carlos Cárdenas. I would occasionally end up in his bed when I was too drunk to drive home from Egan's or the Chukker. If John was away, I would double up with his

John Engels and Peter Kruty at a crafts fair, Northport, AL, 1983. (Photo by RGR, courtesy of PWP Archives.)

roommate Paul Johnson, an MFA candidate in Creative Writing. I was also Paul's thesis advisor.

"What Is a Poet?"
In mid-October 1984 Hank Lazer, a professor in the English Department, organized a symposium called "What Is a Poet?" that involved a stellar array of poets including David Ignatow, Denise Levertov, and Louis Simpson, to name those whose work I especially liked. Under my direction some of the students in the Book Arts Program, along with John Wagner from the English Department, printed *On Equal Terms* (1984), a very attractive limited edition of poems by all the participants.

Hank and I often got together to discuss the book, occasionally at Canyon Lake for supper. He was tall and thin with a dashing San Francisco mustache. Plied with good food and wine, he became very flirtatious. I was often tempted to seduce – or try to seduce – him, but I was afraid that if I did, I might lose his friendship. We often met up at lunchtime to swim or work out at the gym on campus.

Collegiate Press Conference
In the fall I was busy organizing the first "Collegiate Press Conference," which was held between October 31 and November 3, 1984. I brought together printers who also taught at presses located in colleges and universities.

Item 40. Could I Ask You Something?   709

D. Steven Corey from the Gleeson Library at the University of San Francisco
served as moderator, and Sandra Kirshenbaum, publisher of *Fine Print*, gave
the keynote address. I will never forget Sandy's remarks at the closing dinner.
She compared fine press books to racehorses, recalling that people worried
about horses becoming obsolete after the invention of the automobile. Just
as there continued to be a market for racehorses, there would always be a
market for finely printed books.

There were also two observers: W. Thomas Taylor, who spoke about selling collegiate press books, and Frank Mattson from The New York Public
Library, who spoke about collecting them for public institutions.

In order to make the conference available to all the printers who wanted
to attend, I enlisted the help of several book arts enthusiasts in Tuscaloosa
to host some of the attendees in their homes. I was reunited with many of
the printers I had met during my travels throughout the States, such as Betsy
Davids of Rebis Press, Wesley Tanner of Arif Press, and Richard Bigus of
Labyrinth Editions.

Fusilli con Broccoli Rabe e Gorgonzola
Pasta with Broccoli and Gorgonzola

Serves 8

When Brad and I were in New Orleans for the Jazz festival, Luca made this pasta dish in Mark Flynn's kitchen. It was a quick and tasty way to feed a lot of people.

    1 pound fusilli pasta
    ½ pound broccoli rabe
    ¼ pound gorgonzola cheese
        Salt and freshly ground black pepper to taste
    4 heaping tablespoons crème fraîche
        Freshly grated Parmigiano-Reggiano cheese on the side

Rinse broccoli and cut into bite-size pieces. Include leaves. Cook pasta according to instructions on the package. Three minutes before the pasta is ready, add broccoli and its leaves to the pasta water. Put Gorgonzola cheese and crème fraîche in a large serving bowl. Mix together without creaming. Drain pasta and broccoli and add to sauce. Add salt and pepper. Serve with Parmigiano-Reggiano cheese on the side.

Item 40. Could I Ask You Something? 711

Pollo alla Diavola
Devil's Chicken

Serves 4

When Luca Steffenoni was staying with Mark and Leisa Flynn in New Orleans before and Brad and I arrived, he prepared this dish. He used a large cast-iron skillet; I use a sauté pan. The dish, as its name implies, is hot and spicy.

    1 whole organic chicken (about 2½ pounds)
    2 teaspoons freshly ground black pepper
    1 tablespoon salt
    2 teaspoons dried red pepper flakes, crushed
    6 tablespoons olive oil, divided
       Juice of 2 lemons, divided
    ½ lemon cut into very thin slices
    6 garlic cloves, crushed
    4 rosemary sprigs (about 4 inches long)

Wash chicken in cold water and pat dry with paper towels. Hang for 30 minutes to air dry. Place the chicken breast side down on a cutting board. With a pair of poultry shears, spilt the bird lengthwise along the backbone. With a boning knife, remove the backbone leaving chicken in one piece. Snip off the wing tips, neck, and tail. Turn chicken over skin side up and slightly flatten it with a meat mallet. With a sharp knife, score breasts, drumsticks, and thighs halfway to the bone in two places. Season with black pepper, salt, and red pepper flakes, rubbing the seasonings into the skin. Put chicken skin side up in a deep dish. Combine 4 tablespoons of the olive oil and the juice of 1 lemon and pour over the bird. Let the chicken marinate in the refrigerator for 1 hour, turning it over every 15 minutes. In a hot sauté pan over medium-high heat, add the remainder of the olive oil. Place the chicken skin side down with a heavy soup pot filled with large stones on top of the chicken. Cook for 15 minutes, then turn the chicken over and add the rest of the marinade, the remainder of the lemon juice, the lemon slices, garlic, and rosemary sprigs and cook for another 15 minutes with the weights on top. The chicken is done when an instant-read thermometer inserted in a thigh registers 165 degrees.

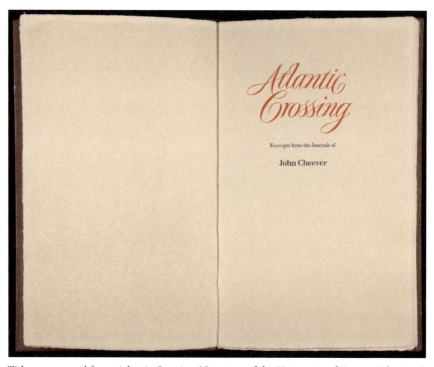

Title-page spread from *Atlantic Crossing*. (Courtesy of the University of Oregon Libraries.)

Item 41. *Atlantic Crossing*
Excerpts from the journals of John Cheever;
with a foreword by Susan Cheever.
24 pages. 30.5 x 19 cm. 90 copies. 1986.

John Cheever

In 1981, the year before Alessandro Zanella and I closed the PWP, Brendan Gill put me in touch with John Cheever. I was in New York during spring break, so I called him during the intermission of a concert at Alice Tully Hall that I was attending with Ben Meiselman. I had read and immensely enjoyed Cheever's short stories and novels, and I noted with pleasure that some were set in Italy. Hoping to interest Cheever in a collaboration, I inquired whether he had any unpublished pieces from that period, specifically one with an Italian setting. He didn't, but not wanting to sound discouraging, he suggested there might be something I could use in the journal he had kept during his family's sojourn in Italy in 1956 and 1957. In particular there was a section

John Cheever, Palo Alto, CA, 1975. (Photo by Dana Gioia, courtesy of the photographer.)

describing their Atlantic crossing that he thought would be complete enough in itself for a small book, and he promised to send it to me.

Unfortunately Cheever died in June 1982 before he had a chance to send the manuscript to me, and I never expected to hear anything more about it. But two years later Brendan called to say that Susan Cheever, while researching her memoir of her father, had come across a section in his journal marked "Send to Gabriel Rummonds." Brendan wondered if I would still be interested in publishing the excerpt. I most certainly was, as it would be a great coup to have a Cheever text for the premier book published with the Ex Ophidia imprint. Soon after, Susan sent me photocopies of the text. It was typewritten – single-spaced with very narrow margins. From the manuscript it seemed that Cheever sometimes left the paper in the typewriter, adding impressions as they occurred to him, and sometimes took the paper out, neglecting to align the margins when he put it back in again. I mention this only because none of the entries were dated, yet it is obvious from the context that they were written over an extended period of time. I decided to use a small type ornament to indicate where the conjectured time breaks appeared in the manuscript.

Typescript page from *Atlantic Crossing*. (Courtesy of The New York Public Library.)

Editing Cheever's Text

Bradley Hutchinson transcribed the text on my computer, and then Brendan and I edited the printout, altering the text as little as possible. At the same time he felt some editing was necessary. Cheever's work at *The New Yorker* had always been edited, and he did not think Cheever would appreciate having the text published if it were not up to his professional standards. In the Ex Ophidia edition Cheever's journal begins thus:

> A stormy Atlantic crossing, like a high fever, may not be worth recounting or possible to recall. In both there are transformations, premonitions of death, prolonged and consuming discomforts, and few memories.

And it ends:

> We reach Naples on a rainy dawn and wait in the railroad station for the train to Rome. This station is very clean with palm trees in urns and the faces of lions, angels, and men with winged brows. We board the train in the rain, and after going through a mountain tunnel we come into a sunny day and a landscape so various, so beautiful, and impressed so on

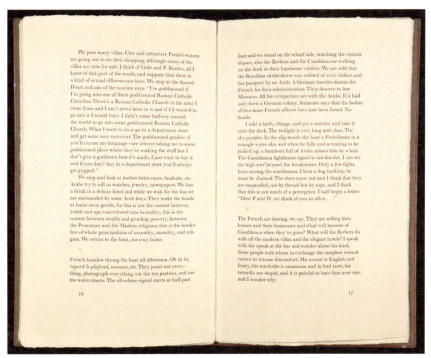

Double-page spread from *Atlantic Crossing*. (Courtesy of the University of Oregon Libraries.)

my memory by postcards, paintings, and the pictures hanging on the walls of the first classrooms I attended that there is a kind of reunion.

For some reason the selection of text that appeared in *Atlantic Crossing* was not included in *The Journals of John Cheever* published by Alfred A. Knopf in 1991.

The Paper

During the summer of 1982, I had established my first face-to-face contact with members of the book arts faculty at the University of Georgia. Three of them – including Charles Morgan, who called me in 1977 about Howard Clark's paper demonstration – had come to the Book Arts Institute, the five-week workshop I coordinated that summer at the University of Alabama. Another of the participants from Georgia was Rick Johnson, whom I often saw in the following years. In addition to teaching graphic design, Rick directed the new paper mill on campus. He was producing by far the best domestic handmade text papers I had seen. Since I was eager to end my dependency on European sources and determined to spare no cost in making this first Ex Ophidia book truly unique, I commissioned him to make the paper for *Atlantic Crossing*. After several tests, Rick and I settled on a paper with a warm brownish tint – Cheever loved the fall, and his family's Atlantic crossing had taken place in October. Rick could make only a small sheet, limited by the dimensions of his mold; however, the size of the paper perfectly suited my needs because I had already decided to print the book in a small folio format on the Albion press. Due to his academic commitments, Rick did not finish making the paper until the summer of 1985.

On one of Rick's visits to Cottondale, he brought along his girlfriend Lynn, who was very attractive and sexy, as well as being a feminist. Occasionally the three of us would go down to the Chukker for beers. One night we were leaning against a wall in the poolroom watching a beer-bellied redneck teach his girlfriend how to play pool. He kept setting up the shots incorrectly. Lynn was furious. She asked the redneck, "Do you want to play a game with me?" He did, adding that since she was a girl he would let her shoot first. She broke the rack and did not stop until she had sunk all the balls before he even had a chance to shoot. As we watched in amazement,

Rick and I kept saying, "Lynn, miss one." But she was on a roll. "He's not going to punch you out, he's going to punch us out if he loses." She ignored our pleas as she cleared the table. The redneck grabbed his girlfriend and said, "Let's get out of this fucking bitch-infested place."

Setting the Type

Michael Bixler was the only source I knew for Monotype Walbaum. Since Michael wouldn't sell fonts, I had to buy the composition from him already set and pass it through the stick later. With few exceptions all my books had extensive optical letterspacing. I would mark the proofs with different colored pencils to represent the brasses, coppers, and different thicknesses of paper that I inserted between the letters. Then Antony O'Hara, who was still working at the Press, would make the adjustments. We usually went through three or four sets of corrections before we were ready to print.

When James and Ann Laughlin came to Tuscaloosa for the "Ezra Pound: The Legacy of Kulchur" symposium, they stayed with me at Canyon Lake.

Tony O'Hara and Gabriel examining the Cheever proofs in the Canyon Lake studio, Cottondale, AL, 1985. (Photo by Ann Laughlin, courtesy of the photographer.)

James tried to get permission for me to print a selection of Pound's unpublished poems. Ann enjoyed watching Tony and me work in the studio and took several photographs of us

Printing the Book

Tony and I didn't get started on the printing until late October 1985. The little inline squares used as ornaments –periods from a typeface called Headline Open – were locked into the form along with the text. After the black ink was rolled on, we removed the ink from the ornaments with a Q-tip dipped in benzene. Then, using the eraser on a No. 2 pencil as a dabber, Tony gently tapped the yellow ochre ink onto the ornaments. That way we were able to print both colors at once without disturbing the form. Of course we had to remember to clean the ornaments before we inked up again in black; but once we had established our printing rhythm, it became quite automatic. Pam Smith, from the Press of the Palace of Governors in New Mexico, and the binder Priscilla Spitler visited us while we were printing. They couldn't believe their eyes when they saw us actually inking with an eraser. In the photo below, we are printing at night, something I had always avoided at the PWP.

Tony O'Hara inking a form for *Atlantic Crossing* in the Canyon Lake studio, Cottondale, AL, 1986. (Photo by Priscilla Spitler, courtesy of the photographer.)

Item 41. Atlantic Crossing

For this book and *Journeys in Sunlight*, we used two-ply pulpboards from the Miller Cardboard Corporation to dampen the paper, and one-ply to dry it down. These pulpboards had a thin film between layers that keeps the moisture uniform.

Golda Laurens did some of her most elegant calligraphy for the title page, which was printed in rust. After the book was printed, the type was redistributed and eventually reused for *Seven Aspects of Solitude*.

Binding the Book

Since the book wasn't illustrated and didn't involve any artists' fees, I decided to use the money that I otherwise would have spent for graphics on the binding. I have always liked full-leather bindings, so I splurged a little on the one for this book. Once more Craig Jensen's understated binding was perfect. Its only ornamentation was a small gold-stamped inline square high up on the spine.

Printing a Prospectus for the Book

Tony and I printed enough copies of a prospectus for *Atlantic Crossing* on the Albion press to enclose with the books for standing-order collectors.

Gabriel, in the Canyon Lake studio, displaying the Cheever book to a newspaper photographer to accompany an article about the publication of the book in the October 3, 1986 issue of *The Tuscaloosa News*, Cottondale, AL, 1986. (Photographer unknown, with permission of *The Tuscaloosa News*.)

This was only the second prospectus I had printed on the handpress in all my years as a printer. Later that year Brad, who was working in the bookseller W. Thomas Taylor's commercial print shop in Austin, Texas, printed a folder of leaflets for me that included a full description of *Atlantic Crossing*. The folders were used to promote the new imprint. Once the prospectus was finished, Tony left for Siena to study Italian.

A Visit from Laure Vernière and Anne Garde

Laure Vernière and her partner, Anne Garde, the photographer with whom she lived in Paris after her divorce from Pucci De Rossi, visited me in Alabama in 1986. Together we retraced Walker Evans's footsteps in and around Tuscaloosa so Anne could capture the essence of the famous photographer's landscapes and people.

Gabriel leaning on the wheel of the standing press in the Canyon Lake studio, Cottondale, AL, 1986. (Photo by Anne Garde, with permission of the photographer.)

Item 41. Atlantic Crossing 721

During Laure's visit she gave a reading of her poetry in one of the seminar rooms in the library. It was well attended by both students in the Creative Writing and Book Arts Programs. She has a deep, husky voice, which immediately draws her listeners into the images and rhythms of her poems.

An Unfortunate Review

The book did not sell well, perhaps because it was not illustrated, but more likely because Doris Grumbach gave it a very negative review in the January 1987 issue of *Fine Print*, describing it as being "like a mouse inhabiting a mansion. It is a monument to self-congratulatory production, a *ding an sich,* within which resides a Giacometti of a text: quiet, thin, slight, its fine words by a master writer echoing somewhat hollowly in these marble chambers."

It has been my experience that a press book, much like a good play on Broadway, loses its appeal when it receives a bad review. No one knows this better than my printing buddy Richard Bigus at his Labyrinth Editions, whose fine work has been frequently and brutally attacked by critics. Unlike me, Richard has always been able to defend himself in eloquent terms. I just sulk.

A Sad Comment

When the book was finished I sent a copy to each of the Cheevers: John's widow Mary and their children, Susan, Benjamin, and Federico. To my recollection I received no thanks or even an acknowledgment of their having received the books.

Pork Chili con Carne

Serves 8

I was now feeding what seemed at times like an army. Because I was so often at school or working alongside Tony and John, there was little time to prepare fancy meals. With so many people to cook for, we often ate stews, such as this pork chili.

16 ounces dried kidney beans, soaked overnight
4 tablespoons olive oil
2 pounds boneless pork ribs, cut into bite-size pieces
4 teaspoons salt, divided
2 teaspoons freshly ground black pepper, divided
1 cup red wine
4 cups beef broth
1 can (28 ounces) Italian peeled and chopped tomatoes with liquid
½ pound white onion, coarsely chopped
2 green bell peppers, sliced into strips about ½ x 3 inches
1 carrot, coarsely chopped
3 celery stalks, coarsely chopped
3 large garlic cloves, quartered
3 tablespoons fresh ginger, finely chopped
4 tablespoons chili powder
4 dried chiles, crushed

Put beans in a large pot with 5 cups of water and soak overnight. Lightly coat the bottom of a large Dutch oven with oil and heat. Brown meat on medium-high. Do not crowd. Cook in two batches if necessary. When browned on all sides, sprinkle with 2 teaspoons of the salt and 1 teaspoon of the pepper. Add wine to deglaze the bottom of the pan. Add broth and tomatoes and stir with a wooden spoon. Add beans and bring the mixture to a boil before turning heat down to medium. Cover and cook for ½ hour. Stir frequently. Add onions. Cover and cook on medium-low for ½ hour. Stir frequently. Add bell peppers, carrots, celery, ginger, and garlic. Cover and cook on medium-low for ½ hour. Stir frequently. Add chili powder,

Item 41. Atlantic Crossing

crushed chiles, and the remaining salt and pepper. Cover and cook on low for 1 hour. Stir frequently. Serve with assorted garnishes: grated goat cheese, chopped Italian parsley or cilantro, thinly sliced scallions, and crème fraîche.

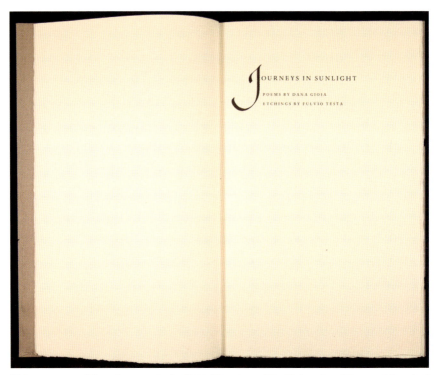

Title-page spread from *Journeys in Sunlight*. (Courtesy of the University of Oregon Libraries.)

Item 42. *Journeys in Sunlight*
Six poems by Dana Gioia.
With three etchings by Fulvio Testa.
28 pages. 33 x 20.5 cm. 90 copies. 1986.

Dana Gioia
Writing a column for the *American Book Collector* not only kept me apprised of what was being printed in the book arts community at large, but also introduced me to several new writers. In the March/April 1984 issue I reviewed *Daily Horoscope* by Dana Gioia, which had been beautifully printed by Kim Merker at The Windhover Press at the University of Iowa: "Gioia's poetry is easy to read; it is like an inner voice unknown to us which surprises us with its aptness, with its immediacy to our lives and feelings." Obviously I admired his poetry a great deal, and soon Dana and I were exchanging letters and planning a book together. In July 1984 he mentioned a group of poems about Italy, "though through years of revision it has ceased

Dana Gioia. (Photo Black Star, courtesy of Dana Gioia.)

to be the real country which originally inspired them and instead what [Wallace] Stevens called 'an Italy of the mind'." Whether real or of the mind, the Italy of Dana's poems is the Italy I loved.

The Worn Steps

But if the vision fails, and the damp air
stinks of summer must and disrepair,
if the worn steps rising to the altar
lead nowhere but to stone, this, too, could be
the revelation – but of a destiny
fixed as the graceless frescoes on the wall –
the grim and superannuated gods
who rule this shadow-land of marble tombs,
bathed in its green sub-oceanic light.
Not a vision to pursue, and yet
these insufficiencies make up the world.
Strange how all journeys come to this: the sun
bright on the unfamiliar hills, new vistas
dazzling the eye, the stubborn heart unchanged.

Fulvio Testa

When Dana sent me the manuscript, I was immediately reminded of Fulvio Testa's small landscape etchings so I mentioned the poems to him. Fulvio, who was now living in New York, was as excited about the project as I was. During one of his visits home to Verona, he asked Luciano Cristini to prepare three plates for him. One thing was sure: if Luciano made the plates, they would be perfect.

Fulvio and Dana came to Canyon Lake in April 1986 so we could work together on the project and celebrate my birthday. Dana gave a poetry reading as well as two talks: one to students in the Creative Writing Program in the English Department, and the other to my printing students on collaborating with authors, which was reminiscent of my talk in Omaha in 1979. My students later printed some of Dana's poems in a small book called *Words for Music* (1987).

I had hoped that Antony O'Hara would still be around when we started to pull the etchings for the book, but the shipment of paper from the

Item 42. Journeys in Sunlight

Fulvio Testa and Dana Gioia in front of the Duomo, Verona, Italy, 1987. (Photographer unknown, courtesy Fulvio Testa.)

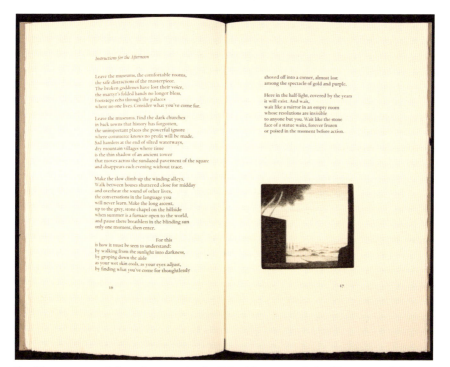

Double-page spread from *Journeys in Sunlight*. (Courtesy of the University of Oregon Libraries.)

Magnani mill was delayed until after he had already left. I was working alone before Cary Wilkins, one of my former students at the university, moved out to Canyon Lake in August to give me a hand at the press.

Cary Wilkins

Cary, who has his own imprint, the Close-Grip Press, stayed with me until we finished printing *Journeys in Sunlight*. He had completed most of his master's project before he graduated, but I let him use the Albion press to finish it. I included a description of Cary's book, *August* by Guy Davenport, in a talk I gave at the Firehouse Art Center in Norman, Oklahoma in 1987. The following is an extract from that talk.

> This is Wilkins's first major book, and, like Davenport, he enjoys the mysterious, often parallel aspect of storytelling and graphic presentation.... Homoerotic overtones permeate Davenport's work in something as subtle as a Cub Scout's pair of shorts. An even more obscure erotic reflection is evidenced in Wilkins's use of, as the width of his book, the length of one character's penis, which is described as 23 centimeters – that is 9 inches for those of you who cannot quickly convert to the metric system.

Cary Wilkins in the Fifth Floor Gallery at the University of Alabama, Tuscaloosa, AL, 1985. (Photo by RGR, courtesy of PWP Archives.)

Item 42. Journeys in Sunlight 729

Pulling the Etchings

I did not have an etching press in my studio, so I was very grateful to Richard Zoellner for letting me use his. Dick, who had befriended Alessandro Zanella and me in 1977, had been a printmaking teacher at the university, but was now retired. He still had his own atelier near campus and offered me the use of it to pull Fulvio's etchings. Luciano made our work a little easier by using extra thin copper for the plates, which minimized the platemark, and I further minimized the impression by dropping the plate into a well in a sheet of heavy Mylar taped to the bed of the press. Cary inked the plates, and I positioned the paper, very much as I had done for my first book in Verona, when I worked side by side with the printers at Luciano's atelier.

Printing the Text

Once we had pulled the etchings for a form, we returned to my studio, where Cary and I would partially dry down the still damp sheets. Then the next day we printed the letterpress on the Albion press. The text was set in Dante. I had purchased several fonts from Harold Berliner's Type Foundry in spite of the negative rumors I had heard from other printers about the poor quality of his type. On the contrary I was very pleased with the way it printed.

Binding the Book

Craig Jensen again did a superb job on the binding aside from one problem over which he had no control. When the first batch of bound books arrived from Texas, I noticed that the bottom tray of the drop-spine box was smudged with a dark blue powder. It turned out that the pigments in the marbled papers used to cover the book boards had not been properly fixed. Not only did they smudge the boxes, but they also smeared in handling. I had foolishly let myself be pressured into commissioning the papers from Paula Gourley, a member of the faculty in the Book Arts Program. Craig and I tried a variety of fixatives without any success and eventually put a distracting glassine wrapper on the book to isolate the fugitive pigments.

The Last Book Printed at the Studio in Cottondale

After *Journeys in Sunlight* was printed, I printed *Seven Aspects of Solitude*, which, in reality, is where this memoir should end.

Praise from Dana Gioia

I knew that my efforts to scrutinize every text I published had finally been appreciated when I read Dana's account of his experience working with me in the April 1989 issue of *Fine Print*:

> Surely one reason why the sumptuous production of *Journeys in Sunlight* complemented the text so well was Gabriel's meticulous attention to every editorial and literary detail. Several of the poems in this sequence were complex and demanding. Gabriel studied the poems with intense care. He also went through the typescript line by line with a professional copy editor's eye and suggested several small changes in punctuation which I immediately adopted. During the planning and printing of the book he phoned me at least twice a month to discuss details of design or production. . . . Gabriel is a printer with strong opinions, and there is no doubt that he controlled every detail in making the actual book, but he always wanted to hear my opinions before making his decisions.

In this sense, I accomplished my aim in taking up printing. The text, whether mine or another's, always came first. I printed primarily to communicate ideas. My whole body of work is more than a mere collection of press books; it is also a testament to the endurance of the handpress as an instrument to disseminate literature in finely printed editions. Who knows what I would have done – or where I would have ended up – if I hadn't been introduced to the handpress by Martino Mardersteig. I could just as easily have started out on the mythical mimeograph machine I often alluded to in my talks about the formative years of the PWP, recalling that some of Jack Spicer's early books were published in mimeograph editions.

A Bittersweet Memory

Beth Dinoff, an occasional book arts student, introduced me to her friend David Ferrill, who was eager to meet me. David and I would occasionally get together at my place for dinner or see a play on campus or take in a movie. On our first date we attended a performance of *The Chalk Garden* in September 1986. We both wore ties and jackets; we looked like a couple of frat brothers. I never seduced David, even though I could see in his eyes and body language that he was open to the idea. I could easily have fallen in love with him, but he was too innocent. Ultimately, I didn't want to introduce him to my lifestyle, only to have him leave me later for someone closer to his own age.

A Miserable Year

After Cary left in December, I was pretty much on my own. All my boys – Brad Hutchinson, Tony O'Hara, and John Coleman – had their own lives to think about. The year 1987 was dreadful. I had no new projects lined up, although I was busy touring the country giving lectures and participating in exhibitions of my work. My relationship with my fellow faculty members was growing more and more unpleasant, even hostile. I was no longer cruising. Against my better judgment I had an on-again-off-again affair with a redneck named Steve Rust, who was in the Army Reserve. We had nothing in common except sex, which in retrospect was mediocre. I put up with him because he was a warm body. He came out to the lake frequently to go swimming and drink beer. He had a truck with a rifle on a rack in the rear window. Standing on the deck, he tried to teach me how to kill water moccasins in the lake. I was a terrible shot. I don't remember actually hitting one.

Two of my brothers, Tom and Bill, came to visit me in September 1987. They were there to cheer me up and to talk some sense into me. They urged me to get rid of the redneck, which I did, but I was still depressed.

Three of the Rummonds boys, Bill, Gabriel, and Tom on the porch of the Canyon Lake house, Cottondale, AL, 1987. (Photographer unknown, courtesy of PWP Archives.)

Visits from *la Piccola Famiglia*

For two and a half weeks in July 1987, Lauren Fishbein visited me in Cottondale. While she was there she single-handedly painted the Typographic Laboratory a warm tan, then painted my office a sage green, a color I have used in all my apartments since. First we got rid of the office furniture. I used two narrow credenzas, one as a desk with a lamp and telephone, and the other behind me and against the wall for teaching materials. There were two chairs, one with rollers for me, and an upholstered one for visitors. Framed double-page spreads from my books adorned the walls. Without the fluorescent lights the office assumed an aura of an aesthete's hideaway.

Later that December Lauren returned to Cottondale to celebrate Christmas with her mother Golda, and her brother Mark, and his wife. Two friends from Italy, Ellen and Carlo Ferrari, also joined us for one of the last festive occasions I hosted before I left Alabama in the fall of 1988.

Item 42. Journeys in Sunlight   733

Risotto Nero di Seppie
Risotto with Cuttlefish

Serves 6

Writing this memoir brought back many vivid recollections of eating out in the Veneto. I have saved this recipe for last, in part because *Journeys in Sunlight* was inspired by travels in Italy and in part because this is a glorious dish to end this account of my life as a printer. It can be made with either cuttlefish or squid. It is served as a first course in the Veneto. It is *never* garnished with grated cheese.

    12 ounces whole cuttlefish or squid
     4 cups fish stock
     6 tablespoons butter
    12 ounces white onion, finely chopped
     2 garlic cloves, finely chopped
     8 ounces Vialone Nano rice
        Salt and freshly ground black pepper to taste
        Ink from cuttlefish or squid *or* 3 packets of ink
    1⅔ cups dry white wine
     2 tablespoons olive oil

Pull head and tentacles and any innards out of the body cavity. Cut heads off below the eyes and set aside for extracting the ink. Rinse and set aside 3 tentacles cut in half for the garnish. Rinse bodies and remove the quill-like bone in sac. Finely chop the bodies and remaining tentacles rinse under running water. Simmer fish stock in a saucepan. Heat butter until it bubbles in a sauté pan. Add onion sauté until but not brown. Increase the heat and add cuttlefish and cook until opaque, about 3 minutes. Add garlic and stir briefly. Reduce the heat to low and add rice. Season and stir to coat rice. Add ink and wine Increase the heat and stir until absorbed. Stir in a ladleful of stock and cook on a fast simmer. When the stock has been absorbed, stir in another ladleful, continuing this for about 20 minutes, or until the rice is *al dente*. Heat the olive oil in a small skillet and quickly fry the tentacles for the garnish.

Loading the PWP equipment on the truck, Cottondale, AL, 1988. (Photo by RGR, courtesy of PWP Archives.)

Postscript: October 1988

When I moved to Cottondale in 1982, I swore I would never again pack up the equipment on which the majority of my books had been printed. But in September 1988 I found myself again taking the presses apart and building shipping crates for them. This time, however, I would not also be at the receiving end anxiously awaiting their arrival. Earlier that summer John Balkwill, one of my former students, put me in touch with his printing associate, Gregor Peterson. Greg subsequently purchased the entire contents of my studio and moved it to his Huckleberry Press in Incline Village, Nevada. At least I was going to be spared the trauma of having to reassemble the presses in a new location. With the help of a small forklift, everything was loaded onto an open eighteen-wheeler flatbed truck and strapped down securely. I last glimpsed the presses as they disappeared over the top of the hill. Then I went into the house and poured myself a stiff drink.

I must, however, confess that I was a nervous wreck until I heard everything had arrived safely. The Plain Wrapper Press and Ex Ophidia had finally run their courses, but the tangible artifacts – the cast-iron handpresses that had so long been at the core of their existence – will persevere. I hope and trust they will serve their new owner and those to follow as well as they served me. I left Alabama and resettled in Tinseltown to be closer to the movie industry. I wanted to write screenplays and distance myself from all the pains and bittersweet pleasures of printing. "Yes, Mr. DeMille, Gabriel is ready for his closeup."

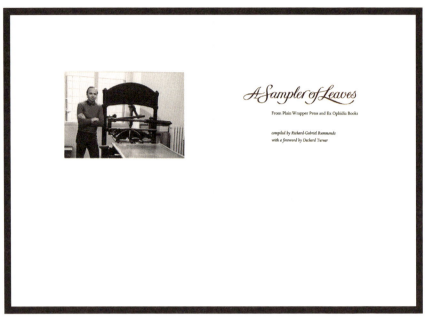

Title-page spread from *A Sampler of Leaves* (1996). (Courtesy of PWP Archives.)

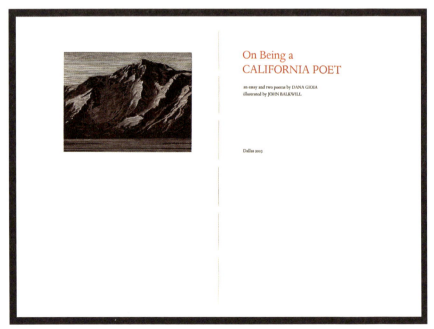

Title-page spread from *On Being a California Poet* (2003). (Courtesy of PWP Archives.)

Afterword: September 2014

Even though I gave up printing in 1988, I was not able to completely extricate myself from it. Here are a few printing-related highlights from the ensuing years.

Books Printed and Published by RGR

Beginning with the first book I printed in Verona, I saved all the seconds and overruns of each edition I printed, about two thousand sheets in all. So many sheets took up a lot of storage space, and Bradley Hutchinson and I decided to put them to good use. From the forty-two items printed at the Plain Wrapper Press and Ex Ophidia we salvaged enough sheets to compile forty sets of *A Sampler of Leaves,* with title-page lettering by Golda Laurens. Each set contained eleven gatherings with illustrations and eleven more with just text. The book measured 48 x 29 cm, ample enough to contain gatherings from three of the largest PWP books. Each gathering was sewn into a brown Fabriano Ingres paper four-page signature, which was in turn enclosed the gathering from the book. The item number and title of the book were printed on the front leaf of the brown wrapper. Craig Jensen bound the books in quarter leather and cloth over boards, as well as making the drop-spine boxes for them.

In April 2003 the Bridwell Library at Southern Methodist University offered me a fellowship to print and publish a book in eighty copies on its Ashendene Albion press. *On Being a California Poet* by Dana Gioia and illustrated by John Balkwill, one of my former Alabama students, was the result. I had a lot of help printing this book. Patricio Gatti came up from Buenos Aires, Argentina; Bradley Hutchinson from Austin, Texas; and Fred and Barbara Voltmer from Danville, California. Again Craig bound it, using patterned papers printed from a woodcut by Lucio Passerini. Lucio, whose studio was in Milan, Italy, was also a printer. Ever since I met him through Garrett Boge at the "Association Typographique Internationale" conference in Rome in 2002, I had hoped that someday he would illustrate one of my books.

Books Written by RGR

Over the years I jotted down notes on handpress printing practices, mostly describing the techniques I used when printing my own books. The resulting handouts, which I gave to participants in the two workshops I gave at the Rochester Institute of Technology in the nineties, were eventually transformed into *Printing on the Iron Handpress*, with illustrations and technical diagrams by George Laws. The book was published by Oak Knoll Press and The British Library in 1998.

This book was followed by *Nineteenth-Century Printing Practices and the Iron Handpress* in two volumes, also published by Oak Knoll Press and The British Library in 2004. Stephen O. Saxe edited the book. I am indebted to a number of libraries in the States and in England who let me use their collections to research this book, in particular Peter Van Wingen and Nigel Roche at the St. Bride Printing Library in London.

Both titles were typeset in Adobe Minion by Bradley Hutchinson and featured custom end papers with a step and repeat pattern using a wood engraving of a handpress cut by John DePol.

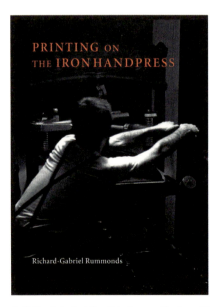
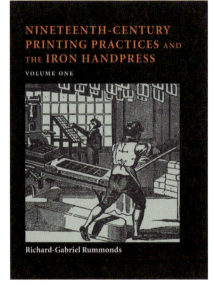

Left: Book jacket for *Printing on the Iron Handpress* (1998). (Courtesy of PWP Archives.)

Right: Book jacket for *Nineteenth-Century Printing Practices and the Iron Handpress* (2004). (Courtesy of PWP Archives.)

Exhibitions of Works by RGR

In 1999 the Biblioteca Civica in Verona mounted an exhibition of the photographs of handpress printers from *Printing on the Iron Handpress*, accompanied by examples of books they had printed. Here are a few of the books that were on display. The University of Oregon loaned *The Wood Beyond the World* printed at the Kelmscott Press in 1894 and *Shelley* printed at the Doves Press in 1914. Martino Mardersteig loaned *De divina proportione* printed at the Officina Bodoni in 1956. The Rochester Institute of Technology loaned *Songs of the Love Unending* printed at the Village Press in 1912.

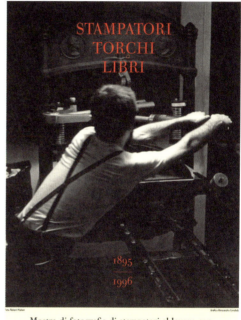

Exhibition poster for "Stampatori, Torchi, Libri" held at the Biblioteca Civica di Verona, Verona, Italy, 1999. Alessandro Zanella is pulling the bar of the PWP Washington press. (Courtesy of Alessandro Corubolo.)

Left: Announcement/mini-catalog for the Milan retrospective. (Courtesy of PWP Archives.)

Right: Gabriel at the entrance to the Biblioteca di via Senato, Milan, Italy, 1999. (Photo by Garrett Boge, courtesy of the photographer.)

The highlight of my career as a printer was the extensive retrospective exhibition of my work titled *Un Tipografo fra Due Culture: Richard-Gabriel Rummonds* (A Typographer between Two Cultures: Richard-Gabriel Rummonds) at the Fondazione Biblioteca di via Senato in Milan, Italy, in September and October 1999.

The exhibition was curated by Alessandro Corubolo and Gino Castiglioni, my old printing buddies from Verona. Friends came from all over the world for the opening.

The following evening a performance of *Cantico dei Cantici* was given in the Teatro di Verdura in the library's inner courtyard. The biggest surprise was when the director announced that this performance was dedicated to the Veronese handpress printer Richard-Gabriel Rummonds. I sat in the front row with Valentina Cortese, one of my idols from Italian cinema, and I had an opportunity to chat with her after the performance.

I have a very melancholy photo of Giorgio Vigna and me taken in the garden of the Biblioteca di via Senato during my retrospective in Milan.

Afterword: September 2014 741

Gabriel and Giorgio Vigna in the garden of the Biblioteca di via Senato, Milan, Italy, 1999. (Photographer unknown, courtesy of PWP Archives.)

Giorgio had not been able to come to the opening, but the next day he joined me to view the exhibition. Nothing remained of our relationship of so many years before. It was as if we were strangers; it was perfunctory. Even so, the affair with him was not a complete failure. He went on to become an internationally known jewelry designer. He had matured artistically during his affair with me in the 1970s. For me, there would never again be another affair so intense. After a few bland pleasantries, he announced he had to go, and I walked him out to the sidewalk. He didn't even have time for a coffee; he hopped on his Vespa and sped away.

Lectures Given by RGR

Between 1988 and 2010 I gave a number of lectures about my work. The last two were the most memorable.

In 1999 Steve Woodall invited me to give a talk as part of the publication celebration for *Printing on the Iron Handpress* at the San Francisco Center for the Book. After the talk, Jonathan Clark and I took a stroll in

Gabriel, San Francisco, CA, 1999. (Photo by Jonathan Clark with permission of the photographer.)

the neighborhood, and he took a series of photographs of me including the one above.

It was quite ironic that I should be selected to give the 2005 J. Ben Lieberman Lecture of the American Printing History Association. Lieberman was a bad hobby printer, and I often belittled his work in print. Delivered in San Francisco, the lecture brought together many old printing friends, such as Jack Werner Stauffacher and Jonathan Clark. I used the occasion to promote my second book and scandalize the audience with the homoerotic aspects of my life as a printer.

In 2010 I was invited to give a talk at the Book Club of California in San Francisco. I thought it might be interesting for the audience to hear about the origins of *The Emperor's Lion* because its author, Cora C. Fletcher, had caused a great furor in Berkeley in 1954, which led to my expulsion from the University of California at Berkeley. My talk was even more risqué than the one I had given for the American Printing History Association in 2005 and surprisingly well received. Many of those present said it was the most interesting and stimulating talk they had heard at the club in a long time. Here are a few excerpts from the review in the *Book Club of California News-Letter* (2010).

Afterword: September 2014 743

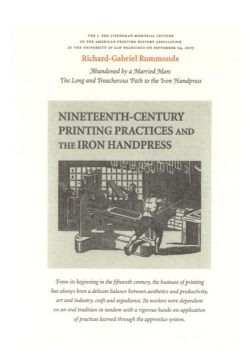

Keepsake for the lecture printed by Bradley Hutchinson. (Courtesy of PWP Archives.)

Gabriel giving his PowerPoint lecture on *The Emperor's Lion* at the Book Club of California, San Francisco, CA, 2010. (Photo by Weldon DeBusk, courtesy of the photographer.)

On November 8, frail Richard-Gabriel Rummonds, 79, supported by a cane, arrived by Amtrak from Port Townsend, Washington. Once behind the podium, his soft voice enthralled all.

. . .

The University kicked out Rummonds, and twenty-two years later from Verona, he confessed to the deception. The Berkeley library catalogue is now digitized. How many entries survive for Cora C. Fletcher's works?

Workshops Given by RGR

David Pankow at the Rochester Institute of Technology invited me to give two workshops on "Problem-Solving on the Cast-Iron Handpress" for their Book Arts Institute. The first was held in October 1991 and the second in June 1992. The short workbook I prepared for these workshops was later expanded into *Printing on the Iron Handpress*.

One of the pleasures of these workshops was sharing my expertise on the iron handpress with other printers, many of them old friends. At breakfast during the second workshop, I got into a discussion about printing on dampened paper with Harry Duncan, Neil Shaver, and Henry Morris. Henry insisted that printing on dampened paper required more ink than printing on dry paper. Harry and I kept telling Henry that the exact opposite was true, but he would not listen to us, so we decided to let ignorant printers wallow in their misconceptions.

In February 2007 Sydney Shep, the director of the collegiate press at Victoria University, invited me to repeat my "Problem-Solving on the Cast-Iron Handpress" workshop at the Australasian Rare Book Summer School in Wellington, New Zealand. There were nine participants, pictured below. Our last project was to print a selection of poems from Bill Manhire's *Nuptials*.

While in New Zealand, I also gave an illustrated lecture at the National Library in Wellington and repeated it at the University of Otago in Dunedin on the South Island.

Tour and Exhibition of "Two Private Presses from Verona"

In 2001 I organized a tour and exhibition of the work of Alessandro Zanella, Gino Castiglioni, and Alessandro Corubolo at five western universities. I traveled with the two Alessandros from Seattle, Washington, to Eugene, Oregon, and with all three printers to San Francisco, California; Reno,

Afterword: September 2014

Wesley Tanner, Gabriel, and Harry Duncan at the 1992 workshop at the Rochester Institute of Technology, Rochester, NY, 1992. (Photo by Diana Thomas, courtesy of the photographer.)

Group photo of participants in the New Zealand workshop, Victoria University of Wellington, Wellington, New Zealand, 2007. Gabriel is second from the left in the front row; Sydney Shep, the workshop coordinator, is the first on the left in the back row. Bill Manhire is leaning against the bar of the press. A selection of poems from his book *Nuptials* was printed during the workshop. (Photo by Les Maiden, courtesy of Victoria University of Wellington.)

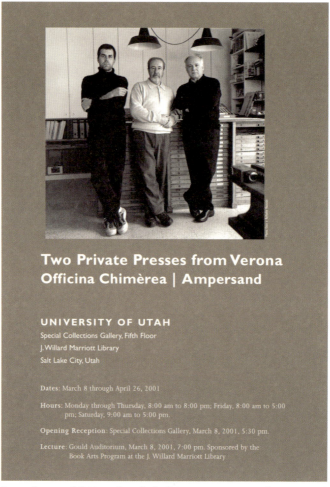

Poster for an exhibition of works by "Two Private Presses from Verona" held at the J. Willard Marriott Library, University of Utah, Salt Lake City, UT, 2001. (Courtesy of Alessandro Corubolo.)

Nevada; and Salt Lake City, Utah. I owed a great deal to these three printers. Alessandro Zanella had been my partner at the PWP, and Castiglioni and Corubolo had been friends and supporters of my work from my earliest days in Verona.

I have always been eager to support other printers of merit. At each venue there was an exhibition of these printers' work. Each university was required to purchase a certain dollar amount of their books. The printers also gave seminars for the students and lectures open to the public.

Afterword: September 2014   747

A Final Note from Gabriel Precio

Many years ago Gabriel Rummonds concocted a fantasy about his death. He said it was the way he wanted to die. He envisioned it to be like the death of one of the characters in his "Miss Findley and Mrs. Johnson and Mnemosyne, the Latter Who Remembered, But Too Late," a short story he wrote in 1953 for Thomas Parkinson's English 141 at the University of California. He pictured himself as Mrs. Johnson:

> She died in the afternoon which was as white as the jasmine she had been picking for the elderly lady next door. She fell dead to the ground, falling like a dancer, tired and aesthetic, falling to the ground and against a Japanese cherry-plum with her hands in her lap and the sun in her eyes. And the elderly lady who had watched this afternoon arabesque gave a cry which stilled the college town. And with her elephant legs and two caned hands, she came out on the porch to watch to the end.

Appendix I

Notes on "The Mr. Wilson Story" by Gabriel Precio

What follows is a draft of "Notes in the Closed Edition." I have silently corrected the spelling, punctuation, and grammatical errors. Additional information is placed between square brackets.

1. The story received its impetus from Schorer's line [the sentence from Henry James]; however, the situation and the physiological significance are quite similar to the noontime picnics Richard and Joan Fisher [a classmate at the University of California at Berkeley] were having in the fall of 1953. He used the same theme again in the Miss Nystrom [a librarian in the SSRS Library] story.

2. Pat Wilson was in charge of the Map Room, which was a separate but connected unit of the SSRS Library. Richard was often assigned to file maps for him, which gave them ample opportunity to chat. Richard's description of Mr. Wilson in the story is quite accurate and true to life. He was a sincere and likeable young man who inspired trust even though by nature he was full of good-natured pomposity. The only serious flaw in the story is that Mr. Wilson would not have been interested in Lucy physically because his sexual preferences lay elsewhere. However, he appeared to be at ease at all times wherever he went and never limited his social life exclusively to other men with similar tastes. We can understand this "flaw" in Mr. Wilson's character when we are aware that Richard is also depicting him as he would have liked him to behave if Richard were Mr. Wilson: he represents a young man who is not shy; who is sophisticated, even in the trivialities of the world; who is capable of complete social integration; and who finds diversion on all levels; who, in short, has all the qualities Richard felt he was lacking.

3. Even though Richard had not yet met Lucy Russell [Dan Russell's wife], he was sure he knew exactly what she would be like because he felt he and Dan Russell [a classmate at Syracuse University] were kindred souls. (Actually, when Richard met her several years later, she turned out to be the exact opposite of what he had expected.) It is her assumed personality he is

weaving into the story. Lucy's character also has the same duality as Mr. Wilson's. On one hand, she represents Richard. Both were shy and had compelling desires to move out of their protective shells and into the world. In addition Richard had a crush on Mr. Wilson, which suggests that the story is a fantasy romance. [It should be noted that Richard always addressed Pat Wilson as "Mr. Wilson" even in private.] However, Mr. Wilson was not interested in Richard sexually, and if he had been, Richard would have been too obtuse to respond. Even if Mr. Wilson had made an advance, Richard (who was a tease, although he was probably unaware to what extent) would have retreated, for he was still afraid to get involved with anyone he liked. But Lucy on the other hand represents the kind of girl Richard was attracted to: a petite, fairly quiet, semi-independent girl, and definitely not intellectually aggressive. Therefore, on a second level, he is creating another fantasy romance where he is Mr. Wilson vicariously enjoying the coming out of Lucy.

4. Picnics were always grand occasions, and he turned them into productions. They were never just a matter of sandwiches and Cokes. They required careful planning of both menu and people, because eating in the open air with someone he was close to was one of the most intimate human exchanges he allowed himself.

5. The setting is the Berkeley hills above the University of California. They were considered "escape territory," and he frequently went there for walks alone, just to get away from the clamor of the university. On other occasions he would take his studies and sit under the trees to read. He liked sleeping in the open air, and more than likely, many days when he planned to study, he slept.

6. The only person Richard could recall having been from Montana was his mother, who in many ways resembled Lucy.

7. Richard liked amusement parks. It is very likely this was one the things Mr. Wilson and Richard chatted about in the Map Room. Richard had first been to the amusement park in San Francisco with his brother Bobby when they were both still in high school. Later, when Richard lived in San Francisco, he and Isabel Freud [a former classmate from the University of California] would occasionally go there. Richard loved the rowdy atmosphere and the trickery.

Appendix I   751

8. The last line has always caused a lot of unfavorable comment, partly because it appears to be out of context with rest of the story. The geranium was one of Richard's favorite private symbols, and he frequently used it to symbolize the introvert, the pure of heart, the common but beautiful life. As hardy as the geranium is, it cannot endure extremely cold weather. In such climates as Montana, it is always taken indoors for the winter. However, when it is strong enough to stand the elements, it is again taken outdoors. Lucy's experience with Mr. Wilson is like those days indoors; one day, she, too, will be able to survive unprotected in a bright and harsh world.

Appendix II

An Aborted Faulkner Project

Whenever plans for the publication of a previously unpublished manuscript by an author of William Faulkner's stature are announced, it is newsworthy. Edwin McDowell first mentioned the proposed University of Alabama/Gorgas Oak Press edition of William Faulkner's unpublished early poetry in the *New York Times* on August 17. 1984. He mentioned that the edition would be limited to one hundred and eighty copies and would cost around $300 a copy. Based on his notice, along with a description of the project in *First Impressions,* the newsletter of the Institute for the Book Arts at the University of Alabama, the entire edition was fully subscribed and had a waiting list before the first line of type had been set.

Leila Clark and Douglas C. Wynn had donated a sizable collection of Faulkner manuscripts to the University of Mississippi at Oxford. The Wynns were interested in seeing a selection from their collection published in a limited fine press edition. Knowing of the fine press publications from the Book Arts Program at the University of Alabama, Thomas Verich, the University of Mississippi Archivist, contacted his old school friend, Gordon B. Neavill, who served as an advisor for the Gorgas Oak Press. Together Verich, Neavill, and I worked out a proposal that would be feasible within an academic structure, because the publication of the book would be undertaken by students in the Book Arts Program. From the outset it was decided that an eminent Faulkner scholar would edit the manuscript, which had been damaged in a fire. It would nevertheless be a literary rather than scholarly fine press book.

Both Verich and the Wynns enthusiastically approved the proposal. Permission was secured from Jill Faulkner Summers, and Judith Sensibar was engaged to edit the manuscripts and write a short note to introduce the text. One cannot imagine my dismay when Verich sent me the manuscript, along with photocopies of the Faulkner typescript on April 18, 1984. Verich requested that we keep a close check on the use of these photocopies, which is why, after I had finished with them, I did not feel justified in keeping a copy of the manuscript in my archive of the project. Sensibar's manuscript was sixty-five pages long. The front matter, which included her long, dull note, occupied twenty of these pages, and thirteen more at the end contained her footnotes and bibliography. I immediately saw that Sensibar and I had different concepts of the project.

Sensibar had completely ignored our instructions that this was to be a literary edition and willfully filled the text full of cumbersome bibliographical apparatus. Two years after we received the manuscript, we were still arguing about how it was going to be printed. I was under a great deal of pressure from James D. Ramer, the dean of the library school, as well as the faculty to get the project started. Curiously enough, I was the only one on the faculty including the pompous Neavill who had bothered to read both the Faulkner typescript and Sensibar's manuscript. I discovered dozens of errors in her transcription, and when I pointed them out, I was accused of attacking an established scholar. In the eyes of the faculty I was an upstart with no scholarly credentials – after all, I had not written a doctoral thesis like the rest of the faculty. Yet I was the only member of that faculty who had ever edited a posthumous manuscript. (I am referring to John Cheever's journals, which I co-edited for my Ex Ophidia edition.)

I felt that by printing the scholarship in grey ink, the flow of reading the text would not be constantly interrupted. To support my point of view Verich consulted James B. Merriwether, another Faulkner scholar. Merriwether wrote to Verich on March 26. 1986, stating that he generally agreed with the position taken by the publisher. Sensibar was unpersuaded and got Mrs. Summers to side with her by withholding permission to publish the text. Legally, however, she could not withhold permission, because she had already assigned the permission to the Gorgas Oak Press, not Sensibar.

The school continued to badger me to get on with the project. We already had the paper on hand, and I finally agreed to order the type for the Faulkner text. Michael Bixler set the type from the marked manuscript that I sent him. The type arrived in galleys with some of the lines set twice. These lines or some of the words in them would be printed in grey. The dean insisted that even if I were right, I must compromise in order to get the book out with the least amount of resistance.

I prepared layouts of the project. My students divided the type into pages and proofed it as part of their classroom work. Then the page proofs were

I

He furrows the brown earth, doubly sweet
To a hushed great passage of wind
Dragging its shadow. Beneath his feet
The furrow breaks, and at its end

He turns. With peace about his head
Traverses he again the earth: his own,
Still with enormous promises of bread
And clean its odorous strength about him blown.

From the shimmering azure of the wood
A blackbird whistles, cool and mellow;
And here, where for a space he stood
To fill his lungs, a spurting yellow

Rabbit bursts, its dulling gold
Muscled to erratic lines
Of fluid fear across the mold.
He shouts. The darkly liquid pines

Mirror his falling voice, as leaf
Raises the clear brown depths to meet its falling self;
Then again the blackbird, thief
Of silence, in a glossy pelf

Inscribes the answer to its life
Upon the white page of the sky:
The furious emptiness of strife
For him to read who passes by.

12

II

The hour comes, on gusts of faint confetti
–The hour comes when day and darkness greet –
Lazily swirled by horns of tin and paper,
Lazily above a frozen stream of street.

The moon stares yellowly through ancient maples.
Through still celestial silver slant slow leaves.
Promises of music question and retreat.
The moon above the maples higher heaves.

And Michael, darkly leaning in a window,
Feels the slow blood of his heart in brain and hand
Marking his life away like drums in music,
In a slow exhaustion of black sand.

This thing that is Michael, sheathing a thought and a vision,
Is only an hourglass of brittle clay
Oblivious, in a window lean with starlight
Of enormous passing pageantries of day.

Shutters in a wind swing sad mosaics
Of shadow on strange indifferent walls.
A flower of music blooms, the flower closes.
Again far music questions him, and falls.

13

Gabriel's typographic layout for a double-page spread for the Faulkner project. (Courtesy of The New York Public Library.)

marked for optical letter spacing and minor adjustments. We still could not proceed with printing, however, until we had Sensibar's approval of the changes I wanted to make in the presentation of the material. The students put a sample form in the press and proofed it in black, blue, and grey, having given it my final approval. Two months after classes started my students were still waiting for Sensibar's go-ahead. The faculty was finally able to exert the necessary pressure on the dean to override any influence I may have had on the project. On November 6, 1986, Ramer wrote Sensibar a very conciliatory letter. Her response on November 19, 1986, so infuriated Ramer that he irrevocably cancelled the project. In Ramer's letter to Douglas Wynn he wrote that he was afraid he had become infected with the virus that plagued the relationship between Sensibar and Rummonds. He found her letter ungracious and imperious, in short, an affront to a person who was seeking a reconciliation.

By December 15 nothing was resolved, because Ramer wrote to both Sensibar and Wynn that the school was withdrawing from the Faulkner project. I doubt that this particular text will ever be published in book format. Perhaps some of the poems will be published in journals, but what the Wynns had conceived as a joyous celebration of their donation of a few unpublished Faulkner poems, albeit rather insignificant in themselves, somehow was turned into a bitter battle of egos over questionable scholarship.

Acknowledgments

A book of this scope, even though innately very personal, could not have been produced without a considerable amount of help.

The Readers
The manuscript was read by Golda, Lauren, and Mark Fishbein, who heroically tried to get me to stick to the point and the truth. Bradley Hutchinson and Chris Borden, who were apprentices at the press in the 1970s and 1980s, helped me clarify the narrative and simplify the technical descriptions. Alessandro Zanella, who worked with me between 1976 and 1982, unraveled many of the perplexing PWP facts and chronology. Both D. Steven Corey at the University of San Francisco and Francis O. Mattson at The New York Public Library looked at the manuscript with the sharp eyes of archivists. Mary Manous began to read the manuscript, but found it overwhelming and gave up on it. It is a better story thanks to all of these readers.

The Editors
The text went through more than sixteen major rewrites – the nightmare of any editor. I was fortunate to have Jill Mason as my first editor. She patiently smoothed out my byzantine sentence structure and gleefully cut much of the superfluous material. I owe the coherence of the text to her. Paul B. Watry at the University of Liverpool, a longtime enthusiast of my work, was the next editor to work on the manuscript. He helped to make it a more interesting read. Paul was followed by Sal Glynn, who tried to put the text into a more coherent form, although I had certain misgivings with his edits, finding them more confusing than helpful. Lauren Fishbein took over after Sal. She unraveled most of Sal's inconsistencies. My last and primary editor, James T. Jones, coaxed the results of all these many revisions into its final form.

Individuals
I want to thank the many individuals who helped make this memoir a possibility. W. Thomas Taylor was the impetus for getting me started. Alessandro

Corubolo, John Richardson, Jr., Tony O'Hara, and Patricio Gatti more than once came to my rescue. Others filled in gaps in the story. John D. Wagner was especially helpful in sorting out the events in Alabama. Carla Bellini Zanella sent me information about her husband's activities after we dissolved the Plain Wrapper Press. Corey Sabourin did additional research in my archives at The New York Public Library. I owe a great debt of appreciation to the individuals who, over the years, collected my work, for without them I would not have been able to produce the books that inspired this memoir.

Institutions and Organizations

Several institutions and organizations made my archive materials in their collections available to me:

New York Public Library and its staff, including William Stingone, Thomas Lannon, Tal Nadan, and Susan Malsbury.

University of Oregon Library and its staff, including James Fox, Bruce Tabb, Marilyn Reaves, and Lesli Larson.

J. Willard Marriott Library, University of Utah and its staff, including Greg Thompson, Madelyn Garrett, Luise Poulton, and Marnie Power-Torrey.

Richard A. Gleeson Library, University of San Francisco and John Hawk.

Scans

I also want to thank the following individuals for supplying scans for the book: Weldon DeBusk, Dennis Letbetter, and Don Myers.

Photographers

A special thanks to all the photographers whose work lavishly embellishes this memoir: Helen Adam, Tony Aiello, Stephen M. Allen, Bekir Arpag, William E. Barksdale, Enzo Bassotto, Carlo Bavangnoli, James D. Birchfield, Garrett Boge, Richard Capp, Luca Carrà, Mario Carrieri, Jonathan Clark, Chip Cooper, Alessandro Corubolo, Kit Currie, Weldon DeBusk, Irwin Dermer, Pucci De Rossi, Golda Fishbein, Lauren Fishbein, Mark Flynn, J.P. Forsthoffer, Isabel Freud, Anne Garde, Reggie Gay, Dana Gioia, Hannes Heldele, Carol Joyce, David Kent, Stephen Kigsley, Mario Lencia, Oliver Livoni, Luciano Luise, Robert Mahon, Les Maiden, Mary Manous, Fred W.

Acknowledgments 759

Maiden, Mary Manous, Fred W. McDarrah, Mirek, Carlo Nanni, Rolf Nelson, Antony O'Hara, Joe Oppedisano, Amanda Ortega, Ruggiero Passeri, Hoke Perkins, Pftzner, Guillermo Ramos, Jürgen Reuter, Nancy Richardson, Federico Rossi, William Rothschild, Thomas Rummonds, Filippo Selden, Priscilla Spitler, Luca Steffenoni, Studio Gulliver, Arto Szabo, Allen Tate, Diana Thomas, Guido Trevisani, Emilio Veclani, Giorgio Vigna, James Weil, Henryk Wieniewski, Alessandro Zanella, Pino Zanfretta.

Providers of Images

A sentimental acknowledgement to all those who let me use images from their personal collections: John Balkwill, Barton Lidicé Beneš, James D. Birchfield, Black Star, Garrett Boge, Steven D. Corey, Alessandro Corubolo, Kit Currie, Muir Dawson, Weldon DeBusk, Irwin Dermer, Winthrop Kelly Edey, Pietro Ferrari, Golda Fishbein, Lauren Fishbein, Miguel Frasconi, Gordon Fraser, James Fraser, Antonino Gammaro, Patricio Gatti, Brendan Gill, Dana Gioia, Carol Joyce, Barbara Knight, Ann Laughlin, Golda Laurens, Montserrat Lehmann, Dietrich Leube, Martino Mardersteig, Leopoldo Messer, Berta Moltke, Mondadori/Getty Images, Paul Moxon, Alessandro Mozzambani, Carlo Nanni, Antony O'Hara, Parvum Photo, Hoke Perkins, Clara Pettitt, Arnaldo Pomodoro, Jack Pooler, Jürgen Reuter, Nancy Richardson, Elfie Rummonds, Roger Selden, Society of Young Publishers, Priscilla Spitler, Jack Werner Stauffacher, Fulvio Testa, Diana Thomas, Time Inc. Picture Collection, Julien Vernière, Laure Vernière, Brooks Walker.

A Special Nod of Appreciation

I want to thank Jameson Irish Whiskey for helping bring many buried memories to the surface.

Credits and Permissions

Grateful acknowledgement is given to the following for permission to publish the texts and photographs. Every effort has been made to identify the copyright holders.

Images Provided by the University of Oregon
Note that the full credit for the University of Oregon should read: Image digitalization courtesy Special Collections and University Archives, University of Oregon Libraries.
All images of PWP and EXO books.

Images Provided by The New York Public Library
Note that the full credit for The New York Public Library should read: Richard-Gabriel Rummonds papers. Manuscripts and Archives Division. The New York Public Library. Astor, Lenox, and Tilden Foundations.
Images on pages 28, 137, 186, 246, 317, 325, 457, 714, 755.

Images Provided by the University of Utah
Note that the full credit for the University of Utah should read: J. Willard Marriott Library, University of Utah.
Images on pages 10, 55, 75 (*left*), 76 (*left and right*), 569.

Image Provided by the University of Wisconsin-Madison
Note that the full credit for the University of Wisconsin-Madison should read: Department of Special Collections, Memorial Library, University of Wisconsin-Madison.
Image on page 680.

Images Provided by Officina Chimèrea
Images on pages 378, 380.

Image Provided by the Pinacoteca de Brera
Image on page 626.

Image Provided by State University at Buffalo
Note that the full credit for State University of New York at Buffalo should read: Photograph of Jack Spicer by Helen Adam, copyright © the estate of Helen Adam. From the Helen Adam Collection, The Poetry Collection of the University Libraries, University at Buffalo, The State University of New York. Page 233.

Image Provided by Nyack Library
Note that the full credit for Nyack Library should read: Nyack Library Local History Image Collection.
Page 30.

Texts
Page 241, "A Song for Gabriel" with permission of Laure Vernière.
Page 353, "The Photograph" with permission of Edmund Keeley.
Page 505, "Sleepiness" with permission of Peter Robinson.
Page 674, "Distant Friends" with permission of Peter Eustace.
Page 692, Excerpt from Dal Vero with permission of John Hollander.
Page 698, "Earth-Orbital" with permission of Abigail Thomas.

Copyrighted Images
Page 68, copyright by Mary Manous 2009
Page 182, copyright by Robert Mahon 1980
Page 260, copyright by Luca Steffenoni 1971
Page 314, copyright by Amanda Ortega 1970
Page 469, copyright by Ruggiero Passeri 2008
Page 478, copyright by Joe Oppedisano 1998
Page 490, copyright by Robert Mahon 1980
Page 497, copyright by Robert Mahon 1980
Page 530, copyright by Luca Steffenoni 1975
Page 548, copyright by Luca Steffenoni 1976
Page 575, copyright by Robert Mahon 1980
Page 576, copyright by Robert Mahon 1980
Page 577, copyright by Robert Mahon 1980
Page 578, copyright by Robert Mahon 1980
Page 603, copyright by Robert Mahon 1980

Credits and Permissions 763

Page 672, copyright by Robert Mahon 1981
Page 692, copyright by Robert Mahon 1984
Page 720, copyright by Anne Garde 1986
Page 744, copyright by Jonathan Clark 1999

Recipes Index

Agnello alle Olive, 501

Agnello coi Finocchio, 595

Antipasto of Shrimp and Squid with Artichoke Hearts, 519

Argentine Meat and Vegetable Stew, 114–115

Arrosto di Maiale al Latte, 681

Baked Alaska, 159

Baked Halibut, 665

Baked Macaroni and Cheese, 532

Beef in Burgundy, 461-463

Beef Rolls with Artichokes, 437

Beef Tolstoy, 35

Boeuf Bourguignon, 461–463

Bollito Misto, 282–283

Braised Beef in Barolo Wine, 541

Braised Lamb Shanks, 583

Braised Leg of Lamb with Juniper Berries, 677

Braised Veal Shanks, 268

Brasato di Agnello al Ginepro, 677

Brasato di Bue al Barolo, 541

Cabbage Stuffed with Meat, 87

Cannelloni con Ripieno di Gamberi, 80–81

Cannelloni Stuffed with Shrimp, 80–81

Carpaccio, 385

Ceviche de Pescado, 53

Chicken Liver Pâté, 158

Coniglio alla Reggiana, 243

Devil's Chicken, 711

English Trifle, 440–441

Filet Mignon with Green Peppercorns, 67

Filet of Sole Stuffed with Crabmeat, 146-147

Filetto al Pepe Verde, 67

Fusilli con Broccoli Rabe e Gorgonzola, 710

Gnocchi di Patate, 473–475

Gnocchi di Spinaci e Ricotta alla Salvia, 622–623

Green Sauce, 284

Herb Pâté, 646

Hunter's-Style Chicken Stew, 602–603

Indonesian Spicy Eggs, 261

Involtini coi Carciofi, 437

Lamb with Black Olives, 501

Lamb with Fennel, 595

Locro de Betty, 114–115

Marsala Custard, 507

Martini, 610

Milanese-Style Saffron Risotto, 495

Mixed Boiled Meats, 282-283

Mussels in White Wine and Herbs, 433

Negroni, 610

Ossobuco alla Milanese, 268

Pasta and Bean Soup, 251

Pasta e Fasioi (Pasta e Fagioli), 251

Pasta Piccante, 311

Pasta with Broccoli and Gorgonzola, 710

Pastissada de Caval (Spezzatini di Cavalo), 221

Pâté aux Herbes, 646

Pearà, 285

Penne with Spicy Tomato Cream Sauce, 311

Pepper Sauce, 285

Philadelphia Cream Cheese Pie, 21

Piccata di Vitello con Limone, 695

Pickled Okra, 647

Pineapple Upside-Down Cake, 533

Polenta with Gorgonzola, 611

Pollo al Forno con Patate, 371

Pollo alla Cacciatora, 602–603

Pollo alla Diavolo, 711

Pomodori con Mozzarella e Basilico, 361

Pork and Chicken Stew, 336

Pork Chili con Carne, 722–723

Pork Loin Braised in Milk, 631

Potato Gnocchi, 473–475

Potato Salad, 460

Prosciutto and Melon or Figs, 360

Prosciutto e Melone o Fichi, 360

PWP Cocktails, 610
Rabbit with Herbs, 243
Radicchio di Verona al Forno, 337
Raw Beef, 385
Raw Fish Appetizer, 53
Risotto Nero di Seppie, 733
Risotto con Zafferano alla Milanese, 495
Risotto alla Pilota, 409
Risotto with Cuttlefish, 733
Risotto with Sausage, 409
Roast Chicken with Potatoes, 371
Roasted Radicchio, 337
Salsa Verde, 284
Saltimbocca alla Romana, 284
Shirred Eggs, 349
Sliced Chicken with Tuna Sauce, 449
Spaghetti con Vongole e Cetrioli, 277
Spaghetti with Clams and Cucumbers, 277
Spezzatini di Maiale e Pollo, 336
Spezzatini di Vitello in Agrodolce, 211

Spinach and Ricotta Gnocchi with Sage
    Sauce, 622–623
Spit-Roasted Songbirds with Polenta, 176–
    177
Steak Tartare, 203
Stinci di Agnello, 583
Stuffed Pork Tenderloin, 687
Sweet and Spicy Veal, 211
Tacchino con Funghi in Panna, 295
Tomatoes with Mozzarella Cheese and
    Fresh Basil, 361
Tramezzini, 610
Turkey with Mushrooms in Cream, 295
Uccellini allo Spiedo con Polenta, 176–177
Veal Scallops with Lemon, 695
Veal with Prosciutto and Sage, 229
Veneto Cornmeal Cookies, 485
Veronese Horsemeat Stew, 221
Zabaglione, 507
Za'leti, 285

General Index

Page numbers in *italics* refer to illustrations.
Page numbers in **bold** refer to main entries.

A

"Abandoned by a Married Man" (RGR), 669–670

"Abandoned by a Married Man" (lecture by RGR
keepsake for, *743*

Aborted Faulkner Project, An, **753–756**

Ackerman, Martin S., 432

Acton, Harold, 664, *570, 570,* 571, 664

Adam, Helen, 233, 758

Adana horizontal-platen press, 57

Adobe Minion, 738

Aesop, 379, 685

Affected Ladies, The (Molière), 11, 393, *393*

After Lorca (Spicer), 238

Agenoux, Søren, 23, *24, 25–26*

Agora Studio, 199, 304

Aguirre Mac-Kay, Mario, 75–76, 102, 106, 108, 333, 376

Aiello, Tony, 155, *155,* 156, 189, 758

Albergo Due Torri, 408, 423

Albion press, 275
Ashendene, 737
Hopkinson & Cope, 223
Luigi Ghisi, 588–589, *589,* 682, *682*

Albus, Anita, 261

Alcorn, John E., 249, 491, 549, 661

Alcorn, Tommy, 249

Alejandro, Father, 69, 72, 79

Alexandra (boutique owner), 371

Alexandria Quartet, The (Lawrence Durrell), 571

Alfred A. Knopf (New York publishing house), 121, 140, 146, 162, 317, 411, 487, 604, 716

Alfred A. Knopf/Random House, 175, 248, 250, 297

Algonquin Hotel, 281

Alitché (*nom de plume* of Laure Vernière), 287, 290

Allen, Beverly, 477

Allen, Donald M., 237

Allen, Dorothy, *135,* 136, 187

Allen, Lewis M., 65, 135, *135,* 136, 187, 191, 224, 373

Allen, Stephen M., 135, 758

Allen Press, The, 135, *136*

Alliance for Progress, 40

All That Is (Salter), 633

Alphabets & Ornaments (Lehner), 435

Altobell, Leonard, 12

"Altro Posto di Lavoro" (Sereni), 468

Alweis, Barbara, 426

Alweis, Frank, 426, 509

Amatruda mouldmade wove paper (*see also* Cartiera Ferdinando Amatruda fu Luigi), 274, 292, 322–223, 365, 367, 458

Ambrosi, Fabio, 267, 329, 591

American Book Collector (magazine), 333, 580, 649, 685, 725

American Institute of Graphic Arts, The, 577

American Printing History Association, 742
keepsake for, *743*

Ampersand (*see* Stamperia Ampersand and Edizioni Ampersand)

Amsterdam Continental Types, 55

Anabase (Saint-John Perse), 589

Anatomia auri (Mylius), *680,* 685

Anderson, Betty, 121, 146

Andrews/Nelson/Whitehead (A/N/W), 131, 136, 145, 183

Androcles and the Lion (Harris), 11
lion costume, *10*

Andy (printer), 62

Anglim, Paule, 568

Anna, S.R.A duchessa d'Aosta (Anna, Duchess of Aosta), 471

Antes, Horst, 320

767

Antony and Cleopatra (Barber), 31
Antúnez, Nemesio, 126
Arche Scaligere, 593
Arena di Verona (Roman amphitheater), 426, 444, 572
Arena di Verona, L' (newspaper), 263
Argus Books, 544
Aricò, Rodolfo, 263, 265–266
Ariel (Plath), 363
Arif Press, 579, 709
Arnoldo Mondadori Editore (Italian publishing house), 267, 490, 504
Arpag, Bekir, 555, 758
Art Market, 294
  invitation for, *294*
"Art of the Printed Book" (conference), 370, 561
Arte Fiera '75, 521,
Arte Fiera '76, 341, 491, 525, 547, *547*, 548
Artichoke Press, The, 566
Arts and Crafts Movement, 560
Ash, Lee, 76, 227
Ashendene Albion press, 737
"Assault on the Book" (lecture by Abe Lerner), 455–456
Assault on the Book (Lerner), 455
Aster (Simoncini Linotype), 102
Aston, Katherine, 89
Atlantic Crossing (Cheever), 645, **712–720**, *712*, *715*
  manuscript page from, *714*
Attenzione (magazine), 517
Atwood, Margaret, 661
August (Davenport), 728
Augustus (ocean liner), 108
Aura (Carruth), 554
Australian Printing Historical Society, The, 376
"Author and Publisher: A Love Story, of Sorts" (lecture by RGR), 370, 561
Ava Gardner: The Secret Conversations (Gardner), 681

B
Bacon, Francis, 411, 414, 415
Baker, Anthony, 377, 597, 599

Baker, Philip, 27, 29, *29*, 30, 123, 134, 158
"Baker Man" (RGR), 704
Bakin, Tony, 193
Balkwill, John, *661*, *662*, *735*, *737*, *759*
Ball, John, 62–63
Ballata delle madri (Pasolini), **222–228**, *222*, *225*, *226*, *229*, 318
Balthazar (Durrell), 117
Barba-Vera, Javier, 42, 72
Barber, Samuel, 31
Barboza, Mario, *70*
Barcham Green Charter Oak paper, 316, 317322
Bareiss, Walter, 618
Bar Gar (*see* Gelateria Pampanin)
Barksdale, William E., 51, 71, 758
Barnes, Djuna, 64, 389, 392, *392*, 396
Baro, Gene, 381
Barret, James Sanford, 552
Barthelme, Donald, 572
Bartolini, Sergio, 427
Baskerville, John, 619
Bassotto, Enzo, 378, 758
bathhouses, 107–108
Baudelaire, Charles, 553
Bauer Alphabets, 55, 185
Bauhaus, 26
Bavagnoli, Carlo, 228, 758
Bayerische Staatsbibliothek, 566–567
Bear, Bebe (fictitious character), 97, 391
Beat poets, 242
Beaumont, Francis, 413–414
Beck, Julian, 26
Becker, David, 577
Beebe, Lucius, 19
Beech, John, 545
Beethoven, Ludwig von, 17
Belacqua Presse, 377, 380
Bellini Zanella, Carla, 673, 758
Bembo (Monotype), 291
Bendinelli, Pino, 454–455
Beneš, Barton Lidicé, 149, 150, *150*, 151, 152–157, 205, 429, 697, 759
Benn, Susan, 545
Benn, Timothy, 545

General Index

Benton, Megan, *640, 644*

Benton, Paul, *644*

Berardinelli, Luigi (Gino), 265, 492, 515, 591–592, 594, 617–618, 653

Berenson, Bernard, 516

Berghammer, Ortwin, 528–530

Berkeley Renaissance (literary movement), 342

Berlioz, Hector, 247

Bernstein, Ben, 45

Berrocal, Miguel, 589

Bertani, Giorgio, 227

Bertaso, Guerrino, 216–217

Berthold, H. (German type founder), 343, 567

Bertram Rota, 334, 545

Bestiario vegetale (Testa), 500

Betti, Laura, 228

Bettini, Bruno, 144–145

Bianchet, Roberto, 308

Biblioteca Capitolare, 427, 482, 620

Biblioteca Civica di Verona, xiv, 271, 379, 452, 560, 739

Biblioteca Comunale (*see* Biblioteca Civica di Verona)

Biblioteca di Milano, 579

"Bicycle Odyssey, The" (Paul Zweig), 181

Bigus, Richard, 709, 721

Binns, Betty, 119

Biondello (character in *The Taming of the Shrew*), 7

Birchfield, James D., 452, 758, 759

Bixler, Michael, xv, 717, 754

Black, Shirley Temple, 571

Blackburn, Bob, 183, 187, 194

Black Hole of Calcutta, 275, 454, 635

Black Star, 759

Black Sun Press, 126

Blake, William, 334, 573

Blanchard, Gérard, 377

Blaser, Robin, 242

Ballata delle Madri (Pasolini), **222–228**, *222, 225, 226,* 229, 318

Blesse, Fred, 139, 152

Blinn, Carol J., 659, 660

Bloomingdale's, 28

Bluest Eye, The (Morrison), 140

Blumenthal, Joseph, 567, 576, 651

Boar's Head Playhouse, 9

Bodoni, Giambattista, 466

Boge, Garrett, 737, 740, 758, 759

Bolognese, Don, 316, 318

Bolognese, Leon, 121, 138

Bomarzo (Ginastera), 521, 522

Boner Grosselli, Lina, 201, 293, 363

"Book Arts Celebration: 50 Years of the Cummington Press" (conference), 134

Book Arts Institute, 633, 645, 707, 716

Bookbindings of T.J. Cobden-Sanderson, The (Tidcombe), 383

Book Club of California, The, 357, 577–578, 742

Book Club of California News-Letter, 742, 744

Bookmaking: The Illustrated Guide to Design & Production (Ash), 76

Book of Job, 573

Boone, Gray D., 516, 519

Borden, Christopher (Chris), 429, 619–620, *620,* 627, 629, 757

Borges, Jorge Luis, 106–107, 112, 183, 198, 209, 254, 313–314, *314,* 315, 317, 318–319, 320–321, 322, 331–332, 333, 339, 581

Borges/Pomodoro book, 334, 335, 336, 339, 340, 355, 357, 366, 367, 411, 414, 416, 466, 509, 521, 548, 550, 564, 569, 579, 614, 651

Borman, Ann, *661, 663*

Bosn' Locker, 234

Botero, Fernando, 414–415

Bottega del Vino (wine bar), 219

Boulevard (journal), 494

Bovary, Emma (fictitious character), 188, *189,* 393

Boyd, Bruce, 234, 235, 237

Bradbury, Ray, 516, 544

Bradford, Tom, 642

Bragantini, Gigi, 209

Braun Menéndez, Armando, 106, *106,* 107, 135, 313, 333

Bremer Presse, 135, 567

Brentano's Bookstore, 545

Bridwell Library, 684, 737

Brinckman, Roderick (known as Sir Theodore Brinckman after he moved to England), 545
British Hand Made Parchment Substitute paper, 511
British Library, The, 191, 413, 738
Brooks, Hadassah, 359, 430, *430*, 478, 509, 510, 559
Brownstone Press, The, 122, 128
Bruckner, D. J. R. (Don), 582
Bryan, 163, 165
Bullock, Wynn, 566
Burgess, Anthony, xv, 411, 412–413, 414, 417, 420, 422, 423, *423*, 424, *424*, 430–431, 439, 440, 441, 509, 544, 563, 667
Burgess, Liana, 417, 423, *424*
Burgess, Paolo Andrea, 417, 423, *424*
Burgess/Tilson book, 421, 432, 435, 479, 494, 509, 522, 549, 550, 569, 691
Burma (cat, a.k.a. Harry), 163, 165
Burnett, Frances Hodgson, 11
Burton, William, 580
Bussola, Giuseppe (Beppe), 257, 274–275, 279
Butler, Frances, 515
Butts, Mary, 64, 389
Bynner, Witter, 389, 396
"By Way of Errata" (Gill), 513
Byrne, John, 545

C
Cabianca, Cristiano, 171, 275, 447
Caffè Filippini, 172, 245, 247
Calcografia Artistica Cristini (*see also* Cristini, Luciano), 194
California job case, 357–358,
Callaway, Nicholas, 405
Caloi, Ennio, 266–267, 305, 329
Calvino, Italo, 517, 586, 649–650, *650, 651,* 652–654, 657, 659, 664
Calvino/Frasconi book, 660, 668, 684, 686
Cambridge School of English, The, 301
Camp Gualala, 85, 87
Campo dei Fiori, 228
Camus, Albert, 170
  Christmas card, 169–170, *170*

Cancerqueen and Other Stories (Landolfi), 568
Cangrande I della Scala, 591
Canson Ingres paper, 103
Cantata de Bomarzo (Mujica Láinez), **520–530**, *520, 523, 528,* 535, 549, 685
  logbook entry, *525*
  Park of Monsters, *524*
Cantata di Bomarzo ((translated into Italian by Tentori Montalto), **534–535**, *534, 536*
Cantatore, Walter, 574
Cantina, La (wine bar), 619
Capogrossi, Giuseppe, 319–320
Capp, Richard, 12, 393, 758, 759
Capurro, Carlos, 70
Cardazzo, Paolo, 319, 320
Cardazzo, Renato, 267
Cárdenas, Carlos, 32–33, *32,* 117, 118, 144, 310, *310,* 522, 540, 613–614, 707
Cardini, Antonia, 430, 582
Carlis, John, 570
Carmelita (Berkeley girlfriend), 18
Carnegie Institute of Technology, 133, 136
Carrà, Luca, 467, 758
Carrieri, Mario, 320, 758
Carrión, Anita, 47, 63
Carruth, Hayden, 554
Carta a mano di Amalfi (McCord), 322
Carter, Benjamin, 588
Carter, Sebastian, 588, 628
Cartiera Ferdinando Amatruda fu Luigi (*see also* Amatruda paper), 322
Cartiere Enrico Magnani (*see also* Magnani paper), 619, 651, 728
Cartiere Fedrigoni (*see also* Fedrigoni paper), 589, 590, 591
Cartiere Miliani-Fabriano (*see also* Fabriano paper), 145, 323, 416, 420, 448, 554, 619
Casa di Giulietta, 172
Casa Frollo, 165
Casanova di Fellini, Il (film), 481
Casati, Franco, 245–246, 271, 300
Cassa di Risparmio di Verona Vicenza e Belluno, 448, 483
Castelvecchio (*see* Museo di Castelvecchio)

General Index

Castiglioni, Gino, *378, 379, 382, 494, 740, 744,* 746

Castleberry, May, 674, 689–690, 697, 702, 706–707, *707*

Catalogue of the Frick Collection, The, 132, 136

Cather, Willa, 516

Cavafy, C.P., 351, 352, *352,* 411

Cave, Roderick, 376–377, 383

Center for Book Arts, 425, 619

Center for Book Arts: The First Decade, 157

Center for the Book, The, 579–580

Cento Amici del Libro, I, 227, 465, 471, 477, 497, 499, 500, 586, 607

Centro per la Formazione Professionale Grafica , 607

Centrum Frans Masereel, 418

Ceroli, Mario, 529–530

Chafetz. Sidney, 640

Chagall, Marc, 491

Challis, John, 127

Chambers, David, 373

Chanin, Margit, 334–335

Chapman, Sam, 394–395

Charlton, Richard, 12

Checklist of Books Printed by Richard-Gabriel Rummonds & Alessandro Zanella at the Plain Wrapper Press, 1966–1980, A (Pettitt), 574

Checklist of Books Printed by Richard-Gabriel Rummonds at the Plain Wrapper Press, 1966–1972, A (RGR), 66

Cheever, John, 515, 713, *713,* 714, 715–716, 754

Cheever, Susan, 714, 721

Chez Panisse, 579

"Chiaroscuro" (Ungaretti), 626

"Chief Joseph of the Nez Perce Indians" (Warren), 577

Chiesa, Carlo, 466–467

Chiesa di S. Stefano, 465

Child, Julia, 439, 461

Child, Paul, 439

Child's View of Secession, A (Barret), 552

"CHI SONO" (RGR), 667

Christiansen, Wanda Rose, 14

Christie, John, 550–551

Christmas Recipe, A (Burgess), **438–441,** *438*

Chukker, The (bar in Tuscaloosa, AL), 557, 703, 704, *707,* 716

cicala e la formica, La (Aesop), 379

Cinque Maggio, Il / Der Fünfte Mai (Manzoni), 506, **624–628,** *624, 628*

Circhi e Cene / Circuses and Suppers (Zanzotto) **476–483,** *476, 481*

Circle Press, 550

"Circus-Cocò" (Zanzotto), 478

"City Coat of Arms, The" (Kafka), 498

Clark, Howard, 554, 716

Clark, Jonathan, 566, 741–742, 758, 763

Clark, Kathryn 551

Clark, Leila, 753

Clarke, Bert, 133

Clavel, Maurice, 380

Clegg, Charles, 19

Clockwork Orange, A (Burgess), 431

Close-Grip Press, The, 728

Cobden-Sanderson, Thomas James, 135, 216–217, 383, 573

"Cobden-Sanderson: Bookbinder" (Cave), 383

Coerr, Wimberley, 46, 53

Coffin, J.E., 76

Cohen, Bernard, 263, 265

Cohen, Edwin, 393, *393,* 394, 406

Cole, John Y., 579

Cole, Maud D., 200

Colegio Episcopal de Buenos Aires Sagrada Corazón de Jesús, *68, 77*

Coleman, John, *656, 657, 662, 700, 702, 704, 706, 707, 722, 731*

Coleridge, Samuel Taylor, 388, 396

"Coleridge adenoidal" (Comberback), 395

Coletta, Assunta, 560

Coletta, Pietro, 560

Collected Poems of Wallace Stevens, The (Stevens), 614

"Collecting Fine Press Printing: Library and Museum Perspectives" (panelist), 674–675

College Department, The, 121

"Collegiate Press Conference, Alabama," 580, 708–709

Colombo, Emilio R., 106

Colombo, Francisco A., 106

Colombo, Osvaldo F., 106

Colophon Club, 578

Colts Armory press, 563

Columbia University, 129

Comberback, S.T., 388, 389, 395, 396

Committee for the American Participation in the Triennale, 689

Communist Party of Italy, 455

Compton, Henry, 683–684

Comune di Verona, 448

Conceria Cecchi, 427

Concerto per ottone e rame di Pucci De Rossi (pamphlet published by Granetto), 288
  invitation for, *288*

Conquest of Mexico, The (opera libretto by RGR), 572

¿Control de la natalidad después del Concilio? (David), *75*

Cooper, Chip, 639, 758

Cooper Union, 132, 491

Cora (model), 9

Corey, D. Steven, vii, 564, 565, *565*, 566, 603, 709, 757, 759

Cornfield, Robert, 303, *303,* 568

Corrado, 309

Corrick's, 17

Corridori, Bruno, 205, 206–207, 209

Corsaro Nero, Il (film), 260

Corsberg, Ken, 97–98

Cortázar, Julio, 112, 415

"Cortes and Montezuma" (Donald Barthelme), 572

Cortese, Valentina, 740

Corticella Paradiso, 454–455

Corubolo, Alessandro (Sandro), 192, *378,* 379, 494, 739, 740, 744, 746, 757, 758, 759

Cottondale, Alabama: Settling In, **632–645**

Cottondale, Alabama: Ex Ophidia, **681–686**

Could I Ask You Something? (Lewis Thomas), 645, **696–702,** *696, 699, 701*

"Count Dracula" (*see also* Guarienti, Luigi) 458, 634

Covre, Isa, 287, 290

Creighton, Sarah, 659

Cristini, Luciano, 144, 194–196, 198, 202, 209, 256–257, 267, 339, 343–344, 351, 366, 402, 500, 726, 729

Crosby, Caresse, 126

Crosby, Harry, 126

Crouse College, 7, *8,* 9

"Cuando no estoy contigo" (translation by RPR of "When I Am Not with You" by Sara Teasdale), 55, 58

Cummington Press, The, 134

"Cummington Press Fiftieth Anniversary Celebration, The" (conference), 134

Cummins, James, 545

Cunard, Nancy, 571

Cupid, 557, 558
  flyer for, *558*

Currie, Kit, 455, 456, 459, 576, 651, 758, 759

D

Dachs, Karl, Dr., 567

Daily Californian, 392

Daily Horoscope (Gioia), 725

Da Lisca, Maria, marchesa, 445, 471

Dal Vero (Hollander), 188, 645, **688–694,** *688, 691*
  excerpt from, 762

Dampening of Hand-Made Paper, The (Blumenthal), 567

D'Annunzio, Gabriele, 194, 524

Dante (Monotype), xiii, xv, 590, 591, 619, 626, 729

Daolio, Fausto, 420

Da Pian, Renato, 355, 420, 566

Da Re, Bruna, 445, 537, 629, *629*

Dark of the Moon (Teasdale), 58

D'Arpini, Paolo (Max), 168, *168,* 169, 201, 205, *206,* 207, 208, 209–210, 213, 287, 293, 443, 535

Daugherty, Robert, 155, 189, 250

Davenport, Guy, 580, 728

David, Jakob, 75

Davids, Betsy, 565, 567–568, 579, 709

General Index

Davis, Scott, 683

Dawson, Muir, 135, 759

Dawson's Book Shop, 455, 561

Dead Man in Deptford, A (Burgess), 412

Dean, Marius, 234–235

DeBusk, Weldon, 189, 387, 743, 758, 759

De Cnodder, Remi, 418

"Dedication, The" (RGR), 348, 670

De Franchis, Amedeo, 143, 200

De Giovanni, Luigi, principe, 145, 165

De gli hecatommithi (Giraldi Cinthio), 529

Deighton, Bell, 545

Delacorte Press, 315

De La Cueva, Domingo, 144, 165, *165*

DeLamonica, Roberto, 699

De Lanux, Eyre, 146

Delia (fictitious character) 214

Demeter, Peter, 216

DeMille, Cecil B., 735

DePol, John, 685, 738

Derby, The (McClure), 348

De re militari (Valturius), 383

Dermer, Irwin, 446, 517, 567, 758, 759

De Rossi, 289, 323, 370, 371, 535

De Rossi, Pucci, 231, 263, 287, *287*, 288, *291*, 294, *296*, 298, 306, 308, 346, 347, 363, 720, 758

De Rossi, Toni, 653

De Stefanis, Giovanni, 607–609

"Destruction of the World, The" (Pettitt), 549

De Vibraye, Tony, conte, 201

Devil, 39, 47, 49

De Vita, Luciano, 521, 522, 525, *525*, 526, 527, 549

Dial Press, The, 303, 352, 411, 568

Diamond Stylus: An Essay on the Combat between Rational Thought and Inner Vision, The (unpublished manuscript by Moskvitin), 175

Diario de un joven norteamericano (Coffin), *76*

Didascalie (Gammaro), 186, **252–260**, *252*, *254*, *257*, *258*, *279*, 313, 435

Didot (European point system), 186, 318

Didot Garamond (Monotype), 304

"Difference of Imagination, A: Guy Davenport in Limited Editions" (unpublished article by RGR), 580

Di Giovanni, Norman, 313, 314–315, 317–318

Dijck, Ger van (*see* van Dijck, Ger)

Dine, Jim, 529

Dinoff, Beth, 730

"Dirty Old Man Sings the Blues, The" (live concert), 704

poster for, *704*

"Distant Friends" (Eustace), 674, 762

Dixon, Arthur, 305, 554, *555*

Dodge, Mable, 389, 396

Dodge Dart '74, 637, 662

Dog Bite: A Dream Narrative, The (Beneš), 128, 136, 145, **148–157**, *148*, *154*, *155*, *157*, *162*, 183, *184*, 186, 188, 201, 205

invitation for, *150*

Donna con la Bocca Aperta, La (Santucci) **486–494**, *486*, *489*, *492*, *493*

Doors of Perception (Harry Duncan), 659

Doris, Mary, 517

Dorothy (character in *The Wizard of Oz*), 11

Double Crown Club (London), 455

Douek, Maurice, 9

Dover Publications (New York publishing house), 119, 435

Doves Bindery, 216–217

Doves Press, 135, 554, 573, 739

Dowd, Miss (fictitious character), 97

Dragon, Ted, 698

Drescher, Jack, 310

DuBois, Blanche (character in *A Streetcar Named Desire*), 443

Duensing, Paul Hayden, 329

Duncan, Harry, xv, 134, 136, 191, 256, 561, *562*, 659–660, 744, *745*

Duncan, Isadora, 5, 389

Duncan, Raymond, 5–6

Duncan, Robert, 342, 390

Duomo (cathedral), 144, *164*

Durrell, Lawrence, 117, 571

Dusel, Philip, 660–661

Dutch Boys, The (*see* van Dijck, Ger, and van der Aa, Theo)

Dwiggins, W.A., 436

E

Eakins Press, The (New York publishing house), 304

"Earth-Orbital" (Thomas), 697–698, 762

Eberhardt, Fritz, *634, 637*

Eberhardt, Trudi, *634, 637*

Éclairs ou lacunes de raison: Trois gravures au burin (portfolio of engravings by Idalie), 305

   invitation for, *305*

"Economics of Printing Limited Editions, The" (article by RGR), 580

"Ecossaise" (Agenoux), 25

Eden Hill Press, 685

Edey, Winthrop Kelly, 30, 32, 33, 42–43, *43,* 759

Ediciones Felmar (Madrid publishing house), 522, 523, 613

Ediciones Paulinas (Buenos Aires publishing house), 120

Editiones Dominicæ, 377, 379

Editorial Francisco de Aguirre (Buenos Aires publishing house), 75, 120

   pressmark, *77*

Edizioni Ampersand, 630

Edizioni del Cavallino, 319

Edizioni Verona, 223

Egan's (bar in Tuscaloosa, AL), 557, 661–662, 702–703, 707

"Ei fu. Siccome immobile" (Manzoni), 627

Eight Parting Poems (RPR), 3, 32, 47, **54–66,** *54, 58,* 76, 103, 104, 206, 668

Elianti, Luciano, 589, 590, 591, 594

Elie Nadelman (Kirstein), 304

Eliot, T.S., 379, 563, 589, 685

Ellingham, Lewis, 242

Elvira Madigan (film), 188

Emecé Editores S.A. (Buenos Aires publishing house), 106

Emo, Barbara, contessa, 453, 570, 664

Emperor's Lion, The (book by Cora C. Fletcher),

386–404, *386, 404, 406,* 408, 418, 577

"Emperor's Lion, The" (short story by Cora C. Fletcher), 65–66, 388, 742

Engels, John, 707, *708,* 708

"English Trifle" (Burgess), 439–440

Enschedé en Zonen, Joh. (Dutch type founder), 456

Enzensberger, Hans Magnus, 572

epistole, Le (Feliciano), 498

Epstein, Lee, 39, 57, 376

"eredita di Mardersteig: i torchi tipografici a Verona, Un' " (article by Castiglioni), 382

Erker-Galerie, 319

Erker-Presse, 319

"Eros • Thanatos," 149

Erskine, Albert, 577

Est modus in rebus (Horace), 381

Etherington, Mary Jane, 426–427, 428

Ettore (D'Arpini's brother-in-law), 168–169

Euripides, xiii

Eustace, Peter, 629, *629,* 674, 762

Evangeliarium purpureum (ninth-century manuscript), 620

evangelios y la crítica, hoy, Los (Zedda), 75

Evans, Walker, 720

Everard Baths, 108

Everson, William, 136, 422

Everybody's Autobiography (Stein), 39

"Evidence, L' " (Alitché, *nom de plume* of Laure Vernière), 290

Ex (private club in Verona), 208

"Excerpt from a Letter" (RGR), 667

"Exiles," 388

Ex Ophidia, 515

F

Fabara, Ricardo, 47, 63

Fabriano paper (*see also* Cartiere Miliani-Fabriano) 169, 200, 214, 254, 323, 324, 344, 404, 436, 441, 466, 490, 597, 599, 737

Fabriano PWP paper, 416–417, 504

Fabriano Umbria paper, 145, 184, 239, 279

Facincani, Mario, 325–327

Factory (Andy Warhol's studio), 128

General Index

Faeries' Garden Theatre, 24

Fagiuoli, Vincenzo, 201

Falck, Alberto, 465, 466–467, 497–498, 500

Falconi, Ugo, 340

Family and Children's Agency, 14, 16

Family Reunion, The (T.S. Eliot), 563

Fantasies and Cold Hard Facts, xv

Farrell, David, 554

Faulkner, William, 702, **753–754**

Favro, Tony, 324

Fawcus, Arnold, 573

Fedrigoni, Gianfranco, 590

Fedrigoni paper (*see also* Cartiere Fedrigoni), 591

Feliciano, Felice, 498

Fellini, Federico, 259, 481

Ferlinghetti, Lawrence, 342

Ferrari, Carlo, 732

Ferrari, Ellen, 732

Ferrari. Enzo, 171, 227

Ferrari, Pietro, 165–166, *166,* 759

Ferrill, David, 730–731

Ferro, Giancarlo, 208–209

Ferrofino, Giovanni, 69

Fiera del Libro per Ragazzi (Children's book fair), 303, 545

Fifty Books 1968, The, 577

Filò (Zanzotto), 481

"Final Soliloquy of the Interior Paramour" (Stevens), 613, 614

Fine Print: A Review for the Arts of the Book (journal), xiii, xvi, 66, 384, 432, 545, 577, 580, 685, 709, 721, 730

"Fine Printing Conference at Columbia University," 564, 621

Fine, Ruth, 500

"First William Story *or* What Happens to Animals Once They Have Been Animals and Found They Are No Longer Interested in Being Animals? They Go Right on Being Animals *or* The Bruce Boyd Story" (RPR), 235

Fishbein, Golda (*see also* Laurens, Golda), 121, 135, 174, 209, 248–250, 292, 293, 297–299, 302–303, 304, 310, 321, 329, 330, 334, 339–340, 346–348, 355–356, 359, 373, 380, 381, 408, 413, 415, 422, 423, 430, 439, 440, 445, *456,* 458, 461, 470, 487, 488, 491, 494, 523, 524, 525, 527, 535–536, 545, 547, 548, 564, 573, 604, 629, 630, 631, 693, 707, 719, 732, 757, 758, 759

photos of, *250, 296, 299, 303, 309, 425, 453, 456, 482, 546, 575, 576,*

Fishbein, Lauren, 297, 298–299, 302, *309,* 310, 346, 373, 374, 375, 424, 426, 446, 453, 535–536, 537, *546,* 732, 757, 758, 759

Fishbein, Mark, 209, 292, 294, *296,* 297, 298–299, 299, 302, 303, *303, 309,* 310, 330, 346, *346,* 377, 381, *381,* 382, *382,* 408, 420, 426, 429, *456,* 536, *546,* 732, 757

Fisher, Joan, 91, 96, 749

Fitzgerald, F. Scott, 581

Fiumi, Lionello, 377

Flaubert, Gustave, 188, *189,* 394

Fletcher, Constance, 387, 388

Fletcher, Cora C., 66, 387–389, 391, 392, 393, 394, 396, 742

Fletcher, John, 413–414

Fleurs du Mal, Les (Baudelaire), 553

Flores-Veloso, Carlos, 42, 72

"Florist, The" (RPR), 667

Flugge, Klaus (London publisher), 549

Flynn, Leisa, 705, 706, 711

Flynn, Mark, 451, *452,* 456, 556, 673, 705, 706, 710, 711, 758

FMR (magazine), 314

Fondazione Biblioteca di via Senato, 740

Fontana (Monotype), xiii

Fontana, Giuseppe, 625–626

Forgeries (thwarted book by Thomas Parkinson), 339, 340–341, 342, 343, 348, 548

Fornaro, Marcello, 330–331, 332, 345, 420, 425, 483

Forsthoffer, J.P. (Joe), 640, 758

Forté, Jobe, 127

Fortune (magazine), 615

Fotosetter (typesetting machine), 140

"Four Meetings" (Henry James), 92

Four Saints in Three Acts (Stein), 13

Fox, James, 758

Franceschin, Mirko, 332
Franco "The Fascist," 298
Franco, Francisco, 143
Frankenstein (fictitious character), 427
Frankfurt Book Fair, 549, 550
Frankfurt Book Fair '81, 527, 549, 552, 652
Franklin, Benjamin, 327
Franklin Mint (publisher), 528
Franks, Susan, 544
Frasconi, Antonio, 649, 651, 654, *654*, 673, 685,
Frasconi, Miguel, 654, 759
Fraser, Gordon F., 26, *27*, 28–29, 134, 158, 162,
    604, 759
Fraser, James Howard, 132, 759
Fraser China, 28, *28*, 30
Fraser's (retail store), 18, 26
Fraser's Inc., 26
Frattini, Flavio, 588
Freud, Isabel (*see also* Hanson, Isabel Freud),
    13–14, *14*, 16–17, 21, 93, 96, 247, 578, 750,
    758
"From Dilettante to Professional: A Metamor-
    phosis" (lecture by RGR) 560–561
Frontier, Robert (Bob), 418
Frost Black printing ink, 151, 153, 186
Fruchter, Norman, 140
Fry, Christopher, 11
Fulgor y muerte de Joaquín Murieta (Neruda),
    126
Fuller, John, 597

G

Gadano, Fabiana, 114
Galería Siglo XX, 46
Galleria Borgonuovo, 367
Galleria d'Arte Moderna, 521
Galleria d'Arte Moderna "a-dieci," 208
Galleria del Cavallino, 319
Galleria del Naviglio, 267
Galleria Ferrari, 171, 227
Galleria Quadrangolo, 574
Galleria Il Segnapassi, 529
Galleria "La Meridiana," 208–210
Galleria Linea 70, 616
Galvagni, Alessandro, 199–200, 208, 471

Gammaro, Antonino, 253, *253*, 254–259, 271,
    279, 280, 281, 435, 436, 439, 759
Gammaro, Linda, *253*
Gammaro, Ninì, 259, 279
Garaldus (Nebiolo typeface), 223
Garamond (Monotype), 264
García, Hugo, *48*, 49, *50*, 51–52
García Márquez, Gabriel, xiv, xv, 69
Garde, Anne, 720, 758, 763
Gardner, Ava, 681
Garnett, Porter, 133
Garrett, Madelyn, 758
Gatti, Patricio, 737, 758, 759
Gatti, Roberto (Robertino), 418, 481, *482*
Gavioli, Angelo, 240, 300, 305
Gay, Reggie, 206, 226, 758
Geldenhuys, Paula (*see also* Nanni, Paula), 401,
    401, 402
Geldzahler, Henry, 427
Géographie du regard (Laure Vernière), 240,
    362–370, *366*, *367*, *370*
Giacometti, Alberto, 721
Gibroni, Olga, 170, 489
"Gide's Unending Search for Harmony"
    (Mann), 161
Gill, Brendan, xv, 500, 509–510, *510*, 513, 515–
    516, 552, 561, 576, *577*, 685, 689, 690, 697,
    702, 706, *706*, 713, 714, 715, 759
Ginastera, Alberto, 46, 521, 523
Ginsberg, Allen, 26, 342
Gioia, Dana, 673, 713, 725, *725*, 726, *727*, 730,
    737, 758, 759
Giraldi Cinthio, Giovanbattista, 529
Glassart Stained Glass, 62
Glaxo, 291, 301
Gleason, Dan, 563
Gleeson Library, Richard A., 564, 565, 566,
    578, 758
globos (*see also* hot-air balloons), 43
Gluck, Christoph Willibald von, 405
Glynn, Sal, 757
Goethe, Johann Wolfgang von, 247, 380, 423,
    625
Goldblatt, Sophie, 299
Goldsmith, Heriberto, 72–73

General Index

Goldwasser, Thomas A., 328
Gómez-Quiroz, Juan, 126
Gorgas Oak Press, 753–754
Gospel According to Jesus Christ, The, 543
Gottlieb, Robert, 162, 411
Goudy, Frederic W., 185
Gourley, Paula Marie, *661, 729*
Goya y Lucientes, Francisco José de, 39
Grace, Princess of Monaco, 425
Graduate School of Library Service, 419, 552, 638
Grand Ole Opry, 554
Granetto, Enrica, 259, 288
Granetto, Luigi (Gigetto), 259, 288, 319
Granetto, Margherita, 259
Grass, Günter, 551
Gray, Jennifer, 429
Gray, Robert, 7
Graziani, Francesco, 427, 482
Grazioli, Rino, 325–327, *378*
"Greed" (RPR), 59
"Green Lift, The" (Denise More, *nom de plume* of RPR), 65
Greenwood Press, The, 15–16, 62, 64, 407, 518
Grolier Club, The, 304, 694
Grossi, Rufino, 78–79
Gross-Smith, Rosalinda (Rosie), *661, 662, 665*
Gruffyground Press, The, 597
Grumbach, Doris, 721
Guadagnin, Amerigo, 585
Guarienti, Francesco, conte (a.k.a. "The Humping Medic"), 458, 634
Guarienti, Luigi, conte (a.k.a. "Dracula"), 458, 634
Gudiño, Marcelo, 75
Guild of Book Workers Journal (journal), 492
Gutenberg, Johann, 355
Guthrie, Woody, 16

H

Haas, Robert, 131, 132, *132*, 133, 136, 139, 184, 185, 191, 379
Haggerty, Michael, 306
Hagstrom, Jack, 134
Hahn, Emily, 149, 151

Hallenstein, Dalbert, 301
Hallo Granja, Wilson, 46
Halsband, Robert, 129
Hamady, Walter, 414
Hammer, Carolyn Reading, 136, 250, 355, 451, 552, 553, 554, *555*
Hammer, Victor, 225, 553, 554
handpress, 130, 136
Hannah, Barry, 660
Hansen, Frank (*see also* Agenoux, Søren), 23
Hanson, Isabel Freud (*see also* Freud, Isabel), 247–248, *248*, 638
Hanson, Lou, 21, 247, *248*
Hard Day's Night, A (film), 122
Hardwick, Elizabeth, 570, 576
Hares, Gladys E., 26, 99, *99*, 146
Harold Berliner's Type Foundry, 729
Harris, Aurand, 11
Harris, Sue, *640*
Harrison of Paris, 557
Harry Ransom Humanities Research Center, 638, 658, 684
Harvard University, 381, 536
Haseloff, Charles, 138
Haste, Jeffrey, 640, *640*, 643, *644*
hat weavers, 46
Hawk, John, 758
Hayez, Francesco, 626
Head (film), 139
Hechscher, August, 567, 576
Heldele, Hannes, 61, 758
Helvetica (typeface), 151
Hendrie, Don, 661
Hendrie, Susan, *640*
Henry, Bill, 141–142, 604–605
Heritage of the Graphic Arts, xviii, 560
Herlitzka, Bruno, 328, 411, 414, 569
Hermanos Cristianos, 74
Hertrich, Elmar, 567
Hilliard Collection, 528–529, 535
Hirschfeld, Al, 581
"History in Fiction" (Renault), 570
Hockney, David, 416, 427
Hofer, Philip, 381
Hoffberg, Judith, 564

Holbein, Hans, the Younger, 435, 436
Holland, Paolo, 300–301
Hollander, John, 689, 691–692, *692*, 762
Horace, 381
Horizon (magazine), 516
Horizon Light (Bauer typeface), 184–186,
207, 215, 240, 254, 264, 274, 279, 316, 343,
357, 367, 402, 527, 700
specimen of, *185*
Hostetler, Susan, 551
Hostmann-Steinberg (German manufacture
of printing ink), 187
hot-air balloons, 43, 175, *175*, 458,
Houghton Library, 381
Houlihan, Philomena, 134–135, 139, 146
Hours Press, 571
House, Glenn, 552, 556, 640, *640*
Huckleberry Press, The, 3, 735
Hudson Review, The (journal), 181
"Humping Medic, The" (*see also* Guarienti,
Francesco), 458, 634
Hunt, Randolph, 426, 427, 428
Hutchinson, Bradley, 454, *454*, 455, *456*, 469–
470, 635, *640*, 644, 655, 657, 672, 692–693,
693, 694, 700, 701, 705, 707, 710, 715, 720,
731, 737, 738, 757

I
I.V.A.T., 171, 356
IBM, 379
I Ching (book of changes), 144
Idalie, Olaf, 292, *293*, 299, *303*, 305, 325, 380,
672
"I Do Believe I Shall Drown This Very Night"
(RPR), 60
IDO-C (Information Documentation on the
Conciliar Church), 111, 113, 180
Iglesia de la Compañía de Jesús, La, 42
Ignatow, David, 708
Ill-Timed Lover, The (RGR), **270–276**, *270*,
272, 274
Images & Footsteps (Paul Zweig), 149, 151,
154, **178–202**, *178*, *181*, 202, 225, 238, 247,
264, 313, 316, 543, 606
Imago Hand Paper Mill, 551

"Imperial friend, I'm writing to resign"
(Parkinson), 341
Importance of Being Earnest, The (Wilde), 245
Impresa Veneta Artigiana Tipografia (see
I.V.A.T.), 171
Information Documentation on the Conciliar
Church (*see* IDO-C)
Ingraham, George, 390–391
Inni di Goethe (Goethe), 380
Institute for the Book Arts, University of Al-
abama, 639–640, 662, 753
Institute of Printing History & Graphic Arts,
194
Interlaken Mills, 149
Interplayers, The, 64, 563
"In the Footsteps of William Morris" (lecture
by RGR), xvii–xviii
Inveresk Paper Company, 513
Irma (prostitute), 247
Isella, Dante, 468
Isolde (German girlfriend), 60–61
Istanbul: Memories and the City (Pamuk), 3
Istituto Salesiano San Zeno (printing trade
school), 291, 607
Istituto Superiore Industrie Artistiche
(I.S.I.A.), 419

J
Jackson Library, University of North Carolina,
Greensboro, 554
James, Henry, 92, 95, 749
Jameson Irish Whiskey, 759
Jänecke-Schneemann (German manufacturer
of printing ink), 187
Janus Press, 554, 597
Jeakins, Richard, 334
newspaper quote about, 334
Jim (high school friend), 5
Jensen, Craig W., 658–660, 672, 701, 719, 729,
737
Jenson, Nicolas, 619
Jinn Handmade Paper, 551
Jodorowsky, Alejandro, 126
Joël, 174
John Ball's Printing Company, 62

General Index 779

Johns, Jasper, 654
Johnson, Paul, 708
Johnson, Richard (Rick), 716
Johnston, Alastair, 515
Johnston, Edward, 135
Jollands, Tim, 415
Jones, James T., 757
Jones, Selwyn, 538
Jonson, Ben, 413
Jouffroy, Manina (*see* Manina)
Journals of John Cheever, 716
Journals of Thomas James Cobden-Sanderson, 1879–1922, The, 383
Journeys in Sunlight (Gioia), 645, 719, **724–730**, *724, 727*
Joyce, Carol, 428, 492, *493,* 494, 573, 659, 693, 758, 759
Jubilee (magazine), 51, *51*
Just Shades (Tate), 661

K
Kafka, Franz, 497, 498, *498*
Kakas, Chris, 559
Kalidasa, 201
Kaplan, Herb, 544
Karl, Anita, 604–605
Katz, Leslie, 304, 576
Kaufmann, Edgar, Jr., 689
Keegan, Daniel José, Father, 69, 79, 80, 83, 105
Keeley, Edmund (Mike), 351, 352, 353, 354, 355, 411, 576, 640, 762
Kees, Weldon, 673
Keleher, Daniel, 581
Keller, Stephan, 551
Kelly, Bob, *8*
Kelly, Jerry, 459
Kelmscott Press, 134, 135, 554, 560, 739
Kelmscott Press and William Morris Master-Craftsman, The (Sparling, et al.), 187
Kelpra Studio, 417
Kennerly, Karen, 303, 352
Kent, David, 31, 758
Kerouac, Jack, 242
Khalil, Mohammed Omar, 184, 190
Kigsley, Stephen, 518, 758

Killian, Kevin, 242
Kinesis Group, 15
King, Ron, 550
King James Bible, 412–413
Kirshenbaum, Sandra, xiii, 580, 709
Kirstein, Lincoln, 304
Kitaj, R. B. (Ron), 569
Klein, Ellen, 657
Klingspor-Museum, 579
Knight, Barbara, 96, 137–138, *138,* 139, 144, 605, 759
Knopf, Alfred A., 162
Kraft paper, 64, 274
Krauthammer Buchhandlung, Robert (Swiss bookseller), 545
Kruty, Peter, 640, *640,* 643, *644, 707, 708*
Kuenz, Jane, 663
Kurosawa, Akira, xiii

L
Laboratory Press, 133
Labyrinth Editions, 709, 721
Lambert, Phyllis Bronfman, 149
Lamentation over the Destruction of the World, A (thwarted PWP book by Pettitt), 549
Landa. Peter, 119
Landolfi, Tommaso, 568
Lannon, Thomas, 758
Larese, Franz, 319–320
Larson, Lesli, 758
Laughlin, Ann, 717–718, 758, 759
Laughlin, James, 129, 568, 717–718
Laurens, Golda (*see also* Fishbein, Golda), 693, 707, 719, 732, 737, 759
Lawrence, D.H., 137
Lawrence, Frieda, 389
Laws, George, 619, 738
Lawson, Alexander, 200
Lazer, Hank, 708
Leardi, Juan Carlos, 73
Lee, Helen, 581
Lee, Marshall, 76
Lefkowitz, Jim, 573
Lefranc & Bourgeois (French printing inks), 422

Legatoria A. Galvagni, 199

Legatoria Piazzesi, 418

Legnaghi, Paolo, 224

Lehmann, Ernest (Ernie), *425, 472*, 542, 544, 564, *758*

Lehmann, Montserrat (Montsie), *542*, 544, 620, *759*

Lehner, Ernst, 435

Leighton, Clare, 381

Lencia, Mario, 308, *308*, 309, *331*, 407, *758*

Léon, Mario, 56

Lerner, Abe, 408, 432, 455–456, *456*, 458, 459, 576, 651

Leslie, Robert L., xviii, 408, 557

Letbetter, Dennis, *758*

Leube, Dietrich, 59–60, *61*, 100, 255, 261, 399, 406, *759*

Levertov, Denise, 708

Lewis Roberts, Inc. (ink manufacturer), 151

Library Fellows of the Whitney Museum of American Art, The, 515, 655, 689, 702

Library of Congress, The, 579

Libreria Galleria Giulia (bookstore and art gallery), 574

Lime Kiln Press, The, 422

Limited Editions Club, The, 129, 408, 580–582

Lionni, Leo, 613, 615–616, *616*, 618, 622, 653

Lionni, Nora, 618

Liparini, Phyllis, 295, 448

Litchfield Summer Theatre, 12

"Little Boy in the Bell Glass, The" (RPR), 65, 391

Little Princess, The (Burnett), 11
  costume sketch, *10*

Littrell, David, 563

Living Theatre, The, 26

Livingston, Mark, 432

Livoni, Oliver, 2, 84, *758*

Loewenstein, Jared, 579

Lofgren, Tom, 17

Long, Don, 358

Long, Nancy Foosaner, 358

Lopes, Brigitte de Almeida, 414

Lorilleux Lefranc (French manufacturer of printing ink), 187

Lorilleux Lefranc Italiana (Italian manufacturer of printing ink), 356

Los Angeles Times Magazine, xiv

Lost Poem, A (Spicer), 304, 328, **338–348**, *338, 342*, 404

Low, Joseph, 141–142, 187, 318, 685

Lowery, Jack, 33

Lucy (fictitious character), 92–94, 97, 749–751

Lui, Lanfranco, 331, 492, 621

Luigi Ghisi Albion press, 588–589, *589*, 644, *644, 672, 681, 682*

Luise, Luciano, 363, 368, *758*

Lynch, Jorge, 73

Lynn (Rick Johnson's girl friend), 716–717

M

Mackenzie-Harris Corporation (type founders), 581, 693

Macy, Helen, 129

Mademoiselle (magazine), 18

Magagnato, Licisco, 591

Magdalen College, 405

Magician of Lublin, The (Singer), 581–582

Magister (Nebiolo typeface), 179

Magnani paper (*see also* Cartiere Enrico Magnani), 184, 264–265, 657, 728

Mahon, Robert, 182, 490, *493*, 497, 573, 575, 576, 577, 578, 603, 672, 692, *758, 762, 763*

Maiden, Les, 745, *758, 759*

Mailer, Norman, 581

Maiorana, Phyllis, 306

Malina, Judith, 26

Malkevicius, Carlos, *70*

Malkevicius, Víctor, *70*

Malsbury, Susan, *758*

Mancini, Franca, 529

Mancini, Piero, 253, 256, *256*, 281

Mandlik, John E., 187

Mandlik Canadian black ink, 422, 436

Mandlik ink (*see* Special Black 42 625 L'press ink)

Manfredi, Alberto, 379

Manhire, Bill, 744

Manina, 144, 366–367

General Index
781

Mann, Thomas, 161

Manous, Mary, 68, 757, 759, 762

Manutius, Aldus, 451, 456, 466

Manzoni, Alessandro, 625, 626, *626*

marbled paper, 105, 274, 374, 729

Marchesini, Renato, 446

Marchetti, Giulio, 619–620

Marconi, Giorgio, 328, 332

Mardersteig, Gabriella, 458, 499

Mardersteig, Giovanni (Hans), xiii–xiv, 129, *130*, 143, 145, 187, 191, 195, 216, 227, 240, 253, 267, 325, 329, 377, 379, 382, 383, 465–466, 498, 499, 500, 561, 567, 590, 625

Mardersteig, Martino, 129–131, *131*, 136, 145, 171, 191, 194, 199, 240, 264, 304, 327, 458, 499, 566, 582, 590–591, 619, 730, 739, 759

Marlborough Fine Art, 415

Marlborough Galleria d'Arte, 320, 325, 328, 332, 411, 416, 432, 569, 574

Marlowe, Christopher, 412

Marsh Marigolds (Baro), 381

Marta (Ecuadorean lover), 51

Martin, Nina, 637–638, 640

Martin, Susanne, *661*

Martín Triana, José María, 522, 586, 613, *613*, 614, 616, 618

Mason, Jill, 757

Massetta, Giovanna, 538, 540, 592, 636

Massetta, Stefano, 537–538, *539*, 540, 540, 592, *593*, 635–636, 669

Master, Syndi Beth, 422, *423*, 424

Master of Fine Arts in the Book Arts Program (*see* MFA in the Book Arts Program)

Master of Library Service, 471

Mathews, Mary, 516, 519

Mattson, Francis O. (Frank), 200, 556, 574, *575*, 709, 757

Max's Kansas City (restaurant), 181

Maybeck, Bernard, 14

Mazda pickup truck, 662

McClure, David, 558, 704

McClure, Michael, 348

McClusky (printer), 390

McCord, Margaret, 322

McDarrah, Fred W., 24, 759

McDonald, Leigh, 703

McDowell, Edwin, 576, 753

McGeorge, Gene, 234

McLain, Raymond Francis, 552

McNab, Charles, 117, 121–122, *122*, 137, 152, 266

McTigue, Bernard (Bernie), 576, 684

Mechanick Exercises (Moxon), 134

Megighian, Alessandro, 420

Meiselman, Ben, 359, *359*, 426, 576, *576*, 713

Mejía, Jorge María, Father, 111

Melcarth, Edward, 276

Merchant Marine, 13

Merker, Kim, 136, 725

Meroni, Paula Veronese, 667

Merriwether, James B., 754

Mersereau, Sydna, 544

Merton, Thomas, 49

Merwin, W.S., 126

Messer, Leopoldo, 70, *70*, 759

Metamorphosis (Picasso), 13

Metropolitan Opera House, 31

Meyer, Howard, 155, 156

Mezzelani, AnnaMaria, 636

MFA in the Book Arts Program, 250, 421, 552, 643, 660, 675

Michael Poems (Faulkner)
   RGR's typographic layout for, *755*

Michahelles, Caroline B., 424, 427, 430–431

Milena (whore), 298

Miller, I., 128

Miller, Kathryn, *640*

Mills, Emilie, 554

Minnie Mouse and the Tap-Dancing Buddha (McClure), 348

Minsky, Richard, 157, 425, *425*, 426

Mirek (Miroslav Zahradka), 205, 207–208, 213–215, 219, *219*, 221, 223–224, 231, 240, 250, 306, 380, 398, 535, 552, 759

Miss Chicken Little (Wilder), 29

"Miss Dowd Story, The" (RPR), 97
   criticism, Corsberg, 97–98

"Miss Findley and Mrs. Johnson and Mnemosyne, the Latter Who Remembered, But Too Late" (RPR), 747

Mitgang, Herbert, 509, 657

Mohawk Superfine Text paper, 672, 691

Molière, 11, 393

Moltke, Berta, 109, 127, *128*, 144–145, 151, 152, 163, 175, 179–180, *180*, 182–184, 188, 190, 193, 194, 196–197, 201, 202, 205, 250, 257, 276, 366, 606, 646, 759

Monasterio Trapense Nuestra Señora de los Ángeles, 71

Mondadori/Getty Images, 759

Monferdin, Gabriella, 543

Monk Bretton Books (Canadian and English bookseller), 544, 545

Montini, Giovanni Battista, 488

Montresor, Beni, 143, 572

"Moor of Venice, The" (English translation of a short story by Giraldi Cinthio), 529

Moore, Neil, 630

More, Denise (*nom de plume* of RPR), 65

Morgan, Charles, 554, 716

Morris, Henry, 744

Morris, Jewell, 553, *553*

Morris, William, xviii, 134, 185, 187, 383, 560, 573

Morris, Wright, 660–661

Morrison, Toni, 140

Morton-Saner, Anthea, 571

Moskvitin, Jurij, 175

Moulin Richard de Bas (manufacturer of French handmade papers, *see also* Richard de Bas paper), 323–324

Mowry, Virginia, 96

Moxon, Joseph, 134

Moxon, Paul, 759

Mozart, Wolfgang Amadeus, 188, 220, 423

Mozzambani, Alessandro, 263, 264, *264*, 759

Mozzo, Arrigo, 172

Mr. Wilson (fictitious character), 92–94, 97

"Mr. Wilson Story, The" (RPR), 92–94, 97 notes on, **749–751**

"Mrs. Bebe Bear and the Announcing Angel's Egg" (RPR), 65, 391

Mrs. Johnson (fictitious character), 747

Mujica Láinez, Manuel (Manucho), 521, 522, *522*, 523–524, 525, 535, 543, 552, 685

Munchkins (characters in *The Wizard of Oz*), 11

Muñoz-Vega, Pablo, Obispo Coadjutor, 50, 69

Murphy, Laurence Parke, 200

Museo di Castelvecchio, 531, 591

Museum of Modern Art, The, 335

"Mushroom Hunt, The" (RPR), 89

Myers, Don, 758

Mylius, Johann Daniel, *680*, 685

N

Nadan, Tal, 758

Nadelman, Elie, 304

Nanni, Carlo, 401, 402, 538, 759

Nanni, Giordano, 571

Nanni, Paula (*see also* Geldenhuys) 538

Napoleon, 346, 626

"Narcissus" (Spicer), 238

National Endowment for the Arts (NEA), 376, 422, 426

NEA (*see* National Endowment for the Arts)

Neavill, Gordon (Barry), *640*, 706, 753, 754

Nedo, Michael, 255, 327

Neighborhood: An Early Fragment from Ray (Hannah), 660

Nelson, Rolf, 29, 127, 759

Neruda, Pablo, 112, 126

New American Poetry, The (Donald M. Allen), 237

Newbauer, John, 128, 152, 376, 576

New Directions (New York publishing house), 129, 568

New Dutch Boys, 296

Newman, Barnett, 265–266

New Orleans Jazz Festival, 705, 706

New York City Opera, 521

New Yorker, The (magazine), 321, 509, 572, 576, 715

New York Public Library, The, 134–135, 157, 200, 317, 333, 355, 376, 425, 557, 574, 576, 578, 684, 709, 758, 761

New York Times, The (newspaper), 128, 411, 509, 576, 657, 753

New York Times Magazine, The, 582

Nicolai de Verona, Johannes, 383

Night Games (film), 571

1945–1965: An Evaluation of Two Decades of Self-Deception (RPR), xv, 49, 65, 78, 83, **88–107**, *88*, *94*, *95*, 146

Nineteenth–Century Printing Practices and the Iron Handpress (RGR), 134, 415, 738
jacket for, *738*

Noe, José, 306, 397

Nolan. Tim, 689

"Norfolk" (Gill), 511

Noritake China Company, 31

North Point Press (San Francisco publishing house), 568

Nothing Like the Sun (Burgess), 412

"Novel in Which It Was Too Tedious to Write the Beginning or the End and So the Middle Will Have to Suffice, A; or the Mr. Wilson Story" (RPR), 92–93

Novoa, Salvador, 521

Nuptials (Manhire), 744

Nyack (New York) Library, 762

Nystrom, Miss, 749

O

Oak Knoll Press, 191, 738

Oakland Tribune (newspaper), 394

O'Brien, Edna, 140

O'Day's Printing Company, 62

Occident (magazine), 17, 65, 96, 234, 342, 376, 387, *388*, 389, 390, 391, 392, 393, 395, 397, 404

Oedipus the King (Sophocles), 29

Officina Bodoni, xiii, 129, 135, 145, 191, 191–200, 240, 325–327, 377, *378*, 477, 499, 567, 582, 589, 739

Officina Bodoni: An Account of the Work of a Hand Press, 1923–1977, (Giovanni Mardersteig), xiv

Officina Chimèrea, 377, *378*, 379, 761

Officina Vindobonensis, *132*, 133

O'Flaherty, Terrence, 19

O'Hanrahan, Alcyone, 391

O'Hara, Antony (Tony), 641, 655, *656, 657,* 662, 664, 693, 700, *700*, 701, 702, 704, 706, 707, 717, *717*, 718, *718*, 719, 720, 722, 726,
731, 757, 758, 759

Old Piermont Methodist Church. 29, *30*

Oliboni, Renzo, 224, 331, 428

Olivetti portable typewriter, 163, 400, 439, 543

On Being a California Poet (Gioia), 736, 737

"On Binding Limited Editions" (article by Carol Joyce), 492

On Equal Terms (various authors), 708

"On Translating Zanzotto" (postscript by Beverly Allen, 477

Oppedisano, Joe, 478, 759, 762

Optima (typeface), 59

Orfeo ed Euridice (Gluck), 405

Orfeo in Paradise (Santucci), 487, 488

Origin of Sadness, The (Morris), 660

Orr, Chris, 549

Ortega, Amanda, 314, 759, 762

Oscar (Láinez Mujica's travelling companion), 523, 524–525

Ossolengo, Roberto, 288

Ossorio, Alfonso A., 697–698, *698*, 699, 701

Ottone e Rame di Pucci De Rossi, 288
invitation for, *288*

Ouroboros Centro di Sperimentazione Musica-Teatro, 685

Overseas Federation of Teachers, The (OFT) (teachers union), 472

Overseas Moving Specialists Inc. (freight forwarding company), 163

P

Pacci dono (portfolio of prints), 209

Padovani, Giovanni, dott., 484

Paesaggi arcaici (book of twelve etchings by Ger van Dijck), 185

Pagan Place, A (Edna O'Brien), 140

Palazzo Da Lisca, 208, 517

Palazzo Guarienti, 144, *160*, 166, 224, 244

Palimpsest (Vidal), 23

Palm Sunday (Vonnegut), 281

Palma, La (restaurant), 173

Palmer, Garrick, 597

Palou, Ricardo, 73–74, 143

Pamuk, Orhan, 3

Panicali, Carla, 328, 411, 414

Pankow, David, 744
Pappagallo, Il (restaurant), 303
Parkinson, Ariel, 26, 328, 339, *339*, 340–341, 344, 345–348, 367, 397, 522, 548, 579
  painting, 63
Parkinson, Chrysa, 339, 346, *346*, 348
Parkinson, Thomas (Tom), 13, 26, 58, 91, 232, 339–341, 343–344, 548, 579
  classes
    English 41B, 13, 58, 747
    English 141, 91, 232
Parra, Nicanor, 126, 129
Parsons, Betty, 188
Parvum Photo, 759
Partch, Harry, 29
Pasetto, Giorgio (Trota), 175, *175*, 308, *308*
Pasini, Roberto (Pat), 585
Pasolini, Pier Paolo, 223, 228, *228*
Passeri, Ruggiero, 469, 759, 762
Passerini, Lucio, 737
Passions and Ancient Days (Cavafy), 352, 411
Pastyme of People, The (book printed by John Rastell), 436
Patchen, Kenneth, 16
"Patient Lover, The" (RGR), 138
Paulinos, 74, 76, 78, 98, 101–102, 179
Paul VI, (Pope) (*see also* Montini), 71, 488
Pausig, Sergio, 653, 654
Payne, Maurice, 694
Peace Corps, 44–45
Pellegrini di terrafirma (Italian translation by Lionello Fiumi of a book by Blanchard), 377
Penumbra (magazine), 138
Peopleology of Richard Rummonds, xv, **82–86**,
Pergamena, La (tannery), 331, 492, 621
Perishable Press, 414
Perkins, Hoke, 454, 759
Perryman, Marcus, 503, *505*, 506
Peters, Othmar, 581
Peterson, Gregor G., 3, 735
Petrillo, Jim, 565, 567–568
Pettitt, Clara, 759
Pettitt, Kenneth, 16, 112, 368, 376, 394–395, *395*, 444, 549, 565, 574, 577, 587

Pettitt, Wade, 587, *587*, 588, 589, *589*
Peyronie's Disease, 566
Pfister, Patrick, 551
Pftzner, 132, 759
Phantom Farm, 443, *443*
Phelps, Lyon, 126
Phoenix Art Museum, 56
Phoenix Too Frequent, A (Fry), 11, *12*
"Photograph, The" (Cavafy), 353
  Keeley's revisions, 353–354, 762
Photograph As Symbol, The (Bullock), 566
"Photographer, The" (RGR), 291, 667
Piano Concerto no. 21 in C (Mozart), 188
Pía Sociedad de San Pablo, 74, 102
Piazza delle Erbe, 170, 172, 176, 405, 439, 528, 593
Piazza Navona, 111, *111*
Piazza Pitti, 685
Piazza San Marco, 530
pica (American point system), 186
Picasso, Pablo, 13, 334
piccola famiglia, la, 310, 370, 536, 545, 732
"Pictures and a Poem" (RPR), 98
Pierpont Morgan Library, The, 129
Pierre (camp counselor), 85
"Pietra, La" (Harold Acton's villa in Florence), 571
Pinacoteca di Brera, 761
Piras, Alberto, 311
Piras, Susi, 311
Pivano, Fernanda (Nanda), 242
Plain Edition (Gertrude Stein's imprint), 65
Plain Wrapper Press
  ephemera
    Camus Christmas card, *170*
    Casati broadside, *246*
    Change of address card, *676*
    Dog Bite invitation, *150*
    Insegnate, *300*
    Invitation to Olaf Idalie's reception, *305*
    "Miss Mattie's Trucking Service," 137
    Serata da Gabriel, *302*
  equipment
    Albion press (Ghisi), 588
    marble-topped table, 245

General Index

standing press, 171
type cabinets, 357, *447*
Poco proof press, 143, *683*
Washington press (Low), 141, *141*
Vandercook proof press, 122
exhibitions,
The New York Public Library, 573, *578*
locations, Cottondale, AL
Canyon Lake, 637
locations, NY
32 Union Square, *116*, 127, 149
444 East 84th Street, 141
48 West 25th Street, 131
locations, Verona
via Carlo Cattaneo, 6, 443, *444, 445*
sign above entrance, *629*
via Duomo, 15, 161, *440*
origin of name, 65
pressmark, 373, 417
"Plain Wrapper Press: A Bittersweet Recollection" (lecture by RGR, 658
Plain Wrapper Press: An Exercise in Frustration, The (tentative title for memoir by RGR), xv
"Plain Wrapper Press: A Retrospective Survey" (lecture by RGR), 561
Plain Wrapper Press: 1966–1988, xv
"Plain Wrapper Press Guidelines for Authors," 561
Plain Wrapper Press Newsletter: One, 313, 341, 366
quote from, 313
Plain Wrapper Press Notebook (proposed publishing plan)
Plain Wrapper Press to Close (letter sent to collectors), 649
Plank, Cybèle, 288, 293, *296*, 346, *346*
Plank, Eva, *296*
Plank, Tania, 288, 293, *296*, 346, *346*
Plath, Sylvia, 363
Plaza Lasso, Galo, 45–46
Pocar, Ervino, 497
Poco proof press (small cylinder press), 143, 163, 169, 205, 206, 208, 210, 217, 246, 288, 304–305, 358, 381, 383, *683*

Poemes (Laure Vernière), 363
"Poem Written in a Copy of Beowulf" (Borges, translated by Alastair Reid), 315
Poems from "The Wall Inside the Mirror (Ritsos), 355
Poesie del tappeto volante (Mozzambani), **262–267**, *262, 266*
Poet Be Like God: Jack Spicer and the San Francisco Renaissance (Ellingham and Killian), 242
Poetry Center of the 92nd Street YM-YWHA, The, 129, 314, 317
Poetry Renaissance (literary movement), 342
Poltroon Press, 515
Pomodoro, Arnaldo, 313, 317, 320, *320*, 321, *320*, 324, 328, 329, 331, 332, 333, 334, 414, 418, 529, 569, 759
Ponte Garibaldi (bridge in Verona), 444
Ponte Pietra (bridge in Verona), 174, 307, 494, 588
Pontificia Universidad Católica del Ecuador, 64
Pooler, Jack, 18, *18*, 19, 26, 349, 759
Post Mediaeval (Berthold typeface), 304, 343, 357, 367, 373, 413, 436, 567, 651, 667
Post, Herbert, 567
Potocki de Montalk, Geoffrey, Count, 567
Potter proof press, 141–142
Pottlitzer, Joanne, 125
Poulton, Louise, 758
Pound, Ezra, 379, 717–718
Power-Torrey, Marnie, 758
Prach, Bob, 8
"Practical Printing and Typography" (demonstration by RGR), 619
Pradella, Luigi, 356
Prado, José J., 73
Prandi, Dino, 247
Prater, Christopher (Chris), 417–418, 569
précieuses ridicules, Les (Molière), 11
Precio, Gabriel, xv, 83, 85, 89, 98, 100, 101, 747, 749
Premio Internazionale Diano Marina (award given to RGR), 333 469
Press in Tuscany Alley, 578

Press of the Palace of the Governors, The, 718

Prima Che Tu Dica "Pronto" / Before You Say "Hello" (Calvino), 645, **648–660**, *648, 655, 658*

Prince and the Pauper, The (Twain), 5

Prince Apartments (apartment complex in Tuscaloosa), 557, 661

"Printing and Publishing on the Handpress" (workshop by RGR), 451, *451*, 554
brochure for, *451*

"Printing Illustrated Books" (workshop by Claire Van Vliet), 662

Printing for Pleasure (Ryder), 57

Printing Office at High Loft, The, 567

Printing of To-day (Simon and Rodenberg), 628

Printing on the Iron Handpress (RGR), 191, 559, 560, 619, 738, 739, 741, 744
jacket for, *738*

Printing with the Handpress (Lewis M. Allen), 187, 224

Printmaking Workshop, The (Bob Blackburn's studio), 183

Private Libraries Association, 373, 376

Private Library, The (journal), 373, 383

Private Press, The (1971) (first edition, Cave), 383

Private Press, The (1983) (second edition, of Cave), 383

Private Press Association, 194, 376

Private Press Books (annual publication), 376, 377, 599

"Problem-Solving and Printing on the Cast-Iron Handpress" (1991), (workshop by RGR), 744

"Problem-Solving and Printing on the Cast-Iron Handpress" (1992), (workshop by RGR), 744

Proceedings of the Fine Printing Conference Columbia University, 64

Professional Press, 390

Pronto Soccorso: The Pucci-Parigi Book (a miscellany by various authors), **286–294**, *286, 290, 296, 297, 299*

"Protreptics to a Portable Apollo" (Boyd), 236–237

Psallidi, Gianni, 325, 328

Psalm XLVI (from the King James Bible)

Purdy, James, 570

Purple Place, 89, *90*, 91, 394

Q

Quadragono Libri (Italian publishing house), 549

Quarterly News-Letter (The Book Club of California), 357, 742

Quartus Series (PWP series title), 344, 404, 477, 479, 498, 511, 590, 628

Quesada, Mario, 574

"Quien ha contemplado la belleza, esta ya desinado a la muerte" (Martín Triana), 615

R

Rabbitt, Thomas, 660

Radiguet, Raymond, 126

Raiff, Stanley, 9, 11

Raimondi, Raymond, 89

Ram Press, The, 131–132

Rame, Le (Italian publisher of limited editions), 589

Ramer, James D., xvii, 552, 553, *553*, 638, 754, 755

Ramos, Guillermo, 41–42, *42*, 44, 47, 49, 53, 443, 759

Rampant Lions Press, 588, 628

Randall, Robert, 487

Randle, John, 415

Randle, Rosalind, 415

Random House (New York publishing house), 119–121, 123, 138, 155, 189, 316, 571, 577

Rare Books and Manuscripts Division, 134

Rashomon (film), xiii

Rastell, John, 436

Rath-dorcha, Ruiseart, 23–24, 25

Reading, W. Gay, 553

Reaves, Marilyn, 758

Rebis Press, 579, 709

Reichardt, Anthony, 415

Reid, Alastair, 313, 315, 613, 614, 618

Reisbord, Coriander, xv

General Index

Reisman, Harriet, 127

Renault, Mary, 570

"Report from Italy: Two Gentlemen of Verona" (article by Weaver), 517

Reprex proof press (cylinder proof press), 103

Resistance, 455

Resistance, Rebellion, and Death (Camus), 170

Re Teodorico (restaurant), 453

"Return of This Native" (lecture by RGR), 578

Requirements for a Goddess (unpublished manuscript by Zetterling), 571

Reuter, Jürgen, 445, 517, 528, *529,* 587, 589, 629, 759

Rexroth, Kenneth, 389

Rhoda (graduate student at the University of Alabama) , 703–704

Ricci, Franco Maria, 314, 333

Richard de Bas paper (French handmade paper), 324, 357, 367, 373, 504

"Richard-Gabriel Rummonds: A Veronese Printer" (article by John Richardson), 357

Richardson, John V., Jr., 332, 355, 356, *356,* 357, 758

Richardson, Nancy, 332, 355, 356, 759

Riding, Laura, 64, 389, 396

Rigoldi, Mario, 369, 528

Rijksmuseum Meermanne-Westreenianum, 579

"Rime of the Ancient Mariner" (Coleridge), 396

Rinaldi, Arturo, 607

RIT *see* Rochester Institute of Technology

Ritsos, Yannis, 355, 640

Riva, Franco, xiv, 327, 379–380, *380,* 465, 481

River, The (Paul Zweig), **602–609,** 602, *605, 607, 608,* 702

Rivera, Harrison, 126, *126,* 127

Rivers, Larry, xviii, 581, 582

Rizzoli Editore (Italian publishing house), 491

Rizzoli International Publications, Inc. (bookstore in New York), 334, 544, 570

Roberge, Oliver, 28

Roberto, (edition printer), 183, 195

Robinson, Jack, 131, 141

Robinson, Peter, 503, *505,* 506, 762

Roche, Nigel, 738

Roches, The, 706

Rochester Institute of Technology (RIT), 200, 256, 408, 738, 739, 744

Rockland Opera Company, 29

Rodenberg, Julius, 628

Rogers, Hoyt, 405, *405*

Rohmer, Bret, 122, 127, 151

Rojas, Ángel, 75

Roman Catholic Church, xvi, 49–50

Rosenstein, Sherry, 331, *331,* 332

Rosenthal, Raymond, 568

Rose Towers (student housing at the University of Alabama), 552, 556

Rossi, Federico, 271, *271,* 272, 276, 277, 646, 759

Rossi, Giuseppe, 481–483, 608

Rota, Anthony, xv, 65, 66, 334, 545 quote in *Fine Print,* 66

Roth, Sylvia, 699

Rothschild, William, 30, 759

Rubin, Mauro, 494, 499, 500, 511, 527–528, 535

Ruggero Olivieri (Italian typesetting company), 264, 291, 304, 590

Rummonds, Christiane, *109*

Rummonds, Dick, 2

Rummonds, Elfie (RGR's sister-in-law), 98, 110, 566, 759

Rummonds, Geraldine *née* Westenhaver (mother), 3, 4, 12, 17, 85, 117, 267, 684 recipes, 21, 85, 87, 460, 532, 533

Rummonds, Newton Price (father), 3, 4, 12, 17 death of, 348

Rummonds, Richard Price, affair with

    Agenoux, Søren, 23

    Baker, Philip, 29

    Boyd, Bruce, 234

    Cárdenas, Carlos, 32

    Dean, Marius, 234

    Isolde, 60

    Léon, Mario, 56

    Leube, Dietrich, 59

    Lofgren, Tom, 17

Marta, 51
Ramos, Guillermo, 41
Russell, Avery, 33
Scaasi, Arnold, 33
Tracy, 13
Catholicism, 4
eroticism, teenage, 5
health, 27, 43
hitchhiking to NY, 19
industrial design, 30–31, 34
  Fraser China, 28, *28*
letters to
  Corsberg, 97
  Hares, Gladys, 99, 103
  Leube, Dietrich, 60
  mother, 161
  parents, 61, 103
life in the seminary, 69–70, 76–77
Mexico
  first trip, 16–17
  second trip, 17
Navy, 13
New Orleans, 19–20
Peace Corps, 44–45
photos of, *2, 4, 8, 14, 22, 29, 31, 38, 44, 50, 84, 93, 396*
printing, allure of, 5–6
residences, Quito
  first house, 40–41, *41*
  second house (Calle Las Casas), 46–47
residences, USA
  1106 Oxford Street, Berkeley, 90
  2317 Virginia Street, Berkeley, 18
  2415 Haste Street, Berkeley, 58, 387
  315 East 69th Street, NY, 32
  65 Carmine Street, NY, 23
  Dwight Way, 234
running away, 13–14
teaching English, 69
Triumph Spitfire, 43–44, 637
theater,
  Children's Theatre, 9, 11
  early interest in, 7,
  Litchfield Summer Theatre, 12
  Sombrero Playhouse, 12

University of California at
  Berkeley, 11–12
Rummonds, Richard-Gabriel
affair with
  Aiello, Tony, 155
  Bricklayer, 174
  Cárdenas, Carlos, 32
  Davis, Scott, 683
  Engels, John, 707
  Halsband, Robert, 129
  Knight, Barbara, 137
  Kruty, Peter, 707
  Phelps, Lyon, 126
  Rivera, Harrison, 126
  Rossi, Federico, 271
  Rust, Steve, 731
  Vigna, Giorgio, 348
  Zanolli, Giorgio, 172
death, fantasy about his, 747
health, 125, 210, 250, 355, 478, 509, 566, 662, 683
letters to
  Moltke, Berta, 113, 127, 151, 152–153, 163, 183, 196, 197–198, 202
  parents, 61, 77–78, 103, 109–110, 118, 157, 188
  Pettitt, Kenneth, 112
  Rummonds, Thomas, 107
  Secon, Paul, 103, 113, 127, 152–153, 163, 196–198, 202
  Simmonds, Harvey, 483
  Sterne, Hedda, 197, 201
  Stuart, Tom, 124–125
  Tate, Allen, 105
logbook entries, 202, 325, 525
photos, Argentina, *70*
photos, Europe, *iv, 169, 190, 206, 220, 231, 239, 249, 260, 272, 289, 296, 344, 356, 359, 369, 375, 398, 403, 405, 407, 430, 431, 442, 446, 453, 456, 479, 490, 494, 522, 530, 539, 546, 547, 548, 550, 587, 589, 630, 740, 741*
photos, New Zealand, *745*
photos, Turkey, *400*
photos, USA

General Index   789

156, *479*, 555, *557*, 575, *577*, 634, 639, 640,
   644, *663*, 664, *681*, 693, *705*, *717*, *719*, 720,
   731, *742*, *743*, 745
prowling, 173, 246, 260, 308–309, 399, 540
residences, Italy
   via Duomo, 15, *160*, 167
residences, USA
   444 East 84th Street, NY, 141–142
   506 East 82nd Street, NY, 121, 297
   socializing, 258–259, 302, 370
     teaching English, 300, 301
       card for, *300*
Rummonds, Robert Newton (a.k.a. The Strawberry Bitch) (brother), 3, *4*, 18, 84–86, 98, 117
Rummonds, Thomas Chester (brother), 3, *4*, 98, 109, 117, 199, 255, 267, 348, 566, 576, 684, 731, *731*, 759
Rummonds, William Lee (brother), 3, 731, *731*
Ruskin, John, 590, 585
Russell, Avery, 33
Russell, Dan, 749
Russell, Lady, 383
Russell, Lord Arthur, 383
Russell, Lucy, 749
Rust, Steve, 731
Ryder, John, 57

S

S.S.R.S. Stories (RPR), 96, 100
Sabourin, Corey, 758
Sacks, Oliver, 297
Sada, Gabriel, 70, *70*
St. Bride Printing Museum, 415, 738
Saint-John Perse, 589
Salamone, Antonio, 168
"Saluto all'alba" (Kalidasa), 201
Salter, James, 633
Sampler of Leaves, A (RGR), *736*, 737
San Francisco Center for the Book, 741–742
San Francisco Chronicle (newspaper), 19, 394
San Francisco Renaissance, 237, 242
Sanguineti, Edoardo, 322
Santa Iglesia Catedral de Quito, 50

Santucci, Luigi, 487, *487*, 488, 489, 491, *494*, 495, 549
Santucci/Tadini book, 498, 573
San Zeno, Basilica of, 246, 531
Sarah Lawrence College, 288, 363, 509, 536
Saramago, José, 543
Sartori, Alessandro (Sandro), 420
Saunders, T.H. (British papermaker), 63
Savidis, George, 351, 352
Savinio, Ruggero, 465, 469, *469*, 470, 499
Saxe, Stephen O., 738
Sayit, Semin, 111
Scaasi, Arnold, 33
Scarlatti, Domenico, 248
Scattergood, Sarah, 44, *45*
Schaeffer, Paul B., 97
Schimmel, Stuart B., 333
Schmoller, Hans, xiv
Scholder, Judith, 139
School for the Book, Urbino (*see* Istituto Superiore Industrie Artistiche)
Schorer, Mark, 91–92, 95–97, 98, 235, 749
   classes
     106A, 91, 100, 235
Schutzmann, Pia, 572
Schwartz, Elizabeth, 5–6, 89
Scobie (fictitious character), 571
Scribner's Monthly (magazine), 92
Scudellari, Robert, 119–121, 188
"Search for Love" (D.H. Lawrence), 137, *137*
Secon, Paul, 103, 109, 127, *128*, 152, 163, 180, 188, 208, 250, 276, 297, 376
Selden, Filippo, 606, 759
Selden. Roger, 605–606, *606*, 608, 616, 702, 759
Selected Fables (Aesop), 685
Selected Poems, 1923–1967 (Borges), 315
Seminario Menor Metropolitano Sagrado Corazón de Jesús, 68, 69
Sensibar, Judith, 753–755
September Elegy (Thomas Parkinson), 548
Serafini, Cataldo, 526, *526*
Sereni, Vittorio, 465, 467, *467*, 468, 469, 490, 499, 504, *505*, 506, 669
Serpa, Robert, 551

Serra, Paolo, 332–333

Sette poesie sassoni (Italian translation by Serra of Borges's *Siete Poemas Sajones*), 332–333

Seven Aspects of Solitude (RGR), 3, 291, 348, 537, 629, **666-672**, *666, 669, 672,* 684, 686, 719, 729

"*Seventy from the Seventies*" (review of an exhibition at the New York Public Library) by Schimmel), 333

Sextet (various authors), 663

Shakespeare, William, 7, 412, 413

Shapiro, Karl, 577

Shark, Bud, 265

Shaw, Ed, 72, 73

Shaw, María, 72, 73

Shaver, Neil, *562,* 744

Shep, Sydney, 744, 745

Shiff, Ben, 581–582

Shiff, Sidney, 580–581

Ship of Sounds, The (Fuller), **596-599**, *596, 596*

Siete Poemas Sajones / Seven Saxon Poems (Borges), 154, 183, 190, 205, 213, 224, 297, **312-335**, *312, 316, 330,* 332–333

dampening paper for, *326*

pressure for, *325*

proof on Barcham Green paper, *317*

Sigovich, Donald, 408, 580–581

Sillari, Judith, 500, 510

Simmonds, Harvey, 304–305, 331, 354, 373, 381, 405, 408, 483, 564, 576

Simon, Oliver, 628

Simons, Anna, 135

Simpson, Louis, 708

Singer, Isaac Bashevis, 581

Single File (Fruchter), 140, *140*

Sistine Chukker, The (painting on the ceiling of The Chukker), 642, *642*

Six Poems (Ungaretti), **502-506**, *502, 504*

note by RGR, 503–504

Six Printers Mottos: A Spectrum Specimen (book with multiple contributors), **450-459**, *450, 457*

Skeptical Press, xv

"Sleepiness" (Ungaretti), 505, 762

Smith, Daniel, 422

Smith, Pamela S. (Pam), 718

Smyth, Elaine, xv

Smyth, Joseph (Joe), 614

Social Science Reference Service (correct name of SSRS), 90

Social Sciences Research Section [*sic*], 101

Società Nebiolo (Italian type foundry), 179

Society of Private Printers, 373

Society of Private Printers: Third Exchange (contribution by RGR), **372-375**, *372, 374*

Society of Young Publishers (SYP), 518, *518, 759*

Sombrero Playhouse (winter stock theater in Phoenix, AZ), 12

Some News and Bits of Gossip from Gabriel (newsletter by RGR), 633

Some Things from Jack (Spicer), **230-242**, *230, 241*

Sommaruga, Renzo, 185, 192, *192,* 193, 195, 196, 199, 201, 213, 223–228, 253, 318, 322, 327, 328, 373, 377

Sonata in E major (Domenico Scarlatti), 248

"Song for Gabriel, A" (Laure Vernière), 241, 762

"Sonnet for Dietrich, A" (RPR), 60

Sophocles, 29

Sorgetti, Marco, 308, *308,* 309

Soulèvement de la vie, Le (Clavel), 380

Southern Methodist University, 684, 737

Spann, Barry, 573

Spark, Muriel, 570

Sparling, Henry Halliday, 187

"Speak, Memory" (Sacks), 297

Special Black 42625 L'press ink (an ink distributed by Mandlik), 187, 422

Spectrum (typeface), 456, 466, 490

prospectus, *457*

Sperisen, Albert, 565, 603

Spiccato Spectres Related Silenticiously (S.S.R.S.), 100

Spicer, Jack, 58–59, 64, 231, 233, *233,* 234, 237–239, 342, 394, 730

letter to RPR, 233–234

Spitler, Priscilla, 718, 759

General Index

791

spyeghel der salicheyt van Elcerlijc, Den, 351

Squassabia, Antonio, 420

"Stadtwappen, Das" (Kafka), 498

Stagioni, Le (Gammero), **434–436**, *434, 436*

Stam, David H., 574, 577

"Stampatore, Torchi, Libri" (exhibition in Verona, 1999), 379, 560

   poster for, *739*

Stamperia Ampersand (*see* Ampersand and Edizioni Ampersand)

Stamperia Ponte Pietra, 377, 381

Stamperia Valdonega, 130, 304, 582, 590, 591

Stanbrook Abbey Press, The, 573

Stanhope press (iron handpress), 348, 636

Starbuck, George, 16

Stark, Lewis M., 135, 200

Starr, Harrison, 13, 15

State University of New York at Buffalo, 233, 762

State University of New York at Purchase, 654

Stauffacher, Jack Werner, 15, *15*, 16, 62, 404, 518, 568, 579, 645, 742, 759

Steffenoni, Luca, 260, 322, 530–531, 537, 547, 548, 705, *705*, 711, 759, 762, 763

Stein, Gertrude, 13, 39, 64, 65, 389, 396

Steinberg, Saul, 188, 698, *690*, 691, *690*, 692, 697

Stella Variabile (Sereni), **464–470**, *464, 468, 468, 470, 471*, 477, 497, 499

"Stemma Cittadino, Lo" (Kafka), **496–500**, *496, 499*

Sterling, Jan, 301

Sterne, Hedda, 146, 188, 203, 691

Steve (Rust), 731

Stevanoni, Riccardo, 545, *546*

Stevens, Wallace , 613, 614, 726

Stewart, Alice McLean, 638

Stingone, William, 758

Stone, Reynolds, 130

"Stop Motion" (Laure Vernière), 364–365

Strápico, Carlos, 543

Strathmore Chroma moldmade paper, 151

Stravinsky, Igor, 521

Strawberry Bitch, The (*see* Rummonds, Robert Newton)

Streetcar Named Desire, A (Williams), 20, 443, 581

Streghette, Le (Mirek), **212–220**, *212, 214*, 247

   invitation for, *218*

Strilko, Anthony, 30–31, *31*, 126

Stuart, Tom, 124

Studio della Quaglia, 653

Studio Gulliver, 442, 759

Studio Immagini (RGR and Testa's proposed art gallery), 307

Studio La Città, 200–201, 263, 265, 268, 275, 287, 306, 307, 320, 543, 589

Studio Marconi, 320, 325, 328, 332, 416, 432, 491

Subject Collections (Ash), 227

Suds, Miss (fictitious character), 97

Suite Lirica / Lyric Suite (Martín Triana), **612–621**, *612, 617, 618, 621*

   type in bed for, *619*

Summers, Jill Faulkner, 753, 754

Sundberg, Alan Frederick, 652–653, 654

Superior Printing Ink Company (American manufacturer of printing ink), 153

Superior press (tabletop vertical platen press), 55, *55*, 56

Sutherland, Sheila, 544

Sutton, Hélène, 200, 263, 265, 266, 267, 275, 320–321, 543

   her etching press, 275

Syracuse University, 7, 9, 11, 58, 89

Syracuse University Children's Theatre, 9, 11

Szabo, Arto, 99, 759

T

Tabb, Bruce, 758

Taddei, Richard, 276

Tadini, Emilio, 487, 491–492 , 549

Tadzio (fictitious character), 615

Tagliabue, Grace, 572

Tagliabue, John, 572

Talleur, Linda Samson, 660, *661, 706*

Tallien: A Brief Romance (Tuten), 569

   proof of illustration for, *569*

Tallone, Alberto, 384

Tallone, Aldo, 384

Tallone, Bianca, 384
Tallone, Enrico, 384, *384*
Taming of the Shrew. The (Shakespeare), 7
Tanner, Wesley B., 579, 709, *745*
Tate, Allen (designer), 48, *48*, 49, 50, 89, 98, 105, 117, 759
Tate, James, 661
"Tatti, I" (Berenson's villa near Florence), 516
Taylor, James, 376
Taylor, W. Thomas, xv, 513, 672, 709, 720, 757
Teague, Phil, 556, 673
Teasdale, Sara, 55, 58
Teatro di Verdura (open-air theater in Milan), 740
Teatro/Laboratorio (experimental theater in Verona)
Tedeschi, Nereo, 292, 328
Tema astrologico (Casati), 245
Ten Poems & Ten Reflections (Max D'Arpini and Bruno Corridori), 200, **204–210**, *204*, *207*, 351
Tentori Montalto, Francesco, 535
terra guasta, La (play by Ariel Parkinson), 345–346, *346*
  invitation for, *347*
Terre, Le, 293
Testa, Fulvio, 263, 304, 306–307, *307*, 324, 348, 381, 387, 399–400, 402, *403*, 404, 409, 439, 440, 500, 509, 510, 514, *514*, 515, 538, 545, 549, 578, 618, 724, 726, *727*, 729, 759
Theatre of Latin America, Inc. (TOLA), 125–126
Then and Now Stories, The (Cora C. Fletcher), 388, 392
"There Is an Inner Nervousness in Virgins" (Spicer), 343
Third Exchange: A Display of Presses (see Society of Private Printers: *Third Exchange*), 373
34th Biennale Internazionale d'Arte, Venice, 651
Thistle Press, 133
Thomas, Abigail, 762
Thomas, Diana, 444, 562, 745, 759

Thomas, Dylan, 15
Thomas, Lewis, 697, *698*, 699
Thomas/Ossorio book, 706
Thompson type cabinet, 128, 142
Thompson, Beth, 683
Thompson, Greg, 758
Thrash, Keith, 556, *556*
Three Poems of Passion (Cavafy), **350–357**, *350*, *354*
Tidcombe, Marianne, 383
Tiger's Eye, The (magazine), 390
Tilcock, Sandy, *661*
Tilson, Joe, 411, 415, 416, 417, 418, 421, 422, *423*, 424, 428, 429, 477, *479–480*, 517
Tilson, Jos, 417
Time Inc. Picture Collection, 759
Tipografo fra Due Culture: Richard-Gabriel Rummonds, Un (PWP retrospective exhibition in Milan in 1999), 740
  mini-catalog for, *740*
TOLA (*see* Theatre of Latin America)
Toninello, Nino, 219–220
Torcolo (restaurant), 466, 473
Tracy (Berkeley girlfriend), 13
Trappist monastery, 51, 111
Trappists, 69, 71
Trattoria al Cacciatore (restaurant), 174
Trattoria Ciccarelli (restaurant), 282
Trattoria La Fontana (restaurant), 567, 583
Tre poesie d'amore (Gammero), **278–281**, *278*, *280*
Trevisani, Guido, iv, 239, 289, 291, 292, 304, 759
Trianon Press, 573
Triumph Spitfire, 43, *44*, 637
Turnbull, William, 568
Turner, Decherd, xv, 638, 684
Tuscaloosa News, The (newspaper), 719, 763
Tuten, Frederic, 569
Twain, Mark, 5
Twinrocker Handmade Paper (paper mill), 554
"Two Gentlemen of Verona" (lecture by RGR), 689
"Two Gentlemen of Verona" (Weaver), 517

General Index
793

"Two Private Presses from Verona" (exhibition), 746
  poster for, *746*
type cabinets, 128, 133, 142, 357, 447, 448, 681, 683, *683*
Typophiles, The, 408, 557, 561, 580, 582
  World Printing Museum Tour, The, 1976), 408, 580

U

Über das Marionettentheater (von Kleist), 630
Umbrella (journal), 564
Ungaretti, Giuseppe, 503, *503*, 505, 506, 589, 626
United States Agency for International Development (USAID), 39
University of Alabama, xvii, 250, 310, 355, 359, 379, 419, 432, 445, 448, 451, 454, 469, 471, 491, 552, 559, 573, 580, 655, 675, 700, 716, 753
  MFA in the Book Arts Program, 250, 421, 552, 643, 660, 665, 675
University of California at Berkeley, 11, 16, 17, 58, 65, 89, 91, 100, 161, 394, 397, 477, 742, 747, 749
University of California at Santa Cruz, 422
University of Georgia, 267, 554, 684, 700, 716
University of Kentucky, 250, 355, 554, 762
University of Mississippi at Oxford, 753
University of Nebraska at Omaha, 134, 370, 561
University of North Carolina at Greensboro, 305
University of Oregon, 310, 684, 739, 761, 758, 761
University of Oxford, 405
University of San Francisco, 564, 578, 584, 587, 603, 709
University of Texas at Austin, 267, 684
University of Utah, The, 684, 761, 758, 761
University of Virginia, 579
University of Wisconsin–Madison, 761
Upiglio, Giorgio, 469, 479–480, 605–606
Upton, Richard, 149

V

Valéry, Paul, 645
Valli, Alida, 111
Valturius, Robertus, 383
Vandercook 14 proof press, 122, *123*, 127, 128, 129, 130, 133, 151, 187
Vandercook proof press, 63
van Dijck, Ger, 144, *164*, 165–171, 185, 199, 205, 207, 227, 304, 351–352, *351*, 535
Van Dijck (Monotype), 693
van der Aa, Theo, 144, *164*, 165–171, 199, 227, 304, 535
van Heek-Scholco (Dutch manufacturer of binder's cloth), 267
Van Vliet, Claire, 554, 564, 597, 662
VanWingen, Peter, 415, 738
Varda, Jean, 15
Varese-style papers (decorated papers), 659–660
Vaughan, Phillip, 557–558
Veclani, Emilio, 166, 759
Velasco, Leandro, 104, *104*, 105
Vera (designer), 33
Verba Edizioni (Milan publishing house), 625
Verich, Thomas, 753–754
Vernière, Jacques, 274–275, 279, 287, 291, 294, 298, 304, 323, 324, 332–333, 346, 363, 367, 368, *368*, 380, 419, 477, 548
Vernière, Julien, 759
Vernière, Laure, 240, 287, 288, 290, 293, 294, 363, *363*, 364–365, 366, 367, 368, 370, 371, 720–721, 759, 762
Verona, Italy: Via Carlo Cattaneo, 6 **442–448**
Verona, Italy: Via Duomo, 15, **160–175**
  via Duomo, *164*
Verona: The Lull before the Storm, **296–310**
Verona and Its Rivers (Ruskin), 590
Verona e i Suoi Fiumi (Ruskin), 538, **584–594**, *584*, *592*, *594*
Vespa, 219–220, **244–250**, *244*
  Casati's new, 271
VGM Gesellschaft für Münzeditionen, 528
Victoria and Albert Museum, 573, 579
Victoria University of Wellington (workshop by RGR), 744, *745*

Vidal, Gore, xviii, 23

Vigiak, Mario (Italian publisher), 549, 574

Viglierchio, Italo Carlos, don, 69

Vigna, Giorgio (Giorgiolino), 344, 345, *345*, 346, 347–348, 355, 358–359, 369, 374, 397, *398*, 399, 400, 401, 402, 403, 405, 406, 407, *407*, 415, 417, 418, 428, *547*, 548, 588, 670, 740–741, *741*, 759

Vigna, Laura, 407

Villa Emo di Fanzolo, La (Palladian villa in the Veneto), 453
  brochure for, *452*

Village Craftsmen (commercial printers), 690

Village Press, 739

Vino Gabrielis, 240

Viper's Tongue Press, The (proposed name for Ex Ophidia), 685

"Visit to Bianca Tallone" (article by RGR, 384

Vittoriale, Il (D'Annunzio's villa on Lake Garda), 524

Vivir para contarla (García Márquez), 69

Voltmer, Barbara, 737

Voltmer, Fred, 737

von Kleist, Heinrich, 630

Vonnegut, Kurt, Jr., 281

von Oppersdroff, Theodor, 550

W

Wagner, John, 702–703, 704, 707, 708, 758

Waiting Room, The (Kees), 673

Walbaum (Monotype), 184, 667, 717

Wald, Stephanie, 175

Waldrep, Shelton, 663

Walker, Bonnie, 199, *199*, 209, 215, *215*, 216–217, 219, 247, 274, 298, 323, 358, 369, 398, 537

Walker, Brooks, 199, *199*, 215, 216, 219, 246, 247, 257, 271, 273, 274–275, 276, 279, 292, 298, 323, 332, 358, 369, 472, 517, 759
  Hélène's etching press, 257

Walker, Emery, 135, 357, 383, 573

"Wall Inside the Mirror, The" (*see Poems from "The Wall Inside the Mirror"*)

Warhol, Andy, 29, 126, 128, 570

Warren, Robert Penn, 576, 577

Washburn, Ted, 62

Washington press (iron handpress), 131, 133, 136, 137, 139, 141, 154, 184, 317
  Washington press (Low's), *iv*, 141, *141*, 155–156, 163, 169, 187, 201, 207, 266, 288, 305, 318, 340, 358, 373, *375*, *442*, 537, 547, 548, 573, 592, 657, 660, *681*

Wasted Land, The (English translation of Ariel Parkinson's play), 354

Watry, Paul B., 757

Way, David J., 133, 136, 187, 193

Wayzgoose II (sponsored by The Australian Printing Historical Society), 376

Weaver, William, 517, *517*, 649, 651

Weil, James, 131, 759

Wescott, Glenway, 557, *557*

West, Mae, 558, 704

Westcott & Thomson (compositors), 140

What Did I Do?: The Unauthorized Autobiography of Larry Rivers (Rivers), xviii

"What Is a Poet?" (symposium), 708

Wheeler, Monroe, 557

"When I Am Not with You" (Teasdale), 55, 58

"When Printing Becomes an Art" (article by Jonathan Clark)

White Albatross Press, 388

White-Haired Lover (Shapiro), 577

White Rabbit Press, 243

Whitney Museum of American Art, 3, 645, 668, 686, 690, 762

Whittington Press, 415

Wickelman, Fred, 142

Wiegang, Willy, 135

Wieniewski, Henryk, 514, 759

Wild Carrot Letterpress, 581

Wilde, Oscar, 245

Wilder, Alex, 29

Wilkins, Cary, 660, *661*, 706, 707, 728, *728*, 729, 731

Will and Testament: A Fragment of Biography (Burgess), 224, **410–432**, *410*, *412*, *421*, *429*, 527

William Morris, Master Craftsman (Sparling),

General Index

187
Williams, Ken, 700
Williams, Tennessee, 20, 443, 570, 581
Williams, Wightman, 134
Wilson, Adrian, 64, 563, 566, 578
Wilson, Frances, 553, *553*
Wilson, Joyce Lancaster, 563, 566, 578
Wilson, Patrick (Pat) G., 101, 749
Wimpheimer, Charles Anthony (Tony), 577
Windhover Press, The, 725
"With Art and Craftsmanship, Books Regain Former Glory" (Bruckner), 582
Wizard of Oz, The (Raiff), 11
Wolde, Ludwig, 135
Wollitz, Ken, 23
"Woman with Her Mouth Open, The" (RGR's translation of Santucci's *La Donna con la Bocca Aperta*), 494
Wong, Judy Ling, 551
Wood, Ann, 603
Wood, Thor, 603
Woodall, Steve, 741
Wooings (Gill), **508–516**, *508*, *512*, *515*
Wookey Hole Mill, 513, 527
Words for Music (Gioia), 726
"Worn Steps, The" Gioia), 726
Württembergische Metallwarenfabrik (WMF), 60
Wynn, Douglas C., 753, 755–756

X

Xilographia Italiana, 357

Y

Yávar, Gerardo, 323–324

Z

Zahradka, Miroslav (*see* Mirek)
Zand (portfolio), 304
Zambonini, Giuseppe, 346
Zanella, Alessandro, 419, 423, 425, 426, 427, 429, 430, 435, 436, 442, 443, 447, 451, 454, 466, 469, 470, 477, 479, 481, 482, 484, 488, 489, 490, 498, 499, 500, 503, 506, 511, 517, 526, 527, 535, 537, 539, 544, 550, 551, 552, 553, 554, 562, 571, 572, 582, 585, 590, 593, 599, 616, 618, 620, 621, 625, 626, 627, 629, 635–636, 649–650, 653, 659, 667, 673, 684, 693, 713, 729, 744, 746, 757, 759
    photos, Europe, *442*, *482*, *490*, *494*, *497*, *551*, *552*, *589*, *593*, *629*, *630*
    photos, USA, *555*
Zanfretta, Angiolina, 631, 636
Zanfretta, Pino 588, 629, *629*, 630, 631, 636, 759
Zanolli, Giorgio ("Hat Shop"), 172, 172, *172*, *173*, *175*, 176, 282, 308, *308*, 346, *346*, 560
Zanzotto, Andrea, 477, 478, *478*, 481, 483, 485, 490
Zapf, Hermann, 185
Zavrel, Stepán, 306–307
Zedda, Silverio, 75
Zetterling, Mai, 571
Zheng, Ting, 673
Zoellner, Richard, 553, 559, 729
Zorzi, Giordano, 279, 280–281, 435
Zucca, Cristina, 430, *430*
Zweig, Francine, 183
Zweig, Paul, xviii, 180, *182*, 183, 188, 190, 193, 586, 603–604, *603*, 606
Zweig/Moltke book, 183, 201, 205, 700